W9-CSN-044

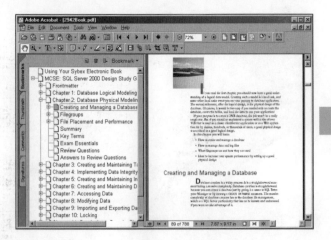

Search through the complete book in PDF.

✔ Access the entire *MCSE: SQL Server 2000 Design Study Guide*, complete with figures and tables, in electronic format.

✔ Search the *MCSE: SQL Server 2000 Design Study Guide* chapters to find information on any topic in seconds.

Use the Electronic Flashcards for PCs or Palm devices to jog your memory and prep last-minute for the exam!

✔ Reinforce your understanding of key concepts with these hardcore flashcard-style questions.

✔ Download the Flashcards to your Palm device, and go on the road. Now you can study anywhere, any time.

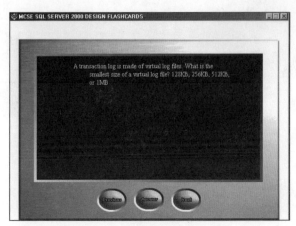

SYBEX

MCSE: SQL Server 2000 Design Study Guide

Exam 70-229: Objectives

SYBEX

PROGRAMMING BUSINESS LOGIC

TUNING AND OPTIMIZING DATA ACCESS

DESIGNING A DATABASE SECURITY PLAN

SYBEX

MCSE:
SQL Server 2000 Design
Study Guide

MCSE:
SQL Server™ 2000 Design
Study Guide

Marc Israel

J. Steven Jones

San Francisco • Paris • Düsseldorf • Soest • London

Associate Publisher: Neil Edde
Acquisitions and Developmental Editor: Jeff Kellum
Editor: Malka Geffen
Production Editor: Elizabeth Campbell
Technical Editors: Scott Warmbrand, Scott Sanford
Book Designer: Bill Gibson
Graphic Illustrator: Epic Studios, Tony Jonick
Electronic Publishing Specialist: Interactive Composition Corporation
Proofreaders: Laurie O'Connell, Nancy Riddiough, Jennifer Greiman, Suzanne Stein
Indexer: Ann Rogers
CD Coordinator: Christine Harris
CD Technician: Kevin Ly
Cover Designer: Archer Design
Cover Photographer: The Image Bank

Library of Congress Card Number: 2001089819

ISBN: 0-7821-2942-0

SYBEX

To Our Valued Readers:

In recent years, Microsoft's MCSE program has established itself as the premier computer and networking industry certification. Nearly a quarter of a million IT professionals have attained MCSE status in the NT 4 track. Sybex is proud to have helped thousands of MCSE candidates prepare for their exams over these years, and we are excited about the opportunity to continue to provide people with the skills they'll need to succeed in the highly competitive IT industry.

For the Windows 2000 MCSE track, Microsoft has made it their mission to demand more of exam candidates. Exam developers have gone to great lengths to raise the bar in order to prevent a paper-certification syndrome, one in which individuals obtain a certification without a thorough understanding of the technology. Sybex welcomes this new philosophy as we have always advocated a comprehensive instructional approach to certification courseware. It has always been Sybex's mission to teach exam candidates how new technologies work in the real world, not to simply feed them answers to test questions. Sybex was founded on the premise of providing technical skills to IT professionals, and we have continued to build on that foundation, making significant improvements to our study guides based on feedback from readers, suggestions from instructors, and comments from industry leaders.

The depth and breadth of technical knowledge required to obtain Microsoft's new Windows 2000 MCSE is staggering. Sybex has assembled some of the most technically skilled instructors in the industry to write our study guides, and we're confident that our Windows 2000 MCSE study guides will meet and exceed the demanding standards both of Microsoft and you, the exam candidate.

Good luck in pursuit of your MCSE!

Neil Edde
Associate Publisher—Certification
Sybex Inc.

SYBEX Inc. 1151 Marina Village Parkway, Alameda, CA 94501
Tel: 510/523-8233   Fax: 510/523-2373   HTTP://www.sybex.com

Software License Agreement: Terms and Conditions

To my wife, Claire, and to our boys, Thibault and Quentin. Love and tolerance are values you share. I love you.

—Marc Israel

Not a day goes by when I do not think of my wife, Tia. For you, my darling.

—Steve Jones

Acknowledgments

Like a piece of software, a book is seldom the work of only one man or woman, but the work of a team of people, aiming at one goal: to teach and bring enjoyment to the future reader. While the author is focused on what to say, dozens of other people are helping him to say it well, from editors to the art crew, in order to publish the best computer book. I would like to acknowledge all the crew who worked with me on this book, beginning with my co-author, Steve. Co-authoring is not an easy task when you sit in the same office, but when 10,000 miles are between both authors, it's a tough challenge. I think trust did it all! And everybody at Sybex trusted us, including Jeff, Elizabeth, Malka, and all those who I do not know but who worked on this book. Be thanked beyond your wildest dreams!

—Marc Israel

This book is my first and was a great experience. It was also more trying and difficult than I had imagined. It would not have been possible without the support and assistance of my wife, Tia, who put up with quite a few late nights and weekends away from her and our children. I also have my mother, Mary Jones, to thank for her limitless enthusiasm and support. Her constant praise helped to keep me going when the writing was slow to appear.

Writing with someone is always a difficult chore and writing when you are physically removed is even more of a challenge. I'd like to thank my co-author, Marc, for his efforts in working with Sybex and myself from half a world away.

I also have to thank the IT staff at IQdestination for putting up with a co-worker who was distracted at times and exhausted at others. Thanks to Adam, Charles, Chris, Corey, Dave, Kevin, Matt, Michael, and Mindy.

—J. Steven Jones

Contents at a Glance

Contents

Chapter 5   **Creating and Maintaining Indexes**   **287**

Table of Exercises

Introduction

Microsoft's Microsoft Certified Systems Engineer (MCSE) track for Windows 2000 is the premier certification for computer industry professionals. Covering the core technologies around which Microsoft's future will be built, the MCSE Windows 2000 program is a powerful credential for career advancement.

This book has been developed to give you the critical skills and knowledge you need to prepare for one of the electives for the MCSE certification program: *Designing and Implementing Databases with Microsoft® SQL Server™ 2000 Enterprise Edition* (Exam 70-229).

This exam is also one of the required exams for the Microsoft Certified Database Administrators (MCDBA). We have chosen to focus on the MCSE track as that is by far the most popular of Microsoft's certification tracks. As of this printing, there were over 400,000 MCSEs, and roughly 20,000 MCDBAs. We will discuss all of the different tracks below.

Since the inception of its certification program, Microsoft has certified over one million people. As the computer network industry grows in both size and complexity, these numbers are sure to grow—and the need for *proven* ability will also increase. Companies rely on certifications to verify the skills of prospective employees and contractors.

Microsoft has developed its Microsoft Certified Professional (MCP) program to give you credentials that verify your ability to work with Microsoft products effectively and professionally. Obtaining your MCP certification requires that you pass any one Microsoft certification exam. Several levels of certification are available based on specific suites of exams. Depending on your areas of interest or experience, you can obtain any of the following MCP credentials:

Microsoft Certified System Engineer (MCSE)   This certification track is designed for network and systems administrators, network and systems analysts, and technical consultants who work with Microsoft Windows 2000 client and server software. You must take and pass seven exams to obtain your MCSE.

Since this book covers one of the MCSE elective exams, we will discuss the MCSE certification in detail in this Introduction.

Microsoft Certified Database Administrator (MCDBA) This track is designed for database administrators, developers, and analysts who work with Microsoft SQL Server. As of this printing, you can take exams on either SQL Server 7 or SQL Server 2000, but Microsoft is expected to announce the retirement of SQL Server 7. You must take and pass four exams to achieve MCDBA status.

The Designing and Implementing Databases with Microsoft® SQL Server™ 2000 Enterprise Edition exam is one of the MCDBA required exams.

Microsoft Certified Solution Developer (MCSD) This track is designed for software engineers and developers and technical consultants who primarily use Microsoft development tools. Currently, you can take exams on Visual Basic, Visual C++, and Visual FoxPro. However, with Microsoft's pending release of Visual Studio 7, you can expect the requirements for this track to change by the end of 2001. You must take and pass four exams to obtain your MCSD.

Microsoft Certified Trainer (MCT) The MCT track is designed for any IT professional who develops and teaches Microsoft-approved courses. To become an MCT, you must first obtain your MCSE, MCSD, or MCDBA; then you must take a class at one of the Certified Technical Training Centers. You will also be required to prove your instructional ability. You can do this in various ways: by taking a skills-building or train-the-trainer class; by achieving certification as a trainer from any of a number vendors; or by becoming a Certified Technical Trainer through the Chauncey Group (www.chauncey.com/ctt.html). Last of all, you will need to complete an MCT application.

As of March 1, 2001, Microsoft no longer offers MCSE NT 4 required exams. Those who are certified in NT 4 have until December 31, 2001, to upgrade their credentials to Windows 2000. Also, Microsoft has retired three other certification tracks: MCP+Internet, MCSE+Internet, and MCP+Site Builder. The topics and concepts that are tested in these certifications have been incorporated into the MCSE and MCSD exams.

How Do You Become an MCSE?

Attaining MCSE certification has always been a challenge. In the past, students have been able to acquire detailed exam information—even most of the exam questions—from online "brain dumps" and third-party "cram" books or software products. For the new MCSE exams, this is simply not the case.

Microsoft has taken strong steps to protect the security and integrity of the new MCSE track. Now, prospective MSCEs must complete a course of study that develops detailed knowledge about a wide range of topics. It supplies them with the true skills needed, derived from working with Windows 2000 and related software products.

The new MCSE program is heavily weighted toward hands-on skills and experience. Microsoft has stated that "nearly half of the core required exams' content demands that the candidate have troubleshooting skills acquired through hands-on experience and working knowledge."

Fortunately, if you are willing to dedicate the time and effort to learn Windows 2000, you can prepare yourself well for the exams by using the proper tools. By working through this book, you can successfully meet the exam requirements.

This book is part of a complete series of Sybex MCSE Study Guides, published by Sybex Inc., that together cover the core Windows 2000 requirements as well as the new Design exams and a number of the electives needed to complete your MCSE track. Study Guide titles include the following:

- *MCSE: Windows 2000 Professional Study Guide,* Second Edition, by Lisa Donald with James Chellis (Sybex, 2001)

- *MCSE: Windows 2000 Server Study Guide,* Second Edition, by Lisa Donald with James Chellis (Sybex, 2001)

- *MCSE: Windows 2000 Network Infrastructure Administration Study Guide,* Second Edition, by Paul Robichaux with James Chellis (Sybex, 2001)

- *MCSE: Windows 2000 Directory Services Administration Study Guide,* Second Edition, by Anil Desai with James Chellis (Sybex, 2001)

- *MCSE: Windows 2000 Network Security Design Study Guide,* by Gary Govanus and Robert King (Sybex, 2000)

- *MCSE: Windows 2000 Network Infrastructure Design Study Guide,* by Bill Heldman (Sybex, 2000)

- *MCSE: Windows 2000 Directory Services Design Study Guide,* by Robert King and Gary Govanus (Sybex, 2000)

- *MCSE: SQL Server 2000 Administration Study Guide,* by Lance Mortensen, Rick Sawtell, and Joseph L. Jorden (Sybex, 2001)

- *MCSE: Exchange 2000 Server Administration Study Guide,* by Walter Glen with James Chellis (Sybex, 2001)

- *MCSE: Exchange 2000 Server Design Study Guide,* by William Heldman (Sybex, 2001)

- *MCSE: Windows 2000 Migration Study Guide,* by Todd Phillips (Sybex, 2001)

 Please visit certification.sybex.com for a complete list of our offerings, including our Virtual Trainers, Virtual Test Centers, and Exam Notes.

Exam Requirements

Candidates for MCSE certification in Windows 2000 must pass seven exams, including four core operating system exams, one design exam, and two electives.

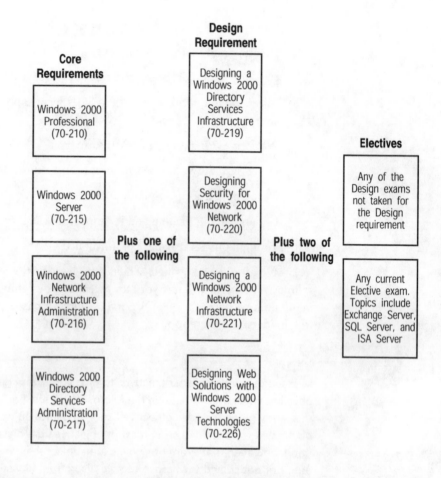

Core Requirements

Windows 2000 Professional (70-210)

Windows 2000 Server (70-215)

Windows 2000 Network Infrastructure Administration (70-216)

Windows 2000 Directory Services Administration (70-217)

Design Requirement

Designing a Windows 2000 Directory Services Infrastructure (70-219)

Designing Security for Windows 2000 Network (70-220)

Designing a Windows 2000 Network Infrastructure (70-221)

Designing Web Solutions with Windows 2000 Server Technologies (70-226)

Plus one of the following

Plus two of the following

Electives

Any of the Design exams not taken for the Design requirement

Any current Elective exam. Topics include Exchange Server, SQL Server, and ISA Server

---

For a more detailed description of the Microsoft certification programs, including a list of current and future MCSE electives, check Microsoft's Training and Certification Web site at www.microsoft.com/trainingandservices.

The *Designing and Implementing Databases with Microsoft® SQL Server™ 2000 Enterprise Edition Exam*

The Designing and Implementing Databases with SQL Server 2000 Certification exam covers concepts and skills required for the support of SQL Server 2000. It emphasizes the following areas:

- Creating and maintaining tables

- Implementing data integrity using rules, constraints, and keys

- Creating and maintaining indexes

- Creating views, defaults, stored procedures, and triggers

- Accessing and modifying data in SQL Server and remote data sources

- Working with data in an XML format

- Using SQL Server utilities to import and export data in bulk

- Developing a security plan for a database

- Understanding locking and its impact on the server

- Tuning SQL Server query performance

If we had to create a single sentence to describe the test, it would be as follows: The exam will test your knowledge of designing, creating, and maintaining a database on SQL Server 2000. To pass the test, you need to fully understand these topics.

Microsoft provides exam objectives to give you a very general overview of possible areas of coverage on the Microsoft exams. For your convenience, this study guide includes objective listings positioned within the text at points where specific Microsoft exam objectives are discussed. Keep in mind, however, that exam objectives are subject to change at any time without prior notice and at Microsoft's sole discretion. Please visit Microsoft's Training and Certification Web site (www.microsoft.com/trainingand-services) for the most current listing of exam objectives.

Types of Exam Questions

In an effort to both refine the testing process and protect the quality of its certifications, Microsoft has focused its Windows 2000 exams on real experience and hands-on proficiency. There is a higher emphasis on your past working environments and responsibilities, and less emphasis on how well you can memorize. In fact, Microsoft says an MCSE candidate should have at least one year of hands-on experience.

Microsoft will accomplish its goal of protecting the exams' integrity by regularly adding and removing exam questions, limiting the number of questions that any individual sees in a beta exam, limiting the number of questions delivered to an individual by using adaptive testing, and adding new exam elements.

Exam questions may be in a variety of formats: Depending on which exam you take, you'll see multiple-choice questions, as well as select-and-place and prioritize-a-list questions. Simulations and case study–based formats are included, as well. You may also find yourself taking what's called an *adaptive format exam*. Let's take a look at the types of exam questions and examine the adaptive testing technique, so that you'll be prepared for all of the possibilities.

For more information on the various exam question types, go to www.microsoft.com/trainingandservices/default.asp?PageID=mcp&PageCall=tesinn&SubSite=examinfo.

MULTIPLE-CHOICE QUESTIONS

Multiple-choice questions come in two main forms. One is a straightforward question followed by several possible answers, of which one or more is correct. The other type of multiple-choice question is more complex and based on a specific scenario. The scenario may focus on a number of areas or objectives.

SELECT-AND-PLACE QUESTIONS

Select-and-place exam questions involve graphical elements that you must manipulate in order to successfully answer the question. For example, you might see a diagram of a computer network, as shown in the following graphic taken from the select-and-place demo downloaded from Microsoft's Web site.

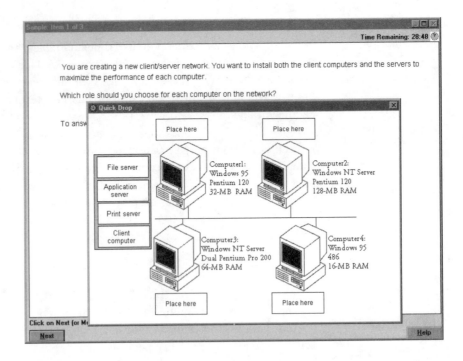

A typical diagram will show computers and other components next to boxes that contain the text "Place here." The labels for the boxes represent various computer roles on a network, such as a print server and a file server. Based on information given for each computer, you are asked to select each label and place it in the correct box. You need to place *all* of the labels correctly. No credit is given for the question if you correctly label only some of the boxes.

In another select-and-place problem you might be asked to put a series of steps or lines of code in order, by dragging item from boxes on the left to boxes on the right, and placing them in the correct order. One other type requires that you drag an item from the left and place it under an item in a column on the right.

CASE STUDY–BASED QUESTIONS

Case study–based questions first appeared in the MCSD program. These questions present a scenario with a range of requirements. Based on the information provided, you answer a series of multiple-choice and select-and-place questions. The interface for case study–based questions has a number of tabs, each of which contains information about the scenario.

ADAPTIVE EXAM FORMAT

Microsoft presents many of its exams in an *adaptive* format. This format is radically different from the conventional format previously used for Microsoft certification exams. Conventional tests are static, containing a fixed number of questions. Adaptive tests change depending on your answers to the questions presented.

The number of questions presented in your adaptive test will depend on how long it takes the exam to ascertain your level of ability (according to the statistical measurements on which exam questions are ranked). To determine a test-taker's level of ability, the exam presents questions in an increasing or decreasing order of difficulty.

Unlike the earlier test format, the adaptive test does *not* allow you to go back to see a question again. The exam only goes forward. Once you enter your answer, that's it—you cannot change it. Be very careful before entering your answers. There is no time limit for each individual question (only for the exam as a whole). Your exam may be shortened by correct answers (and lengthened by incorrect answers), so there is no advantage to rushing through questions.

Microsoft will regularly add and remove questions from the exams. This is called *item seeding.* It is part of the effort to make it more difficult for individuals to merely memorize exam questions that were passed along by previous test-takers.

Exam Question Development

Microsoft follows an exam-development process consisting of eight mandatory phases. The process takes an average of seven months and involves more than 150 specific steps. The MCP exam development consists of the following phases:

Phase 1: Job Analysis Phase 1 is an analysis of all the tasks that make up a specific job function, based on tasks performed by people who are currently performing that job function. This phase also identifies the knowledge, skills, and abilities that relate specifically to the performance area being certified.

Phase 2: Objective Domain Definition The results of the job analysis phase provide the framework used to develop objectives. Development of objectives involves translating the job-function tasks into a comprehensive package of specific and measurable knowledge, skills, and abilities. The resulting list of objectives—the *objective domain*—is the basis for the development of both the certification exams and the training materials.

Phase 3: Blueprint Survey The final objective domain is transformed into a blueprint survey in which contributors are asked to rate each objective. These contributors may be MCP candidates, appropriately skilled exam-development volunteers, or Microsoft employees. Based on the contributors' input, the objectives are prioritized and weighted. The actual exam items are written according to the prioritized objectives. Contributors are queried about how they spend their time on the job. If a contributor doesn't spend an adequate amount of time actually performing the specified job function, his or her data are eliminated from the analysis. The blueprint survey phase helps determine which objectives to measure, as well as the appropriate number and types of items to include on the exam.

Phase 4: Item Development A pool of items is developed to measure the blueprinted objective domain. The number and types of items to be written are based on the results of the blueprint survey.

Phase 5: Alpha Review and Item Revision During this phase, a panel of technical and job-function experts review each item for technical accuracy. The panel then answers each item and reaches a consensus on all technical issues. Once the items have been verified as being technically accurate, they are edited to ensure that they are expressed in the clearest language possible.

Phase 6: Beta Exam The reviewed and edited items are collected into beta exams. Based on the responses of all beta participants, Microsoft performs a statistical analysis to verify the validity of the exam items and to determine which items will be used in the certification exam. Once the analysis has been completed, the items are distributed into multiple parallel forms, or *versions,* of the final certification exam.

Phase 7: Item Selection and Cut-Score Setting The results of the beta exams are analyzed to determine which items will be included in the certification exam. This determination is based on many factors, including item difficulty and relevance. During this phase, a panel of job-function experts determine the *cut score* (minimum passing score) for the exams. The cut score differs from exam to exam because it is based on an item-by-item determination of the percentage of candidates who answered the item correctly and who would be expected to answer the item correctly.

Phase 8: Live Exam In the final phase, the exams are given to candidates. MCP exams are administered by Prometric and Virtual University Enterprises (VUE).

Tips for Taking the SQL Server 2000 Design Exam

Here are some general tips for achieving success on your certification exam:

- Arrive early at the exam center so that you can relax and review your study materials. During this final review, you can look over tables and lists of exam-related information.

- Read the questions carefully. Don't be tempted to jump to an early conclusion. Make sure you know *exactly* what the question is asking.

- Answer all questions. Remember, a guess is better than a blank answer. Also, make sure that you can go back, and if you can't, do not go onto the next question without answering the previous one. On simulations, do not change settings that are not directly related to the question. Also, assume default settings if the question does not specify or imply which settings are used.

- For questions you're not sure about, use a process of elimination to get rid of the obviously incorrect answers first. This improves your odds of selecting the correct answer when you need to make an educated guess.

Exam Registration

You may take the Microsoft exams at any of more than 1,000 Authorized Prometric Testing Centers (APTCs) and VUE Testing Centers around the world. For the location of a testing center near you, call Prometric at 800-755-EXAM (755-3926), or call VUE at 888-837-8616. Outside the United States and Canada, contact your local Prometric or VUE registration center.

Find out the number of the exam you want to take, and then register with the Prometric or VUE registration center nearest to you. At this point, you will be asked for advance payment for the exam. The exams are $100 each and you must take them within one year of payment. You can schedule exams up to six weeks in advance or as late as one working day prior to the date of the exam. You can cancel or reschedule your exam if you contact the center at least two working days prior to the exam. Same-day registration is available in some locations, subject to space availability. Where same-day registration is available, you must register a minimum of two hours before test time.

You may also register for your exams online at www.prometric.com or www.vue.com.

When you schedule the exam, you will be provided with instructions regarding appointment and cancellation procedures, ID requirements, and information about the testing center location. In addition, you will receive a registration and payment confirmation letter from Prometric or VUE.

Microsoft requires certification candidates to accept the terms of a Non-Disclosure Agreement before taking certification exams.

Is This Book for You?

If you want to acquire a solid foundation in SQL Server 2000 Design, and your goal is to prepare for the exam by learning how to use the database program, this book is for you. You'll find clear explanations of the fundamental concepts you need to grasp, and plenty of help to achieve the high level of professional competency you need to succeed in your chosen field.

If you want to become certified as an MCSE, this book is definitely for you. However, if you just want to attempt to pass the exam without really understanding SQL Server 2000, this Study Guide is *not* for you. It is written for people who want to acquire hands-on skills and in-depth knowledge of SQL Server 2000, paying particular attention to the published exam objectives.

How to Use This Book

What makes a Sybex Study Guide the book of choice for over 100,000 MCSEs? We took into account not only what you need to know to pass the exam, but what you need to know to take what you've learned and apply it in the real world. Each book contains the following:

Objective-by-objective coverage of the topics you need to know   Each chapter lists the objectives covered in that chapter, followed by detailed discussion of each objective.

Assessment Test   On the CD you'll find an Assessment Test that you should take. It is designed to help you determine how much you already know about SQL Server 2000. Each question is tied to a topic discussed in the book. Using the results of the Assessment Test, you can figure out the areas where you need to focus your study. Of course, we do recommend you read the entire book.

Exam Essentials   To highlight what you learn, you'll find a list of Exam Essentials at the end of each chapter. The Exam Essentials section briefly highlights the topics that need your particular attention as you prepare for the exam.

Key Terms and Glossary   Throughout each chapter, you will be introduced to important terms and concepts that you will need to know for the exam. These terms appear in italic within the chapters, and a list of the Key Terms appears just after the Exam Essentials. At the end of the book, a detailed Glossary gives definitions for these terms, as well as other general terms you should know.

Review questions, complete with detailed explanations   Each chapter is followed by a set of Review Questions that test what you learned in the chapter. The questions are written with the exam in mind, meaning that they are designed to have the same look and feel of what you'll see on the exam. Question types are just like the exam, including multiple choice, exhibits, select-and-place, and prioritize-a-list.

Hands-on exercises   In each chapter, you'll find exercises designed to give you the important hands-on experience that is critical for your exam preparation. The exercises support the topics of the chapter, and they walk you through the steps necessary to perform a particular function.

Real World Scenarios   Because reading a book isn't enough for you to learn how to apply these topics in your every-day duties, we have provided Real World Scenarios in special sidebars. These explain when and why a particular solution would make sense, in a working environment you'd actually encounter.

Interactive CD   Every Sybex Study Guide comes with a CD complete with additional questions, flashcards for use with a palm device, and the electronic book. Details are in the following section.

 The topics covered in this Study Guide map directly to Microsoft's official exam objectives. Each exam objective is covered completely.

What's on the CD?

With this new member of our best-selling MCSE Study Guide series, we are including quite an array of training resources. The CD offers numerous simulations, bonus exams, and flashcards to help you study for the exam. We have also included the complete contents of the study guide in electronic form. The CD's resources are described here:

The Sybex Ebook for the SQL Server 2000 Design Study Guide   Many people like the convenience of being able to carry their whole study guide on a CD. They also like being able to search the text via computer to find specific information quickly and easily. For these reasons, the entire contents of this Study Guide are supplied on the CD, in PDF format. We've also included Adobe Acrobat Reader, which provides the interface for the PDF contents as well as the search capabilities.

The Sybex MCSE Edge Tests   The Edge Tests are a collection of multiple-choice questions that will help you prepare for your exam. There are four sets of questions:

- Two bonus exams designed to simulate the actual live exam.

- An adaptive test simulator that will give the feel for how adaptive testing works.

- All the questions from the Study Guide, presented in a test engine for your review. You can review questions by chapter, by objective, or you can take a random test.

- The Assessment Test.

Here is a sample screen from the Sybex MCSE Edge Tests:

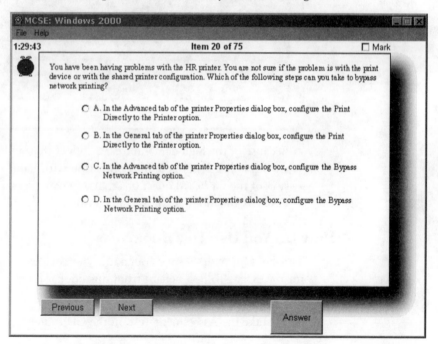

Sybex MCSE Flashcards for PCs and Palm Devices   The "flashcard" style of question offers an effective way to quickly and efficiently test your understanding of the fundamental concepts covered in the exam.

The Sybex MCSE Flashcards set consists of more than 150 questions presented in a special engine developed specifically for this study guide series. Here's what the Sybex MCSE Flashcards interface looks like:

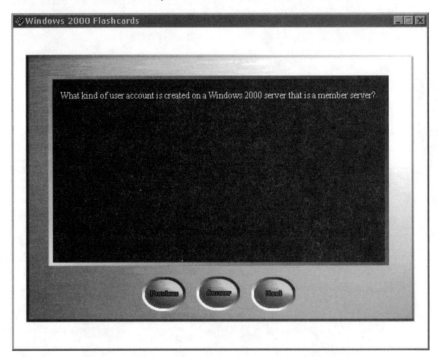

Because of the high demand for a product that will run on Palm devices, we have also developed, in conjunction with Land-J Technologies, a version of the flashcard questions that you can take with you on your Palm OS PDA (including Handspring's Visor).

How Do You Use This Book?

This book provides a solid foundation for the serious effort of preparing for the exam. To best benefit from this book, you may wish to use the following study method:

1. Take the Assessment Test on the CD to identify your weak areas.

2. Study each chapter carefully. Do your best to fully understand the information.

3. Complete all the hands-on exercises in the chapter, referring back to the text as necessary so that you understand each step you take.

To do the exercises in this book, your hardware should meet the minimum hardware requirements for SQL Server 2000. Many of the exercises use the Northwind database, which is included with SQL Server.

4. Read over the Real World Scenarios, to improve your understanding of how to use what you learn in the book.

5. Study the Exam Essentials and Key Terms to make sure you are familiar with the areas you need to focus on.

6. Answer the review questions at the end of each chapter. If you prefer to answer the questions in a timed and graded format, install the Edge Tests from the book's CD and answer the chapter questions there instead of in the book.

7. Take note of the questions you did not understand, and study the corresponding sections of the book again.

8. Go back over the Exam Essentials and Key Terms.

9. Go through the Study Guide's other training resources, which are included on the book's CD. These include electronic flashcards, the electronic version of the chapter review question (try taking them by objective), and the two bonus exams.

To learn all the material covered in this book, you will need to study regularly and with discipline. Try to set aside the same time every day to study, and select a comfortable and quiet place in which to do it. If you work hard, you will be surprised at how quickly you learn this material. Good luck!

Contacts and Resources

To find out more about Microsoft Education and Certification materials and programs, to register with Prometric or VUE, or to obtain other useful certification information and additional study resources, check the following resources:

Microsoft Training and Certification Home Page
www.microsoft.com/trainingandservices

This Web site provides information about the MCP program and exams. You can also order the latest Microsoft Roadmap to Education and Certification.

Microsoft TechNet Technical Information Network
www.microsoft.com/technet
800-344-2121

Use this Web site or phone number to contact support professionals and system administrators. Outside the United States and Canada, contact your local Microsoft subsidiary for information.

Palm Training Product Development: Land-J
www.land-j.com
407-359-2217

Land-J Technologies is a consulting and programming business currently specializing in application development for the Palm Personal Digital Assistant. Land-J developed the Palm version of the Edge Tests, which is included on the CD that accompanies this Study Guide.

Prometric
www.prometric.com
800-755-3936

Contact Prometric to register to take an MCP exam at any of more than 800 Prometric Testing Centers around the world.

Virtual University Enterprises (VUE)
www.vue.com
888-837-8616

Contact the VUE registration center to register to take an MCP exam at one of the VUE Testing Centers.

MCP Magazine Online
www.mcpmag.com

Microsoft Certified Professional Magazine is a well-respected publication that focues on Windows certification. This site hosts chats and discussion forums, and tracks news related to the MCSE program. Some of the services cost a fee, but they are well worth it.

Windows 2000 Magazine
www.windows2000mag.com

You can subscribe to this magazine or read free articles at the Web site. The study resource provides general information on Windows 2000.

Cramsession on Brainbuzz.com
cramsession.brainbuzz.com

Cramsession is an online community focusing on all IT certification programs. In addition to discussion boards and job locators, you can download one of a number of free cramsessions, which are nice supplements to any study approach you take.

Chapter

1

Database Logical Modeling

✓ **Define entities. Considerations include entity composition and normalization.**

- Specify entity attributes.
- Specify degree of normalization.

✓ **Design entity keys. Considerations include FOREIGN KEY constraints, PRIMARY KEY constraints, and UNIQUE constraints.**

- Specify attributes that uniquely identify records.
- Specify attributes that reference other entities.

✓ **Design attribute domain integrity. Considerations include CHECK constraints, data types, and nullability.**

- Specify scale and precision of allowable values for each attribute.
- Allow or prohibit NULL for each attribute.
- Specify allowable values for each attribute.

For many users, database design is a total mystery. Over the years, database management systems became easier to use and were included in office productivity tools. Databases were being created by people unaware of what a database design is. With a system like SQL Server, if the architecture of your database does not follow the rules of relational systems, you will end up with an unusable application.

In this chapter, we will discuss:

- Designing a database system
- The Entity/Relationship model
- The relational model and the normalization process
- The denormalization process

Designing a Database System

Whatever its size, the development of a database system may be split into five stages:

1. Planning and Analysis
2. Conceptual Design
3. Logical Design
4. Physical Design
5. Implementation

This chapter focuses on the first three phases of designing. Phase four is covered in Chapter 2. Phase 5 is discussed throughout the book, since it concerns the development of database objects.

The planning and analysis phase is an investigation phase, during which you are going to gather and analyze needed information. This stage is generally done with the help of users, and is crucial to the second phase.

You should involve users in the analysis phase because you do not know their job as well as they do, and because they should agree that what you are doing will work in the real world. You'll probably encounter difficulties in involving users because they may not have time nor feel concerned. Insist! Explain to them that you are working for them and that the time they invest now with you will prevent lost time later due to an inadequate application. Sometimes, people won't want to meet with you because they are intimidated; they fear to tell you that they dislike computers or fear you are going to use computer words or idioms they won't understand. Users are involved only up to the logical design; they do not need to be concerned about DBMS systems or any computer related information.

The whole process of planning and analyzing information and building a *conceptual design* can be a long and costly one. That's the reason why it's often skipped, which is a huge a mistake! You can compare these two steps to designing a house. Would you think of building your house without blueprints? That's the decision you make if you build a database without analysis and conceptual design. A deficient or even non-existent conceptual design leads to inaccurate logical design and an unusable physical one. Of course, we know the real world is not perfect. The borders between the analysis, conceptual, and logical designs are often blurred. You go from one stage to the other, back and forth. That's why several methodologies or pieces of software will derive a conceptual design from a logical one, helping you to create your logical design step by step.

It's always easier to modify the logical design than the physical one, once it has been implemented. Spend time creating your design! Check it! Make users validate it!

In fact, the conceptual and logical designs will generally be used as communication tools since they present data and functions in an understandable manner, even for the computer illiterate. The conceptual design is roughly made of two distinct models: the data model and the function model. The data model defines the data stored in the database; the function model defines the queries that will be executed on the database.

 Real World Scenario

The New Database Analysis

You are a senior database developer of a medium-size organization and are called to analyze the future vacation and sick leave application for the Human Resources department. As an employee, you probably have ideas about information needed in this kind of application. But, as you are not working for HR, you do not know all of the subtleties of their jobs. The first step is to gather all necessary information, keeping in mind that even minor facts for you could be critical for someone in HR.

You make an appointment with Gary Pinkleton, the HR Manager, to determine the information the HR employees need. Fortunately, Gary is a well-organized guy, and he also invited Joan Winslow, the Office Manager, to the meeting. Each of them prepared a document summarizing the purpose of the application and the information that is needed. Unfortunately, they dislike computers, as do many of the HR employees, and you have to take that into account. They are paper and people oriented! You thank them for the good job they've done, and explain you would like to interview some HR employees in charge of managing vacation and sick leave, just to understand the way they work now. Then you will get back to them to discuss any issues met.

After gathering information through interviews, available documents, artifacts, etc., you have to analyze it. Probably the most important thing at that stage is to keep connected to the real world, being sure the analyzed information is representative of the situation. During the analysis stage, you have to organize, prioritize, and validate information.

Once you have all the necessary, accurate, and validated information, you can create cases to show actions between users and the new system and to describe the states of the system. Being able to identify theses cases will help the conceptual and logical design because it will enhance the *relationships* between specific information.

After a couple of weeks, you meet again with Gary and Joan. You used Microsoft Visio to diagram your entity/relationship model and explain to them how you see things working. They are impressed by the simplicity of the diagram and the fact you clearly understood their need. They are reassured about the new application because you have not talked yet about computers or the way the application is to be implemented, but they can sense how it will work and see that all the necessary information is there.

Because you used what I call a user-oriented approach, they feel reassured about the new computer system and confident in the fact that the application will definitely help them do their jobs. On your side, you know that, as they participate in its design, they are partly responsible for the new system, so it will be easier to implement it in the department.

There is a classic confusion between the conceptual and the logical design. The *ER model* refers to the conceptual design stage and the *relational model* to the logical design stage. The ER model has been very popular because it is easy to derive it to create the relational model. Both models are discussed in the following sections.

The Entity/Relationship Model

Peter Chen first introduced the Entity/Relationship (ER) model in 1977. It has become very popular because an ER model is very simple to create and read, and can be used directly to create a relational model and transform its elements into database elements. The ER model translates your analyzed information into data requirements, and, as stated earlier, is used to facilitate communications between the database architect and the future users of the new system. An ER model is made of three different elements:

- *Entity*, which represents real-world concepts, such as places, objects, events, persons, orders, customers, and so on.

- *Relationship*, which represents associations between objects, such as the fact that a customer may place an order.

- *Attribute*, which describes the entity, such as the invoice date or the customer first name.

In the next pages, you'll notice there is a difference between an entity and an entity instance. An instance is an individual occurrence of an entity. In the relational world, an entity is equivalent to a table and an instance to a row.

Deriving entities, attributes, and relationships from the analysis phase may be an intricate process. What you need to do is to take every sentence of your conceptual model and transform the nouns (subjects) into the entities, the adjectives or nouns (direct objects) into the attributes, and the verbs into the relationships. Well, this may sound a little bit too easy, but in fact, that's a logical process.

Let's look at an example. The HR Manager of your company asked you to consider the following in your database (see previous design scenario sidebar):

- An employee is defined by his/her employee ID, first name, last name, hired date, and department.

- He/she applies for a vacation leave.

With these two statements, you discover two entities: Employee and Vacation Leave, plus five attributes of the Employee entity:

- ID

- First Name

- Last Name

- Hire Date

- Department

You also discover one relationship: applies for (between Employee and Vacation Leave). We do not have enough information to define what a Vacation Leave is, but that's a kind of data we'll need to gather from the HR Manager or any member of his/her team.

Let's take a closer look at how to define entities and attributes first, then how to define relationships between entities.

Defining Entities and Attributes

Microsoft ✓ *Exam* *Objective*	**Define entities. Considerations include entity composition and normalization.**
	▪ Specify entity attributes.

As stated earlier, entities define real-word concepts, and attributes describe precisely these concepts. Peter Chen defines an entity as "a thing that can be distinctly identified." There are two interesting aspects of this definition. First, he describes an entity as being a "thing." It might be better to say an entity can be a thing, a concept, an object, an event, or a person, but on the whole, it is "something." Second, he says that the entity can be distinctly identified. That may be the most important part of the concept. An item that does not have descriptive information and permits its identification is not an entity! So while analyzing a new database application, you should precisely describe and identify an item, so it has every chance to be an entity.

An attribute is a noun or an adjective that identifies or describes an entity. An attribute identifying an entity is called a *key attribute*. An attribute describing an entity is called a *non-key attribute*. For example, the employee ID is a key attribute of the employee entity. On the contrary, the employee's first name is a non-key attribute. We'll see later in this chapter that key attributes play an important role in relationships between entities.

Take the example of your address book. Each address represents a person or an organization you know—that's an instance of the entity. Each address owns different attributes: the contact's first name, last name, address, zip code, city, country, e-mail, phone number, and so on. If you have ever used Microsoft Excel to store that kind of data, you've used the spreadsheet format to create a table. An instance of the entity corresponds to one row of this table and an attribute to one of its columns. From the interview conducted during the analysis phase, you can easily define entities and attributes from all the sentences and information gathered.

Generally, the consultant or anyone in charge of the analysis of the new database creates the entity/relationship diagram representing entities and relationships. In an ER model, each entity is represented by a labeled rectangle. The label is the name of the entity, which should always be a noun. Each entity attribute is listed inside the adequate entity rectangle.

Some ER gurus do not agree on listing the attribute directly on the ER model. In fact, there are different ways to represent entities, relationships, and attributes. The diagrams presented there conform to what is found in different Microsoft publications (official curriculum, books, white papers, and so on.) It may not exactly conform to Peter Chen's ER historic representations, but it's less academic and more understandable for a majority of people.

You can use Microsoft Visio 2000 to create an entity/relationship diagram, and to derive the logical and physical models from that point. Visio 2000 manages metadata directly to automatically generate tables, relationships, triggers, indexes, and so on from the diagrams. All the diagrams in this chapter have been made with Visio 2000 using the Source ER Model template, and all the examples are taken from the Pubs or Northwind databases shipped with SQL Server 2000.

To illustrate this concept of entities and attributes, let's take a look at a part of the Northwind database, which is shipped with SQL Server 2000. While developing the Northwind database, the following have been extracted from the interview with the Purchase Manager of Northwind Traders Inc.:

- Every product is shipped by a specific supplier.

- We have the address, phone number, and fax number of every supplier. This is mandatory information because we must be able to contact them anytime.

- As far as the products are concerned, they are supplied by different suppliers, knowing that one supplier can supply many different products.

- For each product, we store its name, its price, the quantity per unit, the units on stock, and the units on order based on the reorder level, which is different for every product.

- Sometimes, we are forced to discontinue a product because it's no longer produced or we cannot sell it anymore.

From these few statements, we discover two entities: products and suppliers, each of them having different attributes. Figure 1.1 illustrates entities and their associated attributes, plus the relationship.

FIGURE 1.1 Entities/Relationship/Attributes

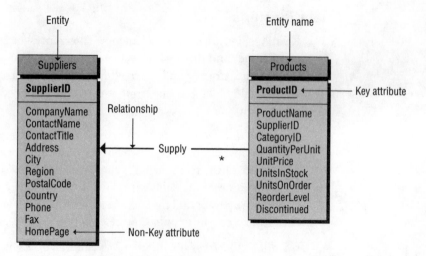

Using this kind of diagram, it becomes easy to communicate with users and have them help you validate your architectural choices. But, as you may have noticed, we find a relationship between both entities and key attributes. Let's now take a look at how we define these keys and relationships.

Defining Relationships and Keys

Microsoft ✓ *Exam* *Objective*

Design entity keys. Considerations include FOREIGN KEY constraints, PRIMARY KEY constraints, and UNIQUE constraints.

- Specify attributes that uniquely identify records.
- Specify attributes that reference other entities.

The purpose of key attributes is to uniquely identify records and to allow relationships to be created between entities. SQL Server allows you to define keys and relationships in the physical model. These elements have to be identified early in the logical modeling process.

Relationships

Relationships are complex elements. They represent associations between entities and bind them with a set of defined rules. As stated earlier, relationships are generally derived from verbs or verb phrases in the conceptual model, but that's only the first step. Relationships carry three other main characteristics:

Direction indicates the source entity. For instance, a customer places an order, so the relationship goes from the customer entity to the order entity. The source of the relationship is often referred to as the parent entity and the destination as the child entity. In the preceding example, the customer entity is the parent and the order entity is the child. A relationship always goes from a parent to one or more children.

Cardinality defines the number of instances of a specific entity that could be associated with an instance(s) of another entity. For example, an employee can apply for one or more vacation leaves. An employee may apply for the first time (one); an older employee may have applied many times (many).

Existence determines the precedence between entities. That is, the entity that must exist before another entity is created. It may be optional or mandatory. For example, the relationship between a vacation leave and an employee is optional: the employee may apply for a vacation leave. But, the relationship between an employee and a department is mandatory: each employee belongs to one department.

A relationship is represented by a line between both entities. The type of line differs depending on the used methodology, the software, your university teacher, the country you live in, the weather. To be honest, there are as many notations as database experts. Let's take three illustrated examples.

Figure 1.2 shows an arrow that indicates the direction of the relationships, labeled with its name and the cardinality on both sides.

FIGURE 1.2   A relationship represented by a direction arrow

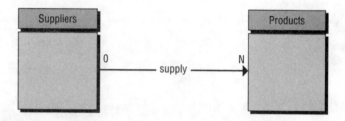

In this association, a supplier may supply many products, which is represented by the "supply" relationship. The character 0 (zero) on the supplier's side indicates that a supplier can exist without related products. The character N (many) on the products side indicates that a supplier may supply many products. The direction of the arrow is natural and goes from one to many.

Figure 1.3 (used by default by Visio 2000) says that the line should be an arrow, with the arrowhead indicating the parent entity (the opposite of the "natural" direction), labeled with its name and cardinality on the child side.

FIGURE 1.3   A default Visio 2000 relationship

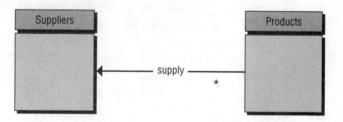

In Figure 1.3, the "supply" relationship represents the same association as the preceding figure. The arrowhead indicates the parent entity, which is the source of the relationship. In fact, you should not see an arrowhead

but a starting point enlarging like a megaphone. The smallest side of the arrowhead indicates the "one" side, while the largest side indicates the "many" side. The asterisk character (*) on the "many" side indicates the cardinality.

In Figure 1.4 (using crow's feet) the vertical bar on the line indicates the "one" side of the relationship and a crow's foot indicates the "many" side. The zero sign on the line indicates this is a one-to-zero-or-many relationship.

The different types of relationships are discussed later in this chapter.

FIGURE 1.4 A relationship using a crow's foot

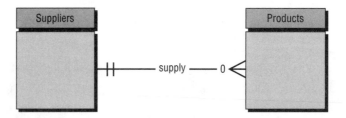

In Figure 1.4, the "supply" relationship is always the same. The double vertical bar indicates the parent side. The first vertical bar next to the Suppliers entity indicates that a supplier must exist for every product (mandatory). The second vertical bar (representing a 1) indicates that one supplier (at most) must exist for every product. The crow's foot next to the Products entity (representing many) indicates the child side. The 0 sign before the crow's foot indicates that it is a one-to-zero-or-many relationship, meaning a supplier can be associated to zero, one, or many products.

On the physical side, SQL Server 2000 offers a diagram functionality that uses different notations. Figure 1.5 shows you the physical implementation of the above example.

FIGURE 1.5   SQL Server 2000 one-to-many relationship

As you can see, the relationship direction is illustrated by a key on the "one" side and an infinity sign (∞) on the "many" side. In the case of a *one-to-one relationship*, the key sign is on both sides, like in Figure 1.6.

FIGURE 1.6   SQL Server 2000 one-to-one relationship

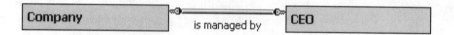

In the above examples, you probably see that direction and existence are quite straightforward characteristics, which can be discovered easily. Cardinality is a little more complex, due to the different types of relationships: one-to-one, one-to-many, and many-to-many.

One-to-One Relationship

A one-to-one relationship (Figure 1.7) occurs when one instance of the parent entity is associated to one (at most) instance of the child entity. For instance, every company has only one CEO, and a CEO cannot be CEO of two different companies. It exists as a one-to-one relationship between the company entity and the CEO entity. In such a relationship, the direction is from the independent entity (the company) to the dependent entity (the CEO).

FIGURE 1.7   A one-to-one relationship

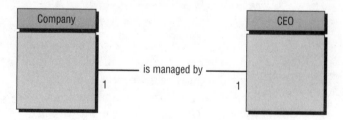

You may wonder what the use is of a one-to-one relationship. In this example, if there is only one CEO per company, why not create only one entity comprising all the necessary attributes? That is definitely the answer that can be given in a majority of cases. But you may decide to logically split information to keep entities small and manageable. This kind of relationship exists to take into account that some decisions are human and not only mathematical.

One-to-Many Relationship

A *one-to-many relationship* (the most frequently used relationship) occurs when one instance of the parent is associated to zero, one, or many instances of the child entity. For instance, a customer may place many orders. In this case, there is a one-to-many relationship between the customer entity and the order entity. The direction of a one-to-many relationship is always from the "one" side entity to the "many" side entity. Figure 1.8 shows a one-to-many relationship.

FIGURE 1.8   A one-to-many relationship

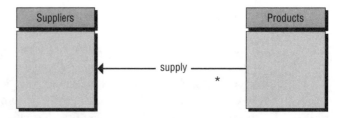

Figure 1.8 is equivalent to Figure 1.3. The asterisk represents the "many" side. In this example, each supplier supplies zero or many products.

Many-to-Many Relationship

A *many-to-many relationship* (Figure 1.9) occurs when one instance of the parent is associated with zero, one, or many instances of the child entity and when one instance of the child entity is associated with zero, one, or many instances of the parent entity. Even if the description may sound intricate, it's quite a common situation. Consider when a customer places an order. He/she can order many products and those products can be on many orders. So, the relationship between the Orders entity and the Products entity is a many-to-many relationship. Many-to-many relationships cannot be directly implemented in a relational database, but must be transformed into at least two one-to-many relationships, as we are going to see in the next sections. In a many-to-many relationship, the direction is arbitrary.

FIGURE 1.9   A many-to-many relationship

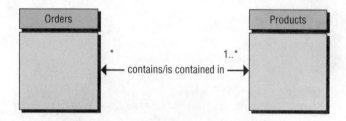

Figure 1.9 shows a many-to-many relationship because an order contains one or many products and a product can be contained in zero, one, or many orders. That kind of relationship has to be resolved by inserting an entity called an association entity. Figure 1.10 shows a solution to our many-to-many relationship.

FIGURE 1.10   A resolved many-to-many relationship

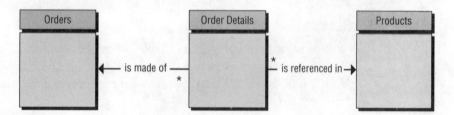

By introducing the Order Details entity, we transform the many-to-many relationship into two one-to-many relationships. The new diagram shows that every order is made of one or many order details, and that each product may be referenced by zero, one, or many order details. As you can see, the original cardinality and existence are conserved by the new entity and relationships. A majority of many-to-many relationships are resolved that way.

Recursive Relationship

A recursive relationship is an epiphenomenon of a one-to-one or one-to-many relationship. A relationship is recursive when the source entity and the destination entity are the same. For example, every employee reports to his/her manager. But the manager is an employee, too. A recursive relationship is illustrated in Figure 1.11.

FIGURE 1.11   A recursive relationship

The previous figure shows that every employee reports to zero, one, or many employees. This kind of relationship is very easy to handle, since it is totally compatible with the relation model and SQL Server 2000.

Keys

Key attributes play a "key" role in relationships and in the relational model. There are two major types of keys: primary and foreign. Let's take a look at what these keys are, what they are used for, and how they are chosen.

Primary Key

The *primary key* is an attribute or a set of attributes identifying unique instances of each entity. For example, the social security number identifies every citizen of a country, or the invoice number identifies every invoice created by a specific company. An entity may have multiple attributes or sets of attributes that identify unique instances of each entity. Each of these attributes or sets of attributes is called a *candidate key*. While an entity can have more that one candidate key, it has only one primary key. The other candidate keys are called *alternate keys*.

If a key is made of multiple attributes, it is said to be composite.

Besides the fact of being an attribute or a set of attributes, a primary key must have the following properties to uniquely identify every instance:

- Every attribute must have a value. That means that no attribute composing the key can be NULL.

- The value of the key must be unique for every instance of the entity. If the key is composite, every group of attribute values has to be unique.

Some experts and gurus say that a primary key cannot be changed. In fact, even if it is not a good practice to permit the modification of a primary key, SQL Server 2000 permits it by default. You can forbid it by using triggers or stored procedure, as we'll discover in the following pages.

The choice of the primary key may be complex and tricky, when no obvious choice is possible or when multiple choices are possible. Let's look at two examples: an employee and a customer. An employee can be identified by different attributes: the combination of his/her first name and last name, his/her employee ID, or his/her social security number. In a small company, the combination of the first and last names could be a good choice, but in a medium or large company with thousands of employees this combination may not be unique. The social security number is a perfect choice for every company because every employee has one prior to his/her hiring. Now, the SSN may not be an identified or a necessary attribute, so having an employee ID automatically attributed by the system could be a good choice. Both attributes are candidate keys.

The customer can be identified by his/her ID or the combination of his/her name, address, and ZIP code, or you can create an increment ID to automatically identify the customer. The ID is not always known at record creation time, and the combination of name, address, and ZIP code creates quite a large key (that is containing too many attributes and too many characters). The last choice is sometimes called an *artificial key* because it has no real meaning to the entity, except being a unique identifier. The need for an artificial key arises when no attributes are really suitable or when the candidate keys seem too large.

SQL Server 2000 addresses the problem of artificial keys with identity property and `UNIQUEIDENTIFIER` datatypes. Read more about this in Chapter 3: Creating and Maintaining Tables.

In general, the primary key is identified in the ER by underlining the name of the attributes that compose the key and optionally listing it at the beginning of the attributes list (if other attributes are listed, of course). As you can see, Figure 1.12 is Figure 1.10 with the primary keys.

FIGURE 1.12 Defining the primary keys

Note that the primary key of the associate entity (Order Details) is a composite key made of the primary keys of both parent entities. This is generally the case in this many-to-many relationship situation, though the primary key could be an artificial key, such as a counter.

SQL Server 2000 proposes to create a primary key through the primary key constraint, enforcing the non-NULL and unique properties of such a key. The creation of a primary key in SQL Server 2000 automatically creates an index. The physical creation of a primary key is discussed in Chapter 4: Implementing Data Integrity.

Primary keys are often noted as "PK" in diagrams. In SQL Server 2000, they are defined with a small yellow key. Every entity should have a primary key. As we see in a following section, this is a basic requirement for the first normal form.

Besides the primary key, the alternate keys can also be identified in the ER diagram and the relational model. An alternate key is a candidate key, so it may share the primary key characteristics: not NULL and uniqueness.

The alternate keys may be enforced in SQL Server 2000 using the unique constraints or unique indexes. The physical creation of a unique constraint is discussed in Chapter 4: Implementing Data Integrity, and the unique indexes are discussed in Chapter 5: Creating and Maintaining Indexes.

Besides the identifying entity instances, the primary key and eventually the alternate keys are used to define relationship source, linked to foreign keys.

Foreign Key

A *foreign key* is an attribute or a set of attributes that identifies the child side of a relationship. A foreign key is in fact the "migrating" primary key (or alternate key) of the parent entity. For example, if a customer entity is identified by a customer ID attribute, that customer ID attribute will be found in the order entity, since a relationship exists between customer and order. In Figure 1.13, the Orders entity is associated by one-to-many relationships with three different entities.

FIGURE 1.13 Primary and foreign keys

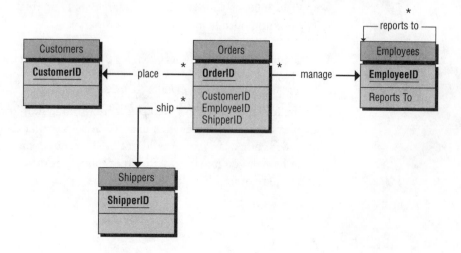

The three non-key attributes of the Orders entity are "migrated" primary keys of the other entities. As you can see, discovering a foreign key is a straightforward process, once you know every primary key and every relationship.

A foreign key is linked to a primary or alternate key. In SQL Server 2000, a relationship is created through declarative integrity, with what is called a constraint. A relationship is created by declaring a foreign key constraint referencing either a primary key constraint or a unique constraint (alternate key) as the source.

To finish with relationships and foreign keys, the last notion is that of the "identifying relationship." This is particularly useful if you use an ER design software like Visio 2000. A relationship is said to be identifying if the primary key of a child entity contains all the attributes of a foreign key. If the primary key of the child entity does not contain all the attributes of a foreign key, then the relationship is non-identifying.

In Visio 2000, as soon as you create an identifying relationship, the foreign key is automatically included in the primary key.

Figure 1.14 shows you an extract of the Entity/Relationship diagram of the Northwind database.

You may be used to more complicated or more complete diagrams due to the fact that only keys are listed here. Adding non-key attributes is a subject of discussion between experts. Some say that they should be included, other say they should not be. Depending on the complexity of your model, you may create different models or different levels allowing the display of non-key attributes.

FIGURE 1.14 An extract of the ER model of the Northwind database

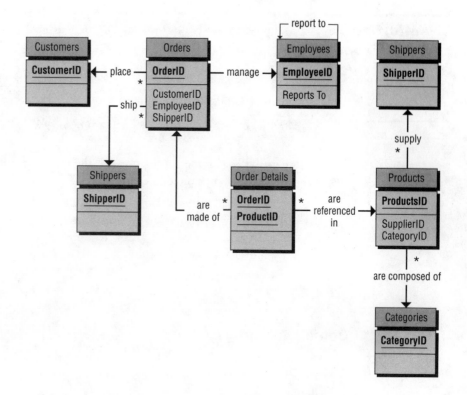

Visio 2000 and SQL Server 2000 let you customize the display of your ER model so that you can declare every attribute but display only the ones necessary to your analysis.

Before switching to the relational model of our database, let's spend some time with integrity. Integrity rules are essential to a database system, assuring that your data is correct and consistent.

Adding Data Integrity Rules

Microsoft ✓ *Exam* *Objective*	**Design attribute domain integrity. Considerations include CHECK constraints, data types, and nullability.** ▪ Specify scale and precision of allowable values for each attribute. ▪ Allow or prohibit NULL for each attribute. ▪ Specify allowable values for each attribute.

Integrity is one of the cornerstones of the relational model and has been over the years incorporated in every RDBMS (Relational Database Management System) on the market. There are four types of integrity:

- Domain integrity

- Entity integrity

- Referential integrity

- Enterprise integrity

Domain Integrity

A *domain* defines the possible values of an attribute. Domain integrity rules govern these values. In a database system, the *domain integrity* is defined by:

- The datatype and the length

- The NULL value acceptance

- The allowable values, through techniques like check constraints or rules

- The default value

For example, if you define that the attribute Age, of an Employee entity, is an integer, the value of every instance of that attribute must be numeric and an integer. If you define this attribute as always positive, then a negative value is forbidden. The value of this attribute being mandatory indicates that the attribute can be NULL. All these characteristics form the domain integrity of this attribute.

Datatypes in a database system can be numerous. Over the years, the storage need pushed RDBMS developers to introduce complex datatypes to handle any case. Generally, datatypes can be divided into four types of attributes:

Character *Character attributes* may have a fixed or a variable length, but the maximum length is precisely defined. For example, a ZIP code may be an attribute of five-character length.

Numeric *Numeric attributes* can be integers of different lengths, or they can be real figures. In a computer, a numeric attribute can be two types of real figures: *floating point* and *fixed point*. For a floating point, the number of decimals is not known and the figure can be rounded to any decimal. For a fixed point, the architect defines the scale, which is the maximum number of decimals, and the precision, which is the maximum number of digits of the number. With these "precise" real figures, no rounding errors can occur. They are very useful for storing money values (for example, storing in the same entity values in dollars, Euros, and yen, up to the fourth decimal) or a precise decimal value.

Note that SQL Server 2000 proposes two "precise" real figures: numeric and decimal. Before SQL Server 7, their internal implementation was a little bit different. Since SQL Server 7, numeric and decimal figures are synonyms.

Special *Special attributes* are, for example, datatypes like Boolean (true or false), GUID (Globally Unique Identifier), or Variant. They may be very useful for minimizing consumed space or providing special features.

We cover these special datatypes in detail in Chapter 3: Creating and Maintaining Tables.

Binary *Binary attributes* can be anything besides character, numeric, and special types, such as a photograph, a sound, a file, a movie, and a binary string. These attributes are stored in the database in their binary format, without any modification. The RDBMS does not know what these binary data are, but knows they are a flow of binary digits.

The datatypes depend precisely on the RDBMS that you are going to use. But you can define in the conceptual model the global datatypes of every attribute, allowing you to define the domain integrity. For example, an attribute value can be implemented as one character allowing two values, Y and N, as a tiny integer allowing only 0 and 1, or as a bit, depending on the available features of your system. But you can define in the conceptual and logical model phases that this attribute has to be Boolean.

Entity Integrity

The *entity integrity* states that every instance of an entity has to be uniquely identified. The existence of the primary key is the core of the entity integrity. If you defined a primary key for each entity, they follow the entity integrity rule.

Referential Integrity

The *referential integrity* rules are enforced by the relationships between entities. As a starting point, the referential integrity rules state that a child instance cannot exist if there is no corresponding parent instance. For example, an order cannot exist without a matching customer, or an order detail cannot exist without the associated order.

Generally, referential integrity is defined by the following:

- You cannot delete a parent instance if one or many associated child instances exist.

- You cannot insert a child instance if the associated parent instance does not exist.

In other words: orphanage is impossible! Unfortunately, in the real world, orphans exist. Referential integrity defines rules to manage orphanage:

- Insert a child instance rule.

- Delete a child instance rule.

- Update a primary key rule.

Insert Rules

The insert rules include the following:

Dependent   A child instance can be inserted only if a matching parent instance exists. This is generally the default rule.

Default   A child instance can always be inserted. If no matching parent exists, then the foreign key is set to the default value or to NULL.

Automatic   A child instance can always be inserted. If no matching parent exists, then one is created automatically.

No Effect   A child instance can always be inserted, even if no matching parent exists. This situation leads to no referential integrity and to data inconsistency!

Customized   A child instance can only be inserted if specific constraints are met. Depending on the existence of the matching parent instance, the custom function will follow the Dependent, the Default, the Automatic, or the No Effect rule.

Delete Rules

Delete rules include the following:

Restrict   A parent instance can be deleted if and only if no matching child instance exists. This is generally the default.

Cascade   The deletion of a parent instance triggers automatically the deletion of all matching child instances.

Default   The deletion of a parent instance triggers the update of the foreign key of all matching child instances to a default or a NULL value.

No Effect   A parent instance can always be deleted, regardless of the existence of child instances. This situation leads to no referential integrity and to data inconsistency!

Customized   A parent instance can only be deleted if specific constraints are met. Depending on the existence of the matching child instance(s), the custom function will follow the Cascade, the Default, or the No Effect rule.

Update Rules

Update rules include the following:

Restrict   A parent instance's primary key cannot be updated if at least one child instance exists. This is generally the default rule.

Cascade   The update of a parent instance's primary key triggers automatically the update of the foreign key of all matching child instances to the new value of the primary key.

Default   The update of a parent instance's primary key triggers the update of the foreign key of all matching child instances to a default or a NULL value.

No Effect   A parent instance's primary key can always be updated, regardless of the existence of child instances. This situation leads to no referential integrity and to data inconsistency!

Customized   A parent instance's primary key can only be updated if specific constraints are met. Depending on the existence of the matching child instance(s), the custom function will follow the Cascade, the Default, or the No Effect rule.

In SQL Server 2000, only the Dependent insert rule, the Restrict or Cascade delete rules, and the Restrict or Cascade update rules can be enforced with foreign key and reference constraints.

 Real World Scenario

Operation Order Issue

As a SQL Server freelance expert, you are called to design the new customer relationship management system of Golf Line Inc., a small company selling golf accessories through direct selling and the Internet. Martha Jarvis, the CEO, wants to know the company's customers better. The golf players generally spend a lot of money on golf accessories, and she wants to be able to know who these people are, what they like and dislike, how much they spend every year, and so on.

You first meet Jon Albert, the in-house IT guy, who explains the different existing systems. The invoicing database is an old Access application, that slows down every day. So, you'll need to incorporate invoicing facilities into the new system. The product database is managed by SQL Server. Every week, the in-house product manager receives new products from different suppliers, and decides with

Martha which products to add to their catalog and those to take out. You'll need to use that product database in coordination with the new application.

After a quick meeting with Martha and Jon, you are hired to design and implement the new system. While designing it, you face classical problems of relationship rules. The first one deals with the Customer/Order relationship. You cannot create an order if matching customers does not exist, and you cannot delete a customer with matching orders.

You think about the Insert order situation. While entering a new order in the system, what happens if the customer does not exist? Sure, the front-end application will force the user to choose the customer first, but that situation could happen during batch inserts. So, the order is entered first and then the customer. If you decide to enforce the Dependant insert rule, the order cannot be inserted. With the Automatic insert rule, a new customer is automatically inserted, allowing the order to be inserted. The last operation is the update of this new customer.

Concerning the delete order, the problem may be a little more complex. Martha told you she wanted to mail people who have not ordered during the last six months, to be able to offer them special discounts and promotions. But at the same time, she told you to get rid of customers who have not been ordering for more than two years. She wants to keep a live database. The problem is simple: if you delete these customers, there will be inaccuracy in the orders, since the customer ID of these customers do not exist anymore. The Restrict delete rule does not work. If you implement the Cascade delete rule, you are going to lose every order the customers placed and paid. So you decide to implement a Customized delete rule: each time a customer is "deleted" for aging reasons, it is moved to an archive table, and the order is not impacted. This solution gives you the advantage of keeping a table of live customers and keeping all the information about the orders.

We all know that there are as many possible solutions to a problem as there are the number of people you are asking for a solution. These rules are there to meet all these possible solutions. Depending on your knowledge of the skills of the architect, on the complexity of your solution, and on the software you are using, you'll choose whatever solution suits you.

Enterprise Integrity

The last type of integrity is *enterprise integrity*, also called *business rules*. These rules, generally implemented through programmatic methods, like stored procedures or triggers on the database server side, define the way the company works. For example, you can state that a customer cannot place a new order if he still owes more than $10,000, or that an order greater than $200,000 has to be approved by the sales manager before being shipped. Enterprise integrity is generally not defined in the data model, but rather in the function model.

The Relational Model and the Normalization Process

Microsoft ✔ *Exam* *Objective*	**Define entities. Considerations include entity composition and normalization.** • Specify degree of normalization.

So far, we have discussed the conceptual model of our database, creating the ER model, entities, relationships, attributes, and attribute properties. It is now time to skip to the logical model, creating what is called the *relational model*. The relational model was first introduced by E.F. Codd in 1970, while he was a researcher at IBM. At that time, this model was revolutionary in the database world. In the relational model, two-dimensional tables represent data. Each table refers directly to an event, a person, and an object, like the entities we were talking about in the previous pages. In this model, a database is a collection of tables.

The organization of these tables is called the *logical model*, or logical view. The *physical model*, or physical view, is the real way data are stored in the database system that may differ from one software to another.

The physical model will be discussed in Chapter 2: Database Physical Modeling.

Going from the ER model to the relational model is very easy, since the first step is only a name change. Table 1.1 gives you the main differences between the main database elements, depending on the model or the formal names.

TABLE 1.1   Name Differences of Database Elements

ER Model	Relational Model	Formal Name	Physical Model
Entity	Table	Relation	Table
Entity Instance	Row	Tuple	Record
Attribute	Column	Attribute	Field

No real formal representation of the logical model exists, except the one proposed by the ER model. So, you just transform entities in a table and attributes in a column, and the diagram remains the same. Let's first take a look at the definition of the relational table.

The Relational Table

A *relational table* matches an ER entity. It defines the logical representation of the data and follows six rules:

Every column is atomic.   This is definitely one important rule as far as relational tables are concerned. Being atomic means that a column contains only one value that cannot be broken into smaller pieces.

Atomicity examples are included in the section "First Normal Form" below.

Each column has a unique name.   Each column matches an attribute, and must have a unique name within a table. Two different columns belonging to two different tables can have the same name.

Every value of a specific column is the same type.   For the relational model, this rule means that every value of a column belongs to the same domain, and respects the domain integrity rule.

There are no duplicate rows.   Each row is identified by a primary key, assuring its uniqueness. This rule states that every row can be accessed just by knowing its primary key.

The rows are unordered.   The physical order of rows is meaningless. This property guarantees that the rows can be sorted in different ways, depending on what you need.

The columns are unordered.   As with the rows, column order is meaningless. This property guarantees you can query the column of a table in the order you wish.

SQL Server 2000, like many other RDBMS, allows you to create tables without primary keys and with non-atomic columns. You can drive your car at 120 MPH downtown, but is it really a good idea? Concerning computer theory, I do not know a lot of things that have lasted more than 30 years, like the relational model. Therefore, it must be a good theory to still be the basis for RDBMS.

As you see, moving from the ER model to the relational model is straightforward if you just follow the previous rules. Nevertheless, while building our logical design, we did not really care about rows. If we start thinking about what happens when we "insert" data into the model, we may discover that we have duplicates, or information redundancy, which is information existing in more than one occurrence. That's where the *normalization* process arrives. Normalizing data is the process of eliminating duplicated data by defining keys and creating new relationships and new entities.

Like ER modeling, the normalization process is mathematical and quite natural. A lot of database architects normalize their data without knowing the formal rules. Once you know them, you may find this process quite complex, but in fact, it's straightforward if you use real-world data.

Each step of the normalization process starts with your logical model and ends with a new, normalized model. Each of these models has a name: First Normal Form, Second Normal Form, and so on. The model can include up to five normal forms (and even six if we consider the Boyce-Codd Normal Form), but it's been a common practice to stop at the Third Normal Form. In addition, the Microsoft Exam does not address normal forms beyond the third. In the following section, we will explain in detail how to get from a non-normalized model to the Third Normal Form and give you hints about the other three forms.

Normal Forms

Normal form theory is based on functional dependency between columns. Column A is said to be functionally dependent on column B if each value of B is associated with only one value of A. For example, an employee's last name is functionally dependent on the employee's ID. Knowing an ID, you are guaranteed to know the employee's last name. In a relational table, every column must be dependent on the primary key. As you will see, this rule governs the normal forms.

Another concept is the *full functional dependency*. This concerns composite keys. Column A is said to be fully functionally dependent on B (B being a composite key) if A is functionally dependent on B and not on any subset of B. In other words, the whole primary key is necessary to accurately identify column A's value. If this value can be identified accurately with only a few columns from the primary key, then A is not fully functionally dependent on the primary key.

Functional dependencies may be represented with the following notation:

B → A

This means A is functionally dependent on B, or knowing a value of B you know the matching value of A.

If A is functionally dependent on B, we also say that A is a *determinant* of B.

The goal of normal forms is to remove redundant data from relational tables by splitting the tables into smaller tables, without losing any data. It is necessary that the decomposition is lossless. That means that you can easily come back to the base table by combining the new created tables with a join.

First Normal Form

A relational table is in First Normal Form (1NF) if:

- It has a primary key.

- Each column is atomic.

- There is no repeating group of columns.

As you can see, the rules have nothing to do with redundancy, but almost follow some of the rules of relational tables. In fact, a table is said to be relational if it is in 1NF.

You should now understand the principle of the primary. So, let's have a quick look at atomicity of columns. Imagine we create a table listing authors and the books they have written. This is shown in Figure 1.15.

FIGURE 1.15   Non-atomic column

au_id	Titles
▶ 172-32-1176	Prolonged Data Deprivation: Four Case Studies
213-46-8915	The Busy Executive's Database Guide; You Can Combat Computer Stress!
238-95-7766	But Is It User Friendly?
267-41-2394	Cooking with Computers: Surreptitious Balance Sheets; Sushi, Anyone?
274-80-9391	Straight Talk About Computers
341-22-1782	<NULL>
409-56-7008	The Busy Executive's Database Guide
427-17-2319	Secrets of Silicon Valley
472-27-2349	Sushi, Anyone?
✱	

The Titles column can contain multiple values. For example, author 213-46-8915 wrote two books. He co-authored one of them with author 409-56-7008 (The Busy Executive's Database Guide). It may become very difficult to query such a table and find information about a specific book. The first solution that comes to mind is to split the Titles column into two columns, as shown in Figure 1.16.

FIGURE 1.16 Repeating group of columns

au_id	Title1	Title2
172-32-1176	Prolonged Data Deprivation: Four Case Studies	<NULL>
213-46-8915	The Busy Executive's Database Guide	You Can Combat Computer Stress!
238-95-7766	But Is It User Friendly?	<NULL>
267-41-2394	Cooking with Computers: Surreptitious Balance Sheets	Sushi, Anyone?
274-80-9391	Straight Talk About Computers	<NULL>
341-22-1782	<NULL>	<NULL>
409-56-7008	The Busy Executive's Database Guide	<NULL>
427-17-2319	Secrets of Silicon Valley	<NULL>
472-27-2349	Sushi, Anyone?	<NULL>

The solution addresses the issue of atomicity, but does not solve the query problem. It may be difficult, for example, to find if a specific title has been written by one or many authors, or to know the number of co-authors of one title. Worse, what if an author writes a third title? Where are you going to store it? Well, you could create a third Title column. But the problem would occur for the fourth, the fifth, and so on. Furthermore, even if you create 20 Title columns, it would be a waste of space for authors who only wrote one or two books.

If you want to put this table in 1NF, you could introduce a new column, title_id, identifying each book, and create a composite primary key (Figure 1.17).

FIGURE 1.17 Table in 1NF

au_id	title_id	Title
172-32-1176	PS3333	Prolonged Data Deprivation: Four Case Studies
213-46-8915	BU1032	The Busy Executive's Database Guide
213-46-8915	BU2075	You Can Combat Computer Stress!
238-95-7766	PC1035	But Is It User Friendly?
267-41-2394	BU1111	Cooking with Computers: Surreptitious Balance Sheets
267-41-2394	TC7777	Sushi, Anyone?
274-80-9391	BU7832	Straight Talk About Computers
409-56-7008	BU1032	The Busy Executive's Database Guide
427-17-2319	PC8888	Secrets of Silicon Valley
472-27-2349	TC7777	Sushi, Anyone?

Now our table is in First Normal Form, since a primary key identifies every row, and every column is atomic. The problems we talked about are now solved: an author can write as many books he wishes, and it's simple to group the table by title to list every co-author.

Let's use a more complex table to uncover problems that could arise with a table in 1NF. The table in Figure 1.18 illustrates the entity described by the following:

- An author writes one or many books.

- Books are published by one publisher only.

- Books may be written by many authors, the royalties being shared amongst co-authors.

- Each publisher's head office is in a particular city.

- Every publisher may publish one or more books.

FIGURE 1.18 Royalties Table in First Normal Form

au_id	title_id	royaltyper	pub_name	city
172-32-1176	PS3333	100	New Moon Books	Boston
213-46-8915	BU1032	40	Algodata Infosystems	Berkeley
213-46-8915	BU2075	100	New Moon Books	Boston
238-95-7766	PC1035	100	Algodata Infosystems	Berkeley
267-41-2394	BU1111	40	Algodata Infosystems	Berkeley
267-41-2394	TC7777	30	Binnet & Hardley	Washington
274-80-9391	BU7832	100	Algodata Infosystems	Berkeley
409-56-7008	BU1032	60	Algodata Infosystems	Berkeley
427-17-2319	PC8888	50	Algodata Infosystems	Berkeley
472-27-2349	TC7777	30	Binnet & Hardley	Washington

The Royalties relational table, shown in Figure 1.18, is already in First Normal Form. Nevertheless, it contains redundant data. For example, the publisher_id or the title is repeated. Redundancy may cause anomalies during data insertion, deletion, or update. For example:

- You cannot insert a new publisher until it has published at least one book.

- If you delete a row, you are deleting information about an author and a book, and you lose information about the publisher.

- If you update the city of a publisher, you have to update every row of the author who has been published by this publisher.

We have to decompose this table to achieve Second Normal Form.

Second Normal Form

A relational table is in Second Normal Form (2NF) if:

- It is in 1NF.

- Every non-key column is fully functionally dependent on the primary key.

In Figure 1.18, the Royalties table is in 1NF but not in 2NF because the columns title and publisher_id depend only on the title_id and not on the key (au_id, title_id). You can easily establish this fact if you study the functional dependencies of the table:

(au_id, title_id)$\rightarrow$ royaltyper

title_id$\rightarrow$ pub_name, city

pub_name$\rightarrow$ city

So, two non-key columns are not fully functionally dependent on the primary key. That is, they do not depend on the entire primary key, but only on one of its subsets. Decomposing a table in 1NF to achieve 2NF is a logical process:

1. Identify all the determinant parts of the primary key and their dependant columns.

2. Create a new table from every determinant and their dependant columns.

3. The determinant becomes the primary key of the new table.

4. Delete the dependant columns from the source table. Do not delete the determinant, since it will become the foreign key.

You may rename the source table if you wish to keep meaningful information. To transform the Royalties table to 2NF, we create a new table, named Titles, with the columns title_id, pub_name, and city. Title_id becomes the primary key of this new table (Figure 1.19).

FIGURE 1.19   The new Titles and Royalties tables in Second Normal Form

title_id	pub_name	city
BU1032	Algodata Infosystems	Berkeley
BU1111	Algodata Infosystems	Berkeley
BU2075	New Moon Books	Boston
BU7832	Algodata Infosystems	Berkeley
PC1035	Algodata Infosystems	Berkeley
PC8888	Algodata Infosystems	Berkeley
PS3333	New Moon Books	Boston
TC7777	Binnet & Hardley	Washington

au_id	title_id	royaltyper
267-41-2394	TC7777	30
472-27-2349	TC7777	30
213-46-8915	BU1032	40
267-41-2394	BU1111	40
427-17-2319	PC8888	50
409-56-7008	BU1032	60
172-32-1176	PS3333	100
213-46-8915	BU2075	100
238-95-7766	PC1035	100
274-80-9391	BU7832	100

Though the tables are in 2NF, update anomalies can still occur. For example:

- You cannot insert a new publisher if you do not know the title_id of at least one of the books published.

- If you delete a row in the Titles table, you lose the information about the publisher at the same time. A publisher may disappear if you delete its last published book referenced in the table.

To avoid these anomalies, the Titles table should be decomposed to achieve the Third Normal Form.

Third Normal Form

A relational table is in Third Normal Form (3NF) if:

- It is in 2NF.

- Every non-key column is functionally dependent only on the primary key. In other words, a non-key column cannot be dependent on another non-key column.

In our example, the Royalties table is already in 3NF because the column royaltyper depends on both columns of the primary key: the royalty percentage attributed to an author depends on the author and on the book. Conversely, the table Titles is in 2NF but not in 3NF because the city column may be determined both by the publisher name (pub_name) and by the primary key. The functional dependencies of the table show this straightforward situation:

title_id→ pub_name

title_id→ city

pub_name→ city

The dependency between title_id and city is called *transitive dependency*. If title_id→ pub_name and pub_name→ city, then title_id→ city.

This relation table is nonetheless in 2NF because city is functionally dependent on the primary key. A table can be decomposed to achieve 3NF by doing the following:

1. Identify all the determinants amongst non-key columns and their dependent columns.

2. Create a new table from every determinant identified and their dependent columns. The determinant becomes the primary key of the new table.

3. Delete the dependent columns from the source table. Do not delete the determinant, since it will become the foreign key.

To achieve Third Normal Form in our example, we create a third table, called Publishers, containing pub_name and city, with pub_name becoming its primary key and deleting city from the Titles table (Figure 1.20).

FIGURE 1.20 Publishers and Titles tables in Third Normal Form

title_id	pub_name
BU1032	Algodata Infosystems
BU1111	Algodata Infosystems
BU2075	New Moon Books
BU7832	Algodata Infosystems
PC1035	Algodata Infosystems
PC8888	Algodata Infosystems
PS3333	New Moon Books
TC7777	Binnet & Hardley

pub_name	city
Algodata Infosystems	Berkeley
Binnet & Hardley	Washington
New Moon Books	Boston

Once in Third Normal Form, all the anomalies we encountered so far disappear:

- You can insert a new publisher even if it has not published a book.

- If you delete a royalty, you are not losing information about the publisher.

- The city of a publisher has to be updated in only one place.

- You may delete a row in the Titles table without simultaneously losing the information about the publisher.

The normalized logical model of our database is illustrated in Figure 1.21. It contains the three tables with the relationships and the keys.

FIGURE 1.21 The normalized logical model

3NF has many advantages. Amongst them, we find:

- Better data consistency.

- Data space is saved, because data occurs only once.

- Fewer anomalies.

In 99.99 percent of cases, 3NF is enough. Having achieved 3NF, you may have achieved higher normalization. Nevertheless, after E.F. Codd defined the first three normal forms, some gurus found issues in it. So, higher normal forms have been introduced. Let's have a very quick look at these higher forms.

Advanced Normalization

The database community generally accepts three other levels of normal forms. These levels concern tables containing at least three columns that are all keys. These normal forms are the following:

Boyce/Codd Normal Form   Boyce/Codd Normal Form (BCNF) is a more precise version of the 3NF. It concerns a table that contains many composite overlapping candidate keys and is based on the concept of determinants. A relational table is in BCNF if and only if every determinant is a candidate key.

Review the definition of determinant and candidate key in the previous pages.

Fourth Normal Form   Fourth Normal Form (4NF) is based on the concept of multivalued dependency (MVD). A MVD can occur in a table containing at least three columns. If one column has multiple rows whose values are matching another column value of a single row, then there is a MVD. A table is in 4NF if it is in BCNF and if every MVD is also functionally dependent.

MVD is noted as ->>. A->>B means A multidetermines B. Given a table with three columns—A, B, and C—if a set of B values matching a pair of A and C values depends only on the A value and not on the C value, then A->>B.

Fifth Normal Form   Fifth Normal Form (5NF) is based on the concept of join dependencies. Join dependency means that if a table is being decomposed into three or more tables, it can be joined again to retain its original state. A table is said to be in 5NF if it cannot be decomposed into smaller tables without the loss of data. In other words, if you add a row to a table that is not in 5NF, and if you decompose this table into smaller tables and join these tables again, the result you obtain contains spurious data.

If you are interested in going further than 5NF, I recommend that you read *An Introduction to Database Systems*, by Chris Date (Addison Wesley, 7th Edition, 1999). It's a little bit academic, but one of the best books on database theory.

You may have thrown your book away after reading the definitions of these last normal forms. This is really complicated material. Lots of database specialists, if not all them, agree on the fact that most of the real-life tables in 3NF are also in 4NF and 5NF, so achieving the 3NF is the only requirement for a database. There may be less than a tenth of a percent of tables that need a real 4NF or 5NF analysis.

3NF guaranties that almost no redundancy remains in your database. But is it a good idea? While the situation is theoretically ideal, it may become unusable due to the number of tables and necessary joins to retrieve specific information. So, while we're at it, let's introduce redundancy into your 3NF database again!

The Denormalization Process

Microsoft ✔ **Exam Objective**

Define entities. Considerations include entity composition and normalization.

- Specify degree of normalization.

The whole database community agrees on the 3NF requirement for a database. Nevertheless, if the result of the 3NF is the total or almost total elimination of data redundancy, it can lead to poor performance. Consider the relational model illustrated in Figure 1.22, directly extracted from the Northwind database.

FIGURE 1.22   Relational model in 3NF

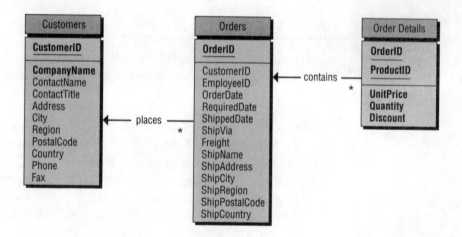

If you want to calculate the total turnover realized with a specific customer, you must write a query that joins the three tables, calculate the amount of every order detail, and total all the amounts. That query will consume quite a lot of CPU time. Now consider adding the field Total-Amount to the table Orders. We obtain the relational model illustrated in Figure 1.23.

FIGURE 1.23 Introducing a redundant calculated field

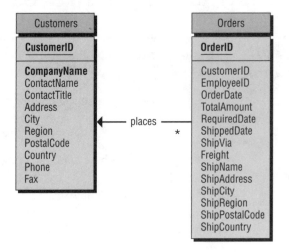

In Figure 1.23, the CompanyName column is required, which is why is it bolded. All the other columns allow the NULL value.

Now, when you want to calculate the total turnover realized with a specific customer, you just have to join two tables and calculate a sum. You could even add a field Total Turnover in the Customers table, if you need frequent access to this information. The global idea of *denormalization* is presented in this example: introducing redundancy to improve data access performance.

While denormalization has advantages, it also has drawbacks, the worst being the maintenance of redundant data. In the previous example, each time an order detail is inserted, the total amount of the order has to be calculated and updated in the order table, or in the customer table if you decided to store it with the customer's data. Data integrity is endangered by denormalization, and update performance may decrease.

Data integrity is endangered because you have to guarantee that the redundant data are up to date. For example, you may decide that the Total Turnover column in the Customers table should be updated every night by a batch process recalculating every value, or that its value should be calculated on the fly and cross-checked every night to correct possible inaccuracies. On the other hand, if you have to update the Customers table each time you insert a new order, you slow your insert query. Is the redundancy worth it?

Denormalization is a dangerous game and is generally more an art than a science. The techniques that are presented in this chapter give you an idea of what you can do with denormalization. Each time you denormalize your model, you must always thoroughly document your choice.

NOTE One last word before switching to the denormalization techniques: some database architects or consultants always denormalize a model or will advise you to do so, because they say that a model in 3NF cannot perform well. This is not necessarily true. Never predict performance problems before implementing the physical model because software and hardware have progressed, and what was true five or six years ago may not necessarily be true today. Also, every database is unique, and what is true for one system may be not be true for another; the volume of data, the number of users, the type of the server, of the network, the software used, and so on could be different. It creates a combination that has to be studied precisely before making any decision concerning de-normalization. Never denormalize before implementing your physical model and the first performance test is under full load.

We will cover the following denormalization techniques in the upcoming sections:

- Adding a redundant column
- Adding a derived column
- Partitioning tables

Adding a Redundant Column

Adding a redundant column is probably the most straightforward and logical denormalization technique. It consists of copying a column in a child table to a parent table. It generally violates the Third Normal Form, but it does help some queries to avoid a join. In the Pubs database, consider the Titles and Roysched tables (Figure 1.24).

FIGURE 1.24 Titles and Roysched tables

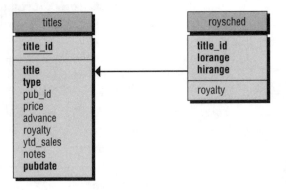

The Roysched table contains the royalty range for each title. For example, if the sales of title BU1032 are between 0 and 5000, then the royalty is 10 percent, and above 5001 it is 12 percent. Now to avoid querying that table, the current value of royalty is inserted in the Titles table. Now, that table is not achieving 3NF anymore because the royalty column is functionally dependent on the title_id and ytd_sales columns. This column is not part of the primary key, so the table is not in 3NF anymore.

With the loss of the 3NF, anomalies can occur. Here are two examples:

- If a user updates the value of the royalty column in the Roysched table, he/she has to update the matching record in the Titles tables; otherwise, data is inconsistent.

- If a user updates the value of the ytd_sales column in the Titles table, he/she has to look for the corresponding royalty value in the Roysched tables to update the royalty column.

To avoid these two situations, it is possible to create an update trigger on each table to track updates of the royalty column of the Roysched table and of the ytd_sales column of the Titles table. The trigger is a piece of code fired during the update of one of the columns. Compared to a single update, the trigger slows the overall update. That loss of performance may be a minor drawback compared to the fact that each time a title is queried, the user retrieves its royalty value without having to query another table or to join that table.

NOTE   Triggers are discussed in Chapter 6: Creating and Maintaining Database Objects.

Adding a Derived Column

Another useful technique of denormalization is the use of derived columns. A *derived column* is a column whose values are calculated from the values of one or many other columns of the same table or other tables. Adding such a column generally violates the 3NF, since this column is functionally dependent on non-key columns.

The simplest example is the computed column: In a Sales table, you store the amount, the sales tax, and the net price, calculated from the amount and the sales tax.

The Titles and Sales table in Figure 1.25 illustrates a more complicated example.

FIGURE 1.25   Titles and Sales table

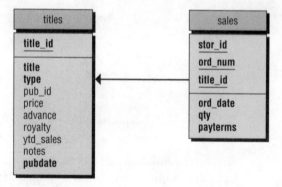

Each time you wish to know the year-to-date sales of a given book, you need to query the Sales table and total the values of the qty column for that book. It may be a long-running query if the sales table is big. To avoid querying that table and totaling the values, the architect introduced the ytd_sales column in the Titles table. Now each time you query the sales of a given book, you just have to query the Titles column. Of course, as for the redundant column, the value of that column needs to be maintained dynamically to be consistent and accurate.

You can add triggers to the Sales table to update the ytd_sales column of the Titles table each time a sales record is inserted, deleted, or updated. This trigger will lower the performance and inserts, deletes, and updates. But again, the performance gain of the data retrieval must outweigh the performance loss of the insert, delete, and update operations.

Partitioning Tables

Partitioning a table is not really a denormalizing technique, but it is worth mentioning because it can address particular performance issues. There are two ways to partition a table: horizontally or vertically.

Vertical Partitioning

Vertical partitioning consists of cutting the table in two or more tables by moving entire columns. Consider the example illustrated in Figure 1.26.

FIGURE 1.26   Vertical partitioning

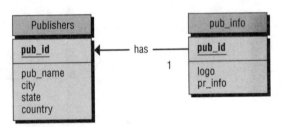

The Publishers table has been split into two tables. One (Publishers) contains all the "basic" information, and the other (Pub_info) contains the logo and the pr_info field. This split has been realized for two reasons:

- There is not a logo and a description for every publisher, so it makes more sense to split mandatory information from optional information.

- The fields in the Pub_info table are large binary objects (BLOB), and the architect may want to store them in another disk or "table space."

SQL Server 2000 allows you to store text and image columns on another filegroup thanks to the clause TEXTIMAGE_ON of the CREATE TABLE statement. See Chapter 2: Database Physical Modeling, for more information on the CREATE TABLE statement.

Another interesting point concerning vertical partitioning is the table width and the number of records per page. In SQL Server 2000, an 8K page contains a certain number of records. The wider the table, the fewer the records per page. The cache hit ratio may increase, the number of I/O per operation may lower, and the SQL Server cache may be well used.

In splitting a table for performance purposes, you should consider keeping the columns that are accessed more frequently in the "master" table and moving the other columns to one or more "slave" tables. Then, a one-to-one relationship between the master and each slave table guarantees the referential integrity.

Horizontal Partitioning

Another classic way of partitioning a table consists of moving a certain number of rows to one or many other tables. This is done during archiving, for example. If you consider a Sales table, you can imagine that every July the sales from July of last year to June of this year are archived. This technique is fine to keep small tables for the transactional system, while still allowing access to the archived data.

A view can be used to simulate a full view of archived and live data. With the new feature of partitioned view of SQL Server 2000, this technique becomes very interesting to achieve scaling out.

Other examples can be found in real-world applications, like splitting customers from prospects, active customers from customers who have not placed an order for more than 12 months, and so on.

Summary

This chapter is the only entirely theoretical one of the book. It may be hard to remember all the terms and concepts we have learned here. But it's the kind of information you will use all your database life long, because you cannot create a good database application without keeping these concepts in mind.

In this chapter, we covered the following:

- Designing a database system

- The Entity/Relationship model

- The relational model and the normalization process

- The denormalization process

Exam Essentials

Know what makes a good database design.   In the exam, you will be judged on your real-world knowledge. Knowing what makes a good database design will enable you to focus on the technical questions and tricks.

Identify entities and attributes.   The basis of ER modeling is the identification of entities and attributes. Having a thorough knowledge of modeling will help you criticize the way a database is designed and will help you to create a good design.

Identify the types of relationships.   Even if one-to-one or one-to-many relationships are obvious, you should know how to manage every type of relationship, even many-to-many.

Know how to define key attributes.   Candidate keys, primary keys, and alternate keys are the identification keys of your entities. Foreign keys are the basis of relationships. Defining them will allow you to enforce entity and referential integrity.

Identify precisely all the integrity types. Integrity is the source of correct data. Know the four types of integrity, what they are used for, and how they can be enforced to design a precise and optimal ER model.

Know how to normalize and denormalize an ER model. You should have no problems with normal forms, at least up to the third. Denormalization techniques are commonly used and can appear in the exam.

Key Terms

Before you take the exam, be certain you are familiar with the following terms:

alternate keys	character attributes
artificial key	Integrity
attribute	key attribute
binary attributes	logical design
business rules	logical model
candidate key	many-to-many relationship
cardinality	non-key attribute
conceptual design	normal form
denormalization	Normal form theory
derived column	normalization process
determinant	Numeric attributes
direction	one-to-many relationship
domain	one-to-one relationship
domain integrity	physical model
enterprise integrity	primary key
entity	referential integrity
entity integrity	Relational Database Management Systems (RDBMS)
ER model	
existence	relational model
fixed point	relational table
floating point	relationship
foreign key	special attributes
full functional dependency	transitive dependency

Review Questions

1. You are a developer for World Wide Importers. You are designing the new shipment tracking system. You print your ER model to show some selected users during the next phasing meeting (see graphic).

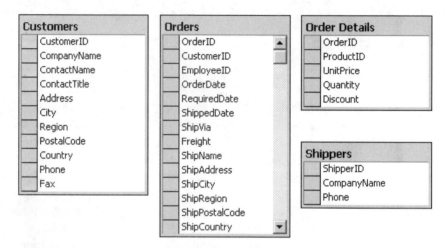

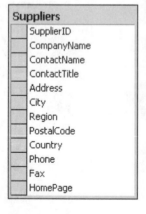

What should you add to your model to ensure a useful meeting with your end-users?

A. Attributes

B. Entities

C. Datatypes

D. Relationships

2. Build a list: As a database consultant, you have been asked to optimize a database model designed by the IT department of an insurance company. The model comprises just entities and attributes. You should follow a certain number of steps before producing an optimized ready-to-implement model. What is the proper sequence of steps to produce this model? Some elements may not be part of the sequence.

	Define primary keys
	Denormalize the model
	Define attributes
	Normalize the model
	Define alternate keys
	Define entities
	Define relationships

3. You are a developer for World Wide Importers. One developer of your team is working on the Products entity. Each product is imported by one supplier only. You need to record information on every product and on every supplier. Your developer shows you the structure of the table he designed and a data sample (see graphics on next page).

	Column Name	Data Type	Length	Allow Nulls
⚷	ProductID	int	4	
	ProductName	nvarchar	40	
	UnitPrice	money	8	✓
	CompanyName	nvarchar	40	
	Address	nvarchar	60	✓
	City	nvarchar	15	✓
	PostalCode	nvarchar	10	✓
	Country	nvarchar	15	✓

ProductID	ProductName	UnitPrice	CompanyName	Address	City	PostalCode	Country
17	Alice Mutton	39	Pavlova, Ltd.	74 Rose St. Moonie	Melbourne	3058	Australia
3	Aniseed Syrup	10	Exotic Liquids	49 Gilbert St.	London	EC1 4SD	UK
40	Boston Crab Meat	18.4	New England Seafood	Order Processing D	Boston	02134	USA
60	Camembert Pierrot	34	Gai pâturage	Bat. B 3, rue des Al	Annecy	74000	France
18	Carnarvon Tigers	62.5	Pavlova, Ltd.	74 Rose St. Moonie	Melbourne	3058	Australia
1	Chai	18	Exotic Liquids	49 Gilbert St.	London	EC1 4SD	UK
2	Chang	19	Exotic Liquids	49 Gilbert St.	London	EC1 4SD	UK
39	Chartreuse verte	18	Aux joyeux ecclésiasti	203, Rue des Franc	Paris	75004	France

As a matter of fact, you discover that the table needs a little extra work. In which normal form is it?

A. First

B. Second

C. Third

D. Boyce-Codd

4. You are developing a new customer care system for an insurance company. Every customer will be assigned a unique customer ID made of a combination of 7 characters and 8 figures. You expect to have over one million customers, each signing an average of 2.5 policies. Furthermore, it is important to track every customer's questions and complaints. You expect over 10 questions and complaints per customer. You want to minimize space used in your database. What primary key are you going to define for the customers table to minimize space and programming tasks?

A. An integer column, defined with an auto-numbering property

B. The customer ID

C. A unique identifier column, designed to generate a new globally unique ID for every row

D. A big integer column, defined with an auto-numbering property

5. You are a database developer for a banking corporation. Recently, one of the counter clerks "lost" a customer. This customer went to the bank for a deposit, but the counter clerk could not find her by her customer ID. In fact, after a few minutes' search, he found her, but with a wrong ID. After looking at the audit tables, it seemed another counter clerk accidentally modified the customer ID. You need to forbid the modification of the primary key to avoid any other "loss" like this. In SQL Server 2000, what is the fastest way to implement this feature, without modifying the existing front-end application?

A. Alter the table to enable the CHECK PRIMARY KEY option.

B. Alter the table to disable the MODIFY PRIMARY KEY option.

C. Add an AFTER UPDATE trigger to the table that rolls back the transaction in case of modification of the primary key value.

D. It is not possible to implement this feature in SQL Server.

6. The database application you developed last year for the insurance company you are working with was performing well, until last month when some users started to complain about some long-running queries. Last month your company acquired another insurance company and inserted all its existing customers and policies into the database, increasing the volume of data by a magnitude of 3. You have been asked to find the cheapest solution to this performance problem before the end of the week. After having analyzed what was happening, you have observed that only 10 percent of the data is used 90 percent of the time. In fact, data older than 2 years are selected only in 0.5 percent of the time. What is the solution you are going to implement?

A. Buy a new RAID 5 subsystem and spread the data all over the disks.

  B. Change the server to a new 4-way machine.

  C. It is not possible to enhance performance before the end of the week. You need more time.

  D. Split the data horizontally and store the archive table on another disk.

7. The database application you developed last year for the regional bank you are working with was performing well, until last month when some users started to complain about some long-running queries. Last month your company acquired another bank and inserted all its existing customers and accounts into the database, increasing the volume of data by a magnitude of 5. You have been asked to find the cheapest solution to this performance problem before the end of the week. After having analyzed what was happening, you have observed that each time an employee was gaining access to a customer record, the system was calculating the amount of money of his account based on all the money transferred since the beginning of the year. What is the solution you are going to implement to hasten the access to the customer record?

  A. Create a stored procedure that calculates the amount on the fly.

  B. Denormalize the customer table to include the calculated amount value, updated through a batch that runs every night.

  C. Index the transfer table to fasten the join with the customers table.

  D. Create a temporary table in tempdb that stores the account's amount and query this table each time a customer is queried.

8. You are helping your town library develop their new computer system to track members, books, and borrowed books. The manager of the library is a computer addict but knows little of ER modeling. She designed a Member table to store every member, assigning each a unique ID. She designed a Book table to store every book of the library, and a Borrowed table to assign every borrowed book to members. Each member can only borrow three books at a time, can

keep them up to four weeks and must bring them back at the same time. The proposed design is illustrated in the following graphic:

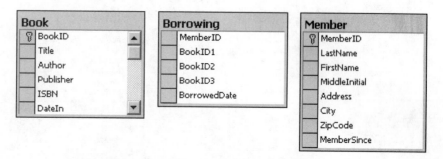

What level of normal form is reached by this model?

A. None

B. 1NF

C. 2NF

D. 3NF

9. You are a SQL Server developer for Northwind Traders. Your users complain about performance of the application when they query the order amount per employee name and per customer name. After a quick investigation, you discover that this is due to the number of tables joined to calculate the amount. Your logical design is represented in the graphic on the next page.

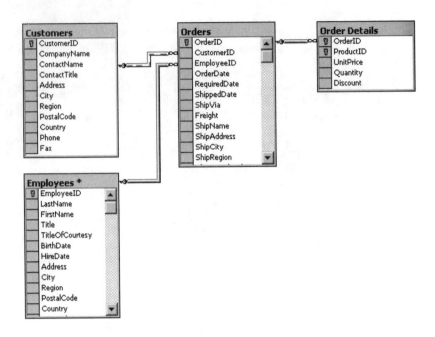

What can you do to optimize this query?

A. Create a new denormalized table containing the employee name, the customer name, and the amount ordered, and create the necessary trigger to maintain this table.

B. Create a stored procedure that performs the needed calculation.

C. Create new indexes on the Order Details table.

D. Create a view on the four tables.

10. You are a database developer for the local university. You need to define a relationship between the students and the courses, knowing a student can attend many courses and one course can be attended by many students. You have the two entities illustrated in the following graphic:

How can you implement this many-to-many relationship?

A. Insert a StudentID attribute in the Courses table and a CourseID column in the Students table.

B. Create a new entity called StudentsCourses containing at least two attributes, StudentID and CourseID, forming the primary key.

C. Insert a StudentID attribute in the Course table.

D. Insert a CourseID attribute in the Students table.

11. One of the developers on your team asked you about a problem he could not address. He needs to represent a hierarchy in the new HR database. Every employee reports to a manager. Managers can report to another manager and so on, up to the CEO. He explains to you that there are five hierarchical levels in the company, so he intends to create five entities representing every level. You think this can lead to many problems, the first being the case of a promotion. A promoted employee has to be moved from one level to an upper level, and that could lead to consistency issues. What is the best solution, using the ER model, to address such a hierarchy?

A. Use two tables, one containing the employee information and one the hierarchy information.

B. It is impossible to address this problem in a relational database.

C. Keep a table for every hierarchical level and develop a series of stored procedures to manage inserts, deletes, and updates.

D. Insert a ReportsTo column in the Employees table and create a recursive relationship.

12. As an independent SQL Server expert, you have been chosen to explain the ER modeling that the developers will to use to model the needed data and business processes to users of the future loyalty management system. You decide to define the basic objects of the ER model. What are they? (Chose three.)

A. Entity

B. Relationship

C. Datatype

    D. Attribute

    E. Property

    F. Columns

13. You are a SQL Server database developer for Northwind Traders. You designed the Products, Categories, and Suppliers table illustrated in the graphic below.

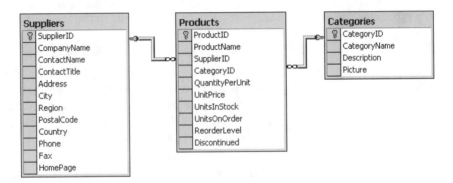

    What is the level of normalization of your model?

    A. 1NF

    B. 2NF

    C. 3NF

    D. BCNF

14. You are designing a new procurement database for a regional bank. While defining the suppliers and orders relationship, you are faced with the choice of what has to be done when a supplier is deleted from the database. You must propose all the SQL Server possible declarative choices to your customer. What are they? (Choose all that apply.)

    A. Restrict: You cannot delete a supplier if it is linked with existing orders.

    B. No Effect: You can delete a supplier even if it is linked with existing orders.

C. Default: All foreign keys are defined to a default value if the matching primary key is deleted.

D. Cascade: Every order is deleted if the linked supplier is deleted.

15. You are a database developer for an insurance company. Every insurance policy is managed by one and only one product manager. One product manager can manage many policies. How can you represent that information in the database?

    A. Include the manager ID in the Policies entity.

    B. Include the policy ID in the Managers entity.

    C. Create a relationship entity formed by the policy ID and the manager ID.

    D. Include the manager ID in the Policies entity and the policy ID in the Managers entity.

Answers to Review Questions

1. D. Attributes and entities are represented in the diagram. End-users do not need to be know about datatypes, but they do need to know about relationships to fully understand the links between entities.

2.

Define primary keys
Normalize the model
Define relationships
Denormalize the model

Defining primary keys first allows you to enforce entity integrity and prepare the normalization process that is based on functional dependency to the primary key. Normalizing the database leads naturally to the definition of relationships. You will then have a 3NF model that you will only need to denormalize if needed.

3. B. Some non-key attributes depend on other non-key attributes. For example, Country depends on the supplier name and product ID. This is a transitive dependency: if you have the product ID, you can find the supplier name, and once you get the supplier name, you can find the supplier country. So, if you know the product ID, you know the supplier country. Country is not functionally dependent only on the primary key, but also on the Company Name.

4. A. For one million rows, the integer is sufficient (it goes up to more than 2 billion) and will consume only 4 bytes per row instead of 15 for the customer ID, 16 for the unique identifier, and 8 for the big integer.

5. C. Options A and B do not exist. C is the only way to do it without modifying the programming logic.

6. D. The 3NF seems to be the problem in the sense that there is too much data in the table and the machine is probably not suited for that volume of data. So, the cheapest solution is to split the table horizontally and store older data on another disk to minimize the volume of data in memory.

7. B. This is a classic problem of heavy calculation on a frequently accessed table. The only solution is to denormalize the table with a column updated through a batch or a trigger, depending on the frequency of inserts and deletes.

8. A. The Borrowing table contains a repeating group. To be in First Normal Form, the table should only contain one BookID column, not three.

9. A. Creating a new table will give the best results since the information will be immediately available. However, the information should be updated through synchronous or asynchronous mechanisms.

10. B. The only way to implement a many-to-many relationship in ER modeling is by creating a new entity made of, at least, the primary keys of the linked entities.

11. D. This is the classical hierarchy problem. In such a case, the only solution is a recursive relationship, which handles the hierarchy.

12. A, B, and D. ER stands for Entity-Relationship, and an entity is made of attributes.

13. B. This is a tricky question. At first sight, the model is in 3NF, but there is a transitive dependency in the Suppliers table: ContactTitle depends on ContactName and not only on SupplierID. You should introduce a Contacts table to be in 3NF.

14. A, B, and D. This is a tricky one. Options A and D are obvious, but B is possible if you do not enforce the foreign key in the Orders table. C is only possible through stored procedures or triggers.

15. A. This is a one-to-many relationship. Each policy can have only one manager ID, so the manager ID must be part of the Policies table.

Chapter

2

Database Physical Modeling

MICROSOFT EXAM OBJECTIVES COVERED IN THIS CHAPTER:

✓ **Create and alter databases. Considerations include file groups, file placement, growth strategy, and space requirements.**

  ▪ Specify space management parameters. Parameters include autoshrink, growth increment, initial size, and maxsize.

  ▪ Specify file group and file placement. Considerations include logical and physical file placement.

  ▪ Specify transaction log placement. Considerations include bulk load operations and performance.

If you read the first chapter, you should now have a good understanding of a logical data model. Creating such a model is a hard task, and some other hard tasks await you on your journey to database application. The second milestone, after the logical design, is the physical design of the database. Of course, it would be too easy if you needed only to create the database, create the tables, and load the data to run your application!

If your purpose is to create a 2MB database, the job won't be a really tough one. But if you intend to implement a system with a size of over 1GB that is used as a classic client/server application or as a Web application hit by dozens, hundreds, or thousands of users, a good physical design is as critical as a good logical design.

In this chapter you will learn:

- How to create and manage a database

- How to manage data and log files

- What filegroups are and how they are used

- How to increase your system performance by setting up a good physical design

Creating and Managing a Database

Database creation is a tricky process: It is a straightforward statement hiding a massive complexity. Database creation is straightforward because you can create a database just by giving it a name in SQL Enterprise Manager or by running a CREATE DATABASE statement. The massive complexity of database creation lies in the database file management, which is a SQL Server particularity that has to be known and understood if you want to take advantage of it.

As is the case for many SQL Server operations, there are two ways to create a database: with SQL Enterprise Manager or with Transact-SQL. Let's take a look at how to create a simple database, then we can go further into its architecture.

Creating a Simple Database

Microsoft ✔ **Exam Objective**

Create and alter databases. Considerations include file groups, file placement, growth strategy, and space requirements.

To create a database with SQL Enterprise Manager, right-click the Databases folder and choose New Database. The Database Properties dialog box appears (Figure 2.1), allowing you to name the database.

FIGURE 2.1 The Database Properties dialog box

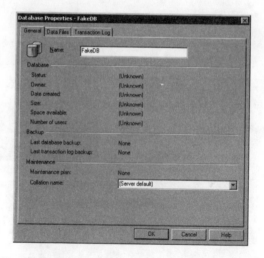

To create a database with Transact-SQL, use the following statement:

```
CREATE DATABASE database_name
```

If you want to create the FakeDB database (as in Figure 2.1), run the following statement in SQL Query Analyzer:

```
CREATE DATABASE FakeDB
```

Of course, with these processes, SQL Server creates a database made of default file size and placements. While this is useful for quick and dirty databases, it is not the brightest idea for the next killer Internet Web site. The default size of the log file is 1MB. The default size of the data file is that of the model database.

Data and Log Files

A SQL Server database is made of at least two physical files: one data file and one log file. The data file contains data and the log file contains the transaction log (Figure 2.2).

It is no longer possible to create a database with the transaction log stored in the data file as it was in versions of SQL Server before SQL Server 7.

FIGURE 2.2 Data and log files

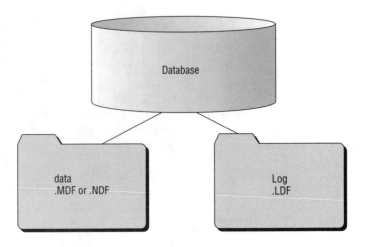

While at least one data file and one log file are needed to create a database, the database can span multiple data files and multiple log files. Database files are of one of these three types:

- *Primary data file* (extension .MDF). A database must have one .MDF file. The primary data file contains the database system tables and user tables.

- *Secondary data file* (extension .NDF). A database can have up to 32,766 .NDF files. The secondary data files contain the user and system data not stored in the primary data file. Secondary data files are optional.

- *Log file* (extension .LDF). A database can have up to 32,766 .LDF files. The log file contains the *transaction log*.

A SQL Server 2000 database can have up to 32,767 files of any type.

In SQL Enterprise Manager, the Database Properties dialog box allows you to define one or more data files and log files. To define a data file while creating a database in the Database Properties dialog box, follow these steps:

1. Click the Data Files tab.

2. Enter a physical file location and file name.

3. Enter an initial file size in MB.

4. Define automatic growing options (they are defined in detail in the "Size and Growth Options" section, later on in this chapter).

To define the log file(s) while creating a database, perform the same actions as for the data file, but on the Transaction Log tab.

By default, data and log files are placed in the C:\Program Files\Microsoft SQL Server\MSSQL\Data folder. If you installed named instances and create the database on a named instance, replace MSSQL with MSSQL$*instancename*.

With Transact-SQL, use the following statement to define the files and their attributes:

```
CREATE DATABASE database_name
ON
    [([NAME = logical_file_name ,]
    FILENAME = 'physical_file_name'
    [,SIZE = size]
    [,MAXSIZE = { max_size | UNLIMITED }]
    [,FILEGROWTH = growth_increment ]) [ ,...n ]]
[ LOG ON
    [([ NAME = logical_file_name ,]
    FILENAME = 'os_file_name'
    [,SIZE = size ]
    [,MAXSIZE = { max_size | UNLIMITED } ]
    [,FILEGROWTH = growth_increment ])[ ,...n ]]]
```

Listing 2.1 creates a 200MB database named FakeDB, composed of one 100MB primary data file, a 50MB secondary file, and a 50MB log file.

Listing 2.1: Create Database statement

```
CREATE DATABASE FakeDB
ON
        ( NAME = FakeDB_data1,
        FILENAME = 'd:\FakeDB_data1.mdf',
        SIZE = 100MB,
        MAXSIZE = 1GB,
        FILEGROWTH = 10MB),
          ( NAME = FakeDB_data2,
            FILENAME = 'd:\FakeDB_data2.mdf',
        SIZE = 50MB,
        MAXSIZE = 1GB,
        FILEGROWTH = 10MB)
LOG ON
        ( NAME = FakeDB_log,
            FILENAME = 'e:\FakeDB_log.ldf',
        SIZE = 50MB,
        MAXSIZE = 2GB,
        FILEGROWTH = 10%)
```

You can generate the database creation script with the Generate SQL Scripts utility, even if you created your database graphically with SQL Enterprise Manager. Right-click the database in SQL Enterprise Manager, then chose All Tasks ➢ Generate SQL Scripts. In the Generate SQL Scripts dialog box, click the Options tab and check the Script database option. The generated script will contain the CREATE DATABASE statement.

Now you know a database is made of at least two files. It is easy to guess the purpose of a data file, but it may be a little more complicated to understand the purpose of the log file. It is essential, however, that you fully understand the way it works and its uses in writing good SQL Server applications.

First of all, every modification in a relational database management system is (or may be) a transaction. A *transaction* is defined by the following properties (referred to as the *ACID* properties):

Atomic   All operations in a transaction are atomic, meaning if one operation fails, the whole transaction fails.

Consistent   Before the transaction, the database was in a consistent state. After the transaction, it is back in a consistent state, but it may have gone through an inconsistent state during the transaction. That is why a transaction must comply with the third property, isolated.

Isolated   A running transaction is isolated from the outside. Locking provides this property.

Durable   Once a transaction is validated (committed), the effects of the transaction remain in the database forever. The transaction log provides this property.

The transaction log records every modification made to a database: from the INSERT, UPDATE, or DELETE operations to the data page allocation or file growth. In the following process, a modification query is any query or operation resulting in the modification of any part of the database: its data or its physical structure. The following shows the overall process (Figure 2.3):

1. The user or the system issues a modification query.

2. The query processor asks the cache manager if the page to update is already in cache. If it is not, it is read from the disk and written into cache.

3. The query processor writes the modification in memory.

4. At the same time, it writes the statement in the transaction log. For example, if the operation is an UPDATE statement, it updates the data in memory and writes the UPDATE statement in the log.

5. Once the query processor has the confirmation that the statement has been written in the transaction log (COMMIT) on the disk, the modification is over.

FIGURE 2.3   Data Read and Write Log process

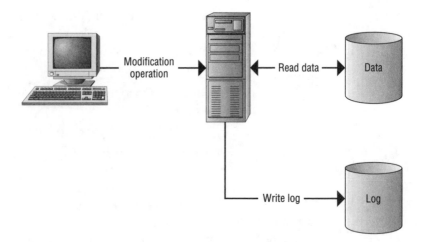

Note that once an operation is finished, its effect remains in the data cache, but the statement is written in the transaction log on the disk. Now, if you consider a one-million-row update is taking place, it is faster to write the statement in the transaction log (one row) than to write each of the one million rows.

The transaction log guaranties the Durable property of every transaction, since it is on disk. Think of your database transaction log as your life insurance. You should protect it. If you lose your data and your transaction log at the same time, you lose your database. But if RAID 1 protects your transaction log, for instance, a disk crash does not affect your system. And, if you lose your data and not your transaction log (because it is on another physical disk), you can recover what's been done since the last back up of your database thanks to your transaction log.

It is beyond of the scope of this book to describe the data guarding protection measures you should take to safeguard your data. This subject is a requirement of exam 70-228: Installing, Configuring, and Administering Microsoft® SQL Server™ 2000 Enterprise Edition. Refer to Sybex's *MCSE: SQL Server 2000 Administration Study Guide* for more information.

Remembering How Queries are Processed

Two things you should always remember while working with SQL: Data modification is always done in memory and the transaction log is constantly written to the disk. Developers often write stored procedures or applications for SQL Server without knowing how queries are processed. The same applies for database architects and database administrators. A thorough understanding of the log functions should be a prerequisite to develop for SQL Server. You do not need to understand how a motor is working to drive a car, but you do not know any Indy car driver who does not know exactly how his engine works. A Certified SQL Developer is equivalent to the Indy car driver. If he does not know how to drive, he will go directly into the wall at the first curve.

There is an important question to ask yourself concerning the use of the database files: If the modification is done in memory and the transaction log is constantly written to the disk, when is the modification written to the disk? The answer is that it depends. In fact, the frequency that data is written back to the disk depends on the activity of the database and the memory available.

Two processes are in charge of writing back dirty pages (pages in memory that contain modified data) to the disk:

- The *checkpoint* process depends on the number of transactions written in the transaction log.

- The *lazy writer* process depends on the available pages in cache.

For many developers and administrators, the checkpoint process depends on a particular database option called recovery interval, which depends on the activity of the database. By default in SQL Server 2000, the recovery interval value is 0, meaning that in case of a failure of SQL Server, each database will recover in less than one minute. If SQL Server stops unexpectedly, the transaction logs will not be well closed, and when SQL Server restarts, all the transactions since the last checkpoint are replayed. This recovery process takes less than one minute per database, with a recovery interval value of 0. But SQL Server bases its evaluation of the "real" recovery process duration on the number of transactions written in the transaction log. So every *n* transactions, the dirty pages are written to the disk but still remain in memory as clean pages.

In the meantime, if the available pages between two checkpoints decrease and fall below a predefined threshold, the lazy writer process flushes pages from the memory to the disk (if they are dirty) to keep the number of available pages always above the threshold. This threshold is approximately 5 percent of the SQL Server cache.

In SQL Server 2000, the cache is unified. This means that there is no distinction between data and procedure cache, which is memory allocated to data and to queries and stored procedures.

Throughout the book, keep in mind that updates, inserts, and deletes all occur in memory. Now that you know how a database works, let's look at the details of its creation and management.

Managing Databases

Microsoft
✓ *Exam*
Objective

Create and alter databases. Considerations include file groups, file placement, growth strategy, and space requirements.

- Specify space management parameters. Parameters include autoshrink, growth increment, initial size, and maxsize.

The CREATE DATABASE statement contains many options. The following pages discuss these options, starting with the filenames, locations, and sizes, continuing with the collation and the shrinking of a database, and finishing with the different possibilities of altering a database.

Filenames

When you define the filename, you also give the file a logical name. The physical name and location are being defined in the Locate Database File dialog box, as in Figure 2.4.

FIGURE 2.4   Defining a physical filename and location

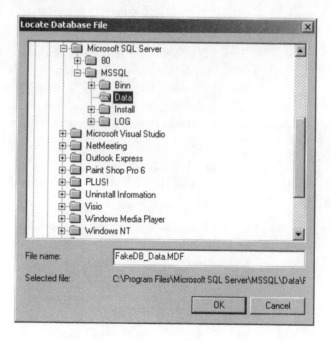

These two names correspond to the NAME and FILENAME clause of the CREATE DATABASE statement. The logical name of the file is used inside the Transact-SQL statement to reference the file. The physical name of the file is used at the operating system level.

You cannot create data or log files in a compressed directory.

The database and logical filenames can be a maximum of 128 characters long. The physical filenames (location and file name) can be a maximum of 260 characters long. Be careful not to create too big a hierarchy of folders to store your data and log files; otherwise, their creation will fail.

These lengths are the max lengths of the name and filename columns in the Sysdatabases and Sysaltfiles tables, which contain information about databases and files.

Size and Growth Options

Each data and log file has three properties controlling their size and their growth options:

- SIZE defines the initial size of the file. In SQL Enterprise Manager, you define size in megabytes. With Transact-SQL, you can specify kilobyte (KB), megabyte (MB), gigabyte (GB) or terabyte (TB), with MB being the default. The size cannot be smaller than the size of the model database (1MB, unless it has been changed).

- MAXSIZE defines the maximum size to which the file can grow. The unit rules are the same for SIZE. MAXSIZE can be UNLIMITED, meaning that the file can grow up to the disk size.

- FILEGROWTH defines the growth increment of the file. It cannot exceed MAXSIZE and can be specified by Transact-SQL in (KB), megabyte (MB), gigabyte (GB), terabyte (TB), or percent (%), with MB being the default. In SQL Enterprise Manager, you can only define the file growth in MB or in percent.

Keep the following pieces of advice in mind when considering these options:

- Always define a "smart" size. It's easy to leave the data file as 1MB and then let it grow. But first file fragmentation will occur, followed by a drop in performance. Both consequences are the results of the file chunk allocation. Each time the system inserts new data, if there is not enough space in the data file, it increases the size of the file, following the FILEGROWTH value. So SQL Server asks the file system to allocate a new chunk of data to the files. That takes time, and the new chunk is not necessarily contiguous to the other allocations. The initial size of the file has to reflect the needed initial size plus the expected growth for the months or years to come.

- Never allow a file to have an unlimited growth. It's better to give a limit, even if it's a very high limit. With an upper limit, you have more efficient space management and can monitor more easily the number of space allocation errors (see the note about errors below).

- Define a "smart" value for FILEGROWTH. For example, if you create a 1GB file, do not define a 1MB file growth value. Instead, define a 50 or 100MB file growth value. Doing so, you limit file fragmentation and minimize the file growth frequency. In general, a value between 5 and 20 percent of the initial size is a good choice.

The CREATE DATABASE statement presented in Listing 2.1 shows different options of file growth. The data files grow by 10MB chunks and up to 1GB. The log file grows by chunks of 10 percent of the actual file size and up to 2GB.

Historically, there is one error that has to be monitored if you defined the maximum size of your file(s): 1105. The error message received is: Could not allocate space for object *objectname* in database *databasename* because the *filegroupname* filegroup is full. With SQL Server 2000, you should also monitor error 9002 if you fixed the maximum size of the transaction log: The log file for database *databasename* is full. Back up the transaction log for the database to free up some log space.

In Exercise 2.1, we'll create a database using Enterprise Manager.

Creating a Database with SQL Enterprise Manager

This exercise will walk you through creating a database with SQL Enterprise Manager, defining files and growing options, and then generating the SQL script.

1. Open SQL Enterprise Manager. Do this by choosing Start ≻ Programs ≻ Microsoft SQL Server ≻ Enterprise Manager.

2. In SQL Enterprise Manager, click the plus (+) sign next to Microsoft SQL Servers to unfold the server groups list.

3. Click the plus (+) sign next to SQL Server Group to unfold the list of server names belonging to the group named SQL Server Group.

4. On the left-hand side of your server name, you should see an icon representing a small server and a white or green disk:

   - If this icon represents a red square in a white disk, your server is stopped. Start it by right-clicking your server name and choosing Start.

   - If this icon represents a green arrow in a white disk, your server is started and you are not connected.

   - If this icon represents a white arrow in a green disk, your server is started and you are connected.

   Click the plus (+) sign next to your server name to unfold the object types list of your server.

5. Right-click the Databases folder and choose New Database.

6. In the Name text box, type **MyFirstDatabase**.

7. Click the Data Files tab. Define an initial size of 10MB, allow a file growth value of 5MB and a maximum file size of 100MB. Do not change the file name and the location.

EXERCISE 2.1 *(continued)*

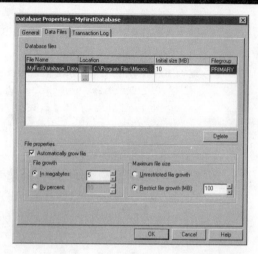

8. Click the Transaction Log tab. Define an initial size of 5MB, allow a file growth value of 1MB and a maximum file size of 50MB. Do not change the file name and location.

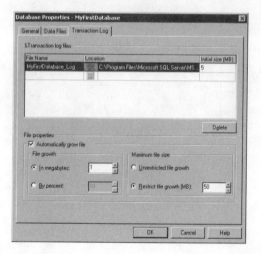

9. Click the OK button.

10. Right-click the Databases folder and choose Refresh.

11. Click the plus (+) sign next to the Databases folder to unfold the databases list.

12. Click MyFirstDatabase to select the database, then right-click MyFirstDatabase and choose View ➤ Taskpad. The taskpad on the right-hand side of SQL Enterprise Manager allows you to check the space allocated.

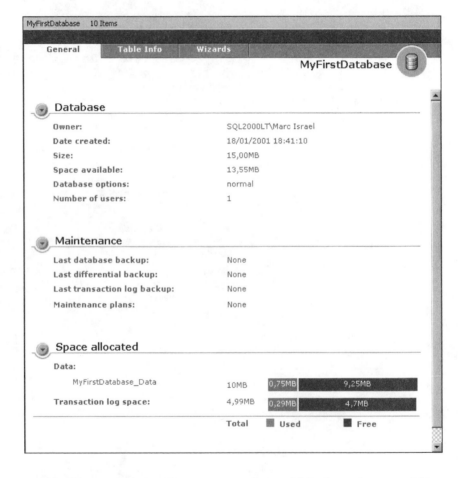

13. Right-click MyFirstDatabase and choose All Tasks ➤ Generate SQL Scripts.

14. Click the Options tab. Activate the Script Database option.

15. Click the General tab and click the Preview button. After a couple of seconds, the Generate SQL Script Preview dialog box appears and presents you with the database creation script. You can copy the script to the clipboard if you wish to analyze it in the Notepad or in SQL Query Analyzer.

16. Click the Close button, then the Cancel button. You can close SQL Enterprise Manager if you wish.

Most of the scripts and queries you'll see in this book can be opened and executed with SQL Query Analyzer or OSQL.

Collation

In versions of SQL Server up to SQL Server 7, the *character set* (or code page) was a server-wide parameter. On a server, every database used the same set of characters. With SQL Server 2000, the character set, sort order, and Unicode collation have been grouped in what is now called a *collation*, which can be defined at the server, database, or even column level. This means that a server can be installed to use the Latin1_General_CI_AS collation (that is code page 1252, case insensitive, accent sensitive), and a specific database can be created with the Modern_Spanish_CS_AS collation. While this feature has many advantages for administrators, such as the possibility to restore a database on a server that has been backed up on another server installed with a different collation, it has some drawbacks for the developers.

In the CREATE DATABASE statement or in the Database Properties dialog box in SQL Enterprise Manager, it is possible to define the collation of the database. Two types of collation names exist: Windows and SQL collation names. Both can be used with the COLLATE clause.

You'll find exhaustive information on collation names in the SQL Server Books OnLine, in the Transact-SQL Reference book, at the COLLATE chapter. Open the Books OnLine by choosing Start ➢ Programs ➢ Microsoft SQL Server ➢ Books OnLine. You'll find the Transact-SQL Reference book in the list on the left-hand side of the window.

You can modify the collation used by a database with the ALTER DATA-BASE statement under strong restrictions:

- You are the only user of the database.

- No schema bound object is dependent on the database collation.

- No name duplicates are created by the altering process.

If the collation choice is a good idea, it should be used cautiously. In fact, a developer will now face two choices: changing collation or using Unicode. In an international environment, Unicode is always a better choice because you do not have to handle character translation. Even if Unicode occupies twice the space (16 bits per character instead of 8 bits with a single-byte character set), you do not have to ensure the proper translation of characters between different collations. Furthermore, collation precedence rules are not easy to manage. Reserve this collation feature only if you have to manage different servers using different locales.

Shrinking a Database and File

While a database can grow automatically, it can also shrink manually or automatically, depending on the options you activated and space usage. Automatic shrinking is one of the many database options that we will see later in this chapter. You can manually shrink databases or files with SQL Enterprise Manager or Transact-SQL.

Automatic Shrinking

Automatic shrinking is not enabled by default on any SQL Server editions but Desktop, regardless of the OS used. Automatic shrinking is quite simple: Every half hour, a special housekeeping process recovers ghost records (records that have been logically deleted) and checks whether a shrink is necessary by analyzing empty space.

If more than 25 percent of a file contains unused space, it is shrunk automatically. The target size is either the initial file size or a size where 25 percent is unused space, whichever is greater.

A file cannot be automatically shrunk to a smaller size than its initial one.

Let's say, as an example, that you've created a 100MB file for your database. This file fills up, and then increases by 10MB chunks. Having reached 150MB, you archive half of the data, resulting in almost 50 percent of unused space. The allocated space is now 82MB. The autoshrink process shrinks the file to 110MB. Note that it's not shrunk to its initial size, because that would result in only 18 percent of free space.

To set this parameter in SQL Enterprise Manager, check the Autoshrink check box in the Database Properties dialog box. With Transact-SQL, use the ALTER DATABASE statement, like in the following example:

```
ALTER DATABASE MyFirstDB SET AUTO_SHRINK ON
```

For those of you who know SQL Server 7, note that SQL Server 2000 no longer uses sp_dboption. In fact, this system-stored procedure is still supported, but only for backward compatibility.

You can disable autoshrink, just by turning OFF the previous option:

```
ALTER DATABASE MyFirstDB SET AUTO_SHRINK OFF
```

It is not a good idea to enable the autoshrink on a production database because this process can occur anytime. As Murphy's Law is always peeping above you shoulder, you can be sure it will occur just in the middle of a very busy day and will exhaust the resources on your server. Just monitor database growth and unused space, and shrink your database only when you need to and only when there is no activity on your server.

To turn on autoshrink, follow these steps (we will use the MyFirstDatabase database):

1. In SQL Enterprise Manager, right-click the MyFirstDatabase folder, and click Properties.

2. Click the Options tab.

3. Check the Autoshrink property and click OK.

Manually Shrinking a Database

A database can be shrunk with the DBCC SHRINKDATABASE statement. To shrink a database, you have to give SQL Server the name of the database you want to shrink and the free space target size, represented as a percentage of the overall target size. The following example shrinks MyFirstDatabase to retain only 20 percent of free space:

```
DBCC SHRINKDATABASE (MyFirstDB, 20)
```

You cannot shrink a database beneath its initial size, though you can shrink a specific file beneath its initial size. The DBCC SHRINKDATABASE statement can only be used to reclaim unused free space after a database growth. The database shrinking process is "lossless," which means that you are not going to lose any data, since you cannot ask for an unreachable free space value. For example, if you have only 20 percent of free unused space in your database, you cannot ask to reach 30 percent.

The shrinking process does not only shrink data and log files, it moves data from one extent to another, or from one file to another one. Starting from the end of each file, the process moves toward the beginning of the file and moves any allocated extent to an unused extent in the same file or in another available file until it leaves the necessary amount of unused space or reaches the initial size of the file.

In the example illustrated in Figure 2.5, 44 percent of the space is used before the shrinking process, leaving 56 percent of the overall size as unused space (there are 18 extents and only eight are allocated). You want to reduce this free space size to 20 percent.

FIGURE 2.5   Shrinking a database file with a target size

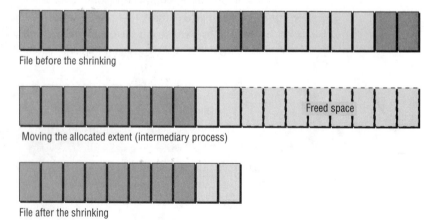

File before the shrinking

Moving the allocated extent (intermediary process)

File after the shrinking

The basic theory behind database shrinking is quite simple, but it becomes more complex when you consider that a database can be made of multiple data and log files. Let's look at an example to understand how the shrinking process works.

Consider the FakeDB database as being made of two 50MB data files that have grown to 100MB each and one log file of 50MB. The primary data file contains 65MB of data, the secondary contains 40MB of data. Consider these three cases:

- You want to shrink the database to 10 percent of free space. The target size allows this value. Considering that SQL Server calculates a target size of 72MB, it shrinks the file by moving the data inside the file because 65MB of used space plus 7MB unused space solves the problem.

- You want to shrink the database to 25 percent of free space. This target is reachable. Considering that SQL calculates that it can shrink the file to 80MB, it will leave 60MB of data in this file and move 5MB to the secondary file.

WARNING   This extent transfer from file to file is possible only if the considered files belong to the same filegroup.

- You want to shrink the database to 40 percent of free space. The primary file will not be shrunk because the target is bigger than the available space.

If you shrink a database, you shrink the log files at the same time. Unfortunately, a log file is not structured like a data file. That means, you cannot "move" transactions around your log file like the system did with the data. It has to be shrunk from the end. The two operations that apply to a transaction log are log truncation and log shrinking:

- Log truncation concerns the deletion of the inactive portion of the log, which are the transactions whose data has been checkpointed. A checkpoint marks the writing of dirty pages to the disk. So, the transactions before this checkpoint are useless (they have to be backed up to be recovered in case of failure of the data disk, and a log backup truncates the inactive portion of the log).

- Log shrinking means that part of the truncated inactive portion of the log can be released to the operating system.

As you will see in the "Space Management" section, a log file is split into virtual log files, whose size and numbers depend on the log file size. A log file can always be shrunk to an integer number of virtual log files. So, if a 1GB log file is made of eight 128MB files, it can be shrunk to 128, 256, 384, 512, 640, 768 or 896MB, depending on its initial size and on the start and end of the active portion of the log.

You may never predict with precision what the file size will really be, but you may get a good idea if you run DBCC SHRINKDATABASE with just the database name, like the following statement:

```
DBCC SHRINKDATABASE('mydb')
```

The result will look like the following:

DbId	FileId	CurrentSize	MinimumSize	UsedPages	EstimatedPages
7	1	25600	25600	10400	10400
7	2	12800	12800	12800	12800
7	3	25600	25600	0	0

The previous table shows the possible results of the size reduction of mydb files. The columns are as follows:

- DbId is the database ID (found in sysdatabases).

- FileID is the file ID (found in sysaltfiles).

- CurrentSize is the current file size in 8KB pages. In the example, the size of file numbers one and three is 200MB, and the size of file number two is 100 MB.

Remember there are 1024KB in 1MB, so there are 128 pages in 1MB.

- MinimumSize is the minimum size of the file, generally its initial size, in 8KB pages. In the example, the files have been created at their current size.

- UsedPages indicates the number of allocated 8KB pages. In the example, file one uses 81.25MB, file two is full, and file three is empty.

- EstimatedPages indicates the minimum size the file could be shrunk to, taking into account the allocated pages. In the example, all files can be shrunk to their used pages.

This result will help you determine if there is any free space in the files, so you could use a suitable value for the DBCC SHRINKDATABASE statement. But if you want to precisely shrink a file, you would use DBCC SHRINKFILE, as we will see in the next section.

You can shrink a database directly in SQL Enterprise Manager:

1. Right-click the database you want to shrink.

2. Click All Tasks ➤ Shrink Database.

3. Define the Maximum Free Space in Files After Shrinking.

4. Check the Move Pages to Beginning of the File Before Shrinking option.

5. Click the OK button.

These options are shown in Figure 2.6. Note that you can schedule the execution of the DBCC SHRINKDATABASE if you enable the Shrink the Database Based on This Schedule option. If you do so, the operation will not be done, but only scheduled.

FIGURE 2.6   Shrinking a database in SQL Enterprise Manager

You have two options when executing the DBCC SHRINKDATABASE statement:

- NOTRUNCATE moves the pages to the beginning of files and does not release the freed extents to the operating system.

- TRUNCATEONLY does not move any data inside the files. The shrinking process starts from the end of the file and frees the unused extents until it reaches the first allocated extent, regardless of the target percent. This option simulates the functioning of the DBCC SHRINKDB of SQL Server 6.5.

In Exercise 2.2, we will shrink a database using Enterprise Manager.

EXERCISE 2.2

Increasing the Size and Shrinking a Database with SQL Enterprise Manager

This exercise will walk you through managing your database size—increasing and decreasing it—with Enterprise Manager.

1. Open SQL Enterprise Manager by choosing Start ➢ Programs ➢ Microsoft SQL Server ➢ Enterprise Manager. In SQL Enterprise Manager, right-click the MyFirstDatabase folder, and click Properties.

2. Click the Data Files tab.

3. In the Space Allocated cell of the first data file, type **20**.

4. Click OK.

5. In SQL Enterprise Manager, right-click the MyFirstDatabase folder, and click All Tasks ➢ Shrink Database.

6. In the Maximum Free Space in Files After Shrinking text box, type **80**.

7. Check the Move Pages to Beginning of File Before Shrinking option.

8. Click OK.

9. Click OK in the dialog box to indicate that the database has been shrunk successfully.

10. In the Taskpad, note that the size of the MyFirstDatabase_Data file has come back to its initial size.

Even though DBCC SHRINKDATABASE is a useful tool to reclaim unused space, it is not powerful enough to free up space in a determined file or to free up space beyond the initial size. The DBCC SHRINKFILE statement will help you to do so.

Shrinking a File

The DBCC SHRINKFILE allows you to shrink a specified data or log file directly to the desired size. For example, if you have a 200MB file in which only 50MB are used, and you want to release 40MB, just run the following line:

```
DBCC SHRINKFILE (myfile, 60)
```

There are two things you should remember when running this statement:

1. You name the file by its logical name, so you must be in the database context before running the statement. Just run USE mydb first.

2. The specified value is the target size in megabytes. If you omit that value and there is enough free space to allow the shrinking, the file is shrunk to its initial size.

The target size may not be reached if there is too much data in the file. In the previous example, if there were 70MB of data, the file would have a size of 70MB instead of the 60MB asked for and without any warning. The Query Analyzer result pane gives you an indication of what has been done with the file.

```
DbId FileId CurrentSize MinimumSize UsedPages EstimatedPages
---- ------ ----------- ----------- --------- --------------
7    1      7680        256         6400      6400
```

The previous table shows the result of the size reduction of myfile. The table contains the following columns:

- DbId is the database ID (found in sysdatabases).

- FileID is the file ID (found in sysaltfiles).

- CurrentSize is the current file size in 8KB pages. In the example, the file is 60MB.

- MinimumSize is the minimum size of the file, generally its initial size, in 8KB pages. In the example, the file has been created with a size of 2MB.

- UsedPages indicates the number of allocated 8KB pages. In the example, there are 50MB of data.

- EstimatedPages indicates the minimum size the file could be shrunk to, taking into account the allocated pages.

You have three options when executing the DBCC SHRINKFILE statement:

- EMPTYFILE allows you to empty the file by moving the data it contains to another file of the same filegroup. After a file has been emptied, it can be deleted with an ALTER DATABASE statement (see below). You do not specify a target size if you want to empty a file.

- NOTRUNCATE moves data at the beginning of the file but does not release the freed space to the operating system.

- TRUNCATEONLY shrinks the file to the last allocated extent and releases the freed extents to the operating system.

The last two options work exactly the same way with DBCC SHRINKFILE as with DBCC SHRINKDATABASE.

To shrink a file directly in SQL Enterprise Manager:

1. Right-click the database you wish to shrink.

2. Click All Tasks ➤ Shrink Database.

3. Click Files.

4. Choose the file in the Database File drop-down box. The system will give you information on the file, as in Figure 2.7.

FIGURE 2.7   Shrinking a file in SQL Enterprise Manager

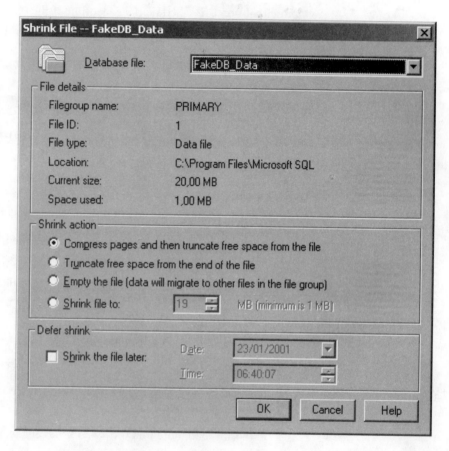

The different options presented in the dialog box correspond to some DBCC SHRINKFILE options:

- Compress Pages and Then Truncate Free Space From the File is the default option. It will truncate the file to the smallest possible size.

- Truncate Free Space From the End of the File corresponds to TRUNCATEONLY.

- Empty the File (Data will Migrate to Other Files in the File Group) corresponds to EMPTYFILE.

5. Click the OK button.

Note that you can schedule the execution of the DBCC SHRINKFILE if you check the Shrink the File Later check box. If you do so, the operation will not be done, but only scheduled.

In Exercise 2.3, we will shrink a file using Enterprise Manager.

EXERCISE 2.3

Shrinking a Database File with SQL Enterprise Manager

This exercise will walk you through shrinking a file using SQL Enterprise Manager.

1. Open SQL Enterprise Manager by choosing Start ➢ Programs ➢ Microsoft SQL Server ➢ Enterprise Manager. In SQL Enterprise Manager, right-click the MyFirstDatabase folder, and click All Tasks ➢ Shrink Database.

2. Click the Files button.

3. Make sure the MyFirstDatabase_Data file is selected in the Database File drop-down box.

4. Select the Shrink File To option and type **80** in the text box.

5. Click OK.

6. Click OK in the dialog box to indicate that the database file has been shrunk successfully.

7. In the Taskpad, note that the MyFirstDatabase_Data file size is now 5MB.

Now that you've seen how to shrink a database, let's take a look at how you can alter a database.

Altering a Database

Altering a database means modifying its file structure by adding, removing, or modifying files, or by changing its name. All three operations can be done through SQL Enterprise Manager or with Transact-SQL. We will focus more on Transact-SQL, since the language is always the primary focus of any process in the exam. SQL Enterprise Manager is mentioned here, as it is the easiest way to do a specific operation. Knowing the statements allows you to understand what's happening behind the curtain. Let's start with file modification.

Modifying a File

Modifying a database file means changing its name, its size, its max size, or its file growth increment. The following example increases the size of the primary file of the FakeDB database:

```
ALTER DATABASE FakeDB
MODIFY FILE
  ( NAME = FakeDB_data1,
    SIZE = 200MB)
```

The size value must be greater than the current file size. Otherwise, you'll encounter error 5039: MODIFY FILE `failed. Specified size is less than current size.`

The following example modifies, in one statement, the database name, max size, and file growth increment:

```
ALTER DATABASE FakeDB
MODIFY FILE
        ( NAME = FakeDB_data1,
          NEWNAME = FakeDB_Primary,
      MAXSIZE = 1.5GB,
      FILEGROWTH = 50MB)
```

The MODIFY FILE clause has a FILENAME property, like in CREATE DATABASE, which allows for the modification of the physical name and location of the file. This property can only be used for tempdb files and take effect when SQL Server is restarted.

All these operations can be realized in SQL Enterprise Manager through the Database Properties dialog box.

1. In SQL Enterprise Manager, right-click the database name.

2. Click Properties.

3. In the Database Properties dialog box, click the Data Files or the Transaction Log tab, depending on the file you want to modify.

4. Select the file you want to modify and modify the necessary properties.

5. Click OK to validate your modification.

Increasing the database size can be done through increasing one or more file sizes by adding new files.

Adding a File

Adding a file to a database is quite a simple process, since it is like creating a file at the time of database creation. The following example adds a file to the FakeDB database:

```
ALTER DATABASE FakeDB
ADD FILE
     ( NAME = FakeDB_data3,
     FILENAME = 'd:\FakeDB_data3.mdf',
     SIZE = 100MB,
     MAXSIZE = 1GB,
     FILEGROWTH = 10MB),
```

You can add a new file to an existing database in SQL Enterprise Manager with the Database Properties dialog box:

1. In SQL Enterprise Manager, right-click the database name.

2. Click Properties.

3. In the Database Properties dialog box, click the Data Files or the Transaction Log tab, depending on the file you want to add.

4. Click the empty File Name cell and type the new file logical name.

5. Define its location in the Location cell, type its size, and choose its growing properties in the File Properties frame.

6. Click OK to validate your addition.

Removing a File

You can remove a file from a database if and only if it is empty. You can empty a file with DBCC SHRINKFILE and the EMPTYFILE property. The following statements empty the third file from FakeDB and remove it:

```
DBCC SHRINKFILE ('FakeDB_data3', EMPTYFILE)
```

```
ALTER DATABASE FakeDB
REMOVE FILE FakeDB_data3
```

You can remove an empty file from an existing database in SQL Enterprise Manager with the Database Properties dialog box:

1. In SQL Enterprise Manager, right-click the database name.

2. Click Properties.

3. In the Database Properties dialog box, click the Data Files or the Transaction Log tab, depending on the file you want to remove.

4. Select the file by clicking its row.

5. Click Delete.

6. Click OK to confirm your choice.

Once you've clicked the OK button, the file is physically deleted and cannot be recovered!

7. Click OK or Cancel to close the dialog box.

Remember you can only remove a file if it is empty. If it contains data, you obtain error 5042: The file 'filename' cannot be removed because it is not empty.

Changing a Database Name

You can change a database name very easily. Two methods exist to do so: ALTER DATABASE and sp_renamedb. The system-stored procedure uses the ALTER DATABASE statement after doing some basic name checks and is kept only for backward compatibility. The following example renames the FakeDB database to TestDB:

```
sp_rename 'FakeDB', 'TestDB'
```

With the ALTER DATABASE statement, the syntax is almost as simple:

```
ALTER DABASE FakeDB MODIFY NAME=TestDB
```

It is not possible to rename a database through SQL Enterprise Manager.

So far, we have seen that a database is composed of data and log files. Let's look closer at these files to uncover their structure.

Space Management

Microsoft Exam Objective

Create and alter databases. Considerations include file groups, file placement, growth strategy, and space requirements.

- Specify space management parameters. Parameters include autoshrink, growth increment, initial size, and maxsize.

A good understanding of SQL Server space management is necessary to write and optimize queries. We have seen that there are three types of files: primary, secondary, and log. While the structure of primary and secondary files is almost the same, the log file is totally different. Let's start with the data files.

Data Files

Each data file is made of 64KB extents. Each *extent* is made of eight 8KB pages. The *page* is the base allocation of a table or an index. Each time you create a table or an index, its data is stored in a page.

Even if a page is 8KB, that is 8,192 bytes, the maximum record length (text, ntext, and image data types excluded) is 8,060 bytes. Furthermore, a record must entirely fit in a page (text, ntext, and image data types excluded).

Figure 2.8 represents a data file, an extent, and a page. All the data files are organized the same way, and all data is stored in pages. As we are going to see, different types of pages exist, depending on the content. As for the extents, the two types are uniform and mixed. Let's have a look first at these extents, then at the pages that compose them.

FIGURE 2.8   Data file, extent, and page

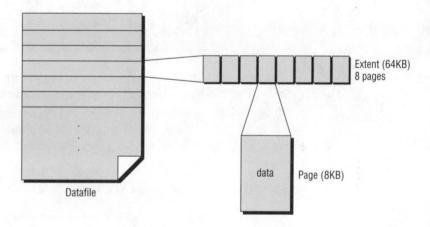

Extents

A *uniform extent* is allocated entirely to one table or index. A *mixed extent* is shared between different tables or indexes. Figure 2.9 represents three extents, two mixed and one uniform extent. Extents one and two are shared between three tables: T1, T2, and T3. Extent three is fully allocated to T1.

FIGURE 2.9 Mixed and uniform extents

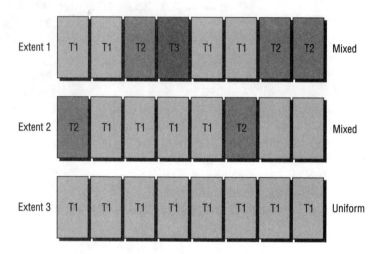

The process of extent allocation is quite simple: At the table or index creation, the first eight pages allocated are in mixed extents. From the ninth page allocation, the table or index is allocated uniform extents. You can observe this phenomenon if you run the sp_spaceused stored procedures in SQL Query Analyzer. Let's create a table to demonstrate the process:

```
CREATE TABLE BigTable(Col1 Char(8000))
```

The BigTable table contains only one column, but as it is a char column, each time you insert a record, that record fills the page. If you run sp_spaceused BigTable, you obtain the following result:

```
Name       rows  reserved  data   index_size  unused
---------  ----- --------- -----  ----------- -------
BigTable   0     0 KB      0 KB   0 KB        0 KB
```

As you can see, for the moment, no page has been allocated yet. Before inserting the first row, let me give you some explanation about the columns:

- Rows contains the number of rows of the table.

- Reserved represents the number of kilobytes allocated to the table.

- Data represents the number of kilobytes allocated to the data.

- Index_size represents the number of kilobytes allocated to the table indexes.

- Unused shows the results of reserved-data-index_size and represents the unused allocated kilobytes.

All of these figures, rows excluded, are multiples of 8KB, since the page is the base allocation.

If you insert one row in the BigTable table, for example:

```
INSERT BigTable VALUES ('FakeData')
```

the result of sp_spaceused is the following:

Name	rows	reserved	data	index_size	unused
BigTable	1	16 KB	8 KB	8 KB	0 KB

As you can see, the table has one row, and two pages have been allocated (16KB are reserved)—one data page and one index page. At the extent level, a data page and an index page are very similar. Nevertheless, an index on BigTable has not been created. So, why has an index page been allocated? This allocation represents the IAM (*Index Allocation Map*), as we are going to see in a few pages.

One important thing to note here is that, besides the index, only one page has been allocated. It has been allocated to the table to store the inserted record. Note that the record is 8000 characters wide, meaning each record occupies one page. If you insert a second row in the BigTable table, the result of sp_spaceused is the following:

Name	rows	reserved	data	index_size	unused
BigTable	2	24 KB	16 KB	8 KB	0 KB

Now the data space used is 16KB, or two pages. If you insert six other records in the table, the sp_spaceused stored procedure will give the following result:

Name	rows	reserved	data	index_size	unused
BigTable	8	72 KB	64 KB	8 KB	0 KB

As you can see, the first eight allocations are made on a page basis. Each time SQL Server needs to assign space to a table, it allocates the first free page in a mixed extent, if any are available. If no free page is available, it allocates a new extent and assigns one page to the table. Things change from the ninth allocation. If you insert the ninth row in the BigTable table, you obtain the following results for the sp_spaceused stored procedure:

Name	rows	reserved	data	index_size	unused
BigTable	9	136 KB	72 KB	8 KB	56 KB

One major modification occurred: One whole extent has been allocated, even if only one page would have been enough. You see the reserved space going from 72KB (eight data pages and one index page) to 136KB, which is a 64KB increase (an extent). In the previous results, we have nine pages in mixed extents (the first eight data pages and the IAM page) and one page in one uniform extent. Subsequently, new pages will be allocated in the uniform extent until it is fully used. Afterwards, a new uniform extent will be allocated, and so on.

This allocation method is used to minimize the allocated space; small tables are allocated only for the necessary pages. It is also used to minimize the number of times the size of a bigger table has to be increased. Each time the table needs space, it is allocated 64KB at one time.

In the previous example, a special kind of index called IAM was mentioned. This index is allocated its own page. We will now look at the different types of pages that exist in a SQL Server database.

Pages

So far, we know that a database is made of extents and pages. Eight different types of pages exist in a database:

Data   The real user or system data rows, except text, ntext, and image data.

Index   Index rows.

Text/Image   Text, ntext, and image data.

IAM   *Index Allocation Map.* Information about extents used by a table or an index.

GAM, SGAM   *Global Allocation Map. Secondary Global Allocation Map.* Information about extents allocation.

PFS   *Page Free Space*. Information about page allocation and the percentage of free space in each page.

BCM   *Bulk Changed Map*. Information about extents that have been modified since the last log backup.

DCM   *Differential Changed Map*. Information about extents that have been modified since the last database differential backup.

The first six of these types of pages are described in the following sections. The last two, totally new to SQL Server 2000, are beyond the scope of this book, since they concern the modification tracking for backup purposes. You can read more about BCM and DCM in the SQL Books Online.

DATA ALLOCATION

A data and index page are composed of three parts:

- The 96-byte header contains information about the page, such as its number, the table, and index it belongs to.

- The data rows space contains the rows of data.

- The row offset table tracks the start byte of each record in the page.

Figure 2.10 represents a SQL Server data page. The first row starts immediately after the header, at byte 96 (the first byte of the page is byte 0, the header is 96 bytes long, and the first available byte is byte 96). This information is stored in the first slot of the offset table.

FIGURE 2.10   A data page

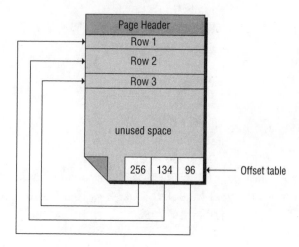

In Figure 2.10, the first row is 38 bytes long. So the second row starts at byte 134. This figure is recorded in the second slot of the offset page, and so on. When SQL Server reads a page, it goes to the header to discover the position of every record in the page.

The position of the records in the page, while sequential at the beginning, may change due to updates, deletes, and inserts. For example, if the second record is updated so its size increases, it will not fit in the space it occupied. It is then stored after the third record, but remains record number two. So the offset table would store, for example, 96, 297, 256. There is now space available between bytes 134 and 255.

Index pages are almost the same, except index entries take the place of data rows. We cover indexes and index storage in Chapter 5: Creating and Maintaining Indexes. Text/Image pages store text, ntext, and image datatypes. We cover these data types and their storage in Chapter 3: Creating and Maintaining Tables.

Database pages can be studied in detail with the DBCC PAGE statement. DBCC PAGE is an undocumented statement that is very useful in understanding data storage. You will not be asked any questions on this statement in the test, but it is a good way to uncover SQL Server storage strategies.

Run the following statement in the SQL Query Analyzer:

```
dbcc traceon(3604)
dbcc page('pubs', 1, 49, 1)
```
you obtain this result:
```
PAGE: (1:49)
------------


PAGE HEADER:
------------


Page @0x19714000
----------------
m_pageId = (1:49)      m_headerVersion = 1    m_type = 1
m_typeFlagBits = 0x0   m_level = 0            m_flagBits = 0x0
m_objId = 1977058079   m_indexId = 0         m_prevPage = (0:0)
```

```
m_nextPage = (0:0)      pminlen = 24          m_slotCnt = 23
m_freeCnt = 6010        m_freeData = 2136     m_reservedCnt = 0
m_lsn = (5:242:2)       m_xactReserved = 0    m_xdesId = (0:0)
m_ghostRecCnt = 0       m_tornBits = -2147483591
```

```
Allocation Status
-----------------

GAM (1:2) = ALLOCATED      SGAM (1:3) = NOT ALLOCATED
PFS (1:1) = 0x60 MIXED_EXT ALLOCATED 0_PCT_FULL
DIFF(1:6)= CHANGED ML (1:7) = NOT MIN_LOGGED


DATA:
-----


Slot 0, Offset 0x631
--------------------
Record Type = PRIMARY_RECORD
Record Attributes =  NULL_BITMAP VARIABLE_COLUMNS
19714631: 00180030 20383034 2d363934 33323237 0...408 496-7223
19714641: 34394143 01353230 00000009 00330005 CA94025.......3.
19714651: 003f0038 0058004e 2d323731 312d3233 8.?.N.X.172-32-1
19714661: 57363731 65746968 6e686f4a 316e6f73 176WhiteJohnson1
19714671: 32333930 67694220 52206567 654d2e64 0932 Bigge Rd.Me
19714681: 206f6c6e 6b726150                    nlo Park

...


OFFSET TABLE:
-------------
Row - Offset
22 (0x16) - 357 (0x165)
21 (0x15) - 448 (0x1c0)
...
2 (0x2) - 272 (0x110)
1 (0x1) - 184 (0xb8)
0 (0x0) - 1585 (0x631)
```

The page number may be different on your SQL Server installation, so if you try to run the DBCC PAGE example statement directly, you may get a different result.

The page header and the different information it contains is returned first. Next you find the user data, starting with the first record of the table. If you ran a SELECT * FROM authors statement, you would see the same record, but presented in a more readable arrangement:

```
au_id        au_lname  au_fname phone
-----------  --------- ---------------------
172-32-1176 White      Johnson   408 496-7223

address           city         state  zip     contract
----------------  -----------  ------ ------  --------
10932 Bigge Rd.   Menlo Park   CA            94025  1
```

The previous record has been presented on two lines for reading purposes, but would appear on one line in SQL Query Analyzer.

From the DBCC PAGE result, you may note the column information is not in the same order physically and logically. This is due to the record structure, which will be explained in Chapter 3.

Finally, the offset table presents the physical location in the page of every record starting from the last one. Note that the first record is not on byte 96 because it moved due to the creation of a clustered index.

DBCC PAGE is not a statement you are going to use every day. It's just a tool in your toolbox that can help you better understand SQL Server data storage.

One final piece of information on record allocation is that if a row is updated, three situations can occur:

- If the size of the row is smaller or equal after the update, then the row stays at the same address.

- If the size of the row is bigger after the update and there is enough space in the page to store it, then the row moves inside the page but its offset index occupies exactly the same space. So, if row number two moves to row number 10 physically in the page, its address will always be stored in the second slot.

- If the size of the row is bigger after the update and there is not enough space in the page to store it, then the row moves to another page, and a forwarding pointer is kept in the page to avoid index update. If row number two was in page 15 and moves to page 23 and becomes, in this page, row number four, then the address 23:4 is stored in the second slot of page 15. If the row moves another time, the forwarding pointer is updated. The indexes remain stable.

If a row is deleted, it remains physically in the page, until the space it occupied is used by another inserted or updated row, or until the household process (the same that shrinks automatically if the option is enabled) runs. It runs every half hour under a normal load, but can be postponed automatically if the server is under a very heavy load.

When a row is inserted, it is inserted in the first available slot in the page, so the physical order of records inside a page does not necessarily reflect the insert order of the records that page contains. A clustered index modifies the behavior of inserts, as we will see in Chapter 5.

ALLOCATION TRACKING

Computers are just machines and they need to be told where they should store information. If you put away the power cable of your laptop in the first drawer of your office desk, you probably store in your memory that you did so. When you need your power cable, your brain tells you automatically that it is in the first drawer. Unfortunately, computers are not so intelligent.

Each time a page or an extent is allocated, SQL Server must record that allocation. The five types of pages that were introduced earlier do the allocation tracking: File header, GAM, SGAM, PFS, and IAM. The first four pages of every file are the header, the PFS, the GAM, and the SGAM (Figure 2.11). These pages manage the file information and allocation. Every table and index has an IAM.

FIGURE 2.11 First four pages of every file

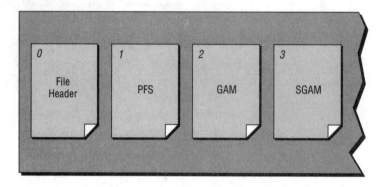

The first page of every data file is its header. It contains information about the file like its size, its max size, its growth increment, etc. You can see this in the following DBCC PAGE result:

```
File Header Data:
-----------------
...
BindingID=10df082a-53e0-4024-809c-140aeb022990  File-
   GroupId=2
FileIdProp=4         Size=128              MaxSize=25600
Growth=10            Perf=0
   BackupLsn=[NULL]
MaxLsn=[NULL]                    FirstLsn=[NULL]
FirstCreateIndexLsn=[NULL]      FirstUpdateLsn=(5:86:1)
FirstNonloggedUpdateLsn=[NULL]  CreateLsn=(5:42:1)
DifferentialBaseLsn=(0:0:0)
DifferentialBaseGuid=00000000-0000-0000-0000-000000000000
MinSize=128          Status=0          UserShrinkSize=65535
```

The second page of every file is the PFS. PFS stands for Page Free Space. It contains information about allocation and fill rate for the first 8,000 pages. If the file has more than 8,000 pages, there is a PFS every 8,000 pages with all the PFS linked together. The PFS allows the system to find the first available page for an insert or for a page allocation. The following result gives the content of a PFS:

```
PFS: Page Alloc Status  @0x190EE000
------------------------------------
(4:0) -(4:3)  =     ALLOCATED   0_PCT_FULL
(4:4) -(4:5)  = NOT ALLOCATED   0_PCT_FULL
(4:6) -(4:7)  =     ALLOCATED   0_PCT_FULL
(4:8) -(4:9)  =     ALLOCATED 100_PCT_FULL  Mixed Ext
(4:10)-       =     ALLOCATED   0_PCT_FULL  IAM Page  Mixed Ext
(4:11)-(4:15) = NOT ALLOCATED   0_PCT_FULL
(4:16)-(4:23) =     ALLOCATED   0_PCT_FULL
(4:24)-(4:127)= NOT ALLOCATED   0_PCT_FULL
```

The first number in every page address represents the file number, the second figure represents the page number. For example, 4:5 means page number five in file number four. In this example, we find out that the four first pages are allocated (header, PFS, GAM, SGAM), that pages four and five are not allocated (in fact, they are reserved for DCM and BCM), and that pages six to seven are allocated. The 0_PCT_FULL information means that less than 1 percent of the page is used. Pages eight and nine are allocated, are in a mixed extent, and are full. Page 10 is an IAM (Index Allocation Map). Pages 11 to 15 (the last five pages of the extent beginning on page eight) are not allocated. Pages 16 to 23 (one full extent) are allocated but almost empty, and all the other pages (from 24 to 127) are not allocated.

The PFS content is presented in a readable way here, but is in reality a bitmap containing one byte per page.

Pages two and three of every data file are reserved for GAM and SGAM. The GAM, or Global Allocation Map, tells you whether an extent (eight contiguous pages) contains allocated pages. Every GAM tracks 64,000 extents. Every bit indicates whether the extension is free or not: 1 means the extent is free, 0 means it is allocated. The SGAM, or Secondary Global Allocation Map, is used with the GAM to show whether an extent is mixed and contains at least one free page. Each extent reference follows the bit pattern indicated in Table 2.1.

TABLE 2.1 GAM-SGAM Usage

GAM	SGAM	Extent
1	0	Free
0	0	Uniform extent or full mixed extent
0	1	Mixed extent with at least one free page

If you run DBCC PAGE on the GAM of a file, you will obtain a result similar to the following:

```
GAM: Extent Alloc Status @0x191200C2
--------------------------------------
(4:0)          - (4:16)       =      ALLOCATED
(4:24)         - (4:120)      = NOT ALLOCATED
```

In this result, ALLOCATED means 0 and NOT ALLOCATED means 1. Extents starting on pages 0, 8 and 16 are allocated, which means they contain at least one page. The others are free. Now, if you run DBCC PAGE on the SGAM of a file, you may obtain the following results:

```
SGAM: Extent Alloc Status @0x1947E0C2
--------------------------------------
(4:0)          - (4:8)        = NOT ALLOCATED
(4:8)          -              =      ALLOCATED
(4:16)         - (4:120)      = NOT ALLOCATED
```

In this result, ALLOCATED means 0 and NOT ALLOCATED means 0 (very logical, isn't it?). So, the first extent (starting on page 0) is full (pages four and five are free, but they are reserved). The second one (starting on page eight) is a mixed extent with some free pages (pages 11 to 15 are not allocated). The third one (starting on page 16) is a full mixed extent or a uniform extent.

Last of all allocation pages, the IAM tracks page allocation for a specific table or index. Every table and every index has at least one IAM. The IAM stores the first eight allocated pages (in mixed extents) and the uniform allocated extents. The following DBCC PAGE result indicates the different allocations for a table:

```
nIAM: Single Page Allocations @0x191A008E
-------------------------------------------
Slot 0 = (3:8)     Slot 1 = (3:10)    Slot 2 = (3:11)
Slot 3 = (3:12)    Slot 4 = (3:13)    Slot 5 = (3:14)
Slot 6 = (3:15)    Slot 7 = (4:8)
```

```
IAM: Extent Alloc Status Slot 1 @0x191A00C2
--------------------------------------------
(3:0)         - (3:8)        = NOT ALLOCATED
(3:16)        -              =    ALLOCATED
(3:24)        - (3:120)      = NOT ALLOCATED
```

The first eight pages have been allocated in file numbers three and four (slot seven is in file four). The extent starting on page 16 is allocated to the table. A single IAM can track 64,000 extents. So, if the table size needs to go beyond that limit, a second IAM is allocated to the table and linked to the first one.

The IAM is very important to every table, since it is the only way to track its page allocations if it does not have a clustered index (see Chapter 5). The IAM address is stored in the sysindexes table. You can see this if you run the following statement:

```
SELECT * FROM sysindexes WHERE id=OBJECT_ID('Customers')
```

If you run the previous SELECT statement in the Northwind database (one of the sample databases installed with SQL Server), you obtain a five-line result set. On line one (indid column value is one), you will find a column named FirstIAM containing the value 0x6E0000000100 (your own value may vary). This is the address of the first IAM page of the Customers table. All the addresses you find in sysindexes are displayed using reverse polish notation. The first four words (6E000000) give you the address in the file, while the last two words (0100) give you its number. You should read addresses from right to left in blocks of two. In our example, the file number is 0001. The page address is 0000006E, that is 110 decimal. We now know that the first IAM page of the Customers table is in file number one on page number 110, and so does the system that tracks the data. Once the system has the IAM, it reads the IAM to discover the allocated pages.

Log Files

Log files have nothing in common with data files. You may have found that the data file structure is complicated, however, log files have a simple structure. The complexity of data files is needed to track all the modifications performed on data. In contrast, the log files are only written to most of the time, truncated some of the time, and never, ever modified, so the structure is simpler.

SQL Server 2000 uses a transaction log called a write-ahead log. Each time a modification is done to any data, the system records a transaction.

The process of working with data and log files is illustrated in Figure 2.3. When a page is modified (remember every modification is done in cache, then flushed to the disk during checkpoints), the transaction is written in the log cache, then to the disk. So, the transaction is written to the log ahead of the data file. That is why it is called a write-ahead log.

The transaction log can be represented as a table containing information on all the modifications that have occurred in a database. This pseudo table contains "log records," which contain the definition of the statement executed on the system. With the undocumented DBCC LOG statement, it is possible to have a readable view of the log using

```
DBCC LOG('Northwind')
```

You obtain the following result (extract):

Current LSN	Operation	Context	Trans. ID
0018:0117:0001	LOP_BEGIN_CKPT	LCX_NULL	0000:0000
0018:0118:0001	LOP_END_CKPT	LCX_NULL	0000:0000
0018:0119:0001	LOP_BEGIN_XACT	LCX_NULL	0000:0edb
0018:0119:0002	LOP_DELETE_ROWS	LCX_MARK_AS_GHOST	0000:0edb
0018:0119:0003	LOP_MODIFY_HEADER	LCX_PFS	0000:0000
0018:0119:0004	LOP_SET_BITS	LCX_PFS	0000:0000
0018:0119:0005	LOP_MODIFY_COLUMNS	LCX_CLUSTERED	0000:0edb
0018:0119:0006	LOP_INSERT_ROWS	LCX_INDEX_LEAF	0000:0edb
0018:0119:0007	LOP_DELTA_SYSIND	LCX_CLUSTERED	0000:0edb
0018:0119:0008	LOP_COMMIT_XACT	LCX_NULL	0000:0edb
0018:011b:0001	LOP_BEGIN_XACT	LCX_NULL	0000:0edc
0018:011b:0002	LOP_MODIFY_HEADER	LCX_PFS	0000:0edc
0018:011b:0003	LOP_EXPUNGE_ROWS	LCX_INDEX_LEAF	0000:0000
0018:011b:0004	LOP_SET_BITS	LCX_PFS	0000:0000
0018:011b:0005	LOP_COMMIT_XACT	LCX_NULL	0000:0edc

In the previous example, the Current LSN and Transaction ID values have been shortened to four characters from eight to allow the information to fit on one line. For example, the LSN 0018:0117:0001 should read 00000018:00000117:0001, and the Transaction ID 0000:0edb should read 0000:00000edb.

Consider the following about the DBCC LOG result:

- It is not the SQL statements that are logged in the transaction log, but the way it is executed by SQL Server. The previous log example has been read after a simple column update. But updating an indexed value may lead to many data and physical structure modifications.

- Each time an operation is done on the system it may be recorded as a transaction. In this case, the transaction ID is recorded in the transaction log to identify the committed transaction. This feature is crucial to the automatic recovery process.

- New log records are always added at the end of the log. No log record can be updated. Log records may be deleted if the transaction log is truncated or backed up.

- Each log record is identified by a unique *Log Sequence Number* (LSN).

For performance and internal management purposes, a transaction log file is divided into virtual log files (Figure 2.12). The number and size of virtual log files depend on the size of the log. SQL Server creates or resizes these log files at the file creation or extension.

The minimum size for a virtual log file is 128KB. The size and the number of virtual log files depend on the initial size of the log and the growth increment value.

FIGURE 2.12   Virtual log files

| Virtual Log 1 | Virtual Log 2 | Virtual Log 3 | Virtual Log 4 |

WARNING

If your transaction log size and growth increment are too small, after a couple of weeks in production, you may find a large number of small virtual log files. These will likely slow down database performance. It is better to choose an initial size close to the biggest needed size and a large growth increment.

Log records are inserted in the file sequentially, starting with the first virtual log. If you truncate the log by backing it up either automatically or manually, the inactive part of the log is deleted. The inactive portion of a transaction log is the portion that contains transactions with entries that have been saved to disk. The system always keeps on disk what is called the minimum recovery log. This is the active portion of a transaction log, the one that will be applied in the event of a failure. The application of these log entries to the database will bring the database back to the state it was in before the failure. The beginning of this minimum recovery log is called the min LSN (see Figure 2.13).

FIGURE 2.13 Transactions and checkpoint

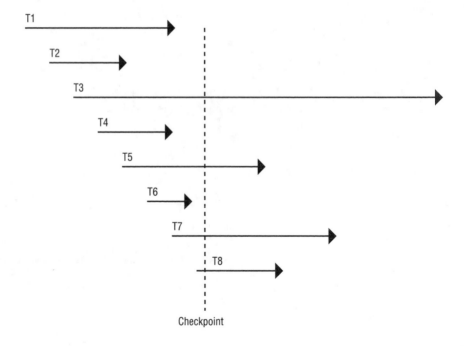

Figure 2.13 represents some running transactions. When the checkpoint process occurs, the committed data is flushed to the disk. In this example, the data modified by transactions T1, T2, T4, and T6 are written to the disk. The one modified by transactions T3, T5, T7, and T8 are not written to the disk because the transactions are still running at checkpoint time. In this case, the min LSN is the first LSN of transaction T3, since it is the oldest running transaction. The transaction log could be truncated up to the min LSN.

The min LSN may be in the middle of a virtual log, like in Figure 2.14, but the start of the logical log is always the start of the virtual log file containing the min LSN.

FIGURE 2.14 Min LSN and virtual logs

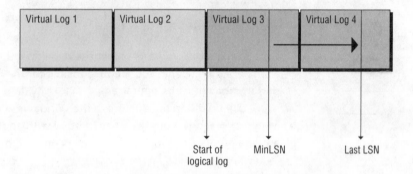

The log file is used in a round-robin fashion: Log records are added to the end of the last used virtual log file. If the end of the physical file is reached, the inserts continue at the beginning of the file, like in Figure 2.15.

FIGURE 2.15 Round-robin log

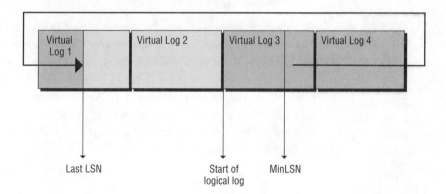

If the inserts reach the start of the logical log, the physical file will grow automatically if it has been configured to do so. If the file growth cannot occur for some reason, the user trying to modify a record and insert rows in the transaction log will receive error 9002: The `log file for database 'database name' is full. Back up the transaction log for the database to free up some log space.`

If the transaction log covers many files, SQL Server fills every file before it goes back to the first virtual log.

 Real World Scenario

The Write-ahead Paradigm

Let's imagine that you are a database developer and administrator for a small regional bank. You are responsible for the SQL Server box. Its performance must be optimized permanently, and you keep an eye every day on different counters of the Windows 2000 Performance Monitor. Recently, your bank has merged with another regional bank, and the number of counter clerks has been multiplied by three, increasing the stress on the server.

You use the Performance Monitor to observe what is happening on the disks. The log disk is used at 100 percent, while the data disk is used at only 65 percent on average, with peaks at 100 percent during the checkpoint process. As you observe, the most severe impact is on the transaction log disk because the application is heavily transactional. Your log disk is an old 7200 RPM SCSI disk, and you decide to upgrade it to a 15K RPM disk.

Having done that after normal work time, the next day you observe that the log disk is used at 60 percent. Your goal is achieved. There are two morals from this scenario: First, the Performance Monitor is the tool to use to discover bottlenecks or potential bottlenecks when you need to analyze what's going on a SQL Server system. Second, the disk capacity of the log, in terms of speed and bandwidth, is crucial to performance. A good hardware design will lead faster to a well performing application.

One last thing concerning the log: Its use depends on the recovery model. If not truncated, it grows indefinitely. In the previous versions of SQL Server, the database option `trunc. log on chkpt.` meant that the log was truncated from time to time, on every checkpoint. This option still exists but it's hidden behind the recovery model. To avoid filling up the log, always adopt one of these two strategies:

- You choose the Simple recovery model so that the log is truncated automatically. This can be done on a development or a test system, never on a production server.

- You choose the Full or Bulk-logged recovery model and schedule the log backup. Each time the log is backed up, its inactive portion is truncated. It is the best practice on a production server. This may mean extra work for the administrator, but also peace of mind in the event of failure!

Database Options

When it is created, there are many options that can be set for a database. Some options are readable and updateable through SQL Enterprise Manager (Figure 2.16), but others can be manipulated only through Transact-SQL.

FIGURE 2.16   The Database Options tab

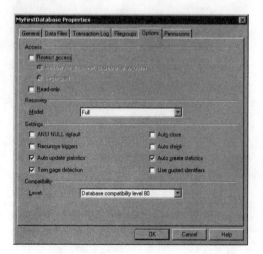

In Transact-SQL, you may modify a database option with the ALTER DATABASE statement or with the sp_dboption stored procedure:

```
ALTER DATABASE database
SET optionspec [ ,...n ] [ WITH termination ]
```

Or

```
sp_dboption [ [ @dbname = ] 'database' ]
        [ , [ @optname = ] 'option_name' ]
        [ , [ @optvalue = ] 'value' ]
```

Table 2.2 gives you the different values of *optionspec*, *option_name*, and the SQL Enterprise Manager equivalent.

TABLE 2.2 Database Options Value

Option Name	Optionspec	Option in SQL Enterprise Manager
ANSI null default	ANSI_NULL_DEFAULT ON | OFF	ANSI NULL default
ANSI nulls	ANSI_NULLS ON | OFF	N/A
ANSI padding	ANSI_PADDINGS ON | OFF	N/A
ANSI warnings	ANSI_WARNINGS ON | OFF	N/A
arithabort	ARITHABORT ON | OFF	N/A
auto create statistics	AUTO_CREATE_STATISTICS ON | OFF	auto create statistics
auto update statistics	AUTO_UPDATE_STATISTICS ON | OFF	auto update statistics
autoclose	AUTO_CLOSE ON | OFF	autoclose
autoshrink	AUTO_SHRINK ON | OFF	autoshrink
concat null yields null	CONCAT_NULL_YIELDS_NULL ON | OFF	N/A

TABLE 2.2   Database Options Value *(continued)*

Option Name	Optionspec	Option in SQL Enterprise Manager
cursor close on commit	CURSOR_CLOSE_ON_COMMIT ON | OFF	N/A
dbo use only	RESTRICTED_USER	Restrict access, Members of db_owner, dbcreator, or sysadmin
default to local cursor	CURSOR_DEFAULT LOCAL | GLOBAL	N/A
merge publish	N/A	N/A
numeric roundabort	NUMERIC_ROUNDABORT ON | OFF	N/A
offline	OFFLINE | ONLINE	N/A
published	N/A	N/A
quoted identifier	QUOTED_IDENTIFIER ON | OFF	Use quoted identifier
read only	READ_ONLY | READ_WRITE	Read-only
recursive triggers	RECURSIVE_TRIGGERS ON | OFF	recursive triggers
select into/bulkcopy	Depending on the Recovery Model	Depending on the Recovery Model
single user	SINGLE_USER | MULTI_USER	Restrict access, Single user
subscribed	N/A	N/A
torn page detection	TORN_PAGE_DETECTION ON | OFF	torn page detection
trunc. log on chkpt.	Depending on the Recovery Model	Depending on the Recovery Model

You can find the complete description of database options in the SQL Server Books OnLine. You open them by choosing Start ➤ Programs ➤ Microsoft SQL Server ➤ Books OnLine.

For the recovery model concerned, Table 2.3 gives the matching values for SELECT INTO/BULKCOPY and trunc.log on chkpt.

TABLE 2.3   Recovery Model and Database Options

Model/Option	SELECT INTO/BULKCOPY	trunc.log on chkpt.
Full/RECOVERY FULL	False	False
Bulk_logged/RECOVERY BULK_LOGGED	True	False
Simple/RECOVERY SIMPLE	False	True

To query the database options, you can run sp_dboption or use the DATABASEPROPERTYEX function. The following stored procedure gives you the options of the Northwind database:

```
Sp_dboptions 'Northwind'
```

The result is:

```
The following options are set:
-----------------------------------
autoclose
select into/bulkcopy
trunc. log on chkpt.
torn page detection
autoshrink
auto create statistics
auto update statistics
```

As you can see, only the SET options are listed. If you want to query a specific option value, the DATABASEPROPERTYEX function is the best way to do it. The result of the following statement is one, since the autoshrink option is set:

```
SELECT DATABASEPROPERTYEX('Northwind', 'IsAutoShrink')
```

You can find the complete list of option names for the DATABASEPROPERTYEX function in the SQL Server Books OnLine.

The following examples show you which statements to run to execute common operations:

- Restrict a database to one user:

```
ALTER DATABASE dbname SET SINGLE_USER
```

- Set a database in read-only mode:

```
ALTER DATABASE dbname SET READ_ONLY
```

- Set a database recovery model to Full:

```
ALTER DATABASE dbname SET RECOVERY FULL
```

- Set a database offline:

```
ALTER DATABASE dbname SET OFFLINE
```

Problems caused by other users occurred in previous versions of SQL Server that may still occur if you use the sp_dboption stored procedure. For example, if you want to set the database to single user, it fails if there is at least another user besides you using the database. When you set an option with the ALTER DATABASE statement, you can specify whether to rollback all running transactions on the database. There are three options that exist:

WITH ROLLBACK IMMEDIATE   All the running transactions are immediately rolled backed and the option is set.

WITH ROLLBACK AFTER *n* SECONDS   All the transactions running after *n* seconds are rolled back and the option is set.

WITH NO_WAIT   If the option cannot be set immediately due to running transactions, the option is not set.

The following statement will rollback all the running transactions and set the Northwind database to single user:

```
ALTER DATABASE Northwind
SET SINGLE_USER
WITH ROLLBACK IMMEDIATE
```

The last point about database options concerns the Level drop-down box you find in the Compatibility section of the Database Properties dialog box in the Options tab (Figure 2.16).

The database *compatibility level* defines the level of SQL grammar that can be used on the database. For example, if you run

```
SELECT
    ProductID,
    Sum(UnitPrice*Quantity*(1-Discount))
FROM [Order Details]
GROUP BY ProductID
```

in the Northwind database, the result set will be sorted in the ProductID column if the database is in compatibility level 60 or 65 and won't be sorted in the ProductID column if it is in compatibility level 70 or 80. If you upgrade your server from SQL Server 7 to SQL Server 2000, all the databases but the master will be in compatibility level 70. The same applies if you upgrade from SQL Server 6.5; all the databases will be in compatibility level 65.

The compatibility level has been designed to minimize the impact of a version upgrade on an existing application. In the previous example, a developer may know that in SQL Server 6.5, the GROUP BY clause sorts the result. So it does not add an ORDER BY clause, and the application works fine. When you switch to compatibility level 80, the result may no longer be sorted, and the application may behave unexpectedly. By lowering the compatibility level, you can upgrade the server without having to upgrade the application first.

The GROUP BY Compatibility Side Effects

I remember a few months ago, encountering a vicious side effect of the compatibility level after an upgrade for one of my customers. This customer was in a hurry to upgrade his SQL Server 6.5 database, so we did not take the time to test every feature of the application. Instead, we tested only the major features, as identified by the customer, after having changed the compatibility level.

A few weeks later the customer called, and while very satisfied with the upgrade, he explained that one report, for different product values, was sometimes giving strange results. In fact, the report was a kind of "cross-table." Products were in rows and monthly sales were in columns. Sometimes, the report was correct, other times the report had only one value for a product row, but each product was repeated twelve times.

The procedure to build this report was quite complicated, using different temporary tables. So, I had to test the procedure step-by-step to understand the flow of the application. After two hours of testing, I decided to analyze some of the SQL queries with the SQL Query Analyzer. I found that depending on the amount of data, the studied period, the number of products, and so on, the query optimizer was either using an order strategy for the GROUP BY clause or a hash-coding one. Adding the ORDER BY clause to the query solved all the problems with this report.

Test your application thoroughly before changing the compatibility level of the databases after an upgrade.

SQL Server 2000 is SQL Server version 8, so the database default compatibility level is eight, except for the upgraded databases. You have to be aware of the inherent risk of a compatibility level change. You will find all the differences between compatibility levels in the SQL Server Books Online if you search for the sp_dbcmptlevel stored procedure.

The master database always has a compatibility level 80.

To query or change the compatibility level of a database, you can use SQL Enterprise Manager or the sp_dbcmptlevel stored procedure. For example,

```
sp_dbcmptlevel 'Northwind'
```

gives you the following result:

    The current compatibility level is 80.

And

    sp_dbcmptlevel 'Northwind', 65

sets the compatibility level of the Northwind database to 65.

At this point, you should have a good understanding of how databases are created and are built. The next section will deal with filegroups. This chapter has talked about files, but filegroups can also be used, for performance or management reasons, to place data on specific disks.

Filegroups

Microsoft ✓ *Exam Objective*

Create and alter databases. Considerations include file groups, file placement, growth strategy, and space requirements.

- Specify file group and file placement. Considerations include logical and physical file placement.

*F*ilegroups are groups of data files, allowing explicit placement of tables, indexes, text, image, and ntext columns. There are two types of filegroups:

Primary   The primary filegroup created by default contains all system tables' allocation and some or all user tables.

User-defined   User-defined filegroups may contain user tables and are created during database creation or modification.

Figure 2.17 represents a database containing four files and three file-groups. The primary filegroup contains one file, the DataFG filegroup contains two files that can be placed on different physical disks, and the IndexFG filegroup contains one file.

FIGURE 2.17   Data files and filegroups

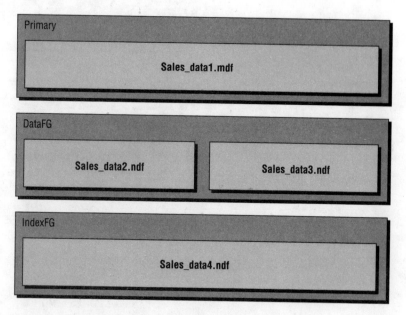

The creation of filegroups is generally driven by performance considerations. Some systems may improve their performance using filegroups by placing different filegroups on different physical devices.

Creating Filegroups

Filegroups are created in SQL Enterprise Manager when you create or alter a database, or with Transact-SQL with the FILEGROUP clause of the CREATE DATABASE or ALTER DATABASE statement.

Figure 2.18 represents the Database Properties dialog box for the Sales database whose structure is shown in Figure 2.17.

FIGURE 2.18 Creating data files and filegroups

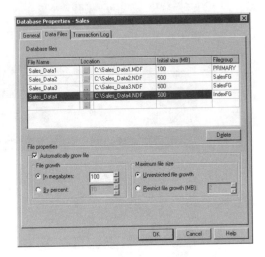

The following is the matching CREATE DATABASE statement:

```
CREATE DATABASE Sales
ON PRIMARY
    (NAME = 'Sales_Data1',
    FILENAME = 'C:\Sales_Data1.MDF' ,
    SIZE = 100,
    FILEGROWTH = 10),
FILEGROUP SalesFG
    (NAME = 'Sales_Data2',
    FILENAME = 'D:\Sales_Data2.NDF' ,
    SIZE = 500,
    FILEGROWTH = 50),
    (NAME = 'Sales_Data3',
    FILENAME = 'E:\Sales_Data3.NDF' ,
    SIZE = 500,
    FILEGROWTH = 50),
FILEGROUP IndexFG
    (NAME = 'Sales_Data4',
    FILENAME = 'F:\Sales_Data4.NDF' ,
    SIZE = 500,
```

```
              FILEGROWTH = 100)
LOG ON (NAME = 'SALES_Log',
        FILENAME = 'G:\SALES_Log.LDF' ,
        SIZE = 500,
        FILEGROWTH = 10%)
```

In this example, files are placed on different physical disks to split I/Os among them. The purpose of the filegroups in this example is to physically separate the data and indexes onto different drives. User data may be placed on the SalesFG filegroup and the indexes on the IndexFG filegroup. Furthermore, as the SalesFG filegroup is made up of two files, the data is evenly distributed on these two files, so the I/Os are split amongst two disks.

By default there is one filegroup marked as "default," and all tables or indexes are placed on this filegroup if not otherwise and explicitly requested. The Primary filegroup is the default filegroup. You can change the default filegroup with SQL Enterprise Manager or Transact-SQL. Figure 2.19 shows the different filegroups of the Sales database and the Default column.

FIGURE 2.19 Filegroups in SQL Enterprise Manager

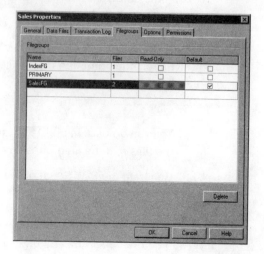

The following is the matching ALTER DATABASE statement that will set the SalesFG to the default filegroup:

```
ALTER DATABASE Sales
MODIFY FILEGROUP SalesFG DEFAULT
```

You can add or remove files to or from an existing filegroup, but you can not change the filegroup to which a file has been allocated once the file has been created.

In Exercise 2.4, we will add a file and filegroup to an existing database.

EXERCISE 2.4

Adding a File and a Filegroup to an Existing Database

1. In SQL Enterprise Manager, right-click the MyFirstDatabase folder, and click Properties.

2. Click the Data Files tab.

3. In the empty File Name line of the Database files table, type **MyFDB_Data2**.

4. At the end of the line, in the Filegroup cell, type **DataFG**.

5. Repeat the operation for the file MyFDB_Data3, and the filegroup IndexFG.

6. Click OK.

7. You can go back in the Database Properties dialog box to note that the files and the filegroups have been created.

8. Generate the SQL Script of the database creation (see Exercise 2.1).

Some other operations are possible with filegroups. You can create a filegroup before allocating any files to it:

```
ALTER DATABASE Sales
ADD FILEGROUP Sales99FG
```

You can remove a filegroup only if it does not contain any files:

```
ALTER DATABASE Sales
REMOVE FILEGROUP Sales99FG
```

You can put a filegroup in read-only mode to disallow any modification to the data while still allowing updates to the system tables. This can be useful in giving access to a read-only database while keeping open the possibility to manage permissions and security access. The following statement puts the SalesFG filegroup in read-only mode, then puts it back into read-write mode:

```
ALTER DATABASE Sales
MODIFY FILEGROUP SalesFG READONLY


ALTER DATABASE Sales
MODIFY FILEGROUP SalesFG READWRITE
```

You must have exclusive access to a database to put one of its files in read-only mode. With exclusive access, no connection can be opened on that database, except yours.

The last thing we will look at concerning filegroup updates is the ability to change a filegroup's name. This operation is very simple, as you can see in the following example:

```
ALTER DATABASE Sales
MODIFY FILEGROUP SalesFG NAME = NewSalesFG
```

You just have to give the old name after the MODIFY FILEGROUP clause and the new one after the NAME = option.

Maintenance and Performance

Filegroups are not easy to use. They require more administrative tasks and more analysis, so you must justify their needs. Filegroups carry with them four particular features:

- The ability to place a table or an index on a particular filegroup.
- The ability to place an image, text, or ntext column on a specific filegroup.

- The ability to assign many files to one filegroup.

- The ability to back up a filegroup on its own.

As a rule of thumb, filegroups may be used in one of the following four cases:

Physically separating tables and indexes   By placing a table on one filegroup and its indexes on another, SQL Server accesses indexes with one thread and the data with another one. The same thing may happen if you put a table in a filegroup made of multiple files, each of them being placed on a different physical disk. If the table is accessed sequentially, the performance may increase. But on the whole, RAID 0, 5, or 0+1 is generally a better solution.

If you split tables and indexes on two different filegroups, each filegroup cannot be backed up independently!

Isolating big tables   You can use filegroups to separate archived data from live data. Archived tables tend to get bigger and bigger. They can have a negative impact on performance if they are among the live data. Imagine having your current sales and last five years' sales data in the same table. If by mistake, you run a SELECT query grouping by product without a date restriction clause, you'll end up with a long-running query. Splitting the table is a good idea. If your archive and current sales tables are in the same filegroup, you may also end up with data fragmentation. A good practice may be to put your archive data in another filegroup or even in another database.

Isolating binary data   Binary data is always a source of questions. Storing images or videos in a database is a major concern for many developers. If you decide to store this kind of data directly in the database, you may end up with some strange data allocation and with a serious performance impact if you do not think about your storage strategy. In the previous section, we talked about pages and extents. Character and numerical data are stored in data pages, while image and text data are stored in text/image pages.

The problem comes from the size of this text/image data. If, for instance, you store employees' names, addresses, phone numbers, and social security numbers *plus* the employees' photographs, their photographs will occupy more space than the character/numeric data. Or, it may be that the image data is used in only 10 percent of the cases, so the image data will "spoil" data space. You can then put this data on its own filegroup. The character/numerical data will be together, and the number of accessed pages may be less than if it were stored with the image data.

Ability to back up a portion of a database   From an administrator's point of view, using a filegroup may help with backup issues. For very large databases, it may not be possible to back up the whole database. Filegroups solve that problem by allowing data backups for only a subset of the database.

Another point is the ability to store a table in a filegroup and back up the filegroup independently from the database. This feature solves the problem people had in SQL Server 6.5 of wanting to back up and restore one table at a time.

While filegroups may be a good way to enhance performance and solve physical data storage issues, data and log file placement should be taken into consideration as well. This is the discussion in the last section of this chapter.

File Placement and Performance

Microsoft Exam Objective

Create and alter databases. Considerations include file groups, file placement, growth strategy, and space requirements.

- Specify file group and file placement. Considerations include logical and physical file placement.

- Specify transaction log placement. Considerations include bulk load operations and performance.

Do you know the difference between a good and a poor database physical design? In most cases, it lies in the file placement and the disk subsystem. Unfortunately for developers, they are not generally asked what they need in a server to run their application. They often have to work with the existing servers in the company.

Powerful Hardware for a Powerful SQL Server

In my humble opinion, file placement and disk subsystems are almost always underestimated. Over the years, Microsoft has been renowned for desktop application but was in the past a poor competitor in the database systems arena. Facing Oracle, DB/2, and Informix was a big challenge, so many developers and administrators saw SQL Server as a "mega" Microsoft Access and a "micro" Oracle system. Many people thought this RDBMS could be as good as Oracle! People also said Windows 2000/SQL servers are small compared to Unix/Oracle boxes and cost only a tenth of the Unix/Oracle solution, so they cannot be that good!

SQL Server is seldom installed on very powerful servers with gigabytes of RAM, eight CPUS, and dozens of disks in RAID 5. The real good news is that if you set up a powerful box for SQL Server, it behaves at least as fast as Oracle and is as reliable. TPC benchmarks show SQL Server is a very powerful solution. Unfortunately for Oracle administrators, it is not as complicated as Oracle and therefore needs less maintenance. Most of the complicated tasks done by Oracle administrators are done automatically by SQL Server. SQL Server administrators spend their time on more "intelligent" tasks. My purpose is not to degrade Oracle administrators, but to have them face reality. If they consider SQL Server as a true RDBMS and dig into what's behind the GUI, they probably will discover a product as complicated and powerful as Oracle.

If you ask for a powerful box with disk resources, RAM, and multiple CPUs, and if you design your physical design efficiently, neither you nor your users will regret it.

When you design a machine to run SQL Server, you take into consideration what types of applications you will be running on it. The choices that you make when designing a system include the hardware for the server as well as the software configuration of file placement. The types of access that are made by the applications will influence the design.

Let's take two basic examples:

- In an OnLine Transaction Processing (OLTP) application, most data is accessed through one or many indexes, and many inserts are performed. The transaction log is heavily used. Given these statements, one could place heavily read tables (like products and categories) on their own fast read-access disk subsystem, heavily inserted tables (like sales and customers) on their own fast write-access disk subsystem, and the log file on a fast write-access disk subsystem with a high availability feature. One possible solution is to put data files on a RAID 5 disk subsystem and the log file on a RAID 1 15K RPM disk subsystem.

- In a Decision Support System (DSS) application, most data is read sequentially, and updates are done by batch. The transaction log is important during batch updates, not during normal day operation. The data could be placed on a RAID 5 disk subsystem and the log on a single fast disk.

These are just a few of the possible solutions. One would need to analyze more precisely the application to decide which is the best disk subsystem to implement.

Data Placement

Performance placement is an important item in the database physical design strategy. It is not only the size of the database that dictates the file placement and the filegroup creation, but also other elements like number of users, number of transactions per second, transaction throughput, and type of operations should be taken into consideration.

Nothing replaces experience, but some rules may help you design a data placement strategy:

Always place data on striped disks   Of course, if your database is 10MB this rule may not apply, and working with one disk may be fine. But the more disks the better. If you know that a SCSI 10K-RPM disk can handle approximately 100 I/O requests per second, you understand that with five disks, you can service 500 I/O requests per second. For SQL Server, the disk throughput is not an issue: The max number of I/O per second is much more important. RAID 0 is the best disk stripping strategy for data files. Unfortunately, it is also risky on a production site. RAID 0+1 may be an answer, or RAID 5, since it's cheaper.

Use hardware RAID rather than filegroups   You can simulate RAID with filegroups and multiple disks, but it is better to spend a little more money on a good RAID controller than recreating RAID with filegroups. With filegroups, you may end up with more problems than solutions. Ask your system administrator to optimize your RAID controller by setting the read/write cache. The Performance Monitor will help you discover the read/write ratio on your disk subsystem and help you to set the controller with the optimal value.

Identify your access patterns   Know how your users access data. Depending on their access patterns, the indexes, and the read/write ratio, you may decide to use multiple filegroups over multiple disks or just use a single filegroup. For example, the reference tables of an e-commerce database system can be placed on a RAID 5 disk subsystem and the frequently updated table on RAID 0+1. If the same database is used internally for just a few hundred inserts per day, all the tables can be placed on a RAID 5 array. Now, if your system is heavily updated, you will need to calculate more precisely the numbers of I/O needed to determine the type of disk system you need, but that subject is beyond the scope of this book.

The purpose of this discussion is not to make your company spend a lot of money on disks, but to make you understand that disk systems and file placement are important to performance and are generally driven by common sense. Work closely with your system administrator to learn about RAID subsystems and their characteristics. As a developer, you probably won't be responsible for disk subsystem choices. But you will be the person who knows precisely the query that ran on the system as well as the access patterns, so your insights are invaluable. Exchange your point of view with your DBA—he will be grateful to you.

Log File Placement

Transaction logs are also stored in files and deserve a little consideration. Furthermore, remember that the database transaction log is its life insurance. If you lose the database, all the transactions remain in the transaction log. As for data files, the following rules may help you choose a good file placement.

Always store the transaction log on its own physical disk   The disk is the most fragile component of a server. If your disk crashes and if you stored both data and log files on the same disk, then you have lost everything, and the only solution you have is to go to your last backup. If you separate your data and log files and you lose your data disk, you may still back up your log and recover all the transactions executed since the last backup.

Even on a small system, always follow this rule. This is a basic security rule. Nobody likes losing his or her work. Separating the data from the log increases your chance to recover your data in case of failure.

Protect your log file disk   If you can afford it, protect your log file by mirroring it. With mirror protection, the other side of the mirror continues to work in case of disk failure, offering high availability to your users.

Use the fastest available disks for your log files   Log files are written most of the time. During batch updates, bulk inserts, or just heavy OLTP operations, log disks are stressed a lot. In this kind of environment, the faster the transactions, the better! With very fast disks (10 or 15K RPM is a must), you are sure that your transactions will be written in a few milliseconds and that the log will not be the bottleneck.

RAID 0 is not useful at all for log files, and RAID 5 has too much overhead. Remember that log files are written sequentially, which means that all writings and readings are sequential. If you spread your file on many disks on a RAID 0 array, only one will be working at a time. And if you use RAID 5, each time you write a new transaction, the system will need to recalculate and write the RAID parity. So a fast RAID 1 system is the best choice.

Summary

In this chapter you learned how to create a SQL Server database design. While discovering key elements, we dug into details to help you understand the hidden complexity of SQL Server.

This chapter particularly focused on:

- Creating and managing a database

- Creating and managing data and log files

- Creating and managing filegroups

- Assessing performance enhancement with filegroups

- Assessing performance enhancement with data and log files placement

Key Terms

Before you take the exam, be certain you are familiar with the following terms:

ACID	lazy writer
Bulk Changed Map	Log Sequence Number
character set	mixed extent
checkpoint	page
collation	Page Free Space
compatibility level	primary data file
Differential Changed Map	secondary data file
extent	Secondary Global Allocation Map
filegroup	transaction
Global Allocation Map	transaction log
Index Allocation Map	uniform extent

Exam Essentials

Know the *CREATE* and *ALTER DATABASE* statements syntax.
Know all the possible parameters of these statements. In the exam, you may find questions on database growth or database creation.

Identify the data usage to design the physical structure of the database.
If you know how data is going to be used, you can choose a RAID system or a multiple disk structure.

Identify performance issues with data file and log placement.   Filegroups, file placement, and transaction log placement can have a dramatic impact on database performance. Make sure you understand the basic principles of file placement.

Know the database options and specifically the recovery model.   Database options have evolved since SQL Server 4.21! Knowing the features offered by the different options and the different recovery models will give you a better understanding of database functionality.

Review Questions

1. You are in charge of the Policies database for an insurance company. When you created the Policies database two years ago, it was 500MB. Then it grew to 1.3GB. Recently, you archived last year's data, freeing almost 40 percent of the database. Nevertheless, the database files still occupy 1.3GB. You would like to recover a part of the freed database space. You want to check if autoshrinking is on. What is the fastest way to check it?

   A. sp_configure Policies, 'autoshrink'

   B. SELECT DATABASEPROPERTYEX('Policies', 'IsAutoShrink')

   C. sp_helpdb 'Policies'

   D. SELECT DATABASEPROPERTY('Policies', 'AutoShrink')

2. As a Microsoft SQL Server DBA, you have been called to analyze the performance loss of the SQL server of an international bank.

This customer is using SQL Server to record every credit card operation. At peak hours, the system handles some 500 transactions per second, but on average is serving around 50 transactions per second. For a couple of days, the system engineer sees the number of transactions decreased to around 40 transactions per second, and the bank has had complaints from major stores in the region that the credit card sales quite randomly take longer than they should. Sometimes, the transaction is very fast, even at peak hours, sometimes it is very slow, even between peak hours.

You take a look a the Performance Monitor and monitor the checkpoint pages/second counter. You discover that every fifteen minutes a checkpoint occurs, the checkpoint uses almost 90 percent of the system resources and lasts around 50 seconds. During that time, the number of transactions falls down to less than 10 per second. Which server options may be responsible for that delay in the checkpoint process?

A. Lazy writes per second

B. Recovery interval

C. Lightweight pooling

D. Priority boost

3. You are working for a international group of consultants. Your office in Kuala Lumpur just sent you a database backup you have restored on your SQL Server test box. It works fine until you try to unite the customer table of your New York database and the customer table of your Kuala Lumpur database. You discover some strange characters in the result. You run the following query in SQL Query Analyzer:

```
SELECT DATABASEPROPERTYEX('CustomersNY', 'Collation')
SELECT DATABASEPROPERTYEX('CustomersKL', 'Collation')
```

You obtain the following result:

```
------------------------------------------------
SQL_Latin1_General_CP1_CS_AS

------------------------------------------------
Thai_CI_AI
```

You discover the accented letters issue is due to a difference in collation between the databases. How can you solve this issue?

A. By installing the Thai collation on the server

B. By modifying the collation of the CustomersKL database

C. By modifying the char and varchar columns of both databases to Unicode

D. By restoring the Kuala Lumpur database while forcing the collation

4. You are a database developer for Northwind Traders. The marketing department ordered a new server for the sales analysis database. The marketing manager explains to you that her department needs to do some thorough analysis of sales data to find customer patterns for the next marketing campaign.

   After gathering user requirements, you analyze the volume of data. The database size will be approximately of 1.5GB, 80 percent of which is occupied by the sales table. For data retrieval performance reasons, this table will be heavily indexed. The database will be primarily used for data reading and calculation. The server on which you will install the database has four disks with two SCSI controllers. How are you going to create the database to maximize performance?

   A.

```
CREATE DATABASE Marketing
ON PRIMARY
    ( NAME = MarketingData,
      FILENAME = N'c:\data\MarketingData.mdf',
      SIZE = 2GB,
      MAXSIZE = 4GB,
      FILEGROWTH = 50MB)
LOG ON
    ( NAME = MarketingLog,
      FILENAME = N'd:\data\MarketingLog.ldf',
      SIZE = 500MB,
      MAXSIZE = 2000MB,
      FILEGROWTH = 50MB)
```

B.

```
CREATE DATABASE Marketing
ON PRIMARY
   ( NAME = MarketingSystemData,
     FILENAME = N'c:\data\MarketingData1.mdf',
     SIZE = 500MB,
     MAXSIZE = 2000MB,
     FILEGROWTH = 50MB),
   ( NAME = MarketingData1,
     FILENAME = N'd:\data\MarketingData2.ndf',
     SIZE = 500MB,
     MAXSIZE = 2000MB,
     FILEGROWTH = 50MB),
   ( NAME = MarketingData2,
     FILENAME = N'e:\data\MarketingData3.ndf',
     SIZE = 500MB,
     MAXSIZE = 2000MB,
     FILEGROWTH = 50MB),
LOG ON
   ( NAME = MarketingLog,
     FILENAME = N'f:\data\MarketingLog.ldf',
     SIZE = 500MB,
     MAXSIZE = 2000MB,
     FILEGROWTH = 50MB)
```

C.

```
CREATE DATABASE Marketing
ON PRIMARY
   ( NAME = MarketingSystemData,
     FILENAME = N'c:\data\MarketingSystemData.mdf',
     SIZE = 2,
     MAXSIZE = 4,
     FILEGROWTH = 1),
FILEGROUP MarketingFG1
   ( NAME = MarketingData1,
     FILENAME = N'd:\data\MarketingData1.ndf',
     SIZE = 2,
     MAXSIZE = 4,
     FILEGROWTH = 1),
```

Shawuti, K.

HOLD ESPECIALLY FOR
(Last Name, First Name)

HOLD UNTIL _4/9_

PICK UP AT *(circle one)*

CEN - White   ECO - Green   MIL - Yellow

ELK - Blue   SAV - Gold   GLE - Che'

HDC - Purple   ILL - Pink

COLLECT AT PICK UP:

Reserve Fee* $_____

I.L.L. Fee $_____

Loaning Library Fee $_____

Photocopy/FAX $_____

TOTAL $_____

FILLED BY: _BC_

Seniors exempt from Reserve Fee

HOWARD COUNTY LIBRARY

GREAT EXPECTATIONS

```
LOG ON
    ( NAME = MarketingLog,
      FILENAME = N'f:\data\MarketingLog.ldf',
      SIZE = 1,
      MAXSIZE = 2,
      FILEGROWTH = 1)
```

D.

```
CREATE DATABASE Marketing
ON PRIMARY
    ( NAME = MarketingSystemData,
      FILENAME = N'c:\data\MarketingSystemData.mdf',
      SIZE = 500MB,
      MAXSIZE = 2000MB,
      FILEGROWTH = 50MB),
FILEGROUP MarketingFG1
    ( NAME = MarketingData1,
      FILENAME = N'd:\data\MarketingData1.ndf',
      SIZE = 500MB,
      MAXSIZE = 2000MB,
      FILEGROWTH = 50MB),
FILEGROUP MarketingFG2
    ( NAME = MarketingData2,
      FILENAME = N'e:\data\MarketingData2.ndf',
      SIZE = 500MB,
      MAXSIZE = 2000MB,
      FILEGROWTH = 50MB),
LOG ON
    ( NAME = MarketingLog,
      FILENAME = N'f:\data\MarketingLog.ldf',
      SIZE = 500MB,
      MAXSIZE = 2000MB,
      FILEGROWTH = 50MB)
```

5. You developed a database for managing the consultants' time and invoicing for a consulting firm. You created the database last year with the following statement:

```
CREATE DATABASE Consultants
ON PRIMARY
    ( NAME = ConsultantsData,
      FILENAME = N'c:\data\ConsultantsData.mdf',
      SIZE = 100,
      MAXSIZE = 200,
      FILEGROWTH = 10)
LOG ON
    ( NAME = ConsultantsLog,
      FILENAME = N'c:\data\ConsultantsLog.ldf',
      SIZE = 50,
      MAXSIZE = 100,
      FILEGROWTH = 10)
```

The data size is now 150MB. You archive 50 percent of the data. You want the database to decrease to its initial size. What statement will you run to do so immediately?

A.

```
DBCC SHRINKFILE(ConsultantsData, NOTRUNCATE)
```

B.

```
ALTER DATABASE Consultants SET AUTO_SHRINK ON
```

C.

```
DBCC SHRINKDATABASE(Consultants, 25)
```

D.

```
DBCC SHRINKDATABASE(Consulants, 100)
```

6. Your database is split onto two disks, as indicated by the following statement:

```
CREATE DATABASE MyDatabase
ON PRIMARY
    ( NAME = MyDatabaseData,
      FILENAME = N'c:\data\MyDatabaseData.mdf',
      SIZE = 100,
      MAXSIZE = 200,
      FILEGROWTH = 10)
LOG ON
    ( NAME = MyDatabaseLog,
      FILENAME = N'd:\data\MyDatabaseLog.ldf',
      SIZE = 50,
      MAXSIZE = 100,
      FILEGROWTH = 10)
```

You need to move the data file from drive C to drive E. Order the following statements correctly to achieve this move. Some statements may be useless.

	ALTER DATABASE MyDatabase
	REMOVE FILE MyDatabaseData
	DBCC SHRINKDATABASE(MyDataBase) EMPTYFILE MyDatabaseData
	ALTER DATABASE MyDatabase
	ADD FILE
	(NAME = MyDatabaseData1,
	FILENAME = N'e:\data\MyDatabaseData1.mdf',
	SIZE = 100,
	MAXSIZE = 200,
	FILEGROWTH = 10)
	DROP FILE MyDatabaseData
	DBCC SHRINKFILE(MyDatabaseData, EMPTYFILE)

7. You are a database developer for Northwind Traders. The ordering management database has been set up on a server with two disks. Data has been placed on the C drive and the log file on the D drive, as shown in the statement below:

```
CREATE DATABASE Orders
ON PRIMARY
    ( NAME = OrdersData,
      FILENAME = N'c:\data\OrdersData.mdf',
      SIZE = 500,
      MAXSIZE = 1000,
      FILEGROWTH = 50)
LOG ON
    ( NAME = OrdersLog,
      FILENAME = N'd:\data\OrdersLog.ldf',
      SIZE = 50,
      MAXSIZE = 100)
```

Your users complain about the slow performance of the ordering application. You discover there is a bottleneck on the C drive due to large read processes. You add one disk to the server (E drive) and would like to split data among the C and E drives. How could you achieve this goal?

A. Create a new data file on the E drive for the Orders database. The system will automatically split data among the two files.

B. Create a new data file on the E drive for the Orders database, then a new filegroup containing the C and E drives. From here, the system will balance new inserts among both drives.

C. It is not possible to achieve this goal without a RAID controller.

D. Define the E and C drives as a RAID 0 partition with the Windows 2000 disk management tool.

8. The transaction log is said to be a write-ahead log. Why?

A. Because transactions are written on disk before the data

B. Because it is only written and cannot be read, except during the automatic recovery process

C. Because transactions are kept in memory ahead of data

D. Because transactions are written in the transaction log before they are finished

9. A power failure occurred while the database was operating. Unfortunately, the UPS did not function properly and did not stop the SQL server in a proper manner. Once power comes back, what do you have to do to your server to recover the transactions that have been committed but not checkpointed?

A. You need to back up the transaction log, restore the database from the last full database backup, and then restore all the transaction logs plus the one you just backed up.

B. Nothing. SQL Server will recover automatically, rolling back pending transactions and rolling forward committed ones.

C. Nothing. All transactions since the last checkpoint are lost, the effects of the others are in the database.

D. Run ROLL FORWARD ALL TRANSACTION.

10. You are a database developer for a winery. You have developed an employee management databases. The database has been created with the following statement:

```
CREATE DATABASE Employees
ON PRIMARY
      ( NAME = EmployeesData,
        FILENAME = N'c:\data\EmployeesData.mdf',
        SIZE = 50MB,
        MAXSIZE = 100MB,
        FILEGROWTH = 5MB)
LOG ON
      ( NAME = EmployeesLog,
        FILENAME = N'd:\data\EmployeesLog.ldf',
        SIZE = 20)
```

One morning, a user calls you to inform you that he received a message reading "Could not allocate space for object." What is the most likely cause of that message?

A. The transaction log is full.

B. The D drive is full

C. The database is corrupted.

D. The data file has reached is maximum size and is full.

11. You created a 1GB database with a 250MB transaction log. After a couple of days in production, you observe that the transaction log size used is almost stable, around 10MB. You decide to monitor activity on the database with the Performance Monitor to check whether there is transactional activity. In fact, a lot of inserts, deletes, and updates are run against the database. What is the most likely cause of the transaction log stability?

A. The transaction log is backed up every day.

B. The recovery model is set to Simple.

C. The recovery model is set to Bulk-logged.

D. The truncate log option is set.

12. You are a developer for World Wide Importers. You are setting up the new ERP database. After having created a 500MB database and a couple of tables, you run the sp_spaceused stored procedure and obtain the following result:

reserved	data	index_size	unused
536 KB	152 KB	280 KB	104 KB

How come the reserved space is not 500MB?

A. SQL Server 2000 is only allocating space when objects need it.

B. This is a display bug corrected by Service Pack 1.

C. This is only the system data reserved space.

D. You may have run the stored procedure in the wrong database.

13. You need to do a maintenance job on the customers database you are managing and developing for a local bank branch. You want to make sure nobody besides you will work on this database. What can you do to prevent other users from using this database?

A. Run `sp_dboption 'single user', on`

B. Run `sp_configure 'single user', on`

C. Run `SET DATABASE Customers SINGLE USER`

D. Run `ALTER DATABASE Customers SET SINGLE_USER`

14. You are managing a SQL server for an Internet Application Service Provider (ASP). The server contains many databases for different customers. Some databases are no longer used. They need to be deleted from the system to reclaim their disk space. You decide to delete Base1, Base2, and Base 3; what statement will you run to achieve the deletion as fast as possible?

A.

```
DELETE Base1
GO
DELETE Base2
GO
DELETE Base3
```

B.

```
EXEC sp_dropdatabase Base1
EXEC sp_dropdatabase Base2
EXEC sp_dropdatabase Base3
```

C.

DROP DATABASE Base1, Base2, Base3

D.

```
DROP DATABASE 'Base%'
```

15. You are a SQL Server developer for a winery. You created a database to track the efficiency of workers during the vine harvest. The database has been created with the next statement.

```
CREATE DATABASE Efficiency
ON PRIMARY
    ( NAME = EfficiencyData,
      FILENAME = N'c:\data\EfficiencyData.mdf',
      SIZE = 200,
      MAXSIZE = 400,
      FILEGROWTH = 10)
LOG ON
    ( NAME = EfficiencyLog,
      FILENAME = N'd:\data\EfficiencyLog.ldf',
      SIZE = 50,
      MAXSIZE = 100,
      FILEGROWTH = 10)
```

You frequently monitor the database and observe the that data file is 380MB. You decide to increase its maximum size to 500MB to avoid any interruption of operation. Which statement will do the job?

A.

```
ALTER DATABASE Efficiency
MODIFY FILE
    (NAME = EfficiencyData,
     MAXSIZE = 500MB)
```

B.

```
ALTER FILE EfficiencyData
    (MAXSIZE = 500MB)
```

C.

```
INCREASE FILE EfficiencyData TO 500MB
```

D.

```
sp_filemaxsize EfficiencyData, 500
```

Answers to Review Questions

1. B. Option A is syntactically incorrect, and the sp_configure stored procedure gives you information about server configuration, not database configuration. C may be correct, but you have to dig into one of the columns to find the information. D is incorrect, first because the DATABASEPROPERTY function is provided in SQL Server 2000 only for backward compatibility and because Autoshrink is not the option's name. D is a tricky possible answer.

2. B. Option A is not a server option. C is responsible for fiber scheduling, and D is responsible for increasing the process priority. There is a direct correlation between the checkpoint process and the recovery interval.

3. C. Option A is irrelevant because all collations are available for SQL Server storage. B will modify future inserted data, not the one stored in the database. D is impossible.

4. D. You use the four disks to create three different data files with three different filegroups for table and index placement. The last disk is for the log.

5. C. Option A shrinks the file but does not release the freed space to the operating system because of the NOTRUNCATE keyword. B sets the autoshrink option to on, but will not immediately shrink the database. In the DBCC SHRINKDATABASE statement, the figure indicates the percentage of free space after the shrink. Twenty-five percent of free space will do the job, because only 75MB (50 percent of 150) remains in the database.

6.

ALTER DATABASE MyDatabase
ADD FILE
(NAME = MyDatabaseData1,
FILENAME = N'e:\data\MyDatabaseData1.mdf',
SIZE = 100,
MAXSIZE = 200,
FILEGROWTH = 10)
DBCC SHRINKFILE(MyDatabaseData, EMPTYFILE)
ALTER DATABASE MyDatabase
REMOVE FILE MyDatabaseData

To move data from one file to another, you have to add a new file if it does not exist, then empty the first file, then drop it.

7. B. SQL Server 2000 automatically balances data I/Os among multiple files belonging to the same filegroup.

8. A. Transaction log records are written to the disk before the associated modified data pages are written to the disk.

9. B. The automatic recovery process rolls forward all committed transactions between the last checkpoint and the crash and rolls back any pending transactions that have not been committed.

10. D. The transaction log has unlimited growth; if its drive was full, the error would have read that the transaction log is full (error 9002). The data file has a defined maximum size. It's likely this file is full.

11. B. Option A could not explain that the log space used is stable; if the transaction log was backed up every day, its size will increase, then decrease. With the bulk-logged recovery model, every transaction is logged, so the transaction log size should increase. The truncate log option does not exist. The existing option is `trunc. log on chkpt.`

12. A. SQL Server is allocated at least 8KB per table and index, and allocates pages as object space needs increase.

13. D. Option A would have been good if it was not lacking the database name. Options B and C are syntactically incorrect.

14. C. Option C is the only option with correct syntax. The others do not exist.

15. A. All the other possibilities do not exist!

Creating and Maintaining Tables

✓ **Create and alter database objects. Objects include constraints, indexes, stored procedures, tables, triggers, user-defined functions, and views.**

- Specify table characteristics. Characteristics include cascading actions, CHECK constraints, clustered, defaults, FILLFACTOR, foreign keys, nonclustered, primary key, and UNIQUE constraints.

✓ **Alter database objects to support replication and partitioned views.**

- Support merge, snapshot, and transactional replication models.

✓ **Troubleshoot failed object creation.**

his chapter focuses on the table, the basic storage object. In this chapter you will learn:

- How to create and manage a table
- How to create and manage datatypes
- How to create and manage table extended properties
- How data is stored and managed

This chapter focuses on table creation and maintenance. All other objects, which are part of the same objectives, are covered in Chapters 4, 5, and 6.

Creating and Altering a Table

Microsoft ✓ ***Exam*** ***Objective***

Create and alter database objects. Objects include constraints, indexes, stored procedures, tables, triggers, user-defined functions, and views.

- Specify table characteristics. Characteristics include cascading actions, CHECK constraints, clustered, defaults, FILLFACTOR, foreign keys, nonclustered, primary key, and UNIQUE constraints.

Troubleshoot failed object creation.

Once you have designed a database and created an Entity/Relationship model, creating the tables will be straightforward. Table creation is a simple process, but can become very complex if you add constraint rules, as we are going to see in the next chapter. In this chapter, we will focus on simple table creation and management.

Creating a Table

A table is a set of rows and columns. Columns define the attributes of our ER model.

Creating a Simple Table

To start with a basic example, let's consider the Customers table of the Northwind database (Figure 3.1).

FIGURE 3.1   The Customer table

The Transact-SQL statement that created this table is shown in Listing 3.1.

Listing 3.1: Creating the Customers Table

```
CREATE TABLE Customers (
    CustomerID nchar (5) NOT NULL ,
    CompanyName nvarchar (40) NOT NULL ,
    ContactName nvarchar (30) NULL ,
    ContactTitle nvarchar (30) NULL ,
    Address nvarchar (60) NULL ,
    City nvarchar (15) NULL ,
    Region nvarchar (15) NULL ,
    PostalCode nvarchar (10) NULL ,
```

```
Country nvarchar (15) NULL ,
Phone nvarchar (24) NULL ,
Fax nvarchar (24) NULL
)
```

This statement is quite simple, but it illustrates the basic table creation. The CREATE TABLE statement has the following syntax:

```
CREATE TABLE tablename
    ({columnname datatype} [NULL | NOT NULL] [ ,...n ]
    )
```

The table creation in SQL Enterprise Manager is even simpler:

1. Open the database folder.

2. Right-click the Tables folder, and click New Table.

The Customers table created in the SQL Enterprise Manager window would look like Figure 3.2.

FIGURE 3.2   The Customer table in Design Mode

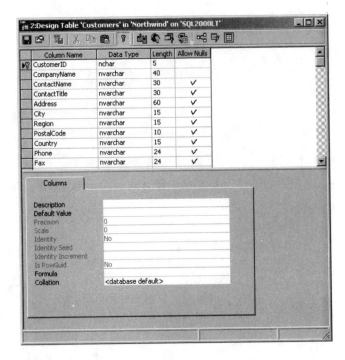

In the Design windows, you find the same characteristics we have in the CREATE TABLE statement:

Column Name

The column name must conform to the rules of the *identifier* (see sidebar below), which identifies every column in a table. Every column name must be unique within a table.

Identifier Rules

A database object name is its identifier. Every name must conform to the rules of the identifier. An identifier must be less than 128 characters. There are two classes of identifier: regular and delimited. The rules are the following:

- Regular
  - The first character must be a letter or the underscore (_) , "at" sign (@), or number sign (#).
  - Subsequent characters must be letters, numbers, underscores, "at" signs, number signs, or dollar signs ($).
  - The identifier cannot be a Transact-SQL reserved key word.
  - The identifier cannot contain space or special characters.
  - Examples include: Customer, @_Balance, and #Test$Mode.
- Delimited
  - The identifier is delimited by double quotation marks (") or square brackets ([]).
  - An identifier that does not conform to regular identifier rules must be delimited.
  - An identifier that conforms to regular identifier rules may be delimited.
  - Examples include: [Order Details], [Color], and "My Table."

Datatype

Every column has a datatype, except the computed columns, as you'll see in a couple of pages. Datatypes are part of entity integrity. Defining an integer column prevents any value except an integer to be stored. SQL Server 2000 has system and user-defined datatypes. They are described in the "Columns and Datatype" section.

Allow NULLs

The value of a specific column may or may not be required. In the Customers table (Listing 3.1), the CustomerID column does not allow NULL values. During an insert, this column must have a value if you want the insert to be successful.

Defining a column as NOT NULL means that a value is required. On the other hand, if you define a column as NULL, it means that a value is not required and, as a consequence, if that column has no value, it will be NULL. In this case, NULL means unknown.

The NULL value plays a significant role in RDBMSs. A NULL value is different from a zero or an empty string. For example, the average of the four following values: one, two, NULL, and three is two, and is not 1.5. In fact, if you ask how many values there are, the system will answer there are only three. NULL does not count! So, the average is two. This is pretty important for count and average function.

In Transact-SQL, if you do not specify the column nullability, i.e. you do not indicate NULL or NOT NULL, its real nullability depends on the ANSI null default database option. To check your database default, run the following:

```
SELECT DATABASEPROPERTYEX('databasename', 'IsAnsiNullDefault')
```

If the result is one, ANSI null default is **on**, if it is zero, the option is off.

To set it on, run the following:

```
ALTER DATABASE databasename
    SET ANSI_NULL_DEFAULT ON
```

To set if off, run the following:

```
ALTER DATABASE databasename
    SET ANSI_NULL_DEFAULT OFF
```

If this option is on, a column allows NULL value by default, unless otherwise defined. If it is off, it does not allow NULL value. In fact, SQL Server 2000 defaults to NOT NULL and the ANSI SQL-92 to NULL, so the option governs the way SQL Server works, on a database basis.

Since there are two other session-wide set options (SET ANSI_NULL_DFLT_ON and SET ANSI_NULL_DFLT_OFF) in addition to the ANSI NULL default database option that may modify SQL Server default behavior, it is best to always specify the column nullability in the CREATE or ALTER DATABASE statements.

EXERCISE 3.1

Creating a Simple Table with SQL Enterprise Manager

This exercise will walk you through creating a table with SQL Enterprise Manager and generating the corresponding Transact-SQL script.

1. Create a database named TestTable of default collation, size, and placement. (See Chapter 2 for directions on how to create a new database with SQL Enterprise Manager.)

2. Once the TestTable database is created, open the TestTable database folder by clicking the plus sign (+) on the left of its name.

3. Right-click the Tables folder, and choose New Table.

4. Fill in the columns description with the information from the following graphic:

Column Name	Data Type	Length	Allow Nulls
▶ MemberID	int	4	
LastName	varchar	50	
FirstName	varchar	30	✔
DepartmentID	int	4	
Phone	char	10	✔

5. Once you have entered the columns' characteristics, click the Save button.

6. In the Choose Name dialog box, type **Members**, then click the OK button.

EXERCISE 3.1 *(continued)*

7. Close the New Table window.

8. Right-click the Members table (in the right pane of the SQL Enterprise Manager window) and choose All tasks ➤ Generate SQL Scripts.

9. Click the Preview button to study the generated script.

10. Close the windows, once finished.

Unique Identifiers

There are many ways to make your table's rows uniquely identified. The IDENTITY and ROWGUIDCOL properties are probably the easiest ones.

Identity

Identity is just the name of SQL Server's auto-numbering property. It allows the creation of automatic incrementing values in columns. It is possible to choose the seed (the first created value) and the increment (the value added automatically to the last one each time a new record is inserted). The following example comes from the Northwind database. The Orders table contains an Identity column starting at one and counting by steps of one:

```
CREATE TABLE Orders (
    OrderID int IDENTITY (1, 1) NOT NULL ,
            CustomerID nchar (5) NULL
)
```

With such a property, the first row will automatically have an OrderID of one, the second of two, and so on.

When you insert a new row, a new identity value is automatically created. If you delete that row, the identity value it used will never be reused automatically by the system. If you run the following script in SQL Query Analyzer:

```
CREATE TABLE Test
    (col1 int IDENTITY(1, 1))
GO
```

```
INSERT Test DEFAULT VALUES
INSERT Test DEFAULT VALUES
DELETE Test WHERE col1=2
INSERT Test DEFAULT VALUES
INSERT Test DEFAULT VALUES
```

```
SELECT * FROM Test
```

You will obtain the following result:

```
col1
---------------
1
3
4
```

As you can see, the value two has been deleted and is not reused. A gap is created since SQL Server always inserts the next available value. If you try to insert an explicit value in an Identity column, you obtain error 8101: An explicit value for the identity column in table 'tablename' can only be specified when a column list is used and IDENTITY_INSERT is ON. As you can see, the IDENTITY_INSERT option can be set to ON to allow explicit inserts in the Identity column. If you run the following script in the SQL Query Analyzer:

```
SET IDENTITY_INSERT Test ON
INSERT Test(col1) VALUES (2)
```

```
SELECT * FROM Test
```

You will obtain the following result:

```
col1
-------------
1
3
4
2
```

Note that value two has been reinserted, not where it was, but at the end of the table. If you want a sorted result set, you need to add the ORDER BY clause to the SELECT statement.

One classic question about identity is generally: How can I know the last identity value inserted? There are three possible answers:

@@IDENTITY This *global variable* returns the last identity value inserted in the current *session* across all scopes. A *scope* is a stored procedure, a trigger, a function, or a batch. For example, an insert in a table fires the table insert trigger, which inserts a record in a table that has an identity column. The INSERT statement and the trigger are in two different scopes. So if you run SELECT @@IDENTITY after the previous INSERT statement, you will obtain the value of the identity generated by the INSERT statement inside the trigger (see Listing 3.2).

IDENT_CURRENT IDENT_CURRENT is a function that returns the last inserted identity value in a specific table in any session and any scope.

SCOPE_IDENTITY SCOPE_IDENTITY is a function that returns the last inserted identity in the current session and scope.

Listing 3.2: Comparisons of @@IDENTITY, IDENT_CURRENT, and SCOPE_IDENTITY

```
SET NOCOUNT ON
GO

IF OBJECT_ID('T1') IS NOT NULL
   DROP TABLE T1
IF OBJECT_ID('T2') IS NOT NULL
DROP TABLE T2
GO

CREATE TABLE T1
      (col1 int IDENTITY(1,1))
CREATE TABLE T2
      (col2 int IDENTITY(250,50))
GO

CREATE TRIGGER InsT1
ON T1
FOR INSERT
```

```
        AS
                INSERT T2 DEFAULT VALUES
        GO

        INSERT T1 DEFAULT VALUES
        SELECT [@@IDENTITY]=@@IDENTITY
        SELECT [IDENT_CURRENT('T1')]=IDENT_CURRENT('T1')
        SELECT [IDENT_CURRENT('T2')]=IDENT_CURRENT('T2')
        SELECT [SCOPE_IDENTITY()]=SCOPE_IDENTITY()
```

If you run Listing 3.2 in SQL Query Analyzer, you obtain the following result:

```
@@IDENTITY
-------------------------------------------
250


IDENT_CURRENT('T1')
-------------------------------------------
1


IDENT_CURRENT('T2')
-------------------------------------------
250


SCOPE_IDENTITY()
-------------------------------------------
1
```

Inserting a record in table T1 inserts a new record in table T2. T1 identity value is one, and T2 identity value is 250. The results show us the following:

- @@IDENTITY returns 250 because it is the last identity value in the current session in any scope.

- IDENT_CURRENT('T1') returns one because it is the last identity value inserted in table T1.

- IDENT_CURRENT('T2') returns 250 because it is the last identity value inserted in table T2.

- SCOPE_IDENTITY() returns one because it is the last identity value inserted in the current session and in the current scope.

If you open a new session (click the New Query button in SQL Query Analyzer or press Ctrl-N) and run the last four SELECT statements of Listing 3.2, you'll obtain the following result:

```
@@IDENTITY
------------------------------------------
NULL

IDENT_CURRENT('T1')
------------------------------------------
1

IDENT_CURRENT('T2')
------------------------------------------
250

SCOPE_IDENTITY()
------------------------------------------
NULL
```

These results show us the following:

- @@IDENTITY returns NULL because in the current session, no identity has been inserted.

- IDENT_CURRENT('T1') returns one because it is the last identity value inserted in table T1, in any session and any scope.

- IDENT_CURRENT('T2') returns 250 because it is the last identity value inserted in table T2, in any session and any scope.

- SCOPE_IDENTITY()returns NULL because in the current session, no identity has been inserted.

If the seed and the increment values are not supplied in the IDENTITY property, their default value is one. So, IDENTITY and IDENTITY(1,1) are synonyms.

A table can have only one identity column. This identity must be an integer so the chosen datatype for the column must be one the following: TINYINT, SMALLINT, INT, BIGINT, DECIMAL(p, 0) or NUMERIC(p,0).

NOTE When defining an identity, you can specify it as NOT FOR REPLICATION. This keyword means that the column will retain its value in the replicated table. When you insert a column in the publishing table, SQL Server automatically assigns the identity value. When the row is replicated, the identity value may change in the subscribing table, unless it has been created with the NOT FOR REPLICATION clause.

If a table has an identity column, you can query it without knowing its name using the IDENTITYCOL keyword. If you run the following SELECT statement:

    SELECT IDENTITYCOL, LastName, FirstName FROM Employees

SQL Server returns the EmployeeID and LastName and FirstName columns because the EmployeeID column is an identity column, and a table can only have one identity column.

Uniqueidentifier

With the advent of mobile computing and disconnected networks, identity does not guarantee uniqueness among multiple sites. Developers needed a "more" unique value to offer the multiple sites uniqueness: The UNIQUEIDENTIFIER datatype and the ROWGUIDCOL property are used to indicate that a column is a *globally unique identifier* (*GUID*). A GUID is a 128-bit number, such as 9CCDD2B9-CC41-4AC9-91CE-7CB4E1F445EB. When automatically generated by the system, it is guaranteed to be unique.

The following statement creates a table with a GUID column:

    CREATE TABLE Company (
        CompanyID uniqueidentifier ROWGUIDCOL NOT NULL ,
        CompanyName nvarchar (40) NOT NULL
)

In this example, the ROWGUIDCOL value is not automatically generated and its uniqueness is not enforced. If you want the value to be computer-generated, you need to use the NEWID() function, like in the following modified example:

```
CREATE TABLE TestCompany (
   CompanyID uniqueidentifier ROWGUIDCOL
     DEFAULT NEWID() NOT NULL ,
   CompanyName nvarchar (40) NOT NULL
)
```

If you insert a row with INSERT Company(CompanyName) VALUES ('Sybex'), and query the content of the table afterwards, you'll obtain the following result:

```
CompanyID                                CompanyName
------------------------------------     ------------
3E9ABF51-9296-4BF0-BD99-F98003550402     Sybex
```

If you insert another record, you'll end up with a totally different GUID value. GUIDs generated with the NEWID function are guaranteed to be unique. In the CREATE TABLE statement, the ROWGUIDCOL keyword is not necessary to create a globally unique identifier. The property is actually enforced by the UNIQUEIDENTIFIER datatype.

EXERCISE 3.2

Creating and Managing a GUID Column

This exercise walks you through creating a table containing a globally unique identifier column.

1. Run SQL Query Analyzer. Do this by choosing Start ➢ Programs ➢ Microsoft SQL Server ➢ Query Analyzer.

2. In the Connect to SQL Server dialog box, type . (dot) in the SQL Server combo box. Choose your authentication method and click OK.

3. Click Query ➢ Change Database.

4. In the SQL Database dialog box, click TestTable and then the OK button.

5. In the Query window, type the following code:

```
CREATE TABLE Company (
   CompanyID uniqueidentifier ROWGUIDCOL
       DEFAULT NEWID() NOT NULL ,
   CompanyName nvarchar (40) NOT NULL
)
```

6. Click Query ➢ Execute. If you do not obtain the message, The com-mand(s) completed successfully, check the statement syntax and run it until you obtain this message.

7. Click Edit ➢ Clear Window.

8. In the Query window, type **INSERT Company(CompanyName) VALUES** (**'Sybex'**), and run the query by clicking Query ➢ Execute.

9. Click Edit ➢ Clear Window, and type **SELECT * FROM Company** to check that the row has been inserted and the GUID has been generated.

10. You can insert other rows of you wish, executing steps eight and nine with different company names, to see varying values of GUID.

With the ROWGUIDCOL property set, the column can be queried with the ROWGUIDCOL keyword in the SELECT statement, like in the following example:

```
SELECT ROWGUIDCOL FROM Company
   WHERE CompanyName='Sybex'
```

UniqueIdentifier and Identity are both used to generate a unique ID for every row. Use Identity whenever you need unique values within a single table and UniqueIdentifier when you need unique values within a group of tables or servers.

Collation

We first met *collation* with the database creation. Each character column of a table can have a different collation, that is, a different character set or sort order, as in the following example:

```
CREATE TABLE Orders (
 OrderID int IDENTITY(1, 1) NOT NULL ,
 CustomerID char(5) COLLATE Latin1_General_CI_AS NULL ,
          EmployeeID int NULL ,
 ShipName nvarchar(40),
 ShipAddress varchar(60) COLLATE Latin1_General_CI_AS NULL ,)
```

In the previous example, the COLLATE keyword introduces the collation used for the column. CustomerID and ShipAddress use the Latin1 _General_CI_AS collation, which is code page 1252, and case-insensitive, accent-sensitive dictionary sort order.

See Chapter 2 for collation and code page definition. You'll find exhaustive information on collation names in the SQL Server Books Online and in the Transact-SQL Reference book, in the Collate chapter.

Note that no collation has been defined for the ShipName column. That means this column uses the database collation. Defining the collation down to the column can be very useful for an international database, but tricky when the time comes for data restitution or management.

Unicode is a Better Choice than Collation

Unicode columns (NCHAR, NVARCHAR, or NTEXT datatypes) and the database default collation is a better choice than creating different collations for different columns. The result with Unicode will be the same; it will assure your use of double the amount of space, but will be easier to manage.

The only interesting case of collation use in columns could come from a database where you lack storage space. But once you use more than one collation, you'll have faced collation precedence rules, which are far from easy. Furthermore, the need for more than one collation generally comes from international data exchange, but using different collations may prevent databases from working well together, or at least may make data exchange more complex. Think twice before going in that direction.

Collation can be implemented directly using the COLLATE keyword in the CREATE TABLE statement for every column needing a different collation, or by using the SQL Enterprise Manager (located in Start ➢ Programs ➢ Microsoft SQL Server), which is an easier and more readable way, as illustrated in Figure 3.3.

FIGURE 3.3 Collation choice in SQL Enterprise Manager

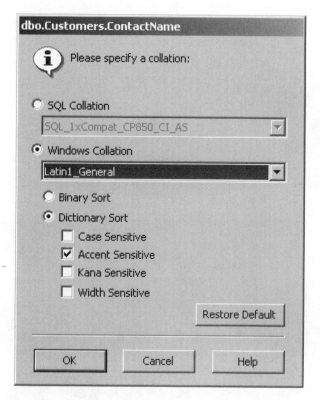

Filegroup

Another point concerning tables is that they can be placed on a specific *filegroup*. In the previous chapter, we met filegroups for the first time. A filegroup is a logical entity containing one or more data files. By explicitly placing a table in a filegroup, you allow that table to be stored in a specific file or files, and then on a specific disk. I see your grin. You're wondering: What's the point of placing a table on a specific disk or file? I'll show you in the following three examples.

The first is the one I call the archive problem. An OLTP database tends to grow indefinitely. But at the same time, it is the main source of data for OLAP databases. The invoicing application inserts fresh data every day in the database and inserts its data every day or so in the company data warehouse. But while the data warehouse needs to keep all the historic data, it's generally not the case for the invoicing database. The problem is then how to handle the historic invoicing records? The answer is archiving. But where to archive? The answer may be: in another filegroup. Figure 3.4 shows two filegroups. The Primary filegroup contains live data and the Historic one contains archived data.

FIGURE 3.4   Four tables and two filegroups

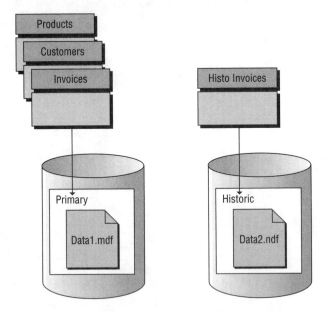

To achieve such file placement, the following statements have to be run:

```
CREATE TABLE Products (…) ON Primary
CREATE TABLE Customers (…) ON Primary
CREATE TABLE Invoices (…) ON Primary
CREATE TABLE [Histo Invoices] (…) ON Historic
```

What is the advantage of such a split? Well, simply to keep the sales table from becoming too big. It's likely that in the invoicing database you do not need paid invoicing older than three months, for example. But you need to keep these invoices for data warehousing purposes. To ease the query of this information and the joins with the Customers and Products table, it is simpler to keep it in the same database. But to avoid old information getting messed up with live data and increasing the fragmentation risk, it's best to put this data in its own filegroup.

The second example concerns the use of multiple threads. Consider that you have the file placement illustrated in Figure 3.5.

FIGURE 3.5   Four files and one filegroup

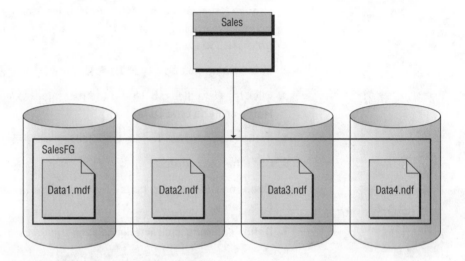

Your SQL server is running on a server with four different physical disks, and the sales data is located on four different files. If you run a query that scans the sales table, SQL Server 2000 can perform parallel scans of the sales table. A separate thread is allocated for every disk containing the table. In the example, four threads will be allocated to scan the Sales table. The same kind of feature could be obtained if a query joins two tables stored on two different disks: a different thread will scan both tables.

The last example concerns another server with a database that is used for a busy Order Entry system. This system inserts over 1,000,000 rows each day into the Orders table along with four to five reads from the Products table for each insert. If the Orders table is placed in its own filegroup on a separate disk drive from the Products table, the read operations will not interfere with the insert operations. A separate thread is used to access each filegroup, and thus, each table.

EXERCISE 3.3

Using Filegroups

This exercise will walk you through creating a database using a new filegroup and a table placed on this filegroup.

1. In SQL Enterprise Manager, right-click the Databases folder and choose New Database. (If SQL Entreprise Manager is not open, open it by choosing Start ➢ Programs ➢ Microsoft SQL Server ➢ Enterprise Manager.)

2. In the Name text box, type **DBFilegroup**.

3. Click the Data files tab. Under the data file row, click in the File Name cell and type **Data2**.

4. In the Filegroup cell for the Data2 file, type **FG1**.

5. Click the OK button.

6. Open the DBFilegroup folder, right-click the Tables folder, and click New Table.

7. Define columns' characteristics as in the following graphic:

Column Name	Data Type	Length	Allow Nulls	
ProjectID	int	4		
Name	varchar	50		
StartDate	smalldatetime	4		
EndDate	smalldatetime	4	✓	
Cost	money	8	✓	

8. Click the Table and Index Properties button.

9. In the Table Filegroup combo box, choose FG1.

10. Click the Close button.

11. Save the table and name it Projects, then close the New Table window.

12. Right-click the Projects table in the right pane of the SQL Enterprise Manager window and choose Open Table ➢ Return all rows.

13. Insert five rows by typing values in the table column.

14. Close the window.

15. Open Query Analyzer, if it is not opened, by clicking Tools ➤ SQL Query Analyzer, and check that you are in the DBFilegroup database.

16. Type **sp_help** '**projects**' and check that it is located on the FG1 filegroup.

In some cases, the performance effect gained by using filegroups can be obtained with RAID 0 (disk striping without parity) or RAID 5 (disk striping with parity). With today's system, consider using RAID disk subsystems first instead of filegroups to enhance performance. If you can afford multiple RAID arrays, then filegroups can even further enhance performance.

The table initial placement on a specific filegroup can be made at table creation. If no specific filegroup is chosen, the default table is placed on the default filegroup.

You are allowed to change the table placement in SQL Enterprise Manager, but that can be a very costly process. As there is no direct way to change the table placement, SQL Enterprise Manager creates a new temporary table on the filegroup, moves all the data to that temporary table, and changes all the referential integrity rules before dropping the source table and renaming the temporary table.

The ON keyword introduces the filegroup name, as shown in the syntax below:

```
CREATE TABLE tablename
( <column_definitions>

) ON filegroupname
```

In SQL Enterprise Manager, the table placement may be defined in the table Properties dialog box, as shown in Figure 3.6.

FIGURE 3.6 Defining the table filegroup

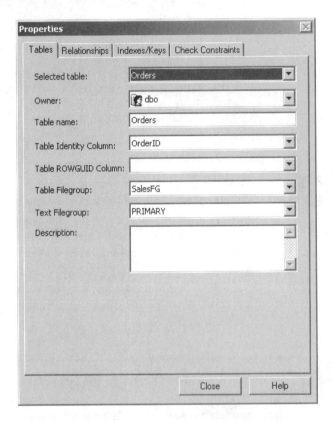

Altering a Table

Microsoft ✓ *Exam Objective*

Create and alter database objects. Objects include constraints, indexes, stored procedures, tables, triggers, user-defined functions, and views.

- Specify table characteristics. Characteristics include cascading actions, CHECK constraints, clustered, defaults, FILLFACTOR, foreign keys, nonclustered, primary key, and UNIQUE constraints.

Alter database objects to support replication and partitioned views.

Troubleshoot failed object creation.

Nobody's perfect, especially when it comes to database structure. Things change, needs change, users change, and therefore database design may change. That's the reason you'll probably have to alter a table. Here we will discuss the standard modifications that can be made to an existing table.

Altering an Existing Column

Changing a column structure obeys very precise rules. While you can find all of them in the Books Online, it's important to remember the following one. The altered columns cannot be:

- Of TEXT, IMAGE, NTEXT or TIMESTAMP datatypes

- The ROWGUIDCOL column

- A computed column or used in a computed column

- A replicated column

- Used in an index, except for character and binary datatype, and if the type is not changed and the size is not decreased

- Decreased in size if values would be truncated (error 8152) or overflow would occur (error 220)

- Used in statistics

- A primary or foreign key

WARNING Many other modifications are allowed from SQL Enterprise Manager, but it is generally because a temporary table is used in the background. So, any other modification than those listed above can be very costly in terms of time and knowledge if done through SQL Enterprise Manager. The methods used by Enterprise Manager may use more resources than you would like, so be careful when making table modifications through Enterprise Manager. While it is nice to use the GUI and have it shield the user from the code required to make the change, there is quite a bit of knowledge that can be gained by making these modifications using T-SQL.

The basic syntax of column alteration is the following:

```
ALTER COLUMN columnname
   { new_datatype [ ( precision [ , scale ] ) ]
[ COLLATE < collation_name > ]
[ NULL | NOT NULL ]
| {ADD | DROP } ROWGUIDCOL }
```

Based on this syntax, you can see there are four types of column alteration.

Change Its Data Type

The new datatype must be implicitly convertible from the old one.

To find out which implicit datatype conversions are allowed, search for the CAST or CONVERT functions in the Books Online. You'll find a table that shows you which implicit datatype conversions are allowed or forbidden.

The following example gives you the initial table and two allowed datatype alterations:

```
CREATE TABLE Altered
(C1 int,
C2 varchar (50))
GO

ALTER TABLE Altered ALTER COLUMN C1 tinyint

ALTER TABLE Altered ALTER COLUMN C2 varchar (25)
```

As you can see, datatypes are demoted here: The INT becomes a TINYINT, and the VARCHAR is reduced to 25 characters. Since this is only possible if no data is lost, you know that datatype promotion, a lossless alteration, is always possible. Datatype demotion is only possible if no data loss occurs.

Change Its Collation

Changing the column collation is definitely not a bright idea if it already contains some data. Changing the collation may change the character set and the sort order, so data may be lost and the result of some query may change.

If you create the following table:

```
CREATE TABLE AlterCollation
(C1 varchar (30) COLLATE Latin1_General_CI_AS,
C2 varchar (30) COLLATE Latin1_General_CI_AS)
GO
```

And insert the following record:

```
INSERT AlterCollation
    VALUES ('prêt-à-porter français', 'prêt-à-porter
    français')
```

When you run SELECT * FROM AlterCollation, you obtain the following result:

C1	C2
prêt-à-porter français	prêt-à-porter français

Now if you change the collation of the second column:

```
ALTER TABLE AlterCollation
    ALTER COLUMN C2 varchar (30) COLLATE THAI_CI_AS
```

And run SELECT * FROM AlterCollation again, you now have:

C1	C2
prêt-à-porter français	pr?t-?-porter fran?ais

The accented letters and special characters have been lost during the collation change because there are no matching characters in the Thai character set.

Test your collation change before running it into production. You could have astonishing results and you will be the first to blame!

Change Its Nullability

Changing the *nullability* is altering a NOT NULL column so that it allows NULL values, or vice versa. If you want a NULL column to disallow NULL values, you must first be sure that your column does not have any NULLs. The following query will help you:

```
SELECT * FROM MyTable WHERE NullColumn IS NULL
```

If the result set is empty, you can change the nullability of the column. If it contains at least one NULL value, you must first update it to change the nullability of the column.

In the following example, you create a table, and then alter it:

```
CREATE TABLE AlterNull
(C1 varchar (30) NOT NULL)
GO


ALTER TABLE AlterNull ALTER COLUMN C1 varchar (30) NULL
```

Note that to change the nullability of the column, you have to specify the datatype even if you do not change it.

Change the Fact That It is a ROWGUIDCOL

The last possible alteration concerns the definition of the ROWGUIDCOL. As seen before, a table can have only one ROWGUIDCOL column. If you want to define or change it, you must first delete any reference to the GUID, then define another UniqueIdentifier column as being the new ROWGUIDCOL. The following statement drops the ROWGUIDCOL property of the Company table.

```
ALTER TABLE Company
    ALTER COLUMN CompanyID DROP ROWGUIDCOL
```

Note it does not drop the column itself. Once the statement is successfully run, the table has no ROWGUIDCOL anymore. It is then possible to add it again:

```
ALTER TABLE Company
    ALTER COLUMN CompanyID ADD ROWGUIDCOL
```

Adding a Column

Adding a column is a straightforward as well as a tricky process. It is straightforward because adding a column is easily done with the ADD keyword in the ALTER DATABASE statement. It is tricky because if the table contains data and the added column does not allow NULL values, it should have a default value.

If you want to store the e-mail address of every employee, you can add a column to the Employees table of the Northwind database by running the following statement:

```
ALTER TABLE Employees ADD Email varchar(40) NULL
```

Pay attention to the fact that we specified that the column should allow NULL values. If you forget that property or ask explicitly for a NOT NULL value, you will obtain the error 4901: ALTER TABLE only allows columns to be added that can contain nulls or have a DEFAULT definition specified. Column 'Email' cannot be added to table 'Employees' because it does not allow nulls and does not specify a DEFAULT definition.

To add a column to a table containing data and fill this column with a default value, use the DEFAULT constraint statement (this constraint is detailed in the next chapter), as in the following example:

```
ALTER TABLE Employees
    ADD Email varchar(40) NOT NULL DEFAULT 'Unknown'
```

If you query the Employees table, with SELECT LastName, Email FROM Employees, you check that every Email value has been initialized with the Unknown value:

```
LastName                 Email
--------------------     ----------------
Davolio                  Unknown
Fuller                   Unknown
Leverling                Unknown
Peacock                  Unknown
Buchanan                 Unknown
Suyama                   Unknown
King                     Unknown
Callahan                 Unknown
Dodsworth                Unknown
```

Dropping a Column

Dropping a column is as simple as adding one, except you cannot drop just any column. You cannot drop a column if:

- It is replicated.

- It is part of an index.

- It is part of a constraint.

- It is bound to a rule.

If your column is not any of the above, then you just have to run the ALTER TABLE statement with the DROP COLUMN clause, as in the following example:

```
ALTER TABLE Employees DROP COLUMN Email
```

Since the beginning of this section, you've encountered different datatypes. Every table column should have a datatype. The next section will deal with the different datatypes provided by SQL Server 2000 and the different features it offers to create and manage your own datatypes.

Columns and Datatypes

A table is made of one or many columns as well as named attributes or fields. In SQL Server 2000, every column must either have a defined datatype or be a computed column.

There are 27 datatypes provided by default by SQL Server; these are called system datatypes. Users can create their own datatypes, based on the system datatypes. Datatypes are used to define the column storage as well as the parameters of stored procedures and user-defined functions, and variables in Transact-SQL scripts. In the following pages, we are going to take a closer look at datatypes and the way they interact with column tables.

System Datatypes

SQL Server provides the base for all other datatypes under the name of system datatypes. Table 3.1 gives you a quick overview of these system datatypes.

TABLE 3.1 SQL Server System Datatypes

Datatype	Min and Max Values	Size	Description
Bigint	-2^{63} to $2^{63}-1$	8 bytes	Integer type new to SQL 2000, allowing storage of large integer values.
Binary	8,000 bytes max	Exact size as defined by the length attribute	Raw Binary data.
Bit		1 byte	Allows storage of Boolean values. Even if it occupies one byte, this byte can be shared among 8 bit columns. Storing from 1 to 8 bit columns consumes only one byte.
Char	8,000 characters max	Exact size as defined by the length attribute	Fixed-length character type.
Datetime	From January 1, 1753 To December 31, 9999	8 bytes	Date and time value.
Decimal	-10^{38} to $+10^{38}+1$	From 5 to 17 bytes, depending on the precision	Synonym to Numeric.

TABLE 3.1   SQL Server System Datatypes *(continued)*

Datatype	Min and Max Values	Size	Description
Float	$-1.79 \ 10^{308}$ to $1.79 \ 10^{308}$	8 bytes	Floating point number.
Image	2GB max	Variable	Often called BLOB, Binary Large Object, this datatype allows the storage of binary data whose size may exceed 8000 bytes.
Int	-2,147,483,648 to 2,147,483,647	4 bytes	Integer.
Money	-2^{63} to $+2^{63}-1$	8 bytes	Monetary data value. Precision goes down to the fourth decimal place (a ten-thousandth).
Nchar	Up to 4,000 characters	Exact size as defined by the length attribute	Fixed-size Unicode character.
Ntext	2GB max - $2^{30}-1$ characters	Variable	Unicode character type.
Numeric	-10^{38} to $+10^{38}+1$	From 5 to 17 bytes, depending on the precision	Fixed precision and scale numeric value.

TABLE 3.1 SQL Server System Datatypes *(continued)*

Datatype	Min and Max Values	Size	Description
Nvarchar	4,000 characters max	Variable	Unicode variable character.
Real	$-3.40\ 10^{38}$ to $+3.40\ 10^{38}$	4 bytes	Floating point numeric value.
Rowversion		8 bytes	Binary data unique within a database.
Smalldatetime	From January 1, 1900 to June 6, 2079	4 bytes	Date and time value with an accuracy to one minute.
Smallint	-32,768 to 32,767	2 bytes	Integer.
Smallmoney	-214,748.3648 to 214,748.3647	4 bytes	Monetary data value. Precision goes down to the fourth decimal place (a ten-thousandth).
Sql_variant		Variable	A universal datatype that stores any other datatype value, except text, ntext and timestamp.
Table		Variable	Type used to store a result set. It is not possible to define a table type column.

TABLE 3.1 SQL Server System Datatypes *(continued)*

Datatype	Min and Max Values	Size	Description
Text	2GB - 2^{30}-1 characters	Variable	Character type.
Timestamp		8 bytes	Synonym of rowversion.
Tinyint	0 to 255	1 byte	Unsigned Integer.
UniqueIdentifier		16 bytes	Globally Unique Identifier.
Varbinary	8,000 bytes max	Variable	Variable-length binary data.
Varchar	8,000 characters max	Variable	Variable-length character data.

System datatypes can be grouped into six families.

Exact Numeric

Integers are represented through four types: TINYINT, SMALLINT, INT and BIGINT. Note that TINYINT is an unsigned value.

NUMERIC and DECIMAL datatypes represent fixed precision and scale numeric values. In SQL Server 2000, both types are synonyms. When you define a column of either type, you must supply the precision and scale. Precision represents the total of digits in the number (from 1 to 38). Scale represents the total of decimal digits in the number. For example, a column of DECIMAL (9, 4) can store numbers containing up to nine digits, with a max of four decimal digits. Values such as 123,456,789 and 12,345.6789 are both valid in this context.

MONEY and SMALLMONEY are used to represent currency values. Note that these monetary datatypes are Euro compatible.

The BIT datatypes may have three values: zero, one, or NULL. This datatype uses a byte that can be shared by multiple byte columns of the same table.

Approximate Numeric

FLOAT and REAL are floating point numbers.

Date and Time

DATETIME and SMALLDATETIME are used to store date and time values.

A DATETIME value is stored as two four-byte integer values. The first integer represents the number of days before or after January 1, 1900. The second integer represents the number of milliseconds after midnight.

A SMALLDATETIME value is less accurate than a DATETIME value. It is stored as two two-byte integer values. The first integer represents the number of days after January 1, 1900. The second one represents the number of seconds after midnight.

Note that it is physically impossible to store a date without a time or a time without a date. Nevertheless, if you only insert a date, the time value will be zero (meaning midnight). If you only insert a time, the date value will be zero (meaning January 1, 1900).

Character Strings

CHAR and VARCHAR are single-byte characters. NCHAR and NVARCHAR are double-byte Unicode characters. These four types are limited respectively to 8,000 and 4,000 characters (8,000 bytes). You have to declare the length of the character string. The default length is one. The CHAR and NCHAR datatypes are fixed-length types. That means that they occupy the whole space even if they are not using it. For example, a CHAR(15) column will always consume 15 bytes, even if it uses only one or two bytes. On the other hand, variable-length types, like VARCHAR and NVARCHAR, use only the space they really occupy plus a two-byte overhead per value.

Use fixed-length strings for values not varying in size, like zip codes, and variable-length strings for values varying in size, like first names or cities.

TEXT and NTEXT types are similar to a Memo field. Each time you need to store a large volume of text (above 8,000 bytes), the TEXT and NTEXT types may be the solution. TEXT and NTEXT fields may be stored in the same data page as the other fields or in one or many separate pages. These storage options are described in the "Table Storage" section.

Binary Strings

BINARY and VARBINARY datatypes are used to store binary strings whose length is less than 8,000 bytes. The same rules apply to binary strings (as far as storage is concerned) and character strings.

The IMAGE type is used to store any binary data that may be larger than 8,000 bytes, like images, video, sound, files, etc.

Storage of BLOBs

Binary Large Objects (BLOBs) are one of the weakest parts of SQL Server. No insert, update, or delete methods exist in SQL Server to handle such data. SQL Server manages their storage intelligently, but leaves the manipulation methods to the client API (OLE-DB, ODBC or DB-Library).

One nice feature has been added to index image columns when they contain files like Microsoft Word documents or Excel spreadsheets. But to store or retrieve this kind of file, it is always necessary to create a temporary storage area. If you need to manage multiple files or multimedia documents, you have to carefully study your needs to decide whether you should store this information in the database or just store their relative path in the database and keep the storage outside of SQL Server.

 For more information on image data management with ADO, look for Managing Long Data Types in the Books Online.

Special

SQL_VARIANT offers the possibility to store almost anything in a column, parameter, or variable. If a column is defined as SQL_VARIANT, some rows may contain integer values, some others character values, and so on. The SQL_VARIANT value is converted to a base datatype to allow manipulation.

The TABLE datatype allows the creation of a temporary result set that can be used as a parameter of a stored procedure or used with table-valued user-defined functions. However, it cannot be used for table columns. It simplifies some operations by avoiding the use of Tempdb.

The TIMESTAMP and ROWVERSION datatypes are synonyms. TIMESTAMP is a little bit tricky in Transact-SQL because it has nothing to see with the SQL-92 timestamp. That's the reason why SQL Server 2000 introduces the new ROWVERSION datatype. In fact, the SQL-92 timestamp is synonymous to the Transact-SQL DATETIME type.

There is a slightly tricky difference between the TIMESTAMP and ROWVERSION datatypes. You can create a timestamp column without defining its name, as in CREATE TABLE T1(C1 char(10), timestamp). In this case, SQL Server creates a column named Timestamp. This behavior cannot be reproduced with ROWVERSION.

The ROWVERSION is used to automatically stamp the version of a row. This kind of column may be used by OLE-DB or ODBC to implement optimistic locking.

The UNIQUEIDENTIFIER, which was described earlier in the chapter, permits the creation of globally unique identifiers among all the SQL servers in the world!

Synonyms

To be SQL-92 compliant, SQL Server offers synonyms to datatypes. Table 3.2 lists all the datatype synonyms that can be used in column, parameter, or variable definition.

TABLE 3.2 Datatype Synonyms

Synonym	System Datatype
binary varying	varbinary
char varying	varchar
character	char
character	char(1)
character(n)	char(n)
character varying(n)	varchar(n)
dec	decimal
double precision	float
float[(n)] for n = 1-7	real
float[(n)] for n = 8-15	float
integer	int

TABLE 3.2 Datatype Synonyms *(continued)*

Synonym	System Datatype
national character(*n*)	nchar(n)
national char(*n*)	nchar(n)
national character varying(*n*)	nvarchar(n)
national char varying(*n*)	nvarchar(n)
national text	ntext

Note that the synonym is used for the creation of the column. Once created, if you generate the SQL Script of the object, the base datatype is used. There is no record that a synonym was used instead of its base data. Synonyms have only been implemented to guarantee the SQL-92 compliancy. They are not available in SQL Enterprise Manager.

User-defined Datatypes

It is possible to create your own datatypes, based on the system datatypes. The advantage of a *user-defined datatype* is to create a repository for developers, so they all use the same datatypes for the same type of columns. For example, you could create a SSN datatype to store social security numbers, so every developer uses the same type of storage.

You can attach a *default* value and a validation *rule* to a user-defined datatype. Once done, the column inherits this validation rule and default value.

The creation of a datatype in Transact-SQL is done with the stored procedure sp_addtype. The following example creates a zip code datatype based on a char(5) system datatype:

```
sp_addtype zipcode, 'char(5)', NULL
```

Note the quotation marks around the system datatype. They are required each time the system datatype has embedded space or a punctuation mark. If forgotten, you will have a syntax error.

The same thing can be done with SQL Enterprise Manager:

1. In SQL Enterprise Manager, open the concerned database folder.

2. Right-click User Defined Data Types and click New User Defined Data Type.

3. Type the name of the new datatype, choose its type, its length and its nullability, then click OK.

FIGURE 3.7   Creating a user-defined datatype with SQL Enterprise Manager

Figure 3.7 shows the User-Defined Data Type Properties dialog box. In this dialog box, besides the four basic characteristics of a datatype (name, type, length, and nullability), you find the attached rule and default and a Where Used button, to know which table columns use this type. Figure 3.8 shows the Where Used window of the ID user-defined datatype of the Pubs database.

FIGURE 3.8 Where Used dialog box

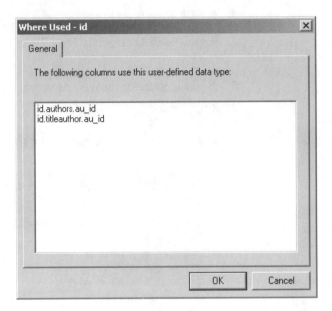

There is no easy way to obtain the same information directly in Transact-SQL, except by querying the Syscolumns and Sysobjects system tables.

It is impossible to create a user-defined datatype based on another user-defined datatype. It must always be based on a system datatype.

Creating and Managing User-defined Datatypes

This exercise will walk you through creating and using user-defined datatypes in a new table.

1. In SQL Enterprise Manager, open the Databases folder, then the TestTable database folder. If SQL Enterprise Manager is not open, open it by choosing Start ➢ Programs ➢ Microsoft SQL Server ➢ Enterprise Manager.

2. Right-click the User Defined Data Types folder and choose New User Defined Data Type.

3. In the Name text box, type **Zipcode**.

4. From the Data Type drop-down box, choose char.

5. In the Length textbox, type **5**.

6. Check the Allow NULLs box and click OK.

7. Repeat steps two through six to create a Phone datatype as a Char(10) allowing Nulls, and an ID datatype as `bigint` not allowing Nulls.

8. Create the following table:

Column Name	Data Type	Length	Allow Nulls
EmployeeID	ID (bigint)	8	
LastName	varchar	50	
FirstName	varchar	30	✓
Address	varchar	100	
Zipcode	Zipcode (char)	5	
City	varchar	30	✓
State	char	2	✓
Phone	Phone (char)	10	✓

9. Name it Employees, save it, and close the window. You can try to enter data in this table to check that the system datatypes are well enforced behind the user-defined datatypes.

Dropping a user-defined datatype is possible if it is referenced in tables, stored procedures, or user-defined functions. The sp_droptype stored procedure does all the work, as in the following example:

```
sp_droptype zipcode
```

In SQL Enterprise Manager, just right-click the datatype you want to delete, click Delete, then click Drop All.

The datatype definition is stored in the Systypes system table.

Computed Columns

Computed columns were first introduced in SQL Server 7. They are virtual columns, not physically stored in the database but still parts of a table structure, and whose values are calculated on the fly. A *computed column* is based on the values of one or many other columns of the same table.

The expression of a computed column can be another column (non-computed), a constant, a function, a global variable, or any combination of these elements connected by arithmetic or Boolean operators. It cannot be a subquery.

The following example creates a Total computed column based on the Price and Qty columns:

```
CREATE TABLE Orders
    (OrderID int NOT NULL,
    CustomerID int NOT NULL,
    ProductID int NOT NULL,
    Price money NOT NULL,
    Qty smallint NOT NULL,
    Total AS Price * Qty)
```

WARNING   Computed columns may generate unexpected behavior. For example, if you create the following column C3 AS C2/C1, if C1 is equal to zero, C3 cannot be calculated and a divide-by-zero error occurs. If this happens, you cannot choose the C3 column in a SELECT statement until you correct the error.

You cannot, of course, insert just any values in the computed column. With the previous table, the following code inserts three records:

```
INSERT INTO Orders(OrderID, CustomerID, ProductID, Price, Qty)
VALUES(1, 1, 1, 12, 5)
INSERT INTO Orders(OrderID, CustomerID, ProductID, Price, Qty)
VALUES(2, 2, 2, 14, 10)
INSERT INTO Orders(OrderID, CustomerID, ProductID, Price, Qty)
VALUES(3, 3, 3, 5, 6)
```

The following is the result of running SELECT * FROM Orders:

OrderID	CustomerID	ProductID	Price	Qty	Total
1	1	1	12.0000	5	60.0000
2	2	2	14.0000	10	140.0000
3	3	3	5.0000	6	30.0000

Remember that the computed column is not stored, so retrieving its values involves some extra CPU work. Computed columns in SQL Server 2000 may be indexed. Chapter 5 describes the indexing rules for computed columns.

EXERCISE 3.5

Creating and Managing Computed Columns

This exercise will walk you through creating and using a computed column in a new table.

1. Open SQL Query Analyzer by choosing Start ➢ Programs ➢ Microsoft SQL Server ➢ Query Analyzer, and check that you are in the TestTable database.

2. Type the following code:

```
CREATE TABLE Royalty
    (AuthorID int NOT NULL,
    TitleID int NOT NULL,
    BookPrice money NOT NULL,
    QtySold smallint NOT NULL,
    Royalty AS
        CASE
            WHEN QtySold<2000 then BookPrice*QtySold*0.06
            WHEN QtySold<4000 then BookPrice*QtySold*0.08
            ELSE BookPrice*QtySold*0.10
        END)
```

3. Execute the code by clicking the Green arrow in the Query Analyzer toolbar.

4. Clear the window by clicking the Clear button in the Query Analyzer toolbar, then type the following statement:

```
INSERT Royalty(AuthorID, TitleID, BookPrice, QtySold)
VALUES (1, 1, 15, 2500)
```

EXERCISE 3.5 *(continued)*

5. Execute the code by clicking the green arrow in the Query Analyzer toolbar.

6. Clear the window, then type and run **SELECT * FROM Royalty** and check that the computed column is displayed with the right result.

A computed column cannot be used as a Default or Foreign Key constraint, which seems quite obvious.

Now that we have seen all the basics of tables and datatypes, let's jump to a totally new subject in SQL Server 2000 called the extended properties. They enable you to create and manage your own properties for your tables and columns.

Extended Properties

New to SQL Server 2000 is the ability to create extended properties. This feature allows the creation of custom properties on almost every database object. An *extended property* is a **SQL_VARIANT** storage area that can be created on databases, users, user-defined datatypes, tables, views, stored procedures, user-defined functions, defaults, rules, columns, parameters, indexes, constraints, and triggers.

If you designed a table in SQL Enterprise Manager, you probably saw an extended property without recognizing it. The Description property (see Figure 3.9) of the Design Table window is an extended property created by default.

FIGURE 3.9   Description of a field

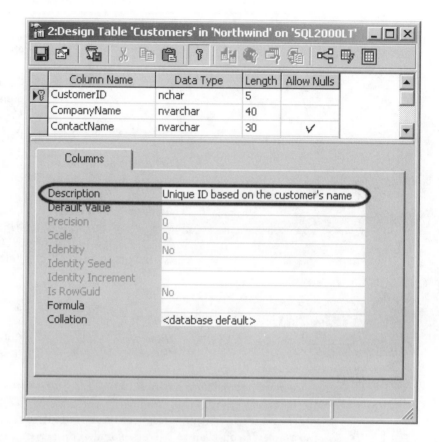

In fact, the Description field is presented in the GUI, but it attaches an extended property to the column only if you fill it.

The management of extended properties in Transact-SQL is not really easy or convenient. Extended properties are managed through three system-stored procedures:

- Sp_addextendedproperty adds a new extended property to a database object.

- Sp_updateextendedproperty updates an existing extended property.

- Sp_dropextendedproperty drops an existing extended property.

These three stored procedures and extended properties are based on three object levels. Table 3.3 shows you the supported objects and levels.

TABLE 3.3 Object Levels

Level 0	Level 1	Level 2
User	Default	N/A
	Function	Column, parameter, constraint,
	Rule	N/A
	Schema-bound function	Column, parameter, constraint
	Schema-bound view	Column, index, INSTEAD OF trigger
	Stored procedure	Parameter
	Table	Column, index, constraint, trigger
	View	Column, INSTEAD OF trigger
User-defined datatype	N/A	N/A

These levels are quite simple to understand if you consider the following example: If you want to add an extended property to a table column, you need to supply the name of the table and of the column, plus the name of the user owning the object (which is the table in this case). We find these levels in the extended properties stored procedure syntax.

If we want to create a Description property for the CustomerID column, as in Figure 3.9, the stored procedure to execute would be:

```
sp_addextendedproperty 'Description',
    'Unique ID based on the customer''s name',
    'user', 'dbo',
    'table', 'Customers',
    'column', 'CustomerID'
```

The real name of the Description property appearing in SQL Enterprise Manager is MS_Description.

Note the level types in this example. They are used as they appear in Table 3.3. If you want to reach a level two object, you must specify the level zero and level one objects as well. The three stored procedures share the same parameters.

Properties are stored in the Sysproperties table.

To know the value of an extended property, you can query the Sysproperties table directly or use the fn_listextendedproperty function. The following example lists the extended properties of all the columns of the Customers table:

```
select * from
    ::fn_listextendedproperty (default,
        'user', 'dbo',
        'table', 'Customers',
        'column', default)
```

The result is the following:

objtype	objname	name	value
COLUMN	CustomerID	MS_Description	Unique ID based...
COLUMN	CompanyName	MS_Description	Name of the Company
COLUMN	ContactName	MS_Description	Name of the primary...

If you run this query on your system, the results may vary, depending on the extended properties you add to the columns.

In the fn_listextendedproperty function, the first parameter is the property name you are looking for. If you specify default, you are asking the system to list every property. You can use default to tell the system that you want every property or object for every parameter. The following statement gives you all the database level properties of the current database:

```
select * from ::fn_listextendedproperty
    (default, default, default,
     default, default, default, default)
```

The next example gives you all the table level properties for all tables in the current database:

```
select * from ::fn_listextendedproperty
    (default, 'user', 'dbo',
     'table', default, default, default)
```

You may be pleased to know that Query Analyzer offers a graphical way to manage extended properties. In the Object Browser, open your database folder, then the User Tables folder. Right-click an object name (table, column, index, and so on) and choose Extended Properties to display the Extended Property dialog box (see Figure 3.10).

FIGURE 3.10 Extended Property dialog box

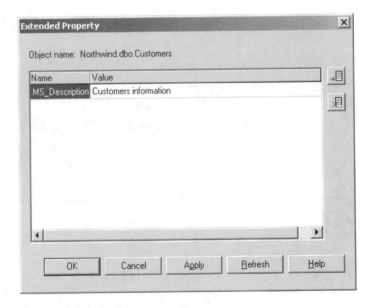

The dialog box illustrated in Figure 3.10 shows the extended properties of the object but not the ones that belong to the object's objects. For example, Figure 3.10 displays the table properties but not the table's column properties.

Extended properties offer a convenient way to store information about database objects. You could use them to store display recommendations for a column, comments for a stored procedure, explanations about development choice for a user-defined function, and so on.

Extended Properties and Metadata

The days of the integration of extended properties in metadata information are gone. The metadata repository offers you the ability to comment on database objects. It would have been nice if the metadata could have retrieved the extended properties information. Unfortunately, it is not the case. Let's hope future development products or future versions of the Microsoft Repository will use extended properties.

Before going into greater details concerning the implementation of declarative integrity rules in the next chapter, the following section lets you in on the secrets of data storage. This information, if not necessary to create tables, gives you insights to SQL Server and helps you to design more intelligent tables.

Table Storage

In Chapter 2, you discovered file, extent, and page allocation. In this chapter, we go a little bit further to understand how SQL Server works to store records. You will discover:

- How records are stored and physically managed

- How text, ntext, and image columns are stored and physically managed

Each time a record is inserted in a table, it goes in an allocated page where the system has enough space to store it. The way the record is physically stored varies depending on the datatypes it is made of. Let's first consider records containing no text, ntext, or image columns.

Record Storage

Records are stored in 8KB data pages. The record max length is 8060 bytes, not including text, ntext, and image columns. You can have a look at Figure 2.10 to remind you of the record allocations within a page. Now, Figure 3.11 shows you the physical storage structure of a record.

FIGURE 3.11 A record's physical structure

A record is divided into five zones:

- The row header, which is 4 bytes long, contains information about the row.

- The fixed-length data zone contains the data of the fixed-length columns (char, int, real, etc.).

- The null block contains the nullability value of every nullable column.

- The variable block contains the stored variable-length data length.

- The variable-length data zone contains the data of the variable length columns (varchar, varbinary, etc.).

Note that the physical structure does not match the column order you defined: Fixed-length columns are grouped together at the beginning of the row, while variable-length columns are grouped at the end of the row. You can check this structure by running DBCC PAGE.

For example, the Authors table of the Pubs database has been created with the following statement:

```
CREATE TABLE authors (
    au_id id NOT NULL ,
    au_lname varchar (40)  NOT NULL ,
    au_fname varchar (20)  NOT NULL ,
    phone char (12)  NOT NULL,
```

```
address varchar (40)  NULL ,
city varchar (20)  NULL ,
state char (2)  NULL ,
zip char (5)  NULL ,
contract bit NOT NULL
)
```

Id is a user-defined datatype corresponding to a VARCHAR(11).

So the physical structure of the records of the Authors table will group columns the following way: Phone, State, Zip, Contract, Au_id, Au_lname, Au_fname, Address, and City. The first record of the Authors table contains the following column values:

au_id	= 172-32-1176
au_lname	= White
au_fname	= Johnson
phone	= 408 496-7223
address	= 10932 Bigge Rd.
city	= Menlo Park
state	= CA
zip	= 94025
contract	= 1

If we query the physical page content with DBCC PAGE, we obtain the following result (excerpt):

```
Slot 0 Offset 0x631
-------------------
Record Type = PRIMARY_RECORD
Record Attributes =  NULL_BITMAP VARIABLE_COLUMNS
194d0631: 00180030 20383034 2d363934 33323237  0...408 496-7223
194d0641: 34394143 01353230 00000009 00330005  CA94025.......3.
194d0651: 003f0038 0058004e 2d323731 312d3233  8.?.N.X.172-32-1
194d0661: 57363731 65746968 6e686f4a 316e6f73  176WhiteJohnson1
194d0671: 32333930 67694220 52206567 654d2e64  0932 Bigge Rd.Me
194d0681: 206f6c6e 6b726150                     nlo Park
```

This gives you the bytes as they are found in the page for the first record (slot 0) at the address 0x631. As you can see, the row data starts at the fifth byte by the phone number (408 496-7223) as we expected, since it is the first fixed-length column. (In Figure 3.11, you can see that fixed-length columns are stored first.) Then we find the state, the zip code, and the contract value.

After the null and variable blocks, the data starts again with the Au_id (172-31-176), since it is the first variable-length column. It continues by the last name, first name, address, and city. All of the records of all the pages follow the same storage rules.

Text, ntext, and Image Storage

Text, ntext, and image columns are managed differently from other columns. As their size can be greater than that of a page, these columns are stored in image pages—and only page pointers are stored in the physical record structure. SQL Server 2000 introduced the new `text in row` option to be able to store text, ntext, and image data directly in the row.

In this section, I will call a BLOB column any text, ntext, or image column.

The behavior of the `text in row` option is straightforward:

- When set to OFF, every BLOB column is stored in an image B-Tree structure, and the address of the root node—a 16-byte address—is stored in the row. If a table has multiple BLOB columns, there are as many pointers as columns.

- When set to ON, every BLOB column is stored in the row if it fits in the page and if its size is less than the predefined maximum size, or it is stored in its own B-Tree structure.

To set this option to ON, use the `sp_tableoption` stored procedure:

```
sp_tableoption tablename, 'text in row', 'on'
```

To set it to OFF, replace ON with OFF. If you set the option with the ON keyword, the BLOB columns will be stored in the row if they are less than 256 bytes long and fit in the page. If you want the maximum length to be different than 256 bytes, you can define it by changing its value from

24 to 7,000, instead of using the ON keyword. The following example tells SQL Server to store the Categories BLOB columns in the row if they are less than 2,000 bytes long:

```
sp_tableoption 'Categories', 'text in row', '2000'
```

Let's see what happens when BLOB columns are stored according to their option values.

Text in Row OFF

By default, BLOB values are stored in their own structures called image pages (see Chapter 2). These pages are arranged in a B-Tree structure to optimize data access.

B-Tree stands for Balanced Tree. Used also in Index storage systems, it is a tree structure whose management algorithm keeps it balanced; that is, the length of every branch (from root to leaf) is the same whatever data you are looking for. There are major differences between balanced and binary trees.

Here's an example illustrating the storage process. The Categories table of the Northwind database has the following structure:

```
CREATE TABLE [dbo].[Categories] (
    [CategoryID] [int] IDENTITY (1, 1) NOT NULL ,
    [CategoryName] [nvarchar] (15) NOT NULL ,
    [Description] [ntext] NULL ,
    [Picture] [image] NULL
)
```

This table has two BLOB columns: Description and Picture, the first one being ntext and the second image. In every row you find two 16-byte pointers. The following result of running DBCC PAGE shows the first record of this table:

```
Slot 0 Offset 0x60
------------------
Record Type = PRIMARY_RECORD
```

```
Record Attributes =  NULL_BITMAP VARIABLE_COLUMNS
191e2060: 00080030 00000001 03000004 35002500 0............%.5
191e2070: 42804580 76006500 72006500 67006100 .E.B.e.v.e.r.a.g
191e2080: 73006500 eb000000 00000000 00005f00 .e.s.........._..
191e2090: 01000100 ec000000 00000000 00005f00 .............._..
191e20a0: 03000100      00                     .....
CategoryID                    = 1
CategoryName                  = Beverages

Description                   = [TextPointer]
------------------------------------------------
TextTimeStamp = 15400960  RowId = (1:95:1)


Picture                       = [TextPointer]
------------------------------------------------
TextTimeStamp = 15466496  RowId = (1:95:3)
```

In the record structure, the CategoryID column is the only fixed-length column, which means that it's before the Null and Variable blocks. Then, after the CategoryName column, you find two addresses: The first one indicates the Description column content is in page 95 in slot 1, and the second one indicates the Picture column content is in page 95 in slot 1.

The BLOB addresses are always 16 bytes long and point to a root node managing the blocks in which the real data is stored. The logical structure of a BLOB column storage is illustrated in Figure 3.12.

FIGURE 3.12   BLOB storage structure

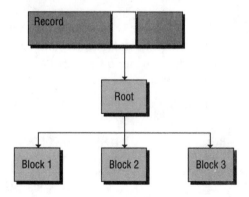

The address points to a root node that contains the pointer to data blocks. If we go to page 95 slot 1, we find the following information:

```
Blob fragment at: Page (1:95) Slot 1 Length: 84 Type: 4
   (LARGE_ROOT_2)

Blob Id: 15400960 Level: 0 MaxLinks: 5 CurLinks: 1

   Child fragment at Page (1:95) Slot 0 Offset: 86
```

This shows us that this slot is occupied by an 84-byte structure (Length: 84 Type: 4 (LARGE_ROOT_2)) indicating the real address of the BLOB content: Child fragment at Page (1:95) Slot 0 Offset: 86. The system finds the content on page 95 at slot 0. The Description value for this row is contained in a single data block.

If we now go to page 95 slot 3, we find the following information:

```
Blob fragment at: Page (1:95) Slot 3 Length: 84 Type: 4
   (LARGE_ROOT_2)

Blob Id: 15466496 Level: 0 MaxLinks: 5 CurLinks: 2

   Child fragment at Page (1:97) Slot 0 Offset: 8080

   Child fragment at Page (1:95) Slot 2 Offset: 10746
```

This root node indicates that the Picture data of the first row is made of two blocks (Child fragments): the first one on page 97 slot 0, and the last one on page 95 slot 2. This structure is illustrated on Figure 3.13.

FIGURE 3.13   First record storage structure of the Categories table

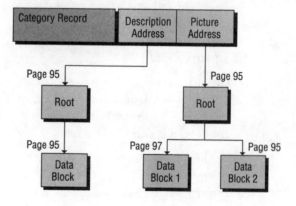

This storage structure is used if the BLOB size is between 64 bytes and 32KB. If the BLOB data is less that 64-bytes long, it is stored in the root node structure. If it is bigger than 32KB, SQL Server creates an intermediate node between the root node and the data block to create a bigger B-Tree structure, as in Figure 3.14.

FIGURE 3.14   Storage structure of a BLOB column whose size is over 32KB

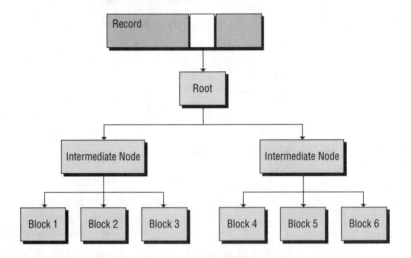

One important fact to note is whatever the size of a BLOB value, the page containing the field content may be shared with other fields' values or nodes. In our previous example, page 95 contains different nodes and different BLOB columns. So, using page space as necessary optimizes BLOB space. The only exception concerns intermediate nodes that are contained in their own page for each row.

Text in Row ON

The sp_tableoption stored procedure allows you to define the limit under which the BLOB data may be placed in the row if there is enough space in the page and above which they are always placed in image pages. Three cases could occur:

There is enough space in the page to hold the BLOB data.   The problem is simple. The BLOB data is handled like a variable string and uses just enough storage space. So if the limit is 2,000 bytes and the text string is 500 bytes long, it will only use 500 bytes.

There is not enough space in the page to hold the BLOB data. This situation could occur because SQL Server evaluates the row size without taking into account the BLOB size. It writes the row and then writes the BLOB data at the end of the row in their definition orders, if there is more than one BLOB column. If there is not enough space in the page to hold the BLOB, SQL Server tries to write the root node structure (72 bytes instead of 84, if it is placed in row) or parts of the root structure (at least 24 bytes). Then the data itself is stored in image pages.

The BLOB data is larger than the defined limit. This situation is quite similar to the previous one. Only the root structure, or parts of the root structure, is written in the row, and the data is stored in image pages.

In the case of multiple BLOB columns in a single table, depending on the BLOB values and on the page available space, some columns may be in row and some may be in image pages.

Filegroups

The last aspect about BLOBs concerns their filegroup location. By default, BLOB data is stored in the table filegroup. The TEXTIMAGE_ON keyword allows storing BLOB columns in a specific filegroup. The following example places the text and image columns of the Categories table in the BLOBFg filegroup, while the table rows are placed in the Primary filegroup:

```
CREATE TABLE [dbo].[Categories] (
    [CategoryID] [int] IDENTITY (1, 1) NOT NULL ,
    [CategoryName] [nvarchar] (15) NOT NULL ,
    [Description] [ntext] NULL ,
    [Picture] [image] NULL
) ON Primary TEXTIMAGE_ON BLOBFg
```

This feature allows you to split BLOB data as well as character and numerical data, while avoiding data external fragmentation. BLOB data is generally larger than the rest of the data, so image page allocation occupies more space, producing big physical gaps between data pages.

Consider placing your BLOB columns on a distinct filegroup if you intend to store a large amount of BLOB data or if you access this data quite infrequently.

Summary

In this chapter you learned how to create and manage database tables. You discovered the details of how tables are structured and created, using system or user-defined datatypes.

This chapter particularly focused on:

- Creating and managing a simple table
- Using row identifiers
- Placing tables or columns on filegroups
- Altering, adding, and dropping table columns
- Understanding system datatypes
- Creating and managing user-defined datatypes
- Creating and managing extended properties
- Data storage

Key Terms

Before you take the exam, be certain you are familiar with the following terms:

B-Tree	GUID
collation	identifier
computed column	identity
default	nullability
extended property	rule
filegroup	scope
global variable	session
globally unique identifier	user-defined datatype

Exam Essentials

Perfectly know the *CREATE* and *ALTER TABLE* statements syntax. Know all the possible parameters of these statements. In the exam you may find tricky questions about table and column creation.

Know how to create automatic identifying columns. Identity and UniqueIdentifier are convenient ways to create automatic columns, and know their limits, advantages, and drawbacks.

Know how to create and bind user-defined datatypes. User-defined datatypes offer a way to set domain integrity. Know how to create and manage them.

Know the image and text datatypes management. Images are binary large objects. Due to their size and type, they cannot be handled like character or numeric data.

Understand the row storage. Tables are stored in pages. A good understanding of data storage helps you comprehend table creation and management.

Review Questions

1. You are one of the database developers working for Contoso, Inc. You are developing the new customer relationship management database. You are working on the customer table, which has the following script:

```
CREATE TABLE Customers (
    CustomerID nchar (5) NOT NULL IDENTITY(1, 1),
    LastName nvarchar (40) NOT NULL ,
    FirstName nvarchar (30) NULL ,
    MiddleInitial nvarchar (3) NULL,
    ContactTitle nvarchar (30) NULL ,
    Address nvarchar (60) NULL ,
    City nvarchar (15) NULL ,
```

```
Region nvarchar (15) NULL ,
PostalCode nvarchar (10) NULL ,
Country nvarchar (15) NULL ,
Phone nvarchar (24) NULL ,
Fax nvarchar (24) NULL ,
CONSTRAINT PK_Customers PRIMARY KEY CLUSTERED
   (CustomerID)
)
```

During your test of the table, you insert 988 test rows in a batch. The last used identity value is 988. You insert a new row, test the identity value with @@identity, and obtain the value 55. What is most likely the cause of this situation?

A. There is a trigger for the insert on the Customers table that inserts a record in another table having a different identity value. The value is given by this insert.

B. The identity column has been reseeded to start at 55.

C. You deleted the row whose CustomerID was 55 and, while you inserted a new customer, SQL Server reused that value to avoid "holes" in the table.

D. The identity value column is corrupted, and you need to run DBCC CHECKIDENT to correct inaccuracies.

2. You are developing an employee database for World Wide Importers. You need to store a short job description for every employee. The length of these job descriptions varies and is less than 500 characters for 90 percent of them, but some can go up to 10,000 characters. What is the best solution for storing the job descriptions while consuming the least amount of space?

A. Use two varchar columns, one with a max length of 2,000 and one with a max length of 8,000. Depending on the real length, you will use one or both columns.

B. Use a varchar column with a max length of 10,000.

C. Use a text column on a separate filegroup.

D. Use an in-row text column.

3. As a freelance SQL Server developer, you have been asked by one of your customers to increase the capacity of part of its ordering system. For the moment, the Orders table is using an identity value as the OrderID. This column is a small integer. You need to change it to an integer to support the increase. Which statement will change the datatype of that column?

   A. `ALTER COLUMN Orders.OrderID integer`

   B. `ALTER TABLE Orders ALTER COLUMN OrderID integer`

   C. `ALTER TABLE Orders (OrderID integer)`

   D. `ALTER COLUMN OrderID integer FROM Orders`

4. You are working as a SQL Server developer for a large retail company. Each time a retail store places an order to the central warehouse, the total order amount has to be calculated from the price and quantity of products ordered. The concerned tables are shown in the following graphic.

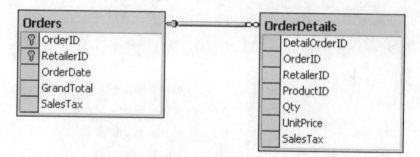

   You want the GrandTotal value to be calculated automatically when the order is validated. What are the three solutions you could use to achieve the expected result?

   A. Make the GrandTotal column a calculated column.

   B. Use an insert trigger to calculate the GrandTotal.

   C. Calculate the GrandTotal in the client application and store it in the table.

   D. Use a stored procedure to perform the insert and calculate the GrandTotal value in the stored procedure.

5. You are currently developing a product management system for Northwind Traders. The product managers need to store one or more photographs of each product for marketing purposes as well as a complete description of every product. For performance reasons, you want to place the products' descriptions and photographs on separate filegroups. From the following scripts, choose the one that best suits this need.

A.

```
CREATE TABLE dbo.Products (
    ProductID int IDENTITY (1, 1)
      NOT NULL PRIMARY KEY,
    ProductName nvarchar (40) NOT NULL,
    SupplierID int NULL,
    CategoryID int NULL,
    QuantityPerUnit nvarchar (20) NULL,
    UnitPrice money NULL,
    UnitsInStock smallint NULL,
    UnitsOnOrder smallint NULL,
    ReorderLevel smallint NULL,
    Discontinued bit NOT NULL,
    ProductDescription ntext,
    ProductPhoto image
  ) ON [PRIMARY] TEXTIMAGE_ON IMAGEFG
```

B.

```
CREATE TABLE dbo.Products (
    ProductID int IDENTITY (1, 1)
      NOT NULL PRIMARY KEY,
    ProductName nvarchar (40) NOT NULL,
    SupplierID int NULL,
    CategoryID int NULL,
    QuantityPerUnit nvarchar (20) NULL,
```

```
        UnitPrice money NULL,
        UnitsInStock smallint NULL,
        UnitsOnOrder smallint NULL,
        ReorderLevel smallint NULL,
        Discontinued bit NOT NULL,
        ProductDescription ntext ON IMAGEFG
    ) ON [PRIMARY]


    CREATE TABLE ProductsPhoto (
    ProductID int
        REFERENCES Products(ProductID),
    ProductPhoto image ON IMAGEFG,
    PhotoLegend varchar(100)
    ) ON [PRIMARY]
```

C.

```
CREATE TABLE dbo.Products (
    ProductID int IDENTITY (1, 1)
      NOT NULL PRIMARY KEY,
    ProductName nvarchar (40) NOT NULL,
    SupplierID int NULL,
    CategoryID int NULL,
    QuantityPerUnit nvarchar (20) NULL,
    UnitPrice money NULL,
    UnitsInStock smallint NULL,
    UnitsOnOrder smallint NULL,
    ReorderLevel smallint NULL,
    Discontinued bit NOT NULL,
    ProductDescription ntext
) ON [PRIMARY] TEXTIMAGE_ON IMAGEFG
```

```
CREATE TABLE ProductsPhoto (
  ProductID int
    REFERENCES Products(ProductID),
  ProductPhoto image,
  PhotoLegend varchar(100)
) ON IMAGEFG
```

D.

```
CREATE TABLE dbo.Products (
    ProductID int IDENTITY (1, 1)
      NOT NULL PRIMARY KEY,
    ProductName nvarchar (40) NOT NULL,
    SupplierID int NULL,
    CategoryID int NULL,
    QuantityPerUnit nvarchar (20) NULL,
    UnitPrice money NULL,
    UnitsInStock smallint NULL,
    UnitsOnOrder smallint NULL,
    ReorderLevel smallint NULL,
    Discontinued bit NOT NULL,
    ProductDescription ntext
      ON IMAGEFG,
    ProductPhoto image ON IMAGEFG
) ON [PRIMARY]
```

6. You ran the following script to create the Suppliers table:

```
CREATE TABLE Suppliers(
    SupplierID int IDENTITY (1, 1) NOT NULL ,
    CompanyName nvarchar (40) NOT NULL ,
    ContactName nvarchar (30) NULL ,
    ContactTitle nvarchar (30) NULL ,
    Address nvarchar (60) NULL ,
```

```
    City nvarchar (15) NULL ,
    State nvarchar (15) NULL ,
    PostalCode nvarchar (10) NULL ,
    Country nvarchar (15) NULL ,
    Phone nvarchar (24) NULL ,
    Fax nvarchar (24) NULL ,
    HomePage ntext NULL
) ON PRIMARY
```

You obtained the following execution error:
`Incorrect syntax near the keyword 'PRIMARY'.`

What is the reason for this error and what can you do to correct it?

A. State is a reserved keyword. Change it to Region and rerun the script.

B. The table Suppliers already exists in the database. Change its name and rerun the script.

C. Primary is a reserved keyword. Put it into square brackets and rerun the script.

D. The `ON PRIMARY` clause should be placed before the closing brackets. Put it inside the brackets and rerun the script.

7. You created the table shown in the following graphic.

Computers			
Column Name	Condensed Type	Nullable	Identity
MachineID	int	NOT NULL	✓
Brand	varchar(30)	NOT NULL	
Processor	varchar(30)	NOT NULL	
RAM	int	NOT NULL	

After a couple of months, you want to reuse the identity value 23, which has been deleted. Choose the required steps from those presented, and place them in the right order to insert new records and reuse the deleted identity value.

Statements	Possibilities
	`INSERT Computers`
	`VALUES(23, 'Compaq', 'Pentium II', 64)`
	`SET IDENTITY_INSERT ON`
	`COMMIT TRAN`
	`UPDATE Computers SET MachineID=23`
	`WHERE MachineID=@@IDENTITY`
	`SET IDENTITY_INSERT Computers OFF`
	`SET IDENTITY_INSERT Computers ON`
	`INSERT Computers`
	`VALUES(DEFAULT, 'Compaq', 'Pentium II', 64)`
	`BEGIN TRAN`

8. You run the following script:

```
CREATE TABLE tblEvents (
    EventID int IDENTITY (1, 1) NOT NULL ,
    EventType nvarchar (10) NULL ,
    EventTitle nvarchar (100) NULL ,
    EventDescription nvarchar (4000) NULL ,
    EventLanguage nvarchar (2) NULL ,
    EventDate smalldatetime NULL ,
    EventEndDate smalldatetime NULL ,
)
```

What happens with the table creation?

A. SQL Server issues a warning and creates the table.

B. SQL Server issues an error and does not create the table.

C. SQL Server issues a warning and does not create the table.

D. SQL Server creates the table without any warning.

9. You are developer for a winery. You create the following table:

```
CREATE TABLE Region (
    RegionID int NOT NULL,
    RegionDescription nchar (50),
)
```

What is the nullability of the RegionDescription column?

A. NULL

B. It depends on the ANSI_NULLS option.

C. NOT NULL

D. It depends on the ANSI NULL DEFAULT database option value.

10. You are a database developer for a regional bank. One of the databases in production contains the Employees table. This table contains a column designed to store the phone extension of every employee. Some of them do not have an extension, so the column allows NULL values. Nevertheless, the telephone system has been changed, and every employee is now assigned an extension. What line of code would you run to modify the Extension column?

A.
```
ALTER TABLE Employees
    ALTER COLUMN Extension Char (3) NULL
```

B.
```
ALTER TABLE Employees
    ALTER COLUMN Extension NULL
```

C.
```
ALTER COLUMN Employees.Extension NULL
```

D.
```
ALTER COLUMN Employees.Extension
    Char (3) NULL
```

11. You want to create the table illustrated in the following graphic. What is the script you are going to use?

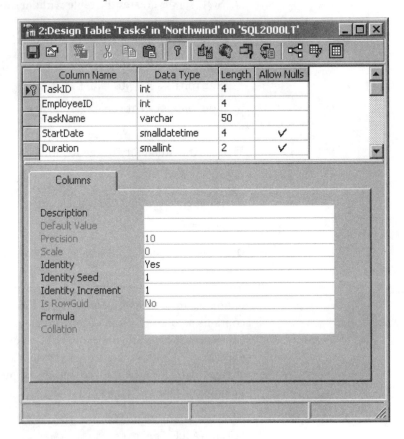

A.

```
CREATE TABLE Tasks (

     TaskID int IDENTITY(1, 1),

     EmployeeID int,

     TaskName varchar (50),

     StartDate smalldatetime NULL ,

     Duration smallint NULL)
```

B.

```
CREATE TABLE Tasks (
  TaskID int IDENTITY(1, 1) NOT NULL
          PRIMARY KEY CLUSTERED,
    EmployeeID int NOT NULL ,
    TaskName varchar (50) NOT NULL ,
    StartDate smalldatetime NULL ,
    Duration smallint NULL)
```

C.

```
CREATE TABLE Tasks (
    TaskID int
          PRIMARY KEY CLUSTERED
          IDENTITY(1, 1),
    EmployeeID int,
    TaskName varchar (50),
    StartDate smalldatetime NULL ,
    Duration smallint NULL)
```

D.

```
CREATE TABLE Tasks (
    TaskID int,
    EmployeeID int,
    TaskName varchar (50),
    StartDate smalldatetime,
    Duration smallint)
```

12. You are a developer for World Wide Importers. You are currently developing a database designed to manage imported products. Some of these products have to be stored at a maximum temperature of -30° C, some may be stored at -18° C, some at 0° C, and some at 4° C. This information has to be stored with each product. You want to minimize the space used by every row. Which datatype are you going to choose for this storage temperature?

A. TINYINT

B. SMALLINT

C. NUMERIC(2,0)

D. INT

13. You are a developer for a winery. A previous developer has created a series of user-defined datatypes that she stored in the model database. All these types are now in each database. In one of the databases, you need to modify a datatype called Telephone. This is a char(10), and you need to change it to varchar(15). Which statement or action will be needed to reach your goal?

    A. ALTER TYPE 'Telephone' varchar(15)

    B. sp_altertype 'telephone', 'varchar(15)'

    C. Alter all tables that use the type, drop it, then recreate it.

    D. sp_changetype 'telephone', 'varchar(15)'

14. You are a database developer for an international law firm. You are working on a new product database for the international offices. The company's headquarters is in San Diego, and it has the following five offices outside of the U.S.: Paris, Singapore, Sydney, Sao Paulo, and Johannesburg. Each of these offices uses their local language. The application you are developing is a brand new one and should accommodate all the company languages without any loss, since all the data will be consolidated in San Diego. Choose two possible solutions to handle this multi-language requirement.

    A. Use Unicode for all character columns.

    B. Use a different collation on each location.

    C. Use the same collation on each location.

    D. Use only text columns.

15. You are working on a new database system for Northwind Traders. The company has ten offices around the world, and each of them will run the new system. Each office can select new products to sell on the foreign markets managed by the other offices. Each product needs to have a unique identifier given automatically by the system across all databases. You decide to use the UniqueIdentifier datatype to offer this uniqueness feature. What column definition will create the ProductID column with the UniqueIdentifier feature?

A. ProductID uniqueidentifier NOT NULL

B. ProductID uniqueidentifer newid()

C. ProductID uniqueidentifier DEFAULT newid()

D. ProductID uniqueidentifier AS newid()

Answers to Review Questions

1. A. The last identity value in any scope is stored in @@Identity. It is likely that the table has a trigger that inserts a new row in another table.

2. D. Option A, while possible, is not convenient for lengthy values. B is impossible since the maximum length of a varchar column is 8,000. C would be possible, but a separate filegroup is useless, because you would consume more space than with the in-row storage. D is the best answer since a majority of rows will have enough space to store the value in the row.

3. B. This is the only correct syntax.

4. B, C, and D. A computed column cannot reference columns in other tables.

5. C. Option A would have been good if only one photograph per product was necessary. B and D are wrong since the test and image column locations are decided with the TEXT_IMAGE ON clause.

6. C. State could be a keyword in a future version of SQL Server, as indicated in the Books Online. It may be a good idea not to use it, even though it will work with SQL Server 2000. If the Suppliers table existed, the error message would not be an incorrect syntax error. The ON PRIMARY clause is after the closing bracket, but PRIMARY should be placed between square brackets because it is a reserved key word (PRIMARY KEY).

7.

Statements
SET IDENTITY_INSERT Computers ON
INSERT Computers
VALUES(23, 'Compaq', 'Pentium II', 64)
SET IDENTITY_INSERT Computers OFF

You cannot insert or update an explicit value in an identity column unless you set the IDENTITY_INSERT option to ON beforehand.

8. A. The maximum length of the record is 8265 bytes, which is bigger than the maximum authorized size of 8060 bytes. Nevertheless, due to the fact that some columns are nvarchar, the table is created with a warning indicating that the insert or update of a row in this table will fail if the resulting row length exceeds 8060 bytes.

9. D. The ANSI_NULLS option concerns only the SQL-92 compliancy behavior of comparison operators. Only the ANSI NULL DEFAULT database option, the ANSI_DEFAULTS, and the ANSI_NULL_DFLT_ON options have an impact on the implicit nullability of columns.

10. A. The right way to alter a column is to alter the table. Options C and D are syntactically incorrect. When you want to alter a column property, like the nullability, you need to redefine all of its current properties. Option B lacks the actual column datatype.

11. B. Option A lacks the primary key and the NOT NULLs; option C lacks the NOT NULL; option D lacks the NOT NULLs, the NULLs, the identity, and the primary key.

12. B. Option A, TINYINT, would be great for space consumption; unfortunately, it is unsigned. Option B, SMALLINT, offers the smallest space consumption, while allowing signed values.

13. C. Unfortunately, you need to make sure the datatype is not used. If you run the sp_droptype stored procedure, SQL Server will give you the list of all the tables using the concerned datatype.

14. A, B. Different languages mean different character sets. The only way to be sure the data is stored and read with the right character set is to use different collations or use Unicode. The only drawback of Unicode is that it uses 2 bytes per character.

15. C. Options B and D are syntactically incorrect. Option A creates the column but does not give an automatic value.

Chapter 4

Implementing Data Integrity

MICROSOFT EXAM OBJECTIVES COVERED IN THIS CHAPTER:

✓ **Create and alter database objects. Objects include constraints, indexes, stored procedures, tables, triggers, user-defined functions, and views.**

- Specify table characteristics. Characteristics include cascading actions, CHECK constraints, clustered, defaults, FILLFACTOR, foreign keys, nonclustered, primary key, and UNIQUE constraints.

✓ **Alter database objects to support replication and partitioned views.**

- Design and create constraints and views.

✓ **Troubleshoot failed object creation.**

The previous chapter focused on table creation. This one defines data integrity, which is the way you implement rules in the table structure to guarantee the data is correct. In this chapter you will learn about:

- Data integrity implementation

- Default values management

- Check rules management

- Primary key and unique constraints

- Foreign key and relationships

Data Integrity

We first met *data integrity* in Chapter 1. Data integrity defines rules for data accuracy and correctness. If, for example, a column is defined with an integer datatype, SQL Server prevents users from entering character data. On the other hand, a developer may design an Age column to prevent negative numbers. These simple rules, which could in certain cases become quite complicated, are data integrity rules.

Integrity Types

Four different types of data integrity are generally accepted in relational databases:

Domain   Domain integrity defines the valid data for a specific column. It is enforced by restricting the datatypes, format, or range of possible values.

Entity   Entity integrity defines each row as unique for each table. In other words, a row can exist only once in a specific table.

Referential   Referential integrity protects the relationship between tables during row inserts, updates, and deletes. Referential integrity may prevent users from:

- Inserting records in a related table if there are no matching records in the parent table

- Deleting records in a parent table if there is at least one matching record in the related table

- Updating the relationship key in a parent table if is there is at least one matching record in the related table

Enterprise   Enterprise integrity defines business rules that describe the processes in your organization.

Integrity Implementation

In every RDBMS, the four previous integrity types can be enforced in two ways:

Declarative Integrity   With *declarative integrity*, integrity rules are part of the table schema. In SQL Server 2000, declarative integrity may be enforced with the following objects and features:

- Datatypes

- Nullability

- DEFAULT constraint

- CHECK constraint

- PRIMARY KEY constraint

- UNIQUE constraint

- UNIQUE indexes

- FOREIGN KEY constraint

Procedural Integrity With *procedural integrity*, integrity rules are defined through external code objects, such as stored procedures or triggers. In SQL Server 2000, procedural integrity may be enforced with the following objects:

- Defaults

- Rules

- Triggers

- Stored procedures

The integrity implementation type you use has an impact on row inserts, updates, and deletes. Declarative integrity rules are always checked before the insert, update, or delete. That means, if one declarative integrity rule is violated, the operation is cancelled before the row has been inserted, updated, or deleted. Procedural integrity rules are generally checked after the insert, update, or delete occurred. The only exception to this last rule concerns INSTEAD OF triggers (see Chapter 6). If there are declarative and procedural integrity rules on a table, declarative rules are checked first and may prevent procedure rules from being checked.

Table 4.1 shows you ways to implement integrity rules.

TABLE 4.1 Implementing Integrity Types

Integrity Type	Declarative Implementation	Procedural Implementation
Domain	Datatype, nullability DEFAULT constraint CHECK constraint	Default Rule
Entity	PRIMARY KEY constraint UNIQUE constraint UNIQUE index	Stored procedure Trigger
Referential	FOREIGN KEY constraint	Stored procedure Trigger
Enterprise	N/A	Stored procedure Trigger

Triggers vs. Constraints

Every time I give a SQL Server programming course, the same question arises. Are constraints better than triggers? There is not a single answer, but the following rules apply any time:

- Always use *constraints* to enforce integrity whenever possible:
  - Enforce domain integrity with CHECK constraints.
  - Enforce entity integrity with PRIMARY KEY or UNIQUE constraints, or a UNIQUE index.
  - Enforce referential integrity with FOREIGN KEY constraints.
- Use triggers only in the following cases:
  - Domain integrity: The column values must be validated against one or many columns in another table.
  - Referential integrity: The needed cascading rule is more complex than the one proposed with FOREIGN KEY constraints. For example, each time a customer is deleted, his orders are moved to an archive table.
  - Whenever the rule that must be applied cannot be done through constraints.

Remember, constraints are part of the table schema. They are checked after AFTER triggers and are more efficient than stored procedures and triggers. So, when you need to enforce data integrity, always think of constraints first.

Declarative integrity is enforced through the CREATE TABLE or ALTER TABLE statements. Integrity rules can be defined at column or a table level. The following items show the different possible cases:

- Column-level constraint definition at table creation:

```
CREATE TABLE tablename
    (columname datatype [ CONSTRAINT constraintname ]
    columnconstrainttype [,...]
```

- Table-level constraint definition at table creation:

```
CREATE TABLE tablename
    (columname datatype [,...],
    [ CONSTRAINT constraintname ] tableconstrainttype
```

- Column-level constraint definition at table modification:

```
ALTER TABLE tablename
   ADD columname datatype [ CONSTRAINT constraintname ]
   columnconstrainttype [,...]
```

- Table-level constraint at table modification:

```
ALTER TABLE tablename
   [ WITH CHECK | WITH NOCHECK ] ADD
   [ CONSTRAINT constraintname ] tableconstrainttype
```

With the CHECK and FOREIGN KEY constraints, specifying WITH CHECK (this is the default) tells SQL Server to check existing values. Specifying WITH NOCHECK tells SQL Server not to check existing values but only check future inserts and updates.

To drop any constraint, use the following statement:

```
ALTER TABLE tablename DROP [CONSTRAINT] constraintname
```

You can disable CHECK and FOREIGN KEY constraints during massive inserts or updates, then re-enable them. To disable one, many, or all constraints, use the following syntax:

```
ALTER TABLE tablename
   NOCHECK CONSTRAINT {ALL | constraintname [,...]}
```

To re-enable one, many, or all constraints use the following syntax:

```
ALTER TABLE tablename
   CHECK CONSTRAINT {ALL | constraintname [,...]}
```

You may have noticed that when creating a constraint, specifying the name is optional. If you do not give a name to your constraint, SQL Server will name it automatically. If you wish to find a constraint name, you can run the sp_helpconstraint stored procedure, as in the following example:

```
sp_helpconstraint authors
```

Note that you have to be in the right database to execute this stored procedure. When you open the SQL Query Analyzer, you may not be in the right database. Check the database drop-down box and choose the right database.

You obtain three different result sets, the first giving the object name (to check you are working on the right object), the second giving the con-

straint list, and the third giving the list of tables referenced by the table
foreign keys:

```
Object Name
------------------
authors


constraint_type            constraint_name ...
------------------------    ------------------------------
CHECK on column au_id       CK__authors__au_id__77BFCB91
CHECK on column zip         CK__authors__zip__79A81403
DEFAULT on column phone     DF__authors__phone__78B3EFCA
PRIMARY KEY (clustered)     UPKCL_auidind


Table is referenced by foreign key
------------------------------------------------------
pubs.dbo.titleauthor: FK__titleauth__au_id__0519C6AF
```

The second result set has more columns than are presented here. You
will find the defined columns for PRIMARY KEY, FOREIGN KEY, and UNIQUE
constraints, as well as the CHECK and DEFAULT constraints.

After defining the integrity basis, let's move to the implementation
details of each integrity implementation type, starting with domain
integrity and the default values.

Default Values

Amongst column characteristics, we find nullability and *default* values. These two features define the value inserted in a column when it is not
specified in an INSERT statement. Three cases can occur when the column
value is not given in the INSERT statement:

- When the column is defined as accepting NULL values and has no
  default value, the column value is NULL.

- When the column is defined as not accepting NULL values and has no
  default value, an error occurs.

- When the column has a default value, whether it has been defined to accept or not accept NULL values, the column value is the default value.

SQL Server 2000 has two ways to implement default values in columns: the default constraint and the default object.

Default Constraint

The default constraint can be created at the time of table creation, added after table creation, or dropped. Each column can only have one default constraint.

TIMESTAMP, IDENTITY, and ROWGUIDCOL columns cannot have a default constraint, since their value definition is already automatic.

Defining the Default Constraint at Table Creation

The default constraint is defined in the CREATE TABLE statement at the column level. The following lines of code give you the basic SQL Server 2000 syntax of the default constraint definition:

```
CREATE TABLE tablename(
    columnname datatype [NULL | NOT NULL]
        [CONSTRAINT constraintname] DEFAULT expression
[,...])
```

The default expression can be a constant; a system function, such as GETDATE(); a system global variable, such as @@trancount; or a user-defined function (see Chapter 6).

The list of system functions can be found in the Books Online in the Transact-SQL Reference book, in the Functions/System functions section. To open the Books Online, choose Start ➤ Programs ➤ Microsoft SQL Server ➤ Books Online. To open a specific book, click on the plus sign (+) next to the book name.

The name of another column cannot be used in the default expression.

Listing 4.1 creates a table with default values.

Listing 4.1: CREATE TABLE Statement with Default Constraints

```
CREATE TABLE Orders (
    OrderID int IDENTITY (1, 1) NOT NULL,
    CustomerID nchar (5),
    EmployeeID int NULL,
    OrderDate datetime NULL
        CONSTRAINT DF_Orders_OrderDate DEFAULT GETDATE(),
    RequiredDate datetime NULL,
    ShippedDate datetime NULL,
    ShipVia int NULL,
    Freight money NULL
        CONSTRAINT DF_Orders_Freight DEFAULT 0,
    ShipName nvarchar (40),
    ShipAddress nvarchar (60),
    ShipCity nvarchar (15),
    ShipRegion nvarchar (15),
    ShipPostalCode nvarchar (10),
    ShipCountry nvarchar (15)
)
```

In this example, the OrderDate column has the current system date and time as its default value, and the Freight column has 0 as its default value. As you can see, defining a default constraint at table creation is rather straightforward.

The CONSTRAINT keyword, which allows you to name the default constraint, remains in the syntax to maintain compatibility with earlier SQL Server versions. If you do not add this word, the constraint will be automatically named by SQL Server as DF_*tablename_columnname_randomnumber*.

In SQL Enterprise Manager, you can define default values directly in the columns' properties (see Figure 4.1).

FIGURE 4.1 Defining a column default value

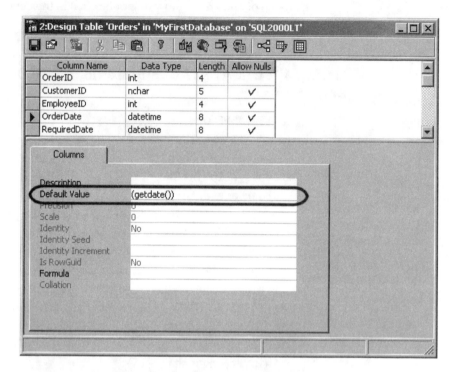

This is equivalent to defining the value in the default value in the
CREATE TABLE statement.

Defining the Default Constraint for an Existing Table

If you want to add a Default constraint to an existing table, two types of
situations can happen:

- You add a default constraint to an existing column.

- You add a new column with a default constraint.

The first case is simple. Adding a default to an existing column is possible only if the column does not already have a default value and is not a
TIMESTAMP, IDENTITY or ROWGUIDCOL. The syntax to add a default constraint to an existing column is the following:

```
ALTER TABLE tablename ADD [ CONSTRAINT constraintname ]
    DEFAULT expression FOR columnname
```

In the previous example, we add a default constraint on the ShipCountry column of the Orders table (see Listing 4.1 for the CREATE TABLE statement of the Orders table):

```
ALTER TABLE Orders ADD DEFAULT 'USA' For ShipCountry
```

Adding this default value does not impact existing rows. It will be applied only to future inserts.

The second case is also simple, but may have side effects. The syntax for adding a new column with a default constraint is as follows:

```
ALTER TABLE tablename ADD columnname datatype
    [NULL | NOT NULL] [ CONSTRAINT constraintname ]
    DEFAULT expression [ WITH VALUES ] [,...]
```

Note the CONSTRAINT keyword is optional. As in the CREATE TABLE statement, SQL Server will automatically name the constraints if no name is specified. The WITH VALUES statement manages the values inserted in existing rows. Table 4.2 shows you the behavior of the new column on existing rows:

TABLE 4.2   Behavior of existing rows with the WITH VALUES keyword

Nullability	WITH VALUES	Behavior for existing rows
NOT NULL	Specified or not	The column is filled with the default value
NULL	Specified	The column is filled with the default value
NULL	Not Specified	The column is filled with NULL

The following example adds the Total column with the default value of 0 to the Orders table:

```
ALTER TABLE Orders ADD Total money NULL DEFAULT 0 WITH VALUES
```

With the WITH VALUES option, the Total column is filled with 0. Otherwise, if the option has not been specified and since the NULL is included in the ALTER TABLE statement, the column would have been filled with NULL values.

Adding a default constraint with SQL Enterprise Manager is done in Design mode: in the right-pane where the table names are listed, right-click the table, and choose Design. You can then add a new column or add a default constraint to an existing column (see Figure 4.1). Note that WITH VALUES cannot be specified in SQL Enterprise Manager, so the nullability of the column specifies the behavior for existing rows.

Default Object

Default objects offer another way of defining a default value for a column. Default objects, called "defaults," have been in SQL Server since the very first version. Defaults are not really part of declarative integrity because they are not part of the table structure; they are actually part of the *database schema*, which is the overall definition of every database object. Defaults play the role of global variables that can be bound, or assigned, to columns or to user-defined datatypes.

The CREATE DEFAULT statement is used to create defaults:

```
CREATE DEFAULT default AS constant_expression
```

Once created, the default can be bound to a column with the following stored procedure:

```
sp_binddefault defaultname, tablename.columnname
```

Or, it can be bound to a user-defined datatype with the following:

```
sp_binddefault defaultname, datatypename [, futureonly]
```

The futureonly flag indicates that the existing columns of the concerned datatype will not inherit the new default value. This flag can only be used when binding a default to a datatype, not to a column.

NOTE DEFAULT constraints are preferred over column-bound default objects. Remember, it's advised to used declarative integrity whenever possible over procedural integrity.

The following example creates a default value named CalifDef and binds it to the ShipRegion of the Order table (see Listing 4.1):

```
CREATE DEFAULT CalifDef AS 'CA'
GO
sp_bindefault 'CalifDef', 'Orders.ShipRegion'
```

The same operation could be done through the Defaults folder of SQL Enterprise Manager. This folder gives you the complete list of defined defaults, allows you to modify and drop existing defaults, and modify or drop existing bindings.

You can drop an existing default by executing DROP DEFAULT *defaultname*, but only if it is not bound to any columns or user-defined datatypes.

To unbind a default from a column, execute the `sp_undbindefault` stored procedure:

`sp_unbindefault` *tablename.columnname*

To unbind a default from a user-defined datatype, run the following:

`sp_unbindefault` *datatypename* [, futureonly]

As for `sp_bindefault`, the `futureonly` flag indicates that all columns using this user-defined datatype are not affected by the unbinding, so they retain their default value.

Note that you cannot bind a default to a column defined with a default constraint or alter the table to add a default constraint to a column having a bound default.

Default Objects vs. Default Constraints

If default objects work like default constraints, you may ask yourself whether defaults are necessary. First, defaults are a backward compatibility feature, which means that they exist in SQL Server 2000 because they were present in previous versions. Second, they allow you to share the same default values among different columns. But their real purpose lies in their datatype binding. Binding a default to a datatype means that when you define a column of that datatype, the column automatically inherits the bound default.

Consider using default objects only when binding to datatypes; otherwise, use default constraints. As a rule of thumb, always consider constraints first!

EXERCISE 4.1

Defining and Testing Default Values

This exercise will walk you through creating a table with different default values, and inserting and selecting records to check the values that have been used.

1. Open the SQL Server Query Analyzer. Do this through the SQL Enterprise Manager by selecting Tools ➤ SQL Query Analyzer or by choosing Start ➤ Programs ➤ Microsoft SQL Server ➤ Query Analyzer.

2. Type the following query to return in Query Analyzer (be sure the Northwind database is selected):

```
CREATE TABLE Events (
    EventID int IDENTITY (1, 1) NOT NULL ,
    EventType nvarchar (10) NOT NULL DEFAULT 'Party',
    EventTitle nvarchar (100) NULL ,
    EventDescription ntext NULL ,
    EventLanguage nvarchar (2) NULL ,
    EventDate smalldatetime NULL DEFAULT GETDATE(),
    EventEndDate smalldatetime NULL DEFAULT DATEADD(day, 1,
GETDATE()),
    EventCreator nvarchar (50) NOT NULL DEFAULT SYSTEM_USER
)
```

3. Highlight these lines with the mouse and press the green arrow or CTRL-E to execute the query.

4. Insert a row by typing the following line of code:

```
INSERT Events DEFAULT VALUES
```

5. Highlight these lines with the mouse and press the green arrow or CTRL-E to execute the query.

6. Select the inserted row by typing the following line of code:

```
SELECT * FROM Events
```

Default values are one part of domain integrity. In SQL Server, you can define constraints and rules to make sure that the data is part of a given range of values or follows a specific format.

Check

Datatypes and default values enforce domain integrity. *Check* rules limit the possible values that can be entered into a column and in doing so, contribute to the domain integrity. Check constraints and rules are the two possible implementations of this feature. Generally, they limit the values allowed by defining:

- A range or ranges of acceptable values

- A list of values

- A pattern to follow, such as a phone number mask or a social security number

Check constraints are a declarative integrity feature and rules are a procedural feature. Both can be bound to columns or to user-defined datatypes. As mentioned for defaults, use check constraints instead of rules except for when defining user-defined datatypes. Let's take a close look now at check constraints.

Check Constraints

Check constraints are part of the table definition. They can be defined at table creation, at table modification, and dropped at any time. They can be disabled or enabled when needed. A column can have more than one check constraint. They are validated in their creation order during inserts and updates.

Check constraints:

- Must evaluate to a Boolean expression, such as a WHERE expression

- Can reference other columns of the same table

Defining a Check Constraint at Table Creation

Check constraints are part of the CREATE TABLE statement and can be defined at column or table level. To reference other columns, the check constraint has to be defined at table level. Column level definition is as follows:

```
CREATE TABLE tablename
   (columname datatype [ CONSTRAINT constraintname ]
   CHECK [NOT FOR REPLICATION] (logical_expression)
```

At table level, the definition is:

```
CREATE TABLE tablename
   (columname datatype [,...],
   [ CONSTRAINT constraintname ]
   CHECK [NOT FOR REPLICATION] (logical_expression)
```

The following listing presents the Orders table with a few different check constraints.

Listing 4.2: CREATE TABLE Statement with Check Constraints

```
CREATE TABLE Orders (
    OrderID int IDENTITY (1, 1) NOT NULL,
    CustomerID nchar (5)
        CHECK (CustomerID LIKE '[A-Z][A-Z][A-Z][A-Z][A-Z]'),
    EmployeeID int NULL,
    OrderDate datetime NULL
        CHECK (OrderDate BETWEEN '01/01/70' AND GETDATE()),
    RequiredDate datetime NULL,
    ShippedDate datetime NULL,
    ShipVia int NULL
        CHECK (ShipVia IN (1, 2, 3, 4)),
    Freight money NULL
        CHECK (Freight>=0),
    ShipName nvarchar (40),
    ShipAddress nvarchar (60),
    ShipCity nvarchar (15),
    ShipRegion nvarchar (15),
    ShipPostalCode nvarchar (10),
    ShipCountry nvarchar (15),
    CHECK (RequiredDate>OrderDate)
)
```

This CREATE TABLE statement generates four column-level constraints and two table-level constraints, as shown by the result from the execution of sp_helpconstraint Orders:

```
constraint_type                     constraint_name
------------------------------      ------------------------------
CHECK Table Level                   CK__Orders__44FF419A
CHECK on column CustomerID          CK__Orders__Customer__412EB0B6
CHECK on column Freight             CK__Orders__Freight__440B1D61
CHECK on column OrderDate           CK__Orders__OrderDat__4222D4EF
CHECK on column ShipVia             CK__Orders__ShipVia__4316F928
```

Note that SQL Server gives the following type of name automatically to the check constraints:

- CK_*tablename_randomnumber* for table level constraints
- CK_*tablename_columnname_randomnumber* for column level constraints

If we take a closer look at Listing 4.2, we see:

- The CustomerID column must follow the pattern [A-Z][A-Z][A-Z][A-Z][A-Z], that must be composed of five letters. For example, ALFKI is a valid value, while A4FK7 is not valid. This kind of check constraint follows the LIKE comparison rules (see Chapter 7 for more on LIKE rules).

- The OrderDate column must be between today and January 1, 1970.

- The ShipVia column must be only one of the four defined values in the list.

- The Freight columns must be a positive number.

- The RequiredDate must be greater than the OrderDate.

As you can see, check constraints referencing more than one column must be declared at table level. If you had tried to define the table level constraints at column level with the following:

```
RequiredDate datetime NULL
     CHECK (RequiredDate>OrderDate)
```

you would have obtained error 8141: Column CHECK constraint for column 'RequiredDate' references another column, table 'Orders.'

Defining a Check at Table Modification

Adding a check constraint to an existing table may not be possible due to existing data. By default, existing data is checked against the new check constraint. If at least one row does not comply with the constraint, the new check constraint creation fails.

You can add a check constraint at column level when defining a new column for the table like this:

```
ALTER TABLE tablename
   ADD columnname datatype [ CONSTRAINT constraintname ]
   CHECK [NOT FOR REPLICATION] (logical_expression) [,...]
```

To define a new check constraint for an existing column, use the following syntax:

```
ALTER TABLE tablename
   [ WITH CHECK | WITH NOCHECK ] ADD
   [ CONSTRAINT constraintname ]
   CHECK [NOT FOR REPLICATION] (logical_expression)
```
The following example adds two constraints to the Orders table:
```
ALTER TABLE Orders
   ADD CHECK (EmployeeID>0)
ALTER TABLE Orders
   ADD CHECK (ShippedDate>OrderDate)
```

As we've seen previously, by default, existing data is checked against the new check constraints. If you want the new constraint to apply only to future inserts and updates, add the constraint with the WITH NOCHECK keyword before the ADD clause.

EXERCISE 4.2

Creating and Using a Check Constraint

This exercise will walk you through modifying a table to add a check constraint and verifying that the constraint is enforced.

1. Open the SQL Server Query Analyzer. Do this through the SQL Enterprise Manager by selecting Tools ➤ SQL Query Analyzer or by choosing Start ➤ Programs ➤ Microsoft SQL Server ➤ Query Analyzer.

2. Type the following query to return in Query Analyzer (be sure the Northwind database is selected):

   ```
   ALTER TABLE Events
   ADD CHECK (EventDate>=GETDATE())
   ```

3. Highlight these lines with the mouse and press the green arrow or CTRL-E to execute the query.

4. Type the following query to return in Query Analyzer (be sure the Northwind database is selected):

```
INSERT INTO Events(EventType, EventTitle, EventDescription,
EventLanguage, EventDate, EventEndDate)
VALUES(DEFAULT, 'This is my Event', 'This will be great
fun', 'US', '12/12/1999', '01/01/2012')
```

5. Highlight these lines with the mouse and press the green arrow or CTRL-E to execute the query.

   You should obtain error 547 because the inserted row conflicts with the check constraint.

6. Type the following query to return in Query Analyzer (be sure the Northwind database is selected):

```
INSERT INTO Events(EventType, EventTitle, EventDescription,
EventLanguage, EventDate, EventEndDate)
VALUES(DEFAULT, 'This is my Event', 'This will be great
fun', 'US', '12/12/2012', '01/01/2012')
```

7. Highlight these lines with the mouse and press the green arrow or CTRL-E to execute the query.

8. Select the inserted row by typing the following line of code:

```
SELECT * FROM Events
```

Rules

Rules are a backward compatibility feature used to define validation rules that can be bound to table columns or to user-defined datatypes. Like default objects, *rules* are created on their own before being bound to another object. The creation of a rule is done with the CREATE RULE statement:

```
CREATE RULE rulename AS condition_expression
```

Once created, the rule can be bound to a column with the following syntax:

```
sp_bindrule rulename, tablename.columnname
```

Or, it can be bound to a user-defined datatype:

```
sp_bindrule rulename, datatypename [, futureonly]
```

The `futureonly` flag indicates that the existing columns of the concerned datatype will not inherit the new rule. This flag can only be used when binding a rule to a datatype, not to a column.

A column can have only one rule bound to it, but you can bind a rule to a column defined with a check constraint. Both will be evaluated, starting with the constraint.

The following example creates a rule for date checking and binds it to the OrderDate columns of the Orders table:

```
CREATE RULE ActiveDate AS
    @Date BETWEEN '01/01/70' AND GETDATE()
AS
sp_bindrule ActiveDate, 'Orders.OrderDate'
```

Expressions used in rules follow the same guidelines as check conditions and are similar to a `WHERE` clause expression, except you cannot reference any other database columns in rules. If you compare the syntax of the `CHECK` statement and a rule expression, two main differences are apparent:

1. The rule expression uses a variable (beginning with an at @ sign) that will be replaced by the column value when attached to the column.

2. A rule expression cannot reference table columns.

The second point is the biggest behavioral difference between check constraints and rules: rules are equivalent to column-level check constraints only! Just as for defaults, check constraints are preferred to rules.

Now that you know how default constraints, defaults, rules, and check constraints work as part of domain integrity checking, let's take a look at entity integrity beginning with primary keys.

Primary Keys

Primary keys form the basic functionality for entity integrity checking. A *primary key* uniquely identifies each row and is formed by one or more columns in the table. In SQL Server 2000, the definition of a primary key automatically creates a unique index on the non-null columns that form the key. A table can have only one primary key (see Chapter 1 for a formal definition of keys).

A primary key can be created during table creation or table modification. You cannot modify an existing primary key in Transact-SQL. The following restrictions apply to the definition of primary key columns:

- All the columns participating in the primary key definition must be defined as NOT NULL.

- In absence of index type specification, the supporting index is clustered (see Chapter 5).

Defining a Primary Key Constraint at Table Creation

The basic definition of the primary key is quite simple, since the only required parameter(s) is the column name(s). The optional parameters are very similar to those of an index. The optional parameters are discussed in detail in Chapter 5.

- Column-level primary key constraint definition:

```
CREATE TABLE tablename
    (columnname datatype [ CONSTRAINT constraintname ]
    PRIMARY KEY [ CLUSTERED | NONCLUSTERED ]
                [ WITH FILLFACTOR = fillfactor ]
                [ON {filegroup | DEFAULT} ] [,...]
```

- Table-level primary key constraint definition:

```
CREATE TABLE tablename
    (columnname datatype [,...],
    [ CONSTRAINT constraintname ]
    PRIMARY KEY [ CLUSTERED | NONCLUSTERED ]
                { ( column [ ASC | DESC ] [ ,...n ] ) }
                [ WITH FILLFACTOR = fillfactor ]
                [ ON { filegroup | DEFAULT } ]
```

A single column primary key can be defined at column level or at table level. A multi-column primary key has to be defined at table level. Listing 4.3 gives you the definition of a single-column primary key definition for the Orders table.

Listing 4.3: Partial CREATE TABLE Statement with Column-level Primary Constraint

```
CREATE TABLE Orders (
    OrderID int IDENTITY (1, 1) NOT NULL PRIMARY KEY,
    CustomerID nchar (5)
    ...
)
```

This statement creates a clustered primary key on the OrderID column, at column level, as shown in the sp_helpconstraint 'orders' execution result:

```
constraint_type          constraint_name        constraint_keys
------------------------  ---------------------- ----------------
PRIMARY KEY (clustered)   PK__Orders__571DF1D5   OrderID
```

As you can see from this result, the default primary key name begins with PK_ followed by the table name and random figures and letters, and the key is supported by a clustered index. We could have given the index a specific name by using the CONSTRAINT keyword, as shown in this example:

```
OrderID int IDENTITY (1, 1) NOT NULL
    CONSTRAINT OrdersPK PRIMARY KEY
```

Listing 4.4 gives you another version of a primary key definition, defined at the table level.

Listing 4.4: CREATE TABLE Statement with Table-level Primary Key Constraint

```
CREATE TABLE Orders (
    OrderID int IDENTITY (1, 1) NOT NULL,
    CustomerID nchar (5),
    EmployeeID int NULL,
```

```
OrderDate datetime NULL
RequiredDate datetime NULL,
ShippedDate datetime NULL,
ShipVia int NULL
Freight money NULL
ShipName nvarchar (40),
ShipAddress nvarchar (60),
ShipCity nvarchar (15),
ShipRegion nvarchar (15),
ShipPostalCode nvarchar (10),
ShipCountry nvarchar (15),
PRIMARY KEY NONCLUSTERED (OrderID) WITH FILLFACTOR=90
)
```

In the above version, the primary key is defined as a non-clustered index with a fillfactor of 90, which means that data pages are filled to only 90 percent.

You can find complete information on indexes in Chapter 5.

Once created, uniqueness of the key is enforced by the index. Trying to insert a duplicate primary key leads to the error 2627: Violation of PRIMARY KEY constraint 'PK_Orders_571DF1D5'. Cannot insert duplicate key in object 'Orders'. The statement has been terminated.

In SQL Enterprise Manager, primary key definition is even simpler. In the Design Table window, select the primary key column (hold the CTRL key to select multiple columns) by right-clicking the columns and choosing Set Primary Key. A small key appears next to the chosen columns, as in Figure 4.2.

FIGURE 4.2 Primary key definition in SQL Enterprise Manager

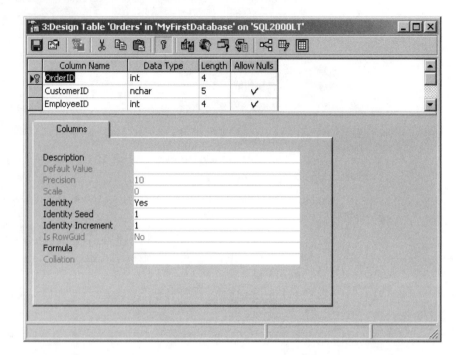

Note that the same operation can be performed in SQL Enterprise Manager.

Creating and Using a Primary Key Constraint

This example will walk you through creating a table with a primary key and using this table to check that the constraint is enforced.

1. Open the SQL Server Query Analyzer. Do this through the SQL Enterprise Manager by selecting Tools ➤ SQL Query Analyzer or by choosing Start ➤ Programs ➤ Microsoft SQL Server ➤ Query Analyzer.

2. Type the following query to return in Query Analyzer (be sure the Northwind database is selected):

```
DROP TABLE Events
GO
```

```
CREATE TABLE Events (
    EventID int NOT NULL PRIMARY KEY,
    EventType nvarchar (10) NOT NULL DEFAULT 'Party',
    EventTitle nvarchar (100) NULL ,
    EventDescription ntext NULL ,
    EventLanguage nvarchar (2) NULL ,
    EventDate smalldatetime NULL DEFAULT GETDATE()
    CHECK (EventDate>=GETDATE()),
    EventEndDate smalldatetime NULL DEFAULT DATEADD(day, 1,
GETDATE()),
    EventCreator nvarchar (50) NOT NULL DEFAULT SYSTEM_USER
)
```

3. Highlight these lines with the mouse and press the green arrow or CTRL-E to execute the query.

4. Insert a row by typing the following lines of code:

```
INSERT INTO Events(EventID, EventType, EventTitle,
EventDescription, EventLanguage, EventDate, EventEndDate)
VALUES(1, DEFAULT, 'This is my Event', 'This will be great
fun', 'US', '12/12/2012', '01/01/2012')
```

5. Highlight these lines with the mouse and press the green arrow or CTRL-E to execute the query.

6. Run the same statement another time by highlighting these lines with the mouse and press the green arrow or CTRL-E to execute the query.

   It conflicts with the primary key constraint since you tried to insert the same EventID and an error is returned.

Defining a Primary Key at Table Modification

You can add a primary key to an existing table, but it can be created only if the values already inserted in the column key are unique.

You can add a primary key while adding a column, at column level:

```
ALTER TABLE tablename
    ADD columnname datatype [ CONSTRAINT constraintname ]
    PRIMARY KEY [ CLUSTERED | NONCLUSTERED ]
                [ WITH FILLFACTOR = fillfactor ]
                [ON {filegroup | DEFAULT} ] [,...]
```

The only way to add a primary key to an existing column is at table level:

```
ALTER TABLE tablename
    ADD
    [ CONSTRAINT constraintname ]
    PRIMARY KEY [ CLUSTERED | NONCLUSTERED ]
                { ( column [ ASC | DESC ] [ ,...n ] ) }
                [ WITH FILLFACTOR = fillfactor ]
                [ ON { filegroup | DEFAULT } ]
```

The same parameters are used in table modification as in table creation. The following example drops the existing primary key and adds a new primary key to the Orders table:

```
ALTER TABLE Orders DROP CONSTRAINT PK_Orders_571DF1D5
GO
ALTER TABLE Orders ADD PRIMARY KEY(OrderID)
```

If you run this statement and duplicate values exist in the column, you will first encounter error 1505: CREATE UNIQUE INDEX terminated because a duplicate key was found for index ID 1. Most significant primary key is '1', and then error 1750: Could not create constraint. See previous errors. The statement has been terminated.

Using a primary key constraint is the preferred technique to implement a primary key in a table. But, as discussed in Chapter 1, a table can also hold alternate keys. These keys can be implemented as unique constraints, as we see in the next section.

Unique Constraints

As their name implies, *unique* constraints enforce the uniqueness of rows. While a table can have only one primary key constraint, it can have many unique constraints. That is the first difference between primary key and unique constraints. The second difference concerns nullability. Unique constraints can be created on columns defined as NULL. Nevertheless these columns cannot contain more than one null value, because two null values are considered equal as far as unique constraints are concerned. As primary keys, unique constraints can be referenced by foreign key constraints to define relationships.

Defining a Unique Constraint at Table Creation

Unique constraint creation syntax is equivalent to the primary key creation syntax:

- Column-level unique constraint definition:

```
CREATE TABLE tablename
    (columname datatype [ CONSTRAINT constraintname ]
    UNIQUE [ CLUSTERED | NONCLUSTERED ]
        [ WITH FILLFACTOR = fillfactor ]
        [ON {filegroup | DEFAULT} ] [,...]
```

- Table-level unique constraint definition:

```
CREATE TABLE tablename
    (columname datatype [,...],
    [ CONSTRAINT constraintname ]
    UNIQUE [ CLUSTERED | NONCLUSTERED ]
        { ( column [ ASC | DESC ] [ ,...n ] ) }
        [ WITH FILLFACTOR = fillfactor ]
        [ ON { filegroup | DEFAULT } ]
```

As with primary keys, a single-column unique constraint can be created at column or table level, and a multi-column unique constraint can only be created at table level.

Listing 4.5 gives you an example of one column-level unique constraint and one table-level constraint.

Listing 4.5: CREATE TABLE Statement with Unique Constraints

```
CREATE TABLE Customers (
    CustomerID nchar (5) NOT NULL PRIMARY KEY CLUSTERED,
    CompanyName nvarchar (40) NOT NULL ,
    ContactName nvarchar (30) NULL ,
```

```
        ContactTitle nvarchar (30) NULL ,
        Address nvarchar (60) NULL ,
        City nvarchar (15) NULL ,
        Region nvarchar (15) NULL ,
        PostalCode nvarchar (10) NULL ,
        Country nvarchar (15) NULL ,
        Phone nvarchar (24) NULL UNIQUE,
        Fax nvarchar (24) NULL ,
        UNIQUE NONCLUSTERED (CompanyName, ContactName)
)
```

The two unique constraints created in Listing 4.5 are named UQ followed by the table name and a random number, as shown in the partial result of the sp_helpconstraint 'customers' procedure execution:

```
constraint_type          constraint_name          constraint_keys
---------------------    ---------------------    ----------------
UNIQUE (non-clustered)   UQ_Customers_6FE99F9F CompanyName, ...
UNIQUE (non-clustered)   UQ_Customers_70DDC3D8 Phone
```

Note that both constraints are non-clustered. Even though when we defined the unique constraint on the Phone column, the type of index was not explicitly indicated.

Once created, if you try to insert a duplicate value in the column defined as unique, you obtain error 2627: Violation of UNIQUE KEY constraint ' UQ_Customers_70DDC3D8'. Cannot insert duplicate key in object 'Customers'. The statement has been terminated.

A unique constraint is supported by a unique index (see Chapter 5), that enforces the uniqueness of the values. The index name is the constraint name.

Unique constraints can be defined in SQL Enterprise Manager. Open the table in design mode and open its properties window. The unique constraints can be defined in the Indexes/Keys tab, as in Figure 4.3.

FIGURE 4.3 Unique constraint definition in SQL Enterprise Manager

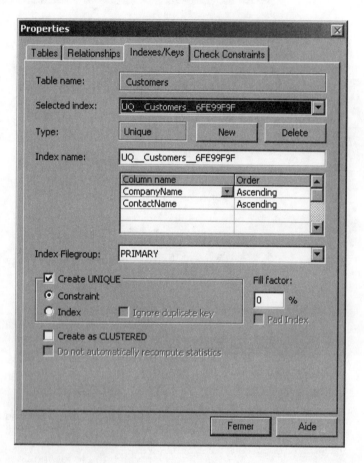

Note that uniqueness of a column or of a group of columns can be enforced through a constraint or an index. The only difference between them is the ability to define a relationship with the constraint. Unique indexes alone can not be defined as part of a relationship.

EXERCISE 4.4

Creating and Using a Unique Constraint

This exercise will walk you through creating a table with a unique constraint and inserting records to check that the constraint is correctly enforced.

1. Open the SQL Server Query Analyzer. Do this through the SQL Enterprise Manager by selecting Tools ➢ SQL Query Analyzer or by choosing Start ➢ Programs ➢ Microsoft SQL Server ➢ Query Analyzer.

2. Type the following query to return in Query Analyzer (be sure the Northwind database is selected):

```
DROP TABLE Events
GO
CREATE TABLE Events (
    EventID int IDENTITY (1, 1) NOT NULL PRIMARY KEY,
    EventType nvarchar (10) NOT NULL DEFAULT 'Party',
    EventTitle nvarchar (100) NULL UNIQUE,
    EventDescription ntext NULL ,
    EventLanguage nvarchar (2) NULL ,
    EventDate smalldatetime NULL DEFAULT GETDATE() CHECK
(EventDate>=GETDATE()),
    EventEndDate smalldatetime NULL DEFAULT DATEADD(day, 1,
GETDATE()),
    EventCreator nvarchar (50) NOT NULL DEFAULT SYSTEM_USER
)
```

3. Highlight these lines with the mouse and press the green arrow or CTRL-E to execute the query.

4. Insert a row by typing the following lines of code:

```
INSERT INTO Events(EventType, EventTitle, EventDescription,
EventLanguage, EventDate, EventEndDate)
VALUES(DEFAULT, 'This is my Event', 'This will be great
fun', 'US', '12/12/2012', '01/01/2012')
```

5. Highlight these lines with the mouse and press the green arrow or CTRL-E to execute the query.

6. Run the same statement another time by highlighting these lines with the mouse and press the green arrow or CTRL-E to execute the query.

It conflicts with the unique constraint since you tried to insert the same EventTitle.

7. Insert another row by typing the following lines of code:

```
INSERT INTO Events(EventType, EventTitle, EventDescription,
EventLanguage, EventDate, EventEndDate)
VALUES(DEFAULT, NULL, 'This will be great fun', 'US',
'12/12/2012', '01/01/2012')
```

8. Highlight these lines with the mouse and press the green arrow or CTRL-E to execute the query.

The row is inserted even if EventTitle is NULL.

9. Run the same statement one more time by highlighting these lines with the mouse and press the green arrow or CTRL-E to execute the query.

It conflicts with the unique constraint since you tried to insert another null value in the EventTitle column.

Defining a Unique Constraint at Table Modification

You can add a unique constraint to an existing table, but it can be created only if the values already inserted in the column forming the constraint are unique.

You can add a unique constraint while adding a column at column level:

```
ALTER TABLE tablename
   ADD columname datatype [ CONSTRAINT constraintname ]
   UNIQUE [ CLUSTERED | NONCLUSTERED ]
        [ WITH FILLFACTOR = fillfactor ]
        [ON {filegroup | DEFAULT} ] [,...]
```

The only way to add a constraint to an existing column is at table level:

```
ALTER TABLE tablename
   ADD [ CONSTRAINT constraintname ]
   UNIQUE [ CLUSTERED | NONCLUSTERED ]
        { ( column [ ASC | DESC ] [ ,...n ] ) }
        [ WITH FILLFACTOR = fillfactor ]
        [ ON { filegroup | DEFAULT } ]
```

The same parameters are used in table modification as in table creation. The following example drops the existing unique constraint and adds a new unique constraint to the Orders table:

```
ALTER TABLE Customers DROP CONSTRAINT
    UQ_Customers_70DDC3D8
GO
ALTER TABLE Customers ADD UNIQUE(Phone)
```

If you run this statement and there are duplicate values in the column, you will first receive error 1505: CREATE UNIQUE INDEX terminated because a duplicate key was found for index ID 2. Most significant primary key is '1', and then error 1750: Could not create constraint. See previous errors. The statement has been terminated. Note that these two errors are the same as the errors for primary key creation failure.

Unique and primary key constraints are useful where enforcing entity integrity. The last type of declarative integrity we are going to discuss is referential integrity with foreign key constraint.

Foreign Keys and Relationships

Foreign keys and relationships have been discussed theoretically in Chapter 1. In SQL Server 2000, relationships are declaratively defined with *foreign key* constraints. As with all other constraints, a foreign key can be created at table creation or added afterwards.

Figure 4.4 shows three tables of the Northwind database and the two relationships between these tables.

FIGURE 4.4   Relationships and keys in the Northwind database

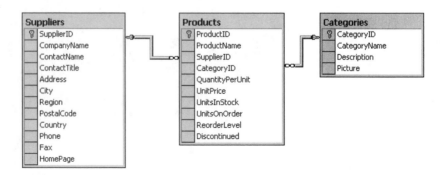

A foreign key constraint can reference columns defined as the primary key or unique constraints only, and only in the same database. A foreign key behaves like a check constraint, since it limits its values to that of the primary key or unique column values to which it is linked. In Figure 4.4, a new product can be inserted only if its supplier ID already exists in the Suppliers table.

Defining a Foreign Key Constraint at Table Creation

A foreign key can be defined on one or more columns. A one-column foreign key can be declared at column or table level in the CREATE TABLE statement. A multi-column foreign key can only be declared at table level:

- Column-level foreign key constraint definition at table creation:

```
CREATE TABLE tablename
   (columname datatype [ CONSTRAINT constraintname ]
   [ FOREIGN KEY ]
        REFERENCES ref_table [ ( ref_column ) ]
        [ ON DELETE { CASCADE | NO ACTION } ]
        [ ON UPDATE { CASCADE | NO ACTION } ]
        [ NOT FOR REPLICATION ] [,...]
```

- Table-level foreign key constraint definition at table creation:

```
CREATE TABLE tablename
(columname datatype [,...],
   [ CONSTRAINT constraintname ]
   FOREIGN KEY [ ( column [ ,...n ] ) ]
        REFERENCES ref_table [ ( ref_column [ ,...n ])]

        [ ON DELETE { CASCADE | NO ACTION } ]
        [ ON UPDATE { CASCADE | NO ACTION } ]
        [ NOT FOR REPLICATION ]
```

Listing 4.6 creates the relationships between the Products and the Suppliers tables and between the Products and Categories tables with column-level constraints.

Listing 4.6: CREATE TABLE Statement with Foreign Key Column-level Constraints

```
CREATE TABLE Products (
    ProductID int IDENTITY (1, 1) NOT NULL ,
    ProductName nvarchar (40) NOT NULL ,
    SupplierID int NULL REFERENCES Suppliers (SupplierID),
    CategoryID int NULL REFERENCES Categories (CategoryID),
    QuantityPerUnit nvarchar (20) NULL ,
    UnitPrice money NULL,
    UnitsInStock smallint NULL,
    UnitsOnOrder smallint NULL,
    ReorderLevel smallint NULL,
    Discontinued bit NOT NULL,
    )
```

The FOREIGN KEY keyword is optional in column-level foreign key constraints, as you can note from the previous example.

The same result can be obtained with table-level constraints, as shown in Listing 4.7.

Listing 4.7: CREATE TABLE Statement with Foreign Key Table-level Constraints

```
CREATE TABLE Products (
    ProductID int IDENTITY (1, 1) NOT NULL ,
    ProductName nvarchar (40) NOT NULL ,
    SupplierID int NULL,
    CategoryID int NULL,
    QuantityPerUnit nvarchar (20) NULL ,
    UnitPrice money NULL,
    UnitsInStock smallint NULL,
    UnitsOnOrder smallint NULL,
    ReorderLevel smallint NULL,
    Discontinued bit NOT NULL,
    CONSTRAINT FK_Products_Categories
      FOREIGN KEY (CategoryID)
```

```
      REFERENCES Categories (CategoryID),
   CONSTRAINT FK_Products_Suppliers
      FOREIGN KEY (SupplierID)
      REFERENCES Suppliers (SupplierID)
)
```

The brackets around the column name in the FOREIGN KEY clause are mandatory, even if the foreign key is defined on one column. If you forgot them, the system will fire an incorrect syntax error.

The columns referenced by the foreign key statement have to be primary keys or members of a unique constraint, otherwise you obtain error 1776 at creation: There are no primary or candidate keys in the referenced table 'Categories' that match the referencing column list in the foreign key 'FK__Products__Categories'.

As with other constraints, the CONSTRAINT keyword and the name definition are not compulsory.

The following shows the result of running sp_helpconstraint for the table created in Listing 4.5:

```
constraint_type   constraint_name         del_act     upd_act
---------------   ---------------------   ----------  ----------
FOREIGN KEY       FK_Products_Categories  No Action   No Action
FOREIGN KEY       FK_Products_Suppliers   No Action   No Action


status_enabled   status_for_replication
--------------   ----------------------
Enabled          Is_For_Replication
Enabled          Is_For_Replication


constraint_keys
------------------------------------------------------------------
CategoryID REFERENCES Northwind.dbo.Categories (CategoryID)
SupplierID REFERENCES Northwind.dbo.Suppliers (SupplierID)
```

This result is given in three different blocks because it could not fit in one block on the page.

If we take the first foreign key, we read that there is no delete or update action. That means that cascading updates and deletes are not enforced. The constraint is enforced (enabled), and it is not defined for replication.

We have seen in Chapter 1 that a foreign key protects the creation of orphans; that is, it is impossible to insert a row in a child table if it has no corresponding row in the parent table. In the previous example (Listing 4.6), if you try to insert a new row in the Products table and give a CategoryID that does not exist in the Category table, you obtain error 547: `INSERT statement conflicted with COLUMN FOREIGN KEY constraint 'FK_Products_Categories'. The conflict occurred in database 'Northwind', table 'Category', column 'CategoryID'. The statement has been terminated.`

In error 547, SQL Server tells you whether the constraint is column or table level. In the Product and Category example, SQL Server recognized a COL-UMN FOREIGN KEY. If the foreign key has been defined on two or more columns, it would have returned TABLE FOREIGN KEY, and would not have referenced the concerned column.

As far as cascading updates and deletes are concerned, they are not enforced by default. That means that to protect orphans, the primary key of the referenced table cannot be updated if it is referenced by foreign keys, and that a parent row cannot be deleted if it has a least one corresponding child row.

If you try to update the primary key, you receive error 547 again, but with a slightly different message: `UPDATE statement conflicted with COLUMN REFERENCE constraint 'FK_Products_Categories'. The conflict occurred in database 'Northwind', table 'Category', column 'CategoryID'. The statement has been terminated.`

If you try to delete a parent row, you receive error 547 again: `DELETE statement conflicted with COLUMN REFERENCE constraint 'FK_Products_Categories'. The conflict occurred in database 'Northwind', table 'Category', column 'CategoryID'. The statement has been terminated.`

Creating and Using a Foreign Key Constraint

This example will walk you through creating two related tables and checking the referential integrity rules we've just seen.

1. Open the SQL Server Query Analyzer. Do this through the SQL Enterprise Manager by selecting Tools ➢ SQL Query Analyzer or by choosing Start ➢ Programs ➢ Microsoft SQL Server ➢ Query Analyzer.

2. Type the following query to return in Query Analyzer (be sure the Northwind database is selected):

```
DROP TABLE Events
GO
CREATE TABLE Events (
    EventID int IDENTITY (1, 1) NOT NULL PRIMARY KEY,
    EventType nvarchar (10) NOT NULL DEFAULT 'Party',
    EventTitle nvarchar (100) NULL UNIQUE,
    EventDescription ntext NULL ,
    EventLanguage nvarchar (2) NULL ,
    EventDate smalldatetime NULL DEFAULT GETDATE() CHECK
(EventDate>=GETDATE()),
    EventEndDate smalldatetime NULL DEFAULT DATEADD(day, 1,
GETDATE()),
    EventCreator nvarchar (50) NOT NULL DEFAULT SYSTEM_USER
)
GO
CREATE TABLE Schedule(
    ScheduleID int IDENTITY (1, 1) NOT NULL PRIMARY KEY,
    EventID int NOT NULL,
    StartDate datetime NOT NULL,
    EndDate datetime NOT NULL,
    PartTitle nvarchar (100) NULL,
    CHECK (EndDate>StartDate),
    FOREIGN KEY (EventID) REFERENCES Events (EventID)
)
```

3. Highlight these lines with the mouse and press the green arrow or CTRL-E to execute the query.

4. Insert rows by typing the following lines of code:

```
INSERT INTO Events(EventType, EventTitle, EventDescription,
EventLanguage, EventDate, EventEndDate)
VALUES(DEFAULT, 'This is my Event', 'This will be great
fun', 'US', '12/12/2012', '01/01/2012')
GO
```

```
INSERT Schedule(EventID, StartDate, EndDate)
VALUES (1, '08:00', '10:00')
INSERT Schedule(EventID, StartDate, EndDate)
VALUES (1, '10:00', '12:00')
```

5. Highlight these lines with the mouse and press the green arrow or CTRL-E to execute the query. Type these lines into Query Analyzer:

```
INSERT Schedule(EventID, StartDate, EndDate)
VALUES (2, '08:00', '10:00')
```

6. Highlight these lines with the mouse and press the green arrow or CTRL-E to execute the query.

The INSERT statement conflicts with the foreign key constraint since EventID 2 does not exist.

In the CREATE TABLE statement syntax, you can define a foreign key in the following way:

```
CONSTRAINT FK_Products_Categories
  FOREIGN KEY (CategoryID)
  REFERENCES Categories (CategoryID)
```

Or you can define a foreign key in this way:

```
CONSTRAINT FK_Products_Categories
  FOREIGN KEY (CategoryID)
  REFERENCES Categories (CategoryID)
  ON DELETE NO ACTION
  ON UPDATE NO ACTION
```

Both ways of defining the foreign key gives you the same result: referential integrity is enforced, but cascading updates and deletes are not enforced. Now, enforcing a *cascading delete* means that if a parent row is deleted, all its child rows will be deleted in the same transaction. The same is true when you enforce a *cascading update*: If the parent row is updated, the child keys will be updated as well.

Real World Scenario

The Delete Dilemma

You are a database developer for a midsize manufacturing company. Your job is to develop and support SQL Server databases. The company employs 300 people. This includes 50 administrative employees, 5 product managers, and 25 salespersons who use the order entry application that has been built on top of a SQL Server 2000 database. The model of this database contains an Orders table, a Products table, and an Order Details table. Each order is comprised of one or many order lines, and each line contains the order of one specific product. You enforced referential integrity between these tables to be sure that every order line is part of an existing order and that orders can be placed only on existing products.

Your company will release new products and drop some old ones in a few weeks, and you face the dilemma of organizing the orders containing these old products into your existing database. If you enforced a cascading delete between the Orders and the Order Details tables (to be sure that if a salesman deletes an order, all the related order lines are deleted), a cascading delete cannot be used between Products and Order lines. If you delete an old product, you should not delete the related order lines. The product managers and the marketing employees are using this information to calculate their monthly revenue. Nevertheless, the product managers do not want orders to be placed on these "deleted" products. By enforcing the foreign key constraint on the Order Details table, you can prevent people from deleting these products if they have been ordered at least once.

The NOCHECK keyword is your immediate solution. You drop the foreign key constraint in the Order Details table, then delete or move old products even if they are referenced in orders, and recreate the constraint specifying NOCHECK. New orders can no longer be placed on old products since they are not in the Products table anymore, but old order lines are still there and the revenue figures are accurate. Of course, if you join the Order Details table with the Products table, you should use an outer join to be sure to include orders containing old "deleted" products. In the meantime, the solution is in place and will work fine!

The following clause enforces cascading deletes and updates for the foreign key constraint on the CategoryID column:

```
CONSTRAINT FK_Products_Categories
    FOREIGN KEY (CategoryID)
    REFERENCES Categories (CategoryID)
    ON DELETE CASCADE
    ON UPDATE CASCADE
```

With such a constraint, if somebody deletes category number 2 (CategoryID data type is an integer, so every category is identified by an integer), all the products of that category will be deleted. If a user updates the ID of category number 3, the CategoryID of all the corresponding products will be updated.

Cascading updates and deletes can be enforced with triggers, but constraints are preferred for performance reasons. Nevertheless, triggers offer more possibilities as we will see in Chapter 6.

You cannot create a cascading foreign key constraint if the table has an INSTEAD OF DELETE or UPDATE triggers. If you try, you end up with error 1787: Cannot define foreign key constraint 'FK_Orders_Customers' with cascaded DELETE or UPDATE on table 'Orders' because the table has an INSTEAD OF DELETE or UPDATE TRIGGER defined on it.

Creating a foreign key constraint does not automatically create an index as for primary keys. Since foreign keys are generally used in SELECT statements (refer to Chapter 7) for joining related tables, it is a good practice to create one or more indexes in the foreign key columns. Refer to Chapter 5 for indexing rules.

EXERCISE 4.6

Creating and Using a Cascading Foreign Key Constraint

In this example, you have the opportunity to create two related tables with cascading relationships and to see the cascading mechanism in action.

1. Open the SQL Server Query Analyzer. Do this through the SQL Enterprise Manager by selecting Tools ➢ SQL Query Analyzer or by choosing Start ➢ Programs ➢ Microsoft SQL Server ➢ Query Analyzer.

2. Type the following query to return in Query Analyzer (be sure the Northwind database is selected):

```
DROP TABLE Schedule
DROP TABLE Events
GO
CREATE TABLE Events (
    EventID int IDENTITY (1, 1) NOT NULL PRIMARY KEY,
    EventType nvarchar (10) NOT NULL DEFAULT 'Party',
    EventTitle nvarchar (100) NULL UNIQUE,
    EventDescription ntext NULL ,
    EventLanguage nvarchar (2) NULL ,
    EventDate smalldatetime NULL DEFAULT GETDATE() CHECK
(EventDate>=GETDATE()),
    EventEndDate smalldatetime NULL DEFAULT DATEADD(day, 1,
GETDATE()),
    EventCreator nvarchar (50) NOT NULL DEFAULT SYSTEM_USER
)
GO
CREATE TABLE Schedule(
    ScheduleID int IDENTITY (1, 1) NOT NULL PRIMARY KEY,
    EventID   int NOT NULL,
    StartDate datetime,
    EndDate datetime,
    PartTitle nvarchar (100),
    CHECK (EndDate>StartDate),
    FOREIGN KEY (EventID)
        REFERENCES Events (EventID)
        ON DELETE CASCADE
```

3. Highlight these lines with the mouse and press the green arrow or CTRL-E to execute the query.

4. Insert rows by typing the following lines of code:

```
INSERT INTO Events(EventType, EventTitle, EventDescription,
EventLanguage, EventDate, EventEndDate)
VALUES(DEFAULT, 'This is my Event', 'This will be great
fun', 'US', '12/12/2012', '01/01/2012')
GO
INSERT Schedule(EventID, StartDate, EndDate)
VALUES (1, '08:00', '10:00')
INSERT Schedule(EventID, StartDate, EndDate)
VALUES (1, '10:00', '12:00')
```

EXERCISE 4.6 (continued)

5. Highlight these lines with the mouse and press the green arrow or CTRL-E to execute the query.

6. Check that the rows were inserted into the Schedule table by typing the following lines of code:

```
SELECT * FROM Schedule
```

7. Highlight this line with the mouse and press the green arrow or CTRL-E to execute the query.

8. Delete EventID 1 by typing the following statement:

```
DELETE Events WHERE EventID=1
```

9. Highlight this line with the mouse and press the green arrow or CTRL-E to execute the query.

10. Check that the rows were deleted from the Schedule table, thanks to the cascading constraint by typing the following line of code:
```
SELECT * FROM Schedule
```

11. Highlight this line with the mouse and press the green arrow or CTRL-E to execute the query.

Creating a foreign key constraint is far easier in SQL Enterprise Manager. It can be done in two ways: in the table Design Mode or in the Database Diagrams Mode. Let's first have a closer look at the table Design Mode, which lets you define the table characteristics:

1. Open SQL Enterprise Manager by choosing Start ➢ Programs ➢ Microsoft SQL Server ➢ Enterprise Manager. In SQL Enterprise Manager, right-click the table name and choose Design Table.

2. In the Design Table window, click the Manage Relationships button in the toolbar.

3. In the Properties dialog box, click the New button, then choose the Primary Key Table, the primary key column(s), the Foreign Key Table, the foreign key columns, and finally choose the options. The different options presented in the dialog box are identical to those offered in the SQL statement and concern checking existing data, enforcing relationship for replication, and enforcing cascading delete and update.

4. Click the Close button to close the dialog box.

The foreign key is not created until you save the table structure. Figure 4.5 shows the Properties dialog box with the relationship between Customers and Orders tables.

FIGURE 4.5   Relationships between Customers and Orders table

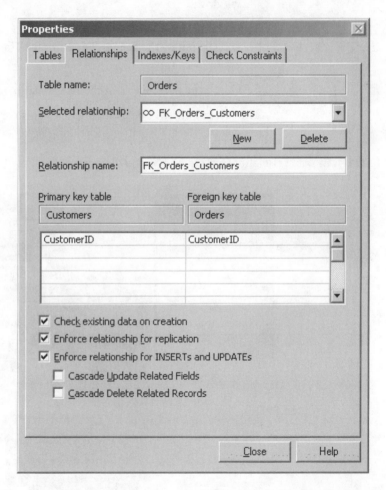

The diagram helps you graphically define the relationship between tables, in the same way that it would be done using Microsoft Access:

1. Open SQL Enterprise Manager by choosing Start ➢ Programs ➢ Microsoft SQL Server ➢ Enterprise Manager. In SQL Enterprise Manager, right-click the Diagrams icon and choose New Diagram.

2. The Create Database Diagram Wizard appears. Click Next.

3. Click the tables you want to add to the diagram and click the Add button to move them into the list box at the right. Click Next, then End.

   All the tables you selected in the wizard appear in the diagram window.

4. In the primary key table, click the primary key column and drag-and-drop it to the foreign key column. The Create Relationship dialog box appears.

5. Check the parameters of the relationship and click OK.

The foreign key will be created when you save the diagram. Figure 4.6 illustrates the Create Relationship dialog box.

FIGURE 4.6   Relationship creation in the diagram

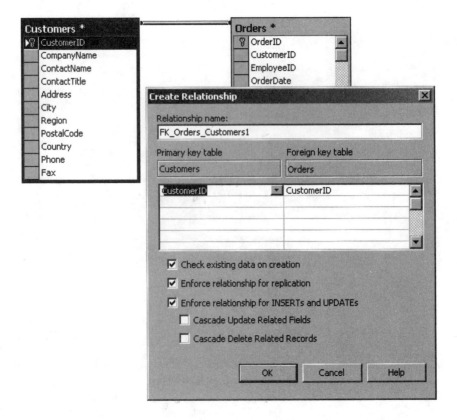

Note that in the graphical interface, in table Design Mode or in the Database Diagram, you have the ability to view and save the script that matches the modification you made. Before saving your modification, click the Save Change Script button on the toolbar. The Save Change Script opens, as illustrated in Figure 4.7.

FIGURE 4.7   Generated modification script

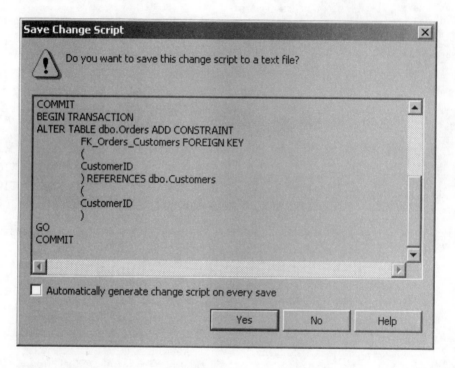

Using this script feature is a very handy way to learn about the ALTER and CREATE TABLE syntaxes.

The NOT FOR REPLICATION clause indicates that the constraint is not enforced during the replication process. Of course, the system can only replicate data stored in the table following the constraint rule. This is true and false: constraints can be disabled for a batch insert or update. To avoid replication of the data that does not respect the constraint, the constraint is enforced for replication by default, meaning the replicated data will be checked against the constraint. If you are sure your data is always valid, you can disable this constraint for replication.

Defining a Foreign Key Constraint at Table Modification

Once tables are created and filled with data, you can change the database structure and may decide to add a foreign key constraint. As with the other constraints, like check or unique, adding a foreign key constraint to existing data means a new rule will be enforced. By default, the foreign key constraint is checked against existing data, but can be disabled if necessary.

A foreign key can be added to a table at column level while adding a new column to the table, or it can be added at table level.

- Column-level foreign key constraint definition at table modification:

```
ALTER TABLE tablename
    ADD columname datatype [ CONSTRAINT constraintname ]
    [ FOREIGN KEY ]
        REFERENCES ref_table [ ( ref_column ) ]
        [ ON DELETE { CASCADE | NO ACTION } ]
        [ ON UPDATE { CASCADE | NO ACTION } ]
        [ NOT FOR REPLICATION ] [,...]
```

- Table-level foreign key constraint definition at table modification:

```
ALTER TABLE tablename
[ WITH CHECK | WITH NOCHECK ] ADD
    [ CONSTRAINT constraintname ]
    FOREIGN KEY [ ( column [ ,...n ] ) ]
        REFERENCES ref_table [ ( ref_column [ ,...n ] )
]
        [ ON DELETE { CASCADE | NO ACTION } ]
        [ ON UPDATE { CASCADE | NO ACTION } ]
        [ NOT FOR REPLICATION ]
```

The following example adds a foreign key to the Orders table to create a relationship with the Products table:

```
ALTER TABLE Products
    ADD CONSTRAINT FK_Products_Categories
    FOREIGN KEY (CategoryID)
    REFERENCES Categories (CategoryID)
```

If the constraint already exists, it has to be dropped first to be recreated, otherwise you'll end up with error 2714: There is already an object named 'FK_Products_Categories' in the database. On the other hand, if some key values exist that do not match the primary key in the related table, then error 547 is fired, disallowing the constraint creation: ALTER TABLE statement conflicted with COLUMN FOREIGN KEY constraint 'FK_Products_Categories'. The conflict occurred in database 'MyFirstDatabase', table 'Categories', column 'CategoryID'.

To avoid error 547, you could have created the constraint with the WITH NOCHECK keyword, like in the following example:

```
ALTER TABLE Products
    WITH NOCHECK ADD CONSTRAINT FK_Products_Categories
    FOREIGN KEY (CategoryID)
    REFERENCES Categories (CategoryID)
```

In this case, some rows in the Products table do not match any row in the Categories table. To isolate these rows, use an outer join with an IS NULL condition on the CategoryID of the Categories table, like in the following example:

```
SELECT Products.*
FROM Products LEFT OUTER JOIN Categories
ON Products.CategoryID = Categories.CategoryID
WHERE Categories.CategoryID IS NULL
```

You will obtain the list of all the products that do not have a matching CategoryID. You can decide to move them to a staging table afterwards or ask the product managers to modify these non-matching CategoryIDs.

Summary

In this chapter you learned to create and alter declarative integrity rules, called constraints.

This chapter particularly focused on:

- Creating and altering default constraints

- Creating and altering check constraints

- Creating and altering primary key constraints

- Creating and altering unique constraints

- Creating and altering foreign key constraints

Key Terms

Before you take the exam, be certain you are familiar with the following terms:

cascading delete	default
cascading update	foreign key
check	primary key
constraint	procedural integrity
data integrity	rule
declarative integrity	unique

Exam Essentials

Identify the differences between declarative and procedural integrity. Integrity can be enforced through declarative constraints or procedural objects. Know the differences between both implementations.

Know precisely how to define a default value. Default constraint and default objects may be used to define default values. Study their differences and know the syntax to create and alter both.

Know precisely how to define check rules. Check constraints and rules may both be used to enforce domain integrity. Study their differences and know the syntax to create and alter both.

Know precisely how to enforce entity integrity. Primary key and unique constraints are used to enforce entity integrity. Take time to discover their differences and the situations they prevent in a table. Know the syntax to create and alter both.

Know precisely how to enforce relationships between two tables. Foreign key constraints are used to enforce relationships between tables. Know the syntax used to define them, including optional elements.

Review Questions

1. You are a SQL Server database developer for a winery. Some of the accountants complain that some orders in the billing system have no CustomerID, but only a Shipping address and the ID of the employee who took the order. When they discover such an order, they have to phone the related sales person and ask him to look for the customer who placed the order. They lose a lot of time with that kind of research. The chief accountant asks you to make this information mandatory in an order. The Customers and Orders table are illustrated below:

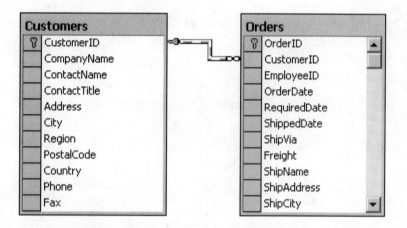

You run sp_helpconstraint Orders in SQL Query Analyzer and obtain the following result:

	constraint_type	constraint_name	delete_action	update_action	status_enabled	s	constraint_keys
1	DEFAULT on column Freight	DF_Orders_Freight	(n/a)	(n/a)	(n/a)	.	(0)
2	FOREIGN KEY	FK_Orders_Customers	No Action	No Action	Disabled	.	CustomerID
3							REFERENCES Northwind.dbo.Customers (CustomerID)
4	FOREIGN KEY	FK_Orders_Employees	No Action	No Action	Enabled	.	EmployeeID
5							REFERENCES Northwind.dbo.Employees (EmployeeID)
6	FOREIGN KEY	FK_Orders_Shippers	No Action	No Action	Enabled	.	ShipVia
7							REFERENCES Northwind.dbo.Shippers (ShipperID)
8	PRIMARY KEY (clustered)	PK_Orders	(n/a)	(n/a)	(n/a)	.	OrderID

How can you solve the problem met by the accountants and make the CustomerID field mandatory?

A. Create a foreign key constraint on the CustomerID column.

B. There is nothing to do, the field is already mandatory.

C. Enable the existing foreign key.

D. Create an `INSTEAD OF INSERT` trigger on the Orders table to check whether the CustomerID entered in the Orders table exists in the Customers table.

2. You are a SQL Server database developer for a hotel. You are testing the new reservation application. While testing, you discover you forgot to create a relationship between the Rooms and the Reservations tables. You decide to modify the Reservations table to enforce a relationship. Which statement do you run to enforce this relationship?

A.

```
ALTER TABLE Reservations
ADD FOREIGN KEY (RoomID)
REFERENCES Rooms(RoomID)
```

B.

```
CREATE FOREIGN KEY
Reservations.RoomID
REFERENCES Rooms(RoomID)
```

C.

```
ALTER TABLE Reservations
ADD CONSTRAINT FK_Reservations_Rooms
FOREIGN KEY RoomID
REFERENCES Rooms(RoomID)
```

D.

```
ALTER TABLE Reservations
ADD RELATION Rooms
ON RoomID
```

3. You are developing a time tracking system for a New York based consulting firm. While continuing to develop, some selected users

test the features you have just finished implementing. All of them tell you it would be great if some fields could already contain the most common values. For example, 90 percent of the customers are in New York city, so they would like the City field to already be filled with "New York City." All the fields and values the user listed could be filled with constant values. What is the fastest way to implement such a feature in SQL Server 2000?

A. Triggers

B. Default constraint

C. Check constraint

D. User-defined datatypes

4. You are a database developer for a Massachusetts insurance company in Boston. You are designing a new database for tracking customers and signed insurance policies. While normalizing your database model, you isolate the primary key for the Customers table. The Customers table has the following structure:

How can you define the primary key on the CustomerID column at table creation?

A.

```
CREATE TABLE Customers (
   CustomerID nchar (5) NOT NULL ,
   CompanyName nvarchar (40) NOT NULL ,
   ContactName nvarchar (30) NULL ,
```

```
        ContactTitle nvarchar (30) NULL ,
        Address nvarchar (60) NULL ,
        City nvarchar (15) NULL ,
        Region nvarchar (15) NULL ,
        PostalCode nvarchar (10) NULL ,
        Country nvarchar (15) NULL ,
        Phone nvarchar (24) NULL ,
        Fax nvarchar (24) NULL
    )
    CREATE PRIMARY KEY Customers.CustomerID
```

B.

```
    CREATE TABLE Customers (
        CustomerID nchar(5) NOT NULL PRIMARY KEY,
        CompanyName nvarchar (40) NOT NULL ,
        ContactName nvarchar (30) NULL ,
        ContactTitle nvarchar (30) NULL ,
        Address nvarchar (60) NULL ,
        City nvarchar (15) NULL ,
        Region nvarchar (15) NULL ,
        PostalCode nvarchar (10) NULL ,
        Country nvarchar (15) NULL ,
        Phone nvarchar (24) NULL ,
        Fax nvarchar (24) NULL
    )
```

C.

```
    CREATE TABLE Customers (
        CustomerID nchar (5) NOT NULL ,
        CompanyName nvarchar (40) NOT NULL ,
        ContactName nvarchar (30) NULL ,
        ContactTitle nvarchar (30) NULL ,
        Address nvarchar (60) NULL ,
        City nvarchar (15) NULL ,
        Region nvarchar (15) NULL ,
        PostalCode nvarchar (10) NULL ,
```

```
    Country nvarchar (15) NULL ,
    Phone nvarchar (24) NULL ,
    Fax nvarchar (24) NULL ,
    ADD PRIMARY KEY (CustomerID)
)
```

D.

```
CREATE TABLE Customers (
    CustomerID nchar (5) NOT NULL ,
    CompanyName nvarchar (40) NOT NULL ,
    ContactName nvarchar (30) NULL ,
    ContactTitle nvarchar (30) NULL ,
    Address nvarchar (60) NULL ,
    City nvarchar (15) NULL ,
    Region nvarchar (15) NULL ,
    PostalCode nvarchar (10) NULL ,
    Country nvarchar (15) NULL ,
    Phone nvarchar (24) NULL ,
    Fax nvarchar (24) NULL
)
GO
ALTER TABLE Customers
ALTER COLUMN CustomerID PRIMARY KEY
```

5. As a SQL Server developer, you are creating a database for a local University to track students and courses. You want to enforce entity and referential integrity rules, as described in the following graphic:

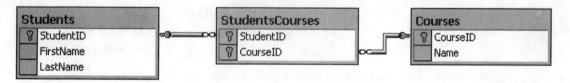

Put the following statements in the right order to create these three tables with the right constraints. Note: Use only relevant items; some may not be useful to obtain the desired result.

| | ```
GO
CREATE TABLE StudentsCourses (
    StudentID int NOT NULL,
    CourseID int NOT NULL ,
    PRIMARY KEY (StudentID, CourseID)
)
``` |
| | ```
ALTER TABLE Students
ADD FOREIGN KEY StudentID
REFERENCES StudentsCourses (StudentID)
``` |
| | ```
CREATE TABLE Students (
    StudentID int NOT NULL ,
    FirstName varchar (50) NULL ,
    LastName varchar (50) NULL ,
    CONSTRAINT PK_Students
    PRIMARY KEY (StudentID
)
``` |
| | ```
CREATE TABLE Courses (
    CourseID int NOT NULL ,
    [Name] char (10) NULL ,
    PRIMARY KEY CLUSTERED (CourseID)
)
``` |
| | ```
ALTER TABLE Courses
ADD FOREIGN KEY CourseID
REFERENCES StudentsCourses (CourseID)
ALTER TABLE Courses ADD PRIMARY KEY CLUSTERED
(CourseID)
``` |
| | ```
ALTER TABLE StudentsCourses
ADD FOREIGN KEY (CourseID)
    REFERENCES Courses (CourseID),
    FOREIGN KEY (StudentID)
    REFERENCES Students (StudentID)
``` |

6. You are a SQL Server developer for an international organization. You need for all your database applications to implement validation rules for some columns. What kind of validation rules can you implement with check constraints? (Choose two.)

   A. Check the value against a defined range of values.

   B. Check the value against values stored in a related table.

   C. Check the value against a defined pattern.

   D. Check the value against the return parameter of a stored procedure.

7. Having normalized your database model, you need a way to implement alternate keys. What is the most efficient way to do that? (Choose one.)

   A. Unique constraints

   B. Primary key constraints

   C. Unique indexes

   D. Nullability

8. One of the programmers on your team comes and shows you the following script that she wrote for a table:

```
CREATE TABLE dbo.Orders (
    OrderID int IDENTITY (1, 1) NOT NULL ,
    CustomerID nchar (5) NULL ,
    EmployeeID int NULL ,
    OrderDate datetime NULL CONSTRAINT CK_OrderDate
CHECK (OrderDate=GETDATE()),
    RequiredDate datetime NULL ,
    ShippedDate datetime NULL ,
    ShipVia int NULL ,
    Freight money NULL CONSTRAINT DF_Orders_Freight
DEFAULT (0),
    ShipName nvarchar (40) NULL ,
    ShipAddress nvarchar (60) NULL ,
    ShipCity nvarchar (15) NULL ,
```

```
      ShipRegion nvarchar (15) NULL ,
      ShipPostalCode nvarchar (10) NULL ,
      ShipCountry nvarchar (15) NULL ,
      CONSTRAINT PK_Orders PRIMARY KEY CLUSTERED
(OrderID),
      CONSTRAINT FK_Orders_Customers FOREIGN KEY
        (CustomerID) REFERENCES dbo.Customers (Cus-
tomerID),
      CONSTRAINT FK_Orders_Employees FOREIGN KEY
        (EmployeeID) REFERENCES dbo.Employees (Employ-
eeID),
      CONSTRAINT FK_Orders_Shippers FOREIGN KEY
        (ShipVia) REFERENCES dbo.Shippers (ShipperID)
)
```

Each time she tries to enter a new row, the system fires an error saying that a conflict occurs on column OrderDate due to the Check constraint 'CK_OrderDate', even if the order date is today's date. What is the cause of the error?

A. The server system date is not on time.

B. You should use the GETUTCDATE() function.

C. GETDATE() gives the century in two digits. This is a Y2K problem.

D. You should not test the value equals GETDATE(), but only its day part.

9. You are a database developer for an e-learning company, providing training over the Internet. You are developing a new identification system for your customers. To enter the training system, each customer must be authenticated. For security reasons, you developed a series of extended stored procedures in C language. One of these functions generates passwords. Each time someone becomes a member, you want the system, using the extended stored procedure, to give the member a password. What is the simplest way to generate and store the password in the Customers table?

A. Use a stored procedure to execute the INSERT statement and call the extended stored procedure.

B. Create an INSTEAD OF INSERT trigger and call the extended stored procedure from the trigger.

C. Create an AFTER INSERT trigger to run the extended stored procedure and generate the password.

D. Create a user-defined function calling the extended stored procedure, and use it as the default value for the password column.

10. As a consultant, you have been called by World Wide Importers, to define their new ordering system. The new system, based on SQL server, will extract data from the legacy database and do some data manipulations before the marketing employees use it. In the model, you design a Suppliers table with the following:

```
CREATE TABLE dbo.Suppliers (
    SupplierID int IDENTITY (1, 1) NOT NULL PRIMARY KEY,
    CompanyName nvarchar (40) NOT NULL ,
    ContactName nvarchar (30) NULL ,
    ContactTitle nvarchar (30) NULL ,
    Address nvarchar (60) NULL ,
    City nvarchar (15) NULL ,
    Region nvarchar (15) NULL ,
    PostalCode nvarchar (10) NULL ,
    Country nvarchar (15) NULL ,
    Phone nvarchar (20) NULL UNIQUE,
    Fax nvarchar (20) NULL UNIQUE,
    HomePage ntext NULL
)
```

After inserting some test rows, you obtain the following error:

```
Violation of UNIQUE KEY constraint
'UQ__Suppliers__31B762FC'. Cannot insert duplicate key in
object 'Suppliers'.
```

Since there are UNIQUE constraints only on the Phone and Fax columns, you know this error is bound to one of these columns. Nevertheless, you are sure you never used the same values twice for Phone and Fax. What is the possible cause of the error?

A. You tried to insert two Null values in Phone or in Fax.

B. You tried to insert a phone number that existed as a fax number in another record, or vice versa.

C. You tried to insert the same phone number twice, but in one you insert spaces that are not considered as characters by the Unique constraint.

D. This is a bug of SQL Server 2000, and you should apply Service Pack 1 to correct it.

11. You are developing a warehouse management database. While interviewing users, it appears that every object has a shelf number. Once an object is moved out of the warehouse, its shelf number should be emptied, but the object remains in the database.

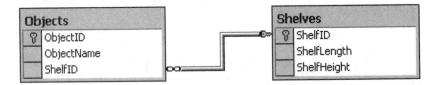

To define that an object has been moved, you decide that its ShelfID will be set to NULL. How can you implement this feature?

A. With a foreign key constraint without cascading option

B. With a foreign key constraint with cascading update and delete

C. With an INSTEAD OF trigger

D. With a default value

12. You are a database developer for a winery. You have been asked to develop a new application to record the work of employees during the vine-harvest. While the employees pick up the grapes, they put them in their assigned basket, then weigh the full basket and go back to their duties. Each weight is recorded with the time and date, and the employee ID. You design the following table to record each weighing:

```
CREATE TABLE weighing(
WeighingDateTime datetime NOT NULL DEFAULT Getdate(),
Weight int NOT NULL DEFAULT 0,
EmployeeID int NOT NULL)
```

You want to be sure that only positive values will be entered into the weight column. What is the simplest method to do so?

A. Create a rule and a user-defined datatype; bind the rule to the datatype and alter the table to change the type of the Weight column to the newly created datatype.

B. Write a trigger that checks the Weight value and rollbacks the insert if the value is negative.

C. Write a stored procedure to manage the insert and check the value, and forbid any direct insert.

D. Alter the table to add a check constraint to the Weight column.

13. You are developer for Northwind Traders. You defined the Order details table to create the many-to-many relationship between the Orders and the Products table, as illustrated in the following graphic:

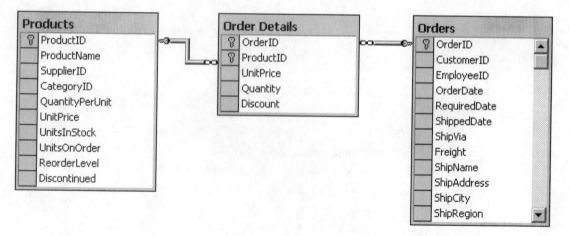

What piece of code will create the Order details table?

A.

```
CREATE TABLE dbo.Order Details (
    OrderID int NOT NULL,
    ProductID int NOT NULL,
    UnitPrice money NOT NULL,
    Quantity smallint NOT NULL,
```

```
        Discount real NOT NULL,
        CONSTRAINT PK_Order_Details
            PRIMARY KEY (OrderID, ProductID),
        CONSTRAINT FK_Details_Orders
            FOREIGN KEY (OrderID)
            REFERENCES Orders (OrderID),
        CONSTRAINT FK_Details_Products
            FOREIGN KEY (ProductID)
            REFERENCES Products (ProductID)
    )
```

B.

```
CREATE TABLE dbo.Order Details (
    OrderID int NOT NULL
            PRIMARY KEY
            REFERENCES Orders (OrderID),
    ProductID int NOT NULL
            PRIMARY KEY
            REFERENCES Products (ProductID),
    UnitPrice money NOT NULL,
    Quantity smallint NOT NULL,
    Discount real NOT NULL
    )
```

C.

```
CREATE TABLE dbo.Order Details (
    OrderID int NOT NULL PRIMARY KEY,
    ProductID int NOT NULL PRIMARY KEY,
    UnitPrice money NOT NULL,
    Quantity smallint NOT NULL,
    Discount real NOT NULL,
    CONSTRAINT FK_Details_Orders
        FOREIGN KEY (OrderID)
        REFERENCES Orders (OrderID),
    CONSTRAINT FK_Details_Products
        FOREIGN KEY (ProductID)
        REFERENCES Products (ProductID)
    )
```

D.

```
CREATE TABLE dbo.Order Details (
    OrderID int NOT NULL,
    ProductID int NOT NULL,
    UnitPrice money NOT NULL,
    Quantity smallint NOT NULL,
    Discount real NOT NULL,
    PRIMARY KEY (OrderID),
    PRIMARY KEY (ProductID),
    FOREIGN KEY (OrderID)
        REFERENCES Orders (OrderID),
    FOREIGN KEY (ProductID)
        REFERENCES Products (ProductID)
)
```

14. Security management is an important issue in your company. For every order, you need to know who inserted it and at what time the insert took place. You know that for security purposes, SQL Server works in integrated mode. All inserts will be done through stored procedures. What table script will reach that goal?

A.

```
CREATE TABLE Orders (
    OrderID int IDENTITY (1, 1) NOT NULL ,
    CustomerID nchar (5) NULL ,
    EmployeeID int NULL
        DEFAULT SESSION_USER
    OrderDate datetime NULL
        DEFAULT GETDATE(),
    RequiredDate datetime NULL ,
    ShippedDate datetime NULL ,
    Freight money NULL ,
    ShipperID int NULL
)
```

B.

```
CREATE TABLE Orders (
    OrderID int IDENTITY (1, 1) NOT NULL ,
    CustomerID nchar (5) NULL ,
```

```
        EmployeeID int NULL ,
        OrderDate datetime NULL ,
        RequiredDate datetime NULL ,
        ShippedDate datetime NULL ,
        Freight money NULL ,
        ShipperID int NULL ,
        UserName varchar (50) NOT NULL
            DEFAULT SYSTEM_USER(),
        InsertDate datetime NOT NULL
            DEFAULT NOW()
    )
```

C.

```
CREATE TABLE Orders (
    OrderID int IDENTITY (1, 1) NOT NULL ,
    CustomerID nchar (5) NULL ,
    EmployeeID int NULL ,
    OrderDate datetime NULL ,
    RequiredDate datetime NULL ,
    ShippedDate datetime NULL ,
    Freight money NULL ,
    ShipperID int NULL ,
    UserName nvarchar (50) NOT NULL
        DEFAULT SYSTEM_USER,
    InsertDate datetime NOT NULL
        DEFAULT GETDATE()
    )
```

D.

```
CREATE TABLE Orders (
    OrderID int IDENTITY (1, 1) NOT NULL ,
    CustomerID nchar (5) NULL ,
    EmployeeID int NULL
    OrderDate datetime NULL,
    RequiredDate datetime NULL ,
    ShippedDate datetime NULL ,
    Freight money NULL ,
    ShipperID int NULL
    )
```

15. You are a SQL Server developer for a winery. You are developing a new invoicing database system. While designing the database, you create a Restaurant table that stores all the restaurants to whom you are selling wine. The code for that table is the following:

```
CREATE TABLE Restaurants (
    RestaurantID int NOT NULL PRIMARY KEY,
    RestaurantName nvarchar (40) NOT NULL ,
    RestaurantOwner nvarchar (30) NULL ,
    Address nvarchar (60) NULL ,
    City nvarchar (15) NULL ,
    Region nvarchar (15) NULL ,
    PostalCode nvarchar (10) NULL ,
    Country nvarchar (15) NULL ,
    Phone nvarchar (24) NULL ,
    Fax nvarchar (24) NULL ,
    HomePage ntext NULL ,
    UNIQUE (RestaurantName, City)
)
```

What does the UNIQUE constraint mean?

A. That every restaurant name must be unique in the table

B. That no two restaurants can have the same name in the same city

C. That no two restaurants can have the same name in two different cities

D. That the restaurant name and the city must not be null

Answers to Review Questions

1. C. With the result of the execution of the `sp_helpconstraint` stored procedure, you see that a foreign key constraint exists on the Orders table to enforce the relationship with the Customers table and that the status-enabled column is set to disabled. The disabled constraint has allowed orders to be inserted without matching CustomerIDs. Re-enabling the constraint will solve the problem.

2. A. The statements in options B and D do not exist. In fact, option C is almost good, except it lacks brackets around RoomID in the `FOREIGN KEY` clause. These brackets are mandatory!

3. B. This feature could be realized with `INSTEAD OF` trigger, but that would involve coding and would not be the fastest way to implement it. Check constraints cannot be used to fill default values. User-defined datatypes linked with default objects could be used, but triggers are not the fastest way. So, default constraints are definitely the fastest way to define default values to specific fields.

4. B. The `CREATE PRIMARY KEY` statement of option A does not exist. The `ADD PRIMARY KEY` of option C is only possible in an `ALTER TABLE` statement, not in a `CREATE TABLE` statement. You cannot add a primary key constraint by altering a column in an `ALTER TABLE` statement as in option D.

5.

```
CREATE TABLE Students (
    StudentID int NOT NULL ,
    FirstName varchar (50) NULL ,
    LastName varchar (50) NULL ,
    CONSTRAINT PK_Students
    PRIMARY KEY (StudentID
)
```

```
CREATE TABLE Courses (
    CourseID int NOT NULL ,
    [Name] char (10) NULL ,
    PRIMARY KEY CLUSTERED (CourseID)
)
```
```
ALTER TABLE StudentsCourses
ADD FOREIGN KEY (CourseID)
    REFERENCES Courses (CourseID),
    FOREIGN KEY (StudentID)
    REFERENCES Students (StudentID)
```

The Students and Courses tables have to be created first in order to create the relationships in the StudentsCourses table.

6. A, C. Option B is not correct because the value can only be compared to other values in the same table. D is not correct because a stored procedure cannot be executed in a check constraint.

7. A. Option C could be the right answer, but unique constraints are enforcing declarative integrity, and it should always be chosen first.

8. D. GETDATE gives you the date and the time in milliseconds. So, between the value given to the column and the time the value is tested against GETDATE(), the milliseconds have changed. You should use the CONVERT function, the DATEPART function, or a range to isolate the date.

9. D. The four options are good, but D is the simplest, since it uses declarative integrity.

10. A. Null values count as "real" values. Two null values are impossible in a Unique column.

11. C. Options A and B will forbid any value besides valid ShelfID. D is irrelevant in the context of an update.

12. D. All the options provide a solution, but D is the simplest because it's declarative integrity and should always be preferred to any other type of integrity.

13. A. Option A is the only one with correct syntax for defining a multi-column primary key. A multi-column primary key can only be defined at table level.

14. C. Option A is wrong because the SESSION_USER function returns a character string and the column is an integer. B is wrong because NOW is not a SQL Server system function. D is wrong because it does not record anything.

15. B. The group RestaurantName, City must be unique, so two restaurants can have the same name if they are not located in the same city.

Chapter

5

Creating and Maintaining Indexes

MICROSOFT EXAM OBJECTIVES COVERED IN THIS CHAPTER:

✓ **Create and alter database objects. Objects include constraints, indexes, stored procedures, tables, triggers, user-defined functions, and views.**

   ▪ Specify index characteristics. Characteristics include clustered, FILLFACTOR, nonclustered, and uniqueness.

✓ **Troubleshoot failed object creation.**

✓ **Create and implement indexing strategies. Considerations include clustered index, covering index, indexed views, nonclustered index, placement, and statistics.**

In the first four chapters, you learned how to create databases and tables. But when it comes time to store and access data in your tables, you need to know how indexes help increase performance and integrity.

In this chapter, you will learn:

- What indexes are and what their advantages are

- How SQL Server accesses data with and without indexes

- What the distribution statistics are and what they do

- How to create and maintain an index

- What fragmentation is and how to solve the problem of data fragmentation

All examples in this chapter use the Northwind database that is supplied with SQL Server 2000.

Definition and Advantages of Indexes

You've probably heard that indexes are the heart of fast data access. In fact, as the database grows, indexes are your guarantee to fast data access. Data access can be fast without indexes, but only if your table is small. If the table contains thousands or millions of rows, data access has to be done through indexes.

In a book, the index helps you to find information about a specific subject you are looking for without having to read the entire book. The same applies to a database index; it helps you to find information about a specific row or rows without having to search through the entire table.

Heaps and Indexes

In Chapter 3, you discovered that table data is stored in 8KB pages. Just after its creation, while the table has no index, the table is called a *heap*. Rows are not stored in any specific order. Figure 5.1 illustrates the Customers table of the Northwind database, stored as a heap.

FIGURE 5.1 A heap

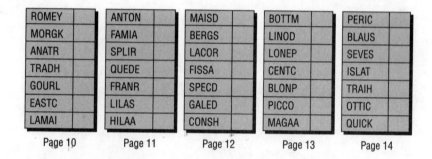

| Page 10 | Page 11 | Page 12 | Page 13 | Page 14 |

When you need to access data in a heap, SQL Server will access the whole table through an operation called *table scan*. SQL scans the whole table to find the needed row or rows. For example, if you run the following query:

```
SELECT * FROM Customers WHERE CustomerID='ROMEY'
```

SQL Server will read all the data pages, even if it finds the row in the first page. SQL Server does not know there is only one 'ROMEY' value, until you create a unique constraint, a unique index, or a primary key constraint on the column. In these three cases, an index is created to support the constraints. This example leads to the two basic functions of indexes. Indexes are used to:

- Increase the speed of data access

- Enforce uniqueness of data

Though indexes have their advantages, they also have drawbacks. The first drawback is that they consume a lot of disk and memory space. Each time you create an index, it will store all index keys, ordered in ascending or descending order and in many levels. The larger the key, the bigger the index. The second drawback is that they cause slower inserts and may cause slower updates and deletes. However, some internal strategies tend to show that indexes have a small negative effect on these operations and may even let them go faster, as you will see in the next few pages.

In SQL Server 2000, indexes are stored as B-Trees. B stands for balanced. Figure 5.2 shows you an index created on the CustomerID column of the Customers table.

FIGURE 5.2 A B-Tree index

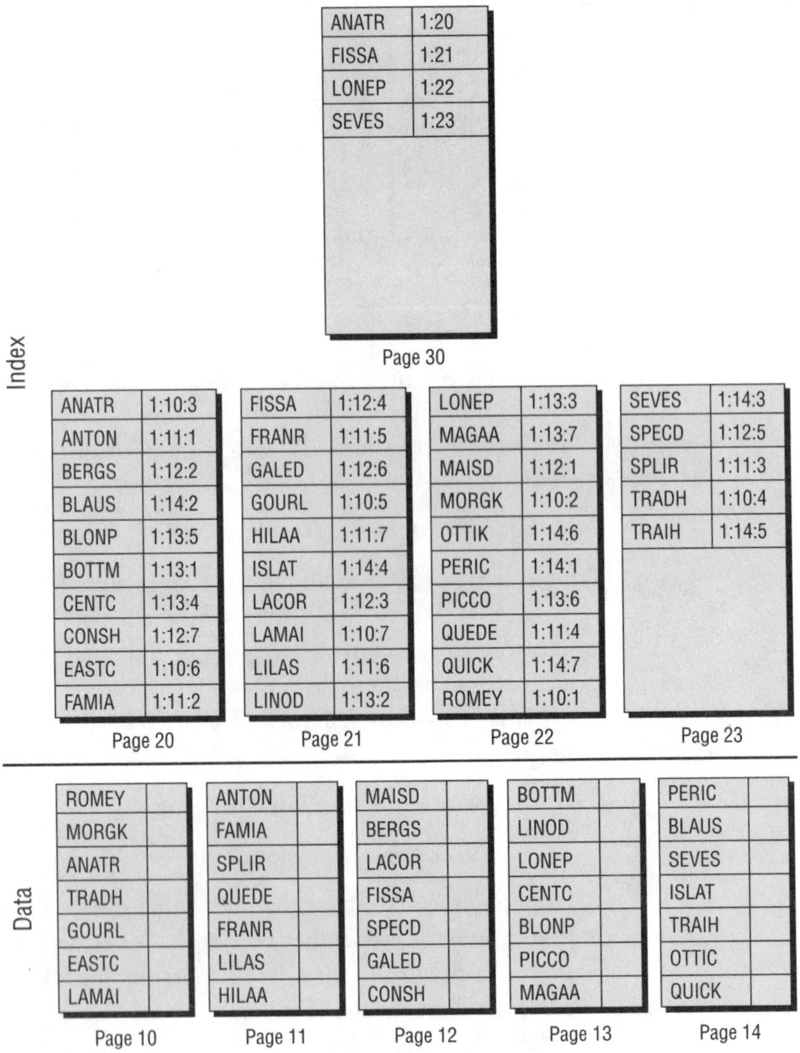

Index	Page 30	
ANATR	1:20
FISSA	1:21
LONEP	1:22
SEVES	1:23

Page 20		Page 21		Page 22		Page 23	
ANATR	1:10:3	FISSA	1:12:4	LONEP	1:13:3	SEVES	1:14:3
ANTON	1:11:1	FRANR	1:11:5	MAGAA	1:13:7	SPECD	1:12:5
BERGS	1:12:2	GALED	1:12:6	MAISD	1:12:1	SPLIR	1:11:3
BLAUS	1:14:2	GOURL	1:10:5	MORGK	1:10:2	TRADH	1:10:4
BLONP	1:13:5	HILAA	1:11:7	OTTIK	1:14:6	TRAIH	1:14:5
BOTTM	1:13:1	ISLAT	1:14:4	PERIC	1:14:1		
CENTC	1:13:4	LACOR	1:12:3	PICCO	1:13:6		
CONSH	1:12:7	LAMAI	1:10:7	QUEDE	1:11:4		
EASTC	1:10:6	LILAS	1:11:6	QUICK	1:14:7		
FAMIA	1:11:2	LINOD	1:13:2	ROMEY	1:10:1		

Data	Page 10	Page 11	Page 12	Page 13	Page 14
	ROMEY	ANTON	MAISD	BOTTM	PERIC
	MORGK	FAMIA	BERGS	LINOD	BLAUS
	ANATR	SPLIR	LACOR	LONEP	SEVES
	TRADH	QUEDE	FISSA	CENTC	ISLAT
	GOURL	FRANR	SPECD	BLONP	TRAIH
	EASTC	LILAS	GALED	PICCO	OTTIC
	LAMAI	HILAA	CONSH	MAGAA	QUICK

Now, if you run the previous query, SQL Server will use the index to find the location of the 'ROMEY' row. In this case, it will go through three pages: 30, 22, and 10, in that order. The next section will go into more detail about accessing data through indexes.

A SQL Server index is a balanced tree in that every branch in the tree has the same length. If you look at Figure 5.2 from top to bottom, you will only cross three pages, where you will find the row you are looking for. Every branch is balanced, and SQL Server keeps the branch balanced.

Some people think B stands for binary. However, a binary tree is not balanced, and in SQL Server, B always stands for balanced!

Note that in Figure 5.2 the data is not sorted. This means that the index needs to recreate a level, called the *leaf level*, containing all the sorted key values and referencing the real position of the record (this level contains pages 20 to 23). In Figure 5.2, the reference is given through a row ID that has the following format: file number:page number:row location. So, ID 1:13:5 indicates the fifth record in page 13 belonging to file number 1. Any other level above the leaf level is called a *non-leaf level* or *intermediate level*. The first level of an index, the one that contains the "entrance door," is called the *root*. The root of an index is made of one page containing the first keys referenced in the pages of the following level.

Index pages are 8KB pages mixed with data pages. See Chapters 2 and 3 for more information on pages.

While all indexes have the same tree structure, SQL Server proposes two types of index: *clustered* and *nonclustered*. These types are described in the following sections.

Clustered Index

In RDBMS, a cluster may mean different things, but in general it refers to two "objects" being considered as one. For example, in Windows 2000 a cluster is a group of two or more servers seen as only one, which is used for fault tolerance and load balancing reasons. In SQL Server 2000, a cluster is an index mixed with a table. The table is part of the index, or the index is part of the table, depending on your point of view.

In SQL Server, once a table has a clustered index, its data is both stored and sorted on the index key. The leaf level of the index is the actual data of the table.

FIGURE 5.3 A clustered index

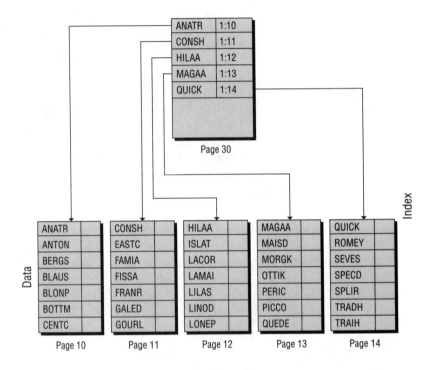

Figure 5.3 illustrates a clustered index created on the CustomerID column of the Northwind's Customers table. As you can see, the leaf level of the index is in fact the data level. The table is part of the index.

As the table is part of the clustered index, only one clustered index can be created on a table.

In SQL Server 2000, a clustered index is a unique index by design, which means that every key should be unique. While duplicates exist in the index, they are made unique by the internal addition of a counter that makes every key unique. Figure 5.4 illustrates this feature. Why did the SQL Server architects implement that feature? Because there are only two ways to reference a record in SQL Server: by its row ID or by its clustered key. The row ID is used when there is no clustered index, and the clustered key is used otherwise.

FIGURE 5.4   A clustered index made unique

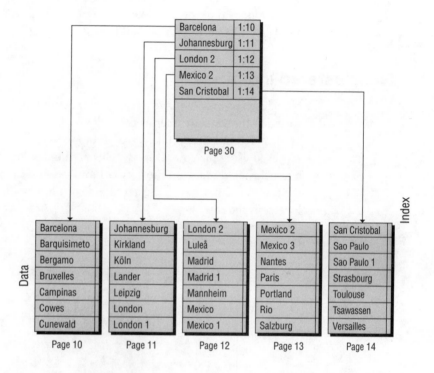

In Figure 5.3, the clustered key was the customerID, which is, by definition, unique. Each value is stored exactly as it is in the index leaf level. In Figure 5.4, for example, suppose the clustered key were changed to the City column. More than one customer can exist in a specific city; for example, Northwind Traders has four customers in Mexico. So, SQL Server added a counter to the duplicates of Mexico, allowing every value to be unique. If a fifth Mexican customer is added, its clustered key would be Mexico 4.

The first of the duplicate values has no counter value. The counter starts after the first duplicate!

The number added to the key value is an automatic counter. It does not appear to the end-user or the developer. It is just maintained internally for identification purposes. With that counter, each clustered key is guaranteed to be unique and can be used as the row's unique reference.

Remember the following rule when working in SQL Server 2000: A record is always located either by its row ID or by its clustered key, depending on the existence of a clustered index. This is an important consideration, as the row ID or key will be stored in the nonclustered index and is used to retrieve the actual data.

Nonclustered Index

Nonclustered indexes have a leaf level that contains all the key values, sorted in the same manner as the index is defined, along with the row ID or clustered index key. The actual data is not stored in the index and is retrieved using the row ID or the clustered index key. Figure 5.5 illustrates a nonclustered index on the City column. As you can see in this example, the table does not have a clustered index (it is a heap) because the row locator is the row ID.

FIGURE 5.5 A nonclustered index on a heap

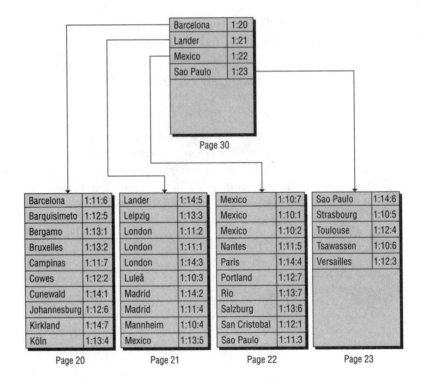

Another example of a nonclustered index on a heap is given in Figure 5.2.

Let's take another example, based on the Customers table. Let's start with the fact that this table has a clustered index on the CustomerID (see Figure 5.3). Now, if we create a nonclustered index on the City column, the result will look like Figure 5.6.

FIGURE 5.6   A nonclustered index on a clustered index

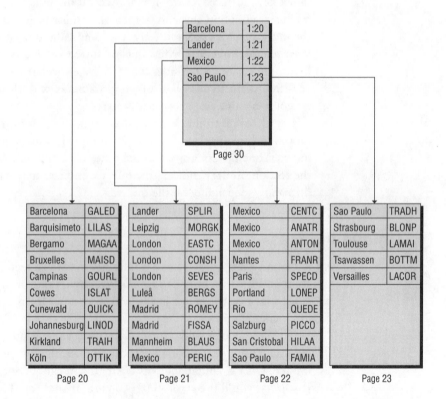

The clustered index key is used a row locator, and it is part of the leaf level of every nonclustered index. This fact leads to another rule in SQL Server: Keep clustered keys as short as possible. Every time you choose a clustered index key, it will be used as a row locator and will be stored at leaf level of every nonclustered index. The larger the clustered key, the bigger the nonclustered indexes. The last thing you want is an oversized index that will increase I/O and reduce performance. The larger the key, the less index data that will fit on each page and the more pages that must be read to find the information.

Composite Indexes

Until now, we've encountered only single-column indexes. An index can be created based on two or more columns. The only restriction is that the index key has to be less than 900 bytes. If the index is composed of only fixed-size columns, the sum of their sizes must be less than 900 bytes. If the index contains variable-length columns, the sum of their maximum size may be more than 900 bytes, but the stored value cannot be over 900 bytes. For example, consider two 500-byte varchar columns. SQL Server 2000 will let you create a *composite index* with these two columns if no column value size exceeds 900 bytes.

Pay attention to the fact that the composite index on (Column1, Column2) is different from (Column2, Column1), and is different from two indexes, one on Column1 and the other on Column2. As you'll see later in the section "Index Choice," the query optimizer may use all these indexes differently, depending on the query.

Unique Indexes

A *unique index* enforces entity integrity. As we've seen in the previous chapter, entity integrity can be enforced by unique or primary key constraints, or by unique indexes. Behind a unique or a primary constraint lies a unique index.

The unique index guarantees that every value is unique in the indexed column, or, in the case of a composite index, that every group of values is unique. Once a unique index is created, you cannot enter duplicate values. If you try, you'll fire error 2601: `Cannot insert duplicate key row in object` `tablename` `with unique index` `indexname`.

Now that you are familiar with the basic terminology and types of indexes, let's take a look at how SQL Server accesses data with or without them.

Accessing Data with and without Indexes

Microsoft
✓ ***Exam***
Objective

Create and implement indexing strategies. Considerations include clustered index, covering index, indexed views, nonclustered index, placement, and statistics.

Depending on the query and on the type of indexes existing on the table, the system may choose to use different data access strategies. The three strategies include:

- Using a heap, when no clustered index exists

- Using a clustered index

- Using a nonclustered index

The following sections describe these three strategies in detail.

Accessing Data with a Heap

When a query accesses a table that does not have a clustered index to pilot the search, a table scan is performed. So, to find data in a heap, SQL Server uses the Index Allocation Map (IAM). The IAM is a page that contains a map of all the extents that contain the data for the table. This data is stored as a bitmap that can quickly be searched. SQL Server uses the IAM page to find the location of data pages. Figure 5.7 illustrates the methodology used by SQL Server. A 1 indicates that the extent is used by the object, and a 0 indicates that it is not used.

FIGURE 5.7   Accessing data with a heap

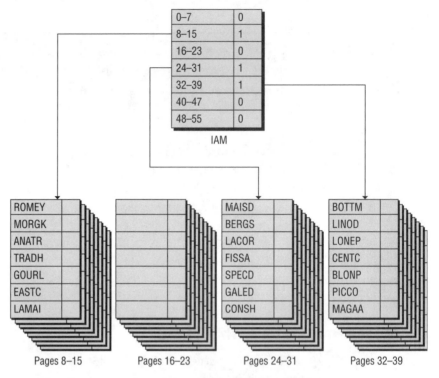

Any query that cannot be driven by an index uses the following methodology. It is broken down in three phases:

1. SQL Server queries the Sysindexes system table to find the address of the FirstIAM page.

2. SQL Server accesses the IAM page and looks for allocated pages and extents.

3. SQL Server accesses data pages and extents as it finds them in the IAM page.

As you can see, the sequence in which the records are sent back to the client is the IAM sequence order, not the inserted order. That's the reason why there is no logic in the record sequence order besides the allocations found in the IAM.

For the Customers table, if you run the following query:

```
SELECT id, indid, firstIAM
  FROM sysindexes
  WHERE id=OBJECT_ID('CustomerCustomerDemo')
```

You obtain the following result for the first row:

```
id            indid  firstIAM
-------- ---- ----------
1189579276  0        0x510100000100
```

The result you receive for the ID and FirstIAM columns may be different as these values are server-dependent.

In this result, note that the Indid value is 0, which indicates that this Sysindexes record refers to a heap.

One of the principal benefits of this strategy is that the scan of the IAM is a Boolean operation, and therefore very fast and reliable. The principal drawback is that the table has to be scanned entirely, even if you need only one record. This could lead to performance problems quite quickly.

This operation can be seen in the query execution plan—the strategy SQL Server is using to execute the query—as a table scan, which is represented by the following icon:

```
Table Scan
Cost: 100%
```

Accessing Data with a Clustered Index

As soon as a table has a clustered index, the IAM is no longer used for data access, but only for maintenance purposes. Data pages are linked together and data is sorted on the clustered index key.

If you run a query like SELECT * FROM Customers, without specifying a WHERE clause, the system will perform a clustered index scan. This operation is similar to a table scan in that all data pages are read. The main difference between a clustered index scan and a table scan is that the result is sorted on the clustered key in the clustered index scan. This occurs because the clustered index scan is not using the IAM, but finds the first page of the table (its address is stored in the Sysindexes table), reads it, and then finds the next page using a pointer to the next page. This pointer is the address of the next data page and is stored at the end of each data page.

In the graphical execution plan in Query Analyzer, the following icon represents the clustered index scan:

```
customers.cidxc...
    Cost: 100%
```

Note that an arrow goes straight through the index icon, meaning this is a scan and not a seek. A seek is a "direct" access to the data, limiting the number of accessed pages (and represented by a bent arrow). A scan accesses every page of the table or the index.

Now, if you want to access specific data in the table using the clustered index, SQL Server will do an index search when you run the following query:

```
SELECT *
  FROM Customers
  WHERE customerid = 'ALFKI'
```

The associated execution plan icon for this search looks like the following:

```
customers.cidxc...
    Cost: 0%
```

Note that the arrow is jagged to indicate that SQL Server is using the index to "seek" specific values. In such an operation, SQL Server finds the root page of the index (the address of this root page is stored in the Sysin-dexes table) and searches the values in the index. Figure 5.8 represents that search.

FIGURE 5.8   A clustered index search

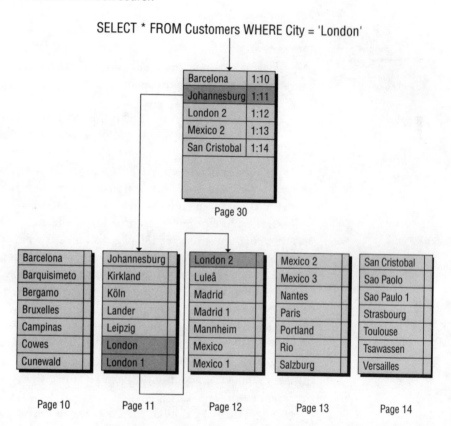

The first operation SQL Server executes is to find the root address in the Sysindexes table. For the Customers table, if you run the following query:

```
SELECT id, indid, root
FROM sysindexes
WHERE id=OBJECT_ID('Customers')
```

You obtain the following result for the first row:

```
id          indid  root
----------- ------ --------------
2041058307  1      0x4B0000000100
```

The results you receive for the ID and FirstIAM columns may be different as these values are server-dependent.

In this result, note that the Indid value is 1, which indicates that this record refers to a clustered index. With a heap, the value is 0. You cannot have both references for the same table in the Sysindexes table, since every table is stored either as a heap or as a clustered index. So, if you go through a Sysindexes table, you'll find some records referencing heaps (Indid = 0) and some referencing clustered indexes (Indid = 1).

The root address is the entrance door of the index. Once SQL Server has the root access, it scans the page to find out what path it has to follow. In the example illustrated in Figure 5.8, you are looking for the London records. London is between Johannesburg and London 2. So, SQL Server knows that the first London record is in page 11, where Johannesburg is the first record. Remember that records are physically sorted on the index key. It accesses page 11, scans it, and finds the first London record. It continues its scan until it does not find any London again. In this example, it reaches the end of the page and goes to the next page (remember that pages are linked), to continue its scan. It stops when it reaches the last London record.

In this particular example, SQL Server had to scan three pages (the root and two data pages) instead of the five that would have been necessary for a full table scan. Now, if you imagine that your table grows to 5,000 pages, SQL Server would just read a couple of pages to find the London records, not all 5,000!

Accessing Data with a Nonclustered Index

When accessing data with a nonclustered index, there is a difference in how the access is performed depending on whether the nonclustered index is created on a heap or over a clustered index. Remember that there are only two ways to locate a record: its row ID in a heap and its clustered key in a table with a clustered index. The method chosen will depend on the structure of the table.

If you drop all indexes on the Customers table and create a nonclustered index on the City column, the execution plan looks like the following when you look for the London records:

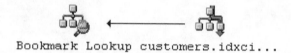

Bookmark Lookup customers.idxci...

The first operation (on the right) is an index seek. The system uses the index to find the records corresponding to the WHERE clause. In the leaf level of the index, it finds the row locator (either a row ID or a clustered key).

When using a search with a nonclustered index, SQL Server queries the Sysindexes table to find the root address of the index, as in the following excerpt of this table:

```
id            indid  root
-----------   ------ --------------
2073058421    2      0x530000000100
```

In this result, note that the Indid value is 2, indicating that it refers to a nonclustered index. Values between 2 and 250 are reserved for nonclustered indexes.

Figure 5.9 illustrates the search process when the table does not have a clustered index (it is a heap).

Once SQL Server has the root address, it scans the root page and finds the page or pages that reference the right value. In the example, London is between Lander and Mexico (alphabetically speaking, of course), so the record reference is to be found in the Lander page, that is, page 21. SQL Server accesses and scans page 21 to find London occurrences. Each time it finds a value of "London," it reads its address and loads the page in memory until it is finished with the searched value.

FIGURE 5.9 A nonclustered index search over a heap

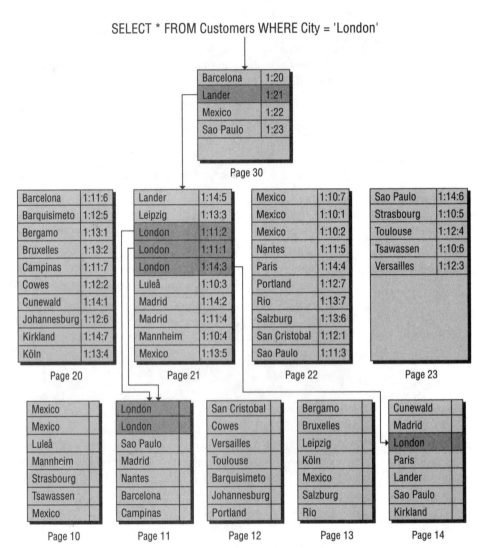

In this example, SQL Server read 4 pages, but performs 5 page accesses. Since there are three occurrences of London, it will access page 11 twice. This counts for two logical accesses, even if this page is physically read only once. If you compare this with the clustered index access example in the previous section, note that there is one additional level here due to the fact that the leaf level of the nonclustered index is above the data page.

Figure 5.10 illustrates the search had there been a clustered index on the CustomerID column.

FIGURE 5.10   A nonclustered index search over a clustered index

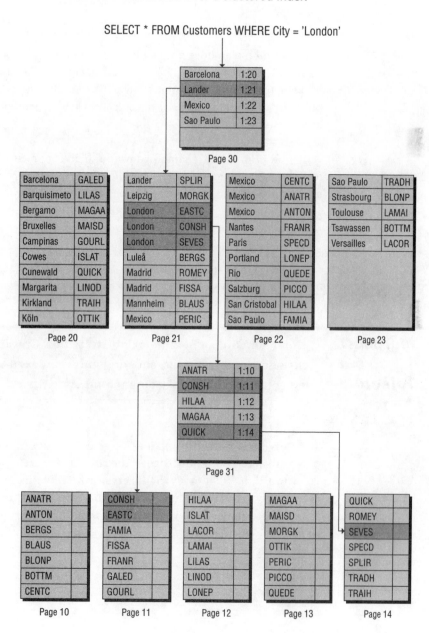

In this example, the nonclustered seek is the same as in Figure 5.9. The difference is that SQL Server finds a clustered key in the nonclustered leaf level and not a row ID. With the clustered key, it uses the clustered index to locate the corresponding record.

The execution plan does not recognize any differences between a nonclustered index seek over a heap and a nonclustered index seek over a clustered index. The last operation is always called Bookmark lookup—the bookmark being the row ID or the clustered key, depending on the existence of a clustered key.

At this point in the chapter, you should have a precise idea of how indexes are used in SQL Server and how they work. One big question remains when it comes time to use them: How does SQL Server choose the right index or indexes to execute a query? The next section answers this important question.

Statistics and Index Choice

Microsoft **✓** *Exam* *Objective*	**Create and implement indexing strategies. Considerations include clustered index, covering index, indexed views, nonclustered index, placement, and statistics.**

A book sometimes contains two or more indexes, one by word and one by theme. Your knowledge of the subject you are looking for guides you toward the right index. SQL Server is faced with the same problem for every query it has to execute. If a table has one clustered index and four nonclustered indexes, how does SQL Server know which index or indexes to use? The *distribution statistics* help the query optimizer to choose the appropriate index.

Distribution Statistics

The index choice is not made with a magic wand or a crystal ball, but with a scientific approach based on distribution statistics. Every index has a distribution statistics zone, stored in the Statblob column of the Sysindexes table.

In previous versions of SQL Server, the distribution statistics were stored in a 2KB page, whatever the size of the index. So, in SQL 6.5, as the table became bigger, the statistics were less accurate as a single 2KB page could not hold an accurate sample of the data distribution. In SQL Server 2000, the distribution statistics are stored in an image column, and its size increases proportionally to the index size for better accuracy. So, in SQL Server 2000, the size of the index does not have any impact on statistics accuracy.

To understand what these statistics are, let's use the Orders table from the Northwind database. If you run the following query:

```
SELECT TOP 24 OrderID, OrderDate
  FROM Orders
  ORDER BY OrderDate
```

You obtain the following result set:

```
OrderID     OrderDate
----------- ------------------------------------------
10248       1996-07-04 00:00:00.000
10249       1996-07-05 00:00:00.000
10250       1996-07-08 00:00:00.000
10251       1996-07-08 00:00:00.000
10252       1996-07-09 00:00:00.000
10253       1996-07-10 00:00:00.000
10254       1996-07-11 00:00:00.000
10255       1996-07-12 00:00:00.000
10256       1996-07-15 00:00:00.000
10257       1996-07-16 00:00:00.000
10258       1996-07-17 00:00:00.000
10259       1996-07-18 00:00:00.000
10260       1996-07-19 00:00:00.000
10261       1996-07-19 00:00:00.000
```

```
10262           1996-07-22 00:00:00.000
10263           1996-07-23 00:00:00.000
10264           1996-07-24 00:00:00.000
10265           1996-07-25 00:00:00.000
10266           1996-07-26 00:00:00.000
10267           1996-07-29 00:00:00.000
10268           1996-07-30 00:00:00.000
10269           1996-07-31 00:00:00.000
10270           1996-08-01 00:00:00.000
10271           1996-08-01 00:00:00.000

(24 row(s) affected)
```

This is an extract of the orders taken between July 7, 1996 and August 1, 1996. Now, count the number of occurrences of every order date.

```
orderdate       # of orderdate
------------    --------------
1996-07-04      1
1996-07-05      1
1996-07-08      2
1996-07-09      1
1996-07-10      1
1996-07-11      1
1996-07-12      1
1996-07-15      1
1996-07-16      1
1996-07-17      1
1996-07-18      1
1996-07-19      2
1996-07-22      1
1996-07-23      1
1996-07-24      1
1996-07-25      1
1996-07-26      1
1996-07-29      1
1996-07-30      1
1996-07-31      1
1996-08-01      2
```

This is a simple view of statistics. When SQL Server sorts and counts the order dates this way, it knows in advance how many orders it will find each time you look for orders taken on a specific date. For example, try running the following query:

```
SELECT *
FROM Orders
WHERE OrderDate BETWEEN '1996-07-15' AND '1996-07-20'
```

SQL Server knows before accessing the data that it will find 6 records. So, it knows that it should access at most 6 data pages if the records are evenly dispatched. The purpose of distribution statistics is based on this simple algorithm: to decide what data access strategy it will use, SQL Server needs to evaluate how many records correspond to the search condition.

In SQL Server, distribution statistics actually go beyond just counting the number of occurrences. First, the statistics should more accurately reflect the reality of data distribution. Second, the distribution statistics zone may not contain all indexed values to spare space, depending on the number of records. There are 830 records in the Orders table, but only 186 values in the distribution zone. (This value is based on a statistics algorithm that goes beyond the scope of this book.) How do you know there are only 186 values in the distribution statistics zone? Thanks to the DBCC SHOW_STATISTICS statement, if you run the following:

```
DBCC SHOW_STATISTICS (Orders,OrderDate)
```

You obtain three result sets similar to the following. The actual results will depend on the your SQL Server. The first result set is the following (extract):

Updated	Rows	Rows Sampled	Steps	Density
Feb 5 2001 10:38PM	830	830	186	1.6926861E-3

This result set indicates that:

- The statistics have been updated for the last time on February 5, 2001.

- The table contains 830 rows.

- All of these rows have been used to calculate the statistics.

- There are 186 values in the statistics (number of steps).

- The average *density* is about 0.17 percent.

Probably the most interesting figure of this result set is the density. If every value were unique, the density would be 1 out of 830, which is 0.12 percent. Here the density of 0.17 indicates that some values exist in two or more occurrences. For example, there were two orders taken on July 8, 1996. As far as density is concerned, the smaller, the better. It indicates that the index is very selective.

If you index a column containing only three different values (for example, Mr., Mrs., Miss), you will end up with a density of 33.3 percent, which is not good and reveals that this index is useless. The index consumes space, but will probably never be used. On the other hand, a unique index has a density of 1 out of the total number of records, which is the best *selectivity* an index can have. Always pay attention to the density of your indexes. If it is above 10 percent, the index is considered useless.

The second result set of running the DBCC SHOW_STATISTICS is the following:

All density	Average Length	Columns
2.0833334E-3	8.0	OrderDate
1.2048193E-3	12.0	OrderDate, OrderID

This is interesting information because the density of the OrderDate alone is 0.2 percent, but paired with the OrderID column it goes down to 0.12 percent. This is a completely normal situation; since the OrderID is the primary key of the table, its density is the best that could be reached on the table.

The last result set may be the most interesting in fully understanding statistics. The following result is an extract of the first rows of this set of data spanning the range from July 4, 1996 through August 1, 1996:

RANGE_HI_KEY	RANGE_ROWS	EQ_ROWS	DISTINCT_RANGE_ROWS
1996-07-04	0.0	1.0	0
1996-07-15	7.0	1.0	6
1996-07-19	3.0	2.0	3
1996-07-25	3.0	1.0	3
1996-08-01	4.0	2.0	4

First of all, note there are only five values in the distribution zone, instead of the 24 values in the table between July 4th and August 1st.

Nevertheless, with the other columns, the system knows exactly how many lines exist between July 4th and August 1st. Let's see how it knows this.

The RANGE_HI_KEY column gives the upper value of a range stored in the distribution page. We know that 1996-07-04 is the upper value of the first range, and that the following value is 1996-07-15. Between these two values, we find seven other values. The RANGE_ROWS column gives this information. There are three values between 1996-07-15 and 1996-07-19, and so on. Now, the EQ_ROWS column gives the number of occurrences of the upper value of the range. In this example, we know there is one 1996-07-04 occurrence, one 1996-07-15, and two 1996-07-19. Last, but not least, the DISTINCT_RANGE_ROWS column gives the number of distinct values within a range. Here, there are six distinct values between 1996-07-04 and 1996-07-15. So, we now know there is one duplicate in this range, since there are seven values among six distinct ones. There is one last column that does not appear in the previous result set, named AVG_RANGE_ROWS, which is the result of RANGE_ROWS/DISTINCT_RANGE_ROWS.

Just with this information, we can figure out the distribution of data in the indexed column. The distribution can be represented the following way:

```
1996-07-04
Seven values and one duplicate
1996-07-15
Three distinct values
1996-07-19
1996-07-19
Three distinct values
1996-07-25
Four distinct values
1996-08-01
1996-08-01
```

When the system is evaluating the number of records concerning orders taken on July 19, 1996 with the distribution statistics, it knows that there are only two records because it found a hit in the statistics. If you are looking for orders taken on July 23, 1996, there is at most one. Between July 19th, and July 25th, there are only three distinct values. So, July 23rd may be one of them, or the record containing the value may not exist. But the system knows that there could not be more than one occurrence.

Index Choice

As you've seen in the previous example about the distribution statistics zone, the system knows quite precisely how data is distributed in the indexed column. Each time a query is run, the first operation performed by the system is an evaluation of the distribution statistics. Let's take a few examples to fully understand what the system does. If you run the following:

```
SELECT *
FROM Orders
WHERE OrderDate BETWEEN '1996-07-19' AND '1996-07-25'
```

SQL Server first checks whether there is an index on the OrderDate column, or a composite index starting with the OrderDate column. In that case, it will evaluate the number of rows that exist in this range. With the estimated execution plan of SQL Query Analyzer, the system gives you back the results shown in the following graphic. To display the estimated execution plan of a query, highlight the query and click the Display Estimated Execution Plan button on the SQL Query Analyzer toolbar.

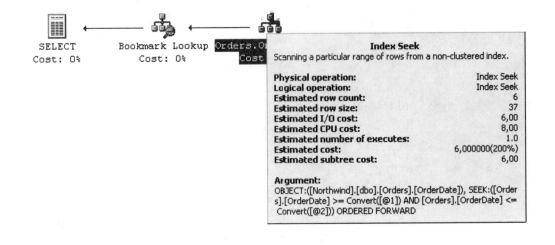

```
Query 1: Query cost (relative to the batch): 100,00%
Query text: SELECT * FROM Orders  WHERE OrderDate BETWEEN '1996-07-19' AND '1996-07-20'
```

			Index Seek
SELECT	Bookmark Lookup	Orders.O...	Scanning a particular range of rows from a non-clustered index.
Cost: 0%	Cost: 0%	Cost	

Physical operation:	Index Seek
Logical operation:	Index Seek
Estimated row count:	6
Estimated row size:	37
Estimated I/O cost:	6,00
Estimated CPU cost:	8,00
Estimated number of executes:	1.0
Estimated cost:	6,000000(200%)
Estimated subtree cost:	6,00

Argument:
OBJECT:([Northwind].[dbo].[Orders].[OrderDate]), SEEK:([Orders].[OrderDate] >= Convert([@1]) AND [Orders].[OrderDate] <= Convert([@2])) ORDERED FORWARD

Here, the Estimated row count is six. This is a good scientific guess: There are two 1996-07-19 occurrences, one 1996-07-25, and three values between them, which add up to six. Easy, isn't it?

Now, if you run the following:

```
SELECT *
 FROM Orders
 WHERE OrderDate BETWEEN '1996-07-19' AND '1996-07-25'
 AND CustomerID = 'FOLKO'
```

SQL Server discovers one index on OrderDate and one on CustomerID. It will then use both and do an intersection between the interim results. The evaluation gives six records for the criteria on OrderDate and 19 for the one on CustomerID. The index intersection is performed like a join between two result sets. In this particular case, SQL Server will use a merge join strategy, resulting in one record.

If you change the AND keyword into an OR keyword, the system may do an index union, or it may prefer to scan the table if it is not too big. In that case, the clustered index scan is chosen because the Orders table is quite small, and it will be faster to scan the table than to use both indexes and join the two result sets. The cost of OR operations is generally high.

Now, what happens if there is no index, and therefore no statistics? The answer is pretty easy: SQL Server cannot work without statistics! So, instead of guessing, it creates a distribution statistics zone without any indexes based on it. If you run the following:

```
SELECT *
 FROM Orders
 WHERE ShipCity='Graz'
```

SQL Server will automatically create a distribution statistics zone for this column, since the ShipCity column is not indexed. To list all the indexes created on the Orders table, run the following:

```
 SELECT name, first, root
 FROM sysindexes
 WHERE id=OBJECT_ID('Orders')
```

You obtain the following result:

name	first	root
PK_Orders	0xF00000000100	0xF10000000100
CustomerID	0xDA0000000100	0xDD0000000100
CustomersOrders	0xDF0000000100	0x920100000100
EmployeeID	0x940100000100	0x970100000100
EmployeesOrders	0x980100000100	0x9B0100000100
OrderDate	0x9C0100000100	0x9F0100000100
ShippedDate	0xA10100000100	0xA40100000100
ShippersOrders	0xA50100000100	0xA80100000100
ShipPostalCode	0xA90100000100	0xAC0100000100
_WA_Sys_ShipCity_797309D9	0x000000000000	0x000000000000

Note the last line. The "index" name is _WA_Sys_ShipCity_797309D9, and its first and root addresses are NULL because this is not an index; it is a distribution statistics zone.

The actual name is randomly generated and may be different on your server.

Statistics created automatically on columns are dropped automatically if they are not used. So, you do not have to bother with them. Just let the system manage them!

You can discover the statistics that exist on a table by running the sp_helpstats system procedure:

```
sp_helpstats 'Orders'
```
You will receive the following result:

statistics_name	statistics_keys
_WA_Sys_ShipCity_797309D9	ShipCity

You can get the same result if you choose Tools ➢ Manage Statistics in SQL Query Analyzer. For the Orders table, the Manage Statistics dialog box is shown in Figure 5.11.

FIGURE 5.11 Manage Statistics dialog box

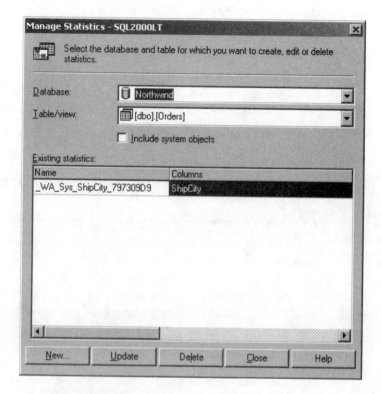

These statistics have been created because the database
    AUTO_CREATE_STATISTICS option is on.

The automatic statistics zones are a great help for SQL Server administrators to discover that some indexes are missing. The only problem with statistics is that they must be up-to-date to be useful.

Statistics Maintenance

What would happen if the statistics were not up-to-date? The answer is quite straightforward: Your index choice may be wrong. Imagine that the statistics have been created while the table contained 1,000 rows, but that the table grew rapidly and now contains more than 100,000 records. The system builds its choice of index on this outdated statistic and may make the wrong decision. To be really useful, the statistics have to be up-to-date.

By default, statistics are updated automatically in SQL Server 2000. To check whether the statistics automatic update is activated in a specific database, run the following:

```
SELECT DATABASEPROPERTYEX('dbname', 'IsAutoUpdate-
   Statistics')
```

If the result is 1, then the statistics are automatically updated when needed. To set the AUTO_UPDATE_STATISTICS option, run the following:

```
ALTER DATABASE dbname SET AUTO_UPDATE_STATISTICS ON
```

To turn if off, run the following:

```
ALTER DATABASE dbname SET AUTO_UPDATE_STATISTICS OFF
```

Avoid using sp_dboption, since this stored procedure is given only for backward compatibility in SQL Server 2000.

As a rule of thumb, it is better to leave this option on. All the statistics will be automatically updated when they become outdated. The update algorithm is entirely managed by SQL Server, depending on the number of updates, deletes, and inserts, and on the number of records in the table. If your table has a one million records and only 100 records change (0.01 percent), the distribution statistics do not have to be updated since this change will not dramatically change the data distribution of the table.

Furthermore, if a table size is over 8MB (1,000 pages), SQL Server will not use all the data to calculate the distribution statistics, but only a sample. All of these features have one purpose: to calculate the most accurate statistics while limiting the impact on performance during their update. So, based on these features, SQL Server will automatically recalculate the statistics when the optimizer finds that they are outdated.

Now, it is possible to enable or disable automatic computation of statistics with the sp_autostats system stored procedure. Run the following:

```
sp_autostats 'Orders'
```

You'll see the automatic statistics setting for the Northwind database and the Orders table:

```
Global statistics settings for [Northwind]:
   Automatic update statistics: ON
   Automatic create statistics: ON
```

```
Settings for table [Orders]
```

Index Name	AUTOSTATS	Last Updated
[PK_Orders]	ON	2001-02-05 22:38:47.693
[CustomerID]	ON	2001-02-05 22:38:47.753
[CustomersOrders]	ON	2001-02-05 22:38:47.803
[EmployeeID]	ON	2001-02-05 22:38:47.833
[EmployeesOrders]	ON	2001-02-05 22:38:47.853
[OrderDate]	ON	2001-02-05 22:38:47.883
[ShippedDate]	ON	2001-02-05 22:38:47.913
[ShippersOrders]	ON	2001-02-05 22:38:47.943
[ShipPostalCode]	ON	2001-02-05 22:38:47.983
[_WA_Sys_ShipCity_797309D9]	ON	2001-03-13 23:54:55.490

If you want to turn off all the automatic statistics for the Orders table, run the following:

```
sp_autostats 'Orders', 'OFF'
```

To turn it on again, run the following:

```
sp_autostats 'Orders', 'ON'
```

Now, you can turn on automatic statistics updates for one specific index, by running the following:

```
sp_autostats 'Orders', 'ON', 'indexname'
```

Here, indexname is the name of the index in question. To turn it off, run the following:

```
sp_autostats 'Orders', 'OFF', 'indexname'
```

The sp_createstats system stored procedure may be used to create statistics for every column of every table of a database. The only columns not affected by this procedure are the non-deterministic columns, the non-precise columns, and those of image, text, and ntext data types (deterministic and precise columns are explained in the "Index on Computed Columns" section). But do not forget that statistics consume space. It is better to do an analysis of the queries run against a database with the Index Tuning Wizard than to create all possible statistics (see Chapter 12 for information on this wizard).

To disable automatic statistics updates, you have the following choices:

- Disable the AUTO_UPDATE_STATISTICS option with the ALTER DATA-BASE statement.

- Use the sp_autostats system stored procedure.

- Use the STATISTICS_NORECOMPUTE of the CREATE INDEX statement (see the next section on creating an index and statistics).

- Use the NORECOMPUTE clause of the STATISTICS UPDATES or CREATE STATISTICS statement.

Once you have disabled automatic statistics update, you need to update them manually. This operation can be done through index maintenance (see the last section of this chapter on fragmentation and index maintenance), or with the UPDATE STATISTICS statement.

The complete syntax of STATISTICS UPDATES is as follows:

```
UPDATE STATISTICS Table | View
        [
            Index
            | ( statistics_name [ ,...n ] )
        ]
        [    WITH
            [
                [ FULLSCAN ]
                | SAMPLE number { PERCENT | ROWS } ]
                | RESAMPLE
            ]
            [ [ , ] [ ALL | COLUMNS | INDEX ]
            [ [ , ] NORECOMPUTE ]
        ]
```

Where the options are defined below.

Table | View   This value is the name of the table or view for which statistics should be updated.

Index | Statistics_name   This value is the name of the index or a comma-delimited list of the statistics kept for the table. If included, then the specific statistics are updated. If this value is not included, statistics for all indexes are updated.

FULLSCAN   This specifies that all rows in the table should be read to compute the statistics distribution. This is the same as specifying

SAMPLE 100 PERCENT. The FULLSCAN and SAMPLE options cannot be used together.

SAMPLE number (PERCENT | ROWS) This option specifies the amount of the table that should be sampled to update the distribution statistics. An integer number is specified in place of the *number* parameter. The sample can be specified as a percentage of the table or an absolute number of rows. SQL Server 2000 has a minimum amount of rows that must be sampled, and if the number specified is too small, it is automatically adjusted.

RESAMPLE This option specifies that the statistics are updated using an inherited sampling ratio. If the ratio is below the minimum, SQL Server automatically adjusts the ratio to the minimum.

ALL | COLUMNS | INDEX This option specifies whether column statistics, index statistics, or all statistics are updated. By default, all statistics are updated.

NORECOMPUTE This option specifies that statistics that become outdated are not automatically recomputed. This is the same as disabling automatic statistics using SP_AUTOSTATS.

The UPDATE STATISTICS statement allows you to perform the following:

- You can update index or column statistics.

- You can precisely calculate the statistics over the whole table (FULLSCAN), or calculate the statistics with a sample.

- You can update the index, columns, or all statistics (all is the default).

- You can disable statistics calculation with the NORECOMPUTE clause.

Here are some examples of a statistics update. The first example will update all the statistics of the Orders table:

```
UPDATE STATISTICS Orders
```

The following statement will update the statistics of the OrderDate index of the Orders table:

```
UPDATE STATISTICS Orders OrderDate
```

The third statement will update the statistics of the OrderDate index, using only a 10 percent sample of the data:

```
UPDATE STATISTICS Orders OrderDate WITH SAMPLE 10 PERCENT
```

Even if you ask for a specific sample percentage, SQL Server may not respect your request if it finds the percentage too small to be representative. Remember, the table must be bigger that 8MB to be sampled. And, even with such a size, too small a sample may not be used! SQL Server decides about the smallest sample possible.

This last example updates the index statistics only and disables their automatic update setting with the following statement:

```
UPDATE STATISTICS Orders WITH INDEX, NORECOMPUTE
```

This statement can be run on a daily or weekly basis if you want to ensure constant statistics accuracy but do not want SQL Server to automatically recompute the distribution statistics.

Now that you have a better understanding of how indexes are used, it is time to examine how to create them.

Creating Indexes and Statistics

Microsoft ✓ *Exam Objective*

Create and alter database objects. Objects include constraints, indexes, stored procedures, tables, triggers, user-defined functions, and views.

- Specify index characteristics. Characteristics include clustered, FILLFACTOR, nonclustered, and uniqueness.

Troubleshoot failed object creation.

Creating indexes or statistics is a straightforward process when done with the CREATE INDEX and CREATE STATISTICS statements. Let's start by looking at how indexes are created.

Indexes

As we've seen in the previous pages, two types of indexes exist: clustered and nonclustered. In addition to these types, different options can be added: uniqueness enforcement, multiple columns, statistics recalculation, and so on. All these choices address a great variety of needs and let the index be tailored to the situation. This section focuses on index creation and option use, starting with basic index creation.

Clustered and Nonclustered Index

The basic CREATE INDEX statement is quite simple:

```
CREATE [ CLUSTERED | NONCLUSTERED ] INDEX index_name
       ON { table | view } ( column [ ASC | DESC ] [ ,...n
] )
[ ON filegroup ]
```

The following statement creates the OrderDate nonclustered index on the Orders table:

```
CREATE INDEX OrderDate ON Orders(OrderDate)
```

As you can observe, the default index is always nonclustered. If you want a clustered index, you have to specify it, as in the following example:

```
CREATE CLUSTERED INDEX idxCustID ON Orders(CustomerID)
```

WARNING A table can have only one clustered index. If you created a primary key constraint on the table, you may have created a clustered index to support the constraint. If you end up with error 1902: Cannot create more than one clustered index on table 'tablename'. Drop the existing clustered index 'indexname' before creating another, it is because you have another clustered index defined on the table and it may be the primary key.

The sp_helpindex system stored procedure gives you the complete list of indexes created on a table. For example, if you run the following:

```
sp_helpindex Orders
```

You obtain the following result:

```
index_name        index_description                  index_keys
----------------  ---------------------------------  ---------------
CustomerID        nonclustered located on PRIMARY    CustomerID
EmployeeID        nonclustered located on PRIMARY    EmployeeID
OrderDate         nonclustered located on PRIMARY    OrderDate
PK_Orders         clustered, unique,                 OrderID
                  primary key located on PRIMARY
ShippedDate       nonclustered located on PRIMARY    ShippedDate
ShippersOrders    nonclustered located on PRIMARY    ShipVia
ShipPostalCode    nonclustered located on PRIMARY    ShipPostalCode
```

You can obtain a more readable result in SQL Query Analyzer by choosing Tools ➤ Manage Indexes. Figure 5.12 shows the Manage Indexes dialog box.

FIGURE 5.12   Manage Indexes dialog box

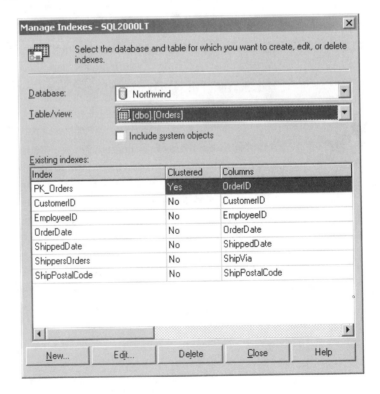

From the previous result set, notice that all indexes are located on PRI-
MARY. That means they have all been created in the primary filegroup (see
Chapter 2 for more information on filegroups). You can place indexes on
a different filegroup than the one used for the table to balance I/Os among
different disks, even if a RAID solution may offer better performance.
Many DBAs love this feature because it allows them control over file
placement.

The CREATE INDEX statement has many options. Among these, we find:

- ASC|DESC

- SORT_IN_TEMPDB

- IGNORE_DUP_KEY

ASC, which is the default, stores the index in ascending order. DESC
stores it in descending order. While it has no effect on search performance,
it may have a positive impact on the ORDER BY clause. The following statement creates an index on the UnitPrice column of the Products table in
descending order (from the most expensive to the cheapest product):

```
CREATE INDEX idxUnitPrice ON Products(UnitPrice DESC)
```

SORT_IN_TEMPDB is useful to improve performance during index creation. The creation of an index occurs in two phases. The first one creates
a temporary result set containing the sorted index key for a nonclustered
index and the sorted data for a clustered index. The second moves this
sorted result set to the final destination of the index. Without the
SORT_IN_TEMPDB option, the temporary result set is stored in the filegroup
of the created index. With the SORT_IN_TEMPDB option, the temporary
result set is stored in the Tempdb database.

The following statement creates a clustered index on the OrderID column of the Order Details table and stores the interim result set in Tempdb:

```
CREATE INDEX idxOrderID ON [Order Details](Orderid)
  WITH SORT_IN_TEMPDB
```

The overall performance can be enhanced if Tempdb is stored on
another set of disks from the current database. During phase 1, reads from
the database won't compete with writes to the interim result, and during
phase 2, writes from the interim result set won't compete with writes to
the final destination. Another positive impact occurs on the extents allocation. They may be more compact, since the interim storage is in another
database.

The only issue you must think of is free space. There should be enough free space to accommodate the interim result, either in Tempdb (with the SORT_IN_TEMPDB option) or in the filegroup (without the SORT_IN_TEMPDB option).

IGNORE_DUP_KEY is a very tricky option. It only concerns what happens during inserts into unique indexes. Without the option, if a duplicate key is found, the entire insert is rolled back. With the option, if two rows contain a duplicate key, the first one is inserted and the second issues a warning, but the insert continues. The intrinsic transactional nature of the insert is violated. Consider the following test tables and index:

```
CREATE TABLE testduplicate(c1 int, c2 varchar(10))
CREATE TABLE test(c1 int, c2 varchar(10))
CREATE UNIQUE INDEX idxc1 ON test(c1)
    WITH IGNORE_DUP_KEY
```

Let's say we insert the same values in the Testduplicate table as with the following:

```
INSERT testduplicate VALUES(1, 'test')
INSERT testduplicate VALUES(1, 'test')
```

And then try to insert these two rows into the test table using the following:

```
INSERT test SELECT * FROM testduplicate
```

We will obtain warning 3604: Duplicate key was ignored, which means one of the two rows has been inserted. If you had created the index without the IGNORE_DUP_KEY option, you would have obtained error 2601: Cannot insert duplicate key row in object 'test' with unique index 'idxc1', and no row would have been inserted in the table. This option can be very convenient when inserting data coming from different sources, but should be used with caution, since you can insert only parts of the result set, and not all the records.

Unique Index

By definition, default indexes allow duplicate keys. If you want to enforce uniqueness, use the UNIQUE clause in the CREATE INDEX statement.

It is better to enforce uniqueness with unique constraints. These constraints build unique indexes in the background, and their major benefit is that they can be used as the source of relationships. Unique indexes cannot be used as the source of relationships.

If you want to enforce uniqueness for the OrderID column of the Orders table, run the following statement:

```
CREATE UNIQUE INDEX uidxOrderID ON Orders(OrderID)
```

As for a non-unique index, the default is nonclustered. If you want to create a clustered unique index, you have to specify it as in the following:

```
CREATE UNIQUE CLUSTERED INDEX uidxOrderID ON
    Orders(OrderID)
```

If duplicate values are found during the index creation phase, the creation will fail with error message 1505: CREATE UNIQUE INDEX terminated because a duplicate key was found for index ID *index-number*. Most significant primary key is 'keyvalue'. You have to find, delete, or update duplicate values before creating the unique index. Imagine that you imported data from your legacy system, and that you have to check whether duplicates exist and cleanse them before creating the unique index. The following query builds a list of duplicate OrderID values:

```
SELECT OrderID, COUNT(OrderID) FROM Orders
    GROUP BY OrderID HAVING Count(OrderID)>1
```

With the list you can directly access faulty data and correct it.

Composite Index

A composite index is made of more than one column. The following example creates an index based on ShipCountry and OrderDate:

```
CREATE NONCLUSTERED INDEX idxDateCountry
    ON Orders(OrderDate, ShipCountry)
```

You should be aware that the column order is essential in a composite index. Consider the following query:

```
SELECT * FROM Orders
    WHERE OrderDate BETWEEN '1996-07-14' AND '1996-08-14'
```

It may use the `idxDateCountry` index. But the following query cannot use it:

```
SELECT * FROM Orders WHERE ShipCountry='Poland'
```

Now, imagine that you create the index in the opposite order:

```
CREATE NONCLUSTERED INDEX idxCountryDate
   ON Orders(ShipCountry, OrderDate)
```

The first SELECT statement cannot benefit from this index, as the second may. Since the ShipCountry column is the first of the index, a query on only the OrderDate column cannot be driven by this index (order dates are ordered for every country, not overall).

```
SELECT * FROM Orders
   WHERE OrderDate BETWEEN '1996-07-14' AND '1996-08-14'
   AND ShipCountry='Sweden'
```

Depending on the selectivity of the query, and on the search condition, SQL Server will use either the `idxDateCountry` or `idxCountryDate` index. The previous example uses `idxCountryDate` because ShipCountry was more selective than OrderDate. The following query uses `idxDateCountry` because, this time, OrderDate is more selective than ShipCountry:

```
SELECT * FROM Orders
   WHERE OrderDate BETWEEN '1996-07-04' AND '1996-07-05'
   AND ShipCountry like 'F%'
```

These examples show you that two composite indexes on the same columns in different orders may be useful to service different queries. A thorough analysis of the different queries run on your system will help you determine what are the best composite indexes to create.

One last thing to note about a composite index is that one index on (OrderDate, ShipCountry) is different from having two indexes, one on OrderDate and one on ShipCountry. In the first case, the index can be used directly to drive the query. In the second case, both indexes may be used, but an intersection (a kind of join) has to be performed, which lowers the performance.

Index on Computed Columns

SQL Server 7 introduced computed columns (see Chapter 3). SQL Server 2000 introduces indexed computed columns. One of the main advantages of indexing computed columns is the ability to perform a fast search. If not indexed, the results of computed columns are calculated on the fly during query execution. If indexed, the result is stored at the leaf level of the index and recalculated when one of the values of the function is updated.

The results of the computed columns are stored at the leaf level, not in the table. That means that if the index on the computed column is not covering the query (an index is covering a query if all columns defined in the query are part of the index), the value will be calculated on the fly, although it is stored in the index. This rule applies because it costs fewer resources to perform the calculation than to seek the index for the value.

To be indexed, a computed column must comply with a certain number of rules:

- The computed column expression must be deterministic and precise. To know whether a computed column is deterministic, run the following:

```
SELECT COLUMNPROPERTY(OBJECT_ID('tablename'),
  'columnname', 'IsDeterministic')
```

If the returned value is 1, the column is deterministic. If 0, the column is non-deterministic. To know if a computed column is precise, run the following:

```
SELECT COLUMNPROPERTY(OBJECT_ID('tablename'),
  'columnname', 'IsPrecise')
```

If the returned value is 1, the column is precise. If 0, it is not precise.

- The ANSI_NULLS option must be set to ON when the table is created. To check whether it was on at table creation, run the following:

```
SELECT OBJECTPROPERTY(OBJECT_ID('tablename'), 'IsAnsi-
  NullsOn').
```

- The computed column result must not be of text, ntext, or image data types.

Now, six options must be set to ON and one to OFF during index creation and index values modification. The options set to ON are:

- ANSI_NULLS
- ANSI_PADDING
- ANSI_WARNINGS
- ARITHABORT
- CONCAT_NULL_YIELDS_NULL
- QUOTED_IDENTIFIER

The option set to OFF is:

- NUMERIC_ROUNDABORT

All of these options, except ARITHABORT are correctly set by the OLE-DB provider for SQL Server and the ODBC driver of SQL Server. By default, ARITHABORT is set to OFF. If you want to implement indexed computed columns and indexed views, you should set the ARITHABORT option to ON for your server. You can use the following script:

```
DECLARE @value int
SELECT @value=(value | 64)
    FROM spt_values JOIN Sysconfigures
    ON number=config WHERE name='user options'
EXEC sp_configure 'user options', @value
RECONFIGURE
```

If all these seven options are not correctly set, the optimizer will not consider the index created on the computed column.

Fillfactor

The index *fill factor* plays an important role in reducing data fragmentation, as you are going to see in the section "Fragmentation and Index Maintenance." The FILLFACTOR option indicates the percentage of pages that are going to be physically occupied at leaf level. Let's consider the index illustrated in Figure 5.13. This index has a default fill factor, which means the pages are 100 percent full.

FIGURE 5.13   An index with a fill factor of 100

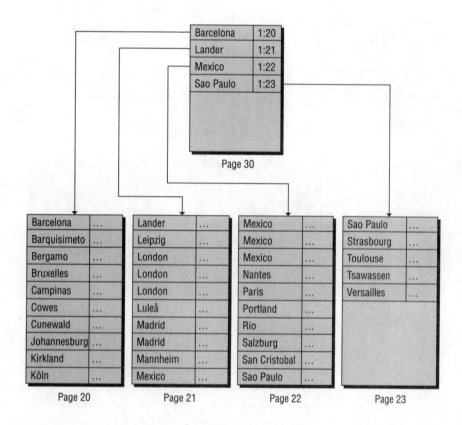

Now, if we create the same index, but with a fill factor of 50, it will look like the one presented in Figure 5.14.

FIGURE 5.14   An index with a fill factor of 50

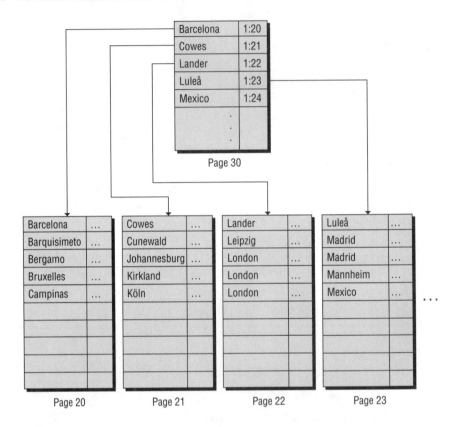

With a fill factor of 50, the pages are half full. The table will occupy more space, but can accept more inserts without incurring page splits (see the section later in this chapter on index fragmentation). If you want to insert the city of Boston, it must fit between Bergamo and Bruxelles. With a fill factor of 100, the page is split in two and the insert is performed. With a fill factor of 50, the insert is performed directly because there is enough free space in the page.

A fill factor of less than 100 is good for tables in which many inserts and updates take place. With such a fill factor, data fragmentation is delayed and may not occur if the index is compacted on a regular basis. On the other hand, if many inserts and updates are performed in an index with a fill factor of 100, data fragmentation occurs frequently, and performance decreases. A good practice is to use a fill factor of around 80. It is a good balance between performance and resource usage.

The following example creates an index on the ShipCountry column of the Orders table with a fill factor of 80:

```
CREATE NONCLUSTERED INDEX idxCountry
    ON Orders(ShipCountry)
    WITH FILLFACTOR = 80
```

The fill factor only applies to the leaf level. The index non-leaf levels are always optimized to leave spaces for at least two index keys. Nonetheless, if you want to apply the same fill factor to non-leaf level, use the PADINDEX option, as in the following statement:

```
CREATE NONCLUSTERED INDEX idxCountry
    ON Orders(ShipCountry)
    WITH FILLFACTOR = 80, PAD_INDEX
```

As a rule of thumb, use a fill factor of 80 for frequently updated indexes, and use a fill factor of 100 for decision support systems or for tables with frequent inserts at the end of the table (for example, an index on an identity column).

If the fill factor cannot be fulfilled exactly, SQL Server will always include excess rows on each page. For example, if 13 records fit on a table, with a fill factor of 50, SQL Server could store 6.5 records on each page, which is impossible. In fact, it will store 7 records on each page, obtaining a real fill factor of 53.8.

Statistics

We've seen in the previous pages that the system was able to generate statistics automatically when no index existed to drive a query. It is possible, though, to create statistics without an index, just to help the query optimizer. Statistics can be created on one or multiple columns. The full syntax is the following:

```
CREATE STATISTICS statistics_name
    ON { table | view } ( column [ ,...n ] )
        [ WITH
            [ [ FULLSCAN
                | SAMPLE number { PERCENT | ROWS } ] [ , ]
    ]
```

```
      [ NORECOMPUTE ]
   ]
```

If you want to create statistics over ShipCountry and EmployeeID, run the following:

```
CREATE STATISTICS statEmpCountry
   ON Orders(EmployeeID, ShipCountry)
```

As for index creation, the system will use a full scan or a sample, depending on the size of the table and the directive you give. The NORECOMPUTE clause indicates that the statistics should not be updated automatically.

Remember, statistics are here to help the query optimizer in its choice. Having statistics on different columns help it to have a better understanding of data distribution, while consuming less space than indexes. Be aware that statistics do not replace indexes. Indexes are still useful to accelerate the query execution. Statistics is just one of the optimization tools that may be used to ease the query execution path.

While indexes are mandatory for performance, they need to be maintained. A database may encounter data fragmentation due to frequent updates, deletes, and inserts. Data fragmentation may decrease the performance. It is time to look at what happens during data modification and what to do to maintain good performance.

Fragmentation and Index Maintenance

Microsoft ✓ *Exam Objective*

Create and implement indexing strategies. Considerations include clustered index, covering index, indexed views, nonclustered index, placement, and statistics.

Even though a lot of action is automated in SQL Server 2000, index maintenance may be a large part of the administration and is directly related to performance. In case of a performance decrease, the DBA and the SQL developers should first think about data fragmentation. Why and when does data fragmentation occur? Because data is updated and rows may move around. We will first look at what happens during inserts, deletes, and updates, and then explain what to do to limit fragmentation and what action to perform to defragment tables.

Fragmentation Types

Fragmentation in SQL Server concerns data files. When a record is deleted, space is freed in the page. When a record is inserted in the middle of a clustered index, or at the leaf level of a nonclustered index, it may cause a page split. When a record is updated, its size may increase and the record may move to another page. All of these situations lead to data fragmentation. In SQL Server 2000, there are two types of fragmentation: internal and external.

Internal fragmentation refers to empty spaces inside pages. *External fragmentation* refers to page links. Figure 5.15 illustrates a classic situation of internal fragmentation.

FIGURE 5.15   Internal fragmentation

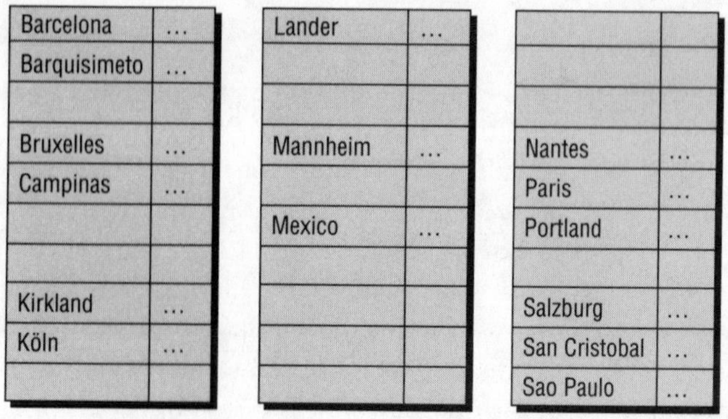

In this example, pages are not fully filled. Space is overused. Defragmenting these pages will lead to less used space, and therefore a better use of I/Os and memory. Remember, pages are moved into memory just as they are moved to disk. If pages are filled at 10 or 20 percent, you will lose 90 or 80 percent of memory, which will be used to store useless bits.

Figure 5.16 illustrates a classic situation of external fragmentation. When a page is split, the new allocation may not be physically close to the split page.

FIGURE 5.16 External fragmentation

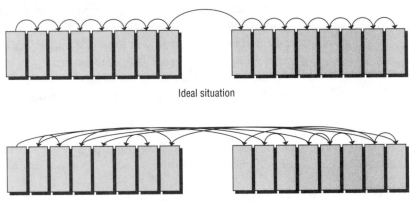

Ideal situation

Fragmented situation

In an ideal situation, pages are linked naturally from left to right, that is, in their storage order. Due to successive page splits, the pages may not be linked in an optimal manner. This situation will lead to performance decrease because the number of pages generally increases, like the number of extents.

The DBCC SHOWCONTIG statement helps you determine external and internal fragmentation. If you run DBCC SHOWCONTIG('Orders'), you may obtain the following result (note that the result may vary from one server to the other):

```
DBCC SHOWCONTIG scanning 'Orders' table...
Table: 'Orders' (21575115); index ID: 1, database ID: 9
TABLE level scan performed.
- Pages Scanned................................: 20
- Extents Scanned..............................: 5
- Extent Switches..............................: 4
- Avg. Pages per Extent........................: 4.0
- Scan Density [Best Count:Actual Count].......: 60.00% [3:5]
- Logical Scan Fragmentation ..................: 0.00%
```

```
- Extent Scan Fragmentation ...................: 40.00%
- Avg. Bytes Free per Page....................: 146.5
- Avg. Page Density (full)....................: 98.19%
```

DBCC SHOWCONTIG works at the leaf level, so all of these results concern the data pages. The explanation of the result is the following:

- Pages scanned shows the number of data pages. Here the table is 20 pages long.

- Extents scanned shows the number of extents used by the table. Here we learn that the table uses 5 extents. This first information tells us there may be external fragmentation, since only 3 pages would be necessary to store 20 pages (8 pages per extent).

- Extents Switches gives the number of times DBCC moved from one extent to the other. In a normal situation, this number is equal to Extent Scanned - 1.

- Avg. Pages per extent gives the average number of pages per extent while traversing the page chain. This value should be as close as possible to 8 (the maximum number of pages per extent if the table is compacted).

- Scan Density represents the value of external fragmentation. Its result is based on the ideal number of extent changes and on the real number of extent changes. The lower the value, the more external fragmentation. This value should always be as close as possible to 100.

- Logical Scan Fragmentation gives the percentage of out-of-order pages. In a normal situation, pages are linked in a right-to-left order, that is, in ascending page number order. If the pages are in this order, the Logical Scan Fragmentation is 0. The higher the value, the more page-to-page fragmentation.

- Extent Scan Fragmentation gives the percentage of out-of-order extents. An out-of-order extent is an extent that is not physically following the previous allocated extent for the object. Again, seeing this figure increase indicates extent-to-extent fragmentation. Allocated extents are not contiguous. This may result in unoptimized I/Os.

- Avg. Bytes Free per Page is the average number of bytes free per page. This number should be as close as possible to 0 if the fill factor is 100; otherwise, you should take the fill factor into consideration. With a fill factor of 80, having an average of 1,600 bytes free per page is a normal situation (20 percent of 8KB).

- Avg. Page Density gives the average page density, taking the row size into account. This value should be as close as possible to 100. The Avg. Bytes Free per Page and Avg. Page Density average numbers give a good overview of internal fragmentation.

If the previous example, we have a page density of 98.19 percent, that indicates there is no real internal density (due to the row size, there is always a little extra space in pages). On the other hand, a scan density of 60 percent and an extent scan fragmentation of 40 percent indicates external fragmentation. If we defragment the table (you will discover the statements to use to defragment a table in the next couple of sections) and run DBCC SHOWCONTIG again, we get the following result:

```
DBCC SHOWCONTIG scanning 'Orders' table...
Table: 'Orders' (21575115); index ID: 1, database ID: 9
TABLE level scan performed.
- Pages Scanned................................: 20
- Extents Scanned..............................: 3
- Extent Switches..............................: 2
- Avg. Pages per Extent........................: 6.7
- Scan Density [Best Count:Actual Count].......: 100.00%
[3:3]
- Logical Scan Fragmentation ..................: 0.00%
- Extent Scan Fragmentation ...................: 0.00%
- Avg. Bytes Free per Page.....................: 146.5
- Avg. Page Density (full).....................: 98.19%
```

As you can see, scan density is now 100 percent and scan fragmentation is 0. Data pages and extents are now contiguous.

Inserts

Inserts may cause leaf level fragmentation. A clustered index is particularly sensitive, where the leaf level contains the data pages. Figure 5.17 represents that kind of situation.

FIGURE 5.17 Page split

In this example, you want to insert the Barstow record between Barquisimeto and Bergamo. Unfortunately, the page is full and there is no free space for the new record. The page is split in two; a new page is allocated where there is enough space, the first half of the records remains in the page, and the second half goes to the new page. Enough space is now available for the insert. In this example, the insert takes place in the first page but could occur in the second, depending on the insert value.

The problem that arises here is the fact that the new page will be allocated wherever there is space in the file, and that could be far away from the original page. If inserts occur randomly, you'll end up with a lot of external fragmentation, as well as internal fragmentation since the page will be half full.

Updates

Update management has always been a subject of long discussions between RDBMS nerds. There are many types of physical update strategies, the two major ones being in-place and out-of-place updates. SQL Server always tries to do in-place updates to avoid moving the record around and updating the indexes. But in the case of size increase, it may not be possible to leave the record in the same page. In that case, to minimize the impact of out-of-place updates, SQL Server uses forwarding pointers.

FIGURE 5.18   Use of a forwarding pointer

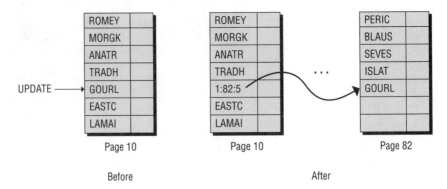

Figure 5.18 illustrates what happens when a row is updated and needs to be moved due to a size increase. SQL Server leaves the new address of the record at its old address. This avoids the need to update the indexes referencing the record. In this example, the address of the GOURL record is always 1:10:5, since it was in fifth position of the tenth page of the first file. When SQL Server arrives at this address, it knows it must go to 1:82:5.

This feature avoids updates that would have a negative impact on performance. With one, two, or dozens of indexes on the previous table, the row locator is stable. The only problem is created when SQL Server scans the table because a lot of external fragmentation occurs. For a transactional system in which update performance is really the top priority, this feature guarantees homogeneous performance.

Deletes

While inserts may have a negative impact on external and internal fragmentation, and updates may have a negative impact on external fragmentation, deletes have a negative impact on internal fragmentation, creating "holes" in data pages. To manage deletes, SQL Server 2000 uses a "phantom" strategy. It does not physically delete the data from pages, but marks the space for deletion.

If a new insert or update reclaims space, the mark-for-deletion space can be reused. Otherwise, every half-hour, a background cleansing process reclaims deleted space.

Figure 5.15 shows a situation in which records have been deleted and internal fragmentation is occurring. If this situation is not a problem on a short-term basis, it overuses space and can dramatically impact I/O performances on a long-term basis. In Figure 5.15, a record has been deleted between Barquisimento and Bruxelles. But this space may have been used by a "short" record, and may not be used by new records. The Avg. Bytes Free per page and Avg. Page Density values of the DBCC SHOWCONTIG indicate internal fragmentation. Keep in mind that pages are as-is in memory. So, if they are 50 percent free, you double your memory need. The more compact the pages, the better.

You should monitor the internal and external fragmentation very closely to be sure that every page is filled and correctly linked.

What to Do Now

You now understand how inserts, deletes, and updates lead to data fragmentation. Luckily, SQL Server proposes three ways to defragment data files:

- DBCC INDEXDEFRAG

- DBCC DBREINDEX

- CREATE INDEX WITH DROP_EXISTING

DBCC INDEXDEFRAG defragments the leaf level of all types of indexes, and deals with internal and external fragmentation. It guarantees that pages are linked in the physical order (see the ideal situation in Figure 5.16) and compacted. Nevertheless, it does not allocate new pages, but simply reshuffles existing pages. So, a heavily fragmented index will not really benefit from this statement.

The syntax of this statement is:

```
DBCC INDEXDEFRAG
    ( { database_name | database_id | 0 }
        , { table_name | table_id | view_name | view_id
    }
        , { index_name | index_id }
    )    [ WITH NO_INFOMSGS ]
```

The following code defragments the PK_Orders index of the Orders table:

```
DBCC INDEXDEFRAG (Northwind, Orders, PK_Orders)
```

At the end of this statement execution, SQL gives you the number of pages it analyzes, and the number of pages it moved and removed, if necessary.

DBCC INDEXDEFRAG has one major advantage: It is an online statement, holding locks for a very short period of time because it's using small transactions instead of one big transaction like other statements (you'll learn more about locks in Chapter 10). You can then defragment an index while users are connected to the database without disturbing normal operations. Its major drawback is that it has an online operation and is not as efficient as a DBCC DBREINDEX or a CREATE INDEX WITH DROP_EXISTING.

DBCC DBREINDEX can be used to rebuild and then defragment any or all indexes of a table, and possibly change the index fill factor. The following shows you its syntax:

```
DBCC DBREINDEX
    ([ 'database.owner.table_name'
      [ , index_name
        [ , fillfactor ]
      ]
    ]
    )[ WITH NO_INFOMSGS ]
```

The following statement rebuilds the PK_Orders index of the Orders table:

```
DBCC DBREINDEX ('Northwind..Orders', PK_Orders)
```

The following statement rebuilds all the indexes of the Orders table:

```
DBCC DBREINDEX (Orders, '')
```

Note that the database name is not given in the previous statement, which means the database on which the statement is executed is the database the connection is using.

The WITH DROP_EXISTING clause of the CREATE INDEX statement allows an index to be dropped and recreated in the same statement. This has a major advantage if you are running this statement on a clustered index, because the nonclustered index may not be rebuilt. Imagine you just ran a CREATE INDEX WITH DROP_EXISTING without modifying the key. As the clustered key is the row locator, if it does not change, the nonclustered index remains unchanged, too. If you had to run DROP then CREATE INDEX to recreate the index, the nonclustered indexes would have been rebuilt during the clustered index destruction (the row locator is changed) and rebuilt again during the clustered index creation.

The following statement recreates the OrderDate index of the Orders table:

```
CREATE INDEX OrderDate
   ON Orders(OrderDate)
   WITH DROP_EXISTING
```

You can modify your index structure during a DROP_EXISTING operation, with the exception of transforming a clustered index to a nonclustered index, which is impossible.

You can schedule the defragmentation of your indexes on a regular basis, either by programming a DBCC DBREINDEX or DBCC INDEXDEFRAG operation, or by using the Database Maintenance Plan Wizard. Listing 5.1 creates a stored procedure that you can execute to reindex all the tables of a database.

Listing 5.1: Reindexing All Tables

Run this script in the master database to be able to run the procedure from any databases.

```
CREATE PROCEDURE sp_reindex_all_tables
AS
DECLARE reindex_cursor CURSOR
    FOR
    SELECT name FROM sysobjects WHERE type = 'U'
OPEN reindex_cursor
DECLARE @tablename sysname
FETCH NEXT FROM reindex_cursor INTO @tablename
WHILE (@@FETCH_STATUS <> -1)
BEGIN
    EXECUTE ('DBCC DBREINDEX (''' + @tablename + ''',
'''')')
    FETCH NEXT FROM reindex_cursor INTO @tablename
END
DEALLOCATE reindex_cursor
```

Summary

In this chapter, you learned how indexes were used by SQL Server, as well as how to create and maintain them to reach expected performance. This chapter particularly focused on:

- What indexes are and how they are structured

- How data is accessed with and without indexes

- What statistics are and how SQL Server chooses what index to use

- How to create and maintain indexes and statistics

Key Terms

Before you take the exam, be certain you are familiar with the following terms:

clustered	leaf level
composite index	nonclustered
density	non-leaf level
distribution statistics	root
external fragmentation	selectivity
heap	table scan
intermediate level	unique index
internal fragmentation	

Exam Essentials

Know the syntax for *CREATE INDEX* statements. Know all the possible parameters of these statements, and especially focus on the different index types and the fill factor.

Understand index impact on performances. Index plays a major role in query performance. A thorough understanding of this role is mandatory.

Know and understand the role of statistics.   Distribution statistics are the only scientific way SQL Server has to guess the right indexes to use for a query. You should understand the functioning of statistics.

Know how to defragment an index.   Fragmentation can have a negative effect on data access. You should understand the two fragmentation types and how to limit them.

Review Questions

1. You are a database developer for Northwind Traders. One of your users complains that the following query is very time consuming:

   `SELECT * FROM Customers WHERE Country = 'Finland'`

   The Customers table structure and the execution plan are shown in the following graphics.

What can you do to improve the execution of the query without modifying the table structure and existing indexes, but knowing that the primary key is clustered?

A. Add a clustered index on the Country column.

B. Add a nonclustered index on the Country column.

C. The clustered index is already used, so the table may be fragmented. You should defragment it.

D. Create a table containing the customers from Finland, and create a partitioned view above.

2. You need to optimize the execution of the following queries:

```
SELECT * FROM Customers
    WHERE City LIKE 'R%' AND CompanyName like 'V%'
SELECT * FROM Customers
    WHERE CompanyName LIKE 'A%'
```

The table structure is shown in the following graphic. The primary key is nonclustered.

Customers		
Column Name	Condensed Type	Nullable
🔑 CustomerID	nchar(5)	NOT NULL
CompanyName	nvarchar(40)	NOT NULL
ContactName	nvarchar(30)	NULL
ContactTitle	nvarchar(30)	NULL
Address	nvarchar(60)	NULL
City	nvarchar(15)	NULL
Region	nvarchar(15)	NULL
PostalCode	nvarchar(10)	NULL
Country	nvarchar(15)	NULL
Phone	nvarchar(24)	NULL
Fax	nvarchar(24)	NULL

What index or indexes would you create to optimize speed while minimizing space consumption?

A. One clustered index on (City, CompanyName)

B. One clustered index on CompanyName and one nonclustered on City

C. One nonclustered index on CompanyName and one clustered on City

D. One clustered index on (CompanyName, City)

3. You are developer for World Wide Importers. You try to optimize data access to the Products table. These past weeks, this table's size has increased by 300 percent due to the merge with a new company. You decide to create a unique clustered index on the ProductID column to increase seeks on productID and to ensure the uniqueness of the IDs. While creating the index, you receive the following error message:

```
CREATE UNIQUE INDEX terminated because a duplicate key was
found for index ID 1
```

What can you do to create the index?

A. Run the CREATE INDEX statement with the IGNORE_DUP_ROW option.

B. Run the CREATE INDEX statement with the IGNORE_DUP_KEY option.

C. Delete duplicate keys and run the CREATE INDEX statement again.

D. Create a UNIQUE constraint with the WITH NOCHECK option.

4. Your customers complain about a performance decrease when querying the invoice table. This performance decrease began approximately 2 weeks ago, without any logical explanation concerning the size increase of the database. In fact, the table has increased 3 percent, but the performance decreased by 50 percent.

You run `DBCC SHOWCONTIG` on the Invoice table and obtain the following result:

```
DBCC SHOWCONTIG scanning 'Invoices' table...
Table: 'Invoices' (325576198); index ID: 1, database ID: 13
TABLE level scan performed.
- Pages Scanned.............................: 912
- Extents Scanned...........................: 205
- Extent Switches...........................: 314
- Avg. Pages per Extent.....................: 4.4
- Scan Density [Best Count:Actual Count].....: 56.00% [115:205]
- Logical Scan Fragmentation ...............: 34.00%
- Extent Scan Fragmentation ................: 25.00%
- Avg. Bytes Free per Page..................: 1673.2
- Avg. Page Density (full)..................: 79.57%
```

You think that fragmentation may be the issue. What statement can you run to defragment the table?

A. DBCC DEFRAG('Invoices')

B. DBCC DBREINDEX ('Invoices', '')

C. DBCC INDEXDEFRAG('Invoices')

D. DBCC REINDEX('Invoices')

5. You are a database developer for a regional bank. You have just received a new server for customer accounts management. The main table of the accounts management database is the Movements table that records every account movement, debit, and credit. You need to optimize data access to this table. You analyzed table usage and discover that 70 percent of the time the table is written and 30 percent of the time it is read. Reads are always related to a specific account, meaning a banking officer needs to check all the movements of specific accounts. The number of records increases approximately 1 percent every day. What type of index or indexes seems to be the more convenient for this table?

A. A nonclustered index on the Account Number

B. A clustered index on the Account Number with a fill factor around 90 percent

C. A clustered index on the Movement Number and a nonclustered index on the Account Number

    D. A clustered index on the Account Number with a fill factor of 50 percent

6. Your company has just merged with another one. As part of your job as the SQL Server developer, you have been asked to consolidate the customers' information. Fortunately, both companies share the same type of information. The CustomerID for each customer is generated by a hashing function that uses the customer name and zip code as parameters to calculate a unique ID. You create a database with both tables, CustomersA from your company and CustomersB from the other company. You calculate the unique CustomerID for each table. You now have two tables each containing hundreds of thousands of rows uniquely identified by the hashed CustomerID. You will perform the insert process from CustomersB into CustomersA with the following statement:

```
INSERT CustomersA SELECT * FROM CustomersB
```

How could you guarantee that no duplicates will appear in CustomersA? (Choose the best answer.)

    A. Create a UNIQUE constraint on CustomersA(CustomerID) before the insert.

    B. Enforce a PRIMARY KEY constraint on CustomersA(CustomerID).

    C. Create a UNIQUE index on CustomersA(CustomerID) with the IGNORE_DUP_KEY option.

    D. Create an INSERT trigger on CustomersA to check whether each inserted row is unique and rejects duplicates.

7. You created the Order Details table with the following script:

```
CREATE TABLE [Order Details] (
    OrderID int NOT NULL,
    ProductID int NOT NULL ,
    UnitPrice money NOT NULL
        CONSTRAINT DF_Order_Details_UnitPrice DEFAULT (0),
    Quantity smallint NOT NULL
        CONSTRAINT DF_Order_Details_Quantity DEFAULT (1),
```

```
Discount smallint NOT NULL
   CONSTRAINT DF_Order_Details_Discount DEFAULT (0),
Total as (UnitPrice*Quantity*(1-Discount/100)),
CONSTRAINT PK_Order_Details
PRIMARY KEY CLUSTERED (OrderID, ProductID)
)
```

You create an index on the Total column to perform a fast seek on the Total column. Once created, you realize that this index is never used by queries. What are the possible causes of this behavior? (Choose two.)

A. The Total column is non-deterministic.

B. The Total column is not precise.

C. The ANSI_NULLS option was not set to ON during table creation.

D. The ARITHABORT option was not set to ON during index creation.

8. You try to run the following statement on the Customers table:

```
CREATE CLUSTERED INDEX cidx ON Customers(CustomerID)
```

And obtain the following error:

```
Cannot create more than one clustered index
```

What is the most possible cause of this error?

A. The primary key constraint already created a clustered index.

B. You have reached the maximum of 250 indexes.

C. The foreign key constraint already created a clustered index.

D. There is already a clustered index on the CustomerID column. You are not allowed to create two indexes on the same column.

9. You are developer for Northwind Traders. You created the Suppliers table illustrated in the following graphic.

Suppliers		
Column Name	**Condensed Type**	**Nullable**
SupplierID	int	NOT NULL
CompanyName	nvarchar(40)	NOT NULL
ContactName	nvarchar(30)	NULL
ContactTitle	nvarchar(30)	NULL
Address	nvarchar(60)	NULL
City	nvarchar(15)	NULL
Region	nvarchar(15)	NULL
PostalCode	nvarchar(10)	NULL
Country	nvarchar(15)	NULL
Phone	nvarchar(24)	NULL
Fax	nvarchar(24)	NULL
HomePage	ntext	NULL

Which statement will create a nonclustered composite index on the CompanyName and City columns?

A. `CREATE INDEX ON Suppliers(CompanyName, City)`

B. `CREATE COMPOSITE INDEX idxCompCity ON Suppliers(CompanyName, City)`

C. `CREATE INDEX idxCompCity ON Suppliers.CompanyName, Suppliers.City`

D. `CREATE INDEX idxCompCity ON Suppliers(CompanyName, City)`

10. The users of the ordering system for World Wide Importers complain about the response time when they query customers' information. The database name is Orders, and the table they are querying is named Customers. You test some of their queries. On one of them, the execution plan indicates outdated statistics on an index. You want to ensure that this situation won't occur anymore. Which statements do you execute to make sure statistics will be updated automatically in the future? (Choose two.)

A. `UPDATE STATISTICS 'Customers'`

B. `sp_autostats 'Customers', 'ON'`

C. `sp_dboption 'Orders', 'auto create statistics', ON`

    D. `ALTER DATABASE Orders SET AUTO_CREATE_STATISTICS ON`

11. Before launching the new Products database into production, you want to ensure that all server and database options are correctly set. Your first concern is about distribution statistics. Which of the following can you run to check that the automatic statistics update is set? (Choose two.)

    A. `sp_dboption 'Products', 'auto update statistics'`

    B. `sp_dbproperty 'Products', 'AutoUpdateStatistics')`

    C. `sp_configure 'Products', 'auto update statistics'`

    D. `SELECT DATABASEPROPERTYEX('Products', 'IsAutoUpdateStatistics')`

12. You are a database developer for Northwind Traders. You led the team that developed the new shipping system. In that database, you have Orders and Shippers tables as illustrated in the following graphic:

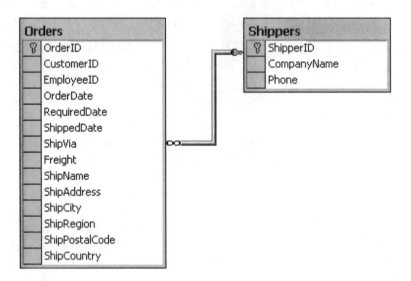

For the past couple of days, users have complained about response time when they query orders shipped by some suppliers. The size of the Orders table has been multiplied by 10 in the past couple of weeks. You think that some index statistics may be outdated or some index may be missing. What can you run to quickly check the last update date of all indexes and statistics on the Orders table?

A. sp_autostats 'Orders'

B. sp_helpstats 'Orders'

C. sp_statistics 'Orders'

D. sp_helpindex 'Orders'

13. You are developer for a regional bank. You have put in production a new customer relationship management system a couple of weeks ago. Some customers complain about the response time when they query some customer accounts. You think it may be a problem of missing indexes. You want to know quickly which indexes are missing. What can you run to get this information?

A. sp_helpindex 'Accounts'

B. sp_statistics 'Accounts'

C. sp_helpstats 'Accounts'

D. sp_indexes 'Accounts'

14. You created a new employee management system for a regional bank. The Employee table and indexes script is the following:

```
CREATE TABLE dbo.employee (
    emp_id int NOT NULL ,
    fname varchar (20) NOT NULL ,
    minit char (1) NULL ,
    lname varchar (30) NOT NULL ,
    job_id smallint NOT NULL
      CONSTRAINT DF_employee_job_id DEFAULT (1),
    job_lvl tinyint NULL
      CONSTRAINT DF_employee_job_lv DEFAULT (10),
    pub_id char (4) NOT NULL
```

```
        CONSTRAINT DF_employee_pub_id DEFAULT ('9952'),
   hire_date datetime NOT NULL
        CONSTRAINT DF_employee_hire_date DEFAULT (get-
date()),
     CONSTRAINT PK_emp_id
       PRIMARY KEY (emp_id)

)


CREATE INDEX idxfname ON Employee(fname)
```

Almost every time you run a query with or without a WHERE condition, you obtain the execution plan shown in the following graphic:

What is the most possible cause of these full table scans?

A. The index statistics are outdated.

B. There are not enough indexes to service the queries.

C. You need to force the index in queries.

D. The indexes are outdated.

15. You are a developer for a winery. You developed a new production management system. This application has been live for a couple of weeks now, and you want to ensure that everything is running smoothly. You query different system tables and discover in Sysindexes an object called _WA_Sys_Region_7B905C75. You are sure you have not created this object. What is it and who created it?

    A. It is an index automatically created by the system on the Region column.

B. It is a distribution statistics zone automatically created by the system on the Region column.

C. It is a temporary table automatically created by the system to perform an ordering operation on the Region column.

D. It is a temporary index created by the system to service a query that has been made on Washington state.

Answers to Review Questions

1. B. The execution plan shows an index scan and not an index seek. Furthermore, the scan is done on the primary key, not on the Country column. Creating an index on the Country column will definitely enhance performance.

2. D. Even if the clustered key is quite large, this index will offer the best performance while not occupying lots of space. Option A would not be useful because CompanyName may not be used alone. Options B and C may be good solutions, but will consume more space than option D.

3. C. The IGNORE_DUP_ROW option is no longer supported in SQL Server 2000. The IGNORE_DUP_KEY option applies only when INSERT statements try to insert duplicate keys; it does not solve the problem of duplicate keys existing in the table. The WITH NOCHECK option cannot be used with UNIQUE constraints.

4. B. This is a tricky question. The DBCC INDEXDEFRAG statement can be used to defragment this table, but you should indicate the database and the index name in the statement. Options A and D do not exist.

5. B. A clustered index on the Account Number will help reads, since all the records concerning a specific Account Number are close to each other. The fill factor of 90 percent will allow inserts during the week (5 percent size increase in five days), while limiting page splits.

6. C. The IGNORE_DUP_KEY option forbids duplicates on the column while leaving unique values to be inserted. It removes the atomicity of the INSERT statement, but allows fast inserts.

7. C and D. The Total column is deterministic and precise. It is only made of precise number values (money and value). If the Total column would not have been deterministic or precise, the index would not have been created. Both options presented should be set to allow index usage.

8. A. There can be only one clustered index per table. When creating a primary key, you can ask for a clustered index. That's probably why you cannot create this clustered index.

9. D. In option A, the index name is missing. In option B, COMPOSITE is not a keyword. Option C is syntactically incorrect.

10. B and D. Option A will update statistics immediately but does not guarantee that statistics will be up-to-date in the future. Option C would have been good, but there is a syntax error, because the ON keyword should have been placed between quotes. So, the only way to make sure statistics will be automatically updated is to set the AUTO_CREATE_ STATISTICS option on the database and on each index of the table.

11. A and D. The stored procedure in option B does not exist. The procedure in option C exists, but concerns only server-wide options. The auto update option is a database option.

12. A. Sp_autostats is the only stored procedure that gives you the last update date for every index and that may set the automatic update feature on or off.

13. C. Sp_helpindex and sp_indexes give you only the list of existing indexes. Sp_statistics gives you the list of existing statistics; but with the result set given, you cannot distinguish between indexes and distribution statistics zones. Only sp_helpstats gives you the

list of distribution statistics zones, which lets you discover the columns that have been queried without the support of indexes.

14. B. A table scan indicates that there are not enough indexes to service the query. So, more indexes should be created in accordance with the WHERE conditions.

15. B. If the auto_create_statistics option is set, SQL Server creates distribution statistics zones when no indexes are available to service the query, to know the statistical distribution of a specific column.

Chapter

6

Creating and Maintaining Database Objects

✓ **Enforce procedural business logic by using stored procedure transactions, triggers, user-defined functions, and views.**

- Specify trigger actions.
- Design and manage transactions.
- Manage control of flow.
- Filter data by using stored procedures, triggers, user-defined functions, and views.

✓ **Troubleshoot and optimize programming objects. Objects include stored procedures, transaction, triggers, user-defined functions, and views.**

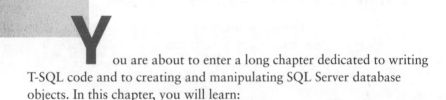

You are about to enter a long chapter dedicated to writing T-SQL code and to creating and manipulating SQL Server database objects. In this chapter, you will learn:

- How to create, use, and manage views
- How to create, use, and manage stored procedures
- How to create, use and manage user-defined functions
- How to create, use, and manage triggers

Views

Microsoft ✓ *Exam Objective*

Create and alter database objects. Objects include constraints, indexes, stored procedures, tables, triggers, user-defined functions, and views.

- Specify schema binding and encryption for stored procedures, triggers, user-defined functions, and views.

Troubleshoot failed object creation.

Alter database objects to support replication and partitioned views.

- Design a partitioning strategy.
- Design and create constraints and views.

Manage data manipulation by using views.

Enforce procedural business logic by using views.

- Filter data by using views.

Defining views can be very simple, but managing and using them can become quite complex. A lot of rules govern view creation and usage. This section focuses on view creation, modification, and usage, starting with the definition and advantages of views.

Definition and Advantages of Views

A *view* is essentially a named SELECT statement. It acts as a table, but does not contain any data. It relies on the data stored in the underlying table. Like a table, a view can be queried, and data can be inserted, deleted, and modified through a view.

FIGURE 6.1   A simple view

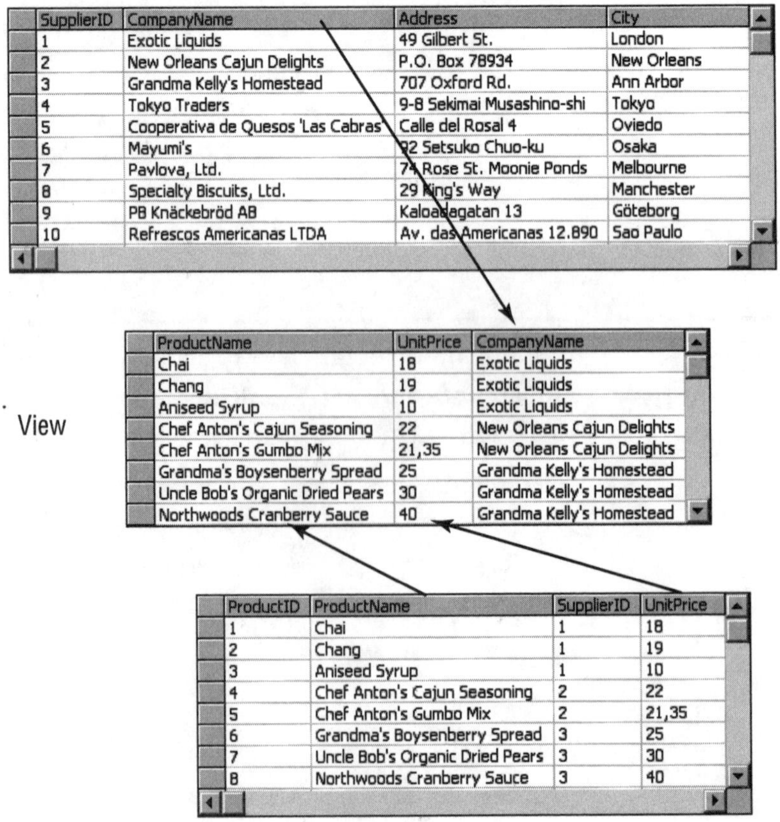

View

In Figure 6.1, the view is relying on the Suppliers and Products tables of the Northwind database. The SELECT statement used to create the view is as follows:

```
SELECT CompanyName, ProductName, UnitPrice
    FROM Suppliers INNER JOIN Products
    ON Suppliers.SupplierID = Products.SupplierID
```

As you can see, if you know how to write a SELECT statement (see Chapter 7), you know how to create a view.

Views can be used in the following situations:

Mask data complexity   A view can join many tables or perform a calculation, which makes it easy to query and access data. A normalized database is sometimes difficult to use due to the number of tables to query. Views can mask this normalization. Views can also be used to combine result sets coming from different servers. The users do not know data is coming from different servers, but this feature helps increase performance by scaling out the application. For example, a server can contain data from the U.S., another one from Europe, and a third one from Asia. A view can combine the data from these three servers.

Provide a security mechanism   Views can be designed with a WHERE clause, or with specific join and column selections to restrict the data available to users. For example, a sales table may contain the region. Different views can be created to ensure each salesperson has access only to his or her sales region. It is better to manage security at a view level (or at a stored procedure level), than at a column level.

Performance enhancer   Views are stored SELECT statements that can be dozens of lines long. Using a view avoids running the query from the client application. Furthermore, the view is already parsed, so running a view is generally faster than running the query it contains directly. Last, but not least, it isolates the application from the data, providing the possibility of changing the query if needed, without modifying the application.

Creating and Altering Views

Troubleshoot and optimize programming objects. Objects include stored procedures, transaction, triggers, user-defined functions, and views.

Creating a view is a straightforward process if you know how to write a SELECT statement. The full syntax is as follows:

```
CREATE VIEW [<db_name>.][<owner>.]view_name [(column[
    ,...n ])]
    [ WITH {ENCRYPTION|SCHEMABINDING|VIEW_METADATA}[
    ,...n]]
    AS
    select_statement
    [ WITH CHECK OPTION ]
```

The various sections are described below:

The *SELECT* Statement

As you can see, a view contains a SELECT statement and a few parameters, if needed. The SELECT statement must follow some restrictions; the SELECT statement cannot:

- Contain ORDER BY clause, unless there is a TOP clause in the select list
- Contain COMPUTE or COMPUTE BY clauses
- Contain the INTO keyword
- Reference a temporary table or a table variable

The following lines of code create the view illustrated in Figure 6.1:

```
CREATE VIEW vwProducts
AS
SELECT ProductName, UnitPrice, CompanyName
FROM Suppliers
    INNER JOIN Products
    ON Suppliers.SupplierID = Products.SupplierID
```

If you try to sort the result set by product name by running the following script:

```
CREATE VIEW vwProducts
AS
SELECT ProductName, UnitPrice, CompanyName
FROM Suppliers
    INNER JOIN Products
    ON Suppliers.SupplierID = Products.SupplierID
ORDER BY ProductName
```

You obtain error 1033, The ORDER BY clause is invalid in views, inline functions, derived tables, and subqueries, unless TOP is also specified. You have to add the TOP clause to make this view creatable:

```
CREATE VIEW vwProducts
AS
SELECT TOP 100 PERCENT CompanyName, ProductName, UnitPrice
FROM Suppliers
    INNER JOIN Products
    ON Suppliers.SupplierID = Products.SupplierID
ORDER BY ProductName
```

The code for the view is stored in the Syscomments system table. You can query this table directly, but it is easier to use the sp_helptext stored procedure. If you run the following:

```
sp_helptext vwproducts
```

The result produced is:

```
Text
------------------------------------------------------------
CREATE VIEW vwProducts
AS
SELECT TOP 100 PERCENT CompanyName, ProductName, UnitPrice
FROM Suppliers
    INNER JOIN Products
    ON Suppliers.SupplierID = Products.SupplierID
ORDER BY ProductName
```

This result is the same code that was used to create the view.

The *ENCRYPTION* Option

If you develop an application that you are going to sell and install at your customers' sites, you may want to protect your intellectual property. All objects containing code, such as views, can be encrypted. In the previous examples, by using the sp_helptext or by querying the Syscomments system table, you could discover the text of the code used to create the view. If you want to protect your code, you can encrypt it with the ENCRYPTION option. The following example creates the view and encrypts it:

```
CREATE VIEW vwProducts
WITH ENCRYPTION
AS
SELECT CompanyName, ProductName, UnitPrice
FROM Suppliers
    INNER JOIN Products
    ON Suppliers.SupplierID = Products.SupplierID
```

When you query its text with the sp_helptext stored procedure, SQL Server's answer is: The object comments have been encrypted. In the same way, if you try to generate the script of an encrypted view, either with SQL Query Analyzer or with SQL Enterprise Manager, SQL Server will answer that the view code cannot be generated: /****** Encrypted object is not transferable, and script can not be generated. ******/.

The *SCHEMABINDING* Option

The SCHEMABINDING option is useful to protect your view definition against any structure modifications of the underlying table. Once a view is created with the SCHEMABINDING option, the underlying tables cannot be dropped and cannot be altered if it affects the view definition. For example, a column could be added to the table, but a column used in the view cannot be dropped. Consider the following view:

```
CREATE VIEW vwProducts
WITH SCHEMABINDING
AS
SELECT CompanyName, ProductName, UnitPrice
FROM dbo.Suppliers
```

```
INNER JOIN dbo.Products
ON Suppliers.SupplierID = Products.SupplierID
```

The Suppliers and Products tables cannot be dropped or altered freely. If you try to remove a column by running the following:

```
ALTER TABLE Products DROP COLUMN UnitPrice
```

The result is the error 5074, `The object 'vwProducts' is dependent on column 'UnitPrice'`.

In the CREATE VIEW statement, two-part names are used (owner.object). This is mandatory with the SCHEMABINDING option.

If you use the SCHEMABINDING option, you have to define every column in the select list; you cannot use the * symbol. If you try, you obtain error 1054, `Syntax '*' is not allowed in schema-bound objects`.

The *VIEW_METADATA* Option

The VIEW_METADATA option is useful when you use a view through DBLIB (DB-Library), OLE DB, or ODBC. In the normal case, each time a client application queries a view or a table through any of these interfaces, it needs first to retrieve *metadata* about this view or table. Metadata is information about the view's properties, such as a column name or type. To be able to manipulate or display the retrieved information correctly, the client application needs to know as precisely as possible the structure of the object it will be using.

When you query a view created with the default options, SQL Server queries the tables constituting the view to retrieve the metadata from the base tables. With the VIEW_METADATA option, SQL Server does not query the table metadata, but instead sends the view metadata back to the client. The main benefit for the client is the ability to create an updateable client-side cursor, based on the view. Generally, client-side cursors based on views are not updateable. The VIEW_METADATA option opens new possibilities for client development.

You can find more information on OLE DB, ODBC, DB-Library, and client-side cursors in the SQL Server Books OnLine.

The *With Check Option* Option

This last option is probably the most useful. To understand it, let's look at a quick example. Suppose you have a Customers table containing a State column. You create a view that selects only customers from California with:

```
CREATE VIEW CustomersCAView
AS
SELECT * FROM Customers WHERE state='CA'
```

Using this view, if you need to update one of the California customers, you can run the following statement:

```
UPDATE CustomersCAView SET state='OR' WHERE
    CustomerID='LETSS'
```

The update occurs without any problem, and when you query the view again, the LETSS customer is not present anymore. This seems normal, since you modified the state for a customer. This can become really annoying, however, for users that perform data access through this view.

By default, you can update any record through a view, and make it disappear, because the WHERE condition applied to the view does not select the data anymore. You can insert data in the table through the view that does not comply with the view WHERE condition. In other words, the view restricts data access but not data updates and inserts! To avoid this situation, you can use the WITH CHECK OPTION option:

```
CREATE VIEW CustomersCAView
AS
SELECT * FROM Customers WHERE state='CA'
WITH CHECK OPTION
```

This option guarantees that the data updated or inserted through the view complies with the WHERE condition.

If you run the previous update, and if the view has been created with the WITH CHECK OPTION option, you obtain error 550, The attempted insert or update failed because the target view either specifies WITH CHECK OPTION or spans a view that specifies WITH CHECK OPTION and one or more rows resulting from the operation did not qualify under the CHECK OPTION constraint.

This option guarantees users cannot eject rows out of the view. It should be used whenever you intend to update or insert data through views.

Using Views

When the time comes to use views, two types of operations are possible: data retrieving and data updating. A view is a pseudo table, so wherever you can use a table, you can also use a view. While this statement is true with SELECT operations, it may be false with INSERT, UPDATE, or DELETE operations, depending on the view. Let's have a look at using views in these two types of situations.

Retrieving Data

Retrieving data is probably the simplest way to use a view. In a SELECT statement, views are like tables. As we've seen at the beginning of this section, views can be useful in restricting or facilitating data access. With views, users have access to the data through a dedicated path.

A Trainer's Point of View

One of the most frequent quandaries students have when learning how to program SQL Server concerns view performance. This is a trivial quandary since everybody sees the two SELECT statements. If you create the following view:

```
CREATE VIEW CustomersCA
    AS
    SELECT * FROM Customers WHERE State='CA'
```

And run the following statement:

```
SELECT * FROM CustomersCA WHERE City = 'San Francisco'
```

People assume that SQL Server runs the "real" statement as follows:

```
SELECT * FROM (SELECT * FROM Customers WHERE State='CA')
    WHERE City = 'San Francisco'
```

They also assume that SQL Server first selects California customers and then filters the result to return only those in San Francisco. In fact, SQL really runs the following statement:

```
SELECT * FROM Customers WHERE State='CA' AND City = 'San
    Francisco'
```

This is an important concept as it means that if indexes exist they will be used accordingly, and that the view is not executing an "internal" SELECT statement (defined in the view) whose result set will be used by the "external" SELECT statement (run by the user). A view does not slow performance, but it is not a stored procedure and should not be directly seen as a performance enhancer. Unlike stored procedures, views are not pre-compiled, as you will discover in the "Stored Procedures" section later in this chapter.

A view can be used in a SELECT statement wherever a table can be used. The rule is as simple as that. It is not so simple, however, when you need to update data.

Updating Data

By default, a view based on one or many tables is updateable. That means you can update, delete, or insert data in the underlying table(s) through the view, as you would do directly to the table. Nevertheless, some restrictions apply:

- If the view is based on two or more tables, the UPDATE, INSERT, and DELETE statements cannot affect more than one table. In other words, if the view is based on more than one table, you cannot run a DELETE statement, and all the columns referenced in the INSERT and UPDATE statements should belong to the same underlying table. If you try to execute a query that affects more than one table, you fire error 4405, View or function 'viewname' is not updatable because the modification affects multiple base tables.

- You cannot update, insert, or delete data in a view created with the DISTINCT clause. If you try, you'll fire error 4404, View or function 'viewname' is not updatable because the definition contains the DISTINCT clause.

- You cannot update, insert, or delete data in a view using grouping functions. If you try, you obtain error 4403, `View or function 'viewname' is not updatable because it contains aggregates.`

- You cannot update, insert, or delete data in a view if it contains calculated columns. If you try, you'll fire error 4406, `Update or insert of view or function 'viewname' failed because it contains a derived or constant field.`

- Your insert, update, or delete operation may fail because of column or table constraint or of column properties. For example, if a table contains a non-NULL column, which has no default value, and if it is not used in a view, you won't be able to insert a new row in this table through the view, since you won't be able to define a value for this column.

All of these rules have existed for years (they were already there in SQL Server 4.2 on OS/2). In SQL Server 2000, all of these restrictions can be avoided with the INSTEAD OF triggers. We will come back to INSTEAD OF triggers in the "Triggers" section later in this chapter.

Indexed Views

One of the brand-new features in SQL Server 2000 is the ability to index views, and, in doing so, materialize views.

WARNING   Indexed views are only available in SQL Server 2000 Enterprise Edition and in SQL Server 2000 Developer Edition.

Normally, view is usually just a query—a kind of pseudo table—in that it does not store data, it accesses the data stored in the base tables. When you index a view, the view result set is stored in the database, and updated dynamically. The main advantage of *indexed views* lies in one word: performance. Here are a few examples that illustrate the performance gains that can occur with indexed views:

- If the view you are querying is grouping data from a table or calculating averages and sums, base data is accessed and thousands or even millions of records are aggregated. If you index this view and then access it, the aggregates will have already been calculated and you may retrieve only a few hundred rows.

- When you query a view that is using multiple tables and performing complex and numerous joins, the system will need to join the different tables. This query time can be very long. If you index this view, all the joins will have already been resolved and you can access the data directly. This view becomes a kind of super-index that spans across multiple tables.

From these two examples, you can see that indexed views are in fact a decision support feature, designed to enhance SELECT query performance.

Indexed views have been designed to offer SQL Server developers the same features Oracle has offered with its *materialized views*. It was with materialized views that Oracle obtained the top TPC-D benchmarks in the world. TPC-D is an industry benchmark for data warehousing databases. Microsoft also obtained a benchmark using indexed views. Without indexed views, SQL Server queries would have needed to access the base data, while Oracle was using its materialized views to avoid accessing base data. After a complaint from Microsoft, the Transaction Processing Performance Council (www.tpc.org) decided to remove the TPC-D benchmark and introduced two specific benchmarks for decision support systems: TCP-H and TPC-R. You can find more information on TPC benchmark on the TPC Web site at www.tpc.org.

An indexed view stores the view result set in the database. The view can be viewed as a super index, but indexed views are generally more complex than indexes. When data is updated in the base table, SQL Server needs to update the data in the indexed view as well, and this update could negatively impact performance. Always consider indexed views only when SELECT performance is much more important when compared to updates, deletes and inserts performance.

The first index created on a view should be a clustered index. View data will then be sorted on the clustered key and made unique by the addition of an internal counter (see the "Clustered Index" section in the previous chapter), accelerating data retrieval. Furthermore, the following conditions must apply:

- The ANSI_NULLS, QUOTED_IDENTIFIERS, ANSI_PADDING, ANSI_WARN-INGS, ARITHABORT, and CONCAT_NULL_YIELDS_NULL options should be set ON during the view creation.

- The NUMERIC_ROUNDABOUT option should be set OFF during the view creation.

- The ANSI_NULLS option needs to be set to ON during the base table creation.

- The view references only tables and not other views.

- All the referenced tables should belong to the same owner and be in the same database.

- The view must be created with the SCHEMABINDING option.

- UNION, TOP, ORDER BY, COUNT(*), MAX, MIN, STDEV, STDEVP, VAR, VARP, CONTAINS, FREETEXT, COMPUTE, COMPUTE BY, HAVING, CUBE, and ROLLUP keywords are not authorized.

- The view cannot contain text, ntext, or image columns.

- Functions used in the view must be deterministic (see the "Index on Computed Columns" section in the previous chapter).

- All table and function names must be referenced using two-part names: *owner.name*.

Aside from these items, the index creation is exactly identical to a normal view created on a table. Since the first index is a clustered index, all data columns will be stored in data pages (leaf level of the clustered index) and only index keys will be stored in the non-leaf levels.

COUNT(*) is not allowed in an indexed view. But you can count the number of rows with the new COUNT_BIG function that is allowed.

After the clustered index is created, you can create nonclustered indexes as well. The clustered index is needed to store the view data. Nonclustered indexes will be used as any other nonclustered index—to enhance data access. Once you've indexed a view, the "virtual" side of the view becomes real: the view contains data, even if this data is extracted from base table.

To learn more about clustered and nonclustered indexes, refer to the previous chapter, dedicated to indexes.

Partitioned Views

One of the most exciting additions to SQL Server 2000 is the *partitioned view* feature, which opens the gate to parallel processing among a number of servers in a server farm. This means that data can be spread out on multiple servers and merged on-the-fly, if needed, by a query. The idea behind partitioned views is that the resources of one server are intrinsically limited, but you can add as many servers as you need to increase the scalability of your application. You can spread data on your various servers, and, once you reach a performance limit, add a new server to increase the performance by distributing the workload.

Let's use an example to illustrate partitioned data. Suppose the number of rows in your Customers table is increasing fast. You want to split this table into three smaller tables: customers from Northern America (USA and Canada), customers from Europe (UK, France, and Germany), and customers from Asia (Japan, Thailand, and China). You place each of these tables on a different server, as in Figure 6.2, and create on each server a Customers partitioned view to access all customers' information.

FIGURE 6.2   A partitioned view

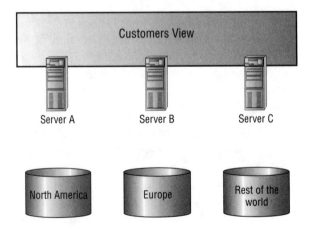

When a user queries the Customers view, the SQL Server that executes the view knows where to find the data because it is a partitioned view. It then sends the query to the necessary servers and merges the result sets. Let's further develop the example illustrated in Figure 6.2. The Customers view is created from the three tables with the following script:

```
CREATE VIEW Customers
AS
SELECT * FROM ServerA.MyCompany.dbo.CustomersAmerica
UNION ALL
SELECT * FROM ServerB.MyCompany.dbo.CustomersEurope
UNION ALL
SELECT * FROM ServerC.MyCompany.dbo.CustomersAsia
```

One important fact to note about partitioned views is that the table is partitioned horizontally into non-overlapping parts. In the above example, the table CustomersAmerica contains only customers from America, but no customers from Europe or elsewhere. A view is considered partitioned if the data from the different tables it unions does not overlap!

To ensure that the data does not overlap and that SQL Server can guarantee it is not overlapping, the individual tables need to contain CHECK constraints. One or more columns from the original table are used to partition the data over the different servers. These columns are called *partitioning columns*. A partitioning column needs to follow some strict rules:

- The column value should be validated by a CHECK constraint using only the following operators: BETWEEN, AND, OR, <, <=, >, >=, and =. Note <> and ! are not allowed in a CHECK constraint if the column has to be a partitioning column.

- The column is NOT NULL.

- The column is part of the table primary key.

- The column is not a calculated column.

- Only one CHECK constraint exists on the column.

Furthermore, the tables need to follow some rules, too:

- The table cannot have indexes on computed columns.

- The table primary keys should be defined on the same columns.

- The SET ANSI_PADDING of all tables constituting the view should be the same.

The following scripts create the partitioning columns of the different Customers tables of our example. Each should be run on a separate server:

```
CREATE TABLE CustomersAmerica(
    CustomerID nchar(5) NOT NULL,
    CompanyName nvarchar(50) NOT NULL,
    ContactName nvarchar(30) NULL,
    ContactTitle nvarchar(30) NULL,
    Address nvarchar(60) NULL,
    City nvarchar(30) NULL,
    Region nvarchar(10) NULL,
    PostalCode nvarchar(15) NULL,
    Country nvarchar(50) NOT NULL
        CHECK (Country IN('USA', 'Canada')),
    Phone nvarchar(24) NULL,
    Fax nvarchar(24) NULL,
    CONSTRAINT PK_Customer_America
        PRIMARY KEY (CustomerID, Country)
)

CREATE TABLE CustomersEurope(
    CustomerID nchar(5) NOT NULL,
    CompanyName nvarchar(50) NOT NULL,
    ContactName nvarchar(30) NULL,
    ContactTitle nvarchar(30) NULL,
    Address nvarchar(60) NULL,
    City nvarchar(30) NULL,
    Region nvarchar(10) NULL,
    PostalCode nvarchar(15) NULL,
    Country nvarchar(50) NOT NULL
        CHECK (Country IN ('UK', 'France', 'Germany')),
```

```
    Phone nvarchar(24) NULL,
    Fax nvarchar(24) NULL,
    CONSTRAINT PK_Customer_Europe
        PRIMARY KEY (CustomerID, Country)
)

CREATE TABLE CustomersAsia(
    CustomerID nchar(5) NOT NULL,
    CompanyName nvarchar(50) NOT NULL,
    ContactName nvarchar(30) NULL,
    ContactTitle nvarchar(30) NULL,
    Address nvarchar(60) NULL,
    City nvarchar(30) NULL,
    Region nvarchar(10) NULL,
    PostalCode nvarchar(15) NULL,
    Country nvarchar(50) NOT NULL
        CHECK (Country IN ('Japan', 'Thailand', 'Japan')),
    Phone nvarchar(24) NULL,
    Fax nvarchar(24) NULL,
    CONSTRAINT PK_Customer_Asia
        PRIMARY KEY (CustomerID, Country)
)
```

These scripts enforce the five column rules and the three table rules. Note that the Country column is part of the primary key. This choice is not a logical one, since logical design guides us to define the CustomerID as the primary key. But, if we want the Country column to be the partitioning column, it needs to be added to the primary key.

If the tables enforce these rules, the view created with the UNION ALL keyword will be a partitioned view if:

- All the columns of constituting tables are referenced in the SELECT statements.

- All the corresponding columns of each SELECT statement are of the same type, precision, scale, and collation.

- Each table column can only be referenced once in the select list.

The Customers view enforces these rules, so it is a partitioned view. Partitioned views are created on different servers along with the tables placed on these servers. OLE DB is the mechanism that is used to communicate between the servers, and the servers are connected as linked servers. If we want to create the partitioned view on each server, all the servers need to be declared as linked servers: ServerA and ServerB are linked server to ServerC, ServerA and ServerC are linked server to ServerB, and ServerB and Server C are linked server to Server A. The linked server definitions need to be created before the partitioned view.

You'll find information about linked servers and how to set them up in Sybex's *MCSE: SQL Server 2000 Administration Study Guide.*

Partitioned views are a great technique for splitting data among different servers. But they are really great when the time comes for inserting, deleting, or updating data in the base table. If the view enforces all the previous rules, SQL Server will automatically update the right table depending on the value given in the query. For example, consider the following insert query:

```
INSERT INTO Customers(CustomerID, CompanyName, Contact-
    Name, ContactTitle, Address, City, Region, PostalCode,
    Country, Phone, Fax)
VALUES('ALFKI', 'Alfreds Futterkiste', 'Maria Anders',
    'Sales Representative', 'Obere Str. 57', 'Berlin',
    NULL, '12209', 'Germany', NULL, NULL)
```

SQL Server will automatically insert the record in the CustomersEurope table. This is due to the partitioning column. Errors 4431 to 4453 are dedicated to dealing with un-updateable partitioned views and all issues that could occur because of the violation of the previous rules.

If you run the following:

```
UPDATE Customers SET Country = 'Canada'
    WHERE CustomerID='ALFKI'
```

SQL Server will automatically move the record from one table to another (and therefore from one server to another).

Partitioned Views are Great, but...

The partitioned view feature is particularly extraordinary when you think of all the work the system has to do. If you needed to program all the necessary cases, you would spend months or invest a lot of money in a transaction monitor. With this feature, Microsoft opens the gate to automatic load balancing in future SQL Server versions. The only drawback concerns all the restriction rules. If you miss one, your view may be created, but it will not be a partitioned view and not all of the automatic features will work. If something is not working with your views, check all the rules; you probably forgot one.

As you have just seen, updates are possible, but there are some restrictions that exist on INSERT, UPDATE, and DELETE statements. INSERT statements are possible only if:

- All the columns declared in the views are referenced in the INSERT statement.

- The DEFAULT keyword is not allowed in the VALUES clause. This rule and the following one disallow a table from containing a column with an IDENTITY property.

- The table does not contain a timestamp column.

- The table does not contain reflexive joins.

UPDATE statements are possible only if:

- The DEFAULT keyword is not allowed in the SET clause.

- The table does not contain a timestamp column.

- The table does not contain reflexive joins.

DELETE statements are possible only if:

- The table does not contain reflexive joins.

If one of these rules is violated, you'll end up with an error whose number is between 4431 and 4453. On the other hand, if you follow all these different rules, you can leverage an extremely powerful feature in SQL Server 2000.

If a view gives you the power to access data wherever it is kept, stored procedures allow you to create complex access and modification methods.

Stored Procedures

Microsoft ✓ ***Exam Objective***

Create and alter database objects. Objects include constraints, indexes, stored procedures, tables, triggers, user-defined functions, and views.

- Specify schema binding and encryption for stored procedures, triggers, user-defined functions, and views.

- Specify recompile settings for stored procedures.

Troubleshoot failed object creation.

Manage data manipulation by using stored procedures.

- Implement error handling in stored procedures.

- Pass and return parameters to and from stored procedure.

- Validate data.

Enforce procedural business logic by using stored procedures.

- Manage control of flow.

- Filter data by using stored procedures.

Troubleshoot and optimize programming objects. Objects include stored procedures, transaction, triggers, user-defined functions, and views.

A database rarely exists on its own. A client application is used to access or to modify data stored in that database. Two possibilities exist to access and update this data: client-side procedures and server-side procedures. With SQL Server, server-side procedures are generally called stored procedures. This section focuses on what stored procedures are, what their benefits are, and how to use them to enhance the performance, security, and functionality of your database application.

Definition and Advantages of Stored Procedures

A *stored procedure* is a batch of Transact-SQL statements stored under a name and executed as a single unit of work. In other languages, like C, Pascal, or Basic, a procedure is usually a set of statements that aim to accomplish one specific goal and can be called from the same program, as a single statement.

In SQL Server, the definition of a procedure is basically the same. A stored procedure can be called from another stored procedure, from a client application, or from a Transact-SQL batch to perform a predefined action. They carry the following inherent advantages:

Fast execution   Stored procedures are precompiled and optimized once, then their execution plan is stored directly in memory, bypassing the parsing, optimization and compilation phase, that an ad-hoc query goes through.

Network load reduction   The client application calls only the stored procedure that is executed on the server. If the client was executing the same operation on its own, it would require many instructions be sent to the server and the results analyzed on the client.

Security mechanism   As with views, a user can be granted permission to execute a stored procedure that updates or retrieves data in a table, while not having to know how to update or retrieve it directly. Stored procedures can shield data access and updates efficiently and easily.

Notes From the Field: Stored Procedures

After all of these years of working with SQL Server, stored procedures are probably the most convenient feature I've ever encountered. They are fast to execute and easy to implement; they have many qualities and no real drawbacks!

The first objects I create after tables and indexes are stored procedures. Even if user-defined functions can replace stored procedures in many cases, they are still number one when the time comes for performance improvement. I do not know a professional solution based on SQL Server that does not contain any stored procedures.

Stored procedures are a must in a SQL Server database. Figure 6.3 shows you why a stored procedure is called "stored."

FIGURE 6.3 Stored procedure compilation process

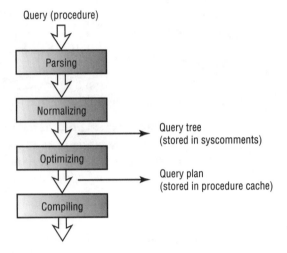

When a stored procedure is created (see the next section for CREATE PROCEDURE syntax), it is parsed and then normalized. The normalization process breaks the query into manageable parts and assembles them into a query tree. For a stored procedure, the query tree is stored in the Syscomments table. The first time the stored procedure is executed, the query tree is optimized and transformed into a query plan that is stored in memory (in the procedure cache). That query plan is compiled and executed. Subsequent execution of the same procedure will use the query plan that is stored in the procedure cache to enhance performance and avoid executing the previous steps.

Stored procedures are definitely a performance enhancer. Most of the work is done on the server, taking advantage of the full server power. Let's now have a look at procedure creation.

Creating and Altering a Stored Procedure

Creating a stored procedure is a straightforward process. SQL Enterprise Manager offers a Create Stored Procedure Wizard for basic insert, delete, or update stored procedures, but most of procedure creation is done through the CREATE PROCEDURE statement:

```
CREATE PROC[EDURE] procedure_name
    [{@parameter data_type} [= default] [OUTPUT]] [ ,...n ]
    [ WITH
            { RECOMPILE | ENCRYPTION | RECOMPILE , ENCRYPTION
    } ]
    [ FOR REPLICATION ]
    AS sql_statement [ ...n ]
```

The most complicated part of the stored procedure creation is the content creation (the sql_statement part). That's where all the intelligence resides. The following procedure, stored in the Northwind database, is a simple example of a stored procedure executing a SELECT statement to retrieve the orders history of a customer given the CustomerID:

```
CREATE PROCEDURE CustOrderHist @CustomerID nchar(5)
AS
SELECT ProductName, Total=SUM(Quantity)
FROM Products P, [Order Details] OD, Orders O, Customers C
WHERE C.CustomerID = @CustomerID
    AND C.CustomerID = O.CustomerID AND O.OrderID =
    OD.OrderID AND OD.ProductID = P.ProductID
GROUP BY ProductName
```

A stored procedure name should follow identifiers rules (See Chapter 3). If its name starts with a single pound sign (#), then the procedure is temporary and local to the connection, which is usable only with the connection used to create it. If its name starts with a double pound sign (##), then the procedure is temporary and global to all connections, that is usable by any connection. SQL Server deletes automatically a temporary stored procedure when the connection used to create it closes.

Parameters are studied in detail in the next section, and the RECOMPILE option is analyzed in the "Executing a Stored Procedure" section later on in this chapter. The ENCRYPTION option encrypts the source code of the procedure to protect intellectual property of its author (see "The ENCRYPTION Option" section earlier in this chapter for more details on encryption).

The FOR REPLICATION option is used for filtering a stored procedure. When replicating a database, you can decide to replicate data and database objects. If a stored procedure is created with the FOR REPLICATION option, it cannot be replicated.

The Strange *FOR REPLICATION* Option

I always thought this option was ill-named. When you use it, the stored procedure cannot be replicated. Just think of it as an option used to indicate that the stored procedure is part of the replication process and executed during replication.

This parameter is reserved for replication stored procedures, which are procedures used during the replication process to filter data to be replicated.

You can use any Transact-SQL statement in a stored procedure, but some limitations exist. The first and most important one is that a stored procedure always ends when the query processor finds a GO.

GO and Batches

GO is not a Transact-SQL statement, but a command used in ISQL (and now OSQL) to run a series of statements. Introduced in the first version of SQL Server, it still plays an important role in certain statements. GO

is said to end a Transact-SQL batch. A *batch* is a series of Transact-SQL statements ended by a GO. The only problem is that historic rules still exist that control statement execution:

- All the statements of a batch are compiled together.
- A syntax error in one statement forbids the execution of the entire batch.
- A batch is not a transaction: if an error occurs, the statements executed prior to the error are not affected.

So, a batch is not a transaction but a unit of work. Now some statements have their own behavior inside of a batch:

- CREATE DEFAULT, CREATE PROCEDURE, CREATE RULE, CREATE TRIGGER, and CREATE VIEW cannot be combined with any other statement inside of a batch.
- You cannot add a column to a table in a batch and reference the new column in the same batch.

With these rules (mainly the first one), you cannot create two views or two defaults without inserting a GO between the two CREATE statements. This has an important impact on the stored procedure creation: you can only create a single view, default, rule, trigger, or other procedure inside a procedure. If you do create one of these objects, it will be the only work performed by the stored procedure.

The second limitation concerns the following statements: ALTER TABLE, CREATE INDEX, CREATE TABLE, All the DBCC statements, DROP TABLE, DROP INDEX, TRUNCATE TABLE, and UPDATE STATISTICS. The object names referenced by these statements should contain the object owner if the stored procedure has to be executed by users besides the procedure creator.

The third and last limitation concerns the SET SHOWPLAN_ALL and SET SHOWPLAN_TEXT statements. They can be used in a stored procedure but should be the only statement of that procedure. Suffice to say this is an unlikely situation!

Stored procedure creation uses a process called *deferred name resolution*, meaning that if a procedure is referencing a table that does not exist at the procedure creation time, the procedure is created without errors. The object names will be resolved at execution time. This feature is really convenient when generating scripts. You may create a procedure and a table in whatever order you choose.

WARNING SQL Server 7 introduced a feature called *compatibility level*, enabling the Transact-SQL grammar level to be "downgraded" to run a script created with a previous version of SQL Server. SQL Server 2000 keeps this feature, its default compatibility level being 80 (SQL Server 2000 is version 8.0). If the compatibility level of a database is 65, a warning is issued if a referenced table does not exist at the stored procedure creation time.

Altering an existing database is another easy process, since the syntax is exactly equivalent to the CREATE PROCEDURE; you just have to replace the CREATE keyword with ALTER. The following example alters the CustOrder-Hist stored procedure:

```
ALTER PROCEDURE CustOrderHist @CustomerID nchar(5)
AS
SELECT ProductName, Total=SUM(Quantity)
FROM Products P, [Order Details] OD, Orders O, Customers C
WHERE C.CustomerID = @CustomerID
   AND C.CustomerID = O.CustomerID AND O.OrderID =
   OD.OrderID AND OD.ProductID = P.ProductID
GROUP BY ProductName
ORDER BY ProductName
```

Last, but not least, you can delete a stored procedure with the DROP PROCEDURE statement, as in the following example:

```
DROP PROCEDURE CustOrderHist
```

A stored procedure may depend on one or many other stored procedures or user-defined functions. If you drop a stored procedure, make sure that it is not referenced by other stored procedures or functions by running the sp_depends system stored procedure.

Using Parameters

One of the main advantages of stored procedures is their ability to accept input and output parameters, as with any other fourth-generation language. A *parameter* declaration has the following syntax:

```
{@parameter data_type} [= default] [OUTPUT]
```

Just as for variables, a parameter's name always begins with an at sign (@) and is of a defined datatype. The minimum declaration is seen in the following example:

```
CREATE PROCEDURE CustOrdersDetail @OrderID int
AS
SELECT ProductName,
   UnitPrice=ROUND(Od.UnitPrice, 2),
```

```
    Quantity,
    Discount=CONVERT(int, Discount * 100),
    ExtendedPrice=ROUND(CONVERT(money, Quantity * (1 -
  Discount) * Od.UnitPrice), 2)
FROM Products P, [Order Details] Od
WHERE Od.ProductID = P.ProductID and Od.OrderID = @OrderID
```

This procedure has one integer parameter called @OrderID. A stored procedure can have up to 2,100 parameters, separated by commas.

Besides its type, a parameter can have a default value. This default value is used if no value is provided for the parameters when the procedure is run. The following declaration of the sp_help system stored procedure has one parameter with a default NULL value:

```
create proc sp_help
   @objname nvarchar(776) = NULL - object name we're after
as ...
```

This stored procedure can be called only with its name, or with its name followed by an object name.

In the previous examples, the parameters were input parameters. If the value of the parameter is modified inside of the procedure, its value is not output to the calling process. The following example creates a stored procedure with an output parameter:

```
CREATE PROC TotalTurnover @total money=0 OUTPUT
AS
SELECT @test=SUM(UnitPrice*Quantity) from [Order Details]
```

The value of the @total parameter, declared with the OUTPUT keyword, is visible outside of the procedure. If you omit the OUTPUT keyword, the @total value will be NULL outside of the procedure, since its value will not be visible outside.

There is another way to return a value from a stored procedure: the RETURN statement. While every parameter can be defined as an output parameter, only one value can be returned with the RETURN statement. Note that only integer values can be returned with the statement, while parameters can be of any datatype. Return values can be trapped with all the classical Application Programming Interfaces (APIs), like DB-Library, Remote Data Objects and ODBC, and ActiveX Data Objects and OLE DB.

Executing a Stored Procedure

A stored procedure can be executed from a client program, another stored procedure, or directly from a Transact-SQL batch. From the client perspective, a stored procedure performs one or many actions and is called just by its name along with any parameters that are needed.

Stored Procedures and SQL Server

Stored procedures have always been part of SQL Server. A SQL Server without stored procedures would be like a good meal without wine (from a Frenchman's perspective): Stored procedures should be seen as the primary data access and modification mechanism. Stored procedures are entirely executed on the server, save network resources, and provide security. Not taking advantage of stored procedures is like filling your formula-one race car with low-octane fuel.

From a server perspective, a stored procedure is just a named set of Transact-SQL statements, seen as a pre-analyzed and compiled batch.

Query Tree and Query Plans

When you run the CREATE PROCEDURE statement, SQL Server analyzes the code of the procedure, parses it, and calculates what is called the query tree (see Figure 6.3). The *query tree* is stored in the Syscomments system table along with the stored procedure source code.

The first time the stored procedure is called by a client program or another stored procedure, the query tree is read from the Syscomments table and is "optimized." Its *query plan*, or *execution plan*, is calculated. This is the most important phase of all. During this phase, SQL Server chooses the right indexes, the table order, the join strategies, and so on. In other words, it chooses how the query is going to be run.

Once the query plan is calculated, it is compiled and passed to the query processor for execution. The query plan is stored in memory, in a zone called the *procedure cache*. This cache is not fundamentally different from the data cache; in fact it is shared with the data cache. It contains every "active" stored procedure. The first time the stored procedure is called, its query plan is brought into the procedure cache. It will remain in this memory area until it ceases to be used and SQL Server needs this memory to allocate to another process. A stored procedure that is used frequently can remain in memory indefinitely.

The query plan can be shared by multiple connections. An execution context is created for every connection for the parameter's substitution.

SQL Server 7 and 2000 introduced the ability of a stored procedure to share its execution plan simultaneously with many connections. In other words, the execution plans became reentrant. This was not possible in previous versions: If two connections wanted to run the same stored procedure at the same time, they needed two distinct execution plans.

You can get an idea of the memory allocation for stored procedures with the DBCC PROCCACHE statement. It gives you information on the number of plans that can be stored, the number currently stored, the number of active procedures, and the size they occupy.

If you want to run tests on whether a stored procedure is useful for performance, free the procedure cache before running it to simulate the worst situation. You free the procedure cache by running DBCC FREEPROCCACHE.

Compiling

The verb *compile* led to much misunderstanding in the past concerning stored procedure. The *compilation* described with the RECOMPILE keyword refers to the optimizing phase. When SQL Server indicates that it is recompiling a stored procedure, it is saying it is recalculating its execution plan.

Recompilation is normally an automatic process, but can be done on demand, depending on the stored procedure. Let's consider the following procedure:

```
CREATE PROC ListCustomer @CustomerID int
AS
SELECT * FROM Customers
    WHERE CustomerID>=@CustomerID
    ORDER BY CustomerID
```

Let's say there are 250,000 rows in the Customers table, with CustomerID values from 1 to 250,000, and a nonclustered index on the CustomerID column. If the first execution of this procedure is done with the customerID value or 249,995, SQL Server will probably choose a query plan using an index, since the number of rows to retrieve is reduced. The query plan stored in the procedure cache is relying on this index.

Suppose another user now executes the same procedure, but with a parameter value of 100. Since a query plan has already been calculated, the same query plan will be reused, which can lead to dramatically poor performance. In fact, with this CustomerID value, a table scan would have been better: Searching more than 249,900 values in an index is more work than scanning the whole table, even if it has to be sorted.

In this situation, it would have been a good idea not to keep the execution plan in memory and to recreate one when needed. So, this procedure needs to be recompiled when the parameter changes, since its execution plan may vary from one execution to another. That's the purpose of the RECOMPILE keyword. If you run the following code, you indicate to SQL Server that it should not keep the execution plan in memory but recreate a new one for each subsequent execution. The code below creates a stored procedure using the WITH RECOMPILE option.

```
CREATE PROC ListCustomer @CustomerID int
WITH RECOMPILE
AS
SELECT * FROM Customers
    WHERE CustomerID>=@CustomerID
    ORDER BY CustomerID
```

You should always validate your decision to recompile a stored procedure by analyzing the estimated execution plan of the query in SQL Query Analyzer with different parameter values. If the plan is always the same, the procedure should not be created with the RECOMPILE clause. If different parameter values lead to different estimated plans, the procedure should be created with the RECOMPILE clause.

You can recompile a procedure when you run it from Transact-SQL with the EXECUTE statement. While this is possible, it is not really convenient, since a procedure call is generally embedded in client code and not made directly from isql or SQL Query Analyzer.

The last discussion of the recompilation process concerns the sp_recompile stored procedure. Used with a table name, it forces every stored procedure and trigger using this table to be recompiled. The following example forces every procedure and trigger referencing the Orders table to be recompiled:

```
sp_recompile 'Orders'
```

This system stored procedure is convenient if you add a new index to a table or new statistics (see Chapter 5 for information on indexes and statistics). Adding this kind of object transforms the way the table is used and may make obsolete the existing query plan.

Running a Procedure

So far, you have seen how to create stored procedures and how SQL Server executes them. If you want SQL Server to run a stored procedure, you have to ask it to do so. This is done in Transact-SQL with the EXECUTE statement.

Generally a stored procedure is called from a client program with a database API like Remote Data Objects or ActiveX Data Objects. You can find information on stored procedure execution with such APIs for Visual Basic or C Language in the SQL Server Books Online.

EXECUTE is not mandatory to run a stored procedure if the procedure is the first instruction of the batch. For example, if you want to run the following lines of code, you need the EXECUTE statement:

```
DECLARE @TO Money
EXECUTE TotalTurnover @TO OUTPUT
SELECT @TO
```

If you omit it, SQL Server fires the error 170, syntax error.

As far as parameters are concerned, they can be called by address or by name. To illustrate this concept, let's take the example of the sp_configure system stored procedure.

```
CREATE PROCEDURE sp_configure   -- 1996/08/14 09:43
    @configname   varchar(35)=NULL - option name to configure
    ,@configvalue  int        =NULL - new configuration value
as ...
```

This procedure has two parameters, @configname, and @configvalue. If you want to modify the lightweight pooling option, you have two possibilities:

```
sp_configure @configname='lightweight pooling', @config-
    value=0
```

or

```
sp_configure 'lightweight pooling', 0
```

In the first syntax, you explicitly name the parameters. In the second syntax, you declare their values in the right order. Note that the following line has the same effect:

```
sp_configure @configvalue=0, @configname=
    'lightweight pooling'
```

Since the parameters' names are given, their orders have no importance. Note that in the last three examples, the EXECUTE statement is not included, implying the stored procedure was the first statement in the batch.

Now if the procedure has a return value, the call is a little bit different. Let's consider the following procedure:

```
CREATE PROCEDURE ListCustOrders @CustomerID nvarchar(5)
AS
IF EXISTS(SELECT * FROM Orders WHERE CustomerID=
    @CustomerID)
BEGIN
    SELECT * FROM Orders WHERE CustomerID=@CustomerID
    RETURN 1
END
ELSE
    RETURN 0
```

In this procedure, if the sought customer has orders, then the procedure returns the corresponding orders as a result set and 1 as the return value of the stored procedure. If the customer did not place orders, the procedure returns 0 as the return value. To query the return value in Transact-SQL, you need to declare a local variable and run the stored procedure using this local variable to indicate where to store the return value, as in the following lines of code:

```
DECLARE @ret INT
EXECUTE @ret=ListCustOrders 'PRINI'
SELECT @ret
```

Note the variable is placed between the EXECUTE keyword and the procedure name. The call is similar to function calls in Visual Basic or the C language.

 Real World Scenario

Performance or Simplicity?

You are the database administrator and lead developer for an insurance company. The board of directors decided that all the mission-critical database applications would now be run on SQL Server. As the lead developer you are in charge of performance tuning and optimizing the applications. Recently, a Microsoft Access application has been upgraded to work with SQL Server. When this application was developed, Access had been chosen for its simplicity, without thinking of the data growth. This application has become over time mission-critical and has been used by dozens of persons and its size is now close to one gigabyte.

The Upsizing Wizard handled the data migration from Access to SQL Server without any problem. Most of the Visual Basic for Application code has been refined to work with a remote database system. Some parts of the application perform well, while others are slower than before the migration. Using the SQL Profiler, you realize that network traffic is very high for these slow parts. Checking the code, you discover this is due to FOR NEXT and DO WHILE loops. You cut and paste this code in SQL Query Analyzer, adapt it to the Transact-SQL syntax, and create stored procedures. Lastly, you change the Visual Basic code so that it just calls the newly created stored procedure. With this change, the network traffic decreases and the actions perform very well.

Stored procedures are not miracles, but you can create miracles with them. Each time you discover huge network traffic as the result of a specific action, or when you see loops with SQL statements in the middle, think about creating a stored procedure. It may require extra work up-front to rewrite the function in Transact-SQL if it has been first written in Basic or any other language, but you'll save a lot of network resources and user time.

Error Handling

No system is perfect. Errors happen all the time. One of the main tasks of the developer is to handle all possible errors to protect users and applications from unwanted behaviors. Error handling has always been a concern in every development project, but is probably the weakest part of Transact-SQL.

First, all errors are not equal from a SQL Server point of view. Some errors cause general failure of the server, while others just stop the statement or warn the user. The following explanation helps you understand why all errors are not equal. An error is composed of many parts:

- An *error number*.

- An error message indicating the apparent cause of the error.

- A *severity level* indicating the kind of problem encountered. There are 25 levels of severity:

  - Less than or equal to 10, the error is only a warning and does not generally stop the execution of the statement.

  - Between 11 and 16, the error is triggered by the user or by a statement written by the user. A syntax error has a gravity of 16, for example. Generally, an error with that severity level stops the statement execution.

  - With a severity of 17 to 19, the error is a system error that stops the statement, but keeps the connection open.

  - Between 20 and 25, the error is fatal and signals a system problem. A problem like a corrupted database causes that kind of error. Such an error stops the statement execution, may close the active connection and may even stop the server.

- A *state code* used by Microsoft Support Engineer to locate the statement that failed in the SQL Server source code. The state code is useless for normal error handling and can be ignored, except when asked for by a support engineer.

As stated above, depending on the severity level, the errors can stop the execution of the statement. A *transaction* is another factor that is affected by the error level. In Chapter 2, we have seen that a transaction is Atomic, Consistent, Isolated, and Durable (ACID). Its atomicity property means that all operations in a transaction are considered as one action. If one statement fails inside a transaction, the whole transaction fails (see Chapter 8 for more information on transactions).

In a stored procedure, the error handling depends on the different factors we have just seen. You should always keep them in mind. Then, the way to program the error trapping and management will almost always be the same: use the @@ERROR system function.

If you used previous versions of SQL Server, system functions beginning with the double "at" sign (@@) were called global variable in the SQL Server documentation. Now called *system functions*, they send back information about the system to the user.

If a statement executes without any error, @@ERROR sends back 0. If it sends back an error number, you can test this value to decide what to do.

All programming APIs (ADO, RDO, etc.) trap these errors along with their numbers and texts.

The following piece of code traps the error in a stored procedure and returns its value to the calling program:

```
CREATE PROCEDURE InsSales
    @stor_id char(4),
    @ord_num varchar(20),
    @ord_date datetime,
    @qty smallint,
    @payterms varchar(12),
    @title_id tid
```

```
AS
DECLARE @err int
BEGIN TRANSACTION
   INSERT INTO sales(stor_id, ord_num, ord_date,
         qty, payterms, title_id)
      VALUES (@stor_id, @ord_num, @ord_date,
         @qty, @payterms, @title_id)
   SET @err=@@ERROR
   IF @err<>0
      GOTO ErrorHandler
   UPDATE titles
      SET ytd_sales=ytd_sales+@qty
      WHERE title_id=@title_id
   SET @err=@@ERROR
   IF @err<>0
      GOTO ErrorHandler
COMMIT TRANSACTION
RETURN 0
ErrorHandler:
ROLLBACK TRANSACTION
RETURN @err
```

In this particular stored procedure, we open a transaction to insert a record into the Sales table of the Pubs database and update the Ytd_Sales of the Titles table on-the-fly. After each of these statements, we test the error number and, if it's different from zero, we jump to the error handler that rolls back the transaction and returns the error number. If the transaction ends normally, it returns zero.

This classical error handler uses the @@ERROR system function and the RETURN statement to send a value back to the calling code. Situations arise where you need more control over what's happening to your code—that's the reason for error message customization. All SQL Server messages are stored in the Sysmessages system table. You can add your own messages to this table, using error numbers over 50,000 with the sp_addmessage system procedure, and then raise your own messages with the RAISERROR statement.

The following statement adds a message to the Sysmessages system table, indicating that the given title_id does not exist:

```
EXEC sp_addmessage @msgnum = 50100, @severity = 16,
  @msgtext = N'The title with the title_id %s does not exist'
```

You can now raise this error in the previous InsSales stored procedure to check first whether the title_id value exists:

```
CREATE PROCEDURE InsSales
    @stor_id char(4),
    @ord_num varchar(20),
    @ord_date datetime,
    @qty smallint,
    @payterms varchar(12),
    @title_id tid
AS
DECLARE @err int
IF NOT EXISTS(SELECT * FROM Titles WHERE
    title_id=@title_id)
BEGIN
    RAISERROR (50100, 16, 1, @title_id)
    RETURN 50100
END
...
```

Note that the custom error message contains one parameter, declared with %s, due to the fact that this is a string parameter. If the parameter had been a signed integer, it would have been declared with %d (C developers recognize printf format options—all these options are defined in the SQL Server Books Online along with the RAISERROR statement definition). You can declare and have any number of parameters in your error message, but know that a message can have a maximum length of 400 characters.

You can also raise system errors with RAISERROR, but this is hardly ever done, since the system will raise errors before you do so!

Stored procedures are a must in SQL Server applications, just as views are necessary to reduce visible complexity. SQL Server 2000 introduced a new feature that may look like a stored procedure or a view, but enhances their functionalities: user-defined functions. Microsoft announced them in SQL Server 7, but we had to wait to SQL Server 2000 to see their implementation.

Transactions

Microsoft ✓ *Exam* *Objective*

Enforce procedural business logic by using stored procedures, transactions, triggers, user-defined functions, and views.

Design and manage transactions.

Troubleshoot and optimize programming objects. Objects include stored procedures, transactions, triggers, user-defined functions, and views.

Everything is a transaction in SQL Server. Each unit of work, each query, and each statement is implicitly a transaction by itself by default. The power of a relational database system is its ability to ensure that each of these transactions is completed in its entirety or that all traces of it are removed from the system.

A *transaction* is defined by the following properties (referred to as the *ACID* properties):

Atomic   All operations in a transaction are atomic, meaning that if one operation fails, the whole transaction fails.

Consistent   Before the transaction, the database was in a consistent state. After the transaction, it is back in a consistent state, but it may have gone through an inconstant state during the transaction. That is why a transaction must comply with the third property, isolated.

Isolated   A running transaction is isolated from the outside. Locking provides this property.

Durable   Once a transaction is validated (committed), the effects of the transaction remain in the database forever. The transaction log provides this property.

SQL Server ensures that every transaction is either completed (called *committed* in SQL Server) or rolled back (removed from the system).

A single statement, however, cannot always perform the amount of work needed for a process. The classic example of this is the transfer of money between two bank accounts. If each statement is a transaction (one statement removes money, and the next one deposits it), then inconsistencies could arise if only one of the statements is completed. Imagine that the first query is executed and money is withdrawn from the first account, but power fails and the server crashes before the second statement, the deposit statement, executes. The funds would be lost!

Fortunately, SQL Server allows the programmer to explicitly declare a transaction and determine whether or not the transaction should be committed or rolled back. By testing for success or failure of a particular process, the programmer can determine if all statements inside the transaction should be marked as completed. Of course, if the server should fail in the middle of a transaction, SQL Server will automatically undo the transaction when it is restarted.

WARNING Be sure that any transaction that is started is either committed or rolled back. An open transaction uses resources and can prevent the transaction log from being backed up!

The structure of a transaction is as follows:

```
BEGIN TRANSACTION [<transaction_name>]
    ➡    [WITH MARK <description>]
...

<T-SQL code>

...

[ SAVE TRANSACTION <savepoint name>]

...

<T-SQL code>

...

<test for errors >
        <if true>
ROLLBACK TRANSACTION [<transaction_name> |
    ➡    <savepoint name>]
        <if false>
COMMIT TRANSACTION
```

This looks complex, but basically the BEGIN TRANSACTION statement starts a transaction. All statements that occur until a ROLLBACK or COMMIT statement will consume resources and hold locks to ensure that the transaction can be completed. The BEGIN TRANSACTION statement allows for the naming of the transaction, which allows nesting of transactions (see the last paragraph in this section) as well as the marking of the transaction. The WITH MARK keywords mark the transaction log and allow a restore of the server up to this point in time.

The SAVE TRANSACTION statement allows the programmer to mark a section of work as completed, although it is not committed. This allows additional statements to proceed and be undone without undoing the work to this point. Suppose a process transferred money between two accounts and then removed additional money from one of the accounts. The transaction could mark a savepoint after the transfer of funds before removing additional money. If there were some business logic that might prevent the removal of money, the transaction could be undone back to the savepoint and then committed. This would allow part of the transaction to be completed. This allows conditional programming within a transaction.

The ROLLBACK TRANSACTION statement will cancel a transaction and undo any work that has been performed by T-SQL statements between it and the BEGIN TRANSACTION statement.

The COMMIT TRANSACTION statement will mark all the work done as completed, and at this point, the transaction is considered complete. If the server crashes after this statement, when it restarts, the work that was performed inside this transaction will be verified as having been performed on the actual data.

Transactions are usually used inside stored procedures when a series of steps must be completed as one unit of work. They are valid, however, in any programming situation, including batches. A transaction can span multiple batches, as you will see in Exercise 10.1. Triggers are executed within a transaction by default. Whatever statement is modifying the table is an implicit transaction that also contains the trigger. A ROLLBACK statement inside a trigger rolls back the data modification statement as well as any transaction that contains it.

One last point about transactions: They can be nested, which allows a transaction to exist inside another transaction. SQL Server allows these transactions to be named, so that the inner transaction can be rolled back or committed without affecting the outer transaction. Nested transactions are very similar to a transaction with a savepoint.

User-defined Functions

Microsoft ✓ **Exam Objective**

Create and alter database objects. Objects include constraints, indexes, stored procedures, tables, triggers, user-defined functions, and views.

- Specify schema binding and encryption user-defined functions.

Troubleshoot failed object creation.

Manage data manipulation by using user-defined functions.

- Implement error handling in user-defined functions.

- Pass and return parameters to and from user-defined functions.

- Validate data.

Enforce procedural business logic by using user-defined functions.

- Manage control of flow.

- Filter data by using user-defined functions.

Troubleshoot and optimize programming objects. Objects include stored procedures, transaction, triggers, user-defined functions, and views.

User-defined functions are the new killer feature for developers. They enhance views and stored procedures, and offer new functionalities that were impossible to achieve on the server side with previous versions of SQL Server. This section focuses on the different types of user-defined functions and on how to create and manage them.

Definition and Advantages of User-defined Functions

A *user-defined function* (UDF) is a named set of Transact-SQL statements used like system functions or views. There are two main types of UDFs:

Scalar   A scalar UDF returns a single value and can be used wherever an expression or variable can be used, for example, in a select list of a SELECT statement, or in the SET clause of an UPDATE statement. A scalar function can be seen as the result of some mathematical or string function.

Table-valued   Table UDFs return a result set and can be used wherever a table or a view can be used (under some limitations). Table-valued UDFs can be referenced in a FROM clause of a SELECT statement, for example. UDFs can be more complex than views and can have parameters.

All the functions are created with the CREATE FUNCTION statement, modified with the ALTER FUNCTION, and dropped with the DROP FUNCTION statement. The different functions share some syntax elements and have their own particularities. The options they share are ENCRYPTION and SCHEMABINDING. These options are equivalent to the same view options. Refer to the "View" section for more information on these options.

Let's now examine the different UDFs and how to create and manage them.

Creating and Altering a UDF

As we have just seen, there are two main types of UDFs: scalar and table-valued. The table-valued UDFs are split into two subtypes: inline and multistatement table-valued.

Scalar UDF

A developer usually thinks of UDFs as functions similar to the mathematical or string-manipulation functions. That's exactly the purpose of *scalar user-defined functions*. They can implement a complex calculation or data manipulation and return one value. For example, you could create a function that calculates the royalty owed to an author, knowing its author_id.

The syntax of such a function is as follows:

```
CREATE  FUNCTION [owner_name.]function_name
   ([{@parameter_name [AS] data_type [=default]} [ ,...n
   ]])
RETURNS scalar_return_data_type
[WITH { ENCRYPTION | SCHEMABINDING } [ [,] ...n] ]
[ AS ]
```

```
BEGIN
    function_body
    RETURN scalar_expression
END
```

The function body can contain any Transact-SQL statement, as in a stored procedure. You can retrieve data from a table, do complex calculations, and so on. The RETURN statement contains the value to return to the calling statement.

The following example calculates and returns the total value of each Order Detail record:

```
CREATE FUNCTION TotalAmount
    (@UnitPrice money, @Quantity smallint, @Discount real)
RETURNS money
AS
BEGIN
    RETURN (@UnitPrice*@Quantity)*(1-@discount)
END
```

This function accepts three required parameters, calculates the total amount, and returns it to the calling statement. The following SELECT statement returns information about order number 10250 and uses the TotalAmount UDF:

```
SELECT
    ProductID,
    Total=dbo.TotalAmount(UnitPrice, Quantity, Discount)
FROM [Order details]
WHERE OrderID=10250
```

The results are:

```
ProductID    Total
-----------  --------------------
41           77.0000
51           1261.4000
65           214.2000
```

As you see, scalar functions are straightforward. They can be more complicated than the previous example, since any Transact-SQL statement can be included in the function body.

Inline Table-valued UDF

An *inline table-valued user-defined function* can be seen as a view with parameters. They execute one SELECT statement, as in a view, but can include parameters, like a stored procedure. The basic syntax is:

```
CREATE FUNCTION [owner_name.]function_name
    ([{@parameter_name [AS] data_type [=default]} [ ,...n
]])
RETURNS TABLE
[WITH { ENCRYPTION | SCHEMABINDING } [ [,] ...n] ]
[AS]
RETURN [(] select-stmt [)]
```

Consider the following SELECT statement:

```
SELECT
    stores.stor_name,
    titles.title
    SUM(sales.qty) AS TotalQty
FROM stores
    INNER JOIN sales ON stores.stor_id = sales.stor_id
    INNER JOIN titles ON sales.title_id = titles.title_id
WHERE stores.stor_id= @stor_id
GROUP BY stores.stor_name, titles.title
```

With the parameterized WHERE clause, the function cannot be transformed into a view. Prior to SQL Server 2000, the only way to store this query in the database was to create a stored procedure. Now, it is the ideal SELECT statement for an inline table-valued UDF:

```
CREATE FUNCTION SalesByBookshop (@stor_id char(4))
RETURNS TABLE
AS
RETURN(
    SELECT
        stores.stor_name,
        titles.title,
        SUM(sales.qty) AS TotalQty
    FROM stores
    INNER JOIN sales ON stores.stor_id = sales.stor_id
    INNER JOIN titles ON sales.title_id = titles.title_id
```

```
    WHERE stores.stor_id= @stor_id
    GROUP BY stores.stor_name, titles.title
)
```

Once created, you simply have to use it:

```
SELECT * FROM SalesByBookShop(7066)
```

The result is:

stor_name	title	TotalQty
Barnum's	Is Anger the Enemy?	75
Barnum's	Secrets of Silicon Valley	50

Inline table-valued are just views with parameters!

Multistatement Table-valued UDF

Multistatement table-valued UDFs are the most complex form of UDF. This type of function builds the result set from one or many SELECT statements. Its basic syntax is the following:

```
CREATE FUNCTION [owner_name.]function_name
    ([{@parameter_name [AS] data_type [=default]} [ ,...n
]])
RETURNS @return_variable
    TABLE ({column_definition | table_constraint} [ ,...n
])
[WITH { ENCRYPTION | SCHEMABINDING } [ [,] ...n] ]
[AS]
BEGIN
    function_body
    RETURN
END
```

The following example creates a contact list from two or three tables, depending on a parameter value:

```
CREATE FUNCTION Contacts(@suppliers bit=0)
RETURNS @Contacts TABLE
    (ContactName nvarchar(30),
    Phone nvarchar(24),
    ContactType nvarchar(15))
```

```
AS
BEGIN
   INSERT @Contacts
      SELECT ContactName, Phone, 'Customer' FROM Customers
   INSERT @Contacts
      SELECT FirstName + ' ' + LastName, HomePhone, 'Employee'
   FROM Employees
   IF @Suppliers=1
      INSERT @Contacts
         SELECT ContactName, Phone, 'Supplier' FROM Suppliers
   RETURN
END
```

The whole idea of multistatement table-valued user-defined functions lies in this example. The function uses a temporary table declared in a table variable. In this example, this table is called @Contacts. Then multiple SELECT statements are run against different tables to insert data in the temporary table. At last the result is returned to the calling statement, like in the following line of code:

```
SELECT * FROM Contacts(1) ORDER BY ContactName
```

Again, this example shows that a multistatement table-valued UDF has the power of a stored procedure and the usage simplicity of a view. This kind of process was implemented with stored procedure and temporary tables stored in the tempdb database prior to SQL Server 2000. Now all the work is done in one function and in memory. This is a dream for developers!

Using UDFs

Depending on the UDF type, the execution call is different. A scalar UDF is always called by a two-component name: *owner.functionname*, like in the following example:

```
SELECT
   ProductID,
   Total=dbo.TotalAmount(UnitPrice, Quantity, Discount)
FROM [Order details]
WHERE OrderID=10250
```

If you omit the owner, dbo in this example, in the function call, you obtain error 195, `'TotalAmount' is not a recognized function name`. A scalar UDF can be used where an expression may be used: in the select list of a SELECT statement, as in the above example, or even in a CREATE TABLE statement. The following code is a custom Order Details table:

```
CREATE TABLE [Order Details] (
    OrderID int NOT NULL ,
    ProductID int NOT NULL ,
    UnitPrice money NOT NULL DEFAULT (0),
    Quantity smallint NOT NULL DEFAULT (1),
    Discount real NOT NULL DEFAULT (0),
    Total AS dbo.TotalAmount(UnitPrice, Quantity, Dis-
count))
```

A table-valued UDF may be called with a one- or two-component name, as in the following example:

```
SELECT * FROM Contacts(1) ORDER BY ContactName
```

Note that if a table-valued function has no parameters, you must still use parentheses:

```
SELECT * FROM Contacts() ORDER BY ContactName
```

WARNING If parameters have default values, they cannot be skipped or ignored in the function call. You have to use the DEFAULT keyword.

You may encounter a strange type of function that starts with two colons (::), as in the following example:

```
SELECT * FROM ::fn_virtualservernodes()
```

This is a system user-defined function. You'll find some of them described in the SQL Server Books OnLine, but the majority are undocumented and used only internally by SQL Server.

This ends this section on user-defined functions. These new objects are extremely useful, fulfilling major needs in database development. The last section concerns another useful object: triggers.

Triggers

Microsoft ✓ Exam Objective

Create and alter database objects. Objects include constraints, indexes, stored procedures, tables, triggers, user-defined functions, and views.

- Specify schema binding and encryption for triggers.

Troubleshoot failed object creation.

Manage data manipulation by using triggers.

- Implement error handling in triggers.

- Validate data.

Enforce procedural business logic by using triggers.

- Specify trigger actions.

- Manage control of flow.

- Filter data by using triggers.

Troubleshoot and optimize programming objects. Objects include stored procedures, transaction, triggers, user-defined functions, and views.

Triggers are as old as SQL Server. In fact, they were one of the features in the first version of SQL Server that made it popular. Like stored procedures, views, and user-defined functions, triggers are pieces of code entirely executed on the server. This section covers their definition and advantages, and then focuses on their different types and usage.

Definition and Advantages of Triggers

A *trigger* is a special form of stored procedure, bound to a table or to a view, and fired automatically by a particular statement. In Chapter 4, we discussed constraints, which are used to enforce different types of data integrity. Triggers are generally used to enforce referential integrity and business rules. While triggers are similar to CHECK constraints, they have one major difference: triggers are reactive while constraints are proactive.

This means a constraint is fired before the effect of the statement takes place, while a trigger is fired after or instead of the firing statement.

Two types of triggers exist:

- AFTER triggers that run after the statements that fired them

- INSTEAD OF triggers that run instead of statements that fired them

Triggers can be used to go beyond declarative referential integrity and to implement more complex rules than those possibly defined with CHECK constraints. Triggers are found in many situations like maintaining denormalized data, complex cascading updates, inserts or deletes, comparing data before and after updates, etc.

A trigger is part of the transaction started by the statement that fired it. So, since a transaction is atomic (see Chapters 2 and 8 for more information about transactions), if the trigger fails, the firing statement fails. If this statement is part of a larger transaction, then the entire transaction fails.

Let's start with AFTER triggers and discuss the way they work and can be implemented.

AFTER Triggers

AFTER triggers can only be created on tables. A table can have any number of AFTER triggers defined for inserts, deletes, and updates. All of them are created with the same syntax:

```
CREATE TRIGGER trigger_name
    ON table
    [WITH ENCRYPTION]
    {
        { {FOR | AFTER} {[INSERT][,][UPDATE][,][DELETE] }
            [WITH APPEND]
            [NOT FOR REPLICATION]
            AS
            [ {IF UPDATE(column)
                [{AND | OR} UPDATE(column)][ ...n ]}
             ]
            sql_statement [ ...n ]
        }
    }
```

Before going further, note the options already discussed with stored procedures. The WITH ENCRYPTION option encrypts the trigger code to protect the intellectual property of its author and forbids reverse engineering the trigger. The NOT FOR REPLICATION option indicates not to fire the trigger if the table is modified by the replication process.

A trigger can be created to react to inserts, updates, or deletes. The same trigger can be created on two or all three of these actions. For example, a trigger can be created for deletes and updates.

The WITH APPEND option has been introduced in SQL Server 7 to allow multiple triggers for the same statement on databases with a compatibility level less than or equal to 65. With SQL Server 7 or SQL Server 2000 databases, WITH APPEND is the default behavior. You can use this option only if you use the FOR keyword and not AFTER, even though they are synonyms.

Triggers are bound to a table. If you drop the table, all the triggers associated to this table are dropped. You can alter a trigger definition with the ALTER TRIGGER statement (same syntax as CREATE TRIGGER) and drop a trigger with the DROP TRIGGER statement:

```
DROP TRIGGER trigger [ ,...n ]
```

Triggers can be nested up to 32 levels. For example, an INSERT trigger that runs an UPDATE statement that fires an UPDATE trigger that runs a DELETE statement that fires a DELETE trigger, and so on. Triggers can be recursive if the database option RECURSIVE_TRIGGERS is turned on with the following command:

```
ALTER DATABASE database_name
SET RECURSIVE_TRIGGERS ON
```

If you want to test whether recursive triggers are on, run the following statement:

```
SELECT DATABASEPROPERTYEX(database,
    'IsRecursiveTriggersEnabled'
```

Triggers working on the same table may be used to check values and modify them on-the-fly. If you implement this behavior, be aware that the recursive triggers option can cause unexpected behavior.

The *INSERT* Trigger

An INSERT trigger is fired on the INSERT statement. That means that when a user inserts a record in the table and the record has been successfully inserted, the trigger is fired. Figure 6.4 illustrates the functioning process of an INSERT trigger.

FIGURE 6.4 The *INSERT* trigger process

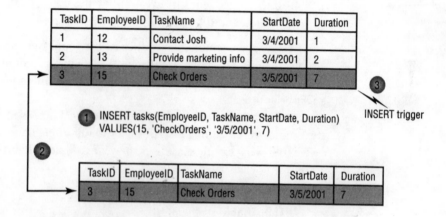

The trigger used in this example is the following:

```
CREATE TRIGGER InsTasks ON Tasks
AFTER INSERT
AS
IF NOT EXISTS(SELECT * FROM Employees E JOIN Inserted I ON
    E.EmployeeID=I.EmployeeID)
BEGIN
    RAISERROR('The Employee does not exist', 16, 1)
    ROLLBACK TRANSACTION
END
```

This triggers a rollback of the insert if the employee ID does not exist.

The same feature could have been realized with a FOREIGN KEY constraint.

The process of INSERT trigger firing is as follows:

1. The user or the system runs an INSERT statement

2. If the record does not violate any constraint, it is physically inserted in the table and in a temporary table called Inserted. This private temporary table has the same structure as the base table and exists only for the duration of the trigger. It isolates the inserted record.

3. The trigger fires.

4. If the trigger ends its execution without errors, the Inserted table is deleted and the record is marked as inserted.

In the code example, the code joins the Employees and the Inserted table to check the employee ID existence. This is a common method of existence checking. The Inserted table contains only the record that has just been inserted.

INSERT triggers are used for existence checking, as in the above example, for cascading inserts, or for maintaining denormalized data. The following example updates the year-to-date column of the Titles table after each sales insert:

```
CREATE TRIGGER InsSales ON Sales
AFTER INSERT
AS
    UPDATE titles
        SET ytd_sales=T.ytd_sales+I.qty
        FROM Inserted I JOIN Titles T
        ON I.title_id=T.title_ID
```

You can imagine other examples: a sales insert fails if the unit in stock count of the ordered products is equal to zero, a book loan fails if the library member has already three books on loan, and so on. Each time insert checks need to be made and go beyond simple CHECK or FOREIGN KEY constraints, INSERT triggers may be the solution.

The *DELETE* Trigger

The process of a DELETE trigger is very close to that of INSERT triggers, with the exception that it uses the Deleted table, which contains the record that has just been deleted, instead of the Inserted table. Figure 6.5 illustrates the delete process, with a firing trigger.

FIGURE 6.5   The *DELETE* trigger process

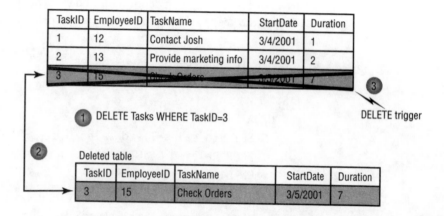

Let's look at an example of a deleted trigger. Support the trigger with the following:

```
CREATE TRIGGER DelTasks ON Tasks
AFTER DELETE
AS
IF EXISTS (SELECT * FROM DELETED WHERE StartDate<=GET-
    DATE())
BEGIN
    RAISERROR('A started task cannot be deleted', 16, 1)
    ROLLBACK TRANSACTION
END
```

This trigger checks the Startdate value and rolls back the transaction if it is before the system date. The process of trigger firing is as follows:

1. The user or the system runs a DELETE statement.

2. If the record does not violate any foreign key constraint, it is physically deleted from the table and inserted into a temporary table called Deleted. This private temporary table has the same structure as the base table and exists only for the duration of the trigger.

3. The trigger fires.

4. If the trigger ends its execution without errors, the Deleted table is deleted and the record is marked as deleted from the base table.

DELETE triggers can be used for existence checking, for cascading deletes, or for maintaining denormalized data. The following example decreases the year-to-date value of the title record if a sales record is deleted:

```
CREATE TRIGGER DelSales ON Sales
AFTER DELETE
AS
    UPDATE titles
        SET ytd_sales=T.ytd_sales-D.qty
        FROM Deleted D JOIN Titles T
        ON D.title_id=T.title_ID
```

As with INSERT triggers, a lot of other examples can be found: if a sales record is deleted, it is moved to a DeletedSales table for statistical purposes; each time a book is brought back to the library, the on_loan column of the Members table is decreased; and so on.

The *UPDATE* Trigger

An update operation can be seen as a delete operation followed by an insert: the old values are deleted and the new ones are inserted. Figure 6.6 shows you the update process.

FIGURE 6.6   The *UPDATE* trigger process

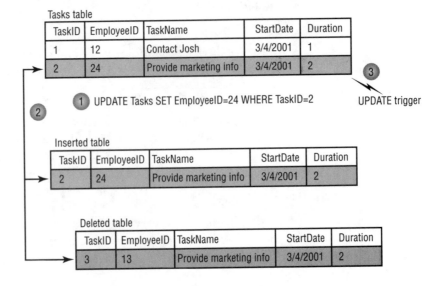

Suppose the trigger looks like the following:

```
CREATE TRIGGER UpdTasks ON Tasks
AFTER UPDATE
AS
IF UPDATE(TaskID)
BEGIN
    RAISERROR('The TaskID cannot be updated', 16, 1)
    ROLLBACK TRANSACTION
END
IF NOT EXISTS(SELECT * FROM Employees E JOIN Inserted I ON
    E.EmployeeID=I.EmployeeID)
BEGIN
    RAISERROR('The Employee does not exist', 16, 1)
    ROLLBACK TRANSACTION
END
```

This trigger first checks that the TaskID column has not been updated. If so, it rolls back the transaction. Then, it checks the employee ID, just as in the INSERT trigger, and rolls back the transaction if it does not exist. The process of UPDATE trigger firing is as follows:

1. The user or the system runs an UPDATE statement.

2. If the record does not violate any constraint, it is physically updated in the table, its old version is inserted into the Deleted table, and its new version is inserted into the Inserted Table.

3. The trigger fires.

4. If the trigger ends its execution without errors, the Deleted and Inserted tables are deleted and the record is marked as updated in the base table.

Like other triggers, UPDATE triggers can be used to maintain data integrity or denormalization.

INSTEAD OF Triggers

SQL Server 2000 introduces INSTEAD OF triggers. This feature, like the user-defined functions, has been awaited for a long time. One of the main drawbacks of AFTER triggers is that they take place after the statement that fires them. You have seen in the previous examples that if the trigger violates the rule enforced in the trigger, it has to rollback the transaction.

Other RDBMSs, like Oracle or DB/2, use AFTER and BEFORE triggers. SQL Server does not propose BEFORE triggers, a kind of trigger that fires before the actual statements modify the base table. As its name implies, an INSTEAD OF trigger is executed instead of the statement that fired it.

INSTEAD OF triggers can be created on tables or on views, but a table or a view can have only one INSTEAD OF trigger per action.

An INSTEAD OF trigger cannot be created on a table that has a foreign key with CASCADE DELETE or CASCADE UPDATE.

When created on a view, an INSTEAD OF trigger enhances the updatability of the view. We've seen that a view can only update, delete, or insert data in one base table at a time. With INSTEAD OF triggers, this limitation disappears. As we are going to see, it is possible with an INSTEAD OF trigger to update any number of tables.

The *INSTEAD OF INSERT* Trigger

Like the AFTER trigger, the INSTEAD OF trigger works with the Inserted table. But the logic is a little bit different:

1. The user or the system runs an INSERT statement.

2. If the record does not violate any constraint, it is inserted only in the Inserted table.

3. The trigger fires and performs any necessary action.

Note first that the record is only inserted in the Inserted table, not in the base table. So there is nothing to rollback if any test in the trigger fails. Second, the INSERT does not really take place in the table. The trigger may decide to insert the record after doing some tests on its values, but if the trigger code does something else, the insert will not be performed. The trigger is executed instead of the base INSERT statement. If the trigger executes an INSERT statement into the table, it is not fired a second time. INSTEAD OF triggers are not recursive!

The following example shows a trigger that tests the quantity of a product in stock before accepting an order:

```
CREATE TRIGGER InsOrdDet ON [Order Details]
INSTEAD OF INSERT
AS
DECLARE @qty int
SELECT @qty=quantity FROM Inserted
IF @qty<=(SELECT UnitsInStock
             FROM Products P JOIN Inserted I
             ON P.ProductID = I.ProductID)
    INSERT INTO [Order Details]
    SELECT * FROM Inserted
ELSE
    RAISERROR('Not enough products in stock', 16, 1)
```

As you can see from this trigger, the INSERT statement in the trigger code is just a normal INSERT SELECT statement, inserting the record already stored in the Inserted table. One major advantage here is that no rollback is required if the units in stock are less than expected.

The *INSTEAD OF DELETE* Trigger

INSTEAD OF DELETE triggers function in the same manner as INSTEAD OF INSERT triggers, but they use the Deleted table:

1. The user or the system runs a DELETE statement.

2. If the record does not violate any constraint, it is inserted only in the Deleted table.

3. The trigger fires and performs any necessary action.

As for the INSTEAD OF INSERT trigger, no action is performed in the table besides what the trigger does.

An INSTEAD OF DELETE trigger cannot be defined on a table enforcing the ON DELETE CASCADE option on a FOREIGN KEY constraint.

The *INSTEAD OF UPDATE* Trigger

INSTEAD OF UPDATE triggers work with the Inserted and Deleted table to store values before and after the update. No data is modified in the base table. The logic is the following:

1. The user or the system runs an UPDATE statement.

2. If the record does not violate any constraint, its old version is inserted in the Deleted table and its new version is inserted in the Inserted table.

3. The trigger fires and performs any necessary action.

As usual, no modification is being made to the table, aside from what is done in the trigger.

An INSTEAD OF UPDATE trigger cannot be defined on a table enforcing the ON UPDATE CASCADE option on a FOREIGN KEY constraint.

The Special Case of Views

INSTEAD OF triggers are useful with views since they can enhance their updatability. Consider the following view found in the Northwind database:

```
CREATE VIEW [Alphabetical list of products]
AS
SELECT Products.*, Categories.CategoryName
    FROM Categories INNER JOIN Products
    ON Categories.CategoryID = Products.CategoryID
    WHERE Products.Discontinued=0
```

If you try to insert a new record into the Products table through this view, you need to define the columns and make sure the category used exists. Now, with an INSTEAD OF INSERT trigger, you may check the existence of the category, create it if it does not exist, and insert the new product as shown in the following example:

```
CREATE TRIGGER InsLP ON [Alphabetical list of products]
INSTEAD OF INSERT
```

```
AS
IF EXISTS(SELECT * FROM Inserted I JOIN Category C
        ON I.CategoryID=C.CategoryID)
    INSERT INTO Products(ProductID, ProductName, SupplierID,
        CategoryID, QuantityPerUnit, UnitPrice, UnitsInStock,
        UnitsOnOrder, ReorderLevel, Discontinued)
        SELECT ProductID, ProductName, SupplierID,
        CategoryID, QuantityPerUnit, UnitPrice, UnitsInStock,
        UnitsOnOrder, ReorderLevel, Discontinued FROM
    Inserted
ELSE
BEGIN
    BEGIN TRANSACTION
        INSERT INTO Category(CategoryName)
            SELECT CategoryName FROM Inserted
        INSERT INTO Products(ProductID, ProductName, SupplierID,
            CategoryID, QuantityPerUnit, UnitPrice,
            UnitsInStock, UnitsOnOrder, ReorderLevel,
            Discontinued)
            SELECT ProductID, ProductName, SupplierID,
            @@IDENTITY, QuantityPerUnit, UnitPrice,
            UnitsInStock, UnitsOnOrder, ReorderLevel,
            Discontinued FROM Inserted
    COMMIT TRANSACTION
    END
```

This version of the trigger is deliberately shortened for the example. To be complete, you should add error handling in the transaction to make sure it is rolled back if an error occurs.

With that trigger on the view, you update both base tables with only one INSERT statement.

Even if a partitioned view is made of multiple tables, it does not need INSTEAD OF triggers to modify the base table, since the partitioned columns determines which table to modify. See the "Partitioned Views" section earlier in this chapter.

As for tables, only one INSTEAD OF trigger can be created per action (insert, update, or delete).

Performance Considerations

Although triggers are a wonderful invention, they can cause dramatic performance loss. Triggers are useful because as part of the database schema, they enforce data integrity directly on the server. Since a trigger will always be part of the base transaction, triggers are guaranteed to be consistent actions. But this guarantee can also lower performance. This is why.

When you modify a record, the trigger fires. Normally, an insert, update, or delete operation takes a few milliseconds. Now since the trigger has been fired, and while it runs, locks are held on the modified record(s). The trigger may update, delete, or insert other records in other tables, acquiring additional locks to do so. As more work is done inside the trigger, the number of locks required increases, as does the contention on the system. The more locks, the longer the transaction and the fewer users that can be supported by the server.

One motto of SQL Server is to keep transactions short. With triggers, you increase the size and the duration of the transactions. Pay very close attention to the execution time of your statements once you add triggers.

On the other hand, triggers are fast: like stored procedures, they are compiled and stored in the procedure cache, and the inserted and deleted tables are stored in the data cache. No I/Os are required to execute a trigger. But again, that may still negatively impact performance. The execution time of the trigger depends on the number of tables and the number of rows impacted by the trigger.

As a rule of thumb:

- Keep triggers short.

- Test, test, and retest triggers' impact on performance.

Never underestimate their impact. If you encounter performance loss and have lots of triggers, finding the statement or trigger that is causing the problem may be a difficult task.

Various Considerations

To finish with triggers, here are some various considerations on triggers you may find helpful for the exam.

A table can have more than one AFTER trigger for a defined action. For example, a table can have three AFTER INSERT triggers. This situation can occur if you created your own trigger, then installed the merge replication (which adds triggers to the table) or published data on the Web with the Web Wizard. These actions could lead to potential problems. With this example, imagine the Web trigger fires first and creates the Web page, then the custom trigger fires and rolls back the transaction. Unfortunately, the creation of the Web page is not a transactional action. So, a Web page has been created with inaccurate information.

Due to situations like this one, it is necessary to be able to change the firing order. SQL Server allows us to choose the first and last trigger to fire, with the sp_settriggerorder system stored procedure. In our previous example, let's consider that triggers are:

- WebTrig for the Web trigger, defined on INSERT, DELETE, and UPDATE

- CustomInsTrig for the custom trigger, defined only on INSERT

- ReplTrig defined on INSERT, DELETE, and UPDATE

If you want WebTrig to be first and ReplTrig to be last, run the following code:

```
EXEC sp_settrigerorder 'WebTrig', 'FIRST'
EXEC sp_settrigerorder 'ReplTrig', 'LAST'
```

Between the first and the last triggers, the trigger order cannot be modified. They are fired in the order SQL Server finds them in the system table.

There is a third parameter for this procedure to define the action on which you are setting the order. For example, a trigger could be the first trigger for INSERT actions but the last trigger for DELETE actions. SQL Server allows precise control of trigger order for the first and last triggers that fire for each action.

In some situations, triggers can become a burden. For example, if you need to import thousands of new rows in a batch job, it may be a good idea to disable the triggers. The ALTER TABLE statement allow you to enable and disable trigger on demand:

```
ALTER TABLE table_name
    { ENABLE | DISABLE } TRIGGER
            { ALL | trigger_name [ ,...n ] }
```

Running the following statement disables all the triggers of the Order Details table:

```
ALTER TABLE [Order Details] DISABLE TRIGGER ALL
```

Run the same statement with ENABLE instead of DISABLE to reenable all triggers.

Summary

In this chapter you learned how to create, manage, and use views, stored procedures, transactions, user-defined functions, and triggers. This chapter particularly focused on:

- Creating and managing views

- Retrieving and updating data through views

- Defining partitioned views

- Creating and managing stored procedures

- Declaring parameters on stored procedures

- Calling stored procedures with and without return values

- Creating and managing user-defined functions

- Understanding the advantages of user-defined functions over views and stored procedures

- Creating and managing AFTER and INSTEAD OF triggers

- Using trigger options

- Managing transactions

Key Terms

Before you take the exam, be certain you are familiar with the following terms:

compilation	partitioned view
encryption	partitioning column
error number	query plan
execution plan	query tree
indexed views	scalar user-defined function
inline table-valued user-defined function	schemabinding
	severity level
materialized view	state code
metadata	stored procedure
multistatement table-valued user-defined function	trigger
	user-defined function
parameter	view

Exam Essentials

Know the *CREATE* and *ALTER VIEW* syntax.   The Exam contains a number of syntax questions. Knowing all the options of CREATE and ALTER VIEW statements is essential.

Understand when a view is updateable.   Updatability of a view is subject to the definitions of its base tables and columns defined. Know the principles of updatability

Know the limitations of views.   SELECT statements used to create the view are subjects to some limitations. Know them well.

Know how to create and alter stored procedures.   Stored procedures are probably the most important objects after tables in a SQL Server database. Many questions in the exam concern stored procedures.

Know how to create and alter user-defined functions.   User-defined functions are new objects replacing or enhancing views and stored procedures.

Understand trigger functioning and limitations. Triggers are fantastic tools to maintain referential integrity or denormalized data. Understand how they work and what their impact is on performance.

Know the differences between *AFTER* and *INSTEAD OF* triggers. INSTEAD OF triggers are new to SQL Server 2000. There are subtle differences between AFTER and INSTEAD OF triggers. Make sure you understand these differences.

Review Questions

1. You are a database developer for Woodgrove Bank. You are working on a new banking system. Each time an account movement is recorded into the Movements table of the banking system,you need to recalculate and store the account balance.

   You have been asked to implement this feature while lowering the impact on the existing application. How can you do that?

   A. Create a stored procedure that inserts the movement and update the balance.

   B. Create a view that joins the Movement and Accounts tables to update both at the same time.

   C. Create a user-defined function that joins the Movement and Accounts tables, and accept the account ID as parameter.

   D. Create AFTER triggers on the Movements table to update the Account table.

2. You are maintaining a SQL Server database for Tailspin Toys. Some users complain that they cannot insert orders where the quantity ordered is above 256. The script that created the table is the following:

```
CREATE TABLE [Order Details] (
    [OrderID] [int] NOT NULL ,
    [ProductID] [int] NOT NULL ,
    [UnitPrice] [money] NOT NULL DEFAULT (0),
```

```
    [Quantity] [tinyint] NOT NULL DEFAULT (1),
    [Discount] [real] NOT NULL DEFAULT (0)
) ON [PRIMARY]
```

You want to alter the datatype of the Quantity column, but when you try to run the dedicate ALTER TABLE statement, you obtain the following error:

`The object 'vwOrders' is dependent on column 'Quantity'`

What can you do to solve this problem, without having any side effect on the applications?

A. Drop the vwOrders view.

B. Alter the vwOrders view so that it has no SCHEMABINDING option.

C. Alter the vwOrders view so that it has no ENCRYPTION option.

D. Drop the Order Details table and re-create it.

3. You are a database developer for a SQL Server 2000 database. Your database tracks employees and customers of the company you are working for. Each person of the database is recorded in the Persons table and each Employee in the Employees table. The schema and links of these tables are shown below:

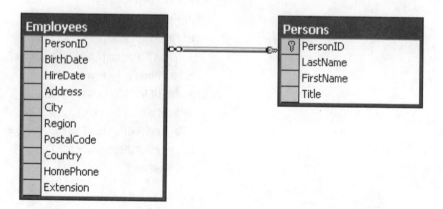

You want to create a stored procedure used to insert a new employee that inserts a new record in the Persons table, then in the

Employees table. What is the best script to preserve transactional integrity?

A.

```
CREATE PROCEDURE InsertEmployee
    (@LastName nvarchar(20),
    @FirstName nvarchar(10),
    @Title nvarchar(30),
    @BirthDate datetime,
    @HireDate datetime,
    @Address nvarchar(60),
    @City nvarchar(15),
    @Region nvarchar(15),
    @PostalCode nvarchar(10),
    @Country nvarchar(15),
    @HomePhone nvarchar(24),
    @Extension nvarchar(4))
AS
    INSERT INTO Persons
        (LastName, FirstName, Title)
    VALUES
        (@LastName, @FirstName, @Title)
    INSERT INTO Employees
            (PersonID, BirthDate,
            HireDate, Address, City,
            Region, PostalCode, Country,
            HomePhone, Extension)
    VALUES(@@IDENTITY, @BirthDate,
            @HireDate, @Address, @City,
            @Region, @PostalCode,
            Country, @HomePhone,
            Extension)
```

B.

```
CREATE PROCEDURE InsertEmployee
    (@LastName nvarchar(20),
    @FirstName nvarchar(10),
    @Title nvarchar(30),
```

```
        @BirthDate datetime,
        @HireDate datetime,
        @Address nvarchar(60),
        @City nvarchar(15),
        @Region nvarchar(15),
        @PostalCode nvarchar(10),
        @Country nvarchar(15),
        @HomePhone nvarchar(24),
        @Extension nvarchar(4))
    AS
        INSERT INTO Persons
          (LastName, FirstName, Title)
        VALUES
          (@LastName, @FirstName, @Title)
        INSERT INTO Employees
              (PersonID, BirthDate,
              HireDate, Address, City,
              Region, PostalCode, Country,
              HomePhone, Extension)
        VALUES(@@IDENTITY, @BirthDate,
              @HireDate, @Address, @City,
              @Region, @PostalCode,
              Country, @HomePhone,
              Extension)
        IF @@ERROR<>0
            ROLLBACK TRANSACTION
    C.
      CREATE PROCEDURE InsertEmployee
        (@LastName nvarchar(20),
        @FirstName nvarchar(10),
        @Title nvarchar(30),
        @BirthDate datetime,
        @HireDate datetime,
        @Address nvarchar(60),
        @City nvarchar(15),
        @Region nvarchar(15),
```

```
                    @PostalCode nvarchar(10),
                    @Country nvarchar(15),
                    @HomePhone nvarchar(24),
                    @Extension nvarchar(4))
        AS
        BEGIN TRANSACTION
          INSERT INTO Persons
             (LastName, FirstName, Title)
          VALUES
             (@LastName, @FirstName, @Title)
          IF @@ERROR=0
          BEGIN
             INSERT INTO Employees
                  (PersonID, BirthDate,
                  HireDate, Address, City,
                  Region, PostalCode, Country,
                  HomePhone, Extension)
                  VALUES(@@IDENTITY, @BirthDate,
                  @HireDate, @Address, @City,
                  @Region, @PostalCode,
                  Country, @HomePhone,
                  Extension)
             IF @@ERROR=0
             BEGIN
                  COMMIT TRANSACTION
                  RETURN 0
             END
             ELSE
             BEGIN
                  ROLLBACK TRANSACTION
                  RETURN 1
             END
          END
          ELSE
```

```
      BEGIN
          ROLLBACK TRANSACTION
          RETURN 1
      END
  COMMIT TRANSACTION
  RETURN 0
```

D.

```
CREATE PROCEDURE InsertEmployee
  (@LastName nvarchar(20),
  @FirstName nvarchar(10),
  @Title nvarchar(30),
  @BirthDate datetime,
  @HireDate datetime,
  @Address nvarchar(60),
  @City nvarchar(15),
  @Region nvarchar(15),
  @PostalCode nvarchar(10),
  @Country nvarchar(15),
  @HomePhone nvarchar(24),
  @Extension nvarchar(4))
AS
BEGIN TRAN
  INSERT INTO Persons
    (LastName, FirstName, Title)
  VALUES
    (@LastName, @FirstName, @Title)
  IF @@ERROR<>0
    ROLLBACK TRAN
  INSERT INTO Employees
        (PersonID, BirthDate,
        HireDate, Address, City,
        Region, PostalCode, Country,
        HomePhone, Extension)
    VALUES(@@IDENTITY, @BirthDate,
        @HireDate, @Address, @City,
        @Region, @PostalCode,
```

```
                    Country, @HomePhone,
                    Extension)
         IF @@ ERROR<>0
                    ROLLBACK TRAN
         COMMIT TRAN
```

4. You are a database developer for A. Datum Corporation. You are gathering data for a national project on personal computer usage. Users are querying this database to find usage patterns based on age, sex, computer brand, and state. All of this data being in different tables in the same database. The data is updated by a batch job every night, so during office hours, the data is only read.

   Users complain that queries are long to run. How could you increase the speed of these queries?

   A. Create views and index these views so users can quickly access the needed information.

   B. Create a stored procedure so user queries do not have to be recompiled.

   C. Create table-valued user-defined functions.

   D. Create temporary tables filled during batch jobs so that users query these tables.

5. You are a database developer for Lucerne Publishing. You have two servers, CORP1 and CORP2, running SQL Server 2000. CORP1 contains national sales data, and CORP2 contains foreign sales data.

   Both Sales data tables contains a column storing the country. You want to create a partitioned view unionizing these two tables, and you want to keep your users from querying base tables but run all their SELECT, INSERT, DELETE, and UPDATE queries on this view. How can you be sure that your view is partitioned and updateable? (Choose three options.)

   A. The partitioning column is part of the primary key.

   B. The partitioning column has a CHECK constraint.

   C. The CHECK constraint of the partitioning column only uses = and <> operators.

D. The column is NOT NULL.

E. The column is deterministic.

6. You are a database developer for a SQL Server 2000 database. Your database tracks employees and customers of the company you are working for. Each customer is recorded in the Persons table and each employee in the Employees table. The schema and links of these tables are shown on the next page:

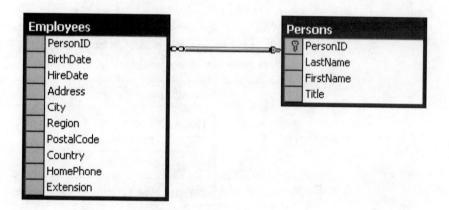

You create the following view to extract employees' information:

```
CREATE VIEW vwEmployees
AS
SELECT PersonID, LastName, FirstName, Title, BirthDate,
HireDate, Address, City, Region, PostalCode, Country,
Extension, HomePhone
FROM Employees
    INNER JOIN Persons ON Employees.PersonID =
Persons.PersonID
```

You want to insert new employees through this view. How can you achieve this result?

A. Create an INSTEAD OF trigger on the vwEmployees view.

B. Create an INSTEAD OF trigger on the Employees table.
Create an INSTEAD OF trigger on the Persons table.

    C. Create a stored procedure that processes the insert.

    D. Create an AFTER trigger on the vwEmployees view.

7. You are developing a customer relationship management system for an insurance company. You need to provide a view unionizing data from different tables, while allowing parameters. You decide to create a multistatement user-defined function. This function will union data from the CorporateCustomers, PrivateCustomers, and Employees tables (in this order).

You want the users to be able to choose whether to include the data from the Employees table. Order the following statements to create this function:

	Possibilities
	INSERT @ListName SELECT CustName FROM CorporateCustomers
	IF @Emp=1
	CREATE FUNCTION ListName (@Emp bit)
	END
	RETURNS TABLE
	BEGIN TRANSACTION
	BEGIN
	RETURNS @ListName TABLE(Name varchar(60))
	INSERT @ListName SELECT FirstName + ' ' + LastName FROM Employees
	COMMIT TRANSACTION
	INSERT @ListName SELECT CustName FROM PrivateCustomers
	RETURN

8. You are a database developer for A. Datum corp. One department of your company gathers information about baseball games. Some users intensively query this database to find information about a specific match or a given team. Besides the match ID or the team ID, the query contains always the same tables and columns. Some users want to join the result set they obtain with other tables. What is the most convenient object you could create to keep users from typing the query every time, while fulfilling their joining needs?

   A. A parameterized stored procedure

   B. A parameterized table-valued user-defined function

   C. A parameterized view

   D. A parameterized scalar user-defined function

9. You are a database developer for Lucerne Publishing. In your organization, you have two servers, CORP1 and CORP2. CORP2 is used for archiving data. Every three months, a batch job extracts data older than three months from the Sales table and moves it from CORP1 to CORP2.

   CORP2 has already been declared as a linked server on CORP1. All the users of your database system are connected to CORP1. You need to provide a seamless access to the archived sales data on CORP02 and merge them with the CORP1 active data.

   What script could you run on CORP1 to achieve this seamless access?

   A.

   ```
   sp_addlinkedserver 'CORP2', 'SQL Server'
   GO
   SELECT * FROM CORP2.Sales S2
      JOIN CORP1.Sales S1
      ON S2.SalesID=S1.SalesID
   ```

   B.

   ```
   CREATE VIEW AllSales
   AS
   SELECT * FROM Sales
   UNION ALL
   SELECT * FROM CORP2.Archive.dbo.Sales
   ```

C.

```
INSERT INTO #ArchievedSales
SELECT * FROM CORP2.Archive.Sales
```

D.

```
sp_addserver 'CORP2'
GO
CREATE PROCEDURE AllSales
AS
SELECT * FROM CORP2.Sales
```

10. You are working for Southridge Video as database developer. You implemented the following stored procedure to return the total sales for a given video title:

```
CREATE PROCEDURE TotalSold
    @title_id varchar(6), @TotalQty int=0 OUTPUT
AS
SELECT @TotalQty=SUM(qty)
    FROM titles INNER JOIN sales
    ON titles.title_id = sales.title_id
    WHERE titles.title_id = @title_id
IF @TotalQty=0
    RETURN 0
ELSE
    RETURN 1
```

How can you call that procedure to return the message 'No sales for that video title' when the sales are null, and 'The total sales for the video number XXX is YYY' when the sales are not null?

A.

```
DECLARE @Title_id varchar(6)
DECLARE @TotalQty int
DECLARE @ret_value int
SET @Title_id='BU1032'
EXEC TotalSold @Title_id,
    @ret_value OUTPUT
IF @ret_value=0
    PRINT 'No sales for that video title'
```

```
    ELSE
        PRINT 'The total sales for the video number ' +
@Title_id + ' is ' + cast(@TotalQty as varchar(10))
```

B.

```
    DECLARE @Title_id varchar(6)
    DECLARE @TotalQty int
    DECLARE @ret_value int
    SET @Title_id='BU1032'
    EXEC TotalSold @Title_id,
        @TotalQty
    IF @ret_value=0
        PRINT 'No sales for that video title'
    ELSE
        PRINT 'The total sales for the video number ' +
@Title_id + ' is ' + cast(@TotalQty as varchar(10))
```

C.

```
    DECLARE @Title_id varchar(6)
    DECLARE @TotalQty int
    DECLARE @ret_value int
    SET @Title_id='BU1032'
    EXEC TotalSold @Title_id,
        @TotalQty OUTPUT, @ret_value
    IF @ret_value=0
        PRINT 'No sales for that video title'
    ELSE
        PRINT 'The total sales for the video number ' +
@Title_id + ' is ' + cast(@TotalQty as varchar(10))
```

D.

```
    DECLARE @Title_id varchar(6)
    DECLARE @TotalQty int
    DECLARE @ret_value int
    SET @Title_id='BU1032'
    EXEC @ret_value=TotalSold @Title_id,
        @TotalQty OUTPUT
    IF @ret_value=0
        PRINT 'No sales for that video title'
    ELSE
```

```
        PRINT 'The total sales for the video number ' +
@Title_id + ' is ' + cast(@TotalQty as varchar(10))
```

11. You are a database developer for a large international organization. SQL Server 2000 is used to store statistics about pages viewed on your corporate Web servers. The database options are default ones. The marketing employees query this database through a series of stored procedure and defined queries.

    The database size has increased fast this past week due to a huge marketing campaign, and the users complains that, depending on the value they used for parameters, some stored procedures are very slow even though the number of rows is approximately the same between two executions.

    What can you do to increase the speed of these procedures?

    A. Update the statistics of indexes used by the slow procedures

    B. Run sp_recompile on the slow procedures

    C. Alter the slow procedure to add the WITH RECOMPILE option

    D. Run DBCC DBREINDEX on the tables used by the slow procedure

12. You are working as a database developer for Woodgrove Bank. Recently, you have been asked to implement a very complicated calculation for loan insurance. This calculation looks for data in different tables based on a customer ID given by the user, joins these tables, performs statistical calculations, and returns one value.

    You will need to use the result of this calculation in SELECT, INSERT, UPDATE, and DELETE statements. What is the most efficient way to implement it?

    A. A scalar user-defined function

    B. A view

    C. A stored procedure

    D. An inline table-valued user-defined function

13. You are a database developer for a SQL Server 2000 database. This database tracks courses, students, and teachers. The database structure is as follows:

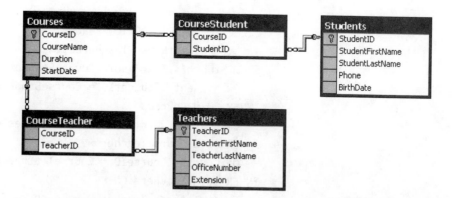

You want to create a view that gives you the list of students, along with the teachers who teach the class they are attending, ordered alphabetically. Which SELECT statement will build that list?

A.

```
SELECT DISTINCT
    StudentLastName, TeacherLastName
FROM Students INNER JOIN CourseStudent
    ON Students.StudentID = CourseStudent.StudentID
INNER JOIN Courses
    ON CourseStudent.CourseID = Courses.CourseID
INNER JOIN CourseTeacher
    ON Courses.CourseID = CourseTeacher.CourseID
INNER JOIN Teachers ON
    CourseTeacher.TeacherID = Teachers.TeacherID
ORDER BY StudentLastName
```

B.

```
SELECT
    StudentLastName, TeacherLastName
FROM Students INNER JOIN CourseStudent
    ON Students.StudentID = CourseStudent.StudentID
INNER JOIN Courses
    ON CourseStudent.CourseID = Courses.CourseID
INNER JOIN CourseTeacher
    ON Courses.CourseID = CourseTeacher.CourseID
INNER JOIN Teachers ON
    CourseTeacher.TeacherID = Teachers.TeacherID
GROUP BY StudentLastName, TeacherLastName
```

C.

```
SELECT DISTINCT TOP 100 PERCENT
    StudentLastName, TeacherLastName
FROM Students INNER JOIN CourseStudent
    ON Students.StudentID = CourseStudent.StudentID
INNER JOIN Courses
    ON CourseStudent.CourseID = Courses.CourseID
INNER JOIN CourseTeacher
    ON Courses.CourseID = CourseTeacher.CourseID
INNER JOIN Teachers ON
    CourseTeacher.TeacherID = Teachers.TeacherID
ORDER BY Students.StudentLastName
```

D.

```
SELECT StudentLastName, TeacherLastName
FROM Students INNER JOIN CourseStudent
    ON Students.StudentID = CourseStudent.StudentID
INNER JOIN Courses
    ON CourseStudent.CourseID = Courses.CourseID
INNER JOIN CourseTeacher
    ON Courses.CourseID = CourseTeacher.CourseID
INNER JOIN Teachers ON
    CourseTeacher.TeacherID = Teachers.TeacherID
ORDER BY Students.StudentLastName
```

14. You are a database developer for Tailspin Toys. You are developing a database system to track purchases made by the product managers. Each time a purchase is made, it should be checked against a budget table and recorded in the Purchases table only if it is under the budget figure.

You decide to implement a trigger on the Purchases table to check the allocated budget to the program manager before acknowledging the purchase. Each Product Manager has only one budget record. You start to write the script of the trigger:

```
CREATE TRIGGER InsPurchases ON Purchases
    FOR INSERT
    AS
```

How do you finish the script to reach your goal? Choose the right statements and put them in the right order. Note that some statements may not be useful.

	Possibilities
	UPDATE Budget
	SET BudgetedAmount = BudgetedAmount-PurchasedAmount
	FROM Inserted I JOIN Budget B
	ON I.ProdManID = B.ProdManID
	IF @@ERROR<>0
	COMMIT TRAN
	IF EXISTS(SELECT *
	FROM Inserted I JOIN Budget B
	ON I.ProdManID = B.ProdManID
	WHERE BudgetedAmount<PurchasedAmount)
	ROLLBACK TRAN
	BEGIN TRAN

15. You are a database developer for Lucerne Publishing. You designed an employee table tracking all the company's employees. The script of this table is below:

```
CREATE TABLE Employees (
EmployeeID int IDENTITY (1, 1) NOT NULL ,
LastName nvarchar (20) ,
FirstName nvarchar (10) ,
DepartmentID int
HireDate datetime NULL ,
Extension nvarchar (4))
```

You want the department manager to view and update only employees of their department. How can you achieve this result?

A. Create a view to filter data horizontally with the SCHEMABINDING option.

B. Create a stored procedure per department and grant the right to the right procedure to each manager.

C. Create a table containing links between DepartmentID and the Manager login ID.

Create a view to filter data horizontally from the Employees table on the Manager login ID with the CHECK_OPTION option.

D. Grant to right to the manager on a row basis.

Answers to Review Questions

1. D. Options A, B, and C, while having advantages, need an update of client application. Only option D meets the expectation of update and minimizing impact on client application.

2. B. The error obtained is due to the fact that a schema-bound view uses the column you need to modify. Removing the SCHEMABINDING option will solve the problem.

3. C. Option A lacks transactional integrity. Option B and D are not syntactically correct.

4. A. For heavy reads, indexed views are a must. In this scenario, the updates are done off-hours, so indexed views will have no negative impact on office-hours operations.

5. A, B, and D. Option C is not good because a partitioning column's CHECK constraint may only use BETWEEN, AND, OR, <, <=, >, >=, and =. Option E is not good either, since the column may not be deterministic.

6. A. A modification through a view can impact only one base table. With an INSTEAD OF trigger, you can capture the modification statement and replace it with your own statement(s). This kind of trigger allows updates on multiple base tables used in views.

7.

CREATE FUNCTION ListName (@Emp bit)
RETURNS @ListName TABLE(Name varchar(60))
BEGIN
INSERT @ListName SELECT CustName FROM CorporateCustomers
INSERT @ListName SELECT CustName FROM PrivateCustomers
IF @Emp=1
INSERT @ListName SELECT FirstName + ' ' + LastName FROM Employees
RETURN
END

This is a multistatement user-defined function. The only tricky statement is the RETURNS. In this kind of statement, you need to define the return table and to use a table variable to store it.

8. B. Parameterized views (Option C) do not exist. A scalar function (Option D) returns one value, so it cannot be joined. A stored procedure can be parameterized but cannot be joined. The only object offering the view feature with parameters is the table-valued user-defined function.

9. B. First, all other options are wrong because they are not using a fully qualified name (four components) to access the table on the remote server. Second, only a partitioned view offers the seamless access to CORP1 users.

10. D. The only difference among the four options is the stored procedure call. If a procedure has a return value, it is always called with the syntax EXEC @variable=procedurename. Then, when you need to output a value, as in this example the @TotalQty value, you need to use the OUPUT keyword after the variable name in the call.

11. C. Given the description of the problem, this problem is caused by a bad execution plan. If you change a procedure parameter and slow the response time, it is generally a problem of bad execution plan choice. This is the kind of procedure you should create with the RECOMPILE option.

12. A. Since this calculation returns only one value, a scalar UDF, a view, or a stored procedure may work well, since inline table-valued UDFs are designed to return a result set, not a single value. Since this calculation needs one parameter (customer ID), only scalar UDF and stored procedures will work (views do not accept parameters). The result should be used in DML statements, so only a scalar UDF fulfills the entire requirement.

13. C. This is a tricky question. First of all, the ORDER BY clause is allowed in a view only with a TOP clause in the SELECT statement. Only option C contains the TOP clause. Second, the DISTINCT clause is compulsory to ensure that no duplicates are retrieved (a student can attend two classes given by the same teacher). Third, with a GROUP BY, we could have avoided duplicates, but we would not be sure that the result is sorted.

14.
```
IF EXISTS(SELECT *
FROM Inserted I JOIN Budget B
ON I.ProdManID = B.ProdManID
WHERE BudgetedAmount<PurchasedAmount)
ROLLBACK TRAN
```

What you have to check is whether the budgeted amount is greater than the PurchasedAmount. If it is, you need to rollback the insert. Remember, the AFTER trigger is part of the transaction that fired it. The needed BEGIN TRANSACTION is implicit.

15. C. You need to filter data horizontally. Unfortunately, there is no known link between the ManagerID and the DepartmentID. You need to first create a table linking the data from both tables and create a view that filters data on the manager login ID.

Accessing Data

MICROSOFT EXAM OBJECTIVES COVERED IN THIS CHAPTER:

✓ Manage result sets by using cursors and Transact-SQL. Considerations include locking models and appropriate usage.

✓ Manipulate heterogeneous data. Methods include linked servers, OPENQUERY, OPENROWSET, and OPENXML.

✓ Extract data in XML format. Considerations include output format and XML schema structure.

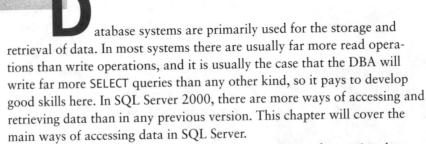

Database systems are primarily used for the storage and retrieval of data. In most systems there are usually far more read operations than write operations, and it is usually the case that the DBA will write far more SELECT queries than any other kind, so it pays to develop good skills here. In SQL Server 2000, there are more ways of accessing and retrieving data than in any previous version. This chapter will cover the main ways of accessing data in SQL Server.

The basic SELECT statement is still the primary way of returning data from the server and is pretty much unchanged from SQL Server 7. This can also be the most complex statement that you will learn in T-SQL, so it pays to develop your skills in this area.

Cursors are still available in SQL Server 2000, and they have not changed substantially since version 7.0 when they were rewritten. This chapter looks at the syntax and structure of cursors with definitions of the options and types of cursors.

Distributed queries have become a feature of SQL Server that is used more now that heterogeneous data sources must be linked together. The concept of linked servers was introduced in SQL Server 7 and allowed a variety of data to be queried from disparate data sources within SQL Server without importing the data. Other database engines could be linked to SQL Server in order to retrieve data from another database and combine it with data inside SQL Server with a single query. Adding, configuring, and using linked servers as well as ad hoc queries are discussed in the third section of this chapter. SQL Server 2000 has also introduced distributed partitioned views that allow a single table to be spread across multiple SQL Servers and accessed through a view as though it were a single table. The method for querying these views is also discussed.

SQL Server 2000 adds an additional method of getting data from the server. XML as a data format has grown in importance over the last few years, and SQL Server 2000 includes the ability to return data in an XML format directly to clients without requiring additional software to reformat the data. XML is increasingly important in e-commerce as more firms seek to exchange data between disparate systems. The last section in this chapter will discuss how to retrieve data and format XML data structures in SQL Server from either a client or directly through a URL.

Only the extraction of data from SQL Server is covered in this chapter. Modifications of data using cursors, Transact-SQL, linked servers, OPENQUERY, OPENROWSET, and OPENXML are covered in Chapter 8: Modifying Data.

The *SELECT* Command

Microsoft ✔ Exam Objective   **Manage result sets by using Transact-SQL.**

The query most commonly written to retrieve data for display or use in some other process is the SELECT query. Mastery of the SELECT command is an important part of any DBA's toolkit. SELECT is also one of the more complicated T-SQL statements since there are so many variables and permutations for its structure. There are some DBAs whose entire job is based on writing SELECT queries for various reports and data retrieval processes. They spend all their time designing and optimizing queries and never worry about any other part of SQL Server.

The tremendous amount of variations of the SELECT statement and a full treatment of it are beyond the scope of this book. There are much better references if you choose to learn more about the SELECT statement and how to write efficient and well-structured queries. Instead, this section will detail the main types of SELECT queries and provide a number of examples. A formal definition of the SELECT statement and its options appears at the end of this section. This chapter assumes that the reader is familiar with the SELECT statement and T-SQL and presents definitions and explanations of the options intended for review but not for initial learning.

Typically, a query that is used to access data is written to provide the information to someone or some application. The SELECT statement is a complex statement with many options, so we will use a series of requirements from a fictional company to get data from the database. This will (hopefully) be more interesting to the reader as well as show how a simple statement can evolve in a business setting.

Single Table *SELECT*

The simplest type of SELECT query involves a single table. In this type of SELECT statement, the query includes the following parts: column list, table name, qualifiers, and order of data. A simple example of this would be one that gets a list of customers:

```
SELECT *
  FROM Customers
```

This statement has only one column in the column list (*) and a table name (Customers) in it. The order of the data returned is in *natural order*, or the order in which the data is stored in the table. The asterisk (*) is a special character in SQL that is used as short-hand notation instead of explicitly listing all column names. For the above statement, this is translated into:

```
SELECT
    CustomerID,
    CompanyName,
    ContactName,
    ContactTitle,
    Address,
    City,
    Region,
    PostalCode,
    Country,
    Phone,
    Fax
  FROM Customers
```

Suppose that we wanted to see a result set with only certain columns that we will use to give to salespeople as a contact list. The salespeople will get the details for each row themselves, so we are only concerned with a few columns. We can explicitly limit the result set to a few columns by only naming those columns that we wish to return. This is called a *vertical partition*. It is called a *vertical partition* because we are blocking information along the vertical axis. Figure 7.1 shows the entire table with the shaded areas representing the blocked information. This query will return a vertical partition of the Customers table that could be used as a contact list.

```
Select
    CustomerID,
    ContactName,
    Phone
From Customers
```

FIGURE 7.1   A vertical partition of the Customers table

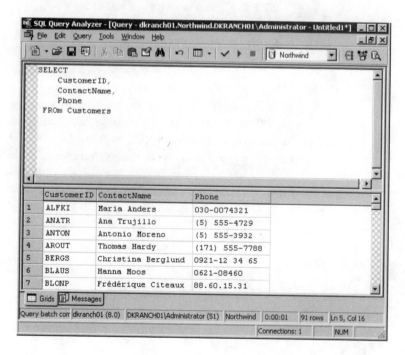

The *ORDER BY* Clause

The ORDER BY clause allows you to order the table by any of the columns. In our example, if we wish to order the list by ContactName, we would do the following:

```
SELECT
  CustomerID,
  ContactName,
  Phone
FROM Customers
ORDER BY ContactName
```

This statement will produce a result set that has the same headers as the previous one, but the rows will be ordered by the ContactName field alphabetically. Here is the first result set (abbreviated):

CustomerID	ContactName	Phone
ROMEY	Alejandra Camino	(91) 745 6200
MORGK	Alexander Feuer	0342-023176
ANATR	Ana Trujillo	(5) 555-4729
TRADH	Anabela Domingues	(11) 555-2167

When an ORDER BY clause is included, the default is to display the data in ascending order. We can alter this by adding a descending (DESC) option to the ORDER BY clause. We can also include multiple column names in the clause to gain more control over the order of the result set. If we wanted to order the results in reverse order (alphabetically) by CustomerID, but in alphabetical order by contact, the query would look like:

```
SELECT
  CustomerID,
  ContactName,
  Phone
FROM Customers
ORDER BY CustomerID DESC, ContactName
```

And the first five rows of the results:

CustomerID	ContactName	Phone
WOLZA	Zbyszek Piestrzeniewicz	(26) 642-7012
WILMK	Matti Karttunen	90-224 8858
WHITC	Karl Jablonski	(206) 555-4112
WELLI	Paula Parente	(14) 555-8122
WARTH	Pirkko Koskitalo	981-443655

If you compare this with the previous result set, you will see that this requirement was satisfied. The results are ordered by the CustomerID column in reverse alphabetical order, and then the results are ordered by the contact name in alphabetical order. The relative positions of the rows returned have been moved to satisfy the SQL statement, and thus the requirements.

Text, ntext, and image columns are not valid in the ORDER BY clause.

In addition to reordering the results, we sometimes wish to limit the results to certain rows that meet some criteria. The next section examines the WHERE clause and its usefulness in qualifying the results.

The *WHERE* Clause

The WHERE clause is used to limit the rows that are included in the result set by specifying certain criteria that each row must meet. The WHERE clause can be thought of as a filter that is applied to the data being retrieved. Each row in the table is run through the filter, and only rows that match the criteria are allowed through the filter.

Now suppose that we are asked to write a series of statements to limit the results to particular countries. These separate queries will be handed out to individual salespeople based on the country. We can use the WHERE clause to qualify which rows will be returned by the server. Let's write the

SQL to get the customers in Finland, which will be given to one of the salespeople:

```
SELECT
  CustomerID,
  CompanyName,
  ContactName,
  Country
 FROM Customers
 WHERE Country = 'Finland'
 ORDER BY Country DESC, ContactName
```

This SQL statement contains a WHERE clause that forces the query processor to evaluate each row and only return those that have a value of "Finland" for the Country column. The complete result set is shown below:

```
CustomerID CompanyName             ContactName       Country
---------- ---------------------- ----------------- -------
WILMK      Wilman Kala             Matti Karttunen   Finland
WARTH      Wartian Herkku          Pirkko Koskitalo  Finland
```

Note that there is a WHERE clause in this statement that filters out all the rows that have a country equal to "Finland" and displays only these rows. The server does not return any rows with different values for Country (we know there are rows with "USA" from a prior example). The result set is limited to, or qualified by, the WHERE clause.

We can include multiple criteria if we wish to limit the result set further. For example, we could limit our result set to the city of Helsinki with the addition of another item in our WHERE clause:

```
SELECT
  CustomerID,
  CompanyName,
  ContactName,
  Country
 FROM Customers
 WHERE Country = 'Finland'
 and City = 'Helsinki'
 ORDER BY Country DESC, ContactName
```

In this statement, we have joined the two qualifications with the keyword AND. We can continue to add as many qualifiers as needed with additional AND statements between the qualifiers.

You can use any valid T-SQL operator in the WHERE clause. Besides the = operator, you can use >, <, != or <>, and LIKE.

Enhancing Performance

One of the things often seen in queries written by less experienced T-SQL programmers is the inclusion of every field in the SELECT clause that is in the WHERE clause. The example above works with the City column included in the WHERE clause, but not in the SELECT list. The two parts of the query are independent and do require any columns to be included in both.

This is mentioned because returning additional columns that are not needed can impact your application in a few ways and is poor programming practice for a couple of reasons. One, this wastes bandwidth. SQL Server is a client/server-based system (even if included in an application that uses more than two tiers). This is an unnecessary use of bandwidth to return columns that are not needed, even if the query is from a local SQL Server.

The second potential problem is poor query performance. The inclusion of extra fields that are not needed can cause the query processor to retrieve data from leaf pages rather than index pages for some queries. Since the amount of data being returned can affect the choices made by the query processor, keeping the data retrieved to a minimum can often speed up query performance, especially in heavily loaded systems.

In addition to limiting the results with a WHERE clause, there are times that we wish to return the results from a table with a different column header. The next section examines this option.

Specifying Aliases

We now have a list to give to our salesperson, but the column headers at the top are not clearly understood by business people. Fortunately, the SELECT statement allows us to change the headers in the query without having to change the underlying table. We can specify an *alias* for any or all of the column names, which this will print out in the result set. Suppose we want to change the headers to look like the following:

```
Customer Code Company            Contact          Country
----------    ------------------ ---------------- --------
WILMK         Wilman Kala        Matti Karttunen  Finland
WARTH         Wartian Herkku     Pirkko Koskitalo Finland
```

We would write the following SQL statement:

```
SELECT
   CustomerID 'Customer Code',
   Companyname as 'Company',
   'Contact' = ContactName,
   Country
   from Customers
   where Country = 'Finland'
   order by Country desc, ContactName
```

If you look closely at the code, you will see that there are three different ways that an alias is being specified. The first is to add a space and then the alias name in quotes after the column name, as seen here:

```
CustomerID 'Customer Code',
```

The second is to place an "as" in between the column name and alias name, as seen here:

```
Companyname as 'Company',
```

The last way places the alias name first with an equality indicator (=) and then the column name, as seen here:

```
'Contact' = ContactName,
```

Any of these ways are valid and will work as expected in SQL Server, but the second way is an ANSI standard and recommended to ensure as much compatibility as possible.

Sometimes we wish to limit the number of rows regardless of whether the rows match the criteria in the WHERE clause. The next section looks at two ways to accomplish this.

Limiting the Number of Returned Results

There are times when the client wishes to have only a limited number of results returned. There are two ways to limit the size of the result set returned from a query: SET ROWCOUNT and TOP.

The SET ROWCOUNT is included for backward compatibility and is not recommended. This is a session option that is set with the syntax SET ROW-COUNT N where N is the number of rows that the client wishes to have returned. All subsequent result sets will be limited to this number of rows until the session ends (the client disconnects) or SET ROWCOUNT 0 is issued. This option is limited to returning a specific number of rows without regard to the total size of the result set.

SQL Server 7 introduced a T-SQL enhancement called TOP that performs the same function as SET ROWCOUNT. However, TOP is an option that is issued inside the SELECT query. There are also two options with TOP. The programmer can specify an absolute number of rows or a percentage of the result set. If the query includes an ORDER BY clause, then the ORDER BY is applied before the TOP operator.

Suppose that we wanted to take the same list generated above, but query the database for customers in the U.S. There are 13 customers located in the U.S., but we do not want to generate a list with more than 7 customers for any one salesperson. We could incorporate the TOP operator to perform this query as follows:

```
SELECT TOP 7
   CustomerID,
   CompanyName,
   ContactName,
   Country
FROM Customers
WHERE Country = 'USA'
ORDER BY Country DESC, ContactName
```

Which returns this result set:

CustomerID	CompanyName	ContactName	Country
SPLIR	Split Rail Beer & Ale	Art Braunschweiger	USA
LONEP	Lonesome Pine Restaurant	Fran Wilson	USA
TRAIH	Trail's Head Gourmet Provisioners	Helvetius Nagy	USA
GREAL	Great Lakes Food Market	Howard Snyder	USA
LETSS	Let's Stop N Shop	Jaime Yorres	USA
LAZYK	Lazy K Kountry Store	John Steel	USA
SAVEA	Save-a-lot Markets	Jose Pavarotti	USA

(7 row(s) affected)

We could generate this same result set using SET ROWCOUNT with the following lines of code:

```
SET ROWCOUNT 7
SELECT TOP 7
    CustomerID,
    CompanyName,
    ContactName,
    Country
  FROM Customers
  WHERE Country = 'USA'
  ORDER BY Country DESC, ContactName
SET ROWCOUNT 0
```

Comparing *SET ROWCOUNT* and *TOP*

When comparing these two options (SET ROWCOUNT and TOP), you see that they both have their place in developing applications. Books Online recommends using TOP, but there are instances where this option does not fit.

The main place where SET ROWCOUNT has an advantage over TOP is in reusing code. The same query that is used to return all rows can be limited to a smaller number of rows with SET ROWCOUNT. If TOP were to be used, then two queries would have to be written to handle the TOP differently from the query that returns all rows.

SET ROWCOUNT is limited to an absolute number of rows, so in those cases where a percentage of the result set is desired, TOP is the only choice. SET ROWCOUNT also suffers from the need to "turn off" this option when complete result sets are needed. Many application developers will forget this, and subsequent queries may be misinterpreted by users who see a limited number of results instead of the complete result set. Also, SET ROWCOUNT only works with absolute numbers. If a percentage of the results is desired, then TOP must be used.

As with most SQL Server tools, the choice of whether to use TOP or SET ROWCOUNT depends on the specific situation.

In Exercise 7.1, you will use a number of queries we just talked about.

EXERCISE 7.1

Single Table Selects

This exercise will walk you through creating a few different single table queries using the various options that have been discussed in the chapter.

1. Open the SQL Server Query Analyzer. Do this through the SQL Enterprise Manager by selecting Tools ➤ SQL Query Analyzer or by choosing Start ➤ Programs ➤ Microsoft SQL Server ➤ SQL Query Analyzer.

   In this example, we want to return a basic contact list from the Customers table in the Northwind database. For this contact list we are interested in the following columns:

   - CustomerID

   - ContactName

   - Phone

   This limited list of rows is a vertical partition that contains the same number of rows as the table, but only the three columns listed.

2. Type the following query to return in Query Analyzer (be sure the Northwind database is selected):

```
SELECT
  CustomerID,
  ContactName,
  Phone
 FROM Customers
```

3. Highlight these lines with the mouse and press the green arrow or CTRL-E to execute the query. You should receive the following results:

```
CustomerID ContactName          Phone
---------- -------------------  ----------
BSBEV      Victoria Ashworth    (171) 555-1212
CACTU      Patricio Simpson     (1) 135-5555
CENTC      Francisco Chang      (5) 555-3392
CHOPS      Yang Wang            0452-076545
COMMI      Pedro Afonso         (11) 555-7647
```

4. Now let's limit the results to those customers that have the owner as the contact. Type the following query into Query Analyzer:

```
SELECT
  CustomerID,
  ContactName,
  Phone
 FROM Customers
 WHERE ContactTitle = 'Owner'
```

5. Highlight these lines with the mouse and press the green arrow or CTRL-E to execute the query. You should receive the following results (results are abbreviated):

```
CustomerID ContactName                     Phone
---------- ------------------------------  --------------
ANATR      Ana Trujillo                    (5) 555-4729
ANTON      Antonio Moreno                  (5) 555-3932
BOLID      Martín Sommer                   (91) 555 22 82
BONAP      Laurence Lebihan                91.24.45.40
CHOPS      Yang Wang                       0452-076545
```

6. Let's now order the results by the phone number so that those customers with similar phone numbers are grouped together. Type the following query into Query Analyzer:

```
SELECT
  CustomerID,
  ContactName,
  Phone
FROM Customers
WHERE ContactTitle = 'Owner'
ORDER BY Phone
```

7. Highlight these lines with the mouse and press the green arrow or CTRL-E to execute the query. You should receive the following results (results are abbreviated):

```
CustomerID ContactName                       Phone
---------- -------------------------------   ----------------
PARIS      Marie Bertrand                    (1) 42.34.22.66
GROSR      Manuel Pereira                    (2) 283-2951
WHITC      Karl Jablonski                    (206) 555-4112
WOLZA      Zbyszek Piestrzeniewicz           (26) 642-7012
LETSS      Jaime Yorres                      (415) 555-5938
TORTU      Miguel Angel Paolino              (5) 555-2933
ANTON      Antonio Moreno                    (5) 555-3932
```

8. Lastly, let's limit the results to the first 20 percent of the results. The previous result set contained 17 rows, so we expect to see 4 rows in the next result set ($17 \times .2 = 3.4$ rounded to 4). Type the following query into Query Analyzer:

```
SELECT TOP 20 PERCENT
  CustomerID,
  ContactName,
  Phone
FROM Customers
WHERE ContactTitle = 'Owner'
```

```
CustomerID ContactName                       Phone
---------- -------------------------------   ----------------------
PARIS      Marie Bertrand                    (1) 42.34.22.66
GROSR      Manuel Pereira                    (2) 283-2951
WHITC      Karl Jablonski                    (206) 555-4112
WOLZA      Zbyszek Piestrzeniewicz           (26) 642-7012
```

Inner Joins

A single table SELECT statement has limited use in relational databases. The power of a relational database comes from its ability to gather information from multiple tables and link the information together. The most common method of linking information in different tables is the *inner join*. An inner join works by comparing columns in two tables and returning the requested information if the values of the columns match.

Since it is easier to explain this with an example, let's suppose that we have a new request from our salespeople. They want to see all of the orders for each customer along with the customer ID, company name, and the date that the order was placed. We could write:

```
SELECT
    Customers.CustomerID 'Customer Code',
    CompanyName as 'Company',
    OrderID,
    OrderDate,
    Country
  FROM Customers, Orders
  WHERE Country = 'Finland'
  AND City = 'Helsinki'
  AND CustomerID = CustomerID
  ORDER BY Country DESC, ContactName
```

However, this statement will actually generate the following error:

```
Server: Msg 209, Level 16, State 1, Line 1
Ambiguous column name 'CustomerID'.
```

The CustomerID column appears in both the Customers and Orders tables, and the query processor does not know which column to use.

In the following query, we have further qualified the column in the WHERE clause that is to be used by including the table name as a prefix to the column name and using a period as a separator. The corrected SQL statement is below:

```
SELECT
    Customers.CustomerID 'Customer Code',
    Companyname as 'Company',
    OrderID,
```

```
    OrderDate,
    Country
FROM Customers, Orders
WHERE Customers.Country = 'Finland'
AND City = 'Helsinki'
AND Customers.CustomerID = Orders.CustomerID
ORDER BY Country DESC, ContactName
```

This returns the following result set:

Customer Code	Company	OrderID	OrderDate	Country
WILMK	Wilman Kala	10615	1997-07-30	Finland
WILMK	Wilman Kala	10673	1997-09-18	Finland
WILMK	Wilman Kala	10695	1997-10-07	Finland
WILMK	Wilman Kala	10873	1998-02-06	Finland
WILMK	Wilman Kala	10879	1998-02-10	Finland
WILMK	Wilman Kala	10910	1998-02-26	Finland
WILMK	Wilman Kala	11005	1998-04-07	Finland

If you run this on your SQL Server, you will likely see the time included with the order date. I deleted this column so that it would fit on the page. Typing the table name in front of each column results in lots of wasted keystrokes, not to mention that it gets rather annoying. Fortunately, T-SQL allows the use of aliases for the table name as well as the column name. Here is the query rewritten with an alias used for each of the tables:

```
SELECT
    c.CustomerID 'Customer Code',
    c.Companyname as 'Company',
    o.OrderID,
    o.OrderDate,
    c.Country
FROM Customers c, Orders o
WHERE c.Country = 'Finland'
AND c.City = 'Helsinki'
AND c.CustomerID = o.CustomerID
ORDER BY c.Country DESC, c.ContactName
```

Using aliases is recommended and actually makes it easier to read your code. You should qualify all columns and tables in every query and use aliases to make it easier. In my queries, I usually develop an abbreviation for each table in the database and tend to use it over and over in all queries. I have colleagues who always alias each table with 'a', 'b', 'c', etc. You can choose whatever method is more comfortable for you.

The ANSI SQL standard specifies that inner joins be qualified in a slightly different manner. Here is the above code rewritten with the ANSI style inner join syntax:

```
SELECT
  c.CustomerID 'Customer Code',
  c.Companyname as 'Company',
  o.OrderID,
  o.OrderDate,
  c.Country
FROM Customers c INNER JOIN Orders o ON  C.CustomerID =
  O.CustomerID
WHERE c.Country = 'Finland'
AND c.City = 'Helsinki'
ORDER BY c.Country desc, c.ContactName
```

In this query, the join between the tables has been moved from the WHERE clause to the FROM clause following the ON keyword. The columns being joined follow the same syntax that is used in the WHERE clause, and multiple qualifications can be specified by separating them from each other with the AND keyword.

Outer Joins

Inner joins require that the qualifying conditions be met for each row to be included in the result set. Outer joins allow all rows from one or more tables to be included in the result set. There are three types of outer joins that can be written in T-SQL: left outer joins, right outer joins, and full outer joins.

Left and Right Outer Joins

The left and right outer joins are very similar and differ only in which table includes all its rows. The left outer join includes all the rows from the table on the left side of the join syntax, while the right outer join is just the opposite. This can be confusing, so let's continue with an example.

Our Finland salesperson is a little bored since there are only two customers in Finland. We are requested to generate a list of customers who have no orders so that our salesperson can try and make some sales by contacting these customers. There are a few ways this could be done, but since we are talking about *outer joins*, we will use an outer join. Starting with the query from above, we will change the inner join to an outer join. We will also remove the existing WHERE clause and add a slightly different one. Here is the code:

```
SELECT
    c.CustomerID 'Cust Code',
    c.Companyname as 'Company',
    o.OrderID,
    o.OrderDate 'OrdDate',
    c.Country
  FROM Customers c LEFT OUTER JOIN Orders o
       ON  C.CustomerID = O.CustomerID
  WHERE o.OrderID Is NULL
  ORDER BY c.Country DESC, c.ContactName
```

In this query, the inner keyword is replaced by left outer in the FROM clause. Since we have specified a *left outer join* and the Customers table is on the left side of this expression, this will generate a list of all customers whether or not there are matching rows in the Orders table. Wherever there is no matching row, SQL Server will return NULL values as placeholders for those columns selected from the Orders table. Matching rows return the data from the Orders table for the OrderID and OrderDate columns. The new WHERE clause merely limits the result set to those rows where a NULL has been placed in the OrderID column so we only see the customers with no orders. The result set looks like this:

Cust Code	Company	OrderID	OrdDate	Country
FISSA	FISSA Fabrica Inter. Salchichas S.A.	NULL	NULL	Spain
PARIS	Paris spécialités	NULL	NULL	France

The *right outer join* works the same way except the table on the right side of the join expression will return all rows. Other than this, the two joins work in the exact same manner.

T-SQL allows an alternate, *legacy syntax* for outer joins in the SELECT statement. Here is the same query rewritten using this syntax:

```
SELECT
   c.CustomerID 'Cust Code',
   c.Companyname as 'Company',
   o.OrderID,
   o.OrderDate 'OrdDate',
   c.Country
  FROM Customers c, Orders o
  WHERE o.OrderID IS NULL
  AND C.CustomerID *= O.CustomerID
  ORDER BY c.Country DESC, c.ContactName
```

Notice that the qualification that was in the ON clause has been moved back to the WHERE clause and the equality symbol has an asterisk (*) added to it on the left side. This is *legacy* syntax for an outer join. While still supported in SQL Server 2000, this syntax can lead to unexpected behavior in complex queries and is not recommended.

Full Outer Joins

The *full outer join* returns all rows from both tables, matching up the rows wherever a match can be made and placing NULLs in the places where no matching row exists. This concept is best explained with an example, so let's examine another request from the Northwind salesperson.

Suppose our salesperson wanted to get a list of cities in which there are customers along with any employees in these cities. In addition, if there is an employee in a city with no customers, this should be included as well. This is a description of a full outer join, where we want to return all rows from both tables, matching the rows up wherever possible.

The following code will implement a full outer join by using the keywords FULL OUTER JOIN between the two tables:

```
SELECT
   c.CustomerID 'Cust Code',
   c.city as 'Cust City',
```

```
    c.country,
    e.firstname,
    e.lastname
FROM employees e FULL OUTER JOIN customers c
    ON e.city = c.city
```

This returns a result set that includes these rows (results are abbreviated):

Cust Code	Cust City	country	firstname	lastname
WHITC	Seattle	USA	Laura	Callahan
WILMK	Helsinki	Finland	NULL	NULL
WOLZA	Warszawa	Poland	NULL	NULL
NULL	NULL	NULL	Andrew	Fuller
NULL	NULL	NULL	Margaret	Peacock

As you can see in this result set, the first row has a match between the employee city and the customer city. The data from each table row is placed in the appropriate column. The second and third rows show rows in the Customers table for which there was no matching row in the Employees table. SQL Server returned the data from the Customers table, but since there was no matching row in Employees, NULLs were returned as placeholders in each of the columns that represent data from the Employees table. The last two rows show NULL values for the columns representing data from the Customers table. Since there were no matching rows in the Customers table for these employees, only the data from the Employees table is included.

In order to fit this result set on the page, the city from the Employees table is not included. We would have to use the names in this result set to query the Employees table for the location of these employees.

Cross Joins

The *cross join* is also referred to as a cross product. You will rarely find a use for this type of join unless you need to generate test data. A cross product can generate quite a bit of data with a single query and is useful to produce large amounts of data. A cross join will generate a result set that includes all combinations of rows from both tables. The number of rows returned is the product of the numbers of rows in each table. Let's look at an example.

Our salesperson is busy calling customers right now, but the purchasing people want a list of all suppliers and categories and every possible combination. Since we are busy, we decide not to ask why they want this data or how they will use it and simply write a cross join query, as seen here:

```
SELECT *
  FROM Suppliers CROSS JOIN Categories
```

There are 29 rows in the Suppliers table and 8 rows in the Categories table. Their product is $29 \times 8 = 232$. This query will return 232 rows, which will include all combinations of suppliers and categories. Notice that there is no need to add a qualifier for this type of join. Since all combinations are being returned, it does not make sense to qualify the join. We could still add a WHERE clause and limit the result set if we choose.

An alternative to specifying a cross join specifically is as follows:

```
SELECT *
  FROM Suppliers, Categories
```

This will return the same result set as the CROSS JOIN query. Often we see complex queries with many tables (usually more than five) that implement a cross join. This is almost always an oversight on the programmer's part in forgetting to include a qualifier between two tables.

When reviewing anyone else's code, the first thing you should check is that all tables are joined together to ensure that no cross products occur.

In Exercise. 7.2, we will look at the various joins.

Joining Tables Together

This exercise will look at various ways that tables in the Northwind database can be joined together.

Suppose that we wish to list each order number along with the quantity purchased and the name of the product for each line item in the order. This is an example of an inner join where we want to return rows that match in all the tables. For this query, we will join two tables together to retrieve the information.

1. Open the SQL Server Query Analyzer. Do this through the SQL Enterprise Manager by selecting Tools ➢ SQL Query Analyzer or by choosing Start ➢ Programs ➢ Microsoft SQL Server 2000 ➢ SQL Query Analyzer.

2. Use an inner join between the Order Details table and the Products table. Type the following query to return in Query Analyzer (be sure the Northwind database is selected):

```
SELECT
    o.OrderID,
    o.Quantity,
    p.ProductName
 FROM [Order Details] o, Products p
 WHERE o.ProductID = p.ProductId
```

3. You should receive the following results (results are abbreviated):

```
OrderID     Quantity ProductName
----------- -------- ------------------------------------
10248       12       Queso Cabrales
10248       2        Tofu
10248       1        Genen Shouyu
10248       10       Singaporean Hokkien Fried Mee
10248       5        Mozzarella di Giovanni
```

Now we wish to find out which customers have never ordered anything. This requires an outer join since we want to return rows from the Customers table that have no match in the Orders table.

4. Use a left outer join to return customers with no matching rows in the Orders table. A WHERE clause is used to limit the results to only the rows that have no match. Type the following query to return in Query Analyzer:

```
SELECT
    c.CustomerID,
    o.OrderId
 FROM Customers c LEFT OUTER JOIN Orders o
   ON c.CustomerID = o.CustomerID
 WHERE o.OrderID IS NULL
```

5. You should receive the following results (results are abbreviated):

```
CustomerID OrderId
---------- -----------
PARIS      NULL
FISSA      NULL
```

Aggregate Operators

Aggregate operators provide a summary of information in a query. The aggregate operations that are supported in SQL Server are:

- SUM
- AVG
- COUNT
- MIN
- MAX

These functions allow the programmer to summarize information using any of the previous mathematical operations.

If we were requested to provide a report that showed how many orders each customer had and the total dollar amount of all orders for that customer, we could write:

```
SELECT
    c.Country,
    c.CustomerID,
    COUNT( o.orderID) 'Total Orders',
```

```
    SUM( od.UnitPrice * od.Quantity) 'Total Sales'
FROM Customers c, Orders o, [Order Details] od
WHERE c.CustomerID = o.CustomerID
AND o.OrderID = od.OrderID
GROUP BY c.CustomerID
```

This query includes three tables, but is very similar to the inner join queries discussed earlier.

In the following sections, we will discuss how to use the aggregate operators, as well as how to group the results using the various aggregate options.

The *GROUP BY* Clause

There is one additional section in this query: the GROUP BY clause. Whenever a non-aggregated field is included in a query, it must be accompanied by the GROUP BY clause and listed in this clause. This tells the query processor where to group the information and provide totals. Without this clause, the query processor returns an error informing the programmer that the field must be included in an aggregate or placed in the GROUP BY clause.

The (abbreviated) results for this query are:

Country	CustomerID	Total Orders	Total Sales
Germany	ALFKI	12	4596.2000
Mexico	ANATR	10	1402.9500
Mexico	ANTON	17	7515.3500
UK	AROUT	30	13806.5000

An improperly structured GROUP BY clause can lead to some misleading results. Be sure that you understand how the data is being summarized in your query. It is easy to misinterpret the results if you do not pay close attention to which fields are included in your GROUP BY clause and in what order. Including an ORDER BY clause can make understanding the results easier.

The *HAVING* Clause

Suppose that we wanted to limit the results to those countries and customers that had spent $10,000 or more and with less than 20 orders. Aggregates can include a HAVING clause for this purpose. A HAVING clause is like a WHERE clause for aggregates. The following query:

```
SELECT
    c.Country,
    c.CustomerID,
    COUNT( o.orderID) 'Total Orders',
    SUM( od.UnitPrice * od.Quantity) 'Total Sales'
 FROM Customers c, Orders o, [Order Details] od
 WHERE c.CustomerID = o.CustomerID
 AND o.OrderID = od.OrderID
 GROUP BY c.country, c.CustomerID
 HAVING SUM( od.UnitPrice * od.Quantity) > 10000
 AND COUNT( o.OrderID) < 20
```

includes the HAVING clause with two qualifications: one for the total sales and one for the number of orders. Only those rows that meet both qualifications in the HAVING clause will be included in the result set.

CUBE and *ROLLUP*

There are also two summary operators that will provide additional data for the aggregate values: CUBE and ROLLUP. These two operators are used with the GROUP BY clause to add additional rows that summarize the totals by groups. CUBE will provide additional summary rows for every combination of group and subgroup that is returned by the query. ROLLUP will provide summary rows in a hierarchical order from the lowest level group to the highest. The number of rows returned by ROLLUP may vary depending on the order of the columns in the GROUP BY clause. Here is an example:

```
SELECT
    c.CustomerID,
    c.City,
    c.Country,
    COUNT( o.orderID) 'Total Orders',
    SUM( od.UnitPrice * od.Quantity) 'Total Sales'
```

```
FROM Customers c, Orders o, [Order Details] od
WHERE c.CustomerID = o.CustomerID
AND o.OrderID = od.OrderID
GROUP BY c.country, c.city, c.CustomerID
WITH CUBE
HAVING SUM( od.UnitPrice * od.Quantity) > 10000
ORDER BY c.country
```

The above query added the City column so that the effects of CUBE and ROLLUP are visible. You can substitute ROLLUP for CUBE to see the effects on the results. These operators are not often used, as the client must be able to distinguish the summary rows from data rows. The summary rows in the result set will have NULLs placed in the columns that are being summarized.

The *COMPUTE* Clause

In addition to the aggregates included in the SELECT list, the COMPUTE clause is included in SQL Server for backward compatibility to produce aggregates as extra result sets. This operator will produce additional result sets that contain the aggregates requested. If our Finland salesperson wanted to see each order for his customers and then the total for all orders, we could use the following query:

```
SELECT c.CustomerID, o.OrderID, (od.quantity * od.unit-
    price) 'total'
 FROM ORDERS o, [order details] od, Customers c
 WHERE c.CustomerID = o.CustomerID
 AND o.OrderID = od.OrderID
 and c.Country = 'Finland'
 COMPUTE SUM( od.quantity * od.unitprice)
```

This query will list each order and the total sales price for this order. After this result set, a second result set is included with the sum of all the orders as a single column.

Books Online recommends that this operator be replaced by the ROLLUP operation or the use of Analysis Services; however, it is still valid T-SQL and should be understood for the exam.

COMPUTE also includes an optional BY keyword that will break the results down into further result sets. The following code:

```
SELECT c.CustomerID, o.OrderID, (od.quantity * od.unit-
  price) 'total'
 FROM Orders o, [order details] od, Customers c
 WHERE c.CustomerID = o.CustomerID
 AND o.OrderID = od.OrderID
 AND c.CustomerID LIKE 'AN%'
 ORDER BY c.customerID
 COMPUTE SUM( od.quantity * od.unitprice) BY c.CustomerID
```

will produce four different result sets, one for each of the customers since the customer is included in the BY clause. After each of these customer result sets, there is a further result set produced by the COMPUTE clause that has the sum of the orders for that customer.

Many client applications cannot handle multiple result sets, so before using the COMPUTE clause in a query, be sure that the application is prepared for multiple result sets. The recommended alternative is to use the ROLLUP option and have the client application decode the single result set.

In Exercise 7.3, we will show you how to use aggregates.

EXERCISE 7.3

Using Aggregates

Aggregates are most helpful in summarizing data for reports. Often a user will want to see the total of some numeric values or the endpoints for date ranges. This exercise will use aggregates to analyze the sales information that is contained in the Northwind database.

1. Open the SQL Server Query Analyzer. Do this through the SQL Enterprise Manager by selecting Tools ≻ SQL Query Analyzer or by choosing Start ≻ Programs ≻ Microsoft SQL Server ≻ SQL Query Analyzer.

   A classic example of an aggregate is generating the total sales revenue for a time period. Suppose that we were interested in knowing the total sales volume by customer for 1997.

EXERCISE 7.3 *(continued)*

2. Write a query that returns the total sales for each customer for 1997. Use the SUM operator to generate the total sales as the quantity of an item purchased multiplied by the unit price. In Query Analyzer, type the following:

```
SELECT
    o.CustomerID,
    SUM( od.Quantity * od.UnitPrice) 'Total Sales'
FROM Orders o, [Order Details] od
WHERE o.OrderID = od.OrderID
AND o.OrderDate > '12/31/1996'
AND o.OrderDate < '01/01/1998'
GROUP BY o.CustomerID
```

3. You should receive the following results (results are abbreviated):

```
CustomerID Total Sales
---------- --------------------
ALFKI      2294.0000
ANATR      799.7500
ANTON      6452.1500
AROUT      6589.0000
```

4. Now, we wish to limit this list to those customers who spent more than $20,000 in 1997. Limit the results from above to those customers with a total sales amount greater than $20,000 using a HAV-ING clause. Type the following in Query Analyzer:

```
SELECT
    o.CustomerID,
    SUM( od.Quantity * od.UnitPrice) 'Total Sales'
FROM Orders o, [Order Details] od
WHERE o.OrderID = od.OrderID
AND o.OrderDate > '12/31/1996'
AND o.OrderDate < '01/01/1998'
GROUP BY o.CustomerID
HAVING SUM( od.Quantity * od.UnitPrice) > 20000
```

5. You should receive the following results (results are abbreviated):

```
CustomerID Total Sales
---------- --------------------
ERNSH      53467.3800
HUNGO      23959.0500
MEREP      26087.1000
QUICK      64238.0000
SAVEA      60672.6400
```

The *UNION* Command

The UNION command is used to join two SELECT queries. It is placed between two queries, and the two result sets are combined and returned to the client as a single result. The results can include or exclude duplicates. Both queries that are included in the UNION must have the same number of columns.

The following query will return a list of cities for both customers and employees:

```
SELECT c.City
  FROM Customers c
UNION
SELECT e.City
  FROM Employees e
```

This list does not have any duplicates included in the results. The UNION operator compiles both result sets and removes any duplicates before sending the data back to the client. If we wanted to see duplicates (and see how many entities are in a city), we could include the ALL option in the UNION command:

```
SELECT c.City
  FROM Customers c
UNION ALL
SELECT e.City
  FROM Employees e
```

This result set will have duplicates included.

The *Distinct* Command

The DISTINCT command is also used to remove duplicates from a single result set in the same manner that UNION removes them from two result sets. If we issue the following query:

```
SELECT DISTINCT e.City
  FROM Employees e
```

we get back a list of cities with no duplicates. If this command is used with multiple columns in the SELECT list, then duplicates are removed from the entire result set, not just the first column listed. Here are the complete results (there are 9 rows in this table):

```
City
----------------
Kirkland
London
Redmond
Seattle
Tacoma
```

Scalars

A *scalar,* also know as a *literal,* is essentially a constant value. There are times when a single value is needed in a result set for some reason. This may be a simple result that returns some value, such as a name, to the user:

```
SELECT 'Steve' as 'Name'
Name

----
Steve
```

We can also use a scalar in combination with a logical test to return some value we specify back in the result set. Suppose we are generating (yet another) sales report and the salespeople want to know only if a customer is a foreign or a domestic customer. We could write:

```
SELECT CASE WHEN c.Country = 'USA'
          THEN 'Domestic'
          ELSE 'Foreign'
        END 'Status',
    c.CustomerID
  FROM Customers c
```

This would return the following (abbreviated):

```
Status    CustomerID
--------  ----------
Foreign   LAUGB
Domestic  LAZYK
Foreign   LEHMS
Domestic  LETSS
Foreign   LILAS
```

In this query, we have combined a CASE expression with a scalar to return one of two values depending on how the CASE is evaluated for each row in the result set.

Subqueries

A *subquery* is a query embedded inside another query. There are many possibilities for subqeuries, so we will cover the three main places that these can appear and that you should be aware of for the exam. You can use a subquery inside the SELECT list in place of a column, in the FROM clause in place of a table, and in the WHERE clause in place of a column or literal qualifier.

Subqueries in the *SELECT* list

When a subquery is used in the SELECT list, it returns data that takes the place of a column. It is rare when this type of query cannot be structured in another way, but it is valid T-SQL syntax. This type of subquery is called a *scalar subquery* since it can only return one value.

If our salesperson wanted a report of all orders with a specific supplier's name prefixed, we could use the following query:

```
SELECT
  ( SELECT ContactName
      FROM Suppliers WHERE ContactTitle = 'Sales Agent'
  ) 'Agent',
  o.OrderID FROM Orders o
```

We would get these results (abbreviated):

```
Agent                              OrderID
--------------------------------------------
Lars Peterson                      10249
Lars Peterson                      10251
Lars Peterson                      10258
Lars Peterson                      10260
```

Subqueries in the *FROM* Clause

When a subquery is used in the FROM clause, this is referred to as a *derived table*. An alias must be specified, and the columns from this query can be used just like the columns in any normal table included in the WHERE clause. The following is an example of this type of query:

```
SELECT a.*, b.*
  FROM Customers a, ( SELECT Ordered, OrderDate, CustomerID
                        FROM Orders) b
  WHERE a.CustomerID = b.CustomerID
```

While not a very efficient or useful query, this does return a list of customers along with their order ID and order date for each of their orders.

Subqueries in the *WHERE* Clause

The last place that subqueries normally occur is in the WHERE clause as part of a qualification. When used as a part of a qualifying statement, a subquery can return a single row, which is used with the >, <, =, and LIKE operators. If the subquery returns multiple rows, then it would be part of an IN operator and take the place of a comma-delimited list.

There is a special type of subquery called a *correlated subquery* that can be used in the WHERE clause. This subquery, also called the inner query, is correlated when it is reevaluated for each row that is passed through the outer query. The subquery is said to be correlated like the results from the subquery correlate directly to the row being evaluated in the outer query. This is probably better explained with two examples; the first is a subquery in the WHERE clause that is not correlated. Here is a query that lists the order ID and date for all orders placed by customers in the U.S.:

```
SELECT o.OrderID, o.OrderDate
  FROM Orders o
  WHERE o.CustomerID in ( SELECT CustomerID
                            FROM Customers c
                            WHERE Country = 'USA'
                                    )
```

This subquery will return the same number of rows containing the same data for each row that is evaluated from the outer query. If the row in the outer query has a customer ID that matches a customer ID returned by the subquery, the row is returned in the result set.

This next query shows customers and the order that directly proceeded a late order:

```
SELECT CustomerID, OrderID
 FROM Orders o
 WHERE OrderDate = ( SELECT max( OrderDate)
                       FROM Orders o1
                       WHERE o1.CustomerID = o.CustomerID
                       AND o1.RequiredDate < o1.ShippedDate)
```

In this query, the subquery returns different results depending on which row is being evaluated in the outer query. The inner query cannot even be evaluated without having some data from the outer query. This subquery is correlated to the outer query by Customer ID.

SELECT: By the Book

This chapter has examined each of the sections and many of the options of the SELECT statement. The formal syntax for the SELECT statement is as follows:

```
SELECT statement ::=
    < query_expression >
    [ ORDER BY { order_by_expression | column_position [ ASC
    | DESC ] }
        [ ,...n ]     ]
```

```
        [ COMPUTE
            { { AVG | COUNT | MAX | MIN | SUM } ( expression ) } [
    ,...n ]
            [ BY expression [ ,...n ] ]
        ]
        [ FOR { BROWSE | XML { RAW | AUTO | EXPLICIT }
                [ , XMLDATA ]
                [ , ELEMENTS ]
                [ , BINARY base64 ]
            }
    ]
        [ OPTION ( < query_hint > [ ,...n ]) ]

< query_expression > ::=
    { < query_specification > | ( < query_expression > ) }
    [ UNION [ ALL ] < query_specification | ( <
    query_expression > ) [...n ] ]

< query_specification > ::=
    SELECT [ ALL | DISTINCT ]
        [ { TOP integer | TOP integer PERCENT } [ WITH TIES ]
    ]
        < SELECT_list >
    [ INTO new_table ]
    [ FROM { < table_source > } [ ,...n ] ]
    [ WHERE < search_condition > ]
    [ GROUP BY [ ALL ] group_by_expression [ ,...n ]
        [ WITH { CUBE | ROLLUP } ]
    ]
    [ HAVING < search_condition > ]
```

This definition of the SELECT statement shows the outline of the SELECT with its options first. Inside this SELECT, there is a placeholder for the *<query_expression>* that is defined in the second section. This in turn, includes a placeholder for the *<query_specification>*, which is defined in the third section.

Some of these options will be discussed in later sections, like the FOR section, which applies to XML formatted data, and the INTO clause, which is a method for inserting bulk data into a table. For more detailed explanations of the other options, Books Online or a reference devoted to T-SQL is recommended.

Functions for Transforming Data

SQL Server 2000 includes a number of functions for changing the values of a column, scalar, or variable. These functions can be grouped into various categories depending on their datatypes. Since this chapter is assuming you have some familiarity with T-SQL, Tables 7.1 through 7.3 list the functions and provide a description of each. More detailed information on these functions is available in Books Online.

TABLE 7.1 General Functions

Function	Description
ISDATE(exp)	Returns 1 if exp is a valid date
ISNULL(exp1,exp2)	Returns exp2 if exp1 is NULL, otherwise exp1 is returned
ISNUMERIC(exp)	Returns 1 if exp is a number type
NULLIF(exp1, exp2)	Returns NULL if both expressions are equivalent

TABLE 7.2 String Functions

Function	Description
ASCII(char)	Returns the ASCII value of a character.
CHAR(int)	Returns the character value for an ASCII integer value.
CHARINDEX(string1, string2, start)	Returns the starting position for string1 in string2 optionally starting at position start.
DIFFERENCE(string1, string2)	Returns the difference between the SOUNDEX values of string1 and string2.

TABLE 7.2 String Functions *(continued)*

Function	Description
LEFT(string, int)	Returns the first int characters from string.
LEN(string)	Returns the length of the string.
LOWER(string)	Returns the string passed in with all characters converted to lowercase.
LTRIM(string)	Returns the string with all blank spaces from the left side of the string removed.
NCHAR(int)	Returns the UNICODE character represented by int.
PATINDEX(string1, string2)	Returns the starting position of string1 in string2. Wildcards may be used in string1.
QUOTENAME(string, char)	Returns a Unicode string with the delimiter char added to make the input string a valid Microsoft® SQL Server™ delimited identifier. If no second parameter is passed, char defaults to the square bracket.
REPLACE(string1, string2, string3)	Searches string1 for string2 and replaces string2 with string3.
REPLICATE(string, int)	Returns a string with int number of char repeated.
REVERSE(string)	Returns the reverse of a character expression.
RIGHT(string, int)	Returns the int number of characters from the right side of the string.

TABLE 7.2   String Functions *(continued)*

Function	Description
RTRIM(string)	Returns the string with all blank spaces from the end of the string removed.
SOUNDEX(string)	Returns a four-character code that can be used to evaluate how similar this string is to another.
SPACE(int)	Returns int number of spaces.
STR(float, length, decimal)	Converts a numeric value to a string.
STUFF(string, start, length, char)	Removes length characters from string starting with character start and replaces them with char.
SUBSTRING(string, start, int)	Returns a portion of the string string starting at position start and continuing for int characters.
UNICODE(Unicode string)	Returns the numeric value of the first character of a UNICODE expression.
UPPER(string)	Returns the string passed in with all characters converted to uppercase.

TABLE 7.3   Date and Time Functions

Function	Description
DATEADD(*datepart, int, date*)	Returns a date based on adding (or subtracting) an interval from *date*. The interval type (days, hours, etc.) is specified by *datepart* and the length of the interval is specified by *int*.

TABLE 7.3 Date and Time Functions *(continued)*

Function	Description
DATEDIFF(*date1, date2*)	Returns the difference between two dates.
DATENAME(*datepart, date*)	Returns a character string that represents the *datepart* of *date*.
DATEPART()	Returns the specific part of the date as an integer.
DAY(*date*)	Returns the numeric day of the week for *date*.
GETDATE()	Returns the current server date and *time*.
GETUTCDATE	Returns the datetime value that represents the current Universal Time Coordinate. Calculated based on the server time zone and the current time.
MONTH(*date*)	Returns the numeric month number of *date*.
YEAR	Returns the numeric year number of *date*.

There are number of other functions that can be used to gather system information, get configuration information, etc., which are available in SQL Server. For a detailed description of all these functions, see Books Online.

Cursors

Microsoft ✔ *Exam* *Objective*

Manage result sets by using cursors and Transact-SQL.

*C*ursors are programming constructs that derive their functionality from procedural programming languages. They simulate a table structure, derived from a result set, and allow the programmer to access the data row by row. The programmer can also perform operations on the underlying data in the existing table. While useful and even essential in some areas, cursors are not recommended for most solutions. The row-by-row nature of a cursor is fundamentally opposed to the set processing that is the basis and strength of SQL Server.

A good description of a cursor might be a temporary table that you define based on a query, but a table that you can only access one row at a time without requiring the computation of a new primary key for each row. You can retrieve all the values from that row, but each row must be retrieved separately. In order to store two rows' worth of data, you must have twice as many variables as you have fields in the cursor.

While ANSI SQL includes the concept of cursors in the SQL standard, you should avoid using them whenever possible. There are usually set-oriented approaches that are both more efficient and quicker to execute.

Cursors can be used to update data as well as retrieve it row by row, but cannot be used to insert data. They can be used as a temporary storage area for a set of data that is protected from changes. Certain configuration options can either ensure that changes to the underlying data show up in SQL Server or that the data is "frozen" when the cursor is declared.

While most situations should not require a cursor, there are times that a cursor is needed and indeed may be the most efficient method of processing a set of data. In the following sections, I will describe a few examples of cursor usage and then provide a more detailed definition of the various cursor parameters and options.

Using a Cursor

Printing reports is usually the function of a front-end application, but there are times when SQL Server will be needed or just used to produce a formatted report. Reporting is a classic example of where T-SQL will be unable to produce the desired output because the report does not conform to the structure of most result sets. In the Northwind database, we have customers and orders in separate tables. Suppose our sales manager wanted a customer history report in the following format:

```
Customer:ALFKI - Alfreds Futterkiste
     Order:10643 (Aug 25 1997)
     Order:10692 (Oct  3 199)
     Order:10702 (Oct 13 199)
Customer:ANATR - Ana Trujillo Emparedados y helados
     Order:10625 (Aug  8 1997)
     Order:10759 (Nov 28 199)
Customer:ANTON - Antonio Moreno Taquería
     Order:10507 (Apr 15 1997)
     Order:10535 (May 13 199)
     Order:10573 (Jun 19 199)
     Order:10677 (Sep 22 199)
     Order:10682 (Sep 25 199)
Customer:AROUT - Around the Horn
     Order:10453 (Feb 21 1997)
     Order:10558 (Jun  4 199)
     Order:10707 (Oct 16 199)
     Order:10741 (Nov 14 199)
     Order:10743 (Nov 17 199)
     Order:10768 (Dec  8 199)
     Order:10793 (Dec 24 199)
```

This report would be extremely difficult to produce using T-SQL and its set-oriented statements. The grouping and ordering of the data is difficult enough without trying to produce the formatting that indents the order and places it directly below the customer data. There are a few ways to implement this report (Temp tables, lots of UNIONs, etc.) without a cursor, but they would not be easier or simpler.

The code in Listing 7.1 will produce the previous report.

Listing 7.1: Sales Report Using a Cursor

```
DECLARE rpt CURSOR FOR
 SELECT c.CustomerID, c.CompanyName, o.OrderID, o.Order-
Date
   FROM Customers c, Orders o
   WHERE c.CustomerID = o.CustomerID
   AND c.CustomerID LIKE 'A%'
   AND DatePart( year, o.OrderDate) = 1997

DECLARE @cid char( 8),
    @cname char( 40),
    @ordid char( 8),
    @orddt datetime,
    @old char( 8)

OPEN rpt

FETCH NEXT FROM rpt INTO @cid, @cname, @ordid, @orddt
SELECT @old = ' '

WHILE @@fetch_status = 0
 BEGIN
   IF @old = @cid
     BEGIN
       PRINT '    Order:' + rtrim( @ordid) + ' (' + cast(
@orddt as CHAR( 10)) + ')'
     END
     ELSE
     BEGIN
       PRINT 'Customer:' + rtrim( @cid) + ' - ' + rtrim(
@cname)
       PRINT '    Order:' + rtrim( @ordid) + ' (' + cast(
@orddt as CHAR( 11)) + ')'
       SELECT @old = @cid
     END
```

```
    FETCH NEXT FROM rpt INTO @cid, @cname, @ordid, @orddt
END
CLOSE rpt

DEALLOCATE rpt
```

This code is relatively simple and short and works in the following manner. In the first six lines, the cursor is declared and the server creates the structure internally. If you run the following lines:

```
SELECT c.CustomerID, c.CompanyName, o.OrderID, o.OrderDate
  FROM Customers c, Orders o
  WHERE c.CustomerID = o.CustomerID
  AND c.CustomerID LIKE 'A%'
  AND DatePart( year, o.OrderDate) = 1997
```

you will get a result set that looks exactly like the cursor. The next statement declares a series of variables that will hold the individual field values from each row in the cursor. One extra variable is declared that is used to control the formatting. The following line from Listing 7.1 is required and allows the program to access the cursor:

```
OPEN rpt
```

Cursors can be opened and closed as many times as needed, though the program can only access the cursor when it is "open."

The following line retrieves the first row of data from the cursor and places it into the variables that were previously declared:

```
FETCH NEXT FROM rpt INTO @cid, @cname, @ordid, @orddt
```

Once the data is stored in these variables, then it can be used in whatever operations are needed (in this case, PRINT statements).

The following lines from Listing 7.1 construct a loop that moves through each line of the cursor and determines what is needed as output based on the data that it finds in the local variables:

```
WHILE @@fetch_status = 0
  BEGIN
      PRINT '    Order:' + rtrim( @ordid) + ' (' + cast(
  @orddt as
  CHAR( 10)) + ')'
    END
    ELSE
```

```
        BEGIN
          PRINT 'Customer:' + rtrim( @cid) + ' - ' + rtrim(
        @cname)
    PRINT '    Order:' + rtrim( @ordid) + ' (' + cast( @orddt as
CHAR( 11)) + ')'
              SELECT @old = @cid
          END
        FETCH NEXT FROM rpt INTO @cid, @cname, @ordid,
        @orddt
    END
```

Note that there is a FETCH statement inside the loop. This is extremely important! Without this FETCH, the loop would continue to run indefinitely as no new data would be retrieved and @@FETCH_STATUS would never change. When a program calls a FETCH statement, it causes the row indicator within a cursor to move and updates @@FETCH_STATUS.

I cannot count the number of times that I have written or reviewed cursor code that neglected a FETCH inside the loop. I finally learned to check for its existence before I do any other troubleshooting.

The last two lines close the cursor and then remove it from memory. It is important to note that once the cursor is deallocated, it is literally removed from the server and cannot be accessed again. A new cursor could be declared with the same structure and data, but it would be a different cursor. If a process is working on a particular row inside the cursor and the cursor is deallocated, the location from which the last FETCH statement was made is lost. Declaring a new cursor with the same structure (or based on the same query) would start processing from the first row. If you intend to work with the same cursor later in a batch or script, then you can close it to conserve resources. When it is needed, another OPEN command will open the cursor for access at the same point where it was closed.

Cursor Declaration

Now that we have explained how a cursor can be used, let's look at the formal declaration of a cursor. There are a number of different cursor types and options that can be used in SQL Server, each one creating a slightly different cursor that is suited to different types of operations. The complete syntax for the declaration of a cursor is as follows:

```
DECLARE <cursor_name> CURSOR
[LOCAL | GLOBAL]
[FORWARD_ONLY | SCROLL]
[STATIC | KEYSET | DYNAMIC | FAST_FORWARD]
[READ_ONLY | SCROLL_LOCKS | OPTIMISTIC ]
[TYPE_WARNING]
FOR
    [ SELECT statement ]
[ FOR UPDATE [ OF column list [ a, b, .., n]]]
```

The cursor name should conform to the standard SQL Server object identifier naming rules. Each of the sections is described below along with an explanation of its effect on the cursor:

[**LOCAL | GLOBAL**] This is an optional argument that controls the scope of the cursor. By default, if this is omitted, the **default is to create a local cursor** database option controls whether the cursor is declared LOCAL or GLOBAL.

LOCAL cursors are visible only within the batch, stored procedure, or trigger in which they are declared. They can only be referenced by variables within these constructs, though they can be assigned to an OUPUT parameter from a stored procedure and assigned to a cursor variable in the calling program. A LOCAL cursor is deallocated implicitly when the batch, stored procedure, or cursor ends.

A GLOBAL cursor has a scope that includes the current connection and may span multiple batches, stored procedures, or triggers. The cursor name can be referenced from any point in the current connection. The cursor will only be implicitly deallocated when the connection closes.

Cursors consume resources and may cause locking problems if held open too long. GLOBAL cursors are especially prone to cause performance problems on shared resources. Be wary of using GLOBAL cursors and holding them open for too long. It is a good habit to deallocate the cursor as soon as it is no longer needed.

[**FORWARD_ONLY | SCROLL**]   This option has an effect on how the cursor behaves with regard to accessing the data within the cursor. FORWARD_ONLY means that the program that uses the cursor can only move from the beginning row to the ending row in that direction. Once a row has passed (in logical order), it can no longer be accessed. This option is generally faster for performance since the server need not provide a mechanism for moving in both directions.

SCROLL cursors allow the programmer to move in both forward and backward directions through the cursor. The movement in this type of cursor does not need to be a row at a time. Any row can be accessed with a FETCH statement by using the options available with this command.

There are additional resources required for scroll cursors since the entire dataset must be maintained until the cursor is destroyed. If backward movement is not required in the cursor, do not declare the cursor with SCROLL.

[**STATIC | KEYSET | DYNAMIC | FAST_FORWARD**]   These options control how the cursor interacts with the data on which it is based as well as how SQL Server stores the cursor internally.

STATIC cursors consist of a temporary copy of the data from the underlying sources. This type of cursor is implemented as a temporary table in Tempdb, where the data is copied from the SELECT statement into Tempdb. Changes to the underlying data are not reflected in the cursor. This type of cursor is also not updateable.

KEYSET cursors also use Tempdb, but only to store the key values that identify the rows in the underlying data. The main feature of this type of cursor is that changes to non-key values are reflected in the cursor. This allows the most up-to-date information about non-key fields to be available inside the cursor. Inserts as well as changes to key values are not reflected in the cursor unless the update is performed through the cursor and the WHERE CURRENT OF clause is used. Deletes of rows cause @@FETCH_STATUS to be set to -2.

DYNAMIC cursors are essentially views of the underlying data source and reflect all changes to data made outside the cursor. Absolute fetches are not supported in this type of cursor.

FAST_FORWARD cursors are forward-scrolling, read-only cursors that have performance enhancements to make them the fastest type of cursor to use. These cursors are non-updateable (hence read-only) and cannot be used when SCROLL, FOR_UPDATE or FORWARD_ONLY are used.

[READ_ONLY | SCROLL_LOCKS | OPTIMISTIC]   READ_ONLY cursors act as the name implies. No updates are allowed through this cursor.

SCROLL_LOCKS cursors ensure that updates made as the program moves through the cursor are guaranteed to succeed. This is because SQL Server locks the rows as they are read into the cursor, thereby preventing any changes by other users and conflicts from occurring.

The OPTIMISTIC option is used when locks on the rows read into the cursor are not wanted or needed. If an update or delete is made to a row in the cursor that was changed by another source, the update or delete in the cursor will fail. It is an optimistic strategy that assumes the data will be the same and updates can occur, but there are no guarantees.

WARNING   SCROLL_LOCKS cursors can cause contention problems with other users. Since each row in this cursor is locked in the underlying table, other users cannot access these rows until the cursor is deallocated.

[TYPE_WARNING]   This option specifies that a message be sent to the client if the server changes the type of cursor from what was submitted. If the client specifies options that require the changing of the cursor from one type to another, this controls whether an informational message is sent to the client.

[SELECT statement]   This query is any valid SELECT statement that follows the rules for the particular database in which the cursor is being declared. This query is the defining statement in the declaration and determines the size and width of the cursor. The number of fields in the column list of the query will set the width of the cursor and determine the fields that are available inside the cursor. The WHERE clause in the SELECT statement (or lack of one) will determine how many rows will populate the cursor.

FOR UPDATE [OF *column 1, column 2, .., n*] This option specifies columns in the cursor that are updateable. If no column list is included, then all columns are updateable. Otherwise, only those columns specifically listed are updateable.

This option is covered in Chapter 8: Modifying Data.

Retrieving Data from the Cursor

Once the cursor has been declared, the data inside the cursor is retrieved using the FETCH command. Each time this statement is issued, it returns a single row of data into local variables. These variables must match the data types of the columns included in the cursor, and there must be the same number of variables in the fetch statement as there are columns in the cursor.

The formal syntax of FETCH is as follows:

```
FETCH
    [ NEXT | PRIOR | FIRST | LAST
        | ABSOLUTE { n | @Nvar}
        | RELATIVE  { n | @Nvar}
    ]
```

The keywords are defined in Table 7.4.

TABLE 7.4 FETCH Options

OPTION	Description
NEXT	Returns the next row from the cursor moving forward
PRIOR	Returns the prior row in the cursor moving backward
FIRST	Returns the first row from the cursor
LAST	Returns the last row in the cursor
ABSOLUTE	Returns the nth row from the cursor where n is counted from the first row
RELATIVE	Returns the nth row from the cursor starting from the current row (n may be negative)

Each execution of FETCH will set the value of the global variable @@FETCH_STATUS depending on the results of the FETCH statement. If the next row is retrieved without any error, this variable will be set to 0. Table 7.5 lists the values that result from the FETCH statement.

TABLE 7.5   FETCH Result Codes

Result Code	Description
0	No errors occurred. The specified row was retrieved.
-1	FETCH failed or row is beyond the result set (EOF or BOF).
-2	Row is missing.

Distributed Queries

Microsoft ✓ Exam Objective   **Manipulate heterogeneous data. Methods include linked servers and OPENROWSET.**

Only the retrieval of data using linked servers and OPENROWSET is discussed in this section. The modification of data is discussed in Chapter 8: Modifying Data.

*D*istributed queries are being used more and more as data spread across various systems must be gathered together for a single query. SQL Server 7 introduced the concept of linked servers, which allowed a variety of data sources to be queried as though the data were stored in a table on the same system. SQL Server 2000 still uses the linked servers for heterogeneous data sources and allows ad hoc queries as well using the OPENROWSET function. Both of these methods for accessing data will be discussed in the following sections.

Supporting very large databases with heavy transaction loads was a design goal of SQL Server 2000. Distributed partitioned views were enhanced to allow updates and create a federation of database servers.

With a federation of database servers, data from a table is spread across all servers in the federation, but is queried and updated as though the data were in a single table on a single server. By distributing this load, SQL Server 2000 is capable of supporting the loads of even the largest systems.

Linked Servers

Manipulate heterogeneous data using linked servers.

The concept of a *linked server* was introduced in SQL Server 7 as a way to allow SQL Server developers to incorporate data stored in other systems into queries. This concept existed in previous versions of SQL Server, but was limited to remote procedure calls and servers that supported a limited set of protocols. With SQL Server 7, this was expanded to any OLE DB source for which a driver was installed on the server. Spreadsheets, dBase, and Excel files were all accessible from within SQL Server by adding a link to the particular data source. The following OLE DB providers have been tested with SQL Server 2000:

- Microsoft OLE DB Provider for SQL Server
- Microsoft OLE DB Provider for ODBC
- Microsoft OLE DB Provider for Jet version 4.0
- Microsoft OLE DB Provider for DTS Packages
- Microsoft OLE DB Provider for Oracle version 2.6
- Microsoft OLE DB Provider for Microsoft Directory Services
- Microsoft OLE DB Provider for Microsoft Indexing Service
- Microsoft OLE DB Provider for DB2

These data sources can either expose their data as a rowset or return data from a query as a rowset. If the remote data source has a database engine that can return a rowset, the section of the query that deals with the remote data source is sent to that engine for processing. For OLE DB sources that do not have an engine, such as Excel or text files, the OLE DB provider is responsible for executing the query and returning the rowset.

SQL Server registers information about the location of the data source, the drivers needed, and any security information (name, password) that is needed to access the server. The data source is then queried from within a database using a four-part name for the object being queried. This name is in the form:

```
linked_server_name.catalog.schema.object_name
```

The parts are defined here:

linked_server_name   This is the friendly name that is registered in sysservers.

catalog   The catalog is analogous to the database in SQL Server. This is the location within the remote data source in which the object is located.

schema   This is equivalent to the owner of the table.

object_name   This is the name of the table or other structure being queried.

This four-part name is the same fully qualified name structure that can be used for any local table in a SQL Server database. If these parts are not included, the server defaults to the local server, the catalog to the current database, and the schema to *dbo*.

Adding a linked server is accomplished with the sp_addlinkedserver system stored procedure. This procedure takes a series of parameters to register the remote server on the local system. The stored procedure format is:

```
sp_addlinkedserver [ @server = ] 'server'
    [ , [ @srvproduct = ] 'product_name' ]
    [ , [ @provider = ] 'provider_name' ]
    [ , [ @datasrc = ] 'data_source' ]
    [ , [ @location = ] 'location' ]
    [ , [ @provstr = ] 'provider_string' ]
    [ , [ @catalog = ] 'catalog' ]
```

The parameters are described here:

@server   This is the local name for the linked server that will be used in queries.

@srvproduct This is the product name of the OLE DB data source being added as a linked server. If this is SQL Server, then the remaining parameters do not need to be specified.

@provider This is the unique programmatic identifier of the OLE DB provider being used for the data source.

@datasrc This is the name of the data source as required by the OLE DB provider. For SQL Servers it is the name of the remote server, such as server\instance.

@location This is interpreted by the OLE DB provider as the location of the data source, and varies by provider.

@provstr This is the OLE DB connection string specific to the provider.

@catalog This is the catalog to be used when making a connection to the remote data source. It is the database name in SQL Server.

The values that are required for the parameters will vary depending on the type of OLE DB data source being added as a linked server. If our fictional company had a remote SQL Server named NEO that needed to be added as a remote server, we would execute the following code:

```
EXEC sp_addlinkedserver @server='NEO_REMOTE', @srvprod-
   uct='',
      @provider='SQLOLEDB', @datasrc='NEO'
```

This would add the remote server NEO, which we would then access as NEO_REMOTE, for the linked server name along with the other three parts of the name needed for a query.

For an Excel spreadsheet, however, the parameters are much different. A path is needed as well as a name for the range of rows and cells that will be accessed. The name for the range is created from within Excel and is not needed to register the linked server, but is needed in any queries to this linked server. A sample stored procedure call to register the Sales_History.xls spreadsheet on the local server would be:

```
EXEC sp_addlinkedserver 'Sales_History',
   'Jet 4.0',
   'Microsoft.Jet.OLEDB.4.0',
   'c:\Sales_History.xls',
   NULL,
   'Excel 5.0'
```

The local name is set to the same name as the spreadsheet, but this is for convenience. It is not required. In fact, the local name need not look anything like the remote name of the data source for any of the providers.

Security in a linked server environment is handled by storing information about remote logins on the local server. The remote logins can be mapped directly to local logins, or a single account can be chosen for all queries sent to the linked server. One last alternative is to allow the current login's credentials to be "passed through" to the linked server. Keep in mind that no matter which method is chosen for security, the linked server manages its own permissions and will only allow access to those objects that the remote login has permission to access.

Adding a remote server login is accomplished with the `sp_addlinkedsrvlogin` system stored procedure. Its format is as follows:

```
sp_addlinkedsrvlogin [ @rmtsrvname = ] 'rmtsrvname'
    [ , [ @useself = ] 'useself' ]
    [ , [ @locallogin = ] 'locallogin' ]
    [ , [ @rmtuser = ] 'rmtuser' ]
    [ , [ @rmtpassword = ] 'rmtpassword' ]
```

These parameters are defined here:

@rmtsrvname The local name of the linked server. This is the same as the @server parameter for `sp_addlinkedserver`.

@useself Either True or False. If True, then local SQL Server logins use their own credentials and @rmtuser and @rmtpassword are ignored. If False, then @rmtuser and @rmtpassword are used for the login specified in @locallogin.

@locallogin This is the login on the local SQL Server for which this mapping is valid. If NULL, then all local logins are mapped with @rmtuser and @rmtpassword.

@rmtuser The username used to connect to the remote server. This parameter defaults to NULL.

@rmtpassword The password used to connect to the remote server for @rmtuser.

If different login mappings are needed for different users, then this stored procedure must be run separately for each mapping. Suppose our salesperson is named Morpheus, but he has no user account on the linked server

Trinity. We have been given a login on Trinity for Morpheus to use, but the login name is Morpheus2 and the password is matrix. We can add a mapping for Morpheus with the following stored procedure call:

```
exec sp_addlinkedsrvlogin 'Trinity', 'false', 'Morpheus',
    'Morpheus2', 'matrix'
```

The *OPENROWSET* Function

Microsoft ✓ Exam Objective	Manipulate heterogeneous data using OPENROWSET.

Registering a linked server is not difficult but can be time consuming and is a cumbersome way to gain access to a data source that may be needed for only a single query. SQL Server 2000 provides an alternative method of accessing remote data sources with the OPENROWSET function. This function allows ad hoc access to the remote data source within the FROM clause of a SELECT query just as any other table. It may also be referenced as the target of an INSERT, UPDATE, or DELETE clause if the OLE DB provider supports this functionality. The syntax of this function is:

```
OPENROWSET ( 'provider_name'
    , { 'datasource' ; 'user_id' ; 'password'
        | 'provider_string' }
    , { [ catalog. ] [ schema. ] object
        | 'query' }
    )
```

The parameters are described here:

provider_name   The friendly name of the OLE DB provider as stored in the registry.

datasource   The name of the data source. This could be the filename or the server name.

user_id   A username that is used to log in to the remote data source.

password   The password to be used with *user_id* to log in.

provider_string   The provider-specific connection string for initializing the connection.

catalog   The initial catalog to be accessed.

schema   The name of the schema or object owner.

object   The name of the object being queried.

query   The specific query to be run to return a rowset.

Suppose that our salesperson for Finland maintains an Access database table of calls that have been made each week. The sales manager requests that we query this Access spreadsheet and compare the orders with calls made to customers. Since our salesperson uses the CustomerID column in his call log, we copy the Access database to the SQL Server and issue this query:

```
SELECT o.CustomerID, o.OrderID, a.CallTime, a.CallDate
FROM Orders o INNER JOIN
   OPENROWSET('Microsoft.Jet.OLEDB.4.0',
    'c:\MSSQL\Data\calllog.mdb';'admin';'pwd', Calls)
    AS a
ON o.CustomerID = a.customerID
```

This query will perform an inner join on the local Access database against our Orders table in Northwind.

If access to a data source is needed more than a handful of times, the source should be registered with SQL Server. This allows SQL Server to optimize the connection process.

Heterogeneous Data Access

As powerful and useful as relational database systems are, a tremendous amount of data is still stored in other formats. Excel spreadsheets seem to contain most of the data in every company in which I have worked; I often find some of the most valuable information is kept updated in this format. It is also difficult, if not impossible, to get business people to stop using their spreadsheets and perform all data updates in SQL Server.

In prior versions of SQL Server, this data would have to be converted and loaded into the SQL Server after every update or an employee would be forced to manually input the updates into the Excel spreadsheet as well as some SQL Server applications. Neither of these is a good solution and usually results in the spreadsheet and the SQL Server database holding different information most of the time.

Both linked servers and OPENROWSET provide an excellent alternative to either of these methods by allowing queries against SQL Server to include the data in these alternate formats without any duplication of data. By registering a linked server against an Excel spreadsheet (or other format), queries that require this information can always be assured of receiving the most up-to-date data.

Distributed Partitioned Views

In traditional SQL Server views, if a UNION operator is included in the view definition, the view is not updateable. A *distributed partitioned view* is a special view that includes a union of data from multiple servers but is allowed to be updated if it meets certain criteria. Updates are discussed in Chapter 8, and this section will look at what a distributed partitioned view is, how to create one, and how to incorporate a distributed partitioned view into a query.

In Figure 7.2, the structure of a distributed partitioned view is shown. The view is called vCustomers and contains data from the Northwind.Customers table for those customers whose CustomerID starts with A or B. The data that is in this view is actually distributed across two servers, ServerA and ServerB, with each server holding a portion of the data. The data on each server is stored in a table that has a check constraint to ensure that only data that is supposed to be stored on this server is stored here. The distributed partitioned view combines the data from all these servers and presents it as a single view. The query processor load for this data is distributed across multiple servers, which increases the performance and scalability of this data.

FIGURE 7.2   Distributed partitioned view structure

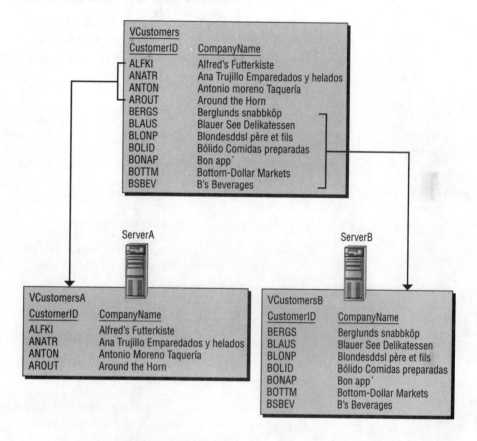

There are a few steps to create a distributed partitioned view. We will show you how to do it in Exercise 7.4.

Creating a Distributed Partitioned View

This exercise requires at least two SQL Servers (or two instances on one server) to complete. To create a distributed partitioned view, follow these steps:

1. Open the SQL Server Query Analyzer. Do this through the SQL Enterprise Manager by selecting Tools ➤ SQL Query Analyzer or by choosing Start ➤ Programs ➤ Microsoft SQL Server ➤ SQL Query Analyzer.

2. First you must create tables on each server with check constraints that will limit the data stored in each table. Connect to ServerA and type the following query (be sure the Northwind database is selected):

```
CREATE TABLE vCustomerA
  (CustomerID char( 10) PRIMARY KEY
          CHECK (substring( CustomerID, 1, 1) = 'A'),
    CompanyName varchar( 100))
```

3. Highlight these lines with the mouse and press the green arrow or CTRL-E to execute the query.

4. Connect to ServerB by choosing File ➢ Connect from the Query Analyzer menu and logging into ServerB.

5. Type the following query into the Query Analyzer window for ServerB (be sure the Northwind database is selected).

```
CREATE TABLE vCustomerB
  (CustomerID char( 10) PRIMARY KEY
          CHECK (substring( CustomerID, 1, 1) = 'B'),
   CompanyName varchar( 100)
   )
```

6. Highlight these lines with the mouse and press the green arrow or CTRL-E to execute the query.

   Notice that each of these tables contains a CHECK constraint on the primary key to limit the data in that table to the *horizontal partition* that is supported by that server.

7. Once the individual tables have been set up, each server must create a link to the servers with the other horizontal partitions. In this case, ServerB would have to be linked on ServerA, and ServerA would have to be linked on ServerB. This allows each server to communicate with the other servers for a query against the view that is made on that server. Steps 8 through 10 will link the servers together.

8. From the Query Analyzer window connected to ServerA, ServerA registers ServerB using the following script (change the login information to match your servers):

```
EXEC sp_addlinkedserver @server='ServerB',
@srvproduct='',
        @provider='SQLOLEDB', @datasrc='SERVERB'
EXEC sp_addlinkedsrvlogin 'ServerB', 'True'
```

9. Highlight these lines with the mouse and press the green arrow or CTRL-E to execute the query.

10. From the Query Analyzer window connected to ServerB, ServerB registers ServerA using the following script (change the login information to match your servers):

```
EXEC sp_addlinkedserver @server='ServerA',
@srvproduct='',
        @provider='SQLOLEDB', @datasrc='SERVERA'
EXEC sp_addlinkedsrvlogin 'ServerA', 'True'
The last step involves creating the partitioned view.
```

11. Type the following code into the Query Analyzer window connected to ServerA and highlight it with your mouse. Press the green arrow or press CTRL-E to execute this code.

```
CREATE VIEW vCustomers AS
    SELECT * FROM Northwind.dbo.vCustomerA
UNION ALL
    SELECT * FROM ServerB.Northwind.dbo.vCustomerB
```

12. Type the following code into the Query Analyzer window connected to ServerB and highlight it with your mouse. Press the green arrow or press CTRL-E to execute this code.

```
CREATE VIEW vCustomers AS
    SELECT * FROM Northwind.dbo.vCustomerB
UNION ALL
    SELECT * FROM ServerA.Northwind.dbo.vCustomerA
```

A query that incorporates vCustomer can be run from either ServerA or ServerB, and the same data is returned. This view can be incorporated into any query in the same manner as any other table or view.

The distributed partitioned view technology has also been incorporated into the query processor. Whichever server the query is run on will only query the other servers if it needs data from that server. A query that only looked for customers starting with a B would only query ServerB, even if this query is run on ServerA. An examination of the execution plan will show that remote queries are only sent to the appropriate servers.

SQL Server 2000 and XML

SQL Server 2000 introduced *Extensible Markup Language (XML)* support for the first time as a part of the SQL Server feature set. While available as an add-on for SQL Server 7, this functionality has been enhanced and extended in SQL Server 2000 and includes a number of features to make data access very easy. The addition of XML data retrieval brings with it a new syntax and method of formatting data that is very different from the traditional row and column structure, which has characterized SQL Server in the past.

XML is a tag-based markup language—similar to HTML—that delimits and describes sections of the data using tags. These tags are not, for the most part, predefined as HTML tags are. Instead, XML tags are defined by the user and will change from data set to data set. Hence the *extensible* part of the XML acronym. Here is an example of an XML document:

```
<Customers CustomerID="ALFKI" CompanyName="Alfreds
    Futterkiste" ContactName="Maria Anders"
    ContactTitle="Sales Representative" Address="Obere Str.
    57" City="Berlin" PostalCode="12209" Country="Germany"
    Phone="030-0074321" Fax="030-0076545"/>
```

A set of XML data is called an *XML document*. In the example above, the document contains one element, `<Customers>`, with a series of attributes: `CustomerID`, `CompanyName`, etc. This XML document has an implicit Document Type Definition (DTD), which defines the elements and attributes of an XML document. The DTD is similar to the table definition in a relational database.

Some additional terminology is necessary in order to understand how XML data can be accessed in SQL Server:

XSL The *Extensible Stylesheet Language (XSL)* is similar to the Cascading Style Sheets (CSS) used in HTML. XSL provides a way to describe how an XML document is to be formatted or displayed.

XPATH *XML Path Language (XPATH)* is a standard language that has been defined by the World Wide Web Consortium (W3C) to navigate through an XML document. SQL Server supports a subset of this standard.

Templates *Templates* are XML documents that contain one or more SQL statements that specify queries (SQL or XPATH queries) executed using the template rather than through a URL.

IIS *Internet Information Server (IIS)* is the Web server that is supplied with Windows NT and Windows 2000. It is a client-server program, similar to SQL Server, that provides data access through the HTTP protocol.

URL A *uniform resource locator (URL)* defines a location for a particular resource. Web pages are commonly specified using a URL as the path to some particular page. SQL Server 2000 integrates with IIS to provide access to SQL Server through a URL.

XML is well suited for a variety of data-related applications, especially those that require the integration of disparate systems. It is, however, a complicated topic, with an almost infinite variety of ways that it could be integrated into a particular system. Readers are advised to consult additional reference materials to learn more about XML. This chapter presents a brief introduction to XML and how XML-formatted data can be retrieved using SQL Server.

In the following sections, will discuss using XML with the SELECT statement and accessing SQL through a URL.

Using *SELECT* with XML

Microsoft Exam Objective	Extract data in XML format. Considerations include output format and XML schema structure.

There are a number of methods for retrieving data in XML format, though the simplest one is using a standard SELECT statement. As noted in the "SELECT: By the Book" sidebar in this chapter, the SELECT syntax includes a FOR XML clause that will return data as XML rather than a standard recordset. When using this form of the SELECT statement, there are three different modes for returning the data as well as three different options. Table 7.6 lists the modes and Table 7.7 lists the options along with a description of each.

TABLE 7.6   FOR XML Modes

Mode	Description
RAW	This mode transforms each row in the recordset into an XML element with the identifier *row*. Each non-NULL column is mapped into an attribute of the element.
AUTO	This mode allows SQL Server to format an XML document in a logical way, based on the table schema. Each row becomes an element, with each column becoming an attribute.
EXPLICIT	This mode requires the query to specify how the XML document will be formed. Additional columns must be introduced into the query that will determine how different elements will be nested together.

TABLE 7.7 FOR XML Options

Option	Description
XMLDATA	When this option is included, the XML Data Schema is returned along with the XML document as an inline schema, prepended to the document.
ELEMENTS	This option is only available in AUTO mode. When included, the columns of the recordset are returned as sub-elements rather than attributes.
BINARY BASE64	When this option is specified, binary data is returned as BASE64 encoded. If using the RAW or EXPLICIT mode to retrieve binary data, this option must be specified. In AUTO mode, the binary data is returned as a reference only.

Here are a few examples that should better explain how XML data is transformed from a relational schema. The first example is a couple of rows from the Northwind database:

```
SELECT CustomerID, CompanyName, ContactName, Country
FROM Customers
WHERE CustomerID LIKE 'BL%'
```

```
CustomerID CompanyName                 ContactName        Country
---------- --------------------------- ------------------ -------
BLAUS      Blauer See Delikatessen     Hanna Moos         Germany
BLONP      Blondesddsl père et fils    Frédérique Citeaux France
```

Now, here is the same data with the FOR XML AUTO option added.

```
SELECT CustomerID, CompanyName, ContactName, Country
FROM Customers
WHERE CustomerID LIKE 'BL%'
FOR XML AUTO
```

```
<Customers CustomerID="BLAUS" CompanyName="Blauer See
Delikatessen"
   ContactName="Hanna Moos" Country="Germany"/>
```

```
<Customers CustomerID="BLONP" CompanyName="Blondesdds1 père et
fils"
  ContactName="Frédérique Citeaux" Country="France"/>
```

This result set is returned as a single row in Query Analyzer. It has been reformatted to fit this page.

Note that the table name is listed as the element (first item in the tag) and repeated for each row. Each column header becomes an attribute, with the value of the column for that row becoming the value of the attribute.

Now, I will add the XML Data Schema to the query:

```
SELECT CustomerID, CompanyName, ContactName, Country
 FROM Customers
 WHERE CustomerID LIKE 'BL%'
 FOR XML AUTO, XMLDATA
<Schema name="Schema7" xmlns="urn:schemas-microsoft-
  com:xml-data" xmlns:dt="urn:schemas-microsoft-
  com:datatypes">
  <ElementType name="customers" content="empty"
  model="closed">
    <AttributeType name="CustomerID" dt:type="string"/>
    <AttributeType name="CompanyName" dt:type="string"/>
  </ElementType>
<customers CustomerID="BLAUS" CompanyName="Blauer See
  Delikatessen" ContactName="Hanna Moos" Country="Ger-
  many"/>
<customers CustomerID="BLONP" CompanyName="Blondesdds1
  père et fils" ContactName="Frédérique Citeaux" Coun-
  try="France"/>
```

This result includes the schema references at the beginning for the namespace (xmlns) and the datatypes (xmlns:dt) that were used to create this document.

If the RAW mode is used, then the same result set looks slightly different:

```
SELECT CustomerID, CompanyName, ContactName, Country
 from Customers
 WHERE customerid LIKE 'BL%'
 FOR XML RAW
```

Results:

```
<row CustomerID="BLAUS" CompanyName="Blauer See
  Delikatessen"/>
<row CustomerID="BLONP" CompanyName="Blondesddsl père et
  fils"/>
```

If the XMLDATA option is used, then the same schema information from the above example will be prepended to the result set. The row identifier will still remain at the beginning of each row.

The EXPLICIT mode is much more complicated than any of the other two modes. When this is specified, the query must follow a specific format to ensure that the XML document is valid. The other two modes return *well-formed* XML documents, which have no open tags in improperly nested elements.

In order to tell the server how to nest the data, two columns are prepended to the result set. The first column is an integer and must be called Tag; it will store the tag number of the current element. The second column is called Parent and stores the tag number of the parent element. The rest of the rowset corresponds to the columns of data that are to be transformed into elements and attributes. They must be named in the following manner: *<element>!<tag_number>!<attribute_name>*. The last item required for EXPLICIT mode is that the children must immediately follow their parent.

With all of these constraints, it is not likely that you will use EXPLICIT mode very often. However, it is an area that you may be tested on when you take the exam. Be sure that you understand how this mode works and what its requirements are.

In the cursor example, we produced a report in the following format:

```
Customer:ALFKI - Alfreds Futterkiste
    Order:10643 (Aug 25 1997)
    Order:10692 (Oct  3 199)
    Order:10702 (Oct 13 199)
Customer:ANATR - Ana Trujillo Emparedados y helados
    Order:10625 (Aug  8 1997)
    Order:10759 (Nov 28 199)
Customer:ANTON - Antonio Moreno Taqueria
    Order:10507 (Apr 15 1997)
```

This same type of formatting can be achieved using the EXPLICIT mode of a SELECT statement. Actually, two SELECT queries are needed and are joined by a UNION ALL to include any duplicates:

```
SELECT 1 as Tag,
        NULL as Parent,
        Customers.CustomerID as [Customer!1!CustomerID],
        Customers.CompanyName as [Customer!1!Company-
    NameD],
        NULL as [Order!2!OrderID],
        NULL as [Order!2!OrderDate]
FROM Customers
UNION ALL
SELECT 2,
        1,
        Customers.CustomerID,
        Customers.CompanyName,
        Orders.OrderID,
        Orders.OrderDate
FROM Customers, Orders
WHERE Customers.CustomerID = Orders.CustomerID
ORDER BY [Customer!1!CustomerID], [Order!2!OrderID]
FOR XML EXPLICIT
```

If you run this query in Query Analyzer without the FOR XML EXPLICIT, you will see a normal result set with a series of NULLs for each top-level element. The details under each top level are complete rows that will be used to fill out the nested elements in the XML document.

The easiest way to view the XML documents is with Internet Explorer 5 or higher. If you access any of these queries through a URL (or you can retrieve the results from ADO and display them), you will see a nicely formatted and indented XML document. We'll discuss how to do this in the next section.

EXERCISE 7.5

Extracting Data In XML Format

This exercise will reformat the two queries in Exercise 7.2 to return the data in an XML format.

1. Rewrite the first query in Exercise 7.2 to return XML data using the AUTO option.

```
SELECT
    o.OrderID,
    o.Quantity,
    p.ProductName
 FROM [Order Details] o, Products p
 WHERE o.ProductID = p.ProductId
 FOR XML AUTO

XML_F52E2B61-18A1-11d1-B105-00805F49916B
--------------------------------------------------------
<o OrderID="10248" Quantity="12">
  <p ProductName="Queso Cabrales"/>
</o>
<o OrderID="10248" Quantity="10">
    <p ProductName="Singaporean Hokkien Fried Mee"/>
</o>
<o OrderID="10248" Quantity="5">
  <p ProductName="Mozzarella di Giovanni"/>
</o>
```

2. Rewrite the second query from Exercise 7.2 to return data using the RAW mode and including the XMLDATA option.

```
SELECT
    c.CustomerID,
    o.OrderId
 FROM Customers c LEFT OUTER JOIN Orders o
    ON c.CustomerID = o.CustomerID
 WHERE o.OrderID IS NULL
 FOR XML RAW, XMLDATA
```

Accessing SQL Server through a URL

SQL Server 2000 integrates with IIS to provide access to SQL Server data. This data is returned in an XML format and queried using the same types of T-SQL code that was presented in the prior section. The setup for IIS to allow this access is made easier with a menu option—Configure SQL XML Support In IIS—that is created when SQL Server is installed. The details are explained in Books Online and are beyond the scope of this text.

Once you have configured IIS to integrate with SQL Server, there will be a virtual root created that is accessible using a URL. Data can be accessed using this URL in a few different ways. SQL queries can be appended to the URL as a parameter named sql. The value of this parameter will be the query that is to be executed. An example of this type of data retrieval is with the following URL:

```
http://MyServer/Nwind?sql=SELECT+CustomerID+FROM+Customers+FOR+XML+RAW&
    root=ROOT
```

Here *MyServer* is the name of the IIS Server. The query is reformatted to conform to the requirements of HTTP requests.

When setting up the IIS integration, be sure to check the Allow URL Queries option.

There are a few different methods of using a URL to extract data from SQL Server. The following sections will examine how template files can store queries on the server, XSL can be used to reformat the result sets, and will briefly discuss XPATH queries.

Template Files

Specifying SQL queries in the URL is cumbersome as well as a possible security risk. A malicious user could possibly alter the query in the URL to retrieve data that they are not intended to view. An alternative to specifying a query in the URL is to incorporate the query into a template file. A template file is a physical file that is placed in a folder on the IIS server. This template folder will have been configured when IIS was configured and will be the virtual root for the template virtual name.

Template files are specified in the following format:

```
<ROOT xmlns:sql="urn:schemas-microsoft-com:xml-sql"
        sql:xsl='XSL FileName' >
  <sql:header>
    <sql:param>..</sql:param>
    <sql:param>..</sql:param>...n
  </sql:header>
  <sql:query>
    sql statement(s)
```

```
    </sql:query>
    <sql:xpath-query mapping-schema="SchemaFileName.xml">
      XPath query
    </sql:xpath-query>
  </ROOT>
```

Table 7.8 defines the various options when using template files.

TABLE 7.8 Options of the Template File

Option	Description
ROOT	This is the top-level element added to an XML fragment to create an XML document. This name is arbitrary and can be replaced with any name. This tag includes the namespace declaration, which provides a reference for the schema of this document.
<sql:header>	This tag holds header values. At the current time, only SQL parameters can be included in this section.
<sql:query>	This refers to any SQL queries that are to be executed. Multiple queries can be placed in the same template file.
<sql:xpath-query>	This section is for any XPATH queries that are to be executed.

The template is then accessed through a URL, like in Listing 7.2.

Listing 7.2: XMLTemplate1.xml

```
<ROOT xmlns:sql="urn:schemas-microsoft-com:xml-sql">
  <sql:query>
    SELECT CustomerID
    FROM   Customers
    FOR XML AUTO
  </sql:query>
</ROOT>
```

This file is saved in the template folder and accessed through the following URL:

```
http://MyServer/Nwind/template/XMLTemplate1.xml
```

The results of this URL request will be an XML document that looks the same as that which was returned from the above example when the query was passed into the URL. Multiple SQL queries can be placed in the file, and they will each be executed and returned as a single XML document.

Each SQL query is a separate transaction. If a single statement fails, processing will continue with the next query.

Templates are not limited to SQL queries; they can also execute stored procedures. And with either queries or stored procedures, the templates can include parameters that will be substituted into the query or stored procedure call when the template is accessed.

Suppose that our Finland salesperson has now returned to us and requested that we provide him two reports on sales; one of these reports is an order history report for a given customer, and the second report is a list of products along with their respective categories. Our salesperson wants these two reports to be generated together, as they are used for a weekly report. In order to provide these reports to the salesperson, we will use a template file that contains the two queries, one of which will be a stored procedure and is the other a SQL query. The file is shown in Listing 7.3.

Listing 7.3: XMLTemplate2.xml

```
<ROOT xmlns:sql="urn:schemas-microsoft-com:xml-sql">
  <sql:header>
  <sql:param name="CustomerID">WARTH</sql:param>
  </sql:header>
  <sql:query>select c.categoryname, p.productid, p.product-
name FROM
    products p, categories c where c.categoryid =
    p.categoryid</sql:query>
  <sql:query>exec CustOrderHist @CustomerID</sql:query>
  </ROOT>
```

The two SQL statements are stored in XMLTemplate2.xml in the template directory. It is similar to the previous template file, but there is an additional section after the root header that is the `<sql:header>` section. In this section, there is a single parameter defined as CustomerID. The value of WARTH that is between the two `<sql:param>` tags is the default value that will be used in the stored procedure query if there is no value passed in with the URL.

Below are two URL strings and the results that will follow each for comparison; one contains a parameter value and one does not.

```
http://MyServer/Nwind/template/XMLTemplate2.xml
http://MyServer/Nwind/template/XMLTemplate2.xml?Cus-
    tomerID=WILMK
```

XSL

Extract data in XML format applying XSL to format the result. Returning an XML document is useful when the data will be used by another process. But if the data will be used directly as a report, the formatting of an XML document is not very useful. Fortunately, the SQL XML integration with IIS allows for the use of XSL templates to change the formatting. An XSL template is a stylesheet that implements a formatting language for XML documents.

To apply an XSL file to an XML document retrieved by a template, there are a few things that must be changed. The XSL file must be added to the template file in the root declaration. Using the XMLTemplate1.xml file from above, Listing 7.4 is the addition of a couple other fields and XSLStyle1.xsl.

Listing 7.4: XMLTemplate1.xml

```
<ROOT xmlns:sql="urn:schemas-microsoft-com:xml-sql"
              sql:xsl='XSLStyle1.xsl'>
  <sql:query>
    SELECT CustomerID, CompanyName, Country
    FROM   Customers
    FOR XML AUTO
  </sql:query>
</ROOT>
```

The contents of XSLStyle1.xsl are shown in Listing 7.5.

Listing 7.5: XSLStyle.xsl

```xml
<?xml version='1.0' encoding='UTF-8'?>
<xsl:stylesheet xmlns:xsl="http://www.w3.org/1999/XSL/Transform"
  version="1.0">

    <xsl:template match = '*'>
        <xsl:apply-templates />
    </xsl:template>
    <xsl:template match = 'Customers'>
      <TR>
        <TD><xsl:value-of select = '@CustomerID' /></TD>
        <TD><B><xsl:value-of select = '@CompanyName' /></B></TD>
        <TD><B><xsl:value-of select = '@Country' /></B></TD>
      </TR>
    </xsl:template>
    <xsl:template match = '/'>
      <HTML>
        <HEAD>
            <STYLE>th { background-color: #CCCCCC }</STYLE>
        </HEAD>
        <BODY>
          <TABLE border='1' style='width:300;'>
            <TR><TH colspan='3'>Customers</TH></TR>
            <TR><TH >CustomerID</TH><TH>CompanyName</TH><TH>Coun-
try</TH></TR>
            <xsl:apply-templates select = 'root' />
          </TABLE>
        </BODY>
      </HTML>
    </xsl:template>
</xsl:stylesheet>
```

This stylesheet contains a section called `<xsl:template>` that looks for an XML element called `Customers`. When it finds it, HTML code is applied to this element. This code creates the row of a table with a different cell for three different columns. Below this section, there is an HTML template that contains a single table that specifies two rows. The first row contains the table header (Customers) and the second row contains the column headers (CustomerID, CompanyName, and Country). In the space where the third row would be is a tag that marks the place where one of the <xsl:template> sections will be substituted. For our query, we will return a series of elements called Customers, and so the second <xsl:template> section will be placed here for each element that is returned called Customers. This will result in a row for each row the query returns. The results are shown in Figure 7.3.

FIGURE 7.3 Transformation of an XML result set using an XSL stylesheet

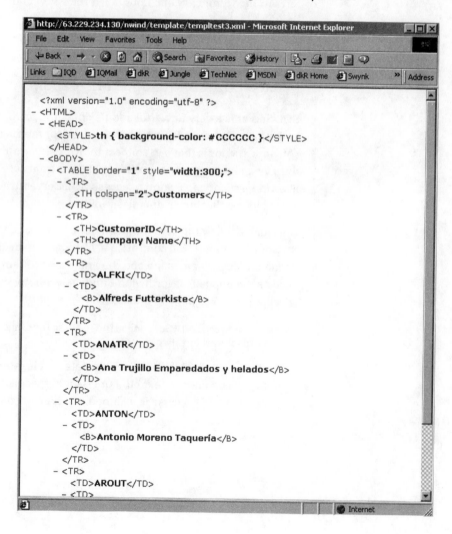

XPATH

XML Path Language (XPATH) is a graphical navigation language for moving through an XML document. Each document has a series of elements and attributes that may be nested underneath one another. This nesting produces a tree-like structure similar to the one shown in Figure 7.3. Once you can visualize an XML document in this fashion, then XPATH will make more sense. Each node in this structure has a parent and children. XPATH allows the selection of a node, or subnode, by specifying the path to that node. For example, if a programmer wanted to refer to the Contact Name node, then the XPATH query would be:

```
/Customer/Contact Name
```

Practical Uses of SQL XML Integration

SQL Server is a very powerful and flexible product, but it has limitations. One such limitation is the need for the client to include software and logic that can connect to SQL Server, submit a query, retrieve a result set, and then reformat that result set as necessary. By allowing a client application to access SQL Server using a URL, the client-side application is greatly simplified.

One such use of XML data retrieved directly from a SQL Server is as the source for an HTML control on a Web page. If an application needed to display an image and the images were kept in the database, such as the images in Northwind.Employees.photo, the data could be specified in a Web page in the following manner:

```
<img src="http://MyServer/nwind?sql=select photo from
    Employees where EmployeeID=1">
```

When there is no FOR XML clause, the data that is returned as the content type defaults to text/html unless it is specified as some other type. If the FOR XML clause is included, the type defaults to text/xml.

Summary

This chapter has examined a number of ways in which data can be retrieved from SQL Server.

- The SELECT statement can be one of the simplest or most complex statements in the T-SQL language. This chapter should not, however, be the sole source of information about the SELECT statement. Readers are encouraged to consult other sources for more details about how the SELECT statement can be used. This chapter provided an overview of a number of different types of SELECT statements including:

  - Single table

  - SELECT using WHERE, ORDER BY, and TOP

  - Joins

  - Aggregates

  - Subqueries

- A cursor is a programming construct that works differently from most other T-SQL functions. A cursor primarily works with a single row at a time, in contrast to most SQL operations that work with a set of rows. A cursor must be explicitly declared along with variables to hold the values from each column as the rows are retrieved from the cursor. A cursor can be updateable or read-only, and movement through the cursor can be limited to a forward direction only or movement both forward and backward.

- Distributed queries are becoming more important as databases grow and different data sources must be incorporated into queries. SQL Server includes three methods of accessing distributed data. Linked Servers are remote data sources that are registered in SQL Server. Once registered, these data sources can be accessed using queries made in the local database. Ad Hoc queries are handled with the OPENROWSET function.

- Distributed partitioned views were developed to allow SQL Server to scale across multiple database servers. To use this technology, a table is horizontally partitioned across multiple servers and then a view is created on each server that implements a UNION across all the horizontal partitions. This technology builds on and requires that each server be linked to the others using SQL Server Linked Servers.

- The ability to work directly with XML formatted data is an integral part of SQL Server 2000. T-SQL has been enhanced to return XML documents directly from SELECT queries in a variety of formats. AUTO and RAW are the most often used and easiest to use. These modes return well-formed XML documents in a format that maps directly to the relational format.

- In addition to using T-SQL to retrieve data as XML, SQL Server 2000 is integrated with IIS to allow access to SQL Server using a URL and HTTP. Queries can be embedded in a URL or saved in template files, which are then referenced in the query. Not only XML documents, but formatted result sets can be retrieved from a URL query. The application of an XSL stylesheet to a query or template allows the programmer to specify how the results are formatted. XPATH is a navigational language that can be used to access some portion of an XML document. In order to use XPATH, the programmer must have a thorough understanding of the XML schema for the particular relational schema being queried.

Exam Essentials

Know the different parts of the *SELECT* statement.   Each part of the SELECT statement contains different options. Know how each one changes the statement and affects the results.

Know the different types of joins and how to use them.   There are five types of joins. Be sure to understand how each one returns data from the joined tables as well as both types of syntax that can be used to specify the joins.

Know how to use aggregates in a *SELECT* statement. Aggregates group data together using different mathematical operators. Remember that a grouping must be specified if there are non-aggregate columns included in the query.

Understand how a subquery can be used. A subquery is a query embedded inside another query. The embedded query can be correlated or not correlated. A subquery can also create a derived table for use in the outer query.

Understand cursors and how they can be used to process data a single row at a time. Cursors are built from a query and then accessed a single row at a time using the FETCH statement. Understand the different types and their effects on concurrency.

Know what a distributed query is and the different types. Linked servers are registered remote data sources that are accessible using the four-part name. Understand OPENROWSET and its format for querying a remote data source. Distributed Partitioned Views allow a table to be spread across multiple SQL Servers. Know how these views are created and accessed.

Understand how data can be returned from SQL Server in an XML format. The SELECT statement includes a FOR XML clause, and you should understand the different options for this clause.

Keep in mind that SQL Server can be accessed using a URL. Understand how SQL Server is integrated with IIS. Know the different methods of accessing data within a URL.

Know how to reformat data returned from a URL query. XSL stylesheets are used to reformat data. Understand their options and use.

Key Terms

Before you take the exam, be certain you are familiar with the following terms:

aggregate operators	linked server
alias	literal
correlated subquery	natural order
cross join	outer join
cursors	right outer join
derived table	scalar subquery
distributed partitioned view	scalar
distributed queries	subquery
Extensible Stylesheet Language (XSL)	templates
	URL
full outer join	vertical partition
horizontal partition	well formed
inner join	XML
Internet Information Server (IIS)	XML document
left outer join	XML Path Language (XPATH)
legacy syntax	

Review Questions

1. You are charged with writing reports for the president of the company. He has requested that you present him with a list of customers who have spent at least $50,000 with the company. Which query would accomplish this?

A.
```
SELECT c.customerID
  FROM Orders o, [Order Details] od
  WHERE o.ordered = od.ordered
  AND sum( od.quantity * od.unitprice) > 50000
```

B.
```
SELECT o.customerID, sum( od.quantity * od.unitprice)
  FROM Orders o, [Order Details] od
  WHERE o.orderid = od.orderid
  GROUP BY o.customerid
  HAVING SUM( od.quantity * od.unitprice) > 50000
```

C.
```
SELECT o.customerID
  FROM Orders o, [Order Details] od
  WHERE o.orderid = od.orderid
  GROUP BY o.customerid
  HAVING SUM( od.quantity * od.unitprice) > 50000
```

D.
```
SELECT o.customerID
  FROM Orders o, [Order Details] od
  WHERE o.orderid = od.orderid
  GROUP BY o.customerid
  HAVING SUM( od.quantity * od.unitprice) > 50000
```

2. You are asked to generate a report for a client. The client requests specific formatting, and you determine that a cursor is needed and that forward and backward movement through the cursor will be needed. Which cursor declaration would best fit these needs?

    A.
    ```
    DECLARE report_cursor FORWARD_ONLY FOR

            SELECT ordered, orderdate, requireddate,
    shippeddate

                FROM orders
    ```

    B.
    ```
    DECLARE report_cursor SCROLL FOR

            SELECT ordered, orderdate, requireddate,
    shippeddate

                FROM orders
    ```

    C.
    ```
    DECLARE report_cursor SCROLL FOR

            SELECT ordered, orderdate, requireddate,
    shippeddate

                FROM orders

                FOR UPDATE OF orderdate
    ```

    D.
    ```
    DECLARE report_cursor FAST_FORWARD FOR

            SELECT ordered, orderdate, requireddate,
    shippeddate

                FROM orders
    ```

3. Which of the following queries will return the most expensive 10 percent of products?

    A.
    ```
    SELECT TOP 10 ProductID, UnitPrice

      FROM products

      ORDER BY UnitPrice
    ```

B.

```
SELECT TOP 10 percent ProductID, UnitPrice
  FROM products
  ORDER BY UnitPrice DESC
```

C.

```
SELECT TOP 10 PERCENT ProductID, UnitPrice
  FROM products
```

D.

```
SELECT TOP 10 PERCENT ProductID, UnitPrice
  FROM products
  ORDER BY UnitPrice
```

4. The customer database in your company has two tables that contain customers and orders. You wish to return a list of all customers and their orders. If a customer has no orders, then only the customer information should be returned. Which query will perform this operation? (Select all that apply.)

A.

```
SELECT c.CustomerID, c.CompanyName, o.OrderID, o.Order-
Total
  FROM Customers c, Orders o
  WHERE c.CustomerID = o.OrderID
```

B.

```
SELECT c.CustomerID, c.CompanyName, o.OrderID, o.Order-
Total
  FROM Customers c, Orders o
  WHERE c.CustomerID *= o.OrderID
```

C.

```
SELECT c.CustomerID, c.CompanyName, o.OrderID, o.Order-
Total
  FROM Customers c, Orders o
  WHERE c.CustomerID =* o.OrderID
```

D.

```
SELECT c.CustomerID, c.CompanyName, o.OrderID, o.Order-
Total
   FROM Customers c LEFT OUTER JOIN Orders o
   ON c.CustomerID = o.OrderID
```

5. You are the DBA for Super Duper Kids Toys, Inc. and have been asked to format a report that lists all current products along with their prices. Each product receives a new price that is discounted based on the classification type of the product. You determine that a cursor is the best way to carry out this task. Place the following statements in the correct order. (Use only those statements that are necessary.) Assume that @t, @p, and @y have already been defined.

	OPEN cproducts
	DEALLOCATE cproducts
	FETCH NEXT FROM cproducts INTO @t, @p, @y
	DECLARE cproducts CURSOR FOR
	SELECT ProductID, UnitPrice, ToyType
	FROM ToyProduct
	END
	SELECT @t 'Product',
	CASE
	WHEN @y = 1 THEN @p * .9
	WHEN @y = 2 THEN @p * .85
	ELSE @p * .8
	END 'Price'
	WHILE @@FETCH_STATUS = 0
	BEGIN
	FETCH NEXT FROM cproducts into @t, @p, @y

6. Which T-SQL statement is an example of a correlated subqeury?

A.

```
SELECT c.customerID
  FROM customers c
  WHERE c.CustomerID = ( SELECT CustomerID
                          FROM Orders o
                          WHERE o.orderID = 10020
                        )
```

B.

```
SELECT c.customerID
  FROM customers c, ( SELECT CustomerID
                        FROM Orders o
                        WHERE o.orderID = 10020 ) o
  WHERE c.CustomerID = o.CustomerID
```

C.

```
SELECT o.OrderID
  FROM Orders o
  WHERE o.OrderID = ( SELECT MAX( OrderID)
                        FROM Orders o1
                    )
```

D.

```
SELECT o.OrderID
  FROM Order o
  WHERE o.OrderID = (
            SELECT MAX( OrderID)
              FROM Orders o1
              WHERE o.CustomerID = o1.CustomerID
        )
```

7. You are the DBA for the Super Spammers E-mail Company and you are in charge of upgrading the database. The Customer table has grown so large and is queried so often that you decide to distribute the load across a federation of four database servers and use distributed partitioned views to access the data. What is the best method for distributing the data on each of your four servers?

   A. You place the first third of Customers on one server, the second on another server, and the last third on the third server. All new customers will be added to the fourth server.

   B. You create four vertical partitions of the Customers table, balancing the column sizes as best you can, and place a vertical partition on each server.

   C. You create four horizontal partitions based on the primary key and place one horizontal partition on each server.

   D. You place the most often accessed rows on one server and evenly distribute the data on the other three servers.

8. You are the Report Writing DBA for Data Integrators, Inc., a company that specializes in converting and combining data from different sources for its clients. You have received an Excel spreadsheet from a client who needs this data added to a report that uses the database. This is a one-time change to this report. Which of the following methods are the easiest way to add this data to the report? (Choose all that apply.)

   A. Create a distributed partitioned view that includes the database and the spreadsheet, and rewrite the report using this view.

   B. Create a linked server for the Excel spreadsheet, and rewrite the report to include the linked server.

   C. Rewrite the report to use a query that uses the OPENROWSET function with the Excel spreadsheet.

   D. Create a view of the Excel spreadsheet using the SCHEMABINDING function.

9. Which of the following items would correctly execute the queries stored in the file Samples.xml with the CustomerID parameter set to "ALFKI"?

A.

```
http://MyServer/Nwind/template/XMLTemplate2.xml?Cus-
tomerID=First
```

B.

```
http://MyServer/Nwind/XMLTemplate2.xml?CustomerID=ALFKI
```

C.

```
http://MyServer/Nwind/template/XMLTemplate2.xml?Cus-
tomerID=ALFKI
```

D.

```
http://MyServer/Nwind/template/XMLTemplate2.xml?Set+
CustomerID+=+ALFKI
```

10. You are the DBA for the ABC Software Company, and one of your developers brings you the following query:

```
SELECT e.name, e.email, s.region, e.age > 35
    FROM email_list e, s.state, i.income_bracket
    WHERE s.region = 'East'
```

He reports that this query is running very slowly and returns more data than he expects. The query should return a list of those customers' names and e-mails who are older than 35 and live in the East region. Which of the following changes will fix this query?

A.

```
SELECT e.name, e.email, s.region, e.age > 35
  FROM email_list e, s.state, i.income_bracket
  WHERE e.state = s.state
  AND s.region = 'East'
  AND i.lower > 50000
```

B.

```
SELECT e.name, e.email, s.region, e.age > 35
 FROM email_list e, s.state, i.income_bracket
WHERE e.state = s.state
            AND s.region = 'East'
```

C.

```
SELECT e.name, e.email, s.region, e.age
 FROM email_list e, s.state, i.income_bracket
WHERE e.state = s.state
AND s.region = 'East'
AND e.age > 35
```

D. Don't change the query. There is nothing you can do.

11. You are the DBA for a small company and have recently been asked to provide access to data through a URL. You decide that the best way to provide this data is by using the SQL XML Integration with IIS in SQL Server 2000. Each client uses the same data but requires the data to be formatted differently. Which tool should you use to reformat the data for each client?

    A. Provide separate XPATH queries for each client.

    B. Use separate XSL stylesheets for each client.

    C. Use separate template files for each client.

    D. Use separate URLs for each client.

12. You are tasked with developing a strategy for providing the clients of your company with data in XML documents. You decide to use the XML features of SQL Server 2000 to accomplish this task. The documents are simple documents that retrieve the data based on a parameter. How can you provide your clients this data? (Select all that apply.)

    A. Create a series of URLs with embedded queries and explain to the client how to change the parameter values.

B. Create a series of SELECT queries using the FOR XML clause and send these to your client with explanations on how to change the parameter values.

C. Create a series of template files and the associated URLs and explain to the client how to change the parameter values.

D. Create a series of queries that join together data with an XML document using the OPENROWSET function. Explain to the client how to change the parameter values.

13. You are the Report Writing DBA for Data Integrators, Inc., a company that specializes in converting and combining data from different sources for its clients. You have been asked to create a report that will combine sales data from an Access database with customer data stored in SQL Server to display the total sales for each customer. You need to add to the following code those items that are required for the return of the total sales amount and date of the most recent order. (Only include those items that are needed).

```
SELECT c.CustomerName



FROM Customer C, INNER JOIN
OPENROWSET('Microsoft.Jet.OLEDB.4.0',
    'c:\Orders.mdb';'admin';'pwd', Orders)
    AS a
ON o.CustomerID = a.customerID


```

(See next page for options.)

Choices:

,SUM(a.OrderAmount)
,MAX(a.OrderDate)
MIN(a.OrderDate)
GROUP BY c.CustomerName
WHERE c.CustomerID = a.CustomerID
GROUP BY c.CustomerName, a.OrderDate, a.OrderAmount

14. You are the DBA for the ShirtOutlet.com company. One of your developers is having trouble with a query and brings it to you. She needs to display all possible combinations of polo shirt styles and their colors. There are 5 styles stored in the PoloStyle table and 8 colors stored in the PoloColor table. Which query will return this data?

A.
```
SELECT *
 FROM PoloStyle s, PoloColor c
 WHERE s.StyleID = c.ColorID
```

B.
```
SELECT *
 FROM PoloStyle s FULL OUTER JOIN PoloColor c
 ON s.StyleID = c.ColorID
```

C.
```
SELECT *
 FROM PoloStyle s LEFT OUTER JOIN PoloColor c
 ON s.StyleID = c.ColorID
```

D.
```
SELECT *
 FROM PoloStyle s, PoloColor c
```

15. As the primary DBA for your company, you are being asked to clean up a number of reports that developers have written for your company. Many of these reports are raw queries that are exported to Excel and have different column names for the same information, i.e. CustName and CustomerName for the name of the customer in two different reports. How can you standardize the names of the columns in all the reports?

A. Rename all columns in the database to have standard names for each type of data.

B. Use a standard alias for each type of data in the queries that generate the reports.

C. Rewrite all queries to look for each type of data in a single table so the column name is always consistent.

D. Rewrite all queries to use self-joins to standardize the column names.

Answers to Review Questions

1. C. This query returns a list of customers who have spent $50,000 or more. Option A is not a valid query. The aggregate cannot appear in the WHERE clause unless it is in a subquery. B will return the list of customers and the amounts they spent, but the question did not ask for the amounts. D returns all customers.

2. B. This type of cursor allows movement (scrolling) both forward and backward. Options A and D only allow forward movements. C will allow scrolling, but updates were not specified.

3. B. Option B orders all products from most expensive to least and then returns the top 10 percent of these products. Option A returns the 10 least expensive products, C returns the first 10 percent of products, and D returns the 10 percent least expensive products.

4. B, D. Both Options B and D are left outer joins that return all customers whether or not they have orders. If they do, the order information is returned. Option A only returns customers with orders. Option C returns all orders whether or not they have a customer.

5.

```
DECLARE cproducts CURSOR FOR
    SELECT ProductID, UnitPrice, ToyType
    FROM ToyProduct
OPEN cproducts
FETCH NEXT FROM cproducts INTO @t, @p, @y
WHILE @@FETCH_STATUS = 0
BEGIN
SELECT @t 'Product',
    CASE
        WHEN @y = 1 THEN @p * .9
        WHEN @y = 2 THEN @p * .85
        ELSE @p * .8
        END 'Price'
        FETCH NEXT FROM cproducts into @t, @p, @y
    END
DEALLOCATE cproducts
```

The cursor declaration comes first and then the cursor must be opened before any rows can be processed. The first action after opening the cursor is to FETCH a row and then loop through the cursor as long as @@FETCH_STATUS is equal to zero. Inside the loop, the select occurs that determines a price based on the type and a new FETCH statement is called to move the cursor to the next row. After all processing is complete, the cursor should be deallocated.

6. D. The code in option D is the only correlated subquery. Each row in the outer query causes a different evaluation of the inner query.

7. C. Distributed partitioned views require that the data be horizontally partitioned based on the primary key and placed on each server.

8. B, C. You can use either linked servers or the OPENROWSET option to access date in an Excel spreadsheet. A distributed partitioned view cannot access non-SQL Server data, and there is no such thing as an OPENEXCEL function.

9. C. If you used this URL, you would be able to execute the queries stored in the Samples.xml file.

10. C. The first and second queries are not valid. The problem in the original query is that two tables are being joined using a cross join. The third query includes the e.state = s.state clause, which eliminates the cross join. The age qualification is also moved from the column list to the WHERE clause.

11. B. The best answer for formatting changes is to use XSL to reformat data rather than different queries.

12. A, B, and C. Each of these methods, using embedded queries in URLs, SELECT statements with FOR XML, and template files will work. The OPENROWSET function is not used for working with XML documents.

13.

SELECT c.CustomerName
,SUM(a.OrderAmount)
,MAX(a.OrderDate)
FROM Customer C, INNER JOIN

OPENROWSET('Microsoft.Jet.OLEDB.4.0',
    'c:\Orders.mdb';'admin';'pwd', Orders)
    AS a

ON o.CustomerID = a.customerID
GROUP BY c.CustomerName

The requirement for the most recent order is asking for the MAX() OrderDate in the table. The SUM() is also asked for in the requirements. No WHERE clause is needed since an INNER JOIN clause is included, and the GROUP BY clause only needs those columns that are not being aggregated.

14. D. When all possible combinations of two tables are requested, a cross join is needed. This can be specified using CROSS JOIN in the query or by not qualifying the join between two tables.

15. B. The use of column aliases is the best solution for standardizing the column names output in various queries.

Chapter

8

Modifying Data

MICROSOFT EXAM OBJECTIVES COVERED IN THIS CHAPTER:

✓ Retrieve, filter, group, summarize, and modify data by using Transact-SQL.

✓ Manage result sets by using cursors and Transact-SQL. Considerations include locking models and appropriate usage.

✓ Manipulate heterogeneous data. Methods include linked servers, OPENQUERY, OPENROWSET, and OPENXML.

The last chapter examined the various ways that data can be extracted from SQL Server. This chapter covers the ways that data can be manipulated in SQL Server. Data can be added to SQL Server, changed once inside a database, or removed if it is no longer needed. Much of the material in this chapter builds on the previous chapter. It is recommended that you have a thorough understanding of the SELECT statement and other ways that data is retrieved before reading this chapter.

There are three primary Transact-SQL statements available to manipulate data. The INSERT, UPDATE, and DELETE statements each work very much like the SELECT statement and will be examined in detail in this chapter.

In addition, cursors can be used to update data that is in the underlying table of the cursor. This chapter will examine how a cursor can be created and used in the manipulation of data.

Both linked servers and the OPENROWSET command can be used to update remote data sources. In addition, distributed partitioned views are updateable in SQL Server 2000. This chapter will look at ways that data that does not reside in the local SQL Server can be changed through Transact-SQL.

XML can also be used to submit an update to the SQL Server. With the OPENXML command, an XML document can be used in data manipulation queries.

The *INSERT* Statement

Microsoft
✓ **Exam**
Objective

Retrieve, filter, group, summarize, and modify data by using Transact-SQL.

The INSERT statement is the way that most data is added to a database in SQL Server. Whenever new data is needed, the INSERT statement provides the flexibility to add data to tables in a variety of ways. Like most other SQL commands, this statement can work with sets of data and insert a large number of rows into a table with a single line of code.

This section will look at the two formats of the INSERT statement that add single rows of data to a table. The multiple row format of the INSERT command will then be presented.

Single Row Insert

There are three formats for inserting a single row into a table:

- Explicit values can be specified.

- A SELECT query can be used that returns a single row.

- A stored procedure can be called that returns a single row in a single result set.

The format for all methods is similar and the syntax for each is presented in Listing 8.1.

Listing 8.1: INSERT Statement

```
INSERT [ INTO]
{ table_name WITH ( < table_hints > [ ...n ] )
}
{ [ ( column_list ) ]
    { VALUES ( { DEFAULT | NULL | expression } [ ,...n] )
    | derived_table
    | execute_statement
```

Each section of this statement is explained below:

table_name This is the name of the table that will receive the new row.

table_hints The following hints are allowed:

> FASTFIRSTROW
>
> HOLDLOCK
>
> PAGLOCK
>
> READCOMMITTED
>
> REPEATABLEREAD
>
> ROWLOCK
>
> SERIALIZABLE
>
> TABLOCK
>
> TABLOCKX
>
> UPDLOCK

These are the same table hints that can be used to influence the query optimizer. A thorough discussion of these is given in the "Query Hints" section of Chapter 12.

column_list This is an optional section. If included, then all columns that receive values are listed here. Columns not listed here must allow NULL values or have a default value bound to the column.

derived_table This can be any valid SELECT statement that returns a result set of the proper size to satisfy the INSERT statement.

Since an insert using a query or a call to a stored procedure is primarily used to insert multiple rows, these will be covered in the next section.

When inserting a single row into a table, the programmer can explicitly list the values that will be inserted into each column using the VALUES clause. This approach provides the programmer with complete control over the values placed in each column. If there is a default value defined for any columns, the keyword DEFAULT can be used in place of an explicit value to allow SQL Server to insert the appropriate default value.

In Exercise 8.1, we will insert a single row into a database.

All the exercises in this chapter will use the Northwind database that is included with SQL Server 2000.

EXERCISE 8.1

Inserting a Single Row

In this exercise, we will add two new rows to the [Order Details] table. Each row will be added using a different form of the INSERT statement.

1. Open the SQL Server Query Analyzer. Do this through the SQL Enterprise Manager by selecting Tools ➤ SQL Query Analyzer or by choosing Start ➤ Programs ➤ Microsoft SQL Server ➤ SQL Query Analyzer.

2. In the Query Analyzer, type the following query to add a row:

```
INSERT [Order Details]
  (OrderID, ProductID, UnitPrice, Quantity, Discount)
VALUES
  (10248, 14, 20, 2, 0)
```

3. Be sure the Northwind database is selected in the database drop-down box, and press the green arrow on the toolbar or CTRL-E to execute the query. You should receive the following results:

```
(1 row(s) affected)
```

The [Order Details] table in the Northwind database has default values bound to a few of the columns, so we will populate one of these columns using the default value.

4. Type the following in Query Analyzer:

```
INSERT [Order Details]
  (OrderID, ProductID, UnitPrice, Quantity, Discount)
 VALUES( 10248, 15, DEFAULT, 1, 0)
SELECT *
  FROM [Order Details]
  WHERE OrderID = 10248
```

EXERCISE 8.1 *(continued)*

5. Highlight these lines with the mouse and press the green arrow or CTRL-E to execute the query. You should receive the following results:

```
(1 row(s) affected)

OrderID    ProductID   UnitPrice    Quantity Discount
---------  ----------  -----------  -------- ------------------
10248      14          20.0000      2        0.0
10248      15          .0000        1        0.0
```

The UnitPrice column has a default of 0 bound to it. This column is listed in the column list section, and the keyword DEFAULT is used in the VALUES clause to populate this field with the default value.

The second row in this result set is the one that was just inserted.

Inserting a Single Row with Selected Columns

Not every column must be included in an INSERT statement if the table meets certain criteria. If a column is defined as an identity field, it should not be included in the INSERT statement unless additional T-SQL statements are executed before the statement. This situation is covered in the next section.

The other situations where a column may be omitted from the INSERT statement are when the column either allows NULL values or has a default value bound to the column. In these situations, SQL Server will automatically insert the default value for the column if it is omitted. If no default value is bound to the column, then a NULL will be placed in this field. If the column does not allow NULL values and does not have a default value specified, SQL Server will not perform the insert and will return an error to the calling program.

In Exercise 8.2, we will insert values for selected columns.

EXERCISE 8.2

Insert Selected Columns

In this exercise, we will insert a new row into the Products table. This table allows NULL values in all fields except the ProductID, ProductName, and Discontinued fields. ProductID is also an identity field.

1. Open the SQL Server Query Analyzer. Do this through the SQL Enterprise Manager by selecting Tools ➤ SQL Query Analyzer or by choosing Start ➤ Programs ➤ Microsoft SQL Server ➤ SQL Query Analyzer.

2. Type the following query (be sure the Northwind database is selected):

```
INSERT Products
  (ProductName, Discontinued)
  VALUES
  ( 'SQL Server Book', 0)

SELECT ProductID, ProductName, SupplierID, UnitPrice,
Discontinued
  FROM Products
  WHERE ProductName = 'SQL Server Book'
```

3. Highlight these lines using your mouse and press CTRL-E. You should see something like the following:

```
ProductID    ProductName          SupplierID  UnitPrice  Discontinued
-----------  -------------------  ----------  ---------- ---------------
78           SQL Server Book      NULL        .0000      0
```

Only a few selected columns are included in the result list to save space. There are three columns in the results that were not in the INSERT statement. The ProductID column is an identity column, so SQL Server calculates and includes its value automatically. SupplierID allows NULL values and has no default, so it receives a NULL value. UnitPrice allows NULL values, but has a default of 0 bound to this column, so it receives a 0 value.

Inserting Single Rows with an Identity Field

An *identity column* is a special column in SQL Server that holds an integer value (TINYINT, SMALLINT, INT, or BIGINT) that is automatically incremented by SQL Server with each insert. When the column is defined, the initial value as well as the amount of each increment is included in the definition. Only one column in a table can be defined as an *identity column*. Since SQL Server automatically calculates the identity value, the identity column should not be included in any INSERT statements.

SQL Server does not guarantee that identity values are unique. If you wish to ensure that every value in a table is unique, an index enforcing this requirement must be created.

If an explicit value is required for the identity field, SQL Server does provide a mechanism for inserting this data. There is a property that allows a programmer to disable the automatic insertion of identity values. This property is the IDENTITY_INSERT property and can be set to either ON or OFF using the SET command. Once the property is set to ON, an INSERT statement can include the identity field in the column list and supply an explicit value for this column in the VALUES clause. The syntax is as follows:

    SET IDENTITY_INSERT <table_name> [ON | OFF]

This property should be set immediately before a statement that will supply a value for the identity column and reset immediately after. Only one table on each SQL Server can have this property enabled at a time. If a user attempts to set this property for another table while it is already set, an error is returned.

Exercise 8.3 will show you how to insert identity values.

EXERCISE 8.3

Inserting Identity Values

The Categories table in the Northwind database has the CategoryID field defined as an identity column. This exercise will explicitly insert a new row with an explicit value for this column.

1. Open the SQL Server Query Analyzer. Do this through the SQL Enterprise Manager by selecting Tools ➤ SQL Query Analyzer or by choosing Start ➤ Programs ➤ Microsoft SQL Server ➤ SQL Query Analyzer.

2. Enable the IDENTITY_INSERT property for the Categories table with the following query (be sure the Northwind database is selected):

   ```
   SET IDENTITY_INSERT Categories ON
   ```

3. Highlight these lines using your mouse and press the green arrow on the toolbar or press CTRL-E. You should see something like the following:

   ```
   The command(s) completed successfully.
   ```

4. Type the following query to insert the new row with an explicit value for the CategoryID column.

   ```
   INSERT Categories
     ( CategoryID, CategoryName, Description)
     VALUES
     ( 9999, 'SQL Products', 'Products that work with SQL
   Server.')
   ```

5. Highlight these lines using your mouse and press the green arrow on the toolbar or press CTRL-E. You should see something like the following:

   ```
   (1 row(s) affected)
   ```

6. Disable the IDENTITY_INSERT property for the Categories table with the following query:

   ```
   SET IDENTITY_INSERT Categories OFF
   ```

7. Highlight this line using your mouse and press the green arrow on the toolbar or press CTRL-E. You should see something like the following:

   ```
   The command(s) completed successfully.
   ```

Inserting Multiple Rows

Often a set of data needs to be inserted into a table. Perhaps the user needs to quickly seed a new table with some values from another table or some data needs to be copied. It is quicker and easier to use a single INSERT statement with a query or stored procedure than to run a series of INSERT statements, each adding one row.

When multiple rows are inserted using a query, all the inserted rows are automatically encapsulated within an implicit transaction. If there is a problem with a single row and it cannot be inserted, then no rows are inserted and the transaction is rolled back. If a series of INSERT statements are run, the programmer must explicitly create a transaction and perform error checking after each insert to ensure that all rows are added. Inserting multiple rows works exactly like inserting single rows with the exception that the VALUES clause cannot be used. Either a SELECT query or a stored procedure must be called to insert a set of rows. This set could be a single row, which would allow these two methods to behave in the same manner as if the VALUES clause were used. The column list in the INSERT clause is optional, though the same restrictions that applied to single row inserts apply here as well. All constraints and rules are also applied.

The DEFAULT keyword cannot be used in either the SELECT query or in the stored procedure, so values must be supplied for all columns if there is no column list explicitly specified. A NULL value can be explicitly specified as a scalar in the queries column list, or it can be returned by the query as part of the result set. Of course, the column that is being populated by the NULL value must still be defined to allow NULLs. Exercises 8.4 and 8.5 will walk you through adding multiple rows to a table using a query and a stored procedure.

EXERCISE 8.4

Using a Query to Insert Multiple Rows

This exercise will add a duplicate row to the Products table for each existing row with a new ProductID value and a price that is reduced by 20 percent.

1. Open the SQL Server Query Analyzer. Do this through the SQL Enterprise Manager by selecting Tools ➢ SQL Query Analyzer or by choosing Start ➢ Programs ➢ Microsoft SQL Server ➢ SQL Query Analyzer.

2. Type the following query to insert the new rows (be sure the Northwind database is selected):

```
INSERT Products
  ( ProductName, SupplierID, CategoryID,
    QuantityPerUnit, UnitPrice, UnitsInStock,
    UnitsOnOrder, ReorderLevel, Discontinued
  )
SELECT ProductName, SupplierID, CategoryID,
    QuantityPerUnit, UnitPrice * .8, UnitsInStock,
    0, 0, 1
  FROM Products
```

3. Highlight these lines using your mouse and press the green arrow on the toolbar or press CTRL-E. You should see something like the following:

```
(78 row(s) affected)
```

Each product that was in the Products table is now listed twice: once at its original price and once at 80 percent of its price.

EXERCISE 8.5

Using a Stored Procedure to Insert Multiple Rows

This exercise will use a stored procedure that returns multiple rows to insert rows into a table. We will create a table and then populate it with a series of rows based on an existing stored procedure.

1. Open the SQL Server Query Analyzer. Do this through the SQL Enterprise Manager by selecting Tools ➤ SQL Query Analyzer or by choosing Start ➤ Programs ➤ Microsoft SQL Server ➤ SQL Query Analyzer.

2. Create the report table using the following query (be sure the Northwind database is selected):

```
CREATE TABLE Rpt_Emp_Sales_By_Country
(    Country VARCHAR( 15),
     LastName VARCHAR( 20),
     FirstName VARCHAR( 10),
     ShippedDate DATETIME,
     OrderID INT,
     SaleAmount MONEY
)
```

3. Highlight these lines using your mouse and press the green arrow on the toolbar or press CTRL-E. You should see something like the following:

```
The command(s) completed successfully.
```

4. Insert the sales data for 1997 by typing the following query:

```
INSERT Rpt_Emp_Sales_By_Country . . .
 EXEC dbo.[Employee Sales by Country] '01/01/1997',
'01/01/1998'
select * from Rpt_Emp_Sales_By_Country
```

5. Highlight these lines using your mouse and press the green arrow on the toolbar or press CTRL-E. You should see something like the following (the results are abbreviated and the time was removed from the ShippedDate column):

Country	LastName	FirstName	ShippedDate	OrderID	SaleAmount
USA	Callahan	Laura	1997-01-16	10380	1313.8200
USA	Fuller	Andrew	1997-01-01	10392	1440.0000
USA	Davolio	Nancy	1997-01-03	10393	2556.9500
USA	Davolio	Nancy	1997-01-03	10394	442.0000

6. Cleanup the database and remove the table with the following query:

```
DROP TABLE Rpt_Emp_Sales_By_Country
```

7. Highlight this line using your mouse and press the green arrow on the toolbar or press CTRL-E. You should see something like the following:

```
The command(s) completed successfully.
```

The *UPDATE* Statement

Microsoft Exam Objective

Retrieve, filter, group, summarize, and modify data by using Transact-SQL.

Once data is stored in SQL Server, it can be changed using the UPDATE statement. This command allows the user to specify that data in a specific table be changed to new values based on qualifications that are included in a WHERE clause, just like the WHERE clause in a SELECT statement. Like the INSERT statement, the UPDATE statement can only affect one table at a time, though multiple rows may be involved. Unlike INSERT where the simplest form adds a single row, the simplest UPDATE statement will update all rows in a table.

This section will examine how various forms of the UPDATE statement can be used to change data that is stored in a table.

Updating All Rows

An UPDATE statement contains an *implicit transaction*, so all rows affected by the UPDATE statement will be changed or none will be. If the server fails in the middle of a transaction, then all the changes will be undone when the server restarts.

The simplest UPDATE statement is one that sets all rows in a column of a table to the same expression. This form of the UPDATE statement has no qualifications and is in the form:

```
UPDATE <table_name>
    SET <column_name> = <expression>
```

The expression in this statement can be a variable, a constant, or an expression. Exercise 8.6 shows a practical application of this type of update.

EXERCISE 8.6

Update All Rows

This exercise will update all rows of the Products table to a single expression using two different forms of the UPDATE command.

1. Open the SQL Server Query Analyzer. Do this through the SQL Enterprise Manager by selecting Tools ➢ SQL Query Analyzer or by choosing Start ➢ Programs ➢ Microsoft SQL Server ➢ SQL Query Analyzer.

2. Set all prices equal to a constant value with the following query (be sure the Northwind database is selected):

```
BEGIN TRANSACTION
```

```
UPDATE Products
 SET UnitPrice = 10

SELECT ProductID, ProductName, UnitPrice
 FROM Products

ROLLBACK TRANSACTION
```

3. Highlight these lines using your mouse and press the green arrow on the toolbar or press CTRL-E. You should see something like the following:

```
(312 row(s) affected)

ProductID    ProductName                        UnitPrice
-----------  --------------------------------   ----------------
1            Chai                               10.0000
2            Chang                              10.0000
3            Aniseed Syrup                      10.0000
```

After running this code, the results show that every row in the Products table has the UnitPrice column set to 10. The ROLLBACK TRANSACTION command restores the original values.

4. Now let us reduce all prices by 10 percent using the UPDATE command. Type the following query into Query Analyzer:

```
BEGIN TRANSACTION
UPDATE Products
  SET UnitPrice = UnitPrice * 0.9

SELECT ProductID, ProductName, UnitPrice
 FROM Products

ROLLBACK TRANSACTION
```

5. Highlight the lines of code above using your mouse and press the green arrow on the toolbar or press CTRL-E. You should see something like the following:

```
(312 row(s) affected)

ProductID    ProductName                        UnitPrice
-----------  --------------------------------   ----------------
1            Chai                               16.2000
2            Chang                              17.1000
3            Aniseed Syrup                      9.0000
4            Chef Anton's Cajun Seasoning       19.8000
5            Chef Anton's Gumbo Mix             19.2150
```

Updating a Set of Rows

Modifying all the rows in a table using an UPDATE statement is not something that is common in most tables. Usually a set of rows with some common elements will need to be updated. In order to update only a portion of a table, the UPDATE statement needs to be qualified so it will affect only those rows meeting the qualification.

In the same manner as the SELECT statement, which was covered in Chapter 7, the UPDATE statement can include both a FROM clause and a WHERE clause to limit the rows that are affected by the statement to those that match the WHERE clause. The FROM clause allows tables other than the table being updated to be used to make qualifications.

Only a single table can be directly affected using the UPDATE statement.

The syntax of the UPDATE command is as follows:

```
UPDATE <table_name>
SET <column_name> = <expression>
[ FROM <table_list>]
[ WHERE <search_condition>
```

The FROM and WHERE clauses behave exactly like they do in a SELECT statement. Aliases and table hints can be used along with derived tables, subqueries, or any other valid form of these clauses as presented in Chapter 7.

When including tables in the FROM clause, the table being updated can be added to this list so an alias can be specified.

In Exercise 8.7, we will update a set of rows.

EXERCISE 8.7

Updating a Set of Rows

1. Open the SQL Server Query Analyzer. Do this through the SQL Enterprise Manager by selecting Tools ➢ SQL Query Analyzer or by choosing Start ➢ Programs ➢ Microsoft SQL Server ➢ SQL Query Analyzer.

2. Reduce the price of products from Tokyo Traders by 10 percent by typing the following query (be sure the Northwind database is selected):

```
BEGIN TRANSACTION
UPDATE Products
 SET UnitPrice = UnitPrice * 0.9
 FROM Suppliers s
 WHERE s.SupplierID = Products.SupplierID
 and s.CompanyName = 'Tokyo Traders'

SELECT ProductID,
    ProductName,
    QuantityPerUnit,
    UnitPrice
 FROM Products

ROLLBACK TRANSACTION
```

3. Highlight the lines of code above using your mouse and press the green arrow on the toolbar or press CTRL-E.

This code reduced the price of the two products from Tokyo Traders by 10 percent. Here are the values before and after this statement is run (the result set is abbreviated):

ProductID	ProductName	QuantityPerUnit	UnitPrice
9	Mishi Kobe Niku	18 - 500 g pkgs.	97.0000
10	Ikura	12 - 200 ml jars	31.0000
74	Longlife Tofu	5 kg pkg.	10.0000

ProductID	ProductName	QuantityPerUnit	UnitPrice
9	Mishi Kobe Niku	18 - 500 g pkgs.	87.3000
10	Ikura	12 - 200 ml jars	27.9000
74	Longlife Tofu	5 kg pkg.	9.0000

Updating Multiple Columns

Updating a set of rows can be useful in many situations; however, a programmer may often want to update multiple columns in a table. T-SQL includes the ability to update more than one column in a single statement. Each column being updated follows the same format of

`<column_name>` = `<expression>`

with these phrases being separated by commas, just like the column expressions in the SELECT statement are separated by commas. All columns in a table, or a subset of the columns can be updated, but only a single table's columns can be updated directly with each statement.

In Exercise 8.8, we will update multiple columns.

EXERCISE 8.8

Updating Multiple Columns

1. Open the SQL Server Query Analyzer. Do this through the SQL Enterprise Manager by selecting Tools ➤ SQL Query Analyzer or by choosing Start ➤ Programs ➤ Microsoft SQL Server ➤ SQL Query Analyzer.

2. The following query will reduce the price of the products from Tokyo Traders, reduce the number on order to zero, and mark these items as discontinued. Type the following query in Query Analyzer (be sure the Northwind database is selected):

```
BEGIN TRANSACTION
UPDATE Products
 SET UnitPrice = UnitPrice * 0.9,
     UnitsOnOrder = 0,
     Discontinued = 1
 FROM Suppliers s
 WHERE s.SupplierID = Products.SupplierID
 and s.CompanyName = 'Tokyo Traders'

SELECT ProductID,
    ProductName,
    UnitPrice,
    UnitsOnOrder,
    Discontinued
 FROM Products

ROLLBACK TRANSACTION
```

3. Highlight these lines using your mouse and press the green arrow on the toolbar or press CTRL-E.

The before and after results are:

ProductID	ProductName	UnitPrice	UnitsOnOrder	Discontinued
9	Mishi Kobe Niku	97.0000	0	1
10	Ikura	31.0000	0	0
74	Longlife Tofu	10.0000	20	0

ProductID	ProductName	UnitPrice	UnitsOnOrder	Discontinued
9	Mishi Kobe Niku	87.3000	0	1
10	Ikura	27.9000	0	1
74	Longlife Tofu	9.0000	0	1

Updating a View

A view can be updated in addition to directly updating a table, though there are a few restrictions to using an UPDATE in this fashion.

- The view and the columns being updated must be defined as updateable.

- The definition of the view must contain at least one table in the FROM clause.

- The columns being updated cannot be derived columns.

- The UPDATE statement can only affect a single base table in the view.

- Any columns from the base table that are included in a view can be updated and are updated using the name of the column defined in the view.

- If the view definition contains aggregates, then it is not updateable. The exception to this is if aggregates appear in a subquery and are not affected by any update operations.

If a view meets these conditions, it can be used in an UPDATE statement like any other base table. All of the above examples could have used a view in place of a table.

Distributed partitioned views are also updateable and are a key part of building a large scalable SQL Server database.

The *DELETE* Statement

Microsoft
✓ **Exam**
Objective

Retrieve, filter, group, summarize, and modify data by using Transact-SQL.

The fourth statement that can be used to modify data in T-SQL is DELETE. This command removes rows from a table in the same way that UPDATE can be used to modify the data in a row.

Deleting All Rows

Like the UPDATE statement, the simplest DELETE statement is one that affects all rows. When there is no qualification included, the DELETE statement will remove all rows from a table or view. The syntax for the DELETE statement is:

DELETE <*table_name*>

Executing this statement will remove all rows from the table or view. Just as an UPDATE statement can only affect one base table, the DELETE statement can only be issued against a view if the view contains a single table.

On large tables, deleting all rows may take a large amount of time since each deletion is logged in the transaction log. It is usually quicker to issue a *TRUNCATE TABLE* <*table_name*>.

In Exercise 8.9, we will remove all rows from a table.

Remove All Rows From a Table

This exercise will remove all rows from the Order Details table. This operation is encapsulated inside a transaction so the deletion is not permanent.

1. Open the SQL Server Query Analyzer. Do this through the SQL Enterprise Manager by selecting Tools ➢ SQL Query Analyzer or by choosing Start ➢ Programs ➢ Microsoft SQL Server ➢ SQL Query Analyzer.

2. Delete all rows from the Order Details table with the following query (be sure the Northwind database is selected):

```
BEGIN TRANSACTION
DELETE [Order Details]
SELECT * FROM [Order Details]
ROLLBACK TRANSACTION
```

3. Highlight these lines using your mouse and press the green arrow on the toolbar or press CTRL-E. You should see something like the following:

```
(2154 row(s) affected)

OrderID     ProductID    UnitPrice      Quantity Discount
----------- -----------  -------------- ----------------------

(0 row(s) affected)
```

The SELECT statement in this batch will not return any rows since they are all deleted by the DELETE statement. The ROLLBACK TRANS-ACTION will restore the deleted rows.

Deleting a Set of Rows

Usually a process that needs to remove data from a table will only remove a subset of the rows in the table. Rarely will the entire table be emptied of data. The DELETE statement allows the programmer to specify a subset of data that is to be removed.

In the same manner as the SELECT statement, which was covered in Chapter 7, the DELETE statement can include both a FROM clause and a WHERE clause to limit the rows that are affected by the statement to those that match the WHERE clause. The FROM clause allows tables other than the table being updated to be used to make qualifications.

Only a single table can be directly affected using the DELETE statement.

The syntax of the DELETE command to delete a set of rows is as follows:

```
DELETE <table_name>
 [ FROM <table_list>]
 [ WHERE <search_condition>
```

The FROM and WHERE clauses behave exactly like they do in a SELECT statement. Aliases and table hints can be used along with derived tables, subqueries, or any other valid form of these clauses as presented in Chapter 7.

When including tables in the FROM clause, the table being updated can be added to this list so an alias can be specified.

In Exercise 8.10, we will delete of set of rows.

EXERCISE 8.10

Deleting a Set of Rows

This exercise will remove only order details for a single order and a single customer. Each set of code is encapsulated inside a transaction so the deletion of data is a temporary event.

1. Open the SQL Server Query Analyzer. Do this through the SQL Enterprise Manager by selecting Tools ➤ SQL Query Analyzer or by choosing Start ➤ Programs ➤ Microsoft SQL Server ➤ SQL Query Analyzer.

2. Remove the order details for OrderID = 10248 by typing the following query into Query Analyzer (be sure the Northwind database is selected):

```
BEGIN TRANSACTION
DELETE [Order Details]
 WHERE OrderID = 10248
```

```
SELECT *
 FROM [Order Details]
 WHERE OrderID = 10248
ROLLBACK TRANSACTION
```

3. Highlight these lines using your mouse and press the green arrow on the toolbar or press CTRL-E. You should see something like the following:

```
(2 row(s) affected)

OrderID     ProductID   UnitPrice         Quantity Discount
----------- ----------- ----------------- --------------------

(0 row(s) affected)
```

4. Remove all the order details for Customer ALFKI by typing the following query into Query Analyzer (be sure the Northwind database is selected):

```
BEGIN TRANSACTION

DELETE [Order Details]
 FROM [Order Details] od, Orders o
 WHERE o.CustomerID = 'ALFKI'
 AND o.OrderID = od.OrderID

SELECT *
 FROM [Order Details] od, Orders o
 WHERE o.CustomerID = 'ALFKI'
 AND o.OrderID = od.OrderID

ROLLBACK TRANSACTION
```

5. Highlight these lines using your mouse and press the green arrow on the toolbar or press CTRL-E. You should see something like the following (the results are abbreviated):

```
(12 row(s) affected)

OrderID     ProductID   UnitPrice   Quantity Discount
----------- ----------- ----------- --------------------

(0 row(s) affected)
```

Modifying Data inside a Cursor

Microsoft
✓ **_Exam_**
Objective

**Manage result sets by using cursors and Transact-SQL.
Considerations include locking models and appropriate
usage.**

In Chapter 7, cursors were presented as a construct that allows a
process to deal with a single row of data at a time in a procedural fashion.
In this section, we will examine how the data inside a cursor can be
changed using the cursor.

We will only cover managing result sets using cursors in the following
sections.

Declaring an Updateable Cursor

If the default values are used when declaring a cursor, then the cursor will
not be updateable. SQL Server assumes that cursors are, by default, not
updateable. When declaring the cursor, the UPDATE keyword must be
included in the declaration. Optionally, a list of columns that are
updateable can be included. If a column list is included, then only those
columns listed are updateable. The syntax for declaring an updateable
cursor is similar to that presented in Chapter 7:

```
DECLARE <cursor_name> CURSOR
[LOCAL | GLOBAL]
[FORWARD_ONLY | SCROLL]
[STATIC | KEYSET | DYNAMIC | FAST_FORWARD]
[READ_ONLY | SCROLL_LOCKS | OPTIMISTIC ]
[TYPE_WARNING]
FOR
    [ SELECT statement ]
[ FOR UPDATE [ OF column_list [ a, b, .., n]]]
```

The last line of this declaration includes the FOR UPDATE clause and optionally a column list. By including this clause, SQL Server understands that the cursor is being used for a *positional update* of the data in the base table. This means the current row in the cursor is mapped to a single row in the underlying base table, and the mapped row is the row that is modified.

The OF `column_list` part of the clause is optional. If this is not included, then all the columns of the cursor are updateable. If the column list is included, then only those columns listed are updateable.

Be sure that the UPDATE statement is updating the correct table from the cursor declaration. There are many cases where the same column name from two different tables may be used to form the cursor.

Updating Data within a Cursor

The UPDATE statement used to modify the base table actually references the base table and must conform to all rules for UPDATE statements, but the row is qualified using the cursor rather than the standard WHERE clause. The syntax for this statement is as follows:

```
UPDATE <table_name>
    SET <column_name> = <expression>
    WHERE CURRENT OF <cursor_name>
```

This statement looks very similar to the UPDATE statement presented in Chapter 7, but the WHERE clause is qualified by the cursor rather than any logical operations. When this statement is executed, it will update the row of the table that corresponds to the row that is currently pointed to by the cursor. If the cursor was not declared as updateable or the column being updated was not included in the column list, then an error will be returned.

Columns in a table that are not included in the cursor may be updated, provided that the OF `column_list` clause is not specified.

In Exercise 8.11, we will modify data using a cursor.

EXERCISE 8.11

Modifying Data Using a Cursor

This exercise will use a cursor to update the CompanyName in the Customers table.

1. Open the SQL Server Query Analyzer. Do this through the SQL Enterprise Manager by selecting Tools ➤ SQL Query Analyzer or by choosing Start ➤ Programs ➤ Microsoft SQL Server ➤ SQL Query Analyzer.

2. Declare the cursor by typing the following query (be sure the Northwind database is selected):

```
DECLARE MyCursor CURSOR
FOR
 SELECT
   c.CustomerID,
   c.Companyname,
   c.contactname,
   o.OrderID,
   o.OrderDate
 FROM Customers c, Orders o
 WHERE c.CustomerID = o.CustomerID
 FOR UPDATE
```

3. Highlight these lines using your mouse and press the green arrow on the toolbar or press CTRL-E. You should see something like the following:

```
The command(s) completed successfully.
```

4. Open the cursor and retrieve a row with the following query:

```
OPEN MyCursor

DECLARE
    @cid VARCHAR( 8),
    @c VARCHAR( 80),
    @o INT,
    @od DATETIME,
    @cn VARCHAR( 80)

FETCH NEXT FROM MyCursor INTO @cid, @c, @cn, @o, @od
SELECT @cid
```

5. Highlight these lines using your mouse and press the green arrow on the toolbar or press CTRL-E. You should see something like the following:

```
---------
VINET

(1 row(s) affected)
```

6. Update the Customers table with the following query:

```
BEGIN TRANSACTION
UPDATE Customers
 SET CompanyName = 'q'
 WHERE CURRENT OF Mycursor
```

7. Highlight these lines using your mouse and press the green arrow on the toolbar or press CTRL-E. You should see something like the following:

```
(1 row(s) affected)
```

8. Cleanup the database, retrieve the results, and rollback the transaction with this query:

```
DEALLOCATE MyCursor

SELECT *
 FROM Customers

ROLLBACK TRANSACTION
```

9. Highlight these lines using your mouse and press the green arrow on the toolbar or press CTRL-E. The result of this update will be seen near the bottom of the result set. Here is an abbreviated result set with the updated row.

CustomerID	CompanyName	ContactName	ContactTitle
VICTE	Victuailles en stock	Mary Saveley	Sales Agent
VINET	q	Paul Henriot	Accounting Manager
WANDK	Die Wandernde Kuh	Rita Müller	Sales Representative

Modifying Data Using XML

Microsoft ✓ *Exam Objective*

Manipulate heterogeneous data. Methods include linked servers, OPENQUERY, OPENROWSET, and OPENXML.

In Chapter 7, the methods that SQL Server 2000 provides for retrieving data in an XML format were presented. However, this is only half of the XML capability of SQL Server 2000. The ability to update data stored in SQL Server using an XML data source is presented in this section.

Modifying Data Using *OPENXML*

The method chosen by SQL Server 2000 that allows modification of data using an XML data source is *OPENXML*. This function provides a view of the XML data that looks like a standard SQL Server rowset. This rowset can be used in place of any other rowset in SELECT statements. This includes SELECT statements used for INSERT, UPDATE, and DELETE statements.

In order for an XML data source to be used in T-SQL statements, the document must be parsed and stored in memory in SQL Server in a tree representation. This tree representation includes information that SQL Server needs to know about the various nodes so it can prepare a rowset view of the data. SQL Server includes a new stored procedure, *SP_XML_PREPAREDOCUMENT*, that will convert an XML document into the internal SQL Server representation.

SP_XML_PREPAREDOCUMENT

OPENXML cannot work with the native text format of an XML document. The information about how the various nodes of an XML document are related is needed to provide the proper rowset view. SP_XML_PREPAREDOCUMENT converts a text-based XML document into a form that SQL Server can use.

Elements, attributes, text, comments, and anything else stored in the XML document as a discrete piece of information is a node.

SQL Server parses and creates an internal representation of the document built in memory. The internal representation is a view of the XML document in a tree-like structure of the nodes in the document. The tree structure includes elements, attributes, text, comments, and any other nodes. Consider the XML document in Listing 8.2:

Listing 8.2: XML Authors

```
<ROOT>
<Customers customerid="ALFKI" contactname="Maria Anders"
Phone="030-0074321">
        <Orders orderid="10643" orderdate="1997-08-
25T00:00:00"/>
        <Orders orderid="10702" orderdate="1997-10-
13T00:00:00"/>
</Customers>
<Customers CustomerID="ANATR" ContactName="Ana Trujillo"
Phone="(5) 555-4729">
        <Orders OrderID="10308"/>
</Customers>
</ROOT>
```

The internal tree representation of this document is similar to Figure 8.1.

FIGURE 8.1   Tree Representation of Prepared XML Document

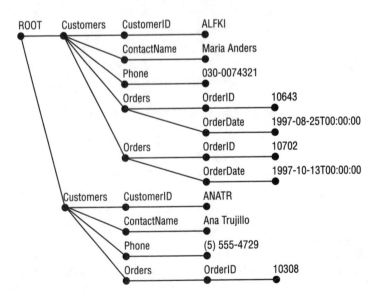

This stored procedure then returns a *handle* for the internal representation of the XML document for use by other processes. The syntax for this stored procedure is as follows:

```
SP_XML_PREPAREDOCUMENT hdoc OUTPUT
    [, xmltext][ , xpath_namespaces]
```

The parameters of this stored procedure are defined as follows:

hdoc   This is an integer that is returned to the calling program as a handle to the internal representation of the XML document. Any process that needs to access the internal representation of the XML document needs to refer to the document using this handle.

xmltext   This is the actual XML document stored as a text parameter. This can be CHAR, NCHAR, VARCHAR, NVARCHAR, TEXT, or NTEXT. If no parameter is passed or its value is NULL, then a representation of an empty XML document will be created.

xpath_namespaces   This parameter specifies that namespace *Uniform Resource Identifiers (URIs)* that are used in the XPATH expressions in OPENXML. These expressions specify the row and column mappings for each node. Its default value is <root xmlns:mp="urn:schemas-microsoft-com:xml-metaprop">.

Once this stored procedure has completed, OPENXML can be used to convert this XML document stored in memory to a row and column view, which can be used in T-SQL statements.

After processing an XML document that was created in memory with SP_XML_PREPAREDOCUMENT, you should always remove the document with SP_XML_REMOVEDOCUMENT. This will free the resources for other processes.

Using *OPENXML*

Once the document is parsed and stored in memory, the OPENXML function can be used to provide a rowset view of the XML document. The basic syntax for OPENXML is as follows:

```
OPENXML(idoc INT [in],row_pattern nvarchar[in],[flags
    byte[in]])
    [WITH (schema_declaration | table_name)]
```

OPENXML has the following definitions for each parameter:

idoc   This is the integer handle that refers to the internal representation of the XML document. This is returned by SP_XML_PREPAREDOCUMENT.

*row*_pattern   A XPATH pattern that identifies the nodes to be processed as rows.

flags   Indicates the type of mapping that is to be used between the XML data and the rowset. This parameter also determines how extra columns should be filled. The default is 0, and here are the possible values:

0   Default

1   Use an attribute-centric mapping. In this mapping, the attributes of elements will map to columns of the same name. If the names are different, then the column_patterns must be specified in the schema declaration.

2   Use an element-centric mapping. May be combined with an attribute-centric mapping. This maps element names to column names.

schema_declaration   This is an optional clause that provides for the specific mapping between the nodes in the XML document and the resulting rowset. The schema declaration will be in the form:

`column_name column_type [column_pattern | meta_property]`

where the parameters are defined as follows:

- `column_name` is the name of the column in the result set.

- `column_type` is the datatype of the column in the result set.

- `column_pattern` is an optional XPATH pattern that maps a specific node to a column. If this parameter is not specified, then the mapping defaults to the attribute- or element-centric mapping specified by the `flags` parameter.

- `meta_property`, if specified, defines the column as holding information provided by the metaproperty. These properties allow you to extract information about the XML node such as namespace or relative position.

table_name   An optional parameter that can be given in place of a schema declaration. This is the name of an existing table that holds the desired schema of the result set.

If no WITH clause is included, then the results of the OPENXML function are returned as an *edge table*. An *edge table* can represent the fine-grained structure of an XML document in a single table. The columns of the *edge table* are defined in Table 8.1.

TABLE 8.1   Edge Table Columns

Column	Description
id	A BIGINT. This is a unique identifier for the row. A value of 0 is used for the root and negative values are reserved.
parentid	A BIGINT. Identifies the parent of the row. The parent is not necessarily the parent element from the XML document. It depends on the node type. If this is a text node, then the parent may be an attribute row.
nodetype	An INT. This identifies the node type. A value of 1 is used for Element nodes, a value of 2 for Attribute nodes, and a value of 3 for text nodes.
localname	A NVARCHAR. This gives the local name of the element or attribute. This is set to NULL if the document object does not have a name.
prefix	A NVARCHAR. This is the namespace prefix of the node.
namespaceuri	A NVARCHAR. The namespace URI of the node. If NULL, then no namespace is present.
datatype	A NVARCHAR. The actual datatype of the element or attribute row. Otherwise this is NULL. The type is taken from the inline schema or inferred by SQL Server.
prev	BIGINT. The XML ID of the previous sibling node.
text	NTEXT. This holds the attribute value or element content in text form.

The following sections will discuss the three data modification statements using OPENXML.

Inserting Rows with *OPENXML*

Since OPENXML returns a rowset that looks like the rowset from any other table or view, it can be used in an INSERT statement in the same manner as a table or view. The only restriction is that the INSERT statement must use a SELECT query for the source data, as this is the type of statement that is used with OPENXML.

In Exercise 8.12, we will insert a row using OPENXML.

EXERCISE 8.12

Inserting Data with *OPENXML*

This exercise will add a new customer using OPENXML.

1. Open the SQL Server Query Analyzer. Do this through the SQL Enterprise Manager by selecting Tools ➢ SQL Query Analyzer or by choosing Start ➢ Programs ➢ Microsoft SQL Server ➢ SQL Query Analyzer.

2. Prepare the internal representation of the XML document and insert the new row by typing the following query (be sure the Northwind database is selected):

```
DECLARE @idoc int
DECLARE @doc VARCHAR(1000)
SET @doc ='
<ROOT>
<Customer CustomerID="STAR" ContactName="Michael Jordan"
  CompanyName="Bulls">
</Customer>
</ROOT>'
--Create an internal representation of the XML document.
EXEC SP_XML_PREPAREDOCUMENT @idoc OUTPUT, @doc

INSERT Customers ( CustomerID, ContactName, CompanyName)
SELECT *
FROM OPENXML (@idoc, '/ROOT/Customer',1)
     WITH (CustomerID  varchar( 5),
           ContactName varchar( 20),
           CompanyName varchar( 20)
                )

SELECT * FROM Customers

EXEC SP_XML_REMOVEDOCUMENT @idoc
```

3. Highlight these lines using your mouse and press the green arrow on the toolbar or press CTRL-E. You should see something like the following:

```
CustomerID CompanyName                ContactName          ContactTitle
---------- -------------------------- -------------------- -------------
SPLIR      Split Rail Beer & Ale      Art Braunschweiger   Sales Manager
STAR       Bulls                      Michael Jordan       NULL
SUPRD      Suprêmes délices           Pascale Cartrain     Accounting
```

Updating Rows with *OPENXML*

In the same manner as the INSERT statement, the XML document can be used in an UPDATE statement to modify data. The OPENXML result looks like any other table and is included in the FROM clause of the UPDATE statement.

In Exercise 8.13, we will update data using OPENXML.

Updating Data with *OPENXML*

This exercise will modify the customer added in Exercise 8.12. The CompanyName field will be changed.

1. Open the SQL Server Query Analyzer. Do this through the SQL Enterprise Manager by selecting Tools ➢ SQL Query Analyzer or by choosing Start ➢ Programs ➢ Microsoft SQL Server ➢ SQL Query Analyzer.

2. Prepare the internal representation of the XML document and perform the update by typing the following query (be sure the Northwind database is selected):

```
DECLARE @idoc int
DECLARE @doc VARCHAR(1000)
SET @doc ='
<ROOT>
<Customer CustomerID="STAR" ContactName="Michael Jordan"
  CompanyName="Chicago Bulls">
</Customer>
</ROOT>'
--Create an internal representation of the XML document.
EXEC SP_XML_PREPAREDOCUMENT @idoc OUTPUT, @doc
```

```
UPDATE Customers
  SET CompanyName = b.CompanyName
FROM OPENXML (@idoc, '/ROOT/Customer',1)
    WITH (CustomerID  varchar( 5),
          ContactName varchar( 20),
          CompanyName varchar( 20)
              ) b
WHERE Customers.CustomerID = b.CustomerID

SELECT * FROM Customers

EXEC SP_XML_REMOVEDOCUMENT @idoc
```

3. Highlight these lines using your mouse and press the green arrow on the toolbar or press CTRL-E. You should see something like the following: (Results are abbreviated. This portion of the results will be near the bottom of the result set.)

```
CustomerID CompanyName             ContactName          ContactTitle
---------- --------------------    --------------------  ---------------
SPLIR      Split Rail Beer & Ale   Art Braunschweiger   Sales Manager
STAR       Chicago Bulls           Michael Jordan       NULL
SUPRD      Suprêmes délices        Pascale Cartrain     Accounting
```

Deleting Rows with *OPENXML*

The DELETE statement is very similar to the UPDATE statement when using OPENXML. A FROM clause must be included for the OPENXML rowset to participate in the delete operation.

In Exercise 8.14, we will delete rows using OPENXML.

Deleting Data with *OPENXML*

This exercise will remove the customer added in Exercise 8.12.

1. Open the SQL Server Query Analyzer. Do this through the SQL Enterprise Manager by selecting Tools ➢ SQL Query Analyzer or by choosing Start ➢ Programs ➢ Microsoft SQL Server ➢ SQL Query Analyzer.

EXERCISE 8.14 *(continued)*

2. Prepare the internal representation of the XML document and delete the customer with the following query (be sure the Northwind database is selected):

```
DECLARE @idoc int
DECLARE @doc VARCHAR(1000)
SET @doc ='
<ROOT>
<Customer CustomerID="STAR" ContactName="Michael Jordan"
  CompanyName="Bulls">
</Customer>
</ROOT>'
–Create an internal representation of the XML document.
EXEC sp_xml_preparedocument @idoc OUTPUT, @doc

DELETE Customers
 FROM OPENXML (@idoc, '/ROOT/Customer',1)
     WITH (CustomerID  varchar( 5),
           ContactName varchar( 20),
           CompanyName varchar( 20)
                ) b
 WHERE Customers.CustomerID = b.CustomerID

SELECT * FROM Customers

EXEC SP_XML_REMOVEDOCUMENT @idoc
```

3. Highlight these lines using your mouse and press the green arrow on the toolbar or press CTRL-E. You should see something like the following in the query analyzer: (Results are abbreviated. This portion of the results will be near the bottom of the result set.)

CustomerID	CompanyName	ContactName	ContactTitle
SPLIR	Split Rail Beer & Ale	Art Braunschweiger	Sales Manager
SUPRD	Suprêmes délices	Pascale Cartrain	Accounting

Note that the row with a *CustomerID* of *STAR* has been deleted.

Data Modification Using *OPENXML*

OPENXML appears to be a cumbersome method of modifying data stored in SQL Server, and in many cases it is. There are a number of places, however, that this technique is much easier to use than any other.

Suppose that you work for a company that specializes in e-mailing newsletters, product specials, etc., and are contracted by various firms to send e-mails on their behalf. These firms send you periodic data feeds that contain the e-mail address, name, and other pertinent information about their customers to whom you are sending e-mails. The feeds you receive are incremental and contain both new and updated information for customers.

If you were to receive these feeds in a text format, you would have to devise an import routine to move this data into a table, scrub the data, perform update and inserts against your existing customer tables, and hope the data is sent in the same format each time.

By receiving this data as XML, the document can be validated against a known scheme, which prevents any processing if the document does not conform to the accepted schema. The document can then be submitted directly to the SQL Server using INSERT and UPDATE statements with OPENXML to add this information to your database. The self-describing nature of XML would also ensure that if columns were ordered differently, the process would be unaffected.

Using Distributed Queries to Modify Data

Microsoft ✓ Exam Objective

Manipulate heterogeneous data. Methods include linked servers, OPENQUERY, OPENROWSET, and OPENXML.

In Chapter 7, we looked at distributed queries and how they can be used to access data stored in a variety of formats. Chapter 7 was concerned with including remote data sources in a query executed in the local

SQL Server. The same techniques for retrieving data can be used to modify the data, if the provider for the data source supports data modification. Since not all providers allow modifications, the documentation for each provider will have to be checked manually.

There are two basic types of distributed queries: those using linked servers and those using the *OPENROWSET* function. We will examine how data modification statements change using each of these remote data sources.

Modifying Data Using Linked Servers

Assuming that it is supported, the process for modifying data in a linked server is the same as a data modification for a local data source with one exception. The table being referenced by the modification statement must be specified in the fully qualified, four-part notation that was presented in Chapter 7. This notation is in the form:

```
linked_server_name.catalog.schema.object_name
```

where parts are defined as follows:

linked_server_name   This is the friendly name of the server that is registered in sysservers.

catalog   The catalog is analogous to the database in SQL Server. This is the location within the remote data source in which the object is located.

schema   Equivalent to the owner of the table.

object_name   This is the name of the table of other structure being queried.

Other than this restriction, the INSERT, UPDATE, and DELETE statements are formed and used exactly as they would be for a local data source. All of the updates presented in this chapter to this point, could be specified with the same four-part, fully qualified notation. The server would be the local server, the catalog would be "Northwind," and the schema "dbo." If we had another SQL Server or Access database that was registered as a linked server, the only change to the queries would be to substitute the remote server name in place of the local server.

Modifying Data Using *OPENROWSET*

When using the OPENROWSET function to modify data in remote data sources, the queries are structured the same way as they are for local tables. The difference is that in place of the name of a local table, the entire OPENROWSET function call is used. While not as readable as the other types of statements presented in this chapter, the structure of the T-SQL statement is the same.

In Exercise 8.14, we will modify data using OPENROWSET.

EXERCISE 8.15

Modifying Data with *OPENROWSET*

This exercise will modify data in an Access database using the OPENROWSET function. To complete this exercise, Access 97 or Access 2000 is needed.

1. Start the Access program and create a blank database called c:\db_test.mdb.

2. In this database, create a new table with three fields:

   Field: CustomerID, Type: Text, Length: 10

   Field: CallTime, Type: Number

   Field: CallDate, Type: Date/Time

3. Save the table by pressing the Save icon on the toolbar or choosing File ➤ Save from the menu. Name the table "Calls."

4. Close the Access program.

5. Open the SQL Server Query Analyzer. Do this through the SQL Enterprise Manager by selecting Tools ➤ SQL Query Analyzer or by choosing Start ➤ Programs ➤ Microsoft SQL Server ➤ SQL Query Analyzer.

6. Insert rows into the database using OPENROWSET by typing the following query (be sure the Northwind database is selected):

```
INSERT OPENROWSET('Microsoft.Jet.OLEDB.4.0',
   'c:\db_test.mdb';'admin';'', Calls)
  (CustomerID, CallTime, CallDate)
   select c.CustomerID, 10, getdate()
    from Customers c
    where c.CustomerID like 'B%'
```

EXERCISE 8.15 *(continued)*

7. Highlight these lines using your mouse and press the green arrow on the toolbar or press CTRL-E.

8. Start the Access program and open the Calls table. There will be eight rows of data in this table as shown below.

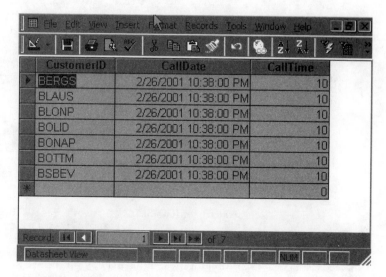

9. Close the Access program.

10. Type the following code into Query Analyzer (Access should be closed).

```
UPDATE OPENROWSET('Microsoft.Jet.OLEDB.4.0',
   'c:\db_test.mdb';'admin';'', Calls)
SET CALLTIME = 20
WHERE CustomerID = 'BOLID'
```

11. Highlight these lines using your mouse and press the green arrow on the toolbar or press CTRL-E.

12. Start the Access program and open the Calls table. The row with the CustomerID = 'BOLID' will have a calltime of 20 as shown on the next page.

EXERCISE 8.15 *(continued)*

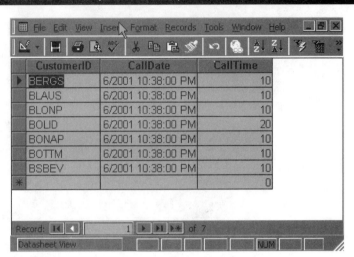

13. Delete a row from the table by typing the following code into Query Analyzer (Access should be closed):

```
DELETE OPENROWSET('Microsoft.Jet.OLEDB.4.0',
   'c:\db_test.mdb';'admin';'', Calls)
 WHERE CustomerID = 'BOLID'
```

14. Highlight these lines using your mouse and press the green arrow on the toolbar or press CTRL-E.

15. Start the Access program and open the Calls table. The row with the CustomerID = 'BOLID' will no longer be in the table as shown below:

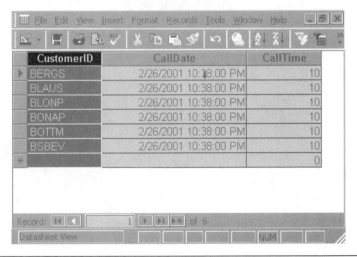

Summary

This chapter has examined various ways in which data in a SQL Server database can be modified. The following topics were covered in this chapter:

- INSERT is the T-SQL statement that adds rows of data to a table. This statement can use a VALUES clause to add single rows or a SELECT query to add multiple rows.

- UPDATE is the T-SQL command that modifies the existing data in a table. This statement can affect all rows or be qualified with a WHERE clause in the same manner as a SELECT statement.

- DELETE is the T-SQL statement that removes rows of data from a table. This statement can also be qualified with a WHERE clause in the same manner as the UPDATE or SELECT statements.

- OPENXML is a function that provides a view of an XML document that is in the same row and column format as other result sets. This can be used in the FROM clause of T-SQL statements in place of a table or view. This chapter presented examples of INSERT, UPDATE, and DELETE statements.

- Linked servers and OPENROWSET distributed queries allow data to be modified if the provider supports this function. Linked server updates are the same as local updates using a fully-qualified table name. OPENROWSET queries substitute the OPENROWSET function for the table name that is being updated.

Key Terms

Before you take the exam, be certain you are familiar with the following terms:

edge table	Uniform Resource Identifiers (URIs)
handle	SP_XML_PREPAREDOCUMENT
OPENXML	SP_XML_REMOVEDOCUMENT
positional update	

Exam Essentials

Understand the different forms of the INSERT statement. This statement can be used with a VALUES clause, a SELECT statement, or a stored procedure call. Understand how to use each form.

Know how defaults are used with *INSERT*. Be sure you understand the difference between an implicit default and an explicit default.

Know the different forms of an *UPDATE* statement. The UPDATE statement only affects a single table, but can include other tables to provide values for the update or qualify the rows affected.

Know how to delete rows from a table. The DELETE statement is similar to the UPDATE statement in its structure. Also understand how TRUNCATE TABLE is different from DELETE.

Understand what an updateable cursor is. A cursor can be used to update rows. You should be aware of the syntax for declaring this cursor and how to structure the UPDATE statement.

Know how the *OPENXML* function works. OPENXML requires the document to be parsed and stored in memory. Know how to prepare and remove the document from memory. Understand how OPENXML transforms an XML document.

Review Questions

1. As a SQL Server consultant, you are asked to add data to a client's database. The source data is in an XML format, and the client offers to have the data manually typed into an Excel spreadsheet. You reply this is not necessary because you can directly work with the XML document. Which two SQL Server tools would you choose?

   A. SP_XML_PREPAREDOCUMENT

   B. OPENQUERY

   C. OPENXML

   D. SP_XML_OPENDOCUMENT

2. You are the DBA for an Internet retailer and you need to reduce the prices of all products by 10 percent. Which statement will accomplish this goal?

   A.
   ```
   UPDATE Products
     SET UnitPrice = 10 Percent UnitPrice
   ```

   B.
   ```
   UPDATE Products
     SET UnitPrice = UnitPrice * .9
     WHERE ProductID IS NOT NULL
   ```

   C.
   ```
   UPDATE Products
     SET UnitPrice = UnitPrice * .9
     WHERE ProductID = 10
   ```

   D.
   ```
   UPDATE Products
     SET UnitPrice = UnitPrice - ( UnitPrice * .1)
   ```

3. A developer brings you a query that is designed to insert a row into the Customer table. His application does not always have values for all columns, but all columns have a default value. How can he structure the INSERT statement?

   A.
   ```
   INSERT Customers ( Name, CID, *) VALUES ( @c, @id,
   DEFAULT)
   ```

   B.
   ```
   INSERT Customers ( Name, CID) VALUES (@c, @id)
   ```

   C.
   ```
   INSERT Customers ( Name, CID) VALUES (@c, @id) WITH
   DEFAULT
   ```

   D.
   ```
   INSERT Customers DEFAULTS EXCEPT (Name = @c, CID = @id)
   ```

4. A developer has accidentally run the following code:

```
BEGIN TRANSACTION
  UPDATE Products
    SET UnitPrice = .6
```

He had been asked to reduce the price of each product by 40 percent and update orders placed after Jan 1, 2001 with the correct unit price. Place the following code in the correct order to complete this task. Only include those steps that are needed.

	BEGIN TRANSACTION
	UPDATE Products SET UnitPrice = UnitPrice * .6
	ROLLBACK TRANSACTION
	COMMIT TRANSACTION
	UPDATE Products SET UnitPrice = (UnitPrice * 1.66) * .6
	UPDATE Products SET UnitPrice = UnitPrice * .4
	UPDATE Orders SET UnitPrice = UnitPrice * .4
	SELECT UnitPrice = UnitPrice * .4
	UPDATE Orders SET UnitPrice = UnitPrice * .6

5. You are the DBA for Super Duper Kids Toys, Inc. and have been asked to reduce the price of all current products. Each product receives a new price that is discounted based on the classification type of the product. You determine that a cursor is the best way to carry out this task. Place the following statements in the correct order (Use only those statements that are necessary). Assume that @y and @p have already been defined.

	OPEN cproducts
	DEALLOCATE cproducts
	FETCH NEXT FROM cproducts INTO @y, @p
	END
	FETCH NEXT FROM cproducts into @y, @p
	UPDATE ToyProduct

	SET UnitPrice = CASE
	    WHEN @y = 1 THEN @p * .9
	    WHEN @y = 2 THEN @p * .85
	    ELSE @p * .8
	    END
	    WHERE CURRENT OF cproducts

	DECLARE cproducts CURSOR FOR
	  SELECT ToyType, UnitPrice
	  FROM ToyProduct
	FOR UPDATE

	WHILE @@FETCH_STATUS = 0
	BEGIN

6. Which query below will delete only those rows from the Orders table that have no child rows in the OrderLine table?

A.

```
DELETE Orders
 WHERE OrderLine.OrderID Is NULL
```

B.

```
DELETE Orders
 FROM OrderLine
 WHERE OrderLine.OrderID Is NULL
```

C.
```
DELETE Orders
 FROM OrderLine ol, Orders o
 WHERE o.OrderID = ol.OrderID
```

D.
```
DELETE Orders
 WHERE OrderID NOT IN
       ( SELECT OrderID from OrderLine)
```

7. You are the DBA for the Super Spammers E-mail Company and have completed an upgrade of the database. The Customer table is now distributed across a federation of four database servers and accessed using a distributed partitioned view called vCustomers. ServerA holds customers with last names beginning with A-F, ServerB holds customers with last names beginning with G-M, ServerC holds customers with last names beginning with N-T, and ServerD holds customers with last names beginning with A-F. Which statement below will update the status of all customers whose last name begins with a J?

A.
```
UPDATE Customer
  SET Status = 1
  WHERE ServerB.Customer.LastName = 'J'
```

B.
```
UPDATE vCustomers
  SET Status = 1
  WHERE LastName = 'J'
```

C.
```
UPDATE vCustomers
  SET Status = 1
  WHERE LastName LIKE 'J%'
```

D.
```
UPDATE ServerB.vCustomers
  SET Status = 1
  WHERE ServerB.Customer.LastName = 'J'
```

8. You are the Report Writing DBA for Data Integrators, Inc., a company that specializes in converting and combining data from different sources for its clients. You have been asked by a client to import data in their Access database and then update the database with the current date and time. Which query below can accomplish this task?

A.
```
UPDATE OPENROWSET('Microsoft.Jet.OLEDB.4.0',
  'c:\datafeed.mdb';'admin';'', Clients)
  SET TimeStamp = GETDATE()
```

B.
```
UPDATE 'c:\datafeed.mdb'..Clients
  SET TimeStamp = GETDATE()
```

C.
```
DECLARE @a int
SELECT @a = OPENROWSET('Microsoft.Jet.OLEDB.4.0',
  'c:\datafeed.mdb';'admin';'', Clients)
UPDATE @a
  SET Timestamp = GETDATE()
```

D.
```
UPDATE LINKED_SERVER('Microsoft.Jet.OLEDB.4.0',
  'c:\datafeed.mdb';'admin';'', Clients)
  SET TimeStamp = GETDATE()
```

9. You are the report-writing DBA for Data Integrators, Inc., a company that specializes in converting and combining data from different sources for its clients. You have received an XML

document from one of your clients, who informs you that all future data files will be in this format. How should you import this data?

A. Use OPENXML with an INSERT statement.

B. Use OPENROWSET with an INSERT statement.

C. Use OPENXML with OPENROWSET to create a derived table in an INSERT statement.

D. Use OPENXML with SCHEMABINDING.

10. When working with an XML document inside SQL Server, a programmer must complete a process before querying the server using OPENXML. Another process should also be performed when the query is complete. Which two functions are used for these processes?

A. SP_XML_OPENDOCUMENT

B. SP_XML_REMOVEDOCUMENT

C. SP_XML_DESTROYDOCUMENT

D. SP_XML_READDOCUMENT

E. SP_XML_PREPAREDOCUMENT

11. The fastest way to delete all the rows in a table is with which statement?

A. DELETE *table_name*

B. DELETE ALL *table_name*

C. TRUNCATE TABLE *table_name*

D. TRUNCATE ALL *table_name*

12. You are the DBA for a company that has received a list of products to remove from your database as an XML document. Which three statements would you use to complete this task? Assume that the XML document is stored in the @doc variable and any other variables needed have been declared.

A.
```
EXEC SP_XML_READDOCUMENT @idoc OUTPUT, @doc
```

B.

```
EXEC SP_XML_PREPAREDOCUMENT @idoc OUTPUT, @doc
```

C.

```
DELETE Products
  FROM OPENXML (@idoc, '/ROOT/Product',1)
     WITH (ProductID  varchar( 5)
                ) b
  WHERE Product.ProductID = b.ProductID
```

D.

```
DELETE OPENXML (@idoc, '/ROOT/Product',1)
     WITH (ProductID  varchar( 5)
                ) b
```

E.

```
EXEC SP_XML_REMOVEDOCUMENT @idoc OUTPUT, @doc
```

F.

```
EXEC SP_XML_DELETEDOCUMENT @idoc OUTPUT, @doc
```

13. You have been asked to insert a series of rows into the Categories table. There is an identity field in this table called CatID. Which two T-SQL statements are needed to complete this operation?

A.

```
INSERT Categories (CatID, CatName)
  SELECT ID, Name FROM TempCat
```

B.

```
INSERT Categories (CatName)
  SELECT Name FROM TempCat
```

C.

```
SET IDENTITY_INSERT Categories ON
```

D.

```
SET IDENTITY_INSERT Categories OFF
```

14. You have received a list of five product names to insert into the Products table. This table has an identity field called ProdID, and the name field is called ProdName. Each product name is stored in a different variable. Which INSERT statements can you use? (Select all that apply.)

A.

```
INSERT Products (ProdName)
  SELECT @a, @b, @c, @d, @e
```

B.

```
INSERT Products (ProdName)
  VALUES(@a, @b, @c, @d, @e)
```

C.

```
INSERT Products (ProdName)
  VALUES(@a)
INSERT Products (ProdName)
  VALUES(@b)
INSERT Products (ProdName)
  VALUES(@c)
INSERT Products (ProdName)
  VALUES(@d)
INSERT Products (ProdName)
  VALUES(@e)
```

D.

```
INSERT Products (ProdName)
  SELECT @a
  UNION
  SELECT @b
  UNION
  SELECT @c
  UNION
  SELECT @d
  UNION
  SELECT @e
```

15. You have a linked server called RemoteData defined on your local SQL Server. After using your Northwind database to test some data modification statements, you delete all the data in your local Products table. Which statement will restore your Products table to its original form?

A.

```
UPDATE Products
 FROM RemoteData.Northwind.dbo.Products
```

B.

```
INSERT Products
 FROM RemoteData.Northwind.dbo.Products
```

C.

```
INSERT Products
 SELECT *
  FROM RemoteData.Northwind.dbo.Products
```

D.

```
INSERT Products
 SELECT *
  FROM RemoteData.Products
```

Answers to Review Questions

1. A, C. The OPENXML function works with an XML document after it has been parsed and stored using SP_XML_PREPAREDOCUMENT.

2. D. Since the question specifies all rows should be altered, the UPDATE statement should not have any qualifications. The SET statement should include a mathematical expression that takes the existing price and returns a price that is 10 percent less. The PERCENT keyword is not a valid expression.

3. B. If a column has a default value and the INSERT statement does not specify an explicit value, the column should not be included. If the default is explicitly included in the VALUES clause, the column name must be specified.

4.

```
ROLLBACK TRANSACTION
```
```
BEGIN TRANSACTION
```
```
UPDATE Products
  SET UnitPrice = UnitPrice * .6
```
```
UPDATE Orders
  SET UnitPrice = UnitPrice * .6
```
```
COMMIT TRANSACTION
```

The code that was presented was incorrect and needs to be undone, so a rollback of the update is needed first. The next two statements should be wrapped in a transaction and should be UPDATE statements that replace the existing unit price with a price that is 60 percent of the original.

5.

```
DECLARE cproducts CURSOR FOR
  SELECT ToyType, UnitPrice
  FROM ToyProduct
FOR UPDATE
```

```
OPEN cproducts
```

```
FETCH NEXT FROM cproducts into @y, @p
```

```
WHILE @@FETCH_STATUS = 0
```

```
BEGIN
```

```
UPDATE ToyProduct
```

```
SET UnitPrice = CASE
      WHEN @y = 1 THEN @p * .9
      WHEN @y = 2 THEN @p * .85
      ELSE @p * .8
      END
      WHERE CURRENT OF cproducts
```

```
FETCH NEXT FROM cproducts into @y, @p
```

```
END
```

```
DEALLOCATE cproducts
```

The cursor declaration is first, and then the cursor must be opened before any rows can be processed. The first action after opening the cursor is to FETCH a row and then loop through the cursor as long as @@FETCH_STATUS is equal to zero. Inside the loop, the update should occur and a new FETCH statement is called to move the cursor to the next row. After all processing, the cursor should be deallocated.

6. D. The last statement deletes those rows in Orders for which a corresponding row in OrderLine is not found. The other queries do not meet this requirement.

7. C. Only the UPDATE statement with the LIKE operator will update all customers whose last name begins with J.

8. A. The OPENROWSET can be used in a query in any place that a table name would be used. The format for an UPDATE statement using OPENROWSET is the same as that for any other UPDATE statement.

9. A. The OPENXML function will transform the XML document into a rowset that can be used in an INSERT statement.

10. B, E. Before an XML document can be read using OPENXML, it must be parsed into an internal representation using SP_XML_PREPAREDOCUMENT. After processing, it should be removed using SP_XML_REMOVEDOCUMENT.

11. C. The TRUNCATE TABLE statement is faster than DELETE.

12. B, C, and E. First, a document must be parsed using SP_XML_PREPAREDOCUMENT; then it can be queried using OPENXML. The DELETE statement must reference the Products table and use the OPENXML query to qualify the products to be deleted. Afterward, the SP_XML_REMOVEDOCUMENT procedure should be called.

13. A, C. Only the SET IDENTITY_INSERT ON statement is required along with the INSERT statement.

14. C, D. To insert multiple rows that are stored in variables, five separate INSERT statements are required using the VALUES clause. Alternatively, a UNION can be used to combine all these variables into a rowset with five rows.

15. C. The insert from a linked server requires the four-part naming to be specified; otherwise, this uses the same format as an INSERT from a local table.

Chapter

9

Importing and Exporting Data

MICROSOFT EXAM OBJECTIVES COVERED IN THIS CHAPTER:

✓ Import and export data. Methods include the bulk copy program, the Bulk Insert task, and Data Transformation Services (DTS).

In any RDBMS, a great deal of loading and extraction of data is required outside of any applications that are built to work against the database. Whether seeding values for a table or creating a set of data to transfer to another system, a DBA must be able to move large quantities of data in and out of SQL Server.

SQL Server 2000 includes a variety of tools that can be used to load a large set of data from a non–SQL Server source or extract a set of data to send to a remote source. These same tools can also be used to move data from SQL Server to SQL Server, database to database, or even from table to table. SQL Server 2000 still includes the *BCP (bulk copy program)*, which has been included for many versions. In SQL Server 2000, the T-SQL language has been enhanced with the *BULK INSERT* command, which allows access to the BCP program from within a batch of T-SQL commands. The *Data Transformation Services* utilities, introduced in SQL Server 7, have been substantially enhanced to provide additional methods of transferring data in and out of SQL Server.

Bulk Copy

SQL Server includes two utilities for the bulk copying of text data: BCP and BULK INSERT. These two utilities are designed for the movement of data into and out of SQL Server quickly. Each is discussed below.

BCP

This is the legacy method for the loading or extraction of data and has been included with SQL Server for a number of versions. BCP is a separate program called, appropriately, bcp.exe, which is installed in the

MSSQL\BINN folder and is run from a command prompt. Since this program is run from a command prompt without a GUI, it is called a *command line utility*.

This utility was written to import and extract data between SQL Server and a data file. The data file can be in a text format, or it could be in a binary format that is understood by SQL Server, called *native format*. The utility can also be run in an *interactive mode* with minimal options specified, or it can be automated with the additional text files that are described in the following "BCP Syntax" and "Using Format Files" sections.

Since this is a command line utility, it lends itself to being scripted in a number of ways. The SQL Agent can be used, an ordinary batch or CMD file along with the Windows NT AT command can be used, or it can even be called from any program that supports shell access to the operating system.

BCP Syntax

The BCP program includes a number of options, which are specified as command line parameters. The syntax and options are as follows:

```
BCP
{[[database_name.][owner].]{table_name | view_name} |
  "query"}
      {IN | OUT | QUERYOUT | FORMAT} data_file
[-m max_errors]
[-f format_file]
[-e err_file]
[-F first_row] [-L last_row] [-b batch_size]
[-n]
[-c]
[-w]
[-N]
[-V (60 | 65 | 70)]
[-6]
[-q]
[-C code_page]
[-t field_term]
```

```
[-r row_term]
[-i input_file]
[-o output_file]
[-a packet_size]
[-S server_name[\instance_name]]
[-U login_id]
[-P password]
[-T]
[-v]
[-R]
[-k]
[-E]
[-h "hint [,...n]"]
```

BCP options are case sensitive, so -N and -n are different parameters and interpreted differently. Each option is described below.

database name   This is the name of the database that contains the table or view that is the target of the copy operation. If no database is specified, then BCP operates in the default database for the login.

owner   This is the owner of the table or view specified for the copy operation. If no owner is specified, the table or view must be owned by the login or SQL Server 2000 will report an error.

table_name, view_name, or query   An entire table or view can be specified here to move all of the data into or out of the table or view. If this is a load of data and a view is specified, then only a single table in the view can be loaded and a format file is needed.

If a query is specified, then QUERYOUT must also be included and the copy operation must be an extraction. Loads of data cannot specify a query. The query must be enclosed in double quotes and anything that is quoted inside the query is specified using single quotes. If multiple result sets are returned by the query, only the first result set is copied to the output file.

IN | OUT | QUERYOUT | FORMAT   Only one of these options can be specified. The IN and OUT parameters specify the direction of the transfer with IN being a load of data into SQL Server and OUT being an extraction of data to a text file. QUERYOUT is specified when copying data out from a query. FORMAT will create a format file that matches the option specified (-n, -c, -6, -N, or -w). The -f option must also be included with FORMAT.

data_file   This is the name of the file that contains the source data for a load or is the destination for an extraction. The name should include the path (if not in the current directory) and is limited to 255 characters.

-m ***max_errors***   This is the maximum number of errors that can occur before the bulk copy operation is cancelled. Each row that cannot be copied for any reason is bypassed and counts as an error. The default for this parameter is 10.

-f ***format_file***   The format file is the name of an additional text file that contains information about the columns of data and their formats in the text file. The name should include the path to the file.

For loads of data, this file must exist and maps each column in the source data file to a column in SQL Server in the table or view. For extractions of data, this file can be created and the user is prompted for formatting information. If this option is not used and none of the parameters -c, -n, -6, -N, or -w is included, BCP will prompt the user for formatting information.

-e ***error_file***   This is the name of a file in which to store the rows that are not imported. Error messages are sent to the user's workstation. If this option is not included, no error file is created.

-F ***first_row***   This specifies which row in the source data to start copying. The default is row 1, which is the first row in the source.

-L ***last_row***   This specifies which row in the source data is the last row to copy. The default is 0, which specifies the last row.

-b ***batch_size***   If this option is not specified, BCP attempts to copy all rows as part of one batch and one transaction. This parameter allows the user to specify smaller batches of data, each of which would be its own transaction. This cannot be used with the -h option.

-n   This parameter specifies that the data in the text file is stored in a binary format native to SQL Server. Using this option will not prompt for formatting information for the columns.

-c   This option specifies that the data being copied is stored in the text file in a character format. The user is not prompted for formatting information. Each field is assumed to be a char datatype with the tab character as the field separator and the newline character as the row terminator.

-w   This parameter specifies that the copy operation will use Unicode characters. The user is not prompted for formatting information. Each field is assumed to be a nchar datatype with the tab character as the field separator and the newline character as the row terminator. This parameter cannot be used with SQL Server 6.5 and below.

-N   This option will transfer data using the database datatype for non-character data and Unicode characters for character data. This offers a speed advantage over the -w option and is designed for moving data from one SQL Server to another. The user is not prompted for formatting information, and this cannot be used with SQL Server 6.5 and below.

-V (60 | 65 | 70)   This option will perform the bulk copy operation using datatypes from an earlier version of SQL Server. This option should be used in conjunction with the -c or -n options.

-6   This parameter performs the copy using SQL Server 6.0 or 6.5 datatypes. This option is supported for backwards compatibility and should not be used. The -V option should be used instead.

-q   This option will execute the SET QUOTED_IDENTIFERS ON statement before beginning the copy of any data. This should be used when the table or view name contains a space or a quotation mark. The entire three-part name should be enclosed in double quotation marks.

-C *code_page*   This parameter specifies the code page of the data in the data file. This option is supported for backward compatibility. Instead of including this parameter, a collation should be specified for each column in the format file or in interactive BCP.

-t *field_terminator*   This parameter specifies the field terminator in the data file. The default is \t (the tab character).

-r *row_terminator*   This parameter specifies the row terminator in the data file. The default is \n (newline character).

-i *input_file*   This parameter specifies an input file that contains the answers to the command prompt questions asked by BCP in interactive mode.

-o *output_file*   This is the name of an output file that receives the output from the BCP utility.

-a *packet_size*   This parameter specifies the packet size in bytes of the data that is being sent to and from the server. This parameter overrides the server option set with SP_CONFIGURE. The parameter can range from 4096 to 65535 and defaults to 4096. An increased packet size can improve performance, but if the requested size cannot be sent, the default is used.

-S *server_name[\instance_name]*   This parameter specifies which server the utility should log into to perform the copy operation. For SQL Server 2000 servers, the instance name can be specified. If no instance is specified, the default instance is used. If this parameter is not sent, then the utility attempts to connect to the default instance on the local machine.

-U *login_id*   This parameter specifies the login ID that is used to connect to the SQL Server.

-P *password*   The parameter specifies the password for the login ID. If this parameter is not at the end of the command prompt line, then the user is prompted for a password. If this parameter is included at the end of the command prompt and no password is specified, then a NULL password is sent.

-T   This option specifies that the BCP utility connect to the SQL Server using a *trusted connection*. The utility will use the network credentials of the user running the utility. The –U and –P parameters are not required with –T.

-v   This parameter returns the BCP version number and copyright information.

-R   This parameter specifies that the currency, date, and time data is copied using the format that is set in the local computer's locale setting. By default the local computer's settings are ignored.

-k   This parameter ensures that empty columns retain a NULL value during the copy operation, rather than using any default values specified for the columns.

-E   This option specifies that values for an identity column are inserted into the table in the identity column, if they exist. If identity values are present in the data file, but –E is not specified, then they are ignored. If the data file does not contain identity values for the table, a format file should be used to specify that the identity column should be skipped when inserting data. SQL Server 2000 will automatically assign the identity values using the identity column seed and increment.

-h "*hint* [,...*n*]"   This parameter specifies a hint that should be used during the bulk copy operation. This parameter cannot be used with SQL Server 6.5 or lower. The available hints are:

ORDER (*column* [ASC | DESC] [, ...*n*]   This hint specifies the sort order of data in the data file. The performance of the operation can be improved if the data being loaded is sorted according to the clustered index. By default, BCP assumes that all the data in the data file is unordered.

ROWS_PER_BATCH = *n*   This hint specifies the number of rows per batch. By default, all the rows in the copy operation are assumed to be in a single batch.

KILOBYTES_PER_BATCH = *n*   This hint specifies the approximate number of kilobytes that should be sent per batch. By default, the number is unknown and the batch size is set with the –b parameter or the ROWS_PER_BATCH hint.

TABLOCK   This hint will cause a table lock to be acquired and held for the duration of the copy operation. This hint can significantly improve performance of the operation since there will be no lock contention. Multiple clients can load the table if there are no indexes on the table and TABLOCK is specified. By default the table lock on bulk load option determines the locking behavior.

CHECK_CONSTRAINTS   This hint specifies that any check constraints on the destination table are checked during the copy operation. By default, these constraints are ignored.

FIRE_TRIGGERS   This hint specifies that any triggers on the destination table will execute during the copy operation. By default, no insert triggers are executed.

Using Format Files

If the data file and the SQL Server table are in different formats, with different column names or orders, then a *format file* must be used. This file is used to specify the specific columns and orders that map the data file to the SQL Server.

SQL Server can automatically generate this file when BCP is used in interactive mode. The user will be prompted for each column's storage type, prefix length, field length, field terminator, and row terminator. Once all columns are specified, the user is prompted, as shown below, to specify whether or not to save a format file and the filename. The default filename is bcp.fmt.

```
Do you want to save this format information in
   a file? [Y/N] y
Host filename: [bcp.fmt]
```

Once this format file is saved, it can be used for future transfers of data, in or out of SQL Server, between the same table and a data file of similar format.

If an existing format file is specified using the −f parameter, then BCP does not prompt the user for the column information.

A format file can be created by hand or edited to reflect changes in the data structure of the text file. The format file itself is a text file of tab-delimited information that looks like the following format.

FIGURE 9.1   Sample format file

```
8.0
11
1    SQLNCHAR    2   10    " "  CustomerID     SQL_Latin1_General_CP1_CI_AS
2    SQLNCHAR    2   80    " "  CompanyName    SQL_Latin1_General_CP1_CI_AS
3    SQLNCHAR    2   60    " "  ContactName    SQL_Latin1_General_CP1_CI_AS
4    SQLNCHAR    2   60    " "  ContactTitle   SQL_Latin1_General_CP1_CI_AS
5    SQLNCHAR    2   120   " "  Address        SQL_Latin1_General_CP1_CI_AS
6    SQLNCHAR    2   30    " "  City           SQL_Latin1_General_CP1_CI_AS
7    SQLNCHAR    2   30    " "  Region         SQL_Latin1_General_CP1_CI_AS
8    SQLNCHAR    2   20    " "  PostalCode     SQL_Latin1_General_CP1_CI_AS
9    SQLNCHAR    2   30    " "  Country        SQL_Latin1_General_CP1_CI_AS
10   SQLNCHAR    2   48    " "  Phone          SQL_Latin1_General_CP1_CI_AS
11   SQLNCHAR    2   48    " "  Fax            SQL_Latin1_General_CP1_CI_AS
```

The first line of the format file contains the version number of BCP to be used. The following below:

```
8.0
```

specifies SQL Server 2000. This number follows the same format as the major and minor version number of SQL Server.

The second line of the format file will determine the number of columns that exist (or should be created) in the data file. The number specified in the following parameter:

4

must match the number of columns for all subsequent rows.

Each additional line in the data file will contain a series of data elements that describe a field in the data file. A tab separates each piece of information, and each line must contain the same number of columns. The data columns that are allowable are listed in Table 9.1.

TABLE 9.1 Format File Column Descriptors

Column	Description
Data File Field Order	This is the position of the field within the data file. The first field is 1 and each additional field is incremented by one.
Data File Datatype	The type of data structure being stored in this particular field. The datatype should be SQLCHAR for character format files. For native files, then use the default datatype. A list of types is listed in Table 9.2.
Prefix Length	This is the number of prefix characters for the field. Legal numbers are 0, 1, 2, and 4. SQL Server has a set of default values for each datatype, data file format, and column nullability. A list of these values is given in Table 9.3.
Data File Data Length	This field is the maximum length of the data stored in this column. The list of lengths for the various datatypes is given in Table 9.4.
Terminator	The *field terminator*. The terminator should be enclosed in double quotation marks. A list of terminators is given in Table 9.5.

TABLE 9.1   Format File Column Descriptors *(continued)*

Column	Description
Server Column Order	This is the column number of the data in the SQL Server table.
Server Column Name	This is the name of the column as stored in SQL Server.
Collation	This is the collation that is used to store character and Unicode data in the data file.

TABLE 9.2   Format File Datatypes

SQL Server Datatype	Format File Datatype
char	SQLCHAR
varchar	SQLCHAR
nchar	SQLNCHAR
nvarchar	SQLNCHAR
text	SQLCHAR
ntext	SQLNCHAR
binary	SQLBINARY
varbinary	SQLBINARY
image	SQLBINARY
datetime	SQLDATETIME
smalldatetime	SQLDATETIM4
decimal	SQLDECIMAL
numeric	SQLNUMERIC
float	SQLFLT8
real	SQLFLT4
int	SQLINT
bigint	SQLBIGINT
smallint	SQLSMALLINT
tinyint	SQLTINYINT
money	SQLMONEY
smallmoney	SQLMONEY4
bit	SQLBIT
uniqueidentifier	SQLUNIQUEID
sql_variant	SQLVARIANT
timestamp	SQLBINARY

TABLE 9.3 SQL Server Prefix Lengths

SQL Server Data Type	Native Format NOT NULL	NULL	Character Format NOT NULL	NULL
char	2	2	2	2
varchar	2	2	2	2
nchar	2	2	2	2
nvarchar	2	2	2	2
text	4	4	4	4
ntext	4	4	1	1
binary	1	1	2	2
varbinary	1	1	2	2
image	4	4	4	4
datetime	0	1	1	1
smalldatetime	0	1	1	1
decimal	1	1	1	1
numeric	1	1	1	1
float	0	1	1	1
real	0	1	1	1
int	0	1	1	1
bigint	0	1	1	1
smallint	0	1	1	1
tinyint	0	1	1	1
money	0	1	1	1
smallmoney	0	1	1	1
bit	0	1	0	1
uniqueidentifier	1	1	1	1
timestamp	1	1	2	2

TABLE 9.4 SQL Server Field Lengths

Datatype	Character Format	Native Format
char	Length defined for the column	Length defined for the column
varchar	Length defined for the column	Length defined for the column
nchar	Twice the length defined for the column	Length defined for the column

TABLE 9.4   SQL Server Field Lengths *(continued)*

Datatype	Character Format	Native Format
nvarchar	Twice the length defined for the column	Length defined for the column
text	0	0
ntext	0	0
bit	1	1
binary	Twice the length defined for the column + 1	Length defined for the column
varbinary	Twice the length defined for the column + 1	Length defined for the column
image	0	0
datetime	24	8
smalldatetime	24	4
float	30	8
real	30	4
int	12	4
bigint	19	8
smallint	7	2
tinyint	5	1
money	30	8
smallmoney	30	4
decimal	41*	*
numeric	41*	*
uniqueidentifier	37	16
timestamp	17	8

TABLE 9.5   Field Terminators

Terminator	Code
Tab	\t
Newline character	\n
Carriage return	\r
Backslash	\\
Null terminator (no visible terminator)	\0

TABLE 9.5 Field Terminators *(continued)*

Terminator	Code
Any printable character (control characters are not printable, except null, tab, newline, and carriage return)	(*, A, t, 1, and so on)
String of up to 10 printable characters, including some or all of the terminators listed earlier	(**\t**, end, !!!!!!!!!!, \t-\n, and so on)

EXERCISE 9.1

Using the BCP Utility

In this exercise, you will use the BCP utility to import data from a text file.

1. Open a Command Prompt by choosing Start Programs ➢ Run and typing **Cmd** in the text box. Press Enter, and a Command Prompt window should open.

2. Type the following (replacing *dev_sjones* with the name of your server):

   ```
   bcp Northwind.dbo.Customers out c:\Cust.txt -Sdev_sjones
   -T -c
   ```

3. You should see something like the following:
   ```
   Starting copy...

   91 rows copied.
   Network packet size (bytes): 4096
   Clock Time (ms.): total          40
   ```

4. Now choose Start Programs ➢ RUN, type **NOTEPAD C:\Cust.txt** in the edit box, and press Enter. The Notepad program should run and display the Customers table in a text format as shown in Figure 9.2.

FIGURE 9.2   The Northwind Customers Table

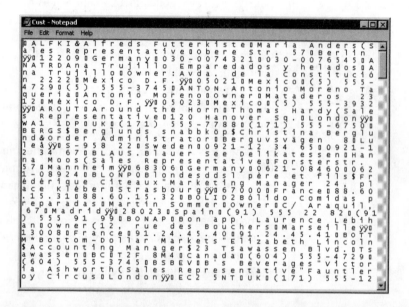

 Real World Scenario

Working with Mainframes

You are a DBA working for a utility company that has compiled a great deal of legacy data stored in mainframe computers. There is a billing database that contains customer information and is used to generate bills for customers. Recently the company has begun to install automated equipment to gather usage information from customers. The new automated equipment is designed to send the data back to the data centers. The format of the data being sent is complex, and it is decided that a server process will be written to receive the data and store it in a SQL Server.

You must ensure this data gets written to the billing database on the mainframe each night. Before you automate the transfer, you must also load the current customers into the SQL Server so the automated equipment can match its information against the existing customer records. You receive a text file of customer information from the mainframe.

Since SQL Server 2000 has been chosen as the server platform, you examine the list of tools available. The bulk copy utilities seem to be the easiest tools to work with and you decide to use them. To load data from the mainframe, you choose the BCP program to copy the data into the table in SQL Server. You decide to load 1,000 rows at a time to ensure that if there is a failure, the work done to date is not lost. This process is run from Query Analyzer one time to load the data for the automated equipment.

Since security is a concern on the mainframe and getting access to the billing database is difficult, you talk to the programmers for this database and they agree to import data if you can generate a text file of data each night. You use BCP to copy out information from the usage database using a query operation. The query copies all rows that have changed since the previous day based on a datetime column that is updated by the server process. This process is scheduled using the SQLAgent to run each night.

BULK INSERT

SQL Server 2000 contains an enhancement to the T-SQL language that allows the execution of a bulk copy program from within the server. This command is very similar to the BCP program, but allows you to execute a bulk copy operation from within a T-SQL batch.

Unlike the BCP program, only members of the Sysadmin or Bulkadmin fixed server roles have permission to run the BULK INSERT command. Applications run by users not part of either of these roles would not be able to execute the BULK INSERT command.

The syntax and parameters are described below.

BULK INSERT Syntax

```
BULK INSERT
 [ [ 'database_name'.] [ 'owner' ].] { 'table_name' FROM
  'data_file' }
 [ WITH
  (
  [ BATCHSIZE [ = batch_size ] ]
  [ [ , ] CHECK_CONSTRAINTS ]
```

```
[ [ , ] CODEPAGE [ = 'ACP' | 'OEM' | 'RAW' | 'code_page'
  ]]
 [ [ , ] DATAFILETYPE [ =
                    { 'char' | 'native'| 'widechar' |
  'widenative' } ] ]
[ [ , ] FIELDTERMINATOR [ = 'field_terminator' ] ]
  [ [ , ] FIRSTROW [ = first_row ] ]
  [ [ , ] FIRE_TRIGGERS ]
  [ [ , ] FORMATFILE = 'format_file_path' ]
  [ [ , ] KEEPIDENTITY ]
  [ [ , ] KEEPNULLS ]
  [ [ , ] KILOBYTES_PER_BATCH [ = kilobytes_per_batch ] ]
  [ [ , ] LASTROW [ = last_row ] ]
  [ [ , ] MAXERRORS [ = max_errors ] ]
  [ [ , ] ORDER ( { column [ ASC | DESC ] } [ ,...n ] ) ]
  [ [ , ] ROWS_PER_BATCH [ = rows_per_batch ] ]
  [ [ , ] ROWTERMINATOR [ = 'row_terminator' ] ]
  [ [ , ] TABLOCK ]
)
]
```

Each of these options is very similar to the same option for the BCP program. They are described below.

database_name   This parameter is the name of the database containing the table that is receiving the data. This allows insertion into a table in a database other than the current connection's database.

owner   This parameter is the name of the owner of the table or view that is being inserted into. This parameter is optional if the user performing the bulk insert owns the table. Otherwise an error is returned.

table_name   This parameter is the name of the table or view that will receive the data from the copy operation. Bulk insertion into views follows the same restrictions as the standard T-SQL INSERT statement.

data_file   This parameter is the name of the source data file, including the path. This must be a valid path from the SQL Server computer. Universal Naming Convention (UNC) paths are allowed.

BATCHSIZE *= nn*   This parameter specifies the number of rows in a batch. Each batch is treated as a single transaction with all rows being inserted or rolled back. The default is all rows in a single batch.

CHECK_CONSTRAINTS   If this parameter is included, then any constraints on the destination table are checked. These constraints are not checked by default.

CODEPAGE = '*code_page*'   This parameter specifies the code page of the data in the source file. This parameter is only needed if character data in the source data file contains characters with values greater than 127 or less than 32.

DATAFILETYPE   This parameter specifies the format of the source data file. The following are the four possible values:

CHAR   This is the default format. This option should be chosen if the source data file contains standard character data.

NATIVE   The source data file is in SQL Server native format. Use this format when the BCP utility was used to create the data file with the −n option.

WIDECHAR   This option is selected when the source data file contains character data with Unicode characters.

WIDENATIVE   This option works the same as **NATIVE** except the character and text data in the source file contains Unicode characters. The data file should have been created with the BCP utility and the −n option.

FIELDTERMINATOR   This parameter specifies the character that is used to delimit fields. The default is the tab character.

FIRSTROW   This specifies the row in the source data at which to begin the copy operation.

FIRE_TRIGGERS   If this parameter is specified, then any **INSERT** triggers on the destination table will fire. By default, **INSERT** triggers on the destination table do not execute.

FORMATFILE = '*format_file*'   This parameter allows the specification of a format file for the bulk insert operation. This format file follows the same format as a format file for the BCP utility. The details on the format of this file can be found in the section "Using Format Files."

KEEPIDENTITY   When this parameter is specified, SQL Server will insert the identity values in the source data file into the destination table. If this parameter is not given, then SQL Server will automatically assign the identity values. If the source file does not contain the identity values, then a format file must be used to skip the identity column.

KEEPNULLS   This parameter specifies that empty columns in the source data file should keep a NULL value in the destination table.

KILOBYTES_PER_BATCH   This parameter can be used to specify the approximate number of kilobytes per batch. The default is unknown.

LASTROW   This parameter is used to specify the last row of data in the source file that should be inserted. The default is 0, which indicates that all rows should be copied.

MAXERRORS   This parameter specifies the maximum number of errors that can occur before the bulk insert operation is terminated. Any row that cannot be imported is counted as an error and not inserted into the destination table. The default for this parameter is 10.

ORDER {*column* ASC | DESC [,...*n*]}   This parameter specifies how the source data file is sorted. If the data is sorted in the same order as the clustered index, then insert performance can be dramatically improved. If there is not a clustered index on the table, this parameter is ignored.

ROWS_PER_BATCH   This parameter specifies the number of rows in the source data file that should be included in each batch. This can be used only if the BATCHSIZE parameter is not specified. By default, all the rows in the source data file are included in a single batch.

ROWTERMINATOR = '*term*'   This parameter specifies the character that is used to delimit one row from the next in the source data file. The default is the newline character (\n).

TABLOCK   This parameter specifies that a table lock be obtained and held for the duration of the bulk insert operation. A table can be loaded in parallel from multiple client machines if it has no indexes and TABLOCK is specified.

Exercise 9.2 will examine how the BULK INSERT command can be used to import a text file into SQL Server.

EXERCISE 9.2

Using *BULK INSERT*

In this exercise, you will use the BULK INSERT command to import a text file into SQL Server.

1. Open Wordpad by choosing Start ➢ Run ➢ Wordpad.

2. Enter the following information in the Wordpad program, separating each city from its team with a tab:

```
Denver      Broncos
San Diego       Chargers
Kansas City     Chiefs
Seattle     Seahawks
Oakland     Raiders
```

3. Save this file to your local drive as c:\BulkInsertTest.txt by pressing the Save icon on the toolbar or choosing File ➢ Save from the menu.

4. Open the SQL Server Query Analyzer. Do this through the SQL Enterprise Manager by selecting Tools ➢ SQL Query Analyzer or by choosing Start ➢ Programs ➢ Microsoft SQL Server ➢ SQL Query Analyzer.

5. Type the following query (be sure the Northwind database is selected):

```
CREATE TABLE BulkInsertTest
(  City char( 20),
   Team char( 20)
)
```

6. Highlight these lines using your mouse and press the green arrow on the toolbar or press CTRL-E. You should see something like the following:

```
The command(s) completed successfully.
```

7. Now type the following query below the previous one:

```
BULK INSERT BulkInsertTest FROM 'c:\BulkInsertTest.txt'

SELECT  * FROM BulkInsertTest
```

8. High light these lines using your mouse and press CTRL-E. You should see something like the following:

```
(5 row(s) affected)

City                    Team
-------------------- ----------------------
Denver                  Broncos
Kansas City             Chiefs
Oakland                 Raiders
San Diego               Chargers
Seattle                 Seahawks

(5 row(s) affected)
```

Data Transformation Services

Data Transformation Services is a subsystem that is included in SQL Server 2000 and is designed for the movement and manipulation of data between formats and platforms. This subsystem can implement very simple data copy operations that are similar to the BCP utility. It can also build very complex data extraction, scrubbing, and insertion routines that perform complex tasks such as loading a data warehouse, archiving old data, or simulating replication between heterogeneous data sources.

This subsystem includes *DTS connections* that allow access to data in various formats, *DTS tasks* that can transform data or perform some action, and the ability to link these items together into a workflow using constraints. The entire collection of tasks, connections, and constraints is called a *package*.

A complete description of the DTS environment and its capabilities is beyond the scope of this book. This chapter will describe the basics of DTS and the new tasks devoted to the transfer of data, along with examples of how these tasks can be used.

The DTS Environment

Data Transformation Services is a utility that allows a programming environment to develop a process that performs some task and a run-time environment to execute this process. The run-time environment allows the execution of a process, called a *package*, from a command prompt on the server. The programming environment is introduced below, but readers are advised to consult Books Online or another text that is devoted to DTS to learn the full scope of its capabilities.

The programming environment is primarily a GUI-based development tool called the DTS Designer that allows a programmer to develop a package that will perform some task. When creating a new package, the programmer is presented with a template package that looks like Figure 9.3.

FIGURE 9.3 Blank DTS package

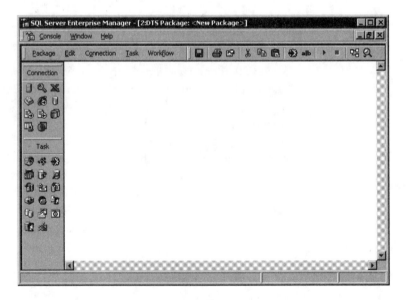

This environment consists of three toolbars: one for connections, one for tasks, and one for the development environment. The development package designer space is the empty white area in the right-hand side of the window. The tasks and connections can be added to the package using the menu at the top or by dragging one of the items from the toolbar onto the designer space. Once an item has been added to the package, then double clicking the object can set its properties and options.

By default, all the tasks that are added to the package execute in parallel when the package is run. Tasks can be arranged into a workflow, however, by arranging the tasks in a sequence. Once each task completes, it returns a success or failure code. The DTS package allows linkages between tasks that execute the next task based on a success code, a failure code, or either code.

If multiple tasks share the same connection, then they will execute in serial rather than parallel. If they are set up with two different connections, even if both connections point to the same data source, they will execute in parallel.

Connections

Connections are sources or destinations for data. Included with SQL Server 2000 are a series of connections for SQL Servers, Access databases, Excel spreadsheets, text files, and other sources of data. A package must contain a connection if it is to manipulate or copy data. These connections are built upon the OLE-DB technology from Microsoft, which allows access to a wide variety of data stored in a great many formats.

A connection can be added to the package by dragging it from the toolbar onto the package designer space. Once it has been added to the designer, various properties can be set that depend on the type of data source selected. SQL Server, for example, requires the server name, user ID and password, and database to be selected for the connection. Excel sources require the path and name of the file along with the username and password under which the file may be saved. The following connections are included with SQL Server 2000:

SQL Server   Allows connections to SQL Servers versions 6.x, 7, and 2000.

Access Databases   Allows connections to Microsoft Access databases through the JET engine.

Excel Spreadsheets   Allows access to data stored in Excel spreadsheets.

DBase 5 Databases   Allows access to data stored in dBase format.

HTML   Allows access to data stored in an HTML file.

Paradox   Allows access to Paradox databases.

Text File   Two connections are provided. One for text files that serve as a source of data and one for text files that act as a destination.

Oracle   A generic Oracle database connection is included.

Data Link   Provides a connection to data where the connection information is stored in a UDL file.

Other   Allows access to any data source for which an ODBC driver is installed on the local machine. This source requires a DSN to be set up to connect to the data source.

Tasks

Tasks are units of functionality that can be used to complete various processes. Each different process that DTS is capable of completing has its own task. These tasks can be added to a package and linked together to perform almost any type of data transfer, manipulation, or extraction.

Tasks are added to the DTS environment using the menu bar or by dragging and dropping a task from the toolbar onto the designer surface. Many tasks require connections, and the DTS designer will ask for the source and destination connections. Once the task has been added to the package, then it can be configured to meet the programmer's needs.

SQL Server 2000's DTS environment includes the following tasks:

FTP Task   This task allows file transfers to and from FTP servers.

ActiveX Script Task   This task allows the execution of an ActiveX script written using VBscript or Jscript.

Transform Data Task   This task will perform a copy of data between two connections. A table or a query can be used to extract the data from the source, and this task specifies the mappings between columns, any data transformations that occur, and other options that are available for transferring data.

Execute Process Task   This task allows any Win32 task or application to be run from within the DTS environment. Parameters may be passed to the process and an exit code received.

Execute SQL Task   This task will execute any SQL script that is entered against a connection.

Data Driven Query Task   This task is similar to the Transform Data Task, but is much more flexible. Each row that is processed can be processed using one of four different SQL statements depending on the result of an ActiveX script.

Copy SQL Server Objects Task   This task allows the copying of any SQL Server object(s) from one SQL Server to another. The user can select which objects are copied—whether data, indexes, permissions, etc. are copied with the objects.

Send Mail Task   This task will send mail using a MAPI provider.

Bulk Insert Task   This task works exactly like the BCP and BULK INSERT commands described earlier in this chapter.

Execute Package Task   This task allows the execution of another package from within this package. This allows the reuse of a package, similar to the way stored procedures allow the reuse of T-SQL code.

Message Queue Task   This task allows the sending or reading of messages from a Microsoft Message Queue.

Transfer Error Messages Task   This task allows the transfer of user defined error messages between SQL Servers. These are error messages that are created using the SP_ADDMESSAGE stored procedure.

Transfer Databases Task   This task will transfer an entire database from one SQL Server to another. The task allows the copy or move of the database and specifies the destination files.

Transfer Master Stored Procedures Task   This task will transfer stored procedures in the master database from one SQL Server to another.

Transfer Jobs Task   This task allows the transfer of SQLAgent jobs from one SQL Server to another.

Transfer Logins Task   This task allows the transfer of logins on one SQL Server to another.

Dynamic Properties Task   This task allows the setting of the package properties at runtime based on a query, an .INI file, a constant, or a variety of other values. The properties being set can be existing properties of the package or any of the objects within it, or new properties that are added to the package as global variables.

Once the tasks are added to a package, they can be connected together in a *workflow*. The programmer can select two tasks and then right-click in the DTS Designer or select Workflow from the menu and choose the type of workflow to implement. An arrow will appear between the two tasks that represents the direction of the workflow. The following are the three choices given in the DTS Designer:

On Completion This type of workflow is always followed when the package is executed. When the first task completes, the second is started, regardless of whether the first task succeeded or failed. This workflow is represented with a blue arrow.

On Success This path is only followed when the first task in the workflow returns a success code. This workflow arrow is green in color.

On Failure When the first task returns a failure error code, regardless of the reason for the error, the second task is executed. If the first task is successful, then this workflow is not followed. This workflow is represented with a red arrow.

When a package executes, by default, all the tasks run in parallel. The package is assigned a certain number of threads, and all tasks not assigned in a workflow will execute on one of these threads as soon as it is available. If a workflow is implemented, then the designer can control the order in which the tasks are completed. This allows a package to create a table and then insert data into the table if the creation succeeded. If the creation failed, however, the programmer might not want the rows to be inserted.

Packages

A collection of connections, tasks, and their workflows is known as a *package* in DTS. While each individual task in a package can be executed from within the DTS designer, most often the entire package will be executed using the DTSRUN command line utility. These programs can use the package GUID, but usually these packages are named and saved in one of four different formats. Each format has its own benefits and drawbacks as described below.

If the package is saved in SQL Server, it is as a binary large object (BLOB) field in msdb.sysdtspackages. Each time the package is changed and saved again, it is given a new version and added to this table. A DBA must manually delete old versions of a package. By default, the most recent version of a package is executed.

The package can also be saved to the SQL Server *Meta Data Services*. Meta Data Services are designed to allow the tracking of packages and their execution as well as the sharing of meta data between DTS and any other applications that can access it.

If the package is saved to Meta Data Services, the various protection options for the package are not available. If security is important, then this format should not be chosen.

The package can be saved to an operating system file in one of two formats. The first is as a *structured storage file* that can be copied across the network just like any other operating system file. This allows the sharing of packages without requiring them to be stored in SQL Server. All versions of the package are saved in the same file, though each version can be edited separately.

Once a package with multiple versions is saved in a structured storage file, the individual versions cannot be deleted. Only the entire file can be deleted. Avoid saving packages in this format if the need to branch versions is required.

The other operating system file format that packages can be saved to is a Visual Basic file format. Packages saved in this format can be edited using Microsoft Visual Basic version 5, Service Pack 3 or later. These packages can be executed from Visual Basic or incorporated into other applications.

Exercise 9.3 will walk you through creating a package in DTS that will duplicate the functionality of Exercise 9.2

EXERCISE 9.3

Using DTS

In this exercise, you will use DTS to import a text file.

1. Open the DTS Designer. Do this through the SQL Enterprise Manager by highlighting Data Transformation Services and selecting Action ➢ New Package or by right-clicking Data Transformation Services and selecting New Package from the pop-up menu.

2. Add a SQL Server connection to the designer surface by dragging the SQL Server icon onto the designer, or selecting Connection ➢

Microsoft OLE DB Provider for SQL Server from the menu. Enter the following options:

1. Select New Connection and type **MyConnection** in the edit box.

2. Enter your server name in the Server box. If you are running Enterprise Manager from the SQL Server machine console, you can leave this as (local).

3. If your server supports NT Authentication, you can leave this radio button checked. Otherwise, select Use SQL Server Authentication and enter the username and password of a user that has permissions to add data to the Northwind database.

4. Select Northwind in the Database drop-down box. Your Connection Properties dialog box should look similar to the one in the following graphic.

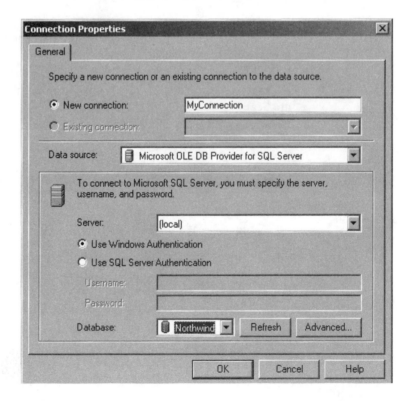

3. Add a Bulk Insert task to the package by dragging this icon onto the designer surface or selecting Task ➢ Bulk Insert Task from the menu. Enter the following properties:

   1. In the Description edit box enter **BulkInsertTest**.

   2. The Existing Connection box should have MyConnection in it.

   3. From the Destination Table drop-down box, select the [Northwind].[dbo].[BulkInsertTest] table. If this is not visible, please go back and complete Exercise 9.2.

   4. In the Source Data File edit box, enter **c:\BulkInsertTest.txt**. If you did not complete Exercise 9.2 to create this file, please complete steps 1, 2, and 3 from Exercise 9.2.

4. Your text file dialog box should look like the following:

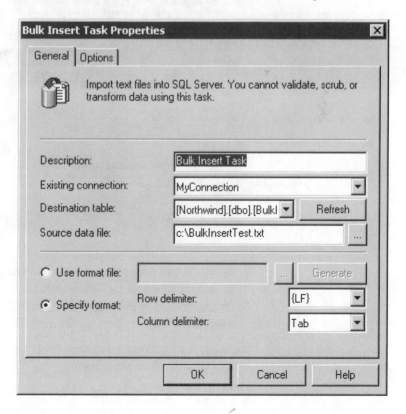

5. Save the package by pressing the floppy disk icon on the top tool-bar or selecting Package ➢ Save from the menu. Enter a name for the package and click OK. Leave the Location drop-down box set to SQL Server.

6. Execute the package by clicking the green arrow on the top toolbar or selecting Package ➢ Execute from the menu. The package should run, and you should get two dialog boxes that look like the following:

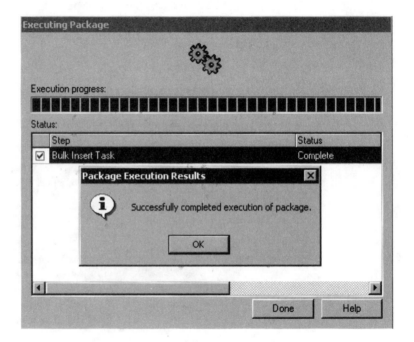

7. Close the two dialog boxes and open Query Analyzer through SQL Enterprise Manager by selecting Tools ➢ SQL Query Analyzer or by choosing Start ➢ Programs ➢ Microsoft SQL Server ➢ SQL Query Analyzer.

8. Select the Northwind database from the Database drop-down box and enter the following query:

```
SELECT * FROM BulkInsertTest
```

9. Highlight these lines using your mouse and press the green arrow on the toolbar or press CTRL-E. You should receive the following output. There are two sets of data, one from Exercise 9.2 and one from this exercise.

```
City                    Team
--------------------    ----------------------
Denver                  Broncos
Kansas City             Chiefs
Oakland                 Raiders
San Diego               Chargers
Seattle                 Seahawks
Denver                  Broncos
Kansas City             Chiefs
Oakland                 Raiders
San Diego               Chargers
Seattle                 Seahawks

(10 row(s) affected)
```

Summary

This chapter has examined various ways in which data in a SQL Server environment can be inserted or extracted from the server in bulk.

- BCP is a command line utility that has been included in quite a few versions of SQL Server. It allows the bulk insert or extraction of data between a text file and SQL Server. Format files can be used to specify mappings between the SQL Server table and the text file.

- The T-SQL language in SQL Server 2000 includes the BULK INSERT command, which operates very similar to the BCP program. It allows the insertion of data into a SQL Server table from a text file. This command can share format files with the BCP program.

- Data Transformation Services is a utility included in SQL Server 2000 that moves and manipulates data between data sources. This utility includes a programming environment that allows a user to develop a package that can include a variety of tasks, processes, and workflow sequences. These packages can be stored in SQL Server or operating system files and are executed using the command line utility DTSRUN.

Key Terms

Before you take the exam, be certain you are familiar with the following terms:

BCP	field terminator
BULK INSERT	DTS connections
Data Transformation Services	DTS tasks
command line utility	package
native format	tasks
interactive mode	workflow
trusted connection	Meta Data Services
format file	structured storage file

Exam Essentials

Understand how the BCP.EXE utility can be used. The BCP utility has been included with SQL Server for a number of versions. It is widely used as an import and extraction utility.

Know the limitations of BCP. The BCP utility can only move data between SQL Server and a text file. This text file can be in a character format or a binary format native to SQL Server.

Understand what the *BULK COPY* T-SQL Extension does. The BULK COPY command performs the same function as the BCP utility, but it can only import data. The options are the same as those for BCP.

Know what Data Transformation Services (DTS) is and how it is used in SQL Server. DTS is a utility that allows the manipulation of data between a variety of data sources. It includes connections to work with different formats of data as well as different tasks to move this data around.

Review Questions

1. You are the DBA for a mass e-mail company and often receive lists of names and e-mails from your clients. Each client sends his or her data in a different format, but each always sends the same format. You use the BCP program to import this data into your e-mail table. Which of the techniques listed below can make importing this data easier?

   A. Changing the BCP batch size for each client to 1,000

   B. Using a single format file that you edit for each client

   C. Using a separate format file for each client, customized to that client's data file

   D. Using an INSTEAD OF trigger to reformat the data received from each client

2. You have received a large data feed from the mainframe programmers in your company. This feed has 26 data files, each one containing a list of customers separated by the first letter of the customer's last name. Which BCP option will speed the importing of this data into SQL Server when using multiple machines?

   A. -f *format_file*

   B. -b *batch_size*

   C. -a *packet_size*

   D. -h "TABLOCK"

3. You are the DBA for OnlineCatalogs, Inc., a Web service provider that places a company's catalogs on the Internet. One of your clients sends you his catalog in a text file with the column headers of the data on the first line of the file. You decide to use the BULK INSERT command to import this data file into SQL Server; however, you do not want to import the column headers as a row of data. Here is the first line of T-SQL code you write:

   ```
   BULK INSERT Products FROM 'c:\Products.txt'
   ```

What options do you need to include to import this file? (Assume no formatting changes are needed.)

A. FIRE_TRIGGERS

B. FIRSTROW = 2

C. LASTROW = 2

D. BATCHSIZE = 100

4. ABC Manufacturing Corporation is a highly automated industrial company. Most assembly lines automatically report information to your SQL Server database. Which tools can you use to extract this information for reporting to the manufacturing supervisors? (Select all that apply.)

A. DTS

B. BCP.EXE

C. BULK INSERT

D. BULK EXTRACT

5. You are the DBA for the Data Integrators Company and in charge of building DTS packages that move data between various systems. One of your clients requests that you build a package that copies data from SQL Server to an Excel spreadsheet and then e-mails the spreadsheet to a user. Place the following tasks in the order required to complete this task. Include only those tasks that are needed.

A. Add the BEGIN TRANSACTION task to the package.

B. Add a Data Transform task from SQL Server to the Excel Spreadsheet to the package.

C. Add a connection for the SQL Server to the package.

D. Add the COMMIT TRANSACTION task to the package.

E. Add and configure a Send E-mail task to the package that attaches the spreadsheet to the e-mail.

F. Add a connection for the Excel spreadsheet to the package.

G. Add a workflow constraint between the Excel spreadsheet and the Send E-mail task.

6. As a DTS package designer, you must often send packages from the corporate network to remote field offices. These packages can be installed and run by trained employees at these locations, but not all locations have network connections to your server. How can you send these packages to your remote users?

   A. Save each package in the Structured File Format and e-mail them to your users.

   B. Save each file on your SQL Server and have the users execute them directly from your SQL Server.

   C. Save each file to the Meta Data Services on your SQL Server and send the meta data to your remote users through e-mail.

   D. Save each package in Visual Basic format and send this to your users through e-mail.

7. As the DBA for Bulk E-mailers, Inc, you often receive large data files to import into SQL Server. Occasionally, one of these files is extremely large and the import does not complete due to a network error. When this happens, you must restart the entire import. Which option for the BULK INSERT command can prevent you from losing the work done to date by the server in the event of a network error?

   A. MAXERRORS

   B. BATCHSIZE

   C. ROWS_PER_BATCH

   D. FORMATFILE

8. A format file can be used to perform which of the following functions for the BCP.EXE utility? (Select all that apply.)

   A. Rearrange columns between the data file and the SQL Server table.

   B. Change the collation of an individual column.

   C. Insert Identity values into the table.

   D. Determine the starting row to import in the data file.

9. Which utility can be used to transfer data from an Access database to SQL Server?

   A. BCP.EXE

   B. BULK INSERT

   C. BULK INSERT with a format file

   D. DTS

10. You are the DBA for a company that stores its products in a few tables. The schema for these tables is shown in the graphic below:

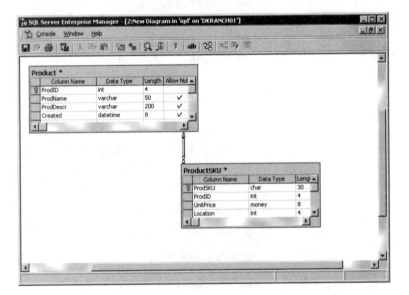

You need to import data that is sent from your manufacturers in a text file into these tables. The manufacturer sends you a single file with each row containing the following information:

- ProdID

- ProdName

- ProdDescr

- ProdSKU
- UnitPrice
- Location

What is the best way for you to import this information?

A. Create a view of both tables and insert the data using the BULK COPY command.

B. Create a view of both tables and insert the data using the BCP.EXE program.

C. Create a DTS package that reads the file once and imports the data into the Product table and then reads the file a second time and imports the data into the ProductSKU table.

D. Create a DTS package that reads the file and imports the data into the Product and ProductSKU tables at the same time.

Answers to Review Questions

1. C. Creating a separate format file for each client that can be reused for each import makes importing the data easy.

2. D. If the TABLOCK hint is specified on each client, a table lock is obtained and parallel loads occur very quickly.

3. B. Since the first row contains the column headers, we want to skip importing this row. The FIRSTROW option will start the import at line 2, which is the first line of data.

4. A, B. Both A and B are tools that can extract data from SQL Server. C is an import utility only, and D is not a valid utility in SQL Server.

5. C (or F), F (or C), B, E, G. Options A and D are not valid tasks. The two connections to the data source must be added before the Data Transform task and the Send E-mail task must be added before the workflow constraint.

6. A, D. Both of these methods create and operating system file that can be e-mailed to the remote users. Options B and C would require network connectivity from the remote user's site to your server, which is not available for all sites.

7. B or C. Either of these can be used to prevent the loss of work during an import by specifying the size of a transaction.

8. A, B, C. All of these items are specified using a format file. Option D is specified by a command line parameter passed to the BCP program.

9. D. Only DTS can transfer between Access and SQL Server. The other utilities only work with text data files.

10. C. Since the data must be moved from a single file to two different files, the BULK COPY command and the BCP utility cannot complete this in one step. DTS is the best choice, though two different steps are needed to ensure that the data in the Product table is imported first. The foreign key between the two tables necessitates this.

Chapter

10

Locking

✓ Manage result sets by using cursors and Transact-SQL.
  Considerations include locking models and appropriate usage.

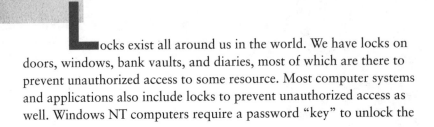

Locks exist all around us in the world. We have locks on doors, windows, bank vaults, and diaries, most of which are there to prevent unauthorized access to some resource. Most computer systems and applications also include locks to prevent unauthorized access as well. Windows NT computers require a password "key" to unlock the computer.

In SQL Server 2000, as in most relational database systems, locks are crucial in ensuring that data loss and integrity can be maintained. All these multi-user systems include some method of locking that prevents one user from overwriting or interfering with another user's actions.

Imagine that there is a paper ledger used to track the sales for a company. There are two people that are assigned to enter sales numbers in this ledger and each enters the numbers in the same way: They read the existing sales total in the ledger, the current sale is added to this total, and the new total is written in the ledger. When these two people get busy, there is the potential that one of these users will overwrite another's entry and data will be lost. Suppose that person A reads the current total as $100. Person A now looks at the current sale, which is $10 and adds these two numbers together. While person A is adding the numbers, person B looks at the ledger and reads $100 also. Person B then starts his own addition using his current sale number of $25. While person B is adding his numbers, person A erases the $100 in the ledger and writes $110. Person B now completes his addition and erases the ledger entry and enters $125. The total should be $135 at this point, but data has been lost.

SQL Server 2000 seeks to prevent this occurrence by using locks to control access to data. The database server implements different types of locks that are designed to ensure that only one person can change a particular piece of data at a time and that data integrity is maintained. SQL Server 2000 has a system of locking that balances the need to protect data against conflicting modifications while allowing as much *concurrency* as possible.

This chapter will examine how locks are implemented in SQL Server 2000 and their effects on the behavior of the server as well as ways that the behavior can be modified.

The Lock Manager

SQL Server 2000 has a *lock manager* that controls and manages the locking process. The lock manager is responsible for acquiring locks for different processes, managing the interaction of the different lock modes, escalating these locks if necessary, and releasing them as soon as possible to avoid contention problems with other processes. The lock manager must avoid releasing locks too soon as transactional integrity must be maintained, depending on the isolation level that is set for the database. If they occur, the lock manager must also resolve deadlock issues.

The lock manager changes its behavior based on the *transaction isolation level* that has been set. There are four levels that are specified by the ANSI and ISO standards groups, which are supported by SQL Server 2000. These are listed in Table 10.1. The isolation level is set to READ COMMITTED by default, but can be changed for any individual transaction using the SET TRANSACTION ISOLATION LEVEL command.

TABLE 10.1   Transaction Isolation Levels

Level	Description
READ UNCOMMITTED	This is the lowest level of isolation, and is also known as "dirty read." This allows a user to read any data on a page, even if some of it has been marked or changed by a transaction in progress. If the transaction were to be rolled back, the second process might have retrieved data that does not exist in the system. A process that is reading data does not acquire shared locks.
READ COMMITTED	This is SQL Server 2000's default isolation level. A process at this level will never read data that is changed but not committed. A process will acquire shared locks when reading data. If a process revisits a row of data inside a transaction, it may have changed or new rows may have appeared.

TABLE 10.1   Transaction Isolation Levels *(continued)*

Level	Description
REPEATABLE READ	This level works in the same manner as READ COMMITTED, but ensures that if a row of data is revisited within a transaction, the data cannot be changed, but new rows may appear. This level will hold shared locks until the transaction completes.
SERIALIZABLE	The serializable level is the highest level of isolation. When set at this level, SQL Server will behave as though it is a single user system for each user, at the expense of contention problems between users. This level adds to REPEATABLE READ by preventing new rows from appearing within a transaction.

The lock manager tries to prevent problems from occurring between multiple users of a system. The main problems that can occur are:

- *Lost updates*
- *Uncommitted dependencies*
- *Inconsistent analysis*
- *Phantom reads*

Each of these items is a basic problem that can result when multiple users or processes are attempting to modify a shared system of data.

Lost updates occur when a situation like the one described in the introduction take place. The update made by person A was "lost." All transaction isolation levels prevent lost updates.

An uncommitted dependency is a "dirty read." One process or user is retrieving data that was changed by another, but the change has not been committed and may be "undone" or rolled back. The READ COMMITTED level prevents inconsistent analysis from occurring.

Inconsistent analysis can result when one process retrieves a set of data and finds one result, but gets a different result when a second retrieval is performed. These two retrievals must be within the same transaction. The REPEATABLE READ isolation level prevents inconsistent analysis.

Phantom reads occur when a process retrieves data in two different operations, but gets more or fewer rows in one of the operations. These are due to an INSERT or DELETE operation between the two retrieval operations. The SERIALIZABLE isolation level prevents phantom reads.

Lock Modes

The SQL Server 2000 architecture implements different lock modes that prevent access to data, as well as protect the users from receiving inaccurate information. The different types of locks can be changed from one type to another on the same resource as needs of the transaction change. Various options and hints (discussed later in this chapter) can be included in applications or set on the server to change the way that SQL Server implements each type of lock. The isolation levels listed previously also affect the way these lock modes are used by a transaction. Table 10.2 lists the modes of locks that exist in SQL Server 2000.

TABLE 10.2   SQL Server 2000 Lock Modes

Type	Lock Code	Description
Shared	S	A shared lock is a read lock that notifies other processes that the data is being read. No changes are possible to data with shared locks, but other processes or users can acquire their own shared locks to read the same data.
Intent Shared	IS	An intent shared lock indicates that a transaction intends to acquire a shared lock on a resource at a lower level than the intent shared lock is held.
Intent Exclusive	IX	An intent exclusive lock indicates that a transaction will seek exclusive locks on a resource at a lower level than the intent exclusive lock is being held.

TABLE 10.2 SQL Server 2000 Lock Modes *(continued)*

Type	Lock Code	Description
Shared with Intent Exclusive	SIX	This type of lock is used when a transaction needs to read some of the resource at a lower level than the shared with intent exclusive lock and will require shared locks. The transaction will also require intent exclusive locks on some of the resource at a lower level to perform a data modification.
Update	U	An update lock is a lock that notifies other processes that a data modification statement is coming. This will be upgraded to an exclusive lock when the actual data is changed.
Exclusive	X	Exclusive locks prevent any other user or process from accessing the resource. All data modifications require an exclusive lock before the data can be changed.
Schema Stability	Sch-S	Schema stability locks are used when a query is being compiled. This prevents any schema from being performed but does not block any other type of lock.
Schema Modification	Sch-M	Schema modification locks are used when a portion of the schema is being modified.
Bulk Update	BU	Bulk update locks are acquired on a table that is the target of a bulk copy operation. This prevents other transactions from accessing the table, but multiple bulk update locks can be acquired by other bulk copy operations in order to load the table in parallel.

Each type of lock is implemented when a particular event occurs. SQL Server can adjust the locking dynamically based on server conditions and its own estimates of how efficient each type of lock may be. Since locking more resources than needed can cause contention problems, each lock is held for as long as it is needed to ensure transactional integrity and then released. Each lock is described below with more detail about its behavior and implementation.

Shared Locks

A shared lock exists to protect the reading of data. This allows a process to access data without the data being changed or lost during the access. A resource can have any number of shared locks on it at one time. These locks do not interfere with one another.

The length of time that a shared lock is held depends on the transaction isolation level. If the isolation level is set to READ REPEATED or SERIALIZABLE, then the shared locks are held until the end of the transaction. If the level is READ COMMITTED, then the locks are only held as long as the server takes to read a page of data. If the query is scanning the table, then the lock is held until a shared lock is acquired on the next page.

Intent Locks

Intent locks are not really locks that are acquired on an object. An intent lock serves as a flag that a transaction needs a lock. These locks prevent another process from gaining an exclusive lock on the resource while the process is waiting. Intent locks are acquired at a higher level than that of the lock they will be changed into. If a transaction requires a lock at a row or page level, an intent lock will be placed on the entire table to prevent another process from gaining a table lock and blocking the process with the intent lock. This also helps performance, as the server need not examine every row or page when attempting a table lock. Just the intent locks need to be examined.

There are three types of intent locks: intent shared, intent exclusive, and shared with intent exclusive. An intent shared lock tells the server that the transaction needs to acquire shared locks on some of the resources at a lower level. An intent exclusive lock indicates that a transaction needs to change some of the data in the resource at a lower level and will need exclusive locks on the data being modified. A shared with intent exclusive lock is a combination that signifies the transaction needs to read as well as modify some of the resources at a lower level. Only one shared with intent exclusive lock can be placed on the higher-level resource, though other intent shared locks from other transactions can exist on the lower-level resources.

Update Locks

Update locks exist to prevent deadlocks on resources that are being modified. Typically the first process acquires a shared lock on the resource being modified. A second process also may acquire a shared lock on the same resource. As each attempts to convert the lock to an exclusive lock, it must wait for the other process to release its shared lock. This results in a deadlock. SQL Server prevents this by acquiring an update lock on the resource and then converting this to an exclusive lock when the data modification occurs or to a shared lock if no update occurs. Only one process can hold an update lock on a resource at a time.

Update locks are not only used for updates. Any data modification statement that reads the data prior to a modification will use an update lock. Conversion to an exclusive lock is still required before the actual data modification takes place.

Exclusive Locks

An exclusive lock is the most restrictive type of lock SQL Server implements. When an exclusive lock has been set on a resource, only the process that acquired the lock may access the resource for reading and/or modification. No other locks of any kind can be acquired on the resource for the duration of the exclusive lock.

When the actual data modification is actually made to a row, an exclusive lock is always required.

Schema Locks

A schema lock is used to ensure that schema modifications cannot occur while some process needs the schema to remain constant. There are two types of schema locks. The schema modification lock is used when the schema for a table is being changed. This prevents another process from modifying the same schema at this time. A schema stability lock is used when a query is being compiled. These locks do not prevent any shared, intent, or exclusive locks from being acquired; they only prevent schema changes on the table.

One other lock similar to the schema locks is the bulk update lock. This type of lock is used when a bulk copy operation is being performed and the TABLOCK hint has been specified.

Latches

In addition to these locks, SQL Server also uses latches, which are essentially lightweight locks. Latches are used when managing access to the internal data structures of SQL Server, such as pages of data, index pages, and text pages. The latches ensure the physical integrity of the data by controlling the access to the actual data structures. They also enhance performance, as the overhead of latches is lower than that of locks.

Levels of Locking

Each of these types of locks can be applied at various levels or granularities. These granularities are at different levels in the database and arranged in a hierarchy. Each different level at which a lock can be applied is described below, arranged in increasing levels of the hierarchy.

Row   A row is the lowest level of lock. A row lock protects a single row of data in a table on a single page. Other rows on the same page of data are not affected.

Page   A page lock affects all rows on a single 8KB page of data.

Extent   An extent lock affects a complete extent, or eight data pages. Since an extent can contain pages from different objects, this type of lock can affect more than one object.

Table   A table lock affects all rows in the table.

Database   This type of lock is held on the entire database and all objects within the database.

The entire database is locked with a shared lock whenever a process has an open connection to that particular database. This shared database lock prevents major changes like a database being dropped or detached from the server.

There is also another type of lock that does not necessarily fit in the hierarchy, but exists to prevent a specific problem.

Key Range Locks   A key range lock is a lock that prevents phantom reads and allows serializable transactions. These locks are held on individual rows and the ranges between rows. By holding a lock on a range, inserts or deletions in the range are prevented, thus ensuring no phantom reads.

Transactions and Locking

A transaction in SQL Server ensures either that all work done by a single statement or a group of statements is completed, or that none of the work is performed. The classic example of this involves the transfer of money between two bank accounts. One account is marked with a decrease of funds and the second account is marked with the corresponding increase of funds. Together, these two changes are a transaction. If only one of them is performed, then money is being either created or lost, neither of which is an acceptable situation. If only one of these transactions occurs, then that transaction must be undone as soon as the second transaction fails. This ensures that all funds are accounted for and the bank will still be in business next week.

SQL Server ensures that all the statements within a transaction will be completed or not done at all. One way in which the integrity of all data can be maintained during a transaction is through the use of locks. Locks prevent changes to the data until the transaction is either committed (all changes are written to the database) or rolled back (all changes are removed and the database is in the same state as it was prior to the start of the transaction). This ensures that one transaction cannot interfere with another. These locks, however, cause a few side effects to the system, the first of which is *blocking*.

Blocking

Blocking is a natural occurrence in any system where one process can prevent another from using some resource. In SQL Server, when one process locks a resource and another object needs to use the same resource, the second process must wait until the locks are released. In this situation, the first process blocks the second process. Blocks are the result of contention in SQL Server when many processes are trying to access the same resource. Blocks are not necessarily the sign of a problem in the system, though they can cause contention issues if they exist for extraordinary lengths of time.

SQL Server tries to minimize the amount of blocking that occurs by acquiring the lowest level of lock that it needs to complete a transaction. SQL Server will estimate the amount of data that is affected by a particular transaction and then decide which level of lock is required to perform the work. If SQL Server needs to update all rows in a table, then a table lock is the most efficient type of lock because until all rows are modified, none of the rows can be unlocked. Rather than acquiring a lock on each row or page of the table, a single table lock can be implemented with less resources and time, which will allow the transaction to complete quicker.

If SQL Server finds that it did not estimate well and large numbers of locks are being acquired at one level, it can perform *lock escalation*. Lock escalation occurs when the server changes from one level of lock to another. A single lock at a higher level is more efficient and quicker to both acquire and release. Higher-level locks, however, cause more contention issues because less data is available to other processes while the locks are being held. SQL Server tries to balance the efficiency of high-level locks with the lower contention of lower-level locks.

Deadlocks

Occasionally, two processes will both be performing transactions and they will block each other. When this occurs, neither process can proceed because it needs a resource that is being locked by the other process. This situation is called a *deadlock* and cannot be resolved without one process being terminated. In this situation, SQL Server will usually choose one process as the *deadlock victim* and terminate it. All work done by the deadlock victim is rolled back and its locks released. This allows the other process to complete its transaction.

A description of a deadlock would be as follows: Suppose that one transaction needs to update the prices in the Products table and any orders that are pending. This process begins to lock pages in the Products table and starts performing updates. At the same time, a second transaction is updating the orders to mark pending orders as completed and reads the current price from the Products table to complete its update. The second transaction is locking pages in the Orders table, but reaches a point where it cannot continue until the first transaction releases its locks on the Products table. The first transaction, however, also cannot complete until the second process releases its locks on the Orders table. This situation results in a standstill, or deadlock. Once SQL Server recognizes this condition, it will choose a deadlock victim and roll back that transaction's work. The client for that transaction will receive the following error message:

```
Server: Msg 1205, Level 13, State 50, Line 1
Transaction (Process ID 51) was deadlocked on {lock}
resources with another process and has been chosen as the
deadlock victim. Rerun the transaction.
```

In this message, whichever process was chosen as the deadlock victim is reported using its system process ID (SPID). SQL Server will usually choose the process that submitted the last statement and caused the deadlock.

One way in which deadlocks can be controlled is through the use of the SET DEADLOCK_PRIORITY option, which can be set to low or normal. If this option is set to LOW by a transaction, the transaction will terminate when a deadlock occurs, even if it is not the transaction that completed the deadlock. Exercise 10.1 creates a deadlock condition and uses the SET DEADLOCK_PRIORITY option to force the first transaction to terminate.

EXERCISE 10.1

Create a Deadlock Condition in SQL Server

This exercise will deliberately create a deadlock condition.

1. Open the SQL Server Query Analyzer. Do this through the SQL Enterprise Manager by selecting Tools ➢ SQL Query Analyzer or by choosing Start ➢ Programs ➢ Microsoft SQL Server ➢ SQL Query Analyzer.

2. Type the following query into Query Analyzer (be sure the Northwind database is selected):

```
SET DEADLOCK_PRIORITY LOW
BEGIN TRANSACTION
UPDATE Customers
 SET Region = 'CO'
```

3. Highlight these lines with the mouse and press the green arrow or press CTRL-E to execute the query. You should receive the following results:

```
(92 row(s) affected)
```

4. Open a second query window by pressing CTRL-N or selecting File ➢ New from the menu. Type the following query into Query Analyzer (be sure the Northwind database is selected):

```
BEGIN TRANSACTION
UPDATE Orders
  SET EmployeeID = 8
```

5. Highlight these lines with the mouse and press the green arrow or press CTRL-E to execute the query. You should receive the following results:

```
(830 row(s) affected)
```

6. Switch back to the first window by selecting Window ➢ 1 from the menu. Type the following query into Query Analyzer:

```
UPDATE Orders
  SET OrderDate = Getdate()
```

7. Highlight these lines with the mouse and press the green arrow or press CTRL-E to execute the query. You should not receive any results and the query should not complete execution.

At this point, the first (current) transaction is being blocked by the second transaction. No deadlock condition has occurred yet.

8. Switch back to the second window by selecting Window ➢ 2 from the menu. Type the following query into Query Analyzer:

```
UPDATE Customers
SET City = 'Denver'
```

9. Highlight these lines with the mouse and press the green arrow or CTRL-E to execute the query. You should receive the following results after a short delay:

```
(92 row(s) affected)
```

10. Switch back to the first window by selecting Window ➢ 1 from the menu. You should see something like the following:

```
Server: Msg 1205, Level 13, State 54, Line 1
Transaction (Process ID 51) was deadlocked on {lock}
resources with another process and has been chosen as the
deadlock victim. Rerun the transaction.
```

Since the DEADLOCK_PRIORITY option was set to low for the first transaction, it terminated as soon as the deadlock condition was detected.

Deadlocks can be tracked using SQL Profiler or Performance Monitor.

Preventing Deadlocks

It is not often that deadlocks are encountered in a new application. Most transactions are implicit, short, and affect a single resource. Once an application starts to mature, however, more complex transactions are usually introduced that contain multiple statements and affect more than one object.

Deadlocks often occur when transactions that use the same resources access these resources in different orders. One way to limit deadlocks is to ensure that transactions that use the same resources all access those resources in the same order.

When developing transactions that will access more than one object, it helps to develop a standard order in which to access all objects. If this is done, then it is unlikely that a deadlock condition will be created.

Locking Options

In SQL Server 2000, a programmer can influence the locking behavior of transactions. There are means of viewing the locking activity on a server in addition to including hints and options in transactions or queries that control or influence the locking behavior. This section will look at some of the other ways that a programmer or DBA can view and change the locking behavior of SQL Server.

Viewing Locks

The first step to controlling the locking behavior in SQL Server is to understand how many and of which types are the locks that are being held in the system. There are two ways that locks can be viewed in SQL Server: through Enterprise Manager or using the SP_LOCK system stored procedure. Each of these methods provides different information that can be used to determine which locks are being applied in SQL Server. Exercise 10.2 examines how Enterprise Manager can be used to view the locks on a system.

EXERCISE 10.2

Viewing Locks with Enterprise Manager

This exercise will allow you to view a snapshot of all the locking activity on your SQL Server.

1. Open the SQL Server Enterprise Manager. Do this by choosing Start ➢ Programs ➢ Microsoft SQL Server ➢ Enterprise Manager.

2. Expand the list of groups by clicking the plus (+) sign next to Microsoft SQL Servers, then expand this group by clicking the plus sign next to the group in which your SQL Sever is registered. Finally, select the SQL Server to which you want to connect by clicking it. Your SQL Server should then have a small green circle on the server icon with a white triangle inside.

3. Expand the folders under the SQL Server by clicking the plus (+) sign next to the server name. Expand the management folder by clicking the plus sign and then expand the Current Activity folder. Your Enterprise Manager should like the one below.

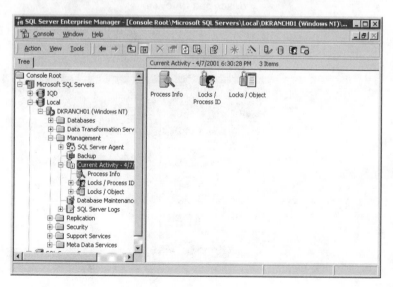

EXERCISE 10.2 *(continued)*

There are three items under Current Activity: Process Info, Locks/Process ID, and Locks/Object. Each of these displays lock information using a different filter.

4. Select Locks/Process ID and click one of the SPID icons below this item. You should see a display like the one below.

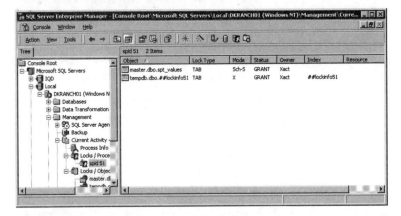

The right-hand pane will display all the locks that are being held on objects by the particular connection that was selected. The columns shown are the same as those returned by SP_LOCK. They are described below.

5. Select Locks/Object and choose one of the objects below this item. Your Enterprise Manager should look like the one below.

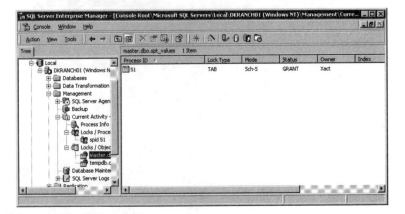

This display shows all of the locks that are being held on the object selected. These columns are also described in Table 10.3.

The other method of viewing lock information is to run the SP_LOCK system stored procedure. Its syntax is given below:

SP_LOCK [@spid1] [, @spid2]

where the arguments are both the *system process ID number*s of one or two processes on the SQL Server. This stored procedure can have none, one, or two parameters. If no parameters are passed, then all lock information about all processes is returned. If one or two system process IDs are passed as parameters, then only locking information for the one or two processes is returned. The result set returned by this stored procedure is given in Table 10.3.

TABLE 10.3   SP_LOCK Result Set

Column	Description
Spid	System Process ID number. The number given to the process by SQL Server and stored in master..sysprocesses.
Dbid	The database ID number. Each database is assigned a unique number on the SQL Server. This number is stored in master..sysdatabases.
Objid	The object ID number. Each object in a database receives a unique ID number in that database. This number is stored in the sysobjects table in each database.
Indid	The index identification number.

TABLE 10.3 SP_LOCK Result Set *(continued)*

Column	Description
Type	The type of lock being applied. The lock types are: DB - Database FIL - File IDX - Index PG - Page Key - Key TAB - Table EXT - Extent RID - Row
Resource	The lock on the resource. This matches the value in Syslockinfo.restext. This is a text description of the resource being locked.
Mode	The lock mode of the requester. The lock modes are listed in Table 10.2.
Status	The status of the lock being requested. The available statuses are GRANT (lock has been obtained), WAIT (blocked by another process), or CNVRT (a lock that is held on a resource is waiting to be converted to another lock).

Lock Isolation Levels

As mentioned in the first section of this chapter, "The Lock Manager," there are four different methods of implementing locking in a relational database. These four levels are ANSI standards that are supported by SQL Server. In SQL Server 2000, the default isolation level is READ COMMITTED. All transactions will behave in a manner consistent with this level by default.

SQL Server 2000 includes a SET option that allows the programmer to change the isolation level for a particular transaction. The syntax for this option is

```
SET TRANSACTION ISOLATION LEVEL <isolation_level>
```

The isolation level is one of the following: READ UNCOMMITTED, READ COMMITTED, REPEATABLE READ, or SERIALIZABLE.

Once this option is run, the isolation level remains in effect for the duration of the connection or until it is changed with another SET command.

Lock Hints

In SQL Server 2000, there are options available that can change the behavior of locking in the server. These *lock hints* are used to force the server to hold locks longer than it otherwise would, or to not acquire any locks at all (and potentially read data that has already been changed). Table 10.4 lists the lock hints that are available for queries. Each of these hints is placed in the FROM clause of a query after the table to which it should apply.

TABLE 10.4 Lock Hints

Hint	Description
HOLDLOCK	Holds a shared lock until completion of the transaction instead of releasing the lock as soon as the required table, row, or data page is no longer required. HOLDLOCK is equivalent to SERIALIZABLE.
NOLOCK	Does not issue shared locks and does not honor exclusive locks. When this option is in effect, it is possible to read an uncommitted transaction or a set of pages that are rolled back in the middle of a read. Dirty reads are possible. Only applies to the SELECT statement.
PAGLOCK	Uses page locks where a single table lock would usually be taken.
READCOMMITTED	Performs a scan with the same locking semantics as a transaction running at the READ COMMITTED isolation level. By default, SQL Server 2000 operates at this isolation level.
READPAST	Skips locked rows. This option causes a transaction to skip rows locked by other transactions that would ordinarily appear in the result set, rather than block the transaction waiting for the other transactions to release their locks on these rows. The READPAST lock hint applies only to transactions operating at READ COMMITTED isolation and will read only past row-level locks. Applies only to the SELECT statement.

TABLE 10.4 Lock Hints *(continued)*

Hint	Description
READUNCOMMITTED	Equivalent to NOLOCK.
REPEATABLEREAD	Performs a scan with the same locking semantics as a transaction running at the REPEATABLE READ isolation level.
ROWLOCK	Uses row-level locks instead of the coarser-grained page- and table-level lock.
SERIALIZABLE	Performs a scan with the same locking semantics as a transaction running at the SERIALIZABLE isolation level. Equivalent to HOLDLOCK.
TABLOCK	Uses a table lock instead of the finer-grained row- or page-level locks. SQL Server holds this lock until the end of the statement. However, if you also specify HOLDLOCK, the lock is held until the end of the transaction.
TABLOCKX	Uses an exclusive lock on a table. This lock prevents others from reading or updating the table and is held until the end of the statement or transaction.
UPDLOCK	Uses update locks instead of shared locks while reading a table, and holds locks until the end of the statement or transaction. UPDLOCK has the advantage of allowing you to read data (without blocking other readers) and update it later with the assurance that the data has not changed since you last read it.
XLOCK	Uses an exclusive lock that will be held until the end of the transaction on all data processed by the statement. This lock can be specified with either PAGLOCK or TABLOCK, in which case the exclusive lock applies to the appropriate level of granularity.

There is also a lock hint available for the bulk data utilities. These hints were discussed in Chapter 9: Importing and Exporting Data. Both the BCP utility and the BULK INSERT T-SQL command support a TABLOCK parameter that will lock the entire table into which data is being copied.

Summary

This chapter has provided a description of the ways that locks are used in SQL Server. The following points were discussed:

- SQL Server contains a subsystem called the lock manager whose function is to manage locks on resources within the server.

- An individual transaction can use one of four different locking methods in processing the transaction. The four methods are:

  - READ UNCOMMITTED

  - READ COMMITTED

  - REPEATABLE READ

  - SERIALIZABLE

- There are a variety of different types of locks that can be acquired on resources in SQL Server. The types are:

  - Shared

  - Update

  - Exclusive

  - Intent shared

  - Intent exclusive

  - Shared with intent exclusive

  - Schema modification

  - Schema stability

  - Bulk update

- Locks in SQL Server can be acquired at different levels of granularity. The levels are nested in a hierarchy that represents increasing amounts of a resource being locked. The levels are:

  - Row

  - Page

  - Extent

- Table

- Database

- Key range

- When a transaction is waiting to acquire a lock on a resource that another transaction holds a lock on, the first transaction is being blocked. If two processes both need a lock on a resource locked by the other and neither can proceed, a deadlock occurs.

- SQL Server 2000 includes lock hints in both queries and the bulk copy utilities that allow the programmer to specify how the server should implement locking.

Key Terms

Before you take the exam, be certain you are familiar with the following terms:

concurrency	phantom reads
lock manager	lock hints
READ UNCOMMITTED	lock escalation
READ COMMITTED	blocking
REPEATABLE READ	deadlock
SERIALIZABLE	deadlock victim
lost updates	System Process ID Number
uncommitted dependencies	(SPID)
inconsistent analysis	

Exam Essentials

Know the four isolation levels supported by SQL Server 2000. There are four ANSI standard isolation levels for transactions that are supported by SQL Server 2000. They are: READ UNCOMMITTED, READ COMMITTED, REPEATABLE READ, and SERIALIABLE.

Know the different types of locks that SQL Server uses. There are six different types of locks that are used in SQL Server 2000. Be sure you know how each one is used.

Know the different granularities at which a lock can be acquired. There are a number of levels at which a lock can be acquired: row, page, extent, table, database, and key range.

Understand how transactions are affected by locking. Locks can cause blocking and deadlocks within transactions.

Know the various lock hints available for queries. There are a number of lock hints that can be used in the FROM clause of a query. Know the effects of each one.

Review Questions

1. Which types of locks are implemented when retrieving data using a SELECT query?

   A. Intent

   B. Shared

   C. Exclusive

   D. Schema stability

2. What is the default isolation level for SQL Server 2000?

   A. SERIALIZABLE

   B. READ UNCOMMITTED

C. REPEATABLE READ

D. READ COMMITTED

3. How can SQL Server 2000's locking behavior be changed? (Select all that apply.)

   A. By starting SQL Server with the -f flag

   B. With the inclusion of a hint in the FROM clause of a query

   C. By running SET TRANSACTION ISOLATION LEVEL

   D. By running SP_LOCK with a parameter

4. Which lock is acquired at the time when a transaction actually modifies data in a row?

   A. Update

   B. Exclusive

   C. Intent

   D. Deliberate

5. What is the maximum number of shared locks that can exist on a single page?

   A. 1

   B. 5

   C. 1,024

   D. No limit

6. You run a query that updates all the rows in an extremely large table called Products. While the query is running, a user calls to tell you that the SQL Server is not responding to his query on the Products table. What is happening?

   A. The user has deadlocked with your update query.

   B. The user is being blocked by your update query.

   C. The user is blocking your update query.

   D. The user's computer has locked up.

7. Key Range Locks are used to prevent _____.

   A. Lost updates

   B. Uncommitted dependencies

   C. Phantom reads

   D. Inconsistent analysis

8. Which type of lock ensures that a table cannot be altered while a query is being compiled?

   A. Schema modification

   B. Schema stability

   C. Shared

   D. Compile

9. You start to import a large text file using the BCP program. Another developer tries to query the table into which you are importing data. Which lock prevents him from querying the table?

   A. Bulk copy locks

   B. Bulk update locks

   C. Update locks

   D. Exclusive locks

10. You try to drop the Test database from your SQL Server, but receive an error that informs you other users are connected to the database. Why can you not drop the database?

    A. The users have open transactions.

    B. The users have exclusive locks on the database.

    C. The users have shared locks on the database.

    D. The users have schema locks on the database.

11. Which lock hint will retain locks on a resource until the completion of a transaction? (Choose two.)

    A. SERIALIZABLE

    B. UPDLOCK

    C. HOLDLOCK

    D. ROWLOCK

12. You run SP_LOCK and receive the following output:

spid	dbid	ObjId	IndId	Type	Resource	Mode	Status
51	6	0	0	DB		S	GRANT
51	1	1977774103	0	TAB		IS	GRANT
52	5	1977058079	1	KEY	(10018e6baefb)	X	GRANT
52	5	1977058079	1	KEY	(0601d808a263)	X	GRANT

   What types of locks is process 51 holding? (Choose two.)

    A. Shared table lock

    B. Shared database lock

    C. Inclusive shared table lock

    D. Intent shared table lock

13. What is a deadlock?

    A. A situation when two processes are both blocking each other from completing and neither can proceed without acquiring a lock on a resource that is locked by the other

    B. A situation when two processes both want to acquire a lock on the same resource

    C. A situation when two processes simultaneously acquire exclusive locks on the same resource

    D. A situation when one process is waiting for another to release a lock on a resource

14. SQL Server acquires a series of row locks to complete a transaction on a table. As the number of locks grows, SQL Server decides to switch the row locks into an extent lock. What is this process called?

    A. Lock alteration

    B. Lock upgrade

    C. Lock escalation

    D. Lock consolidation

15. A phantom read occurs when _____. (Select all that apply.)

    A. A transaction reads a row of data and then sees different data during a second read.

    B. A transaction reads a row of data and then sees a new row during a second read.

    C. A transaction reads a row of data and then the row is deleted during a second read.

    D. A transaction reads a row of data and then is blocked from reading the same data during a second read.

Answers to Review Questions

1. B. Shared locks are used when returning data from a SELECT query.

2. D. The default isolation level is READ COMMITTED.

3. B, C. The locking behavior of SQL Server 2000 can be altered by using a lock hint in the FROM clause of a query or by changing the isolation level of a transaction.

4. B. At the time when the data modification actually takes place, an exclusive lock is required.

5. D. There is no limit to the number of shared locks that can be placed on a page.

6. B. While an update query is being run, it is likely that users trying to access the same table will be blocked.

7. C. Key range locks prevent new rows from being inserted and existing rows from being deleted in a range of data. These are known as phantom reads.

8. B. Schema stability locks ensure that the schema of the objects used in a query is stable while the query is being compiled.

9. B. When a bulk copy operation is started, bulk update locks are acquired on the target table.

10. C. Whenever a user connects to a database, they acquire a shared lock on the database to prevent it from being dropped or taken offline.

11. A, C. Both the SERIALIZABLE and HOLDLOCK hints are equivalent. Both hold locks until the completion of the transaction.

12. B, D. Given the output, process 51 holds a shared database lock on database 6 and an intent shared table lock on object 1977774103 in database 1.

13. A. A deadlock results when two processes each require a lock on a resource already locked by the other to complete.

14. C. When SQL Server changes from a lock at a lower level of granularity to one of higher granularity, it is called lock escalation.

15. B, C. A phantom read occurs within a transaction when there are new rows or missing rows during a subsequent read of the same data.

Chapter

11

Developing a Security Plan

MICROSOFT EXAM OBJECTIVES COVERED IN THIS CHAPTER:

✓ **Control data access by using stored procedures, triggers, user-defined functions, and views.**

- Apply ownership chains.
- Use programming logic and objects. Considerations include implementing row-level security and restricting direct access to tables.

✓ **Define object-level security including column-level permissions by using GRANT, REVOKE, and DENY.**

✓ **Create and manage application roles.**

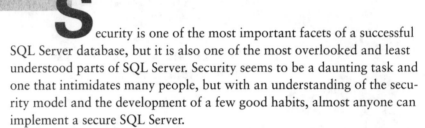

Security is one of the most important facets of a successful SQL Server database, but it is also one of the most overlooked and least understood parts of SQL Server. Security seems to be a daunting task and one that intimidates many people, but with an understanding of the security model and the development of a few good habits, almost anyone can implement a secure SQL Server.

This chapter will examine the security model in SQL Server and explain how this model is applied to control access to the server. This chapter will also examine how the security model affects the objects in a database and how access to these objects can be controlled.

All exercises in this chapter assume that the SQL Server is set up to allow connections using either Windows NT Authentication or SQL Server Authentication.

Overview of SQL Server Security

SQL Server security is a fairly simple model that is based on the same "allow nothing by default" principle that exists in many firewall products. This principle starts by assuming that no one has access to an object or resource in SQL Server. Any access rights must be explicitly granted to a user before they can access the server.

The singular exception to this rule is the "sa" or System Administrator login. This user has rights to all objects in the system.

SQL Server has two levels of security built into the product. The first level is the access needed to connect to the server, and the second level is the database level where access to all the objects in a database is granted. These two levels of security are discussed in the following sections.

Server Access

Imagine that you are starting a new job. On your first day, the office manager gives you a key to the office. This key allows you access into the company's office space whenever you desire to come to work. This key is the equivalent of a *login* in SQL Server. You have access to the outer shell of the company (the building), though not necessarily to any items inside this building.

When you were hired, someone decided that you should be allowed to become a part of the company. This was your *authentication* into the company. SQL Server allows you two different types of *authentication*. A login can be explicitly added to SQL Server, which would be the case with SQL Server *authentication*. Suppose, however, that your office is located in an office building along with a number of other companies. There is a security guard at the entrance to the building, but by virtue of being a part of one company, you are allowed to enter the building and use your key to access your company's office. This is similar to *Windows Authentication*, where as a user of the network, you can be allowed to access SQL Server based on your network login and password.

The Login Process

Before a user can access data in a SQL Server, he or she must first log into the server and be authenticated by SQL Server as being allowed to access the server. The two methods of authentication allowed by SQL Server, as presented above, are Windows Authentication and SQL Server Authentication.

Windows NT/2000 Authentication relies upon the network logon name and password being passed to SQL Server by the NT network. Each user of the network has his or her security credentials presented to a resource automatically when the user attempts to access the resource. When these credentials are presented and accepted, the user has a *trusted connection* to the SQL Server. When using this type of authentication, no login information is required from the user or application; the Windows network automatically handles the login.

The use of Windows NT Authentication for access is always allowed in SQL Server 2000.

SQL Server Authentication does not rely upon the network at all for determining whether a user is allowed to access the server. SQL Server maintains its own database of login names and passwords, which are stored in the master database in the Syslogins table. When this method of authentication is performed, the user must explicitly send a login name and password to SQL Server, or SQL Server will present a dialog box asking the user for the login name and password. Whichever method is used, once SQL Server receives the login name and password, these are compared to the values stored in Master.syslogins table. If there is a match, then the user is logged into the server, otherwise, the user is sent a "failed login" message.

Logins can be added in one of two ways: using T-SQL and using the Enterprise Manager program. Exercise 11.1 will show how Enterprise Manager can be used to add a new login. Exercise 11.5 will show how a login is added using T-SQL.

EXERCISE 11.1

Adding a New Login

1. Open the SQL Server Enterprise Manager. Do this by choosing Start ➢ Programs ➢ Microsoft SQL Server ➢ Enterprise Manager.

2. Expand your SQL Server tree by clicking the plus symbol (+) next to the server name. Select the Security folder and click the plus symbol next to it. Your Enterprise Manager should look like the following:

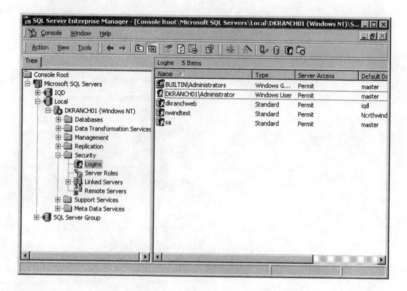

3. Add a new login by right-clicking the Logins icon and selecting New Login or selecting the Logins icon and choosing Action ➢ New Login

from the menu. You should receive a dialog box that looks like the one below:

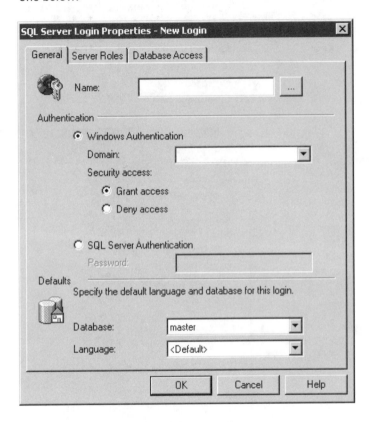

This dialog box contains the information needed to add a new login. The login name, type of login security implemented, and the default database and language are specified here.

4. Enter the following information on this tab:

- Type **Delaney** in the Name edit box for your new login.

- Choose the SQL Server Authentication radio button.

- Type **testpassword** in the Password edit box.

- Select the Northwind database in the default database box.

5. Press the OK button and you will be asked to confirm the password. Reenter **testpassword** in this box and press the OK button.

The new user has now been created and your Enterprise Manager should look like the one below. Note that the new login is listed in the right pane.

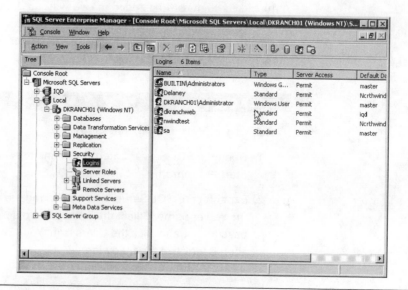

Creating and Managing Database Access

On the first day at your new company, you notice there are a number of filing cabinets around the office. You receive a key to one of these filing cabinets along with your office key. This key gives you access to the data in that one filing cabinet. There are other filing cabinets in your company, but you do not have keys for these and therefore cannot access data in these cabinets. The filing cabinet is similar to a SQL Server database in that there are separate "keys" that allow a user to access a database.

For someone who has logged into SQL Server, a *user* must be created in a database and mapped to a *login* so that data can be retrieved from that database. If access to another database is needed, then a different user must be created in the second database and mapped to the same login. Each database contains a Sysusers table that defines each user and the login to which they are mapped. When a user is added to the database, the server inserts their login ID into this table along with a unique user ID that is generated.

Just like a login can be added in two ways, a database user can be added using T-SQL or Enterprise Manager. Exercise 11.2 shows how to add a user to a database using Enterprise Manager. Exercise 11.5 will show how a user is added using T-SQL.

EXERCISE 11.2

Adding a New Database User

1. Open the SQL Server Enterprise Manager. Do this by choosing Start ➢ Programs ➢ Microsoft SQL Server ➢ Enterprise Manager.

2. Expand your SQL Server tree by clicking the plus symbol (+) next to the server name. Select the Databases folder, the Northwind database folder, and click the Users icon. Your Enterprise Manager should look like the following:

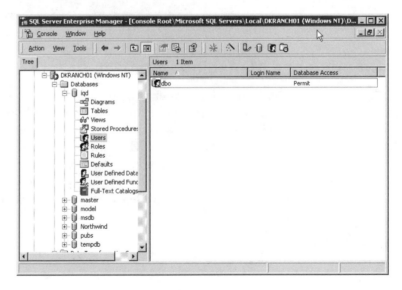

EXERCISE 11.2 *(continued)*

3. Add a new user by right-clicking the Users icon and selecting New Database User or selecting the Users icon and choosing Action ➤ New Database User from the menu. You should receive a dialog box that contains the information needed to add a new database user. The user is mapped to a login name and the various roles this user is assigned to are chosen here.

4. Select the login created in Exercise 11.1. The same name is added to the User Name edit box be default. The username can be changed if you wish. Your dialog should look like the one below:

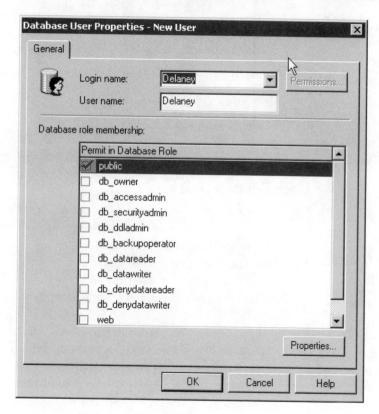

5. Press the OK button and the new user will be added. Your Enterprise Manager should look like the one below:

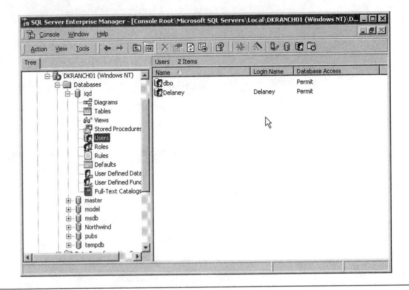

User Defined Roles

Adding users to databases and assigning them rights are simple tasks when working with a new database, but as more and more objects are created, the burden of administering the security for all the users becomes very complex. Rights need to be granted to each user for each object. If you have 10 users in your database and create a new table, you must include all 10 usernames in your GRANT statement to allow everyone access to the table.

Fortunately SQL Server includes a mechanism that can simplify this task: *roles*. The administrator can create a role and add a series of users to this role. Object rights are then granted to the role and all users inherit the rights from the role. A user can be in multiple roles. Roles can also be included in other roles. Roles allow management of users in the same way that groups are used to manage NT users.

The rights that are granted to roles are combined to determine whether a user can access an object. Suppose a user, Delaney, is in the Readers role that has rights to select data from the Books table. Delaney is also a member of the Writers role that has rights to insert data into the Books table. Delaney has combined rights to select and insert data on the Books table.

The DENY permission, however, overrides other rights when combining memberships from multiple roles. Suppose that Delaney is added to the Publishers role that has been denied permission to insert data into the Books table. Delaney will not be allowed to insert data into the Books table even though he has rights to insert from the Writers role. The DENY INSERT permission from the Publishers role overrides the INSERT permission.

Users can be added to roles using both T-SQL and Enterprise Manager. There are a number of stored procedures for managing roles that are listed below.

SP_ADDROLE This procedure adds a new role to a database. The role name is required as a parameter.

SP_DROPROLE This procedure deletes a role from a database. The role name is required as a parameter.

SP_ADDROLEMEMBER This procedure adds a user or another role to a role. The role name that is gaining new members is required along with the username or role name that is being added.

SP_DROPROLEMEMBER This procedure removes a member user or role from an existing role. The role name that is losing members is required along with the name of the user or role that is being removed.

Exercise 11.3 walks through adding a role and a user to the role using T-SQL.

EXERCISE 11.3

Adding a Role and a User

1. Open the SQL Server Query Analyzer. Do this through the SQL Enterprise Manager by selecting Tools ➤ SQL Query Analyzer or by choosing Start ➤ Programs ➤ Microsoft SQL Server ➤ SQL Query Analyzer. Be sure that you log in as *sa* to the SQL Server.

2. Type the following query to add a new role to the Northwind database (be sure Northwind is selected in the database drop-down box):

```
EXEC SP_ADDROLE 'Samples'
```

EXERCISE 11.3 (continued)

3. Highlight these lines and press the green arrow on the toolbar or press CTRL-E to execute the query. You should receive the following results:

New role added.

4. Now type the following query to add a user to this role. The user from Exercise 11.2 will be added to this role.

EXEC SP_ADDROLEMEMBER 'Samples', 'Delaney'

5. Highlight these lines and press the green arrow on the toolbar or press CTRL-E to execute the query. You should receive the following results:

'Delaney' added to role 'Samples'.

Application Roles

Microsoft **Create and manage application roles.**
✔ *Exam*
Objective

SQL Server 2000 includes a second kind of role called an *application role*. This role allows the administrator limited access to data to a specific application. This allows the application to determine how a user can access or modify data within the database. This is useful when the application can be modified to activate the application role in SQL Server.

Application roles have a few differences from user roles. First, application roles have no members. Second, an application role is inactive by default. Once connected to SQL Server, the application runs SP_SETAPP-ROLE to activate the role using the role name and a password. Lastly, all permissions assigned to the current user are removed and only those permissions assigned to the application role are applied.

Permissions are assigned to application roles in the same manner that they are assigned to users or user roles. Exercise 11.4 creates a new role and shows how the permissions are applied.

EXERCISE 11.4

Using Application Roles

This exercise will create an application role and assign it rights. A separate connection will activate the role and demonstrate how permissions work.

1. Open the SQL Server Query Analyzer. Do this through the SQL Enterprise Manager by selecting Tools ➤ SQL Query Analyzer or by choosing Start ➤ Programs ➤ Microsoft SQL Server ➤ SQL Query Analyzer. Be sure that you log in as *sa* to the SQL Server.

2. In the query analyzer, type the following query to create a new table (be sure the Northwind database is selected):

```
EXEC SP_ADDAPPROLE 'AppSample', 'AppPwd'
GO
```

3. Highlight these lines and press the green arrow on the toolbar or press CTRL-E to execute the query. The following results are displayed:

```
New application role added.
```

4. Type the following query to create a new table (be sure the Northwind database is selected):

```
CREATE TABLE AppTest
 ( AppID int,
   AppDesc char( 40)
 )
GO
GRANT SELECT ON AppTest to AppSample
GO
INSERT INTO AppTest VALUES ( 1, 'Sample Application')
GO
SELECT * FROM AppTest
```

5. Highlight these lines and press the green arrow on the toolbar or press CTRL-E to execute the query. The following results are displayed:

```
AppID       AppDesc
----------- ----------------------------------------
1           Sample Application

(1 row(s) affected)
```

EXERCISE 11.4 *(continued)*

No rights are assigned to this table, so normal users, such as the user created in Exercise 11.2, will not have rights to this table. The application role, however, will have SELECT rights to this table.

6. Log into the SQL Server as Delaney by choosing File ➤ Connect from the menu and entering **Delaney** as the login name and **Testpassword** as the password. A blank query window should open.

7. Select the Northwind database and type the following query:

```
SELECT * FROM AppTest
```

8. Highlight these lines and press the green arrow on the toolbar or press CTRL-E to execute the query. You should see the following results:

```
Server: Msg 229, Level 14, State 5, Line 1
SELECT permission denied on object 'AppTest', database
'Northwind', owner 'dbo'.
```

9. Now activate the application role by typing the following query:

```
EXEC SP_SETAPPROLE 'AppSample', 'AppPwd'
```

10. Highlight these lines and press the green arrow on the toolbar or press CTRL-E to execute the query. You should see the following results:

```
The application role 'AppSample' is now active.
```

11. Select the Northwind database and type the following query:

```
SELECT * FROM AppTest
```

12. Highlight these lines and press the green arrow on the toolbar or press CTRL-E to execute the query. You should see the following results:

```
AppID        AppDesc
-----------  ----------------------------------------
1            Sample Application

(1 row(s) affected)
```

Assigning Object Rights

Microsoft
✓ Exam
Objective

Define object-level security including column-level
permissions by using GRANT, REVOKE, and DENY.

Once a user has logged into a SQL Server and chosen a particular
database, the issue of controlling access to data must be addressed. SQL
Server allows a DBA or programmer to control this access at a few different
levels. One way is through the object rights that must be granted to each
user before they can use the object. The second way of controlling access is
through the creation of various objects designed to limit access to data.

This section will look at the various objects that can be used to control
access to data in SQL Server. Each of these objects is used primarily to
implement security according to business rules while the rights granted on
the object determine who can even access the object itself.

Object Rights

There are a number of different types of rights that can be granted to a
user or role. Each type of access for an object requires that a command be
run that explicitly details the access allowed. Rights are granted to users or
roles using the GRANT command. Its syntax is listed below along with a
description of its options.

```
GRANT
    { ALL [ PRIVILEGES ] | permission [ ,...n ] }
    {
        [ ( column [ ,...n ] ) ] ON { table | view }
        | ON { table | view } [ ( column [ ,...n ] ) ]
        | ON { stored_procedure | extended_procedure }
        | ON { user_defined_function }
    }
TO security_account [ ,...n ]
[ WITH GRANT OPTION ]
[ AS { group | role } ]
```

ALL PRIVILEGES | *permission* This is the list of the type of permissions that are being granted. Each permission should be specified in a comma-delimited list. Members of the db_owner role can use the ALL command to grant all rights. The valid permissions depend on the type of object named in the GRANT statement.

Column For objects that have columns, specific columns may be listed. If no column list is included, then the rights default to all columns.

Table | view | stored procedure | extended procedure | user_defined_function This is the name of the object on which rights are being granted.

Security_account This is the name of the user or role who is receiving the rights. This can be a SQL Server user or role as well as a Windows NT user or role. Multiple users can be specified in a comma-delimited list.

WITH GRANT OPTION When this option is included, the user who receives the rights can in turn grant these same rights to another user. This option is only valid for object permissions.

AS {*group | role*} This option is used to specify the group or role that has permissions to grant the rights. When a user is a member of a group that has been given rights to grant permissions and wishes to extend these permissions to users or groups not part of the group or role, this clause is included along with the name of the group or role that has rights to grant permissions.

In addition to being able to grant access to an object, the access can be removed with the REVOKE command. As with Windows NT, the application of a REVOKE command to a user overrides any other rights that the user has been given explicitly or as a member of a group or role. The syntax and explanation of the REVOKE command is given below.

```
REVOKE [ GRANT OPTION FOR ]
      { ALL [ PRIVILEGES ] | permission [ ,...n ] }
      {
          [ ( column [ ,...n ] ) ] ON { table | view }
          | ON { table | view } [ ( column [ ,...n ] ) ]
          | ON { stored_procedure | extended_procedure }
          | ON { user_defined_function }
      }
```

```
{ TO | FROM }
    security_account [ ,...n ]
[ CASCADE ]
[ AS { group | role } ]
```

ALL PRIVILEGES | *permission*   This is the list of the type of permissions that are being granted. Each permission is specified as an item in a comma-delimited list. Members of the db_owner role can use the ALL command to grant all rights. The valid permissions depend on the type of object named in the GRANT statement.

Column   For objects that have columns, specific columns may be listed. If no column list is included, then the rights default to all columns.

Table | view | stored procedure | extended procedure | user_defined_function   This is the name of the object on which rights are being granted.

Security_account   This is the name of the user or role who is receiving the rights. This can be a SQL Server user or role as well as a Windows NT user or role. Multiple users can be specified in a comma-delimited list.

CASCADE   This clause is included when one user needs to remove permissions from a another user as well as any additional users who received rights from this user. This clause is primarily applicable for removing rights from users who received them with the FOR GRANT option in the GRANT statement.

It is preferable to grant rights on objects to roles and assign users to these roles.

The ability to give and remove rights from a user allows most data security to be implemented, but occasionally there is the need to specifically prevent a user from performing an action on an object. The DENY command prevents a specific type of command from being run on an object. The syntax for the DENY command is given below along with explanations of the options.

```
DENY
    { ALL [ PRIVILEGES ] | permission [ ,...n ] }
    {
```

```
                    [ ( column [ ,...n ] ) ] ON { table | view }
                    | ON { table | view } [ ( column [ ,...n ] ) ]
                    | ON { stored_procedure | extended_procedure }
                    | ON { user_defined_function }
              }
        TO security_account [ ,...n ]
        [ CASCADE ]
```

ALL PRIVILEGES | *permission* This is the list of the type of permissions that are being granted. Each permission should be specified in a comma-delimited list. Members of the db_owner role can use the ALL command to grant all rights. The valid permissions depend on the type of object named in the GRANT statement.

Column For objects that have columns, specific columns may be listed. If no column list is included, then the rights default to all columns.

Table* | *view* | *stored procedure* | *extended procedure* | *user_defined_function This is the name of the object on which rights are being granted.

Security_account This is the name of the user or role who is receiving the rights. This can be a SQL Server user or role as well as a Windows NT user or role. Multiple users can be specified in a comma-delimited list.

CASCADE This clause is included when a user needs to remove permissions from a user as well as any additional users who received rights from this user. This clause is primarily applicable for removing rights from users who received them with the FOR GRANT option in the GRANT statement.

Viewing Rights

Rights can also be viewed and managed from the Enterprise Manager program. Once a database is selected, the DBA can view a variety of information. To view the users in a database, select the Users icon beneath a database folder. Double-clicking a user will bring up a dialog box with the username, login name, and role memberships. This dialog box also contains a Permissions button. Pressing this button will display a dialog box like the one in Figure 11.1. This dialog box displays a grid that shows all objects and the type of permissions granted on each object. A green check mark indicates a granted permission, while a red X indicates a denied permission. An empty check box indicates no permissions.

FIGURE 11.1 Database User Permission dialog box

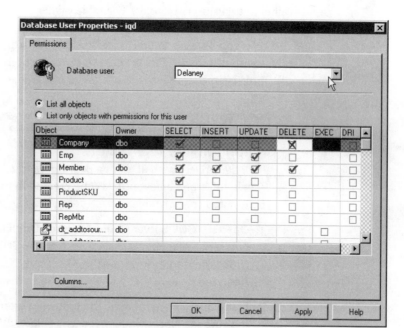

Tables

All data is stored in a table in SQL Server, including system information. When a table is created, only the owner of the table and the owner of the database are allowed to access the table. If other users need to access the table, then they must be explicitly granted access to the table. The rights that can be granted for a table are listed in Table 11.1.

TABLE 11.1 Table Rights

Right	Description
SELECT	SELECT rights allow a user to read from a table.
INSERT	INSERT rights allow a user to add rows to the table.
UPDATE	UPDATE rights allow a user to change rows that exist in a table.
DELETE	DELETE rights allow a user to remove rows from a table.
REFERENCES	REFERENCES rights allow a user to reference foreign keys to the object. Also allows SCHEMABINDING references in views and functions.

Only the owner of the table or the database owner can grant these rights to other users or roles. The table owner or database owner can also revoke the rights.

Tables can be used to limit access to data by storing the data in separate tables with different rights granted to different users. A *vertical partition* of a table is an example of controlling access to data through a table.

EXERCISE 11.5

Granting Rights to a Table

In this exercise, we will grant a user rights to retrieve data from a table. A new table and a new user will be created to prove the rights need to be granted to each table.

1. Open the SQL Server Query Analyzer. Do this through the SQL Enterprise Manager by selecting Tools ➢ SQL Query Analyzer or by choosing Start ➢ Programs ➢ Microsoft SQL Server ➢ SQL Query Analyzer. Be sure that you log in as **sa** to the SQL Server.

2. In the query analyzer, type the following query to create a new table (be sure the Northwind database is selected):

```
CREATE TABLE Security
(    SecureID int,
     UserName char( 20)
)
GO
INSERT Security VALUES ( 1, 'Test')
GO
```

3. Highlight these lines and press the green arrow on the toolbar or press CTRL-E to execute the query.

4. Type the following query to create a new login and grant access to the Northwind database:

```
EXEC SP_ADDLOGIN 'Kyle', 'Test'
EXEC SP_ADDUSER 'Kyle', 'Kyle'
```

5. Highlight these lines and press the green arrow on the toolbar or press CTRL-E to execute the query. You should see the following results:

```
New login created.
Granted database access to 'Kyle'.
```

6. Log into the SQL Server as Kyle by choosing File ➤ Connect from the menu and entering **Kyle** as the login name and **Test** as the password. A blank query window should open.

7. Select the Northwind database and type the following query:

    SELECT * FROM Security

8. Highlight these lines and press the green arrow on the toolbar or press CTRL-E to execute the query. You should see the following results:

    ```
    Server: Msg 229, Level 14, State 5, Line 1
    SELECT permission denied on object 'Security', database
    'Northwind', owner 'dbo'.
    ```

    This table was just created, but no rights on this table were granted to any users. The new user (Kyle) that was created is a part of the public role in Northwind by default, but has no rights to this new table by default. We will now grant rights to this user.

9. Change to the previously opened query window by selecting Window ➤ 1 from the menu. Type the following query:

    GRANT SELECT ON Security TO Public

10. Highlight these lines and press the green arrow on the toolbar or press CTRL-E to execute the query. This statement gives all members of the public role the right to view data in this table.

11. Change to the previously opened query window by selecting Window ➤ 2 from the menu. The following query should still be typed in the window:

    SELECT * FROM Security

12. Highlight these lines and press the green arrow on the toolbar or press CTRL-E to execute the query. You should see the following results:

    ```
    SecureID     UserName
    -----------  --------------------
    1            Test

    (1 row(s) affected)
    ```

Rights to the individual columns within a table can also be granted to users. This has the same effect as a view in limiting access to a vertical partition of the table. The user will only see those columns to which they have been granted rights. Exercise 11.2 walks through granting rights to selected columns.

EXERCISE 11.6

Granting Rights to Selected Columns in a Table

In this exercise, we will grant a user rights to retrieve data from limited columns in a table. A new table will be created to prove the rights need to be granted to each table.

1. Open the SQL Server Query Analyzer. Do this through the SQL Enterprise Manager by selecting Tools ➤ SQL Query Analyzer or by choosing Start ➤ Programs ➤ Microsoft SQL Server ➤ SQL Query Analyzer. Be sure that you log in as *sa* to the SQL Server.

2. In the query analyzer, type the following query to create a new table (be sure the Northwind database is selected):

```
CREATE TABLE Security2
(    SecureID int,
     UserName char( 20),
     Salary money
)
GO
INSERT Security2 VALUES ( 1, 'Test', 100000)
GO
GRANT SELECT ON Security2 (SecureID, UserName) TO Public
```

3. Highlight these lines and press the green arrow on the toolbar or press CTRL-E to execute the query.

4. Log into the SQL Server as Kyle by choosing File ➤ Connect from the menu and entering **Kyle** as the login name and **Test** as the password. A blank query window should open.

5. Select the Northwind database and type the following query:

```
select * from Security2
```

6. Highlight these lines and press the green arrow on the toolbar or press CTRL-E to execute the query. You should see the following results:

```
Server: Msg 230, Level 14, State 1, Line 1
SELECT permission denied on column 'Salary' of object
'Security2', database 'Northwind', owner 'dbo'.
```

When the asterisk (*) is used in a SELECT statement, SQL Server expands this to a list of all columns. Since this user does not have rights to all columns, but only the first two columns, an error is returned.

7. Type the following query:

```
SELECT SecureID, UserName from Security2
```

8. Highlight this line and press the green arrow on the toolbar or press CTRL-E to execute the query. You should see the following results:

```
SecureID     UserName
-----------  --------------------
1            Test

(1 row(s) affected)
```

Views

Microsoft Exam Objective

Control data access by using stored procedures, triggers, user-defined functions, and views.

- Use programming logic and objects. Considerations include implementing row-level security and restricting direct access to tables.

A *view* is essentially a table that is created when the view is accessed. Views provide controlled access to data by limiting which columns or rows from a table (or tables) is available to a user. When a limited set of columns is presented in a view, a vertical partition of the underlying table is created. When a limited set of rows is presented through a view, a *horizontal partition* of data is created.

The object permissions granted on a view are the same ones that are available for tables. These permissions are listed in Table 11.1. There are additional rights that must be implemented in views. The user of the view must have the appropriate rights to the tables that make up the view. The user can have explicit rights granted or can follow an ownership chain (discussed below). Exercise 11.7 shows how rights are granted to a view.

EXERCISE 11.7

Granting Rights to a View

In this exercise, we will grant a user rights to retrieve data from a view. A new view will be created to show how rights are granted to a view. This exercise uses the tables and user from Exercises 11.5 and 11.6.

1. Open the SQL Server Query Analyzer. Do this through the SQL Enterprise Manager by selecting Tools ➤ SQL Query Analyzer or by choosing Start ➤ Programs ➤ Microsoft SQL Server ➤ SQL Query Analyzer. Be sure that you log in as *sa* to the SQL Server.

2. In the query analyzer, type the following query to create a new view (be sure the Northwind database is selected):

```
CREATE VIEW MyView
AS
  SELECT s1.SecureID, s1.UserName, s2.Salary
  FROM Security s1, Security2 s2
  WHERE s1.SecureID = s2.SecureID
GO

SELECT * FROM MyView
```

3. Highlight these lines and press the green arrow on the toolbar or press CTRL-E to execute the query.

4. Log into the SQL Server as Kyle by choosing File ➤ Connect from the menu and entering **Kyle** as the login name and **Test** as the password. A blank query window should open.

5. Select the Northwind database and type the following query:

```
select * from MyView
```

6. Highlight these lines and press the green arrow on the toolbar or press CTRL-E to execute the query. You should see the following results:

```
Server: Msg 229, Level 14, State 5, Line 1
SELECT permission denied on object 'MyView', database
'Northwind', owner 'dbo'.
```

EXERCISE 11.7 *(continued)*

This view was just created, but no rights on this view were granted to any users. The new user (Kyle) that was created is a part of the public role in Northwind by default, but has no rights to this new view by default even though this user has rights to view data in each table. We will now grant rights to this user.

7. Change to the previously opened query window by selecting Window ➢ 1 from the menu. Type the following query:

```
GRANT SELECT ON MyView TO Public
```

8. Highlight these lines and press the green arrow on the toolbar or press CTRL-E to execute the query. This statement gives all members of the public role the right to view data in this table.

9. Change to the previously opened query window by selecting Window ➢ 2 from the menu. The following query should still be typed in the window:

```
SELECT * FROM MyView
```

10. Highlight these lines and press the green arrow on the toolbar or press CTRL-E to execute the query. You should see the following results:

```
SecureID    UserName              Salary
----------- --------------------- -----------------------
1           Test                  100000.0000

(1 row(s) affected)
```

Stored Procedures

Microsoft ✓ *Exam* *Objective*

Control data access by using stored procedures, triggers, user-defined functions, and views.

- Use programming logic and objects. Considerations include implementing row-level security and restricting direct access to tables.

Stored procedures are batches of code that are compiled into a single unit. The user who executes the stored procedure does not know what commands are inside the stored procedure, and cannot change the commands prior to executing the procedure. The stored procedure is essentially a black box that provides the user with certain data (or performs some function) without the user knowing how that data is retrieved or how the function is implemented.

This encapsulation can enforce data security by forcing the user to execute the stored procedure to perform tasks rather than using T-SQL. Since the business logic and rules are contained inside the stored procedure, the integrity of data can be maintained and secured from unwanted modifications.

The only security right that is assignable for stored procedures is the *EXECUTE* right. This allows a user to execute the stored procedure, pass it parameters, and receive results back from the object. Exercise 11.8 shows how rights are granted to a stored procedure.

EXERCISE 11.8

Granting Rights to a Stored Procedure

In this exercise, we will grant a user rights to execute a stored procedure. A new procedure will be created to prove the rights need to be granted to each table. This exercise requires the user from Exercise 11.5.

1. Open the SQL Server Query Analyzer. Do this through the SQL Enterprise Manager by selecting Tools ➤ SQL Query Analyzer or by choosing Start ➤ Programs ➤ Microsoft SQL Server ➤ SQL Query Analyzer. Be sure that you log in as **sa** to the SQL Server.

2. In the query analyzer, type the following query to create a new table (be sure the Northwind database is selected):

```
CREATE PROCEDURE spGetCustomers
AS
  SELECT CustomerID, CompanyName, ContactName
    FROM Customers
RETURN
GO
EXEC spGetCustomers
GO
```

3. Highlight these lines and press the green arrow on the toolbar or press CTRL-E to execute the query. You should receive the following results (results are abbreviated):

```
CustomerID CompanyName                            ContactName
---------- ------------------------------------- --------------
ALFKI      Alfreds Futterkiste                    Maria Anders
ANATR      Ana Trujillo Emparedados y helados     Ana Trujillo
ANTON      Antonio Moreno Taquería                Antonio Moreno
```

4. Log into the SQL Server as Kyle by choosing File ➤ Connect from the menu and entering **Kyle** as the login name and **Test** as the password. A blank query window should open.

5. Select the Northwind database and type the following query:
   EXEC spGetCustomers

6. Highlight these lines and press the green arrow on the toolbar or press CTRL-E to execute the query. You should see the following results:

```
Server: Msg 229, Level 14, State 5, Procedure
spGetCustomers, Line 1
EXECUTE permission denied on object 'spGetCustomers',
database 'Northwind', owner 'dbo'.
```

7. Change back to the first query window by selecting Window ➤ 1 from the menu. This query window should display your server name and database, along with the *sa* user.

8. Type the following query:

   GRANT EXECUTE ON spGetCustomers TO Public

9. Highlight this line and press the green arrow on the toolbar or press CTRL-E to execute the query. You should see the following results:

   The command(s) completed successfully.

EXERCISE 11.8 *(continued)*

10. Change back to the query window that is logged in as Kyle by selecting Window ➢ 2 from the menu. The following query should be typed in the window:

    EXEC spGetCustomers

11. Highlight this line and press the green arrow on the toolbar or press CTRL-E to execute the query. You should see the following results (results are abbreviated):

CustomerID	CompanyName	ContactName
ALFKI	Alfreds Futterkiste	Maria Anders
ANATR	Ana Trujillo Emparedados y helados	Ana Trujillo
ANTON	Antonio Moreno Taquería	Antonio Moreno

Triggers

Microsoft
✔ *Exam*
Objective

Control data access by using stored procedures, triggers, user-defined functions, and views.

- Use programming logic and objects. Considerations include implementing row-level security and restricting direct access to tables.

Triggers are attached to tables and primarily used to enforce referential integrity or business rules. A *trigger* is a batch of code bound to a table that executes in response to a modification of the table. Triggers are discussed in Chapter 6: Creating and Maintaining Database Objects.

Triggers can implement a security plan in a number of ways. Since a trigger will execute whenever a data modification is made on the table, the trigger can contain code that checks business security rules. The business rules may allow or disallow the modification based on other data in the system. This allows much more flexible and granular control of security for the application rather than relying on SQL Server object security at the table or column level.

These objects do not receive rights by themselves, rather, the rights to execute an INSERT, UPDATE, or DELETE statement on a table implicitly allow the user to execute the associated trigger that has been defined for the table. The right to execute the trigger, however, does not extend any permission on other objects that may be referenced in the trigger. If a trigger modifies another table, the ownership chain must remain intact or the user must have rights to modify the table referenced by the trigger. Ownership chains are discussed below in the "Ownership Chains" section.

 Real World Scenario

Using Triggers to Capture an Audit Trail

Imagine that you are the DBA for a financial institution and have been charged with implementing auditing controls on the banking application. You choose to use triggers to ensure that any data modification statements are captured in a separate table. Each INSERT, UPDATE, and DELETE statement fires a trigger that records the user information, current time, and the modification that is occurring.

The main concern is that the data being captured in the auditing table is intact and no user can modify it. You cannot remove all rights from the table for users, however, because they need the ability to add new data to the audit table and read the table for tracking the audits.

To prevent any accidental changes, you decide to create an UPDATE and a DELETE trigger on your audit table. These triggers will rollback any attempts to change the audit data. With these triggers in place, you are assured that all audit data remains intact.

User-defined Functions

Microsoft ✓ *Exam* *Objective*

Control data access by using stored procedures, triggers, user-defined functions, and views.

- Use programming logic and objects. Considerations include implementing row-level security and restricting direct access to tables.

User-defined functions are similar to stored procedures in that they are precompiled scripts of code that the user who executes them cannot change. User-defined functions can be used to enforce security in the same way that stored procedures can be used. A process can be encapsulated in a function so the user cannot alter the process and is unaware of how the process is implemented. For example, a function could be written that provides some type of security encryption. Users of the function are unaware of how the function operates and therefore cannot bypass or change this security. User-defined functions are discussed in Chapter 6: Creating and Maintaining Database Objects.

User-defined functions implement object security in the same manner as stored procedures. The EXECUTE permission must be granted to a user before they can execute the function. Exercise 11.9 shows how execute rights are granted to a user-defined function.

EXERCISE 11.9

Granting Rights to a User-defined Function

In this exercise, we will grant a user rights to execute a function. A new function will be created to prove the rights need to be granted to a user. This exercise requires the user from Exercise 11.5.

1. Open the SQL Server Query Analyzer. Do this through the SQL Enterprise Manager by selecting Tools ➤ SQL Query Analyzer or by choosing Start ➤ Programs ➤ Microsoft SQL Server ➤ SQL Query Analyzer. Be sure that you log in as *sa* to the SQL Server.

2. In the query analyzer, type the following query to create a new function (be sure the Northwind database is selected):

```
CREATE FUNCTION CipherSubst
 ( @PlainText varchar( 80)
 )
RETURNS varchar( 80)
AS
 BEGIN
  RETURN( SUBSTRING( @PlainText, 2, LEN( @PlainText)) +
                SUBSTRING( @PlainText, 1, 1)
                )
 END
GO
select dbo.CipherSubst('PigLatin')
```

3. Highlight these lines and press the green arrow on the toolbar or press CTRL-E to execute the query. You should receive the following results:

```
------------------------------------------------------------
igLatinP

(1 row(s) affected)
```

4. Log into the SQL Server as Kyle by choosing File ➤ Connect from the menu and entering **Kyle** as the login name and **Test** as the password. A blank query window should open.

5. Select the Northwind database and type the following query:

```
SELECT dbo.CipherSubst('PigLatin')
```

6. Highlight these lines and press the green arrow on the toolbar or press CTRL-E to execute the query. You should see the following results:

```
Server: Msg 229, Level 14, State 5, Line 1
EXECUTE permission denied on object 'CipherSubst', database
'Northwind', owner 'dbo'.
```

7. Change back to the first query window by selecting Window ➤ 1 from the menu. This query window should display your server name and database, along with the **sa** user.

8. Type the following query:

```
GRANT EXECUTE ON CipherSubst TO Public
```

9. Highlight this line and press the green arrow on the toolbar or press CTRL-E to execute the query. You should see the following results:

```
The command(s) completed successfully.
```

10. Change back to the query window in which you are logged in as Kyle by selecting Window ➤ 2 from the menu. The following query should be typed in the window:

```
SELECT dbo.CipherSubst('PigLatin')
```

EXERCISE 11.9 *(continued)*

11. Highlight this line and press the green arrow on the toolbar or press CTRL-E to execute the query. You should see the following results:

```
------------------------------------------------
igLatinP

(1 row(s) affected)
```

Ownership Chains

<table>
<tr>
<td>Microsoft
✔ Exam
Objective</td>
<td>Control data access by using stored procedures, triggers, user-defined functions, and views.

▪ Apply ownership chains.</td>
</tr>
</table>

SQL Server 2000 allows objects to build upon other objects; views contain tables, stored procedures can contain views, etc. Each of these objects, however, implements its own security with explicit statements for each object required to grant or deny access to that object. In order to prevent an explicit permission grant or deny statement for each object contained within another object, SQL Server uses *ownership chains* to check the security on an object. An ownership chain is the implicit link between the owners of two objects that access one another. If the same user owns both objects, then an ownership chain is intact. If not, the ownership chain is broken. Ownership chains allow the original owner of the lowest-level objects to retain control over their object.

Each object has an owner that is independent of other objects. When user A accesses object A, user A's permissions are checked to see if the user has been granted the appropriate permissions for object A. If object A then accesses object B, SQL Server first compares the owners of the two objects. If the same user owns both objects, then permissions are not checked on object B. If a different user owns object B, however, then the permissions for access are rechecked for user A against object B.

If different users own two objects, security is checked because the ownership chain is broken. This becomes an issue when different users are creating objects and granting permissions on their own objects in a database. If two different people create objects that each access the other's object, both must grant rights to their object for another user to access the object.

Usually dbo owns all objects in a live database. Broken ownership chains usually are the cause of problems in development databases where multiple people create objects.

Summary

This chapter has presented a description of SQL Server security and how it can be implemented inside a database. The following topics were covered:

- An overview of the SQL Server security model was presented. Allow nothing is the default security setting.

- A brief introduction to server-level security and logins.

- A description of database-level security and users.

- The two types of roles implemented in SQL Server 2000. A description and example of each was presented.

- The chapter examined assigning security using T-SQL commands.

- Object level security for each of the different types of objects was discussed. The chapter also examines how each object can implement data security.

- Ownership chains and their effect on object access when different users own objects in a chain.

Key Terms

Before you take the exam, be certain you are familiar with the following terms:

application role	ownership chains
authentication	roles
authentication	trusted connection
authentication	user
EXECUTE	vertical partition
horizontal partition	Windows Authentication
login	

Exam Essentials

Understand the security model for SQL Server. SQL Server implements an "allow nothing" model by default. All rights to objects must be explicitly granted.

Know how rights on objects are given and removed from users and roles. The GRANT and REVOKE commands are used to give or remove rights from objects. The DENY command prevents a type of action on an object.

Know how tables implement secure access to data. Tables can be used to limit rights to data by splitting data across tables and granting limited rights to each table. Rights can also be granted to specific columns instead of the entire table.

Know how stored procedures implement secure access to data. Stored procedures provide security for data by preventing the user from accessing the underlying tables or views. The user only can access the data that the stored procedure allows them to access.

Know how triggers implement secure access to data. Triggers can be used to validate all changes that are made to a table. This can prevent a user from inappropriately changing data in a way that it should not be changed.

Know how views implement secure access to data. Views provide security for data by limiting those columns that a user can access.

Know how user-defined functions implement secure access to data. A user-defined function can produce a result that is consistent based on its inputs. This prevents users from implementing some function incorrectly. The user is also unaware how the particular function is implemented.

Understand the different types of roles and how they are implemented. SQL Server 2000 databases allow roles to be created that group users together. SQL Server 2000 also allows application roles that are invoked by an application rather than any particular user login.

Understand ownership chains and how they affect the security of objects. SQL Server ensures that a user does not inherit any rights from another user by checking the security of all objects that reference other objects whenever ownership chains are broken.

Review Questions

1. You are the DBA for a large software development company. Each project includes 10 or more developers who are assigned with creating tables and queries to meet business rules. Each developer is assigned to a role that has rights to create objects in their particular database. One of your developers, Jim, has created a table that stores product information, but another developer, Bill, insists the table was not created as he cannot select any rows from this table. What is the problem?

   A. Bill is probably typing the name incorrectly.

   B. Jim did not create the table in the correct database.

   C. Bill is querying the wrong database.

   D. Jim did not grant Bill rights to view the table.

2. Jack creates a table but does not grant any rights to any other user. Jack creates a view on this table and grants Jill SELECT rights

to the view. Jill accesses the data through the view. How can she do this without rights on the table?

A. If rights are granted on a view, the user never needs rights on the tables underneath the view.

B. This is not possible. Jack needs to grant Jill rights to the table.

C. The ownership chain between the table and view is unbroken.

D. Jill is the database owner.

3. You are the DBA for a large corporation. The human resources department has requested access to the Employee table to view address and contact information for all employees. This table also contains salary information that Human Resources employees should not be able to view. What can you do to give Human Resources access to only part of the table? (Choose two.)

A. Create a new role for Human Resources.

B. Grant SELECT rights on the Employee table to the Human Resources role.

C. Grant SELECT rights on the Employee table for the address and contact information columns only to the Human Resources department.

D. Create a view of the entire Employee table and Grant SELECT rights on this view to the Human Resources role.

E. Create a new user that is shared by all Human Resources employees.

4. You are the DBA for the marketing department and have been asked to write a query that can perform a statistical analysis on a series of inputs. Your boss is concerned that users may alter the query to perform their own analysis. What can you do to prevent this?

A. You can create a view that returns the results instead of a query.

B. You can create a user-defined function to calculate the analysis.

C. You can create a stored procedure to calculate the analysis.

D. You can include the FOR ENCRYPTION clause in the query to prevent others from changing it.

5. As a DBA, you want to prevent all the users in the Accounts Receivable department from changing any data in the Invoice table, but they must still be able to view this data. All these users belong to the Account role that has SELECT, INSERT, UPDATE, and DELETE rights on the Invoice table. What can you do?

   A. Remove these users from the Accounting group.

   B. Execute a DENY statement to remove all modification rights from these users.

   C. Execute a GRANT statement that only includes the SELECT permission for these users.

   D. Execute a REVOKE statement to remove all rights from these users.

6. Kyle creates a stored procedure that references a table created by Delaney. Delaney has previously executed the following statement:

   GRANT SELECT, REFERENCES ON MyTable TO Kyle

   Kyle now executes this statement:

   GRANT EXECUTE ON MyProc to Tia

   What will happen when Tia executes MyProc?

   A. She will receive a permissions error on MyTable.

   B. The procedure will execute and return the result.

   C. The procedure will execute and return an empty result set due to a permissions problem.

   D. The procedure will not return an error, but will not execute.

7. You are the DBA for the Super Spammers E-mail Company where a new database and order entry system is being deployed for your sales department. The manager of this department is concerned that his users might use Excel or another tool to enter data into the system. What should you do to prevent this? (Choose three.)

   A. Run a DENY ALL TO Excel statement.

   B. Grant rights to objects to only the OrderEntry role.

   C. Have the developers modify the application to include the password for the OrderEntry role.

D. Create an application role called OrderEntry.

E. Add all users to the OrderEntry role.

8. You are the DBA for a car dealership and have been told that occasionally salespeople try to enter an exceptionally large discount for a car. They must not be allowed to enter more than a 25 percent discount for any car. The manager of the dealership informs you that there are two different applications for entering sales and they cannot be modified in the short term. What can you do to ensure that no discounts greater than 25 percent are entered?

   A. Add a constraint to the Orders table.

   B. Add a user-defined function that calculates the discount.

   C. Add triggers to the Orders table to check for discounts greater than 25 percent and rollback transactions if they exceed this amount.

   D. Add a view on the Orders table that limits the discount to 25 percent.

9. You are a new DBA with a large retailer. A new salesperson starts the same day as you, and their manager asks you to add them to the SQL Server database as a user. He tells you that they should be granted rights to various tables and gives you the following script:

```
-- Cashier
GRANT SELECT, INSERT, UPDATE ON Orders TO <user>
GRANT SELECT ON Products TO <user>
-- Inventory
GRANT SELECT ON Orders TO <user>
GRANT SELECT, INSERT, UPDATE ON Products TO <user>
```

He tells you that this person is a cashier and an inventory person, so they should get all these rights. What can you do to streamline this security implementation?

   A. Separate the two groups of statements into separate scripts.

   B. Create two roles, one for each job type, and grant rights to these roles. Move all users into roles.

C. Create a third script for people performing both jobs.

D. Create an application role for each job and place users into the appropriate role.

10. You add a new employee to SQL Server using the AddLogin dialog box in Enterprise Manager and set their default database to Sales. You e-mail the user their password. A few hours later the user calls to complain that they cannot access the SQL Server and the server is telling them they are not a valid user in the Sales database. What is wrong?

   A. The employee needs to change to the Sales database after they connect.

   B. The employee is connecting to the wrong SQL Server.

   C. The employee is typing the password incorrectly.

   D. You forgot to add the employee as a user in the Sales database.

11. You are the DBA for a large company that has just written a new application called POST for SQL Server. They are concerned that only the POST program be used to access the database, so you create an application role called POST and assign rights to this role for the objects in the database. You add the authorized users to the database, but assign them no rights. A few hours later, you receive a call saying that none of the users can access any data in the database. What is the problem?

   A. The application needs to run SP_ADDAPPROLEMEMBER after connecting to the SQL Server.

   B. The application needs to run SP_ACTIVATEAPPROLE after connecting to the SQL Server.

   C. The application needs to run SP_SETAPPROLE after connecting to the SQL Server.

   D. The application needs to run SP_STARTAPPROLE after connecting to the SQL Server.

12. Charles grants Dave SELECT rights to the Employee table using the WITH GRANT option. Dave then creates a view of the Employee table

and grants Matt SELECT rights to the view and the Employee table. Later Charles decides to revoke the SELECT rights from Dave using this statement:

```
REVOKE SELECT ON Employee FROM Dave
```

What will happen when Matt tries to select data from the Employee table?

A. He will receive a permissions error.

B. He will receive an empty result set.

C. He will receive the result set he expected.

D. He will receive no result set.

13. As the DBA for a large corporation, you have hundreds of users in your SQL Server database. To make administration easier, you have created roles for the different departments that use the database. The sales department has over a hundred users, and their manager is complaining that a dozen salespeople are selling products with extremely large discounts. The manager wants to prevent these salespeople from entering orders, but they should retain all other existing rights. What is the best way to implement this rule?

A. Create a new role and move the dozen salespeople to this role. Give this role the same rights as the other role except for the Orders table.

B. Create a new role and add the dozen salespeople to it. Grant this new role SELECT only rights to the Orders table.

C. Issue a DENY statement for these dozen salespeople individually on the Orders table.

D. Create a new role and add the dozen salespeople to this role. deny modifications on the Orders table for this new role.

14. One of the developers in your company comes to see you with a problem. He has created a table called UserForms with a foreign key that references another table called Forms, which was created by another user. The other user granted him rights to select data from the Forms table. When he tries to create his UserForms table with a foreign key, he receives a permissions error. What is the problem?

A. He needs `insert`, `update`, and `delete` rights on the Forms table.

B. He needs to have cascading rights for `UPDATE` and `DELETE`.

C. He needs `references` rights on Forms to create a foreign key.

D. He needs to own the Forms table.

15. You are the DBA for XXX, Inc. and need to ensure that security is maintained, but IT personnel do not spend an inordinate amount of time administering security. The IT development staff creates tables and stored procedures on the development servers that you must move to the production servers over time. What is the best way to ensure that security is maintained, but problems are kept to a minimum?

    A. Recompile all objects with dbo as the owner.

    B. Create a role for each developer and assign rights to users through these roles.

    C. Create a development role and assign rights to all objects through this role.

    D. Ask each developer to create scripts that grant rights to all roles for all their objects.

Answers to Review Questions

1. D. The most likely explanation is that Jim did not execute a GRANT statement after he created the table. By default, Bill would not be able to see the table.

2. C. If the same user owns a view and the tables underneath the view, the ownership chain is unbroken and rights are only checked on the view. If a different user owns the view than the user who owns the table, the ownership chain is broken and the user of the view must have access to both the view and the table.

3. A, C. To meet this requirement, only grant rights to those columns that are needed. The recommended practice is to create a new role and assign rights to this role.

4. A, B, or C. Option A, B, or C encapsulates the functionality in an object that secures it from user tampering.

5. B. To prevent specific rights that a user has already received as the member of another role, the DENY statement will prevent them from inheriting this right from any other role.

6. A. The ownership chain is broken because Kyle owns one object and Delaney owns another. When Tia executes the stored procedure, SQL Server allows her to execute it because she was granted rights to do so. However, when the stored procedure tries to access the table, the ownership chain is broken and another security check is performed. Since Tia was not granted rights to this table, an error is returned.

7. B, C, D. To allow only a specific application to change data, create an application role and include the password in the application. Assign all rights for objects to this role. No users can be added to an application role.

8. C. Triggers are the best way to enforce a business rule on a table in every circumstance.

9. B. The recommended practice is to create roles and assign object rights to these roles. Users are then assigned to the roles as needed.

10. D. When adding a new login to SQL Server, the login must also be mapped to a user in a database to access the data in that database.

11. C. To use an application role, it must be activated after connecting to the database with the SP_SETAPPROLE stored procedure.

12. C. Unless the CASCADE option is included with the REVOKE statement, rights granted by Dave will not be removed from other users.

13. D. The best way to implement this new security role is to create a new role and deny permissions on the Orders table for this role. By adding the dozen salespeople to this role, the DENY will override their existing permissions on the Orders table. All their other permissions will remain the same.

14. C. In order to create a foreign key that references another user's table, references permissions are needed.

15. A. The easiest way to implement security while preventing problems is to ensure that all objects are owned by one user. This way, no ownership chains are broken.

Chapter

12

Analyzing and Optimizing Data Access

MICROSOFT EXAM OBJECTIVES COVERED IN THIS CHAPTER:

- ✓ Analyze the query execution plan. Considerations include query processor operations and steps.

- ✓ Capture, analyze, and replay SQL Profiler traces. Considerations include lock detection, performance tuning, and trace flags.

- ✓ Create and implement indexing strategies. Considerations include clustered index, covering index, indexed views, nonclustered index, placement, and statistics.

- ✓ Improve index use by using the Index Tuning Wizard.

- ✓ Monitor and troubleshoot database activity by using SQL Profiler.

Developing and deploying an application is merely the first step in what you hope will be its long life. As an application matures and evolves, one area that becomes increasingly important is the analysis and optimization of the queries. The data used by an application will grow and change, and the information used by the query optimizer will change. As this happens, an application's performance may substantially decrease. The database and queries require maintenance to ensure that the application continues to perform as expected.

The analysis and optimization of queries are both an art and a science, and are essential skills for a DBA to learn. Unfortunately it seems that many reference materials devote far more space to learning how to write queries than to teaching one to analyze and improve queries. There are more and more people using SQL Server every year, and Transact-SQL skills are trickling down from DBAs to developers of all levels. However, the knowledge of how to write efficient queries and how to find poorly written ones is limited to relatively few people.

While this text is not designed to cover this topic in detail, it is written to introduce the reader to the *query optimizer* and how SQL Server makes decisions about the execution of queries. The analysis and optimization of queries in SQL Server is covered along with the tools available to the SQL Server DBA. The various options in Query Analyzer, the SQL Server Profiler, and the Stored Procedure Debugger are introduced along with basic instructions on how to use them and when a particular tool can be used in place of another.

The Query Optimizer

Microsoft ✓ **Exam** **Objective**

Analyze the query execution plan. Considerations include query processor operations and steps.

Whenever a query is submitted to SQL Server, the SQL engine must make decisions about how to go about retrieving the data for the user. Inside the SQL Server query processing engine, there is a section of code called the query optimizer whose function is to find the most efficient means of retrieving data at that particular time. This query optimizer compares different possible methods of retrieving the data (called execution plans) and then chooses one. Once this is done, the query engine goes about using this plan to retrieve the data requested by the query.

In any database system, returning data to the client must be done as efficiently and quickly as possible to minimize contention. If the database server spends an inordinate amount of time processing one query, the performance of other queries will suffer. In order for the server to find the most efficient method of satisfying the query, it must spend resources examining the query and comparing different methods of retrieving the data. This overhead, however, is often returned to the user in overall time savings when the most efficient method of satisfying the query is chosen. This is similar to climbing an unfamiliar mountain. If you spend a few minutes with a map comparing different routes, you will likely complete your journey quicker than if you start climbing immediately and decide on the route as you climb. Of course, those who start immediately will get lucky and summit the mountain quicker a few times, but as more and more attempts are made, those who plan will average much quicker times than those who do not.

One of the advantages of stored procedures is that the query plans are usually predetermined. The time required to find an execution plan is eliminated, which can result in a substantial time savings. For many queries, it takes as much time to find an execution plan as it does to execute the query.

There are different types of query optimizers used in various relational database management systems. Microsoft SQL Server uses a *"cost-based"* query optimizer in determining which of the various methods of retrieving data it will pick and send to the query engine. A cost-based optimizer assigns a cost to each method of retrieving data based on the resources required to process the query. Processor time, disk I/O, etc. are all assigned costs based on the number of rows that must be examined in a particular operation. Once the optimizer has assigned the costs, it sums up the total cost for each execution plan that was investigated. Based on the design of the system, the query optimizer chooses an execution plan, which is then sent to the query engine for processing.

SQL Server does not always choose the execution plan with the lowest total resource cost as one might expect. Instead, SQL Server is designed to pick the execution plan that is reasonably close to the theoretical minimum and will return results to the client as quickly as possible with a reasonable cost. The definition of reasonable will change as conditions within the SQL Server and the load changes. This results in a dynamic, efficient query optimizer that delivers some of the best performance in the industry.

Single Statement Optimization

There are basically two types of optimizations that occur: single statement and batch optimizations. This section will deal with the former and the next with the latter. Most of this section is devoted to examining how SELECT statements are processed since this is the basis for most operations within the server. INSERT, UPDATE, and DELETE operations basically consist of determining the number of and which rows are affected. Both of these operations are basically the same as a SELECT statement, so this explanation will apply to them as well.

There are a number of statements in SQL Server that are not SELECT, INSERT, UPDATE, or DELETE operations. Most of these are statements that deal with system level tables, like ALTER, CREATE, etc. Since these are primarily system functions and are not executed as part of an application (in general), this text will not examine how the server satisfies these statements. Also, since these are system statements and it is not recommended that their operation be altered, it would not be productive to spend time examining how they work.

Execution Plans

The steps that the relational engine will go through to satisfy a query make up an *execution plan*. There are two items that all execution plans determine for the relational engine:

- The order in which the source tables are accessed when performing the query

- The method of extraction of the data from these tables

The order in which the tables are accessed is important not for which rows will appear in the result set, but rather for the speed of the joins between the tables. If the first data retrieval from a table can be done quickly and returns a small number of rows, then subsequent join operations have less data to work with and can complete quicker.

The method of data extraction from a table is a fancy way of describing whether an index is used or not. The optimizer will have a few choices for most tables; it can scan the table for rows meeting the qualifications in the WHERE clause, it can use an index, or even use multiple indexes and perform an internal join. If the table is small (with few rows), then it is almost always quicker to use a table scan. If a large number of rows will be returned, but there is an index on columns in an ORDER BY clause, then the index may be quicker.

For queries that include a join, there is a third step that determines the type of join that will be used to combine the information from the various tables. The query optimizer must choose between three types of joins for each pair of tables or result sets that must be joined together.

For any query, there may be any number of execution plans that could satisfy the query. In fact, for complex queries, there may be thousands of possible execution plans that could exist. Instead of examining each plan and assigning a cost to it, the SQL Server will "guess" at which plans will have a cost close to the theoretical minimum cost. SQL Server uses various algorithms to make these guesses and reduce the number of plans that it checks. The SQL Server team has done a good job of building in limitations for the query optimizer to prevent it from spending too much time comparing queries.

I am not sure what "sophisticated" algorithms are, but I am guessing that these are the ones that work well 80-90 percent of the time. Not much detail is available outside of Microsoft, but I can tell you that on the same hardware, a number of queries run faster in SQL Server 2000, so I trust the SQL Server developers made some good choices.

You can view the execution plan for a query in a couple of different ways. You can use the SET SHOWPLAN_TEXT or SET SHOWPLAN_ALL statements, which are described below. You can also view a graphical showplan in Query Analyzer by pressing CTRL-K or selecting QUERY ≻ SHOW EXECUTION PLAN from the menu.

I tend to use the graphical showplan to analyze queries because I think it is easier to read and quickly finds which step consumes most of the resources since the percentage of the resources required is displayed under each step. You can still view the detail for each step by stopping the mouse on each step.

While the optimization of single queries is important for ensuring optimal performance from a SQL Server, there are some additional considerations that must be made for batches of queries. Optimization of batches is discussed in the next section.

Batch Optimization

Optimizing a batch is very similar to optimizing a single query. The same techniques will be used, as the server will execute each statement sequentially in the same order that they are presented in a batch. There are a few key differences that the developer must keep in mind when optimizing a batch that is different from single statements.

If there are conditional statements inside the batch, the developer must be sure that both branches of the conditional statement (TRUE and FALSE) should be optimized to ensure the batch runs as efficiently as possible.

If there are stored procedures called from within the batch, these should be optimized separately as they will comprise a single execution plan for the batch.

One other item to be aware of with batches is that all steps do not take the same amount of time to complete. Profiling the batch is a good way to start analyzing a batch and looking for ways to optimize the code. This involves both determining the time each step takes to execute and the number of times a step may be run. The easiest way to do this in T-SQL is to add a series of SELECT statements in between all code lines. Each SELECT statement returns a result set with the current server time and a text message that identifies where in the batch the SELECT has been placed. This will allow the programmer to find the sections of code that require the most time to execute. These are the sections of code that will make the most difference to the performance of the system if they can be optimized.

Analyzing Queries

<table>
<tr><td>*Microsoft*
✓ *Exam*
Objective</td><td>**Analyze the query execution plan. Considerations include query processor operations and steps.**</td></tr>
</table>

Using *SET* Statements

In order to analyze a query, one must change the behavior of Query Analyzer (or another client tool) to report back information about the query. SQL Server has a number of statements that you can execute on the client to instruct the server to report back information about the batch that can be used to analyze and optimize the query.

The options that pertain to analyzing and optimizing queries are turned on or off by the client and remain in effect for the duration of the connection. To turn off the effects, another SET statement must be issued. If one of these settings is changed within a stored procedure, then it is in effect until changed or until the stored procedure ends. If the stored procedure ends, then the setting defaults to the value that was set before the stored procedure was invoked. The settings also remain at their current value when a stored procedure is invoked. Changing to a different database has no effect on the value of any of these options.

The following options are useful in analyzing and optimizing queries and batches. Each is described below.

- SET FORCEPLAN
- SET NOEXEC
- SET SHOWPLAN_ALL
- SET SHOWPLAN_TEXT
- SET STATISTICS IO
- SET STATISTICS PROFILE
- SET STATISTICS TIME

SET FORCEPLAN

This forces the SQL Server query optimizer to process the join in a query in the same order as the tables physically appear in the FROM clause of the query. This can be used to force the optimizer into different join orders so query plans for each can be compared.

WARNING   Be wary of using this in production code. It restricts the optimizer from examining any query plans that would reorder the table joins.

Syntax

```
SET FORCEPLAN { ON | OFF }
```
Permissions for this option default to all users.

SET NOEXEC

This option does not really report any information that can be used to analyze a query by itself. Instead, this option prevents the execution of the query, allowing only the parsing of the syntax and the creation of the execution plan by the query optimizer.

When you are trying to analyze a query that is extremely long running or contains a very large result set, you will welcome this option. It allows you to perform the same query plan analysis you would otherwise perform without having to wait for the query processor to execute the query. When this option is set, the batch is parsed and the query plan compiled, but the query is not actually run.

Syntax

```
SET NOEXEC { ON | OFF }
```
Permissions for this option default to all users.

For some statements that return a result set (such as SET STATISTICS PRO-FILE), setting this option to ON prevents the information from returning.

SET SHOWPLAN_ALL

This statement will instruct SQL Server not to execute the statements in the batch, but rather to return the detailed information about how the statements are executed. With this information, estimates of the resource requirements are returned as well.

Syntax

```
SET SHOWPLAN_ALL { ON | OFF }
```
This setting applies at run time only, not at parse time.

This statement must be executed within its own batch.

The results from queries executed after SET SHOWPLAN_ALL is set to ON are returned as a specialized result set. The output columns are listed in Table 12.1.

TABLE 12.1   *SHOWPLAN_ALL* Result Set

Results	Description
StmtText	This is the text of the SQL statement for rows that are not of type PLAN_ROW. For type PLAN_ROW, this is a description of the operation that the server would perform to satisfy the request.
StmtID	Statement number in the current batch.
NodeId	The ID of the node in the query.
Parent	The ID of the parent node in the query. The parent is the node that must execute before this node can be executed.

TABLE 12.1   *SHOWPLAN_ALL* Result Set *(continued)*

Results	Description
PhysicalOp	This applies to rows of type PLAN_ROW only. This is the physical algorithm that was applied to the node. (Index Scan, Index Seek, etc.)
LogicalOp	This applies to rows of type PLAN_ROW only. This is the relational algebraic operator that is represented by this node. (Index Scan, Index Seek, etc.)
Argument	This provides additional information about the operation being performed. The contents will depend on the PhysicalOp value.
DefinedValues	This applies to rows of type PLAN_ROW only. This is a comma-separated list of values that are introduced by the operator. This may be computed expressions or internal values needed by the query processor to process the query. The results may be referenced elsewhere within the query.
EstimateRows	This applies to rows of type PLAN_ROW only and is an estimated number of rows that will be output by this operator.
EstimateIO	This applies to rows of type PLAN_ROW only and is an estimate of the I/O cost for this operator.
EstimateCPU	This applies to rows of type PLAN_ROW only and is an estimate of the CPU cost for this operator.
AvgRowSize	An estimate of the average row size in bytes of the rows being passed through this operator.
TotalSubtreeCost	An estimate of the total cost for this operation and all of its child operations.
OutputList	A comma-separated list of the columns being output by this operation.

TABLE 12.1 *SHOWPLAN_ALL* Result Set *(continued)*

Results	Description
Warnings	A comma-separated list of warning messages that relate to this node. Possible messages include "NO STATS():" and "MISSING JOIN PREDICATE." "NO STATS():," with a list of columns, may occur because statistics for the columns were not available and the optimizer had to make a guess. "MISSING JOIN PREDICATE" implies that a join is taking place without a join predicate. This may result in a very long query and the absence of a join predicate should be verified.
Type	Type of the node. For the parent node of the query, this will be the SQL statement type (INSERT, UPDATE, SELECT, DELETE). For other rows that represent some execution step, the type will be PLAN_ROW.
Parallel	Either 0 or 1. 0 means this operator is not running parallel. 1 indicates parallelism is occurring.
EstimateExecutions	An estimate of the number of times this operator will be executed during the current query.

Permissions for this statement default to all users.

SET SHOWPLAN_TEXT

This returns the same information that is returned by SET SHOWPLAN_ALL, but in a more readable format for MS-DOS applications (those returning text output). Only a single column is returned, though multiple result sets are returned.

Syntax

```
SET SHOWPLAN_TEXT { ON | OFF }
```

Results

The result of this statement is a single column result set named StmtText. This is the text of the SQL statement for rows that are not of type PLAN_ROW. For type PLAN_ROW, this is a description of the operation that the server would perform to satisfy the request along with the physical, and optionally the logical, operator. A description may also be included.

Permissions for SET SHOWPLAN_TEXT default to all users.

This statement is used to ask the server to return the execution plan to the client along with the result set.

SET STATISTICS IO

This statement determines whether or not statistical information about the various I/O operations is returned to the client.

Unlike most other SET statements, the output from this statement is not displayed in the results window. Instead, the statistics are sent to the *Messages* tab. The result set is described in Table 12.2.

Syntax

    SET STATISTICS IO { ON | OFF }

TABLE 12.2 *SET STATISTICS IO* Result Set

Column	Description
Table	Name of the table on which statistics are being reported.
Scan count	This is the number of scans that are performed during the query on this table.
Logical reads	This is the number of pages read from the data cache in memory.
Physical Reads	This is the number of pages that are read from the disk.
Read-ahead reads	This is the number of pages that are placed into the data cache (memory) by the read ahead manager for this query.

Permissions default to all users for this statement.

SET STATISTICS PROFILE

This statement determines whether the profile information for ad hoc queries, views, triggers, and stored procedures is displayed. The result set is the same as that for SET SHOWPLAN_ALL with the additional columns that are displayed in Table 12.3.

Syntax

```
SET STATISTICS PROFILE { ON | OFF }
```

TABLE 12.3 *SET STATISTICS PROFILE Result Set*

Column	Description
Rows	This is the actual number of rows that is produced by each operator.
Executes	The number of times this operator was executed.

Permissions default to all users for this statement.

SET STATISTICS TIME

This statement determines whether the server returns the time required (in milliseconds) to the client that the server uses to parse, compile, and execute each statement.

If you have enabled fiber mode (set lightweight pooling), then accurate statistics cannot be reported.

As with SET STATISTICS IO, this information is reported on the messages tab in Query Analyzer rather than in the results pane.

Syntax

```
SET STATISTICS TIME { ON | OFF }
```
Permissions for this option default to all users.

Analyzing the Execution Plan

Once the execution plan for a query is obtained, the easy part of any optimization is complete. The most difficult and time consuming part is performing the analysis of the plan and deciding what steps to take to ensure this query performs as optimally as possible. This is a difficult topic to teach, as it is an art as much as a science. Just as the optimizer will change the execution plan based on a variety of factors, the optimizer must also consider external factors and determine the best optimization at the time. This may not be the same optimization that would be chosen at a later date, but since we cannot predict the future, we must do the best we can.

Since analyzing and optimizing a query is truly an art, this section will explain the basics of examining a query plan, provide hints about what things to look for that can adversely affect performance, and give some suggestions for improving performance.

Query Operations

When you examine an execution plan, the first thing that you should look for is the type of operations that are occurring. There are a variety of operations that can occur and each requires different resources. One cannot say that a particular operation is always more efficient than another since it will depend on the individual query. Instead, we will look at the list of the various types of operations and then discuss their impacts on performance.

Keep in mind that each of these operations can occur in multiple places in the same query. For each table, the query optimizer must choose whether to perform a scan or seek in addition to the order in which to perform the operations.

Table 12.4 lists the various operations that can appear in an execution plan.

TABLE 12.4 Execution Plan Operators

Operation	Description
Bookmark Lookup	An index was used to locate a row that satisfies some portion of the query, but now the query processor must use the ROWID from the index to "lookup" the actual data row. Unless the index can be altered to "cover" the columns needed by the query, this cannot be optimized.

TABLE 12.4 Execution Plan Operators *(continued)*

Operation	Description
Clustered Index Scans	These are the same as a table scan, but since a table with a clustered index has the data ordered as the index, a table scan is the same as a clustered index scan. This is the least desirable operation for a query to perform, especially on a large table (see table scan). Usually if this is occurring, then the columns in the query are either not indexed or the distribution statistics do not lead the optimizer to believe that the index will eliminate enough rows to make more cost effective than scanning the table. Restructuring the query can sometimes eliminate these operations.
Clustered Index Seek	This occurs when the query processor takes advantage of a clustered index to find the rows that satisfy the query. This is an optimal operation for most queries and cannot be optimized further.
Compute Scalar	An expression is being evaluated to produce a scalar result for the query or a scalar that is referenced in another part of the query. Unless you can restructure the query to remove the scalar value, then this cannot be optimized.
Constant Scan	The query requires a constant value in some (or all) rows. A Compute Scalar is usually used to add the constant column to the row(s).
Hash Match	The query processor builds a hash table for each row that is being processed. As subsequent rows are processed, the hash is computed and compared to the hash table for matches. Queries with DISTINCT, aggregates, or UNION often require a hash table to remove duplicates. Unless you can restructure the query to remove one of these conditions, there is no optimization. This type of join requires more memory than the others. This may never be seen on memory-restricted systems.

TABLE 12.4 Execution Plan Operators *(continued)*

Operation	Description
Index Scan	The nonclustered index is being used to locate data rows, but a large number of rows are being returned or the entire WHERE clause cannot be examined with this index. The server reads a part of or the entire index to satisfy the query. Unless you can restructure the query to return fewer rows, this cannot be optimized.
Index Seek	A nonclustered index is being used and the query processor can traverse only a portion of the index to satisfy the query. This is one of the most efficient operations for most queries. Choosing highly selective indexes usually results in the query optimizer choosing this type of operation.
Index Spool	As rows are being scanned, they are placed into a "spool" table that exists in Tempdb. An index is built and as additional scans of the data are needed, this spool table can be used rather than re-reading the input rows. This is an internal optimization for complex queries and cannot be changed.
Merge Join	A merge join occurs when the two inputs contain sorted data and the query processor can merge then together. This is a very efficient operation, but to get this to occur, the joins must be able to take advantage of sorted data. Indexes can be added on join columns or columns included in the ORDER BY clause to get merge joins to occur. This operation may also occur when two or more indexes are used to query a table. The results from each index seek are merged together to obtain a list of data rows that must be read.

TABLE 12.4   Execution Plan Operators *(continued)*

Operation	Description
Nested Loop	Prior to SQL 7, this was the only type of join. In this join, one table is chosen as the inner and scanned for each row of the outer. This is not an efficient operation unless the number of rows is relatively small. Restructuring the query can remove these joins from large queries and provide some gains in performance. If memory is limited on the system, this is probably the only type of join that will be chosen.
Remote Query	Some portion of the query is being submitted to a remote source. If this is a slow portion of the query, the optimization needs to occur on the remote source. Perhaps the data can be moved to SQL Server to allow the server to make its own optimizations.
Sort	This is equivalent to building an index on the result set. While this is an expensive operation, unless you can restructure the query to remove any ORDER BY clauses, there is little that can be done here.
Table Scan	This is the same as a clustered index scan and is performed when the table has no clustered index (is a *heap*). These are usually the least desirable operations to see in any execution plan. This implies that the query processor must read each row into memory and examine it to see if it can be returned by the query. If this is occurring, then adding an index to the table using the column(s) needed for queries can eliminate this from occurring. The main exception to this rule occurs with small tables of less than a few hundred rows. Often SQL Server finds it more efficient to table scan small tables than incur the overhead of reading an index and

TABLE 12.4 Execution Plan Operators *(continued)*

Operation	Description
Table Scan *(cont.)*	then reading the table for data. Try to eliminate table scans using indexes where appropriate, but do not force the server to use one if it consistently chooses a table scan even when indexes exist.

Most of the descriptions and suggestions in the table above require indexes to be altered or the query to be restructured, but these are usually the preferred optimizations. Some of the gains in query performance come from writing well-structured, efficient queries that return the minimum amount of information needed, but most gains in performance are made by choosing good indexes.

The largest gains in query performance will come from ensuring that there are indexes on all tables and that the statistics for these indexes are up to date. These are the two main factors that influence the query optimizer in making decisions about the execution plan.

Many queries are written as SELECT * when only a column or two were needed. Rewriting these queries to return only the values that are needed can provide dramatic performance gains on large result sets. This can cause the query optimizer to choose a table scan over an index seek if all columns are returned, but only an indexed column was needed.

EXERCISE 12.1

Analyzing a Query

In this exercise, we will take a three-table query from Northwind and analyze the execution plan. Since the plan that is chosen may vary based on the system that is running the query, I will present the plan that was chosen on two different systems that were tested. The query text is shown below:

1. Open the SQL Server Query Analyzer. Do this through the SQL Enterprise Manager by selecting Tools ➢ SQL Query Analyzer or by choosing Start ➢ Programs ➢ Microsoft SQL Server ➢ SQL Query Analyzer.

2. Type the following query into Query Analyzer (be sure the North-wind database is selected):

```
SET SHOWPLAN_TEXT ON
GO
SELECT
    c.CompanyName,
    sum( od.Quantity * od.UnitPrice) 'Sales'
  FROM Orders o, Customers c, [Order Details] od
  WHERE o.ShipCountry = c.Country
  and o.OrderID = od.OrderID
  and c.ContactTitle = 'Owner'
  GROUP BY c.CompanyName
```

3. Highlight these lines with the mouse and press the green arrow or press CTRL-E to execute the query. You should receive the following results:

```
StmtText
-------------------------------------------------------------------
SELECT
    c.CompanyName,
    sum( od.Quantity * od.UnitPrice) 'Sales'
  FROM Orders o, Customers c, [Order Details] od
  WHERE o.ShipCountry = c.Country
  and o.OrderID = od.OrderID
  and c.ContactTitle = 'Owner'
  GROUP BY c.CompanyName
```

```
(1 row(s) affected)
```

```
StmtText
-------------------------------------------------------------------
  |--Stream Aggregate(GROUP BY:([c].[CompanyName])
DEFINE:([Expr1003]=SUM(Convert([od].[Quantity])*[od].[UnitPrice])))
      |--Nested Loops(Inner Join, OUTER
REFERENCES:([o].[OrderID]))
          |--Sort(ORDER BY:([c].[CompanyName] ASC))
          |     |--Hash Match(Inner Join,
HASH:([c].[Country])=([o].[ShipCountry]),
RESIDUAL:([o].[ShipCountry]=[c].[Country]))
          |         |--Clustered Index
Scan(OBJECT:([Northwind].[dbo].[Customers].[PK_Customers] AS [c]),
WHERE:([c].[ContactTitle]='Owner'))
          |         |--Clustered Index
Scan(OBJECT:([Northwind].[dbo].[Orders].[PK_Orders] AS [o]))
```

```
      |--Clustered Index
Seek(OBJECT:([Northwind].[dbo].[Order Details].[PK_Order_Details]
AS [od]), SEEK:([od].[OrderID]=[o].[OrderID]) ORDERED FORWARD)
```

(7 row(s) affected)

4. From the second output section we can deduce the following:

- Line 1 shows an aggregate operation occurring, which is unavoidable since the query contains a SUM operator.

- Line 2 includes a nested loop join that is used to perform the grouping operation.

- Line 3 is a sort operation that occurs as an internal operation to prepare the data for grouping.

- Line 4 shows a hash join being made on the Customers.Country field and the Orders.ShipCountry field. There is an index on the Customers table for its field, but not one on the Orders table. This system is not limited by memory, the optimizer feels that there are relatively few rows that will match, and a hash table in memory will find a result set quicker than a nested loop join of the tables.

- Line 5 shows a clustered index scan is occurring on the Customers table. Since there is no index on the ContactTitle field, no index is being used and all rows are being examined to determine which rows match this qualification. This is half of the information needed for the HASH JOIN in line 4. Adding an index on Country would likely change this to a seek operator.

- Line 6 is the other half of the information needed for the HASH JOIN in line 4. There is no index on ShipCountry, so a clustered index scan is needed here as well. Adding an index on ShipCountry would likely change this to a seek operator.

- Line 7 shows a clustered index seek on [Order Details]. Since there is an index on this table, this is an extremely efficient operator. Nothing can be done here to optimize this line.

Optimizing Queries

Microsoft ✓ *Exam* *Objective*

Create and implement indexing strategies. Considerations include clustered index, covering index, indexed views, nonclustered index, placement, and statistics.

There are a few different ways to go about optimizing queries. Indexes and rewriting queries are the most common methods for improving performance, but query hints can also be used to try and force the server to execute a query using a specific method. Keep in mind that query hints can force the server to choose a less than optimal execution plan. Without extensive testing of their use on a particular system, their use is not recommended.

In most systems, relatively few of the total number of queries that are run are used extensively. Most time should be spent on these queries, as they will provide the most overall benefit.

Indexes

If you cannot find another way to write the query to use existing indexes, then adding another index is likely the next best way to improve the efficiency of the query. Whenever an index can be used in a query or a join, the amount of resources the server must consume, both processor cycles and I/O, is reduced.

In order for SQL Server to use an index, the first indexed column must be included in the WHERE clause as part of a qualification. If there are multiple columns in an index, but the first column is not part of the WHERE clause, the index is not considered. However, all the columns in the WHERE clause do not need to be included in the index for it to be chosen. Consider the following query:

```
Select CustomerID
  From Customers C
  Where firstname = 'Joe'
  And lastname = 'Public'
```

This query could be performed in a few different ways by the query optimizer. If there is only an index on FIRSTNAME, then the query optimizer may elect to perform an index seek using this index to find all rows that match 'Joe.' Once this is complete, a bookmark lookup may retrieve the data rows and the optimizer may apply a filter to limit the result set to those that have a LASTNAME of 'Public.'

However if we added an index on LASTNAME as well, then the optimizer could perform the same index seek using the FIRSTNAME index. In addition, a second index seek using the index on LASTNAME could be run and return the rows matching 'Public.' These two result sets could be combined using a merge join to obtain a result set of rows that meet both qualifications. The bookmark lookup would still have to occur to get the actual data rows, but fewer lookups may be needed.

Lastly, the index on FIRSTNAME could be changed to be an index on CUSTOMERID, FIRSTNAME, and LASTNAME. In this case, neither of the columns in the WHERE clause are included as the first column of an index. The index would not be used and a table scan would be chosen.

Of course, none of these execution plans may be chosen by the optimizer to satisfy the query. It depends on a number of factors. The size of the data is a large factor. If there were only 50 rows in this table, then a table scan (or clustered index scan) would probably be chosen by the optimizer regardless of how many indexes are on the table. The cost of reading 50 rows is less than the cost of examining a few query plans.

Also, if this were a large table, but there were relatively few unique values for FIRSTNAME in the table, and the index is nonclustered, the query optimizer may decide on a table scan. Reading a large part of a nonclustered index and then performing the bookmark lookup on the results is not usually as cost effective as a table scan. Nonclustered indexes must be highly selective in order for the query optimizer to choose to use them. Usually an index that does not eliminate 95 percent of the rows, as estimated by the query optimizer, will not be used.

Indexes are not always the solution to an inefficient query. For tables that are accessed often, especially in transactional systems with lots of activity, you should strive to keep the number of indexes on the table under five and preferably limited to two to three. For analytical systems, try to limit the indexes to ten unless there is very little update activity.

Clustered Indexes

There can only be one clustered index on a table, and as a result, it should be chosen carefully. A clustered index is recommended, and by default, the *primary key* is the clustered index. This is probably not the best choice for the clustered index unless this is the only index that will exist on the table. Clustered indexes are best suited for range queries, such as dates or a particular numerical range. When the optimizer detects this type of query, the clustered index is usually chosen.

Clustered Indexes and Primary Keys

One thing that often happens when inexperienced developers build a database is that the primary key usually ends up being created as a clustered index. By default, SQL Server will set up the primary key as clustered, even though this will usually turn out to be a poor choice for the clustered index.

The primary key often contains data that is incremental. A purchase order number, an invoice number, a product SKU, or other identifiers are often the primary key for a table. When data is added to a table, it is all placed in contiguous pages. Not only does this create a hot spot (an area of concentrated data modification in the table) but most queries using these fields will be looking for a single row of data.

A better choice is usually to use a column when querying a range of data. For an invoice table, the payment date or the invoice date might be better choices. Or, if sales were usually grouped into tiers, then perhaps the sale price would arrange the data in ways that are useful to queries searching for a large number of contiguous rows.

Nonclustered Indexes

This type of index works best on large tables when very few rows are being returned. The query optimizer will often choose a nonclustered index that is *highly selective* when the index columns are included in the join statements. When this occurs, SQL Server can find the rows needed in the index very quickly and then get the actual data with a few scans.

If the nonclustered index is not highly selective, however, then it may not be used. The reason for this is that the I/O operations required to repeatedly scan the table for the actual data rows are much more expensive than a single scan through the table. This is why columns that have only a few values, such as gender, are not good choices for nonclustered indexes.

As a rule of thumb, if the nonclustered index can eliminate 95 percent of the rows in a table, it will be used. If not, then another index or a table scan will be chosen. The exception to this may occur if the nonclustered index is a covering index for some queries. If an index includes all the columns in the column list as well as the WHERE clause, then it may be chosen and additional bookmark lookups to retrieve the actual data pages will not be needed.

Foreign Keys are usually good choices for nonclustered indexes. Usually these columns are used in joins.

No matter which type of index you choose, there are a few general guidelines for creating these indexes. First, index those columns that are used often in joins. Next, be sure that the first column of the index is the column that is specified in most joins. If not, the index is useless. If the index will not be used, then it is a waste of space and CPU cycles to both create it and maintain it. Lastly, be sure to analyze your queries and see if the indexes are being used. If not, then perhaps they should be removed and new indexes created.

One last item that can improve performance of queries has to do with the placement of the indexes. SQL Server 2000 allows multiple filegroups of physical files to be associated with a database. Each of these filegroups will be given a logical name inside the database. If these filegroups are on separate physical devices, then placing the nonclustered indexes in a different filegroup than the data for some tables can achieve some performance gains. The performance benefits are difficult to quantify, but with less contention for the index pages, they can be retrieved faster from a separate physical device.

If you have separate physical devices, the log should be placed on a separate physical device than the data. If additional physical devices are available, then heavily used indexes or tables can be moved to these physical devices. Testing of system performance should be completed before and after any changes are made.

EXERCISE 12.2

Optimizing Queries by Limiting the Result Set

This exercise will look at optimizing a two-table join.

1. Open the SQL Server Query Analyzer. Do this through the SQL Enterprise Manager by selecting Tools ➢ SQL Query Analyzer or by choosing Start ➢ Programs ➢ Microsoft SQL Server ➢ SQL Query Analyzer.

2. Type the following query into Query Analyzer (be sure the Northwind database is selected):

```
SELECT *
 FROM [order details] o, Products p
 WHERE o.ProductID = p.ProductId
```

3. Let us show the execution plan for this query by selecting Query ➢ Show Execution Plan from the menu. Then highlight these lines with the mouse and press the green arrow or CTRL-E to execute the query. You should receive the following results on the Execution Plan tab.

EXERCISE 12.2 *(continued)*

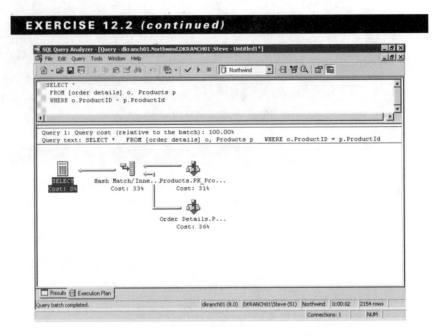

This plan shows a clustered index scan from each table along with a join. Since it is unlikely that all fields are needed from both tables, we can limit the column list to those columns that are needed, and this query may perform better. The following query limits the column list to a few columns.

```
SELECT
    o.OrderID,
    o.Quantity,
    p.ProductID
 FROM [order details] o, Products p
 WHERE o.ProductID = p.ProductId
```

If the second query is executed, the next showplan will be obtained.

SQL Server now uses a nonclustered index scan for the Products table, a much more efficient operation than the clustered index scan since less data must be read.

EXERCISE 12.3

Optimizing a Query by Changing an Index

This exercise will look at a two-way join between the Orders and Order Details tables.

1. Open the SQL Server Query Analyzer. Do this through the SQL Enterprise Manager by selecting Tools ➢ SQL Query Analyzer or by choosing Start ➢ Programs ➢ Microsoft SQL Server ➢ SQL Query Analyzer.

2. Type the following query to in Query Analyzer (be sure the Northwind database is selected):

```
SELECT
    o.CustomerID,
    SUM( od.Quantity * od.UnitPrice) 'Total Sales'
```

```
FROM Orders o, [Order Details] od
WHERE o.OrderID = od.OrderID
AND o.OrderDate > '12/31/1996'
AND o.OrderDate < '01/01/1998'
GROUP BY o.CustomerID
```

3. Let us show the execution plan for this query by selecting Query ➤ Show Execution Plan from the menu. Then highlight these lines with the mouse and press the green arrow or CTRL-E to execute the query. You should receive the following results on the execution plan tab:

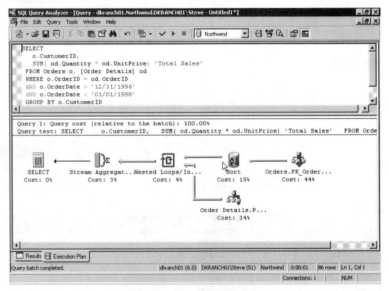

The execution plan shows the server is performing a clustered index scan against the Orders table, a clustered index seek against Order Details, and then uses a Nested Loop join and a Stream Aggregate to return the results. The following indexes exist on these tables:

- Orders

  - PK_Orders (OrderID) Clustered

  - CustomersOrders (CustomerID)

- EmployeeOrders (EmployeeID)

- OrderDate (OrderDate)

- ShippedDate (ShippedDate)

- ShippersOrders (ShipVia)

- ShipPostalCode (ShipPostalCode)

- Order Details

  - PK_Order_Details (OrderID, ProductID) (Clustered)

  - OrderID (OrderID)

  - ProductID (ProductID)

The clustered index seek is extremely efficient for the Order Details table, but we are only concerned with two columns for the Orders table: CustomerID and OrderDate. There is an index on both of these columns separately, but the index on CustomerID is the clustered index. We can change the index on OrderDate to include OrderDate and CustomerID (in that order) with the following code:

```
CREATE
    INDEX [OrderDate] ON [dbo].[Orders] ([OrderDate],
[CustomerID])
WITH
    FILLFACTOR = 80
    ,DROP_EXISTING
ON [PRIMARY]
```

The same query now performs an index scan on the Orders table. Just as in the first query, this change can substantially improve performance for large data sets. Here is the execution plan for the same query after the index change.

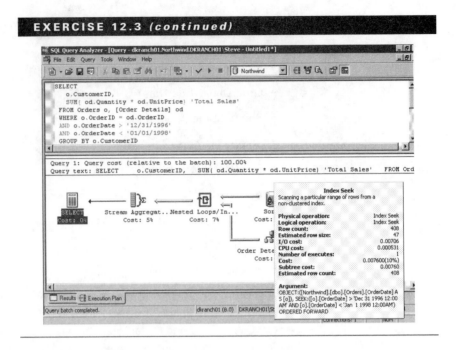

Query Hints

SQL Server does a great job of tuning itself and selecting the optimal join strategies to be used for most queries. There are situations, however, where the programmer or DBA may better understand the data than SQL Server. In these cases, the ability to force the query processor to use a certain strategy is available.

There are four types of hints that can be specified in a query: join hints, index hints, query processing hints, and lock hints. Each of these is discussed below.

Join Hints

These hints are only available when using ANSI-style join syntax. In between the type of join (INNER, LEFT, RIGHT, OUTER) and the word JOIN, the programmer can insert the join method to be used. The valid choices are HASH, LOOP, MERGE or REMOTE. REMOTE is useful when the right table is a remote table and there are less rows in the left table. The join then occurs on the server that contains the right table. An example is below:

```
SELECT c.companyname, o.orderid
  FROM Customers c INNER HASH JOIN Orders o
  ON c.customerid = o.customerid
```

Index Hints

Index hints can force the query processor to choose a specific index for a table when processing the query. The index can be specified by name or ID, and more than one can be included. Specifying index ID 0 will force a table scan. These hints should not be used on a production system unless testing has confirmed that using them will increase performance. The syntax is as follows:

```
SELECT SELECT_list
  FROM table (INDEX {index name | Index ID} {, index name |
  Index ID})
```

Using the index ID is not recommended as these are subject to change as indexes are dropped and recreated. The exception is the clustered index. It is always ID 1.

The hints are enclosed in parenthesis and follow the word INDEX. An example that forces the query processor to use the index on Company-Name is show below:

```
SELECT CustomerID
  FROM Customers (INDEX (CompanyName))
  where CompanyName = 'Old World Delicatessen'
  and City = 'London'
```

Without the hint, this query will use the index on CITY instead.

Query Processing Hints

These hints are placed at the end of the SELECT query following the keyword OPTION. More than one OPTION clause can be used, but only one hint of each type can be used. The different types of hints are described in Table 12.5.

TABLE 12.5 Query Processing Hints

Hint	Description
Grouping Hints	Either HASH GROUP or UNION GROUP to specify how the grouping operations are performed.
UNION Hints	HASH, MERGE, or CONCAT are the types of UNION hints to specify how the different result sets should be combined.
Join Hints	These are the same hints that can be specified in the join clause. This type of hint will override any in the join clause and be applied to all joins.
FAST xx	Where xx is the number of rows. This asks SQL Server to choose an execution plan that will send the first rows back as quickly as possible. This can force the use of a nonclustered index that matches an ORDER BY clause to return the first xx rows quickly and then process the remainder of the result set.
FORCE ORDER	This tells SQL Server to process tables in the same order that they appear in the FROM clause. If there is an outer join, this might be ignored.
MAXDOP xx	Where xx is the max degree of parallelism to use for this query. Overrides the server option.
ROBUST PLAN	This forces the query to choose a plan for the maximum possible row size. Useful when there are large varchar columns.
KEEP PLAN	This will ensure that a query is not recompiled as frequently. Useful when a stored procedure is working with temporary tables, which might cause lots of recompilations.

Lock Hints

Lock hints can be used to control how SQL Server will apply locks in various queries. These hints can impact performance dramatically in heavily loaded systems by requiring or not enforcing locks on the data in tables and indexes. These hints are placed in the FROM clause of a query. Table 12.6 lists the various lock hints and the ramifications of each.

TABLE 12.6 Lock Hints

Hint	Description
HOLDLOCK	Hold a shared lock until completion of the transaction instead of releasing the lock as soon as the required table, row, or data page is no longer required. HOLDLOCK is equivalent to SERIALIZABLE.
NOLOCK	Do not issue shared locks and do not honor exclusive locks. When this option is in effect, it is possible to read an uncommitted transaction or a set of pages that are rolled back in the middle of a read. Dirty reads are possible. Only applies to the SELECT statement.
PAGLOCK	Use page locks where a single table lock would usually be taken.
READCOMMITTED	Perform a scan with the same locking semantics as a transaction running at the READ COMMITTED isolation level. By default, SQL Server 2000 operates at this isolation level.
READPAST	Skip locked rows. This option causes a transaction to skip rows locked by other transactions that would ordinarily appear in the result set, rather than block the transaction waiting for the other transactions to release their locks on these rows. The READPAST lock hint applies only to transactions operating at READ COMMITTED isolation and will read only past row-level locks. Applies only to the SELECT statement.
READUNCOMMITTED	Equivalent to NOLOCK.

TABLE 12.6   Lock Hints (continued)

Hint	Description
REPEATABLEREAD	Perform a scan with the same locking semantics as a transaction running at the REPEATABLE READ isolation level.
ROWLOCK	Use row-level locks instead of the coarser-grained page- and table-level lock.
SERIALIZABLE	Perform a scan with the same locking semantics as a transaction running at the SERIALIZABLE isolation level. Equivalent to HOLDLOCK.
TABLOCK	Use a table lock instead of the finer-grained row- or page-level locks. SQL Server holds this lock until the end of the statement. However, if you also specify HOLDLOCK, the lock is held until the end of the transaction.
TABLOCKX	Use an exclusive lock on a table. This lock prevents others from reading or updating the table and is held until the end of the statement or transaction.
UPDLOCK	Use update locks instead of shared locks while reading a table, and hold locks until the end of the statement or transaction. UPDLOCK has the advantage of allowing you to read data (without blocking other readers) and update it later with the assurance that the data has not changed since you last read it.
XLOCK	Use an exclusive lock that will be held until the end of the transaction on all data processed by the statement. This lock can be specified with either PAGLOCK or TABLOCK, in which case the exclusive lock applies to the appropriate level of granularity.

EXERCISE 12.4

Improving Performance with a Lock Hint

This exercise will look at a two-way join between the Orders and Order Details tables.

1. Open the SQL Server Query Analyzer. Do this through the SQL Enterprise Manager by selecting Tools ➢ SQL Query Analyzer or by choosing Start ➢ Programs ➢ Microsoft SQL Server ➢ SQL Query Analyzer.

2. Type the following query to in Query Analyzer (be sure the North-wind database is selected):

```
SELECT * FROM Customers
```

This query will invoke a shares lock on the Customers table for the duration of the query. Suppose that this is a table with 10 million rows and there is a large amount of insert activity on this table. This simple query can slow down the insert activity with a shared lock.

3. The following query can avoid a shared table lock on the Customers table.

```
SELECT * FROM Customers (NOLOCK)\
```

The addition of the lock hint to this query prevents the SELECT query from obtaining any type of lock on this table. Other users that are updating this table will not be prevented from doing so by this query. The implications of using this hint are that the result set that is returned to the user could potentially be different from the actual data in the table if a change is made to the table during the query.

Using the Profiler to Capture Activity

Microsoft ✓ ***Exam Objective***

Capture, analyze, and replay SQL Profiler traces.
Considerations include lock detection, performance tuning, and trace flags.

In SQL Server 7.0, SQL Server introduced the *Profiler* as a new client tool to "sniff" or "watch" the communications that occur between a client and the server. This tool was substantially enhanced in SQL Server 2000, mainly to allow SQL Server 2000 to become C2 certified. The Profiler is an extremely flexible tool for capturing the processes that are occurring on a SQL Server in real time, the same way that a network analyzer would capture the traffic that is occurring on the network. A picture of the Profiler is shown next.

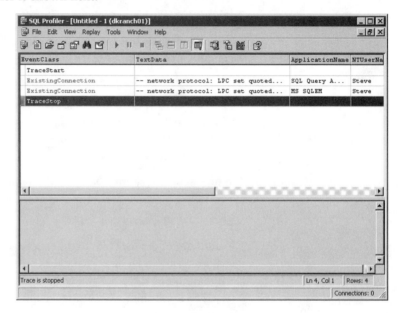

C2 certification is a security rating applied by the NCSA to various computer systems. As of this writing, Windows NT4 and SQL Server 2000 are the only Microsoft products that have received this prestigious rating.

Of all the various uses for the Profiler, performance tuning is one of the few reasons for using this tool most of the time. Rather than a replacement, this tool substantially augments the performance tuning, query analysis, and optimizations that occur. This tool is often the starting point for analyzing queries once an application has been deployed. The Profiler can provide you with information about which queries need to be optimized.

Functions of the Profiler

Microsoft
✓ *Exam*
Objective

Monitor and troubleshoot database activity by using SQL Profiler.

The Profiler can monitor all traffic that occurs between a client and the server and provide details on the queries or statements being executed by the server. The information can be limited to specific workstations, logins, databases, types of statements, or nearly any type of filter that one can imagine. The Profiler also can capture nearly every event that occurs inside SQL Server. There are thirteen classes with hundreds of events that can be added to a trace. Table 12.7 lists the classes of events along with a description of the events under each.

TABLE 12.7   SQL Server Profiler Event Classes

Class	Description
Cursors	Collection of event classes produced by cursor operations
Database	Collection of event classes produced when data or log files grow or shrink automatically
Errors and Warnings	Collection of event classes produced when a SQL Server error or warning occurs (for example, an error during the compilation of a stored procedure or an exception in SQL Server)
Locks	Collection of event classes produced when a lock is acquired, cancelled, released, etc.
Objects	Collection of event classes produced when database objects are created, opened, closed, dropped, or deleted
Performance	Collection of event classes produced when SQL data manipulation (DML) operators execute

TABLE 12.7   SQL Server Profiler Event Classes *(continued)*

Class	Description
Scans	Collection tables and indexes are scanned
Security Audit	Collection of event classes used to audit server activity
Sessions	Collection of event classes produced by clients connecting to and disconnecting from an instance of SQL Server
Stored Procedures	Collection of event classes produced by the execution of stored procedures
Transactions	Collection of event classes produced by the execution of Microsoft Distributed Transaction Coordinator (MS DTC) transactions or by writing to the transaction log
TSQL	Collection of event classes produced by the execution of Transact-SQL statements passed to an instance of SQL Server from the client
User Configurable	Collection of user-configurable event classes

The Profiler can also be set up to gather information from the server directly and store that information without requiring the client to be running. There are a series of stored procedures that allow a user to start, capture, and stop a trace without requiring any client intervention. Once the information is captured, it can be saved and even replayed against this or another server at a later time.

The next sections will examine how the Profiler can be used to gather information about the SQL Server.

Using the Profiler

Microsoft ✓ *Exam Objective*

Capture, analyze, and replay SQL Profiler traces.
Considerations include lock detection, performance tuning, and trace flags.

The SQL Server Profiler literally has thousands of possible options for designing a trace. An entire book could be devoted to this alone, so this text will examine the basics of creating, saving, and replaying a trace file.

Each trace is based on a template trace that includes the events, data columns, filters, and options for a particular type of trace. SQL Server 2000 includes eight filters that each capture a particular type of information. The user can also define their own template files if these are needed. Figures 12.1, 12.2, 12.3, and 12.4 show the various tabs of the Trace Properties dialog box where every option available for a trace can be set.

FIGURE 12.1   Trace Properties General tab

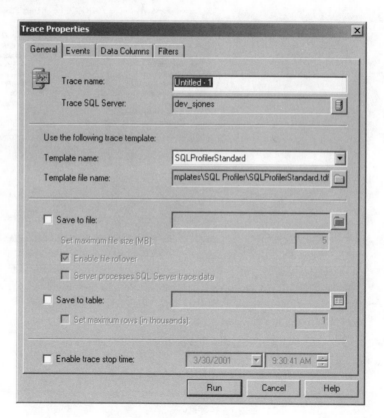

Once a trace is defined, its definition is saved, and it can be run at any time in the future. The trace can also be paused while running if the capture of information needs to be suspended. It can then be restarted at any time. If the activity in the trace is being saved to a file or table, then it can be opened at a later date and the same activity can be replayed against the same or a different database.

FIGURE 12.2 Trace Properties Events tab

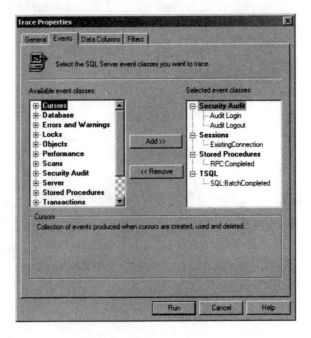

FIGURE 12.3 Trace Properties Data Columns tab

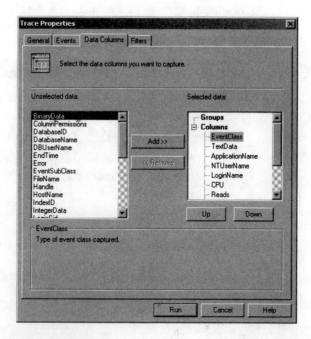

FIGURE 12.4 Trace Properties Filters tab

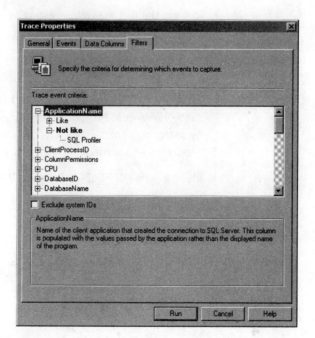

Exercise 12.5 will walk the user through creating a trace, saving the results, and replaying this against a database. Exercise 12.6 will then walk you through replaying the trace against the server.

EXERCISE 12.5

Creating a Trace Using the Profiler

This exercise will create a simple trace, capture activity and save the results, and then replay the activity against a database.

1. Open the SQL Server Query Analyzer. Do this through the SQL Enterprise Manager by selecting Tools ➢ SQL Profiler or by choosing Start ➢ Programs ➢ Microsoft SQL Server ➢ Profiler.

2. Select File ➢ New ➢ Trace.

3. Enter a server name and the appropriate security information in the Connect to SQL Server dialog box.

4. Enter a name for the trace in the Trace Name edit box.

5. Check the Save to File checkbox and enter a filename in which to store the trace data.

6. Select the Filters tab.

7. Expand the DatabaseName event by clicking it, and then click the plus sign by the Like operator.

8. Type **Northwind** in the edit box.

9. Click the Run button and the trace will start.

10. Start Query Analyzer and connect to the Northwind database on the same server that Profiler is connected to in SQL Enterprise Manager by selecting Tools ➢ SQL Query Analyzer or by choosing Start ➢ Programs ➢ Microsoft SQL Server ➢ SQL Query Analyzer.

11. Enter a series of SELECT, UPDATE, INSERT, and DELETE queries in Query Analyzer.

12. Change back to Profiler and select File ➢ Stop Trace when finished.

At this point, the data will be saved in the file that was entered in step 5. Now we wish to replay this trace against a database. If a second SQL Server with the standard Northwind database is available, then it may be used. Otherwise, drop the Northwind database and run the `instnwnd.sql` script that is located in the Install folder under `Microsoft SQL Server\MSSQL`.

EXERCISE 12.6

Replaying a Saved Trace File

1. Open the SQL Server Query Analyzer. Do this through the SQL Enterprise Manager by selecting Tools ➢ SQL Profiler or by choosing Start ➢ Programs ➢ Microsoft SQL Server ➢ Profiler.

2. Select File ➢ Open ➢ Trace File.

EXERCISE 12.5 *(continued)*

3. Select the file that was created in Exercise 12.5.

4. Select Replay ➢ Start to start running the trace file against the database.

Lock Detection with Profiler

Microsoft ✔ ***Exam Objective***

Capture, analyze, and replay SQL Profiler traces. Considerations include lock detection, performance tuning, and trace flags.

One issue that crops up with heavily loaded SQL Server systems is contention for data in certain tables. As the number of users increases, the chances that two users will want the same data at the same time increases as well. Since SQL Server assures users that they receive accurate information and that transactions complete, one user may prevent another user from accessing a table for some period of time.

Without Profiler, these situations would be difficult to detect and resolve. Profiler contains a series of events that can be used to detect blocks or deadlocks. In the Events tab, the following events can be tracked under the Locks class:

- Lock:Acquired
- Lock:Cancel
- Lock:Deadlock
- Lock:Deadlock Chain
- Lock:Escalation
- Lock:Released
- Lock:Timeout

If there are contention problems, then adding these events to a trace along with TSQL:SQL:StmtStarting and TSQL:SQL:StmtCompleted can capture activity that shows how locks are acquired and released by various users. If the table(s) on which contention is suspected are known, a filter can be applied to the trace to limit the amount of information captured.

Lock problems can be verified with Profiler by comparing the time-stamps for when a statement starts and when the lock is acquired. A user that is being prevented from accessing a resource should see a delay between these two events that is longer than the delay that would occur if there were no contention. Once this is determined, perhaps the queries can be rewritten or the application altered to reduce or eliminate the contention.

Lock Detection with Trace Flags

Microsoft
✓ ***Exam***
Objective

Capture, analyze, and replay SQL Profiler traces. Considerations include lock detection, performance tuning, and trace flags.

Monitor and troubleshoot database activity by using SQL Profiler.

An alternative to using Profiler is to enable a *trace flag* for watching lock activity. One of the DBCC commands allows the user to turn on a trace flag, which will instruct SQL Server to report certain debugging information back to the user. The specific trace flag for lock activity is 1209, and the following code turns this flag on:

```
DBCC TRACEON 1209
```

Once this has been turned on, the lock information generated by queries will be reported back to the user. This information can be used to determine if there are contention issues that need to be addressed.

Using the Index Tuning Wizard

Microsoft
✓ ***Exam***
Objective

Improve index use by using the Index Tuning Wizard.

SQL Server 2000 includes a wizard in Profiler to assist DBAs in developing indexes. This tool takes a series of queries and then develops execution plans for the queries based on the tables and indexes that exist on the server. It is at this point that this wizard really provides a great benefit to DBAs. Just as a chess computer considers a wide variety of possible moves before making a decision, this wizard considers the different execution plans that would be generated given different possible indexes that could be added to the tables referenced in the queries. From its analysis, the wizard then provides a list of recommended indexes that would optimize the queries it has analyzed.

There are two ways in which the *Index Tuning Wizard* can be used. It can be fed a single query to analyze or take a workload from the Profiler to analyze a series of queries that actually occurred on the server. Either way, this wizard produces a number of reports that can assist you in creating indexes that may enhance the performance of your application.

WARNING Since the Index Tuning Wizard checks the impact of a wide variety of different possible indexes, a large workload can take a substantial amount of time. It is not recommend that you use a production server to analyze a database. Backup and restore your database to a test server and perform the analysis there.

Exercise 12.7 walks the user through an analysis of indexes using the Index Tuning Wizard.

EXERCISE 12.7

Using the Index Tuning Wizard

This exercise will take a short trace file and analyze it using the Index Tuning Wizard.

1. Create a new trace as outlined in Exercise 12.5.

2. Open the SQL Server Query Analyzer. Do this through the SQL Enterprise Manager by selecting Tools ➢ SQL Query Analyzer or by choosing Start ➢ Programs ➢ Microsoft SQL Server ➢ SQL Query Analyzer.

3. Type the following query to in Query Analyzer (be sure the Northwind database is selected):

```
SELECT
    c.CompanyName,
    sum( od.Quantity * od.UnitPrice) 'Sales'
 FROM Orders o, Customers c, [Order Details] od
 WHERE o.ShipCountry = c.Country
 and o.OrderID = od.OrderID
 and c.ContactTitle = 'Owner'
 GROUP BY c.CompanyName
```

4. Highlight these lines with the mouse and press the green arrow or CTRL-E to execute the query.

5. Switch back to the Profiler and stop the trace by pressing the red rectangle on the toolbar or selecting File ➤ Stop Trace from the menu.

6. Select Tools ➤ Index Tuning Wizard from the menu.

7. Click Next to bypass the splash screen.

8. Enter the connection information to connect to your server.

9. Select Northwind in the database drop-down list and click Next.

10. Select My Workload File and select the file from Step 1. Click Next.

11. Check the boxes next to the following tables:

   - Orders

   - Customers

   - Order Details

12. Click Next, and the wizard will begin its analysis.

13. The next screen will display a list of the recommendations from the wizard. For this query, you should see checks next to the following indexes:

   - PK_Orders

   - PK_Order Details

   - PK_Customers

14. Click the Analysis button to display a series of reports that outline the results from the Index Tuning Wizard.

15. At this point, click Save to save the reports to disk. The Close button returns to the wizard.

16. Clicking Next gives the you the option to apply the recommendations and/or save the script to a file.

Real World Scenario

Using the Index Tuning Wizard

Assume you are the DBA for a company that has a heavily used OLTP application. Prior to the introduction of the Index Tuning Wizard, you would need to examine each query that is being used by an application along with their query plans and try to discern patterns in which columns are used most often. Using a spare server, you would then benchmark the queries, change the indexes, run the benchmarks again and attempt to determine the best indexes to keep for each table. Even a small database could keep you busy for months.

This wizard performs that same task, but does so many times faster. By comparing different possible index columns for a given workload of queries, this tool can save you a tremendous amount of time, as well as provide some justification for why particular indexes are recommended.

When an application appears to be running slow, capture a few small workloads using Profiler. These captures should be at a few different times, with the application performing the tasks that are perceived as slow. This wizard can then be run a few times against the workloads and the results compared. You will likely find that some of the recommendations are good, but some are not. With a little analysis, you can usually find the indexes that provide the most benefit and create these.

As with any performance tuning, be sure to benchmark before and after.

Optimize Stored Procedures and Triggers

Optimizing stored procedures is similar to optimizing a batch or a single query. The first time a stored procedure or a trigger is executed, the source is compiled into an execution plan. This occurs each time the server is restarted, as existing execution plans are lost when the server is stopped.

Since this plan is stored in memory for subsequent executions of the stored procedure or trigger, substantial performance gains can occur on heavily loaded servers if you use stored procedures instead of batched T-SQL code.

While the performance gains by using stored procedures are less pronounced than earlier versions, there are still benefits if you have a large number of diverse queries that are being run on a heavily loaded server. *Autoparametization* and ad-hoc query plan caching have reduced the advantage of stored procedures, but only if these queries are being run quite often. SQL Server will only keep execution plans from these queries in the procedure cache if they are being used.

SQL Server 2000 stored procedure execution plans are re-entrant, which means that more than one user can run the same execution plan at the same time. There are two benefits from this: one, the second call does not need to generate its own execution plan. In v6.5, execution plans were not re-entrant, and two calls to the same procedure at the same time caused one process to generate its own execution plan. The second benefit is that less memory is required to store these execution plans. This allows more execution plans to remain in memory, and allows more memory is available for queries.

If you have an application that receives a load immediately after a server startup (such as a busy Web application), the execution plans of heavily used stored procedures can be preloaded when SQL Server starts by including a call to the stored procedure inside a startup stored procedure.

The methods used for optimizing batches are also useful for optimizing stored procedures. Once all individual statements inside a stored procedure are optimized, there is one last step to perform. Since recompiling the execution plan for any statement is usually an expensive operation, it can be much more expensive for a stored procedure, which contains multiple statements. One aspect of ensuring good performance is to prevent the recompilation of a stored procedure as often as possible.

A stored procedure will be recompiled automatically when any of the following occur:

- Statistics for a table referenced in the stored procedure have been updated.

- The procedure contains mixed DDL and DML statements.

- The procedure references a temporary table created by another process.

SQL Server will automatically recompile the stored procedure. It is best to try and eliminate the last two items by not including these operations in heavily used stored procedures. The first item is controlled by turning off the `Auto Update Statistics` option for the referenced tables. This is not recommended, however, since this is likely out of the control of the programmer.

The Stored Procedure Debugger

SQL Server programming has lagged behind most other integrated development environments (IDEs) in the past primarily because it has lacked debugging features for the programmer to use when troubleshooting their code. There have been third-party debuggers that have been available for a few versions, but nothing was available with the SQL Server tools. That is, until now. With SQL Server 2000, a debugger has been built into Query Analyzer to allow the programmer to step through their code line by line, examine the values of variables, and find problems with the logic that was implemented.

This tool is only available for stored procedures, but with a little creativity, a user can also debug trigger or batch code as well. Triggers can be recompiled as stored procedures, though the programmer will need to simulate the inserted and deleted tables with temporary tables as these tables will not exist in a stored procedure. Batches can also be recompiled as stored procedures to check their logic.

Using the Debugger

The *stored procedure debugger* is integrated into Query Analyzer, but it can only be started from the Object Browser or the Object Search windows. It is hidden at the bottom of these cascading menus or available when you right-click an object in either of these windows. Here are the exact steps to get started:

Object Browser

1. Press F8 to display the Object Browser from within Query Analyzer if it is not visible. It will be a pane on the left side of the application.

2. Use the Object Browser to find the database and then the stored procedure you wish to debug.

3. Select the stored procedure name.

4. Right-click the procedure name and then select Debug from the menu or select Tools ➢ Object Browser ➢ Debug from the menu.

Object Search

1. Press F4 to display the Object Browser from within Query Analyzer if it is not visible. It will be a pane on the left side of the application.

2. Open the Object Search Window.

3. Run a search that finds the stored procedure. When this completes, you should see the stored procedure name in the results (bottom) pane.

4. Select the procedure name.

5. Right-click the procedure name and then select Debug from the menu or select Tools ➢ Object Search ➢ Debug from the menu.

Once you complete either of these procedures, a dialog box will appear that contains the parameters that the procedure uses along with their datatypes and whether they are input or output parameters. The option to set each of these to NULL is also available. Once you enter the parameter values, clicking Execute will open the debugging interface window.

The debugger window consists of five panes and a toolbar. The five panes are the code window at the top, the local variables pane in the left middle window, the middle pane for global variables, the callstack window at the middle right, and the results pane at the bottom (see Figure 12.5). Following are descriptions of each of these panes.

Code pane   Contains the source code of the stored procedure along with a large left margin in which the breakpoints can be placed.

Local variables pane   Contains all the local variables and their values. Updated as values change during stored procedure execution.

Global variables pane   Contains a list of global variables and their values. Updated as the values change. Global variables are variables that SQL Server provides. These start with @@.

Callstack   The list of procedures that were called in order. This allows the user to trace through multiple stored procedures and see the variables and their values at each level.

Results pane   Shows the normal results pane that appears in query analyzer as well as the return value of the procedure.

This debugger works like most modern debuggers. The user can set breakpoints, step through the procedure line by line, execute to a breakpoint or to the cursor, and change the values of variables within the procedure execution. Transactions can be rolled back at the end of debugging rather than be allowed to complete by checking the Auto Roll Back option when the initial dialog box appears with the stored procedure parameters.

FIGURE 12.5   The Stored Procedure Debugger

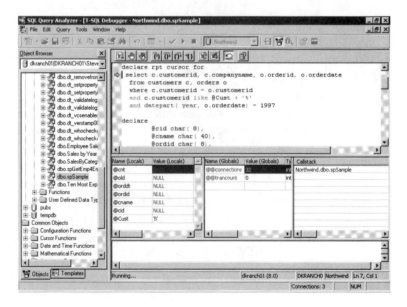

Since the debugger will halt execution of the procedure and hold locks on any resources in use, be careful about using this in a production environment. If there are transactions inside the procedure, the rows involved in the transaction will be locked and unavailable to other users until the transaction completes or is rolled back.

EXERCISE 12.8

Debugging a Stored Procedure

Since the easiest method of learning about the debugger is to see an example, let's walk through the process of debugging a stored procedure. All of the stored procedures included in the Northwind database are single T-SQL statements, so let's use the stored procedure in the following code for this example.

```
create procedure spSample
    @Cust char( 1)
as

declare rpt cursor for
  SELECT c.customerid, c.companyname, o.orderid, o.orderdate
  FROM Customers c, Orders o
  WHERE c.customerid = o.customerid
  and c.customerid like @Cust + '%'
  and datepart( year, o.orderdate) = 1997

declare
    @cid char( 8),
    @cname char( 40),
    @ordid char( 8),
    @orddt datetime,
    @old char( 8),
    @cnt int

-- open the cursor
open rpt

-- get the first row from the cursor and initialize the
locals
FETCH next FROM rpt into @cid, @cname, @ordid, @orddt
SELECT @old = ' '
SELECT @cnt = 1
```

```
    -- loop while there is data
while @@FETCH_status = 0
 begin
   if @old = @cid
   -- if these match, this is the customer
 print the customer
    begin
     print '  Order:' + rtrim( @ordid) + ' (' + cast( @orddt as
char( 10)) + ')'
    end
   else
   -- no match, a new customer
    begin
     print 'Customer:' + rtrim( @cid) + ' - ' + rtrim( @cname)
     print '    Order:' + rtrim( @ordid) + ' (' + cast( @orddt
as char( 11)) + ')'
      SELECT @old = @cid
    end
   FETCH next FROM rpt into @cid, @cname, @ordid, @orddt
   SELECT @cnt = @cnt + 1
  end

-- cleanup the cursor
close rpt
deallocate rpt

return @cnt
```

We want this code to generate a report that looks like the following for the parameter value 'A.'

```
Customer:AROUT - Around the Horn
    Order:10453 (Feb 21 1997)
Customer:ANTON - Antonio Moreno Taquería
    Order:10507 (Apr 15 1997)
    Order:10535 (May 13 1997)
Customer:AROUT - Around the Horn
    Order:10558 (Jun  4 1997)
Customer:ANTON - Antonio Moreno Taquería
    Order:10573 (Jun 19 1997)
Customer:ANATR - Ana Trujillo Emparedados y helados
    Order:10625 (Aug  8 1997)
Customer:ALFKI - Alfreds Futterkiste
    Order:10643 (Aug 25 1997)
Customer:ANTON - Antonio Moreno Taquería
    Order:10677 (Sep 22 1997)
    Order:10682 (Sep 25 1997)
Customer:ALFKI - Alfreds Futterkiste
    Order:10692 (Oct  3 1997)
    Order:10702 (Oct 13 1997)
```

```
Customer:AROUT - Around the Horn
    Order:10707 (Oct 16 1997)
    Order:10741 (Nov 14 1997)
    Order:10743 (Nov 17 1997)
Customer:ANATR - Ana Trujillo Emparedados y helados
    Order:10759 (Nov 28 1997)
Customer:AROUT - Around the Horn
    Order:10768 (Dec  8 1997)
    Order:10793 (Dec 24 1997)
```

There are a couple problems with this report, and the output and logic do not work correctly. When exec `spSample 'A'` is run, no results are returned. There are definitely customers that begin with A and orders for these customers, so some debugging is needed.

Prior to SQL Server 2000, a programmer would likely insert a series of PRINT or SELECT statements inside the procedure that would print out values at various points in the procedure. By running the procedure and observing the results, the programmer could determine where the logical problems in the code were and fix them. This might entail some trial and error to ensure there are enough PRINT statements in the right places.

With SQL Server 2000, we can quickly set up the debugger to trace the execution of the stored procedure.

1. Open the SQL Server Query Analyzer. Do this through the SQL Enterprise Manager by selecting Tools ➢ SQL Query Analyzer or by choosing Start ➢ Programs ➢ Microsoft SQL Server ➢ SQL Query Analyzer.

2. Type the stored procedure code listed above into the Query Analyzer (be sure the Northwind database is selected).

3. Compile the query by pressing the green arrow on the toolbar or pressing CTRL-E.

4. Start the object browser (if it is not started) by choosing Tools ➢ Object Browser ➢ Show/Hide from the menu or pressing F8. Navigate to Northwind ➢ Stored Procedures and select dbo.spSample. The following graphic shows the stored procedure in the object browser after compiling the stored procedure and navigating the tree.

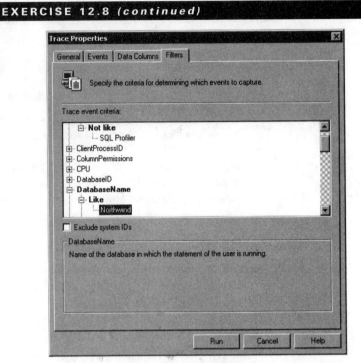

5. To start the debugger, select Debug from the right-click menu and Query Analyzer displays a dialog box that looks like the following. In this dialog box, you can see the input parameters along with their datatypes and whether they are input or output. In the Value box, you can input a value for the parameter or set it to NULL by checking the check box. If you had selected the wrong procedure, you could choose a different one from the drop-down list at the top of the dialog box. The last option is the Auto Roll Back in the lower-left corner. If this procedure were actually changing data, you could check this option to encase the procedure in a transaction that would be rolled back at the end of execution.

EXERCISE 12.8 *(continued)*

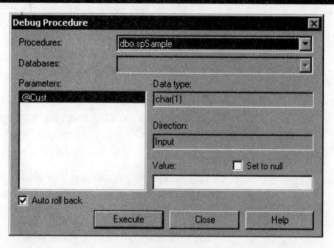

6. For this example, input A in the Value box and click Execute. The window should now look like the next graphic. There are a few things that are worth noting before you begin executing the procedure. First, notice the yellow arrow is set to the first executable line in the procedure. In this case, it is not the DECLARE statement, but rather the query below this line. This is because the cursor line does not execute until the query has been satisfied.

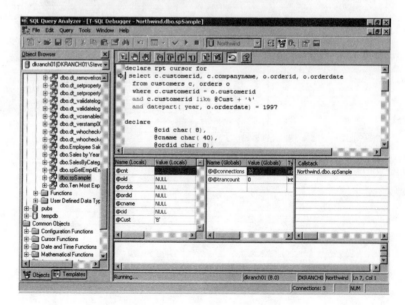

There are a few choices for how to execute this stored procedure. You can execute one line at a time, execute one line at a time but execute all stored procedures called from within this stored procedure as though they were a single line of T-SQL code, set the cursor at a particular line and execute all code prior to that line, or set a *breakpoint* (or more than one) at a particular line and run all code until the breakpoint(s) is reached.

7. For this exercise, click the Step Into button or press F11 a few times and step through the procedure. You will see that the WHILE loop is never entered and the procedure ends quickly.

   This is a problem as there are orders for customers beginning with 'A.' So let's use some additional debugger features to find where the problem is.

   Let's set a breakpoint at the start of the WHILE loop.

8. Place the cursor in the shaded left margin next to WHILE. Then press the F9 button. As you see in the following graphic, a red circle appears in this left margin, which signifies a breakpoint has been set and execution will pause when this section of the code is reached.

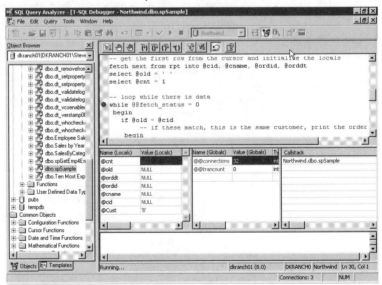

9. Click the Go button (leftmost button) or press F5, and the stored procedure will execute until it reaches the breakpoint. At this point, if you examine the variables, you see that all the variables used in the FETCH statement are still set to NULL. This implies that the cursor has no rows in it.

   At this point, stop and close the debugger, and troubleshoot the cursor by explicitly placing the parameter value in the SELECT statement. Doing this reveals that substituting 'A' for @cust does return an empty result set. The WHERE clause should be changed to AND CustomerID like @CustID + '%'. This query will return a series of rows for @CustID = 'A'.

10. Make this correction in the stored procedure code, recompile the stored procedure, and restart the debugger. The procedure will not work. As you step through the code in the WHILE loop, notice that each time a new *CustomerID* is FETCHed into *@CustID*, a different section of the IF statement is executed.

Summary

Optimizing a query can have a much greater impact on the performance of an application than any other change you can make. Tuning the Windows 2000 or NT Server software or even the SQL Server software can provide incremental improvements in performance. Changing hardware can sometimes dramatically improve performance, but in reality often masks performance problems that will creep back into the system as the data sets grow larger. These improvements tend to pale in comparison with those that come from adding an index or restructuring a query that can provide improvement in query times by orders of magnitude.

This chapter has discussed the following:

- How SQL Server determines the method that will be used to retrieve the data from a query. Inside the SQL Server program, a query optimizer compares its multiple options and then chooses the one that it thinks will complete the quickest at the time. The optimizer that

SQL Server uses is called a cost-based query optimizer. Single statement optimization and batch optimization are very similar. Stored procedures and triggers are optimized in the same way that the query processor handles batches.

- The various options that can be used in analyzing and optimizing Transact-SQL statements. These are turned on and off using the SET statement.

- Analyzing the execution plans of queries requires practice on the part of the DBA to develop proficiency. There are some standard things to look for that will assist the user in finding problems with slow performing queries.

- Optimizing queries is an art as well as a science and requires the DBA to understand the distribution of the data in the system as well as the applications that access the server. Most optimizations will occur from adding indexes. Rewriting queries to use hints or restructuring the query can also provide some performance gains. In using any of these strategies, sufficient testing should be performed to ensure that performance is being increased and not decreased.

- The Profiler allows the tracing of nearly every event that can occur in SQL Server 2000. This tool can be used in analyzing queries by capturing a workload of queries being run against a SQL Server. Once a workload has been saved, it can be run against the Index Tuning Wizard. This will analyze the indexes on the tables used in the workload and make recommendations about which indexes should be added to increase performance.

- The stored procedure debugger is new to the SQL Server tools in SQL Server 2000. It allows a programmer to execute a stored procedure line by line and view the values of variables as the execution proceeds. This is a great tool for assisting the programmer with finding logical errors in code and is available from the query analyzer. This tool can be used against SQL Server versions 2000, v7.x and v6.5 with Service Pack 2.

Key Terms

Before you take the exam, be certain you are familiar with the following terms:

query optimizer	Nested Loop
"cost-based"	Remote Query
execution plan	Sort
Bookmark Lookup	Table scan
Clustered Index Scans	primary key
Clustered Index Seek	highly selective
Compute Scalar	Profiler
Constant Scan	trace flag
Index Scan	Index Tuning Wizard
Index Seek	Autoparametization
Index Spool	stored procedure debugger
Merge Join	breakpoint

Exam Essentials

Understand how the SQL Server query optimizer processes queries. The query optimizer is critical in ensuring performance. Understanding how this engine works can assist you in writing better queries.

Know the various *SET* options and the information they provide. The SET options are useful in analyzing queries. Each can provide valuable information about how SQL Server is processing queries.

Know the different types of indexes. SQL Server allows clustered and nonclustered indexes. A table can only have one clustered index.

Know the different types of hints that can be added to queries. There are four classes of hints that can affect queries.

Understand the functions and use of the Profiler. The Profiler allows a DBA to examine the flow of queries and results between a server and client as well as within the server.

Know how to use the Index Tuning Wizard. This tool can examine a series of queries and provide suggestions for new indexes to improve performance.

Know how to use the stored procedure debugger. This utility allows a programmer to execute a stored procedure line by line and examine the logical flow of the object.

Review Questions

1. The SQL Server query optimizer always chooses the execution plan that will:

   A. Use the least resources

   B. Use the most resources

   C. Return the data the quickest

   D. Return the results in less than 1 minute

2. A developer presents you with the following query, which is running very slow. He mentions that he recently added the Categories table to the query to include the category name with each product.

   ```
   SELECT *
    FROM Products p, ProductType pt, Categories c
    WHERE p.ProdTypID = pt.ProdTypID
   ```

   Which query below would likely improve the performance of this query?

   A.
   ```
   SELECT *
    FROM Products p, ProductType pt, Categories c
    WHERE p.ProdTypID = pt.ProdTypID
    AND c.CategoryID = 5
   ```

   B.
   ```
   SELECT *
    FROM Products p, ProductType pt, Categories c
    WHERE c.CategoryID = p.CategoryID
   ```

C.

```
SELECT *
 FROM Products p, ProductType pt, Categories c
 WHERE p.ProdTypID = 5
 AND pt.ProdTypID = 5
```

D.

```
SELECT *
 FROM Products p, ProductType pt, Categories c
 WHERE p.ProdTypID = pt.ProdTypID
 AND p.CategoryID = c.CategoryID
```

3. As the DBA for Online Distributors, Inc. you are presented with the following query. The users tell you that this query runs very slowly.

```
Select c.customerID, o.ordered
 From Customers c, Orders o
 Where c.customerid = o.ordered
 And c.customerid != 'ALFKI'
 And o.ordered < 2000
```

Which query below would likely run quicker (assume join columns are indexed)?

A.

```
Select c.customerID, o.ordered
 From Customers c, Orders o
 Where c.customerid = o.ordered
 And (c.customerid < 'ALFKI'OR c.customerID > 'ALKFI)
 And o.ordered < 2000
```

B.

```
Select c.customerID, o.ordered
 From Customers c, Orders o
 Where c.customerid = o.ordered
 And c.customerid <> 'ALFKI'
 And o.ordered < 2000
```

C.
```
Select c.customerID, o.ordered
From Customers c, Orders o
Where c.customerid = o.ordered
And (c.customerid > 'ALKFI
And o.ordered < 2000
```

D.
```
Select c.customerID, o.ordered
From Customers c, Orders o
Where o.customerid <> 'ALFKI'
And c.customerID = o.customerID
And o.ordered < 2000
```

4. You wish to capture the activity that is occurring between an application running on your manager's computer and the SQL Server it communicates with. This application is not returning any data from the server, so you decide to use the Profiler to trace all SQL activity from the SQL:StmtCompleted event class. Your manager starts the application and presses a query button, but nothing appears in your Profiler window. What are the likely problems? (Select all the apply.)

   A. Your manager is connecting to another SQL Server.

   B. The application uses stored procedures and not T-SQL.

   C. Your manager is not logging into the SQL Server.

   D. The SQL Server you are profiling is not running.

5. You are the DBA for a company that is building a new database to house their Inventory data. The Receiving table needs to track each incoming shipment of goods using a unique number. You decide to use this unique number as the primary key for this table and implement this as an identity field. What type of index should you use for the primary key?

   A. Clustered

   B. Nonclustered

6. You are the DBA for a large online retailer. Customers have complained that the online catalog takes too long to display in their browsers. This catalog is built dynamically from the database and encompasses eight tables. What is the best course of action that you can take to speed up these queries? (Choose two.)

A. Capture a series of sample queries between the Web server and the SQL Server using the Profiler.

B. Examine each query using SHOWPLAN and STATISTICS IO to determine if the query can be written more efficiently.

C. Add an index to each of the eight tables for each of the columns.

D. Add a single clustered index to each table based on each table's primary key.

E. Run the Index Tuning Wizard against the trace and use its recommendations to add or drop indexes.

7. You are given the following graphical execution plan.

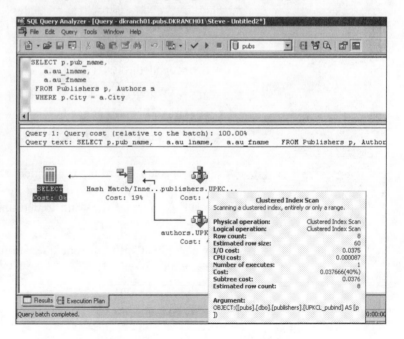

The following script shows the indexes on each table.

```
CREATE UNIQUE CLUSTERED
    INDEX [UPKCL_pubind] ON [dbo].[publishers] ([pub_id])
CREATE UNIQUE CLUSTERED
    INDEX [UPKCL_auidind] ON [dbo].[authors] ([au_id])
```

Which course of action will most likely improve the performance of this query? (Select all that apply.)

A. Add an index on Authors.city.

B. Add an index on Publishers.pub_name.

C. Add an index on Authors.au_lname.

D. Add an index on Publishers.city.

8. Which hint will force the query processor to use a HASH JOIN to return the results?

A. SELECT * FROM Customers c, Orders o WHERE c.customerID = o.ordered USING HASH

B. SELECT * FROM Customers c, Orders o WHERE c.customerID = o.ordered OPTION (HASH JOIN)

C. SELECT * FROM Customers c INNER HASH JOIN Orders o ON c.customerID = o.ordered

D. A hash join will always be used.

9. A client has asked you to rewrite a query that is performing slowly. As you rewrite the query, two different methods of returning the data occur to you, and you want to determine which method runs quicker. How can you do this?

A. Use a stop watch to time one query and then immediately time the second query.

B. Use the SET STATISTICS IO ON command to return the execution plan for each query.

C. Use the SQL Query debugger to determine which query executes quicker.

D. Use the SET STATISTICS TIME ON command to determine which query executes faster.

10. You are the DBA for a retail chain of stores. At your office, a SQL Server receives updates each night from all the stores. Each store has its own login that it uses to send this information to your SQL Server. One store is not sending its updates correctly, and you decide to use Profiler to capture all the activity from this store. You create a new trace and save this activity to a text file. What else should you do before starting this trace?

A. Add the Login Name to the list of data columns captured.

B. Set a filter to capture information for only the particular store's login name.

C. Set a filter to capture information for only the particular store's assigned SPID.

D. Add the SQL:StmtCompleted event to the trace.

11. While you were on vacation, a developer altered a stored procedure that is used to calculate the inventory locations for new products. This procedure should take a product code as a parameter and return an inventory location based on the other products in inventory and the size of the product. None of the applications that use this stored procedure were changed, but inventory is being assigned to the wrong locations. What can you do to solve the problem?

A. Rewrite the stored procedure.

B. Ask the developer to rewrite the stored procedure.

C. Use the stored procedure debugger to trace the logical flow of the procedure and find the problem.

D. Create a new stored procedure that computes the inventory and change the applications to use this procedure.

12. You are the DBA for Super Duper Kids Toys, Inc. and one of your managers is complaining that his sales history report is running too slowly. You execute the query used for the report and receive the following execution plan.

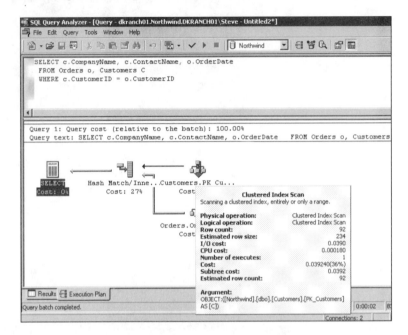

There is only one index on Customers using the CustomerID field and one index on Orders using the OrderID field. What should you do?

A. Add an index on Customers.CompanyName.

B. Add an index on Orders.OrderDate.

C. Add an index on Orders.CustomerID.

D. Add an index on Customers.ContactName.

13. You are the only DBA for a large group of developers in a software development company. To implement some business logic, you decide to use a trigger. This trigger does not appear to be working, and you need to debug the trigger. In what order should you complete the following steps?

	Use the stored procedure debugger to trace the logical flow.
	Build a temporary table to simulate the *Inserted* table.
	Use the Profiler to trace the activity of the trigger.
	Rewrite the trigger as a stored procedure.
	Build a temporary table to simulate the *Deleted* table.

14. You are the DBA for ShirtOutlet.com, an Internet retailer. Good performance is key for your company's databases, and you are tuning a query that is run thousands of times a day. Using the graphical showplan, you find that this query is performing a clustered index scan on a table. You add a nonclustered index to the table on the column being joined, but the query optimizer still performs a clustered index scan. You are sure that using this index would be faster and want to test this scenario. What can you do?

A. Use SET FORCEPLAN ON with the name of your index.

B. Use a query hint to force a hash join.

C. Use an index hint with the name of the nonclustered index.

D. Use the NOLOCK hint to prevent contention issues during this query.

15. As the DBA for a large company, you often export pricing data for your company's products using a SELECT query. While this export is occurring, you need to be sure that no changes are made to the price table. The time required to extract the pricing information must also be minimized. What can you do?

A. Use the TABLOCK query hint.

B. Use the READUNCOMMITTED query hint.

C. Use the FASTxx query hint.

D. Use the ROBUST PLAN query hint.

Answers to Review Questions

1. C. Although SQL Server uses a cost-based query optimizer, it chooses the plan that will return the data the quickest.

2. D. The slowness of the query is due to the cross join that is occurring with the Categories table. Since there is no qualification of this table in the WHERE clause, an implicit cross join occurs. Adding a join between this table and Products will speed up the query.

3. A. Whenever the != operator is used, an index cannot benefit the query and a scan of the table must be performed. Restructuring the query to remove the <> will allow the index to be used for the query. B and C do not return the correct data, and D still requires a table scan.

4. A and C. It is possible that your manager connected to another SQL Server, which would explain the lack of activity. If he had never logged in, then there would also be no activity. If stored procedures were being used, the StmtCompleted event would still be triggered. If SQL Server were not running, you would not be able to run the profiler.

5. B. Since this is an incremental key built using an identity field, it is most efficient to create a nonclustered index for the primary key. A clustered index is better served for a column that will be used in range queries, like a date, or a supplier code.

6. A and E. The key to this question is finding the quickest method to improving performance. Capturing a sample workload and using the Index Tuning Wizard will often be the quickest way to improve performance. Examining each query will be slower, and this should be done when more time is available.

7. A and D. The two columns being used to join this table together are not indexed, so adding an index on these columns will allow the optimizer to perform a seek using the index rather than a scan.

8. B. When specifying a join hint, the OPTION clause is used at the end of the query.

9. D. While the conditions present on the server at the time of the query will affect the time, SET STATISTICS TIME will return the times required to parse, compile, and execute each query.

10. B. To capture activity for a particular store, a filter should be set on that store's login name.

11. C. The stored procedure debugger exists to find trace the execution of a stored procedure and assist a programmer in finding logical errors in the procedure.

12. C. The CustomerID field is used to join the two tables together. Adding an index on this column should improve the performance of this query.

13.

Use the stored procedure debugger to trace the logical flow.
Build a temporary table to simulate the *Inserted* table.
Use the Profiler to trace the activity of the trigger
Rewrite the trigger as a stored procedure.
Build a temporary table to simulate the *Deleted* table.

The stored procedure debugger cannot debug triggers, but the code in the trigger can be rewritten as a stored procedure. Before using the debugger on this procedure, however, temporary tables that simulate the *Inserted* and *Deleted* tables need to be created.

14. C. If you want to force the query optimizer to use a particular index, then an index hint can be used in the FROM clause of a query.

15. A. To prevent any changes from occurring on the table, the TABLOCK hint will lock the table. By acquiring a lock on the entire table, your query will not have any contention issues with other users and complete quicker.

Index

Note to the reader: Throughout this index **boldfaced** page numbers indicate primary discussions of a topic. *Italicized* page numbers indicate illustrations.

S

T

MCSE: SQL Server 2000 Design Study Guide

Exam 70-229: Objectives

SYBEX